# DATE DUE

|  |  |
|---|---|
|  |  |
|  |  |
|  |  |
|  |  |
|  |  |
|  |  |
|  |  |
|  |  |
|  |  |
|  |  |
|  |  |
|  |  |
|  |  |
|  |  |
|  |  |
|  |  |
|  |  |

BRODART, CO.    Cat. No. 23-221-003

# THE ECONOMIC TRANSFORMATION OF THE UNITED STATES, 1950–2000

# THE ECONOMIC TRANSFORMATION OF THE UNITED STATES, 1950–2000

Focusing on the Technological Revolution,
the Service Sector Expansion,
and the Cultural, Ideological, and Demographic Changes

**George Kozmetsky**
and
**Piyu Yue**

**Purdue University Press**
**West Lafayette, Indiana**

Printed in the United States of America

**Library of Congress Cataloging-in-Publication Data**

Kozmetsky, George.
  The economic transformation of the United States, 1950-2000 : focusing on the technological revolution, the service sector expansion, and the cultural, ideological, and demographic changes / George Kozmetsky and Piyu Yue.
      p. cm.
  Includes bibliographical references and index.
  ISBN 1-55753-343-1 (alk. paper)
  1. United States—Economic conditions—20th century. 2. United States—Economic conditions—20th century—Statistics. I. Yue, Piyu. II. Title.

  HC106.5.K69 2005
  330.973'092—dc22

                                        2005003720

*To Ronya Kozmetsky*

# Contents

## PART TWO: ECONOMIC GROWTH OF THE UNITED STATES

### Chapter 3 - Performance of the U.S. Economy

### Chapter 4 - World Oil Price and Its Effect on the U.S. Economy

## PART THREE: DEMOGRAPHIC TRANSFORMATION OF THE UNITED STATES

### Introduction

### Chapter 5 - U. S. Population Estimates and Projections

### Chapter 6 - U. S. Population in the Post Transitional Period

## Chapter 11 - The Evolution of Sectors in the U.S. Economy

## PART FIVE: THE TRANSFORMATION OF THE FINANCIAL SERVICES SECTOR OF THE U.S. ECONOMY

## Chapter 12 - Transformation from Financial Turbulence to Financial Engineering

## Chapter 13 - Changing Portfolio of American Households' Assets

## Chapter 14 - Transformation of U.S. Stock Markets

# FIGURES

# TABLES

# Foreword

This is an important book, which deals with important topics: changes in the size and structure of the U.S. economy from 1950 - 2000 and beyond. This is done in two important ways. The first half covers transformations in the aggregate economy during the remarkable growth that occurred during the post World War II era. The second half deals with the equally remarkable transformations that occurred in the underlying sectors of the economy. As is shown in this book, both the size and the structure of the U.S. economy have seen dramatic changes, and more are forecasted to occur in ways that raise important issues of policy that need to begin to be addressed now.

For illustration we select two graphs from among the many in this book that are used to portray (and forecast) such changes in (a) the aggregate U.S. economy and (b) its underlying structure. We start with Figure 1, which is Figure 5.1 in Chapter 5. Based on U.S. Census Bureau data and forecasts,

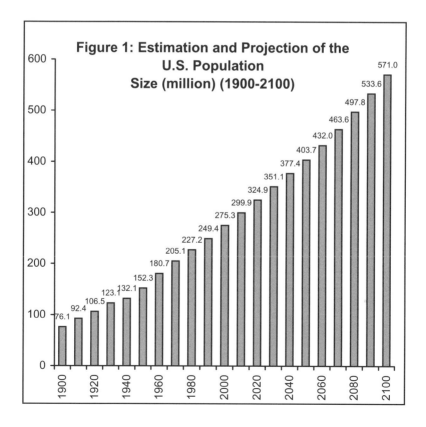

Figure 1: Estimation and Projection of the U.S. Population Size (million) (1900-2100)

this figure shows that total U.S. population increased during this period from approximately 150 million to more than 275 million persons — a gain of some 85%—so that population nearly doubled during this period. As this figure also shows, continuation of this growth will result in a population in excess of 570 million by the year 2100. Thus, by the end of this century population will nearly double to "Asian size" as the U.S. keeps its rank (after China and India) as the third most populous country in the world.

As noted by Drs. Kozmetsky and Yue, about one-third of this steady growth has come from net international migration. Thus, some might suggest stemming the flow of immigrants in order to reduce this growth. However, effects on other variables also need to be considered since, *inter alia,* the remarkable growth in U.S. GDP (Gross Domestic Product) is closely correlated with growth in the labor force which, in turn, is dependent on increases in population.

Based on U.S. Congressional Budget Office data, Figure 2—which is Figure 3.1of the book—brings this out very clearly. In this figure real GDP, which is GDP stated in 1996 dollars, is represented by the wavy line. "Real Potential GDP," represented by the smooth line, is the level of real GDP

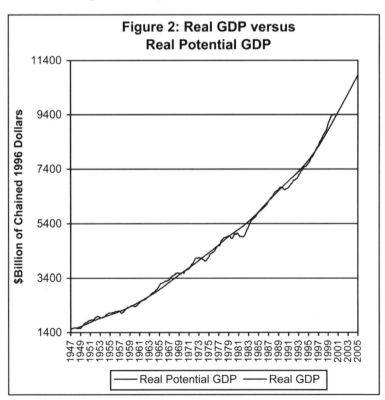

attainable at full employment. As is seen in Figure 2, the two are highly correlated. One can therefore infer that the remarkable increases in real GDP are correlated very highly with growth in the labor force. Hence one can also infer that a halt, or even a substantial slowdown in net immigration would be accompanied by a halt, or possibly even a reversal, in the growth of GDP.

This book contains numerous graphs and tables which, like the above two graphs, are based on reliable data. The results offer both a broad and deepened understanding of what has happened, as well as what is likely to continue to happen, in the U.S. economy.

The material in the book is really a compilation and an extension of many papers, reports, books, etc., which Drs. Kozmetsky and Yue have produced over many years. However, it is woven together in a manner that causes "big picture" issues to emerge without losing sight of supporting detail. We can be grateful to the authors both for their years of research that is drawn together in this book as well as the manner and the perspective in which these materials are presented.

The sector analyses presented in chapters 10-14 help to "fine tune" the results obtained from the aggregate analyses in Volume one. This provides further insight into problems (and prospects) for the future. For instance, one set of sectors is identified as "wealth providers" and another set of sectors is identified as "job providers." These two classifications are pertinent to population and employment issues such as we just examined.

From the standpoint of "wealth providers," the fastest sector growth, by far, is exhibited in finance, insurance and real estate services (e.g., mortgage loans). The fastest growth in "job providers" is exhibited by the retail trades and educational, professional, and social services. The growth in each of these sectors nearly doubled over the period 1950-2000, and this is likely to continue. This has implications for U.S. standards of living. It also has implications for the nature of U.S. export and import activities, with attendant impacts on other countries. It will also impact the quality of the labor force as well as the kinds and amounts of education required in order to be employed.

Fortunately the U.S. is in a position to accommodate demands like these because developments in information technology (including the Internet) are available to vastly extend the nature of the education that can be supplied in order to support the continuing growth in these job producing sectors. This kind of infrastructure will also be available to support and enhance the continuing growth in wealth producers such as finance, insurance, and real estate which depend heavily on the availability of knowledge on changing economic conditions—in the world as well as the U.S.

We earlier noted that this work is the result of a long period of research and joint publication (and related activities) by Drs. Kozmetsky and Yue.

The background of Dr. Yue as a policy analyst at the Federal Reserve Bank of St. Louis provided a good start for these efforts. This has been greatly extended in her joint collaborations with Dr. Kozmetsky. Her background in two cultures has similarly provided a good start for the global and cross-country comparisons that formed a large part of this earlier research. See, for instance, some of their jointly authored monographs such as *Global Economic Competition: Today's Warfare in Global Electronics Industries and Companies* (1997) and *Embracing the Global Demographic Transformation, 1910-2050* (2000).

As is well known, Dr. Kozmetsky was a co-founder of Teledyne (with Henry Singleton) which quickly became a major high tech defense contractor under their direction. Less well known is that this—as well as Kozmetsky's affiliation with Litton Industries—flowed from a marketing survey of the Federal Government which Kozmetsky conducted when he was working with Roy Ash as Controller of the Hughes Aircraft Co. As the latter name suggests, Howard Hughes, its founder, intended this firm to be a supplier of commercial aircraft. However, the results from this marketing survey with its showing of the prospective demand for services from the Federal Government—especially in the area of defense—caused the company to move into defense electronics. It also led to the departure from Hughes of Charles (Tex) Thornton and Roy Ash, who acquired Litton Industries. A new electronics division was introduced at Litton which, under the direction of Dr. Kozmetsky, was renamed the "Computer and Control Division," and helped Litton to become a major defense contractor.

It was at Litton that the meeting between Henry Singleton and George Kozmetsky occurred. Leaving Litton they acquired Amelco Inc., which was subsequently to provide the start from which Teledyne Inc. was formed.

In 1966, with Teledyne well established, George left to become Dean of the College and the Graduate School of Business Administration at the University of Texas. Serving in that capacity from 1966 to 1982, he completely changed (and modernized) the school and its point of view, so that it is now generally ranked among the top 10 schools in each of the numerous rankings that are now in vogue for application to U.S. business schools.

One innovation undertaken at the School by Dr. Kozmetsky was to form a research center named the Institute for Constructive Capitalism which was to have the task of identifying criticisms of capitalism and responding to them constructively (hence, its name). When he left in 1982, Dr. Kozmetsky moved the Institute to the status of a new (separate) entity in the University of Texas system, became its Director, and changed its name to the IC² Institute—where IC² means Innovation, Creativity, and Capital. An example of its activities is represented by the Austin Technology Incubator which (as its name suggests) provides a haven for high-tech start-up companies and which, in turn, undertook related activities that helped to make Austin, Texas, a leading "high tech" center.

Kozmetsky's association with business schools at the University of Texas, and at Carnegie Mellon and Harvard Universities has added to his already extensive background in business and, especially, "high tech" business. This has been further extended by his work with governmental agencies (and activities) at Federal, State, and Local levels. At the Federal level this has taken the form of extensive consulting with the U.S. Department of Defense and the National Aeronautics and Space Agency in order to help them develop their technology transfer programs. California and Texas are among the states where his consulting efforts were directed to helping them develop new, technologically oriented, industrial bases. See his monograph, *Creating the Technopolis* (Ballinger, 1988). Austin, Texas, and Los Angeles, California, have similarly benefited from his advice both informally and in formal consultative (and other) arrangements. Mexico, China, and Russia represent some of the foreign governments where the efforts of Dr. Kozmetsky have ranged from offering advice on the introduction of technology incubators and extended to the development of technopolis-oriented regions within these countries.

Among his many honors, Dr. Kozmetsky (in 1993) received from President Clinton the National Medal of Technology, which is the highest honor the nation awards for technological innovation. To quote from the presentation by President Clinton: Dr. Kozmetsky has "helped bolster our nation's competitive position in world markets…including his efforts toward the establishment of the IC² Institute, the Austin Technology Incubator and the Texas Capital Networks." Paraphrasing further from President Clinton, "his work in developing the IC²-NASA Technology Commercialization Center helps to fulfill the technology policy and NASA administrator David Goldin's program to ensure that the U.S. aeronautics and space programs contribute to the nation's global competitive position."

This book reflects these extensive and varied backgrounds and experiences of its authors as well as the long period of collaborative research that led to this book. It may be read in a variety of ways. One way is to read the chapters in the order in which they are arranged. Another way is to select the chapters that treat topics which are of particular interest to a reader. Still another way is to skim the book while allowing for intermittent pauses to study topics which are found to be of special interest. Indeed, still another way is simply to examine the charts and figures for their portrayal of the important developments that are covered in this book. Any of these ways will prove to be informative. It will also stimulate thought on important topics at a deeper level.

—W.W. Cooper

# Acknowledgments

Our deepest gratitude is to Professor William W. Cooper. With unhesitating faith and support he encouraged us to pursue our long period of collaborative research and joint publication on contemporary issues in economics and business. We would like to convey our appreciation to him for his constructive and detailed comments and suggestions for this book.

Early versions of this book were read and edited by Mr. Jordan Scott. He was very helpful in providing constructive criticism and editorial support for this book. We thank Mr. Kelvin P. Guo for his skill on Excel, which was a great value in collecting data and producing numerous charts and tables for this book. We are grateful to Ms. Margaret Hunt, the managing editor at Purdue University Press, for her editorial and managerial support.

# *Introduction*

The post-World War II period has been extraordinary for the U.S. economy in the sense that the economic system along with American capitalism has been transforming and restructuring dramatically. In the meantime, the U.S. economy has kept growing with only two severe recessions in 1973-1975 and 1981-1982, which were caused by the global oil crises. The longest economic expansion in the post-war era began in 1983; it was interrupted by a mild and brief recession in 1990-1991. The expansion resumed in the second quarter of 1991 and continued into 2000. During this record growth period, the unemployment rate declined to nearly 4% in 2000, which was the target rate for full-employment in the U.S., while the inflation rate remained under 3%, the lowest in forty years. Judged by any historical and contemporary standards, performance of the U.S. economy, particularly in the 1990s, was exceptional.

Entering the 21st century, the U.S. economy evidently slowed down, and its output contracted slightly in the third quarter of 2001. The longest economic expansion in U.S. history had come to an end. In order to stem the current recession, the Fed, the U.S. monetary authority, has aggressively reduced interest rates that led to an economic recovery. The horrific terrorist attacks of September 11, 2001 has been the most devastating single catastrophe in U.S history and caused substantial loss of life, property destruction, and disruption of production, distribution, and transportation. It has also created a lager uncertainty of economic recovery and led to further retrenchment in corporation capital investment and consumer spending.

The economic slowdown depressed corporate profits and increased job cutting by many corporate giants such as General Electric, Proctor & Gamble, Cisco Systems, Intel, Motorola, Lucent, IBM, and Microsoft. In the meantime, following the devastating debacle of Enron, U.S. corporations' accounting and business scandals and bankruptcy dominated newspaper headlines. All these factors further depressed investors' confidence in the U.S. stock market, which started with the collapse of Internet stocks in the middle of 2000 and continued falling to the five-year low in July and October 2002. Wall Street analysts estimated that about $8 trillion was lost in the U.S. stock market in the past two years, including a $2.6 trillion loss in the second quarter of 2002[1].

The destruction of so much wealth in the stock market could force both households and businesses to tighten their belts, cutting spending, saving, and investment in the real economy. Some people predict a double-dip recession and a painfully long downturn of the U.S. economy due to the reverse wealth effects, significant overcapacity in the technology industries, and severely eroded confidence of consumers and investors. The irrational exuberance of the late 1990s has given way to the present irrational pessimism.

Our research on the economic transformation in the United States for the last fifty years indicates that the current difficulties in the U.S. economy and stock markets reflect a transitional process and can be resolved through dynamic forces and factors inherent in the U.S. economic system. We believe that the derailing of the U.S. economy from its potential growth path should be a short-term phenomenon in the continuing economic transformation.

First, the underlying demographic force is supportive to the continuous economic expansion in the United States. The U.S. population is expected to grow at a moderate rate during the next fifty years, while populations in Japan, Russia, and Western European nations are expected to shrink substantially. The growing U.S. population will provide an increasing number of workers and consumers for economic expansion. In 2010, however, the baby boomer generation will be of retiring age, which will raise the share of elderly from 12% in 2000 to 16% in 2020. Still the U.S. population's age structure in the next twenty years will be better than the current situation in Japan, Italy, Germany, France, and U.K.[2] These nations are facing a rapidly rising number of elderly and a declining number of young people. This demographic factor provides a comparative advantage to the U.S. over its peer nations. The unique nature of international immigration has also kept the U.S. population growing and relatively youthful. It provides diversification in race, tradition, culture, religion, skill, and competence; all these factors will continue making contributions to U.S. economic growth.

Second, our research has demonstrated the dynamic process of economic changes in the United States, signifying two principal drivers for economic

---

[1] Rex Nutting, *Will the Bear Move to Main Street?* CBS.MarketWatch.com, July 19, 2002.
[2] See Table 4-2: Age Structure of Selected Nations, 1950-2050, in *Embracing the Global Demographic Transformation*, by George Kozmetsky and Piyu Yue.

development: knowledge-technology innovation and changing American ideology. Particularly we have identified what has been called the *Kozmetsky Effect*, which describes the complexity and dynamics of multi-processes of knowledge-technology innovations. Only through such processes have technology breakthroughs taken place that lead to economic growth. The United States holds superior inherent forces that have engendered many knowledge-technology innovations for the post-World War II era. The Third and Fourth Industrial Revolutions fueled astonishing economic growth and propelled the postindustrial society of the 1940s–1960s into the information technology age of the 1970s–1990s. Based on the technological and human resources invested and built up in the past fifty years, the two principal drivers will continue transforming the U.S. society into the 21st century digital/knowledge society.

Third, our research shows that the sector structure of the U.S. economy has fundamentally changed from the dominance of manufacturing goods to the dominance of providing services. The U.S. workforce has accordingly shifted from low-skill/manual jobs to professional services work. The rise of the "Creative and Innovative Class" has begun to affect all walks of American life. It will have a profound effect on human activities that involve work and leisure. Demand has been increasing for new kinds of goods, products, and services, which not only embody upgraded technological and marketing characteristics, but also are heavily dependent on specific knowledge. Increasing demand for education and continuing education and training, health care, entertainment, insurance, finance, and personal services provides tremendous opportunities to utilize knowledge-technology innovations for creating wealth and prosperity for the majority of Americans.

The knowledge-technology innovation, however, doesn't always produce a nice orderly economy. Witness what was happening in the technology companies of the Internet, B-to-B and B-to-C software, as well as communications equipment, networks and services during 2000 - 2002. There can be so many alternative future courses and utilizations of knowledge-technology innovations that result in exaggerated or faulty expectations of demand, overly built-up industry capacities, and heavy corporate indebtedness. Consequently industrial chaos comes about, which is an inevitable part of the complex process of knowledge-technology innovations. We view the recent years' confusing and difficult situation of the U.S. economy as the contemporary context of Schumpeter's *Creative Destruction*, "that incessantly revolutionizes the economic structure from within, incessantly destroying the old one, incessantly creating a new one. This process of Creative Destruction is the essential fact about capitalism. It is what capitalism consists in and what every capitalist concern has got to live in[3]." In the end, the market force of demand and supply will sort out successes versus failures, and winners versus losers.

In the resulting setting of industrial turmoil, there will occur rapid technological evolution. A kind of balance will be established between creativity and oblivion, between the commercialization of new products, the launching of new startup companies, mergers and acquisitions, and bankruptcies[4].

As Joseph Schumpeter points out, "The fundamental impulse that sets and keeps the capitalist engine in motion comes from the new consumers, goods, the new methods of production or transportation, the new markets, the new forms of industrial organization that capitalist enterprise creates[5]." U.S. corporations, industries, and sectors have systematically engaged in the continuous transformation of the economic system, which creates new technologies and products, opens up new markets, and increases new customers. This transformation has not only moved the U.S. economy from one stage to the next with increasing productivity and capacity to generate wealth and new jobs, but also sustained and flourished from intensified global competition with Japan, Germany, the newly industrialized nations in Asia, and other nations. Consequently, the U.S. economy's competitiveness has improved significantly, and GDP per capita in the U.S. has continuously increased.

We believe that the U.S. economy and American capitalist system hold the key to successfully transforming U.S. society into a digital/knowledge society in the 21st century. This comes about with economic growth through knowledge-technology innovations, and with the conversion of the working class into the creative and innovative class through education and continuing education and training. Accomplishing this transformation will create more wealth and new jobs for the majority of Americans, and at the same time will help increase the wealth of developing nations and make the world safer and more peaceful.

To accomplish such goals requires creative and innovative leadership, great synergy between the private sector and the public sector, and cooperation and collaboration among the industries, corporations, universities, government agencies, organizations, and communities, as well as individual Americans. To engage or not to engage in this inevitable transformation is the choice that all institutions and individuals in the U.S. economic system

---

[3] Joseph A. Schumpeter, *Capitalism, Socialism and Democracy*, New York: Harper, 1975.
[4] Sten Thore, "The Economics of the Information Age: Industrial Turmoil and Rapid Evolution," the IC[2] working paper, 1997.
[5] Joseph A. Schumpeter, *Capitalism, Socialism and Democracy*, New York: Harper, 1975.

must make; they will bear the consequences of success or failure, growing to be a new giant company or going bankrupt, becoming wealthy or remaining poor. Our research provides detailed evidence and data to illustrate the underlying transformation of the U.S. economic system in order to help people understand the scope and depth, as well as the nature of the transformation, before they can make the correct decisions about the future of their businesses and personal lives.

It is believed that yesterday's experiences will shed great insights on today's economic transformation, and today's exercises will help guide the journey in the uncharted sea of tomorrow. Therefore, we shall view the history, present, and future of the U.S. economy as a complex dynamic process. We have investigated the economic transformation in the United States from the contemporary and historical viewpoints, as well as from the theoretical and empirical perspectives. The purpose of our study is to reveal how the U.S. economic system has transformed from one situation to the next, and what kinds of forces have driven the economic transformation. The main emphasis of our research is focused on the time frame from the early 1950s to the beginning of the 21st century.

This book is designed to present the results of our research on the complexity and dynamics of the economic transformation in the United States for the last fifty years. First we provide contemporary and historical contexts to illustrate how two principal drivers, the knowledge-technology innovation and the changing American ideology, play a crucial role in the process of U.S. economic transformation. Recalling human history, one can recognize that major breakthroughs in scientific research and technological innovation always lead to an industrial revolution and an associated distinctive economic transformation. The knowledge-technology innovation has been a driving force for economic growth in all the sectors and industries. As a part of the Fourth Industrial Revolution[6], which started in the middle 1970s and is characterized by technology innovations in computers, genetic engineering, the laser, and still newer industrial material, the present Information Technology Revolution has profoundly changed every facet of U.S. economic, social, cultural, and political life and will continue to do so. Therefore, the economic growth and its driving force become the theme of this first half of this book.

Part One presents different perspectives on economic transformation; Part Two evaluates performance of the U.S. economy during the last fifty years; and Part Three displays the demographic transformation of the United States, which acts as the underlying force for the economic transformation.

Part One consists of Chapter 1 and Chapter 2.

Chapter 1 discusses information technology and its effects on the U.S. economy, including issues related to competitive market, investment orientation, the shifting labor market, deregulation, and rapid organizational changes.

Chapter 1 also provides a review of evolving capitalism in the United States, through which one can observe that changing technology and ideology has driven a seven-stage evolution of capitalism in the United States, from early petty capitalism to the present "institutional capitalism."

The changing American ideology is an invisible asset, bearing great importance on economic development. The United States has successfully converted its invisible and intangible ideology asset into an institutional framework of American capitalism as an infrastructure to support and influence economic transformation. This framework of successful capitalism has integrated everyone, rich and poor, into an economic system that releases aspirations and energies of human beings, and turns the potential of individual creativity and innovation into capital for economic growth and social prosperity. The economic system works cooperatively along with the political system and the moral-cultural system. The three systems of American capitalism are driven by two principal forces, the knowledge-technology innovation and changing ideology. That is why the U.S. economy has successfully transformed in tandem with evolving American capitalism.

Chapter 2 provides different theoretical perspectives on economic growth and its measurements. It has proved to be difficult to use the neoclassical growth theory to deal with knowledge-technology innovations. The economic theories based upon the idea of equilibrium and the methodology of marginal analyses fail to pass historical tests in their explanations of the causes of industrial revolutions and the timing of U.S. economic growth, because rapid technology advances are able to generate some discontinuous and sudden changes in the economy and society that cannot be described by the equilibrium theory. To reveal the complexity of economic growth, we analyze growth phenomena from perspectives of industries and corporations rather than from the viewpoint of the national economy as a whole.

The technology and product life cycle theory in the business world has recognized a more complex growth process that can be described by an S-shaped curve. Our discussion will show that it is the intersection of two S-shaped curves in which more important phenomena of economic growth have been observed and the concept of strategic inflection point is introduced. The strategic inflection point offers exciting opportunities for a hyper economic growth, but at the same time a truly miserable disaster can happen in the seemingly chaotic and turbulent environment. We study the "Kozmetsky

---

[6] W.W. Rostow, *The Greatest Population Spike and After, Reflections of the 21st Century,* Oxford University Press, 1998.

Effect" as an endeavor to search for the mechanism that leads to the creation of the strategic inflection point. The Kozmetsky Effect describes the complex interactive actions among four sub-processes: knowledge, technology, tools, and implementation. The interaction of multiple forces from knowledge, technology, engineering, business, economy, and society leads to the strategic inflection point at the end of the knowledge-technology innovation process.

Part Two consists of Chapter 3 and Chapter 4.

Chapter 3 provides a quantitative presentation of U.S. economic transformation over the last fifty years at the national aggregate level. We illustrate the growing power of the U.S. economy by macro-economic variables, the changing picture of productivity, and the relationship between the unemployment rate and inflation rate. Chapter 4 examines the major external force—the world market for crude oil—and its effects on the U.S. economy.

Part Three presents the demographic transformation in the United States, including estimates and projections of U.S. population size, changes in racial and ethnic groups, international migration, geographic distribution, the changing pattern of fertility and mortality, and the age structure of the U.S. population. Demographic factors always play important roles in the economic transformation that influences and is influenced by population changes. In today's changing economic environment, the educational achievement of workforce and the quality of education and continuing education are decisive factors for turning low-skill workers into highly skilled workers or professionals in order to meet demands of the changed structure of the U.S. economy. The fall of the working class and the rise of the creative and innovative class indicate the depth and scope of this ongoing economic transformation in the United States.

Our research shows that the continuously moderate total fertility rate (TFR), combined with net international migration, allows the United States to avoid a diminishing population size and postpones impending population aging problems, which are threatening many advanced industrial countries like Japan, Germany, Italy, and Russia. The underlying demographic factors in the United States provide a solid foundation for a sustainable economic growth for many years to come.

Up to this point, our analyses focus on the aggregate level of economic transformation, which is viewed through variables of GDP and national income, growing population, labor force and employment, changing unemployment and inflation rates, and improvement in productivity. As discussed in previous chapters, technology revolutions have been driving economic development in stages with shifting leading sectors. Presently, information technology continues to create new leading sectors for the U.S. economy. After all, a nation's economic growth depends on the changing structure of its economy. By shifting away from the sectors and industries with lower growth potential into ones with a faster pace of growth and higher productivity, the economy can generate a higher value of output and contribute to a rising standard of living.

Part Four examines economic transformation by analyzing the changing sector structure of the U.S. economy over the past fifty years. We use historical and present data of the industrial sectors in the U.S. National Income and Product Accounts (NIPA) to reveal the U.S. economy's structure changes. These changes have determined the economic performance from both demand side and supply side. Particularly we will highlight the structure shift by using the latest survey data of the "1997 Economic Census, Core Business Statistics Series" published by U.S. Department of Commerce, which is based on the new North American Industry Classification System (NAICS).

The message delivered by Part Four is that no matter which way one looks at the U.S. economy, either from the aggregate demand or from the industries' supply, the economy has changed its structure drastically, reducing massive material-consumption while increasing massive service-consumption. In response to the shifting consumption pattern, American industries have reallocated their productive capacities by reducing the share of goods-production and increasing the share of services-production. The leading sectors for economic growth in the United States have moved away from the industries associated with the Third Industrial Revolution, such as the automobile, electricity, and chemical industries, to the industries of information technology and services.

There are two chapters in Part Four. Chapter 10 provides a picture of the demand side of the U.S. economy, from which we shall see that increasing consumers' expenditure has become an important source of sustainable economic growth. Investment is also an important component of aggregate demand of the economy. During the 1990s, American corporations increased their purchases of new information-related hardware and software, substantially enhancing the efficiency and productivity of the U.S. economy. U.S. personal savings, however, fell dramatically during the 1990s, and reached a tiny 1% of U.S. disposable income in 2000. Our analyses will show that U.S. disposable income has literally been spent on consumption, while U.S. corporations and governments as well as foreigners have to be responsible for the domestic investment in the U.S.

Chapter 11 presents the structure changes in the supply side of the U.S. economy, with detailed analyses of industries' contributions to gross domestic product (GDP) and employment as well as industries' relative productivity. The goods-producing sector's contributions to the U.S. economy have been significantly declining, while the growth of the services-producing sector is becoming phenomenal. Now, more Americans are delivering services rather than producing goods, and the dominance of the manufacturing sector has been replaced by the increasing dominance of the services sector.

Part Five investigates the transformation of the financial services sector, the most rapidly growing sector in the U.S. economy for the last three decades of the twentieth century. In a modern economy, households directly or indirectly own all economic resources, namely the immense variety of human and property resources, and supply these resources to businesses. The payments, which businesses make in obtaining resources, are flows of wage, rent, interest, and profit to the households. A household's income is partly spent for consumption of goods and services and partly saved, and much of the saving is channeled into investment via a variety of financial institutions and markets.

In the conversion process of moving savings into investments, financial institutions and markets assume the role of intermediaries between borrowers and lenders and provide various financial assets with varying degrees of safety, liquidity, and yield in order to attract lenders or depositors and borrowers. Unlike goods and services, however, financial assets are not directly consumed, they are claims that enable their holders to obtain consumable goods and services should the need arise in the future and the claims are disposed. Changes in financial markets and financial institutions significantly affect the conversion of savings into investments and, therefore, the real economic activities of production and consumption as well as allocation of capital funds to various sectors and types of activities.

Financial service is a vital input for the operation of corporations and government entities. All business enterprises, government agencies, and households are customers of one or more financial services. They act as depositors, investors, borrowers, or pension beneficiaries by using various kinds of financial services in order to transfer, generate, and store wealth. Financial assets constitute significant fractions of the total assets of American businesses and households. Those financial assets include bank deposits, pension plan benefits, insurance policies, mutual fund shares, holdings of government securities, corporation bonds, and equity shares; all of financial assets are liabilities of financial intermediaries and service providers. Therefore, the safety and soundness of the financial services sector become extremely important, which makes the sector one of the most heavily regulated sectors in the U.S. economy despite decades of widespread deregulation.

In Part Five, we present the story of economic growth from a financial view of macroeconomics by looking at the dramatic changes in U.S. financial instruments, financial institutions, and financial markets. We shall review the transformation of U.S. financial services sector in chapter 12, and study the changing portfolio of American households' assets and liabilities in chapter 13. In chapter 14 we discuss the performance of U.S. stock market since 1929.

Part Six, Concluding Remarks, summarizes findings from analyses of the transformation of the sector structure of the U.S. economy. The detailed evidences provided in this volume lead us to rethink the strength of the U.S. economy, to reshape relationship among economic variables, and to believe that the restructuring of the economy for a new phase in the high mass-consumption stage of economic growth is a continuation of the historical development of the United States.

# ECONOMIC GROWTH
## OF THE UNITED STATES

# PART ONE

# PERSPECTIVE ON ECONOMIC TRANSFORMATION

# Chapter 1

## Two Principal Drivers
## for U.S. Economic Transformation

In this chapter we shall address economic transformation in both contemporary and historical contexts to illustrate how the two principal drivers, knowledge-technology innovation and changing American ideology, play a crucial role in the process of U.S. economic transformation. Section 1-1 discusses the current condition of the U.S. economy with an emphasis on information technology innovations and their effects on the economy's structure shifts. Section 1-2 presents a brief view of American ideology, the evolution of U.S. capitalism, and the stages of U.S. economic growth. These discussions serve as a broad, historical backdrop for understanding the economic transformation during the last fifty years.

## 1-1  Information Technology and New Structural Shift

The behavior of the U.S. economy in the 1990s surprised many people who made suppositions in the 1970s and 1980s that capitalism in general and the United States in particular seemed to be running out of gas. At that time, hyperinflation accompanied high unemployment; American corporations lost large shares of the domestic and international markets to the Japanese; oil shocks generated tremendous turbulence in markets around the globe; and poor productivity reduced workers' real wages. To make matters worse, the trade deficit and the national debt of the United States soared.

Some observers and researchers predicted that the decade of the 1990s would see the confluence of two types of cycles. The first is the 500-year cycle noted by Davidson and Rees-Mogg: "The end of each century divisible by five has witnessed a major transition in Western civilization[1]." The second type of cycle is what is known as the 60-year Kondratieff Cycle, named after the Russian economist who first discovered it. "Three depressions have occurred in the past two centuries—in 1814-49, 1873-96, and 1930-39 — roughly 60 years apart. The fourth depression is now due, say the cycle's proponents[2]." These economic cycle models signal a depression of the U.S. economy at the end of the 20th century.

Disregarding for a moment those long-term economic cycles, business fluctuations in the United States for the 1990s were characterized by continuous growth, subdued price inflation, and the longest economic expansion in U.S. history. Specifically, during the global financial crisis of 1997-1998, the economy of Japan, the second largest in the world, was in the middle of a recession; some advanced economies in Europe drastically slowed down; and many economies in Asia and South America as well as Russia were plagued by financial turmoil and fell into negative growth. Under a looming world economic recession, the U.S economy defeated the drag of external forces and continued its ascension in a dangerous global economic environment. During this time, the U.S. lent many troubled nations around the globe a helpful and powerful hand by opening its huge domestic market to foreign goods and services. Exporting to the United States became a powerful resource for many troubled nations to pull their economies out of recession.

At the beginning of the new century, the U.S. economy still grew at 2.3% and 5.7% of the annualized rates of real GDP in first two quarters, with the unemployment rate about 4% and the inflation rate below 3%. Since the third quarter of 2000, economic growth in the United States has declined significantly, as shown in Figure 1-1.

The risks to the U.S. economy were well recognized by the authorities at the Federal Reserve. The Fed wielded its tremendous power by cutting

---

[1] "Future Winners..." by Shlomo Maital, *Across the Board,* December 1991. The author continues: "At the end of the fifth century, Rome fell, signaling a half-millennium economic decline in the Dark Ages. A slow recovery began in 1000 A.D., and the widespread use of gunpowder that began around 1490 signaled five centuries of world growth. As the "era of American predominance" draws to a close, the world is again in jeopardy of economic reversal."
[2] "Future Winners..." by Shlomo Maital, *Across the Board,* December 1991.

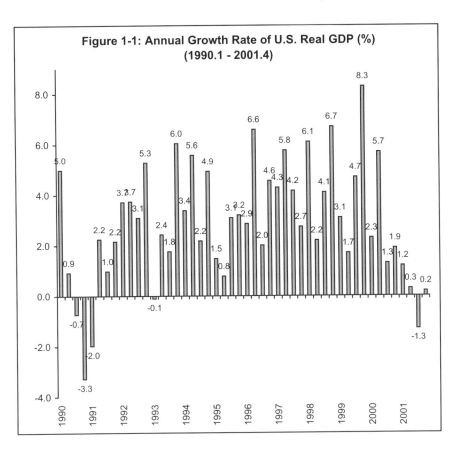

**Figure 1-1: Annual Growth Rate of U.S. Real GDP (%)**
**(1990.1 - 2001.4)**

the federal funds rate eleven times in 2001 with the aggregate rate cut of
4.75 percentage point[3].

This aggressive policy reaction, combined with the Bush Administration's
tax cut, led many people to believe that the U.S. economy will be saved from
a recession. It was predicted that the he U.S. economy would recover by

---

[3] The federal funds rate is the interest rate at which depository institutions lend balances at
the Federal Reserve to other depository institutions overnight. The discount rate is the
interest rate charged by a Federal Reserve Bank on short-term loans to depository institutions. The Federal Open Market Committee (FOMC) determines both the federal funds rate
and the discount rate; all the other interest rates in markets follow them closely. Changes in
these rates can be interpreted as an indicator of monetary policy. Increases in these rates
generally reflect the Federal Reserve's concern over inflationary pressures, while decreases
often reflect a concern over economic weakness. FOMC reduced the federal funds rate from
6.50% to 1.75% in 2001, bring the rate to its lowest level in about 40 years. On 6 November
2002, the Fed slashed interest rates by a shock half-point. The federal funds rate now stands
at a fresh four-decade low of 1.25%.

the middle of 2002 and hopefully return to its 3.0 – 3.5% steady growth pace after 2002. As a matter of fact, U.S. real GDP fell at a 1.3% rate in the 3rd quarter of 2001, and grew by 0.2% in the 4th quarter, with an annual growth rate of 1.1% in 2001 (Figure 1-1).

As Figure 1-1 shows, during the entire decade of the 1990s the United States witnessed three consecutive quarters of decline, Q3 and Q4 in 1990 and Q1 in 1991, plus a minor reduction in Q1 of 1993. Since Q2 of 1993, the U.S. economy has expanded for 32 quarters without interruption. This fact manifests the exceptional performance of the U.S. economy in the 1990s by any historic standards of world economic development. Why did the U.S. economy behave so steadily and so strongly in this recent decade? Alan Greenspan, the chairman of the Federal Reserve, proposes a list of the factors shaping the U.S. economy. Supporting factors include favorable conditions in financial markets with low intermediate- and longer-term interest rates; federal budget-deficit reduction; the increasing productivity and efficiency of American through new technology and innovation, and so on. To support this, Mr. Greenspan made the following comments in 1996 and 1997.

.... Powerful forces have evolved in the past few years to help contain inflationary tendencies. An ever-increasing share of our nation's workforce uses the tools of new technologies. Microchips embodied in physical capital make it work more efficiently, and sophisticated software adds to intellectual capital. The consequent waves of improvements in production techniques have quickly altered the economic viability of individual firms and sometimes even entire industries, as well as the market value of workers' skills[4]....

.... Technological change almost surely has been an important impetus behind corporate restructuring and downsizing. Also, it contributes to the concern of workers that their job skills may become inadequate. No longer can one expect to obtain all of one's lifetime job skills with a high school or college diploma. Indeed, continuing education is perceived to be increasingly necessary to retain a job. The more pressing need to update job skills is doubtless also a factor in the market expansion of on-the-job training programs, especially in technical areas, in many of the nation's corporations[5]....

---

[4] Testimony of Chairman Alan Greenspan before the Committee on Banking, Housing, and Urban Affairs, U.S. Senate, July 18, 1996.
[5] Testimony of Chairman Alan Greenspan before the Committee on Banking, Housing, and Urban Affairs, U.S. Senate, February 26, 1997.

Again, in 1999 he reassessed the situation of technology innovations:

> I have hypothesized before this group on several occasions that
> the synergies that have developed, especially among the
> microprocessor, the laser, fiber-optics, and satellite technologies, have
> dramatically raised the potential rates, not only on new
> telecommunications investments, but more broadly on many types
> of equipment that embody or utilize the newer technologies....
> The newest innovations, which we label information technologies,
> have begun to alter the manner in which we do business and create
> value, often in ways not readily foreseeable even five years age[6].

The following sections illustrate the development of information technology
and examine its effects on the U.S. economy.

## 1-1-1 The Information Technology Revolution

With widely spreading applications, information technology has put down
deep roots in almost all of the sectors of the U.S economy. Myriad innovations brought by information technology have greatly enhanced American
corporations' profitability, efficiency, and competitiveness in perceiving global markets. They have also dramatically altered American workers' expectations regarding their skill levels, training opportunities, job-security, and
wages. Information technology has entered millions of American homes,
shifting consumers' tastes and demands away from material consumption
towards the consumption of services. Today, average Americans are able to
enhance their quality of life by increasing their requests for education and
job-training, cultural and traditional activities, entertainment and travel services, finance and insurance services, health care and medication, etc. As
one of the authors of this text speculated several decades ago,

> .... For the first time, society has the means to reassess itself and to
> choose its destiny instead of drifting into the future on the tide of myths.
> For the first time, it has a technology at its disposal, which will allow it to
> allocate resources for a maximum efficiency directed towards a planned
> purpose. For the first time, society has the ability to reshape its institu-

---

[6] Remarks by Chairman Alan Greenspan, "The American Economy in a World Context," At
the 35th Annual Conference on Bank Structure and Competition of the Federal Reserve Bank
of Chicago, Chicago, Illinois, May 6, 1999.

tions coherently and realistically. The information technology that is now emerging makes all this possible—and more.

.... One facet of information technology, the mass media, has helped to bring society to a point where it demands and expects quick solutions to enduring problems. Another, more sophisticated facet of that technology, the whole cluster of applications built round the computer, has brought society the tools for identifying the causes of these problems, providing solutions, and mobilizing resources. Unfortunately, society does not know how to use those tools.

.... Information technology potentially allows men to move effectively and surely in a world of changing reality. In that future, the authority of management will have a new legitimacy, because it will enable managers to see their role in its social, cultural and economic perspective, and to predict the consequences of their actions with greater certainty than is possible today.[7] ....

We are amazed to see how much the United States and the world as a whole have changed since 1971, when the two authors of the book *Information Technology and Its Impacts* worked out a framework for the effects of information technology. Even though it took three decades to see the authors' vision of those effects become real, the profound impacts of the information technology revolution on business, education, society, community, and government were predicted with a high accuracy.

Information technology has created the telephone, radio broadcasting, television, cable television, VCRs, the cellular phone, PCs, computer networks, telecommunications networks, the Internet, and innovations yet to come. The real information technology revolution might be traced back to the development of microprocessors—the "brains" inside personal computers.

A microprocessor is an integrated circuit built on a tiny piece of silicon containing thousands or even millions of transistors working together to store and manipulate data. The astounding growth of microprocessors is expressed in what is called *Moore's Law*, which states that each new chip contains roughly twice as much capacity as its predecessor, and each chip is released within 18-24 months of the previous chip[8]. In fact, *Moore's Law* quite accurately predicted the revolutionary changes in the semiconductor industry. Figure 1-2 depicts a growth curve for microprocessors produced by Intel Corporation, now the world's

---

[7] *Information Technology and Its Impacts,* by George Kozmetsky and Timothy Ruefli, Graduate School of Business, The University of Texas at Austin, 1971.

[8] In 1965, Intel's president, Gordon Moore, made a memorable observation in his speech about the growth in memory chip performance. This is now known as Moore's Law.

largest manufacturer of microprocessors. Intel's first microprocessor is 4004; it was introduced in 1971, and contained 2,300 transistors. The 8080 microprocessor introduced in 1974 was the brain for one of the first personal computers—the Altair. Microprocessor 8088 was produced for IBM PCs in 1978. The 80286, known as the 286, was the first Intel processor that could run all the software written for its predecessor, and it started the Intel's family of microprocessors 386 and 486. The 386-processor, which was introduced in 1985, contained 275,000 transistors; and the 486 microprocessor was the first one with a mathematical processor built in.

In 1993 Intel released its first-generation Pentium processor, and a series of new Pentium processors hit the market one after another for the next seven years with significantly advanced capabilities and speed. For instance, the Pentium Pro processor, which is designed to fuel a 32-bit server and workstation application, has 5.5 million transistors in the chip. Pentium III, introduced in 1999, incorporated 9.5 million transistors, and was produced by using the 0.25-micron technology. In 2000, Intel released Pentium 4, which contained 45 million transistors and the circuit lines of 0.18 microns, boosting the processing speed to 1.5 gigahertz (or 1.5 billion hertz).

Compared with Intel's first processor 4004 of thirty years ago, which ran at 108 kilohertz (or 108,000 hertz) and contained 2,300 transistors, Pentium 4 has increased speed 13,889 times, and the number of transistors 18,261 times. Pentium 4 processor-based PCs can create professional-quality movies, deliver TV-like video via the Internet, communicate with real-time video and voice, render 3D graphics in real time, quickly encode music for MP3 players, and simultaneously run several multimedia applications while connected to the Internet.

When talking about microprocessors, David K. Allison, a technology historian at the Smithsonian, has ranked the invention of the microprocessor in the same league as the invention of the steam engine, automobile, or airplane.

> The microprocessor has had a kind of transforming quality for civilization. Contrast the microprocessor with its predecessor, the ENIAC, which had 18,000 vacuum tubes. Today, we do something far in excess of that—billions of different components—on something the size of your fingernail. The scale changed everything[9].

---

[9] A History for the Microprocessor, Interviews with Visionaries, http://www.intel.com. The ENIAC computer, the first large-scale general-purpose electronic computer, was built at the University of Pennsylvania's Moore School of Electrical Engineering in 1946. ENIAC is an acronym for "Electronic Numerical Integrator and Computer." The ENIAC is important historically, because it laid the foundations for the modern electronic computing industry. It demonstrated that high-speed digital computing was possible using the then-available vacuum tube technology.

The astonishing speed of the microprocessor's development (illustrated in Figure 1-2) indicates the capability of the information technology revolution to induce the fastest transformation ever seen in any aspect of the economy and society.

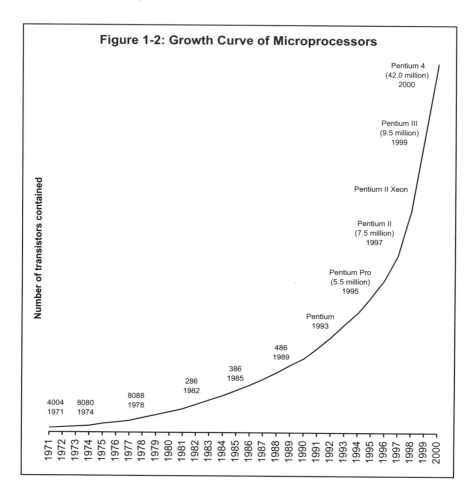

Figure 1-2: Growth Curve of Microprocessors

The information technology sector in the United States soared in the 1990s, and the health of the U.S. economy became increasingly dependent on cutting-edge technology industries. The information-related services industries, in particular, have largely increased their shares in the over-all economy, including such industries as communications, education, health care, computer software, business consulting, managing personal finance, electronic commerce, on-line shopping, on-line auction, on-line broker services, and on-line trading, and so on. Those industries provide renewed energies that fuel economic growth and create more jobs than any industry in the conventional sectors of the economy. The truly phenomenal development of the new applications of information technology is built around computers and the Internet.

Computer purchases by corporations and consumers have accelerated rapidly. The speed of PCs' penetration has overtaken any previous information technology innovations, such as telephone, TV, cable TV, and VCR. According to statistics by Dataquest Inc., in 1998 buyers around the world spent $158.7 billion on 92.925 million PCs, of which the U.S. and European PC market accounted for nearly 65%. Analysts expected manufacturers to ship 158.2 million PCs in 2002, which represents a $253.7-billion PC market worldwide. Affordability and growing relevance of Internet contents most likely were supporting factors for this double-digit PC growth during the 1990s.

Also reported by Dataquest is the fact that the PC industry has made great strides into the home market by making personal computers more affordable for the average consumers. In 1995, only 27% of U.S. households had a PC; that penetration rate increased to 36% in 1996, and 43% in 1997. In 1998, almost 50% of U.S. households had one or more personal computers. Many first-time buyers are from households in the lower socioeconomic levels, showing that the PC is rapidly becoming an affordable, standard household appliance.

A study by a market research firm, Scarborough Research, indicates that the average home PC penetration across the 64 measured markets was 59% in 1999. The number-one computer savvy city is currently Salt Lake City, with 73% of households owning a PC, followed by San Francisco (72%), Washington, D.C. (71%), Seattle (69%), Austin (69%), and Portland, Oregon (69%)[10]. Although the economic slow-down in 2000-2001 depressed the demand for PCs worldwide[11], new PC operating systems by Microsoft, new technology innovations, and major structural shifts in the PC market will insure a future demand for PCs in the global market.

Naturally with expanded computer penetration, home Internet usage is becoming widespread. Dataquest's survey suggests that as many as 37% of U.S. households were connected to the Internet by the middle of 1999.

---

[10] The 30 Hottest PC Penetration Cities, June 06, 2000, http://www.digitrends.net.

[11] A research firm, Gartner Dataquest, reported on July 20, 2001 that worldwide PC sales in Q2 of 2001 fell by 1.9% compared with Q2 2000; it is negative growth in the world PC market for the first time in fifteen years.

According to Computer Industry Almanac Inc., there were over 400 million users[12] worldwide at year-end 2000, up from fewer than 200 million users at year-end 1998. The United States had 134.6 million Internet users or nearly 33% of the world's total at year-end 2000. It was projected that by year-end 2005 there would be about 1 billion Internet users worldwide and over 214 million in the U.S., accounting for 32% of the world's total Internet users. The United States, however, was ranked 4th in terms of Internet users per capita, with 40.6% of the population regular Internet users at year-end 1999. Canada, Sweden, and Finland were the top three, with their Internet users per capita 42.8%, 41.4% and 40.8% respectively.

With more options and contents available on the Internet, people are spending more time on line than ever before. Internet users subscribe to Internet services not only for news and information, but also to buy books, music, computers and consumer electronic products, cars and homes, and other items directly from on-line companies or referred providers. America On Line (AOL), an Internet-based media company, has reported that sales through AOL grew from $12 million to $1 billion in the three-year period of 1998 - 2000. People believe that the Internet will become the ultimate business and personal tool. A web-service firm, Mysite Inc., has posted its "Accurate Demographics of Internet Users[13]," which indicates that 93% of respondents[14] to its survey use their Web browser more than once a day, and 56% use it more frequently than 4 times a day. In terms of primary use, 75% of people use the Internet for personal information, 65% for work, 60% for education, 60% for entertainment and 50% for shopping. Only 10% of respondents have not made online purchases, while 28% buy online once a month and 4% once a week.

While still in its infancy, e-commerce has begun to transform the business landscape. Companies whose business activities are centered on providing information, such as in the banking, brokerage, and publishing industries, have already been profoundly affected by Internet technologies and have been sufficiently motivated to move their businesses on line. Companies in the non-information industries will need to reengineer themselves for the online world, as many small companies have already dramatically outperformed their bigger competitors by adapting more quickly to the new e-commerce environment. The Internet has provided tremendous opportunities for

---

[12] They define an Internet user as any person over 16 years old who uses the Internet on a regular basis at least once a month. These numbers include business, educational and home Internet users.

[13] http://mysiteinc.com/taxfreedom/demographics.html.

[14] Respondents' distribution of geographic location: USA 85%, Europe 7%, Canada 4%, and all other countries 4%.

saving costs and building new revenues. Companies in the conventional industries need to develop their Internet strategies and integrate the Internet into their overall businesses both internally and externally in order to capture those opportunities. Analysts on Wall Street point out, "Any industry that's not going through their Internet strategy, inside and out, is suspect[15]."

## 1-1-2  Effects of Information Technology on the U.S. Economy

Certainly, the effects of the information technology revolution on the U.S. economy are profound. Technology innovations have already generated significant shifts in economic activities, which present unparalleled opportunities as well as unprecedented risks and uncertainties to all the players in the U.S. economy. We characterize the major effects of IT innovations on the U.S. economy into six categories as follows:

## • Technology Innovation Enhances Competitive Market

The increasing use of computers, wireless communication devices, and the Internet allows consumers to access various kinds of information about products and services, and allows corporations to reduce transaction costs and to implement responsive marketing and pricing strategies. The open Internet platform allows any user to communicate with others in the networked global market without national barriers or boundaries.The Internet also provides a great opportunity for small businesses to enter and exit global markets in order to compete with multinational corporations. The limitations of physical distance and geographical locations can be reduced or eliminated via the global communication networks that link customers and producers worldwide. Information technology innovations allow markets to work more efficiently by allocating rare economic resources for their most productive usage. More efficient markets benefit consumers as well as producers, including both conventional businesses and companies in the cutting-edge high tech market. The market efficiency induced by information technology innovations is irreversible, working in both a booming as well as a slowing economy.

Information technology innovations streamline corporations' operations, increase their efficiency, and lower labor and inventory costs. These ben-

---

[15] News (Reuters), Compaq's Shakeup Provides E-Commerce Warning, by Dick Satran, April 20, 1999.

efits are quickly passed on to consumers via declining prices. In the computer and IT product markets, this price deflation was accelerated in the late 1990s, further increasing the competitive pressures in those markets[16]. More efficient companies have a good chance to survive and thrive through the intense global competition. Laggard companies that are locked into old and inefficient technologies have a much hard time competing in the marketplace.

Not only do technology innovations promote market efficiency, they also present some serious challenges to the competitive market. On the one hand, we see many small innovative start-ups grow rapidly and compete vigorously with well-established companies. On the other hand, well-established and well-managed large organizations, like Microsoft, can take full advantage of technology innovations to develop their monopoly power in the market and to edge small competitors out of business. This dilemma cannot be easily resolved through regulatory enforcement, which is illustrated by the marathon lawsuit against Microsoft that was hanging in the court for many years[17]. In short, we recognize that information technology innovations bring, simultaneously, the benefit of a more efficient market and the risk of increasing the potential of monopoly power.

### • Technology Innovation Redirects Investment

Dramatic advances in information technology enable corporations to adopt just-in-time inventory management to reduce costs and inventory fluctuations. A wide variety of tasks that used to require person-to-person contact can now be done via the Internet or other telecommunication networks more quickly and with less cost.

Companies that adopt information- and computer-based technologies show significant reductions in cost, increases in efficiency, productivity, and profitability. This explains why many U.S. corporations invested heavily in various IT innovations during the 1990s. Investment capital has been shifted away from old technologies in order to finance newly produced capital assets that represent cutting-edge technologies. These investments have been geared toward business automation, robotics, innovative production processes,

---

[16] In 2001, consumers could buy a Dell desktop computer with nearly 200 times the speed and memory of Dell's first computer (in 1986) for half the price in inflation-adjusted dollars.

[17] The attorneys for 19 states and the Justice Department sued the company in 1998 alleging it used its monopoly in the operating system market to capture the Net browser market.

fiber optical communication networks, wireless networks, new materials, genetic engineering, human genome, and other emerging technologies. The investment efforts made by American corporations in the 1990s have led to a significant rise in productivity, and will continue to make their contributions to the long-term advance in the standard of living for the majority of Americans. This subject will be covered more thoroughly in Chapter 3 of this book.

In general, an investment decision is made on the basis of expected future returns on capital assets, or essentially the future flow of corporation profits. Companies' expectations on technology investment ran very high during the economic boom of the 1990s, resulting in overspending on computers and other IT products. When an economic slowdown loomed in the middle of 2000, expectations evaporated quickly. Instead of looking for continuously rising profits, American technology companies have witnessed an unprecedented large decline in their profit margin. This was due to a sudden drop in demand for computers, telecommunications equipment and other IT products as well as continuing pressures to lower prices of IT products. Many large corporations dramatically cut their capital spending on information technology, while numerous Internet start-up companies, significant customers of IT products, were verging on the brink of bankruptcy.

This changing reality has brought trouble to even well-established high tech companies, such as Compaq Computer, Lucent Technologies and Cisco Systems. All of these companies suffered from enormous inventories of unsold merchandise and billion-dollar revenue losses. In the telecommunications equipment sector specifically, slumping sales have forced many companies to close assembly lines and lay off thousands workers in order to remain afloat.

Over-investment in too many Internet start-up companies and overspending on IT products were the results of over-speculation on new technologies in the late 1990s of booming business. The current market pessimism regarding technologies was triggered by the burst of many Internet companies in stock markets since the spring of 2000. It has resulted in a large decrease in corporations' spending on computers, telecommunications equipment, and fiber optical network products. Dramatically declining expenditures on information technology by American corporations have been blamed as the origin of the significantly slowing down of the U.S. economy since the middle of 2000; some analysts called this situation an investment recession or the technology sector's recession.

In reality, however, many American corporations have used their invested information technology to reduce transaction costs, to boost efficiency through supply-chain management and just-in-time inventory management, and to improve communications with customers and suppliers. Those benefits from information technology innovations are real and will endure. Investment in intangible capital, such as human skills and creation processes for new information and knowledge, will enable corporations to create new products and services that enhance future prosperity for society. Eventually, the benefits of investing in those technologies that boost creativity, productivity, and profitability will outstrip short-run costs, uncertainties, and risks. With the advent of future technology breakthroughs, the price of computers and other IT products will continue to decline. New applications of innovative technologies should again increase the demand for IT capital equipment. It is foreseeable that new technologies will revive optimism in technology companies and ignite another round of rush for investing in new technologies.

It is clearer than ever before that technology innovation, through directing capital investment, has become a causal factor of the business cycle, playing an important role in both a boom as well as a decline of the U.S. economy.

## • Technology Innovation Shifts the Labor Market

Widely adopted innovative technologies by American corporations, organizations, institutes, and government agencies have shifted the demand for human capital from low to highly skilled workers. Many less-skilled workers have been displaced along with obsolete technologies. In order for these workers to avoid declining wages or unemployment, they must engage in continuing education and training to acquire newly required job skills and competence. Information technology and the Internet have created an entire new labor market that distributes more job opportunities to highly skilled white-collar workers, many of them working on temporary contracts.

As technology rapidly advances, managers and workers at all levels have to update their skills in order to stay competitive. Responding to changing technology and market environment, American corporations have to restructure and streamline their operations more frequently and more radically. Job security becomes the first victim of a corporation's restructuring. Technology giants, such as Lucent and Nortel, have each recently eliminated more than 20 thousand jobs. It is not uncommon for jobs at all levels of a division to vanish without warning. People need to recognize this change in the labor market and be prepared to reallocate their skills. The best preparation is to engage in continuing education and training in order to gain current skill-sets for jobs in the emerging industries of the service sector. There is a huge demand for job skill enhancement, which creates a great business opportunity for the private sector to provide technical and professional training for both employed and unemployed people.

Not only must American workers compete with each other in the domestic labor market, they are also increasingly encountering a fierce competition from workers in many nations around the globe. Job positions requiring a low skill level can be easily relocated from the U.S. to countries in Asia and South America, where workers receive less than one tenth of U.S. wages for the same job. This type of global competition is not limited to lower skill level positions. As the global telecommunications network provides a brand new platform to bring together people who are scattered across the globe, some highly intelligent Indian and Chinese programmers can join a project team without leaving their countries to develop sophisticated computer codes for U.S. companies. The distribution of job opportunities has no longer been confined within national boundaries, and many tasks can be done electronically and transported almost instantaneously across the world.

As more and more nations in the world decide to participate in the global network for economic growth and prosperity, the global competition for jobs of all kinds will be further intensified. Responding to this changing global reality, U.S. governments at all levels and private corporations in all industries need to work together to innovate the American educational system and facilitate continuing education and training in order to develop tomorrow's required talents and workers. The American labor force must stay ahead of the global competition if the United States wants to retain its economic super power status and to strengthen its leadership in global affairs.

## • Technology Innovation Speeds Deregulation

Technology innovations provide the means and methods for companies to organize production in a flexible way in order to comply with industrial regulations, and at the same time to minimize costs, to reduce time to market, and to enhance efficiency and profitability. Innovative technologies have enhanced competition by reducing monopolies in the industries of telecommunications, transportation, electricity, financial service and banking. In return, the competitive market speeds deregulation in those industries to create a more liberalized business environment, which will promote further technology innovation and diffusion.

Innovative technologies also encourage international trade. The Internet creates brand new ways to exchange data, information, ideas, knowledge, goods, and services worldwide. It allows conventionally non-tradable goods, such as service and knowledge, to enter the global market. Technology innovations also enhance a corporation's capability to produce tailored products and services that meet global consumers' needs more precisely and in a timelier fashion. New consumer products and services, along with specialized capital goods, enter the world market through international trade. With the open Internet platform and e-commerce technology, geographic boundaries and market barriers can be reduced or eliminated. It becomes increasingly difficult for one nation or society to isolate its citizens or members from the rest of the world, as news and information can reach out almost everywhere instantly via the Internet. All these changes damp down protectionism worldwide and promote freer international trade. This creates political pressures to deregulate industries and open up national borders to international trade.

A less restrictive regulatory environment enhances a national economy's performance in general, and fosters innovation and diffusion of technologies in particular. It promotes competition in the marketplace and protects workers and consumers by preventing anti-competitive behavior, enforcing pollution control, requiring worker health and safety standards, and protecting intellectual property rights and so on. Those regulations are necessary and important for defending social values of communities and societies. In some cases regulatory changes can force firms to develop new technologies and adopt more-efficient production techniques for reducing pollution and improving safety.

The trend is to move toward a more liberalized regulatory business environment and freer international trade. Clearly, innovative technologies have played an important role in speeding up deregulation processes across the globe.

### • Technology Innovation Enforces a Rapid Organization Change

In the business world, some currently-used management concepts and methods such as divisionalized organization structures, financial control systems, product management, and incentive compensation were actually invented a half century ago by Alfred Sloan, a former President and Chairman of General Motors, who transformed a hodgepodge of business units into the model of a modern business organization[18].

---

[18] Alfred P. Sloan, *My Years with General Motors,* Garden City, N.Y., Doubleday, 1964.

Sloan organized General Motors into five different automobile divisions —Chevrolet, Buick, Oldsmobile, Cadillac, and a division for special parts used by all the divisions—each producing cars in a different price range. Sloan's management strategy and talent boosted GM's market share from 12.7% to 47.5% between 1921 and 1940, while its competitor Ford's share fell from 55.7% to 18.9% in the same time period.

In the modern management science, Sloan's divisions are called the strategic business units of an organization. Many large companies around the globe have adopted Sloan's management approach, building their organizations into the multidivisional hierarchical structure, giving each unit the freedom, authority, and independence to compete for more businesses.

The value chain is another important concept in the modern business world, which is initiated and promoted by Michael Porter, a professor at Harvard Business School[19]. According to the value chain approach, a corporation is viewed as a sequence of systematically divided and discrete activities, each adding value to the whole organization. The sequence or chain includes separate and distinct stages of businesses, such as research and development, market survey, product design, engineering, manufacturing, marketing, sales, distribution, maintenance, and customer service. For management, the value chain is a basic tool for diagnosing competitive advantage and discovering ways to reduce operation costs and to create new values and profits.

Both of these concepts about organizational structure, namely the hierarchical structure of multiple strategic business units and the value chain structure, are about to change. Advanced information technology, a rapidly changing business environment, increasingly intensified global competition, and exploding business opportunities in global markets require American corporations to shift from bureaucracies to networks and from the value chain to an integrated system.

In today's dynamic business world, the conventional hierarchical structure is not flexible enough to fully utilize corporations' capabilities, particularly the intellectual property and special intangible assets of information, ideas, and knowledge. Less restrictive, more fluid, and networked organizational structures are needed for effective decision making in all the strategic business units and across the entire value chain. "The Strategic Business Units (SBUs) of the Alfred P. Sloan era have given way to the creation and effective utilization of Strategic Business Networks (SBNs)[20]."

---

[19] Michael Porter, *Competitive Advantage: Creating and Sustaining Superior Performance,* The Free Press, 1985.
[20] Debra M. Amidon, *Innovation Strategy for the Knowledge Economy, The Ken Awakening,* Butterworth-Heinemann, 1997.

By definition, strategic business networks include not only business units inside the corporation, but also outside partners, suppliers, customers and occasionally competitors. The value chain is also shifting to an integrated innovation value system[21], in which every activity of the corporation is interdependent, though not necessarily in the sequence order. In other words, they are both influencing and influenced by other preceding and following activities in the value chain. A corporation's value is created not only by every distinctive activity, but also through integrating and networking all activities. Collaborations in the networked environment will lead to the creation of new ideas, new knowledge, and ultimate innovation by sharing information, ideas, knowledge, and skills.

Innovative information technologies have also provided American corporations with the means and methods to shift toward a virtual and networking organizational structure. The technology infrastructure, including computers and telecommunications networks, as well as the Internet, has been the backbone that supports all the collaborative activities both inside and outside the organization.

Information technologies now allow for real time interaction among all the SBUs in the networked environment. Information and knowledge gathered in the entire processes of research and development, new product design, engineering, manufacturing, marketing and consumers' acceptance of new products can all be stored in a large database and shared simultaneously by everyone in the enterprise-wide computer network. Collaboration of business activities begins to blur the borderlines along the entire value chain, creating new value and moving the corporation's structure toward a full integration.

This flexible organizational structure provides workers with the freedom to be more creative and productive. People are increasingly working remotely, connected by computers and communication devices. Researchers and workers scattered in different locations can be brought together for a specific project and then quickly moved on to another team that needs a different mix of skills and knowledge. Top managers are able to gather real time information about activity on the factory floor and solve problems without delay. Information technology shortens the communication path from the top to the bottom and vice versa by eliminating many middle management layers. Therefore information technology provides an effective means for organizations to change the conventional hierarchical structure into a flat, agile, networked, and integrated management system with speed and re-

---

[21] Debra M. Amidon, *Innovation Strategy for the Knowledge Economy, The Ken Awakening,* Butterworth-Heinemann, 1997.

sponsiveness; it allows for a more effective and efficient organization that actively capitalizes on the exploding business opportunities at home and abroad.

## • Technology Innovation Changes the Structure of the U.S. Economy

In general, nationwide economic growth depends on the changing structure of the economy, with a shift away from the sectors and industries with lower growth potential into ones with a faster growth pace and higher productivity. This is usually brought about by continuous technology innovations.

In a traditional society, agriculture was the dominating sector; more than 80% of the labor force had to work in fields to produce grains and raise animals to feed its population. Thanks to the industrial revolutions over the past one and a half centuries, only 6.6 million people or merely 11% of the U.S. labor force were needed in the agriculture sector in 1948, while it contributed $24 billion dollars to U.S. nominal GDP, accounting for 8.9%. Fifty years later, there were 3.3 million people working in this sector, accounting for 2.5% of the U.S. labor force, and the agriculture output reached $136 billion dollars (or 1.4% of nominal GDP) in 2000. Clearly the agriculture sector has substantially reduced its role in the national economy in terms of its small GDP and employment shares, while this sector's productivity has increased significantly.

Innovative technologies contribute to the increasing productivity of U.S. agriculture. With widely applied agro-engineering, agrochemical and biotech techniques, crop management, and yield information system and others, fewer agriculture workers have produced adequate high-quality food and agricultural products not only to meet the nutritional needs of the American consumers but also to export to the rest of the world, and at the same time to maintain a quality environment and natural resource base.

Similar but less pronounced than the agricultural situation is what has happened in the manufacturing sector. In 1948, there were 16 million Americans working in factories, accounting for 27% of U.S. workers, with the resulting output contributing nearly 28% of U.S. nominal GDP. In 2000 the percentage of manufacturing workers were reduced to only 14%, and the manufacturing sector's GDP share declined to 16%. The manufacturing output reached $587 billion in 1980 and $1.567 trillion in 2000, representing a 167% increase in twenty years. The number of manufacturing workers, however, declined from 20.2 million to 18.5 million, an 8% drop. As new ideas, new information and knowledge substitute for human efforts and material bulks through innovative technologies, manufacturers have increased their output with fewer workers.

There has recently been a spectacular increase in the services sector in both employment and outputs. American consumers steadily increase their spending on services such as health care, education, entertainment and recreation, travel, hotels, financial services, and insurance, as well as legal, personal and social services. In response to the changing consumer preferences, the services-producing sector has accelerated, with its GDP share increasing from 45% in 1948 to 66% in 2000. About 25 million Americans worked in the services-producing sector in 1948. That number grew to 85 million in 2000, increasing 3.4 times. The services-producing sector includes not only the conventional service industries but also many emerging information-intensive industries, such as wireless communication, e-commerce and interactive services, to meet customers' surging demand for information, news, data, educational needs, music, movie, games and other entertainment.

Recognizing the increasingly vital role of information technology in economic activities and the induced structure shift of the economy, the U.S. Commerce Department has introduced a new national measurement system, known as the North American Industry Classification System (NAICS), to replace the Standard Industrial Classification (SIC) system that existed for sixty years. The new system is in the process of being adopted in the United States, Canada, and Mexico. For the first time, the information sector is identified as a key component in the national economy, along with the sectors of agriculture, mining, utilities, construction, and manufacturing. Professional, scientific, and technical services are also created as major sectors in the new national measurement system. The motivation for those changes in the national economic measurement is clearly stated: "the new system of measurement is organized the way the economy is organized, recognizing the role of new technology and the services that define people's daily lives[22]."

We will keep in mind the above-discussed six major effects of innovative information technologies on the U.S. economy when we move into the next section of this book and review economic transformation in terms of historical perspectives. We believe that based on those significant and profound effects on the economy and society, today's information technology revolution will hold a status similar to that of great industrial revolutions in the history of human civilization.

---

[22] Comments from Kenneth Prewitt, the director of U.S. Census Bureau 1999.

## 1-2   Historical Perspectives on Economic Transformation

Economic transformation is not new; it has been a common and recurrent phenomenon throughout the history of economic and social development. The economic lives of human beings started with the earliest stage of collection economy (hunting and fishing) and then transformed into the stages of cultural nomadic economy, village economy, town economy, and eventually entered the modern metropolitan economy. The movement from one stage to the next represents a great transformation that took hundreds of years to complete. Since the First Industrial Revolution in the last two decades of the eighteenth century, economic transformation has sped up dramatically.

In this section we provide a brief view of American ideology that drives economic transformation, and two kinds of historical perspectives that show ideology and technology working together to shape the landscape of the U.S. economy. Section 1-2-2 presents a brief review on the evolving capitalism system, and the current state of U.S. capitalism. In section 1-2-3, the discussion is on the theory of stages of economic growth, with an emphasis on the crucial role of industrial revolutions and leading sectors in the historical economic transformations. We believe that yesterday's experiences will shed great insights on today's economic transformation, and today's exercises will help to guide the journey in the uncharted sea for tomorrow.

## 1-2-1   American Ideology Promotes Economic Transformation

The economic transformation and evolving capitalism in the United States are based upon the development of such profound ideas and concepts as individualism, democracy, equity and property rights. Any ideology is a collection of ideas or principles that address five basic issues: the individual human being and his/her rights and place in society, the means by which individual rights are to be guaranteed, the mechanism for controlling resources, products and services, the role of government, and finally the organization of science and knowledge[23].

The changing ideology has driven a seven-stage evolution of American capitalism from petty capitalism to security capitalism, which we will review

---

[23] Robert Peterson, Gerald Albaum, and George Kozmetsky, *Modern American Capitalism, Understanding Public Attitudes and Perceptions*, Quorum Books, 1990.

in the next section. The original individualism views a society as no more than the sum of its individuals with equity and property rights. The uses of property and resources for production and consumption are conducted in an open marketplace through competition to satisfy individual desires. The role of government is to respond to crises rather than to engage in planning. Scientists and experts are highly specialized and work well as a part of the society while the society as a whole will take care of itself. Those ideas, however, have undergone, and continue to undergo, radical transformation, affected by economic, political, and ethical values of the American society.

The book *Modern American Capitalism*[24] has described those radical changes in American ideology. Now, it is acknowledged that individualism is augmented and replaced by communitarianism, where the community is more than just the sum of its individuals. Cooperation, the basic phenomenon distinguishing the human species from subhuman species, is recognized as an underpinning factor of any society and its institutions such as marriage, family, school, business, and government. The property right is also augmented as rights of membership in the community known as the United States, which include not only property rights, but also the right to survive, to enjoy income, health care, education, and other rights.

The mechanism of controlling usage of resources and property is changed from unfettered competition to the competitive market with satisfaction of individual desires as well as community needs. Government is becoming an arbiter of community needs, playing the role of coordinating, priority setting, planning, and decision-making regarding the trade-offs confronting society. Finally, the ideology of specialization and fragmentation has given way to the ideology of holism, which is derived from the notion that nature tends to group units of things into a great integrated whole, and the whole system is itself as important as its parts.

U.S. society champions the individual hero and is tolerant of individual failure; it promotes the entrepreneurial spirit and risk-taking behavior. U.S. society strives to give everyone the freedom of creativity, the root of all inventions and innovations, which have engendered industrial revolutions and the evolution of capitalism. Those individuals with brilliant ideas, special intelligence, and managerial skills continuously march toward the next scientific and technological frontier. Their endeavors have raised productivity, efficiency, and quality of products and services. Consequently, those individuals have been highly rewarded spiritually and economically, as society believes that everyone stands to benefit in the long run from the natural

---

[24] Robert Peterson, Gerald Albaum, and George Kozmetsky, *Modern American Capitalism, Understanding Public Attitudes and Perceptions*, Quorum Books, 1990.

meritocracy of brains and talents. That belief has made individuals highly motivated and integrated in the American capitalism system.

America's ideology of democracy promotes equal opportunity and fairness with the belief that everyone should have access to the capitalist system for their livelihood, education, technological gain, innovation, and security. The competitive market works as a powerful glue to integrate all players— large and small companies, great and petty capitalists, producers and customers, employers and employees, large institutional investors and small individual investors—within the capitalist system. This system provides incentive and reward to encourage economic activity and wealth generation; it also sets up explicit and implicit rules via regulations and market principles to guide economic activity and to guarantee community needs and rights of membership for its citizens.

The changing ideas and concepts of America's ideology are a kind of invisible asset, bearing great importance to the economic development. As the author of the book *The Mystery of Capital* indicates, "one of the greatest challenges to the human mind is to comprehend and to gain access to those things we know exist but cannot see. Not everything that is real and useful is tangible and visible[25]." The United States has successfully converted its invisible and intangible ideology assets into an institutional framework of American capitalism, an underlying and complex construct of society.

This framework includes private property rights and a legal system, industrial system, financial system, labor market, education and training institutes, uncoordinated and competitive markets, families and communities. The book *Modern American Capitalism* has examined various definitions of capitalism. The most recent formal definitions identify capitalism as being not only an economic system, but also a political and social system, with four key dimensions of economic, political, social, and technological attributes.

It is important to recognize that an economic system and its transformation do not exist in a vacuum. Rather, the whole capitalist system works as an infrastructure to support and influence economic transformations. For instance, American capitalism promotes the deregulated financial market, which allows freer capital flow and encourages risk-taking and profit-maximizing behaviors. Capital is the lifeblood of the economic system; it is the force that raises productivity of labor and creates the wealth of the nation; it is the cornerstone of economic growth for the rising standard of living of the majority of the population.

---

[25] Hernando de Soto, *The Mystery of Capital: Why Capitalism Triumphs in the West and Fails Everywhere Else,* Basic Books, 2000.

A major function of the capitalist system is to create capital and convert both tangible and intangible assets into capital for wealth generation and economic advance. The private property rights and legal system encourage individuals and corporations to pursue profits and accumulate assets. In the American capitalist system, both tangible and intangible assets are recognized formally. They can readily be traded and used as collateral for credit, a loan, or shares of investment. Savings and assets as well as labor can easily convert into capital to provide fresh lifeblood to the financial system and industrial system for creating profit and wealth. *The Mystery of Capital* has described this ability of Western countries to generate capital as a kind of mystery. The conversion process or the mechanism required to transform savings and assets into productive capital for generating wealth does not exist in the Third World and former communist nations. That is the reason why capitalism triumphs in the West and fails everywhere else, as the author has claimed.

The absence of this process in the poorer regions of the world–where two-thirds of humanity lives–is not the consequence of some Western monopolistic conspiracy. It is rather that Westerners take this mechanism so completely for granted that they have lost all awareness of its existence. Although it is huge, nobody sees it, including the Americans, Europeans, and Japanese who own all their wealth to their ability to use it. It is an implicit legal infrastructure hidden deep within their property systems–of which ownership is but the tip of the iceberg. The rest of the iceberg is an intricate man-made process that can transform assets and labor into capital. This process was not created from a blue-print and is not described in a glossy brochure. Its origins are obscure and its significance buried in the economic subconscious of Western capitalist nations.

In our opinion, it is the institutional framework of capitalism that serves as an infrastructure supporting capital flow, profit maximization, savings and assets conversion, capital generation, and wealth accumulation. This framework of successful capitalism has integrated everyone, rich and poor, into the economic system, releasing aspirations and energies of common people, turning the invisible potential of individual creativity and asset into capital for economic growth and social prosperity. The so-called "mystery of capital" or "the hidden and forgotten process" of Western capitalism gives an example to illustrate the great complexity of capitalism, which can be easily misunderstood as an economic system alone, ignoring the underpinning infrastructure of capitalism in general, and the political system and moral-cultural system in particular.

In the present global wave of modernization, the Third World and former communist nations have adopted many capitalist methods and economic policies, such as market orientation, privatization of sectors and industries, introduction of stock markets, elimination of trade barriers, and the like. These nations have failed to reach their economic goals and are plagued with corruption, financial crises, economic recession and high unemployment. Many people are wondering why capitalism failed to bring prosperity to the Third World as it has done for the advanced Western nations.

We believe that in order to take full economic advantage of capitalism, nations need to build the underpinning infrastructure, namely the economic system along with the political system, and moral-cultural system. It is necessary to turn that "economic subconscious of Western capitalist nations" into a consciousness of understanding capitalism as a complex and integrated system that transforms radically over time. As the authors of *Modern American Capitalism* clearly indicate, American capitalism works

> ....as "a bridge of ideas which a community uses to get values to the real world[26]." In this context, values will simultaneously involve economic, political, and cultural issues and include such concepts as democracy, individualism, equity, and property rights....
>
> When certain attitudes, habits, beliefs, and aspirations do not exist, economic development is not likely to occur. Yet, even when societies lack resources, strong moral-cultural traditions may facilitate economic development. At the same time, however, the economic system may impose certain demands on the moral-cultural system. Beliefs, morals, customs, and so forth may need to be changed if development is to occur[27].

American ideology also encourages the expeditious responses of U.S. society to a changing internal and external environment, which makes American capitalism the most dynamic system in the world. Both economic success and crisis occur frequently in the United States. Some American companies went from being virtually unknown to making billion dollar profits and compensating their executives in hundreds of millions of dollars a year to filing for bankruptcy. American investors lost trillions of dollars in the stock market crashes in 1929, 1987, 1998, 2000, 2001, and 2002.

---

[26] George C. Lodge, "The Large Corporation and the New American Ideology," in *Corporations and the Common Good*, ed. Robert B. Dickie and Leroy S. Rouner, 1986.
[27] Robert Peterson, Gerald Albaum, and George Kozmetsky, *Modern American Capitalism, Understanding Public Attitudes and Perceptions*, Quorum Books, 1990.

Even though economic and political crises repeatedly visit the United States, the American capitalist system continues to survive and prosper through adjusting itself to the changing environment. New laws and regulations are made to serve the social and economic needs of the majority of the population; market rules and principles are adjusted to the changing reality; corporations' behaviors are judged not only by profitability and efficiency, but also by responsibility and accountability to community and society; bad elements of corporate management are punished remorselessly by the market and laws, and removed from the system quickly; public attitudes toward capitalism are shifting more positively; ideas, concepts, and beliefs are transformed accordingly.

The three systems of American capitalism (economic, political, and social) work together and find solutions to any crises and problems on its way forward. That might be the major reason why the U.S. economy has successfully transformed along with the changing American ideology and the underlying infrastructure of capitalism in the United States.

## 1-2-2  Evolving American Capitalism

In business history there are seven stages of capitalism[28]— petty, mercantile, industrial, mature industrial, financial, national, and security capitalism, in which the degree of specialization and control of capital is the foremost changing pattern of businesses. In our opinion, modern American capitalism has moved into a new stage, *"institutional capitalism,"* as a result of responding to the changing reality at home and abroad. In this section we shall briefly review the first six stages of evolving capitalism and explore in more detail the seventh stage, security capitalism, and the new stage, institutional capitalism.

## • Earlier Stages of Capitalism

European immigrants, upon settling in America, opened small businesses and created the first instances of American petty capitalism. The petty capitalists in these town economies were small master handicraftsmen—such as shoemakers, tailors, bakers, and blacksmiths—and storekeepers, retailers, or traveling merchants. Petty capitalists have survived and prospered through

---

[28] Norman S. B. Gras, *Business History of the United States, About 1650 to 1950s*, Edwards Brothers, Inc., 1967.

all the successive stages of capitalism and they still play an important role in the modern economy as the number of small business operations increases significantly year to year.

Mercantile capitalism predominated in the economic affairs of the "Old World" from about 1250 to 1750. Sedentary merchants were the main figures in industrial towns, and they were the first capitalists to exercise control over their contemporaries through the manipulation of capital goods and a managerial system. The First Industrial Revolution created new leading sectors such as machinery-manufactured cotton textile and coke-manufactured iron. By the end of this period, merchant capitalists were giving way to the industrial specialists in iron manufacture, river steam boating, real-estate business and wholesaling. Those specialists had become industrial capitalists in the era of industrial capitalism (1815-1866).

By 1830, the spread of machine and factory systems allowed large-scale private capitalist enterprises to penetrate society quickly. Landless laborers in the countryside flocked to factories for a better life, becoming members of what Karl Marx called the "proletarian" class. During this stage of capitalism, Marx predicted that the capitalist system would unavoidably collapse by 1900. He saw capital as the means of production that would increasingly concentrate ownership in fewer and more powerful hands, leaving the workers increasingly impoverished. Resulting class conflict was inevitable and would lead to a revolution by proletarians who "had nothing to lose but their chains."

As a matter of fact, what occurred is the dramatic reverse of Marx's predictions. Through technology innovations and industrial revolutions, the capitalist system had found a way to dodge the seemingly unavoidable class war between capitalists and laborers into a next stage of capitalism evolution.

## • Stage of Mature Industrial / Financial Capitalism

When specialized business firms found it increasing difficult to make money, industrial capitalists had to change their methods of doing business by diversifying products, integrating functions, such as commodity production, manufacture, transportation, storage, and marketing. They became capitalists in the stage of mature industrial capitalism (1866-1933).

For purposes of increasing efficiency, stability and economy of scale, industrial capitalists organized large business units and many factories by setting up new plants, buying out a competitor, or merging with a competitor.

For instance, the Westinghouse Electric Company had about forty plants, while Woolworth had about 2,000 stores, scattered over the country during the era of mature industrial capitalism. By merging in 1919 with the Standard Oil Company, the Humble Oil & Refining Company of Texas was created, gaining unlimited financial support, a dependable market, and expertise in technology and management[29]. During this mature industrial stage, American conglomerates formed and began to play an important role in the U.S. economy.

Intensified competition had made the well-managed firms succeed and caused poorly managed ones to fail. Even though oligopolistic giants were arising in the industries of iron and steel, oil, and merchandising, many petty capitalistic firms and a few specialized industrial capitalistic companies survived. Big business was becoming a matter of widespread ownership and severe competition to benefit consumers and there seemed less opposition to its existence on the part of the public.

More importantly, productivity began to rise at a rate of 3.5-4.0% compounded annually or doubling every eighteen years in all advanced countries[30]. This unprecedented productivity expansion has increased workers' wages and fringe benefits, resulting in a rise in both standard of living and quality of life for the laboring class.

> ....As a result, Marx's "proletarian" became a "bourgeois." The blue-collar worker in manufacturing industry, the "proletarian" rather than the "capitalist," became the true beneficiary of capitalism and Industrial Revolution. This explains the total failure of Marxism in the highly developed countries....[31].

From 1893-1933, financial capitalism developed and co-existed with mature industrial capitalism. Financial capitalists were the businessmen who received capital from a wide variety of sources and put this capital out in loan and investment. Financial capitalists in the U.S. operated through a range of institutions, such as commercial banks, financial corporations, saving banks, investment bankers, stockbrokers, trust companies, and investment trusts. Those institutions possessed much of the capital that flowed into businesses and influenced or actually controlled the businesses. Under this system, capital and credit were provided and directed into certain economic channels by

---

[29] Norman S. B. Gras, *Business History of the United States, About 1650 to 1950s*, Edwards Brothers, Inc., 1967.

[30] Peter F. Drucker, *Post-Capital Society*, Harper Business, Harper Collins Publishers, 1993.

[31] Ibid.

financial capitalists. Investment bankers participated in the initial public of-fering and underwriting of securities as financial agents for the companies whose securities had been issued.

Financial capitalism encouraged people to save, to invest, and to speculate. It was also related to disastrous results of over-production and over-speculation. Even so, it made a great contribution to wide-spread ownership of securities. Farmers, workers, and others members of U.S. society were becoming the owners of many private businesses as long as they held the company's securities. The crisis of 1929-1933, however, ended the era of financial capitalism with a horrifying stock market crash that was followed by a two-year long decline of the securities and commodities markets.

## • Stage of National Capitalism

National capitalism supplanted the financial capitalism in the early 1930s as a result of the stock market debacle and the resulting economic depression. There was a great danger that the heavy unemployment and private debt, along with the increasing frustration of the laboring, farming, and profes-sional classes, might lead to a revolution resulting in a communistic or social-ist system.

The Roosevelt administration responded to those crises with the New Deal policies of national capitalism to revive the petty capitalists, to help farmers with a high parity-price system, to increase government spending, to create more public works jobs, to set up the minimum wage law of 75 cents an hour, to provide a national insurance plan for elderly and unemployed, and to give the Federal Reserve Board the duty of controlling credit so that businesspeople would be encouraged to invest.

The main purpose of the national capitalist system was to use the na-tional government's power to command capital and credit so as to control private business and keep it in private hands. Private business provided eco-nomic opportunity and liberty for Americans, but was economically insecure under the control of financial capitalists, as was demonstrated by the Great Economic Depression and stock market crash. The government stepped in to restore economic security for Americans, perhaps at the expense of eco-nomic opportunity and liberty.

As the core nature of American capitalism, namely ownership and busi-ness administration or management, remained intact under the national capi-talistic system, America survived the Great Depression without introducing socialism. From the ideological point of view, Americans had proved their determination to believe in and uphold individualism and democracy against fascism, communism, and socialism by transforming their economic, political, and social systems into national capitalism.

As it greatly restricted technology innovations and hampered business initiatives by over-regulations, national capitalism could not allow the situation of government or political administrators in control of business to stay permanently. Political control of private businesses was not consistent with the American genius of freedom of action and the spirit of individual free enterprise. Regulations became so overwhelming and bureaucratic that people prayed for relief. When the economic depression finally ended at the time of the Korean War, the American people were ready to transform their economy and society into the stage of security capitalism (1953-present).

## • Stage of Security Capitalism

In 1953 President Dwight Eisenhower reversed national policies and allowed businesses more freedom to make their own decisions. Private corporations and capitalists underwent fundamental changes in their policies of blindly following the path of maximum profits. They recognized that a public with adequate income was a good market for all kinds of products and services. This fostered a concern for the welfare of U.S. citizens. Instead of government leading the way for economic security, private industries and corporations became a force that brought about economic security for ordinary Americans.

Security capitalism created numerous institutions under the free enterprise system for providing economic security to citizens of all classes. These institutions are collectively influential in social and economic activities, and they have institutionalized America's economic security. Security provisions and institutions include insurance companies, savings banks, investment trusts, mutual funds, pension systems and employee benefits, trade union funds, the law of minimum wage, social security and old age and survivors insurance, and others. Among these institutions there are three—life insurance, mutual funds, and pension funds—that form an interconnected safety net to provide supporting columns to the U.S. economy and society. We shall discuss the three in order.

## (1) Life Insurance

Ordinary people can purchase many insurance policies for life, home, fire, wind, flood, theft, accident, liability, health, disability, and unemployment: anything with value can be insured to help people feel secure economically.

The biggest item on this list is life insurance, which provides a family with replacement of both current and anticipated future income, should an income provider die.

Life insurance reserves represent the required amount to be carried as a liability in the financial statement of an insurer to provide for future commitments under outstanding policies. They are a part of the total financial assets held by U.S. households and nonprofit organizations. For the past fifty-five years, the life insurance reserve has increased twenty fold, from $39.6 billion in 1945, to $130.7 billion in 1970, $220.6 billion in 1980, $391.7 billion in 1990 and $823.5 billion in 2000[32] (Figure 1-3).

For life insurance companies, the reserve is a part of their liabilities; their total financial assets have been much greater than the reserve. For the time period of 1945-2000, total financial assets held by U.S. life insurance companies increased seventy-one fold, from $43.9 billion in 1945 to $200.9 billion in 1970, $464.2 billion in 1980, $1.351 trillion in 1990, and $3.134 trillion in 2000. Total financial assets of other kinds of insurance companies also increased dramatically, from $6.3 billion in 1945 to $869.9 billion in 2000. The total financial assets of all U.S. insurance companies reached 4.003 trillion, or 40.2% of U.S. nominal GDP of year 2000 ($9.963 trillion). With such weight, insurance companies have become a major institutional investor in the domestic and international financial markets.

## (2) Mutual Funds

Mutual funds are booming in the United States. With professional management and diversification of investment, mutual funds are able to minimize risk and provide a regular system of savings for millions of Americans who have accumulated cash and want to share in the profits of capitalist enterprises. Through their purchases of mutual fund shares, individuals with relatively small savings, little knowledge of the stock market, and little time to follow the transactions of trade have become investors in stock markets, and have profited handsomely over the years.

The market value of mutual fund shares has increased spectacularly. In 1945, the market value of all the U.S. mutual fund shares was about $1.2 billion; it rose to $40.4 billion in 1970, $45.6 billion in 1980, $456.6 billion in 1990, $3.106 trillion in 1999, and $3.026 trillion by the end of 2000[33].

---

[32] *Flow of Funds Accounts of the United States*, Board of Governors of the Federal Reserve System, Washington DC 20551, March 9, 2001.
[33] Ibid.

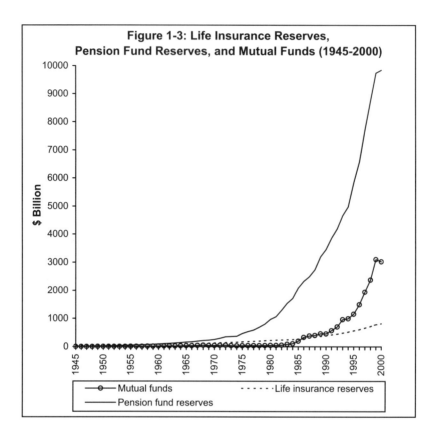

Figure 1-3 displays the growth path of mutual funds, which was about 30.4% of U.S. nominal GDP in 2000. Therefore, the mutual fund industry has become a major institutional investor in the financial market, next to the insurance industry, compared with life insurance companies' total financial assets but not their reserves.

## (3) Pension Funds

Pension funds have become the largest holder of financial assets in the United States, dwarfing the insurance industry and the mutual fund industry combined. Pension fund reserves represent the value of tangible and financial assets held by pension funds, they are the largest component of financial assets held by U.S. households and nonprofit organizations.

Rapid growth of private pension funds and state and local government employee retirement funds has contributed to growth of the pension funds reserves. The U.S. pension funds reserve was about $12.3 billion in 1945, and it increased to $253.8 billion in 1970, $970.4 billion in 1980, $3.460 trillion in 1990, $9.748 trillion in 1999, and $9.847 trillion by the end of the year 2000 (Figure 1-3).

Pension funds are employees' saving plans that allow both employers and employees to put a portion of employees' wages into a special account. This money accumulates until the employee retires and then provides income. Pension funds have become the most important means for today's working people to secure income for their retirement years, and as life expectancy continues to increase, most people can expect to outlive their working lives by many years.

The number of pension plans in the United States has grown significantly, increasing from 442,998 in 1978 to 720,041 in 1997[34]. All pension plans are divided into two categories, defined benefit plans (DB) and defined contribution plans (DC).

A defined benefit plan (DB) is a retirement plan provided by an employer; it specifies how much money will be paid at retirement. An actuary based on investment return, withdrawals from the plan, and other related factors determines the employer's contribution to the plan. A good DB plan typically offers the participant a pension that is comparable to his/her salary prior to retirement and adjusted to meet inflation until death. The plan sponsor, namely the employer, bears financial risks associated with a DB plan investment. Workers also bear some economic risks. When they change jobs or are temporarily unemployed, they will end up with reduced pension benefits. The limited portability of DB plans is a considerable hindrance to labor market flexibility. That may explain the largely declining number of defined benefit plans, from 128,407 in 1978 to 59,499 by 1997.

A defined contribution plan (DC) is a retirement plan provided by an employer; it specifies how much money is contributed with each paycheck. While the percentage of contribution is defined, how much money will be paid at retirement is uncertain due to many other factors. Common versions of defined contribution plans include 401(k), 403(b), and 457 plans. These plans are offered by companies, some nonprofit organizations, public schools,

---

[34] Private Pension Plan Bulletin, Abstract of 1997, Form 5500, Annual Reports, Number 10, Winter 2001, U.S. Department of Labor, Pension and Welfare Benefits Administration, Office of Policy and Research.

some hospitals, and tax-exempt entities, such as states, counties and cities, to allow employees to invest a portion of their pretax wage in a retirement account. The amounts are set aside and the investment earnings grow tax-deferred until withdrawn.

DC pension plans are easily transferable when participants change jobs. It is the participants who bear the risks of inadequate contributions to the plan, a drop in the value of the fund due to falls in asset prices, the risks of low interest rates and high inflation, and other risks. The number of DC pension plans increased rapidly, from 314,591 in 1978 to 660,542 by 1997, reflecting a shift from defined benefit plans toward defined contribution plans. It is a difficult task, however, to evaluate a pension plan as it typically takes more than fifty years to complete a participant's cycle.

## Increasing Power of the Three

On the balance sheet of U.S. households and nonprofit organizations, the pension fund reserve is the largest financial asset, followed by corporate equities, and mutual fund shares. Figure 1-4 presents the three components of financial assets held by households and nonprofit organizations in terms of the percentage of their total financial assets, and Figure 1-5 denotes the same components in terms of the percentage of nominal U.S. GDP.

In 1945, of the total financial assets held by households and nonprofit organizations, life insurance reserves accounted for 7.0%, pension funds reserves accounted for 2.2%, and mutual funds accounted for merely 0.2%. By the end of 2000, pension funds reserves rose to 29.2%, and mutual funds rose to 9.0%, while file insurance reserves decreased to 2.4%. In terms of the percentage of GDP, pension funds reserves increased from 5.5% in 1945 to 104.8% in 1999, the all time high, and slid to 98.84% in 2000, due to the severe drop in the stock market. Similarly, mutual funds' percentage of GDP rose from 0.5% in 1945 to 33.4% in 1999, and dropped to 30.4% in 2000. In the same time period, however, the percentage of GDP for life insurance reserves declined from 17.8% in 1945 to 6.3% in 1985, the lowest percentage, and climbed back to 8.3% by the end of 2000.

During the nineteenth century, the biggest financial need of the average American workers was for life insurance to protect their families in the event of their unexpected death. That was still the case until the end of the 1950s, as shown by the large percentage of GDP share and the large percentage

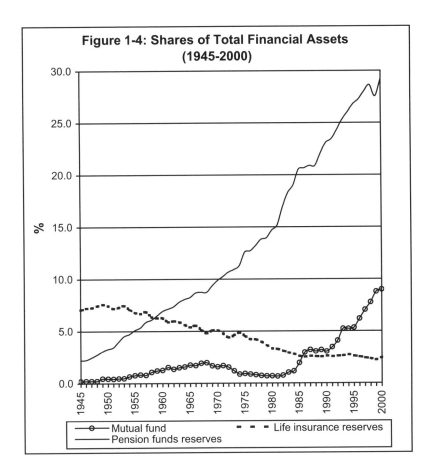

Figure 1-4: Shares of Total Financial Assets (1945-2000)

of the total financial assets of households in life insurance. Since 1960, pension funds reserves have exceeded the life insurance reserves; mutual fund shares have surpassed life insurance reserves since 1986.

Pension funds and mutual funds have become the major source of America's financial security. However, the financial power of life insurance companies should not be underestimated by the slow growth of life insurance reserves. Insurance premiums paid by millions of Americans year after year allow insurance companies to make a variety of investments and accumulate tremendous assets. The total financial assets of all U.S. insurance companies reached 4.003 trillion in 2000, or 40.2% of U.S. nominal GDP of the year.

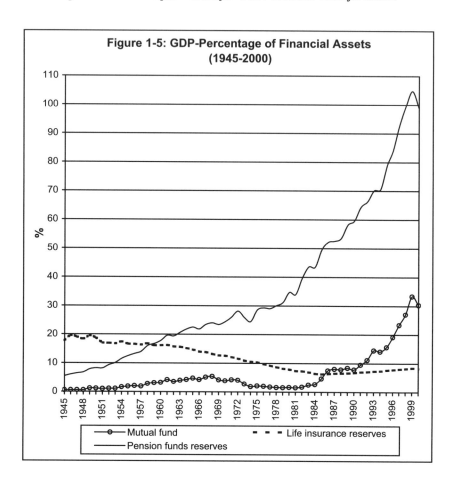

Figure 1-5: GDP-Percentage of Financial Assets (1945-2000)

Among the 75.9 million private wage and salary workers in 1978, there were 42 million workers covered by defined benefit and supplemental pension plans. In 1997, among 106.9 million workers, there were about 68.3 million workers in the private sector who held pension funds plans; the participation rate was 63.8%. Millions of American workers have been the collective owners of pension funds with a trillion dollars of financial assets.

Many financial analysts, portfolio managers, and actuaries are hired to manage pension funds. Even though they are paid high salaries, they are not the owners of pension plans. The true owners of pension funds are the future pensioners. By any conventional definition of capitalism, those millions of workers and future pensioners and the few well-paid pension funds managers are not capitalists at all, but there is a huge amount of capital belonging to them and controlled by them. Peter Drucker describes this peculiar and paradoxical phenomenon as "capitalism without capitalists[35]," and his description may well be applied to such institutional investors as insurance companies, mutual funds and pension funds.

In the current state of American capitalism, the original purpose of providing security for average American workers has been served through purchasing insurance policies and mutual fund shares and by participating in pension plans. These methods, however, far from achieve the goal of a financially secure retirement for all Americans.

Employment-based pensions currently account for a small share of the retirement income received by the majority of Americans. About 80% of elderly Americans rely on Social Security for most of their retirement income, and 40% of the lowest-income Americans depend on Social Security almost exclusively[36]. As a matter of fact, Social Security replaces just one-half of a person's pre-retirement income at the level of $15,000 and only less than 25% of a person's pre-retirement income at the level of $68,400.

Increasing life expectancy and the accelerating costs of long-term care demand a much greater retirement income than what Social Security can provide. It has become increasingly important to encourage working Americans to save and to participate in pension plans in order to be able to count on a secure retirement. Estimated recently, of the 35 million people employed in small companies, 26 million do not have access to retirement plans at work. If those small companies were to offer pension plans and would convince their employees to participate, it is foreseeable that U.S. pension funds will have more room to grow in the future.

## • A New Stage of Institutional Capitalism

It is clear that institutional investors, such as insurance companies, mutual funds, and pension funds, have done what the financial capitalists did in the time period of 1893-1933 to provide, control, and distribute capital in the U.S. economic system. These institutions do not merely provide tools for savings and a secure retirement life; they have become powerful machines them-

---

[35] Peter F. Drucker, *Post-Capital Society*, Harper Business, Harper Collins Publishers, 1993.
[36] Final Report on the National Summit on Retirement Savings, U.S. Department of Labor, June 4-5, 1998.

selves that accumulate capital and generate economic wealth. Never before in U.S. business history have such huge financial assets been concentrated in the hands of a few capitalists as today's institutional investors have enjoyed. We believe that these non-capitalist institutional investors have just opened a new era of "institutional capitalism" for modern American capitalism.

In an earlier stage of capitalism, the process of capital accumulation was confined to small, narrow group of capitalists in society. In this stage of institutional capitalism, this process has spread into almost all groups of society. Millions of workers in the private sector as well as in federal, state, and local governments are involved in capital accumulation and enjoy capital gains via their pension funds and other instruments provided by institutional investors.The majority of Americans depend on a capitalist means of generating wealth to support their standard of living in the present and to secure comfortable lives as retirees. Therefore the safety and health of pension funds and other institutional investments become extremely important.

In the last fifty years, Congress has passed several laws that offer tax benefits and protect private pensions. The Revenue Acts of 1921 and 1926 allow employers to deduct pension contributions from corporate income, and allow for the income of that pension fund's portfolio to accumulate tax-free. To qualify for such favorable tax treatment, pension plans have to meet certain minimum employee coverage and employer contribution requirements.

The Welfare and Pension Plans Disclosure Act in 1959 gave the Department of Labor the power to regulate employee benefits plans to prevent the mismanagement and abuse of plan funds. Congress passed the Employee Retirement Income Security Act in 1974, which divided the responsibilities of the administration of pension plans among three federal government agents, the Labor Department, the Internal Revenue Service of the Department of the Treasury, and the Pension Benefit Guaranty Corporation. The goal of these regulations is to protect the interests of participants and their beneficiaries in employee benefit plans. As a result, pension funds have been institutionalized, monitored, and protected by the federal government. Still, the safety and health of pension funds are not guaranteed and many challenges lie ahead. Since pension funds have only recently emerged as a dominant force in the financial market, and many factors are still not clearly understood.

In the stage of institutional capitalism, the dividing line of capitalist and laboring classes has become blurred. Collectively, millions of workers and employees have become the actual owners of institutional investments that hold enormous pools of money. Dwarfing any capitalists previously in history, institutional investors have become the major source of the capital supporting the U.S. economic system. These pools of capital, however, come from workers' and employees' delayed earnings, and investment gains. Individually, the owners of institutional investments belong to the laboring class and work for salaries and wages.

This is a completely different scenario than the previous capitalist models where the ownership of capital was concentrated in the hands of a very small group of people in the society. Those few people became rich by owning and controlling capital, the means of production. Workers were completely dependent on access to capital for their livelihood, and easily exploited by capitalists who controled the means of production. That was the origin of class conflict in the old capitalist system. Today, widespread capital ownership has made the laboring class itself literally the largest capitalist of the society. Under institutional capitalism, not a single worker or employee, even a top manager of mutual funds or pension funds, could become the capitalist of the past in the scope of their ownership and control of capital. That individual still has to work for a salary and wage to earn his/her living. In fact, institutional capitalism has elevated the laboring class to the affluent middle class as a dominating group, which has greatly contributed to the stability of U.S. society through conciliating the class conflict that was inherent in the old capitalist system.

Individually no one really owns and controls the enormous financial assets of those institutions. The ownership of pension funds simply implies two things. One is that retirees receive their pension as delayed payments of money earned by themselves during their working years and capital gains accumulated over time in their pension accounts. The other is that working people contribute a portion of their income and have an expectation of receiving benefits after retirement. Managers of pension funds and other investment institutions are employees hired to manage the investment portfolios.

Although institutional investors have provided major sources of capital to private corporations, they are not responsible for managing the companies in which they invested. Their primary responsibility is to buy and sell equity shares of corporations from and to each other or to individual investors. The capital market eventually determines success and failure for all investors, either institutional or individual. The financial market has become more important than ever before in this stage of capitalism. As we will show later in this book, the U.S. financial market is subject to large fluctuations over time that create a great risk to institutional investors and, therefore, the average American workers and retirees. The increasing risk of the U.S. financial market is probably the largest inherent threat to the majority of Americans at this stage of capitalism.

The rapid development of institutional investors has only been observed for the last twenty years. We have yet to see the full consequences and effects of institutional capitalism on the economy and society. The emergence of institutional capitalism represents a new stage of science and technology innovation as well as social innovation. It illustrates the capability of modern American capitalism to swiftly respond to changes in technology, demographic force, and the new global reality through creating new organizations in the endless dynamic process that keeps transforming the economy and society.

In the next section we provide another kind of historical perspective on economic transformation. Since economic growth is at the center of any economic transformation, the stages of economic growth become important to understand the dynamic process of economic transformation in both historical and contemporary contexts.

## 1-2-3  The Stages of Economic Growth

In his well-known book, *The Stages of Economic Growth*[37], W.W. Rostow identifies all societies, in their economic dimensions, as lying within one of five categories: the traditional society, the preconditions for take-off, the take-off, the drive to technological maturity, and the age of high mass-consumption. The stage approach explains not only the uniformity in the sequence of modernization but also the uniqueness of each nation's experience.

Even though its application to the formation of economic development policies in the Third World has been under debate,[38] the stage theory clearly

---

[37] W.W. Rostow, *The Stages of Economic Growth*, second edition, Cambridge University Press, 1971.

[38] The main criticism against the stage approach is that it presents a linear conception of history, with an unfavorable implication to the presently under-developed nations that rich countries would be further along the path of progress and poor countries would always fall behind, as all economies are assumed to pass those stages sequentially.

describes the process of economic transformation of Western capitalism in general and American capitalism in particular. The stage theory says that"modern growth is rooted in the progressive diffusion of new technologies on an efficient basis". It reveals how things actually happened at a particular time in the past by analyzing disaggregated economic data for the sectors and sub-sectors. It is within these sectors and industries that new technologies are absorbed into the economy, their spreading effects are generated, and the pattern or the stages of economic growth emerge. The stage theory promotes the idea that economic growth should be measured by the degree of efficient absorption of technologies, rather than using GDP per capita as a measure of the level of growth. As the degree of technology absorption is hardly measured at the aggregate level, the analysis of sectors and industries becomes necessary to study economic growth.

The decisive force to drive economic growth comes from scientific breakthroughs and technological innovations that create the leading sectors during the industrial revolutions. With their high rates of growth, the leading sectors induce growth in associated industries, service productions, international trade and elsewhere. As the scientific breakthroughs and the industrial revolutions in human history occurred sequentially, the stages of economic growth emerged also sequentially in the Western capitalist societies.

The stage theory, however, does not imply that every nation in the world has to follow exactly the identical phases the United States and other advanced nations have followed. The nature of leading sectors and the supporting science and technology innovations tells at what the stage the nation's economy might be. Without efficient absorption of advanced technologies by its leading sectors and the powerful spreading effects, a nation would not leap forward in its economic growth; rather its economy would become locked in one particular stage, or even regress.

Conversely, in the present global modernization wave, the "catching-up" effort may allow late-coming nations to adopt advanced technologies quickly and efficiently. This could produce an economic miracle and shorten or bypass some of the phases that the Western advanced societies had taken. The complexity of the process of economic growth is inherited in the underpinning forces driving economic development and social progress. Those underpinning forces are the emphasis of *The Stages of Economic Growth.*

In any event, the stage theory provides not only a historical backdrop for understanding the economic transformation of the United States, but also an important framework to study economic growth in general. We shall briefly review the stages of economic growth in order.

In a traditional society, the level of productivity is limited by the inaccessibility of modern science and technology; it has to devote a very high proportion of its resources to agriculture, the leading sector of traditional society. The second stage of growth, the preconditions for take-off, is a process of transition, in which modern science has just begun to be applied to the production of agriculture and industry. With more than 75% of its working force in agriculture, the traditional society must shift to a predominance of industry, transportation, communications, and trade. It requires rapid increases in productivity of agriculture and the natural resource extractive industries. Agriculture still plays an important role in the transitional process by supplying income and capital for establishing modern industries. Social overhead capital, mostly in transportation, must be accumulated to enable take-off. Therefore, agriculture and transportation are the leading sectors in the stage of preconditions for take-off.

The First Industrial Revolution brought about the world's first take-off in England more than two hundred years ago. Along with a high-order political desire for modernization, the build-up of social overhead capital and a surge of technological development in agriculture and the extractive industry of natural resources provides stimulus for take-off. During the take-off stage, technologies spread quickly in agriculture and industry. Entire sectors of new industries expand rapidly and yield profits that can be used for reinvesting in new plants or for expanding into new geographic areas. A series of manufacturing industries provide vital components in the take-off process, including the machinery-manufactured cotton textile industry, coke-manufactured iron, and the railroad propelled by Watt's steam engine. The development of railways led to the development of modern coal, iron, and engineering industries. Those industries yield a high growth rate and a large possibility for innovation or for exploitation of newly profitable unexplored resources.

The drive to maturity stage of growth follows the take-off stage. This is "the period when a society has effectively applied the range of (then) modern technology to the bulk of its resources[39]." In this period, the railway revolution is supported by the second Industrial Revolution, which generates new leading sectors, such as steel, shipbuilding, chemicals, electricity and machine tool industries. Those new industries gather momentum to supplant the older leading industries of coal, iron, and textile found in the take-off stage.

As technical maturity is approached, the society enters the age of high mass-consumption. At this stage of growth, real income-per-capita is raised

---

[39] W.W. Rostow, *The Stages of Economic Growth*, second edition, Cambridge University Press, 1971, p. 59.

to a level where a large number of people gain a command over consumption not just for basic food, shelter, and clothing but for higher-grade foods, automobiles, and single-family houses outfitted with radios, refrigerators and other household gadgetry. A new middle-class is created, consisting of professional people, skilled workers, and semi-skilled workers in manufacturing, construction, and transportation. The number of these people increases rapidly and the middle-class, with its increased income and purchasing power, becomes the largest portion of society.

At this stage of mass consumption, resources are increasingly directed to the new leading sectors of production of consumers' durable goods and to the mass diffusion of services. The third Industrial Revolution, characterized by the inventions and innovations of the internal combustion engine, electricity, and modern chemicals, creates new industries, such as automobile, chemical, petroleum, rubber, aeronautic and space industries. During the early years of the third Industrial Revolution, Ford's moving assembly line and the Model-T made the affordable automobile a reality. With its revolutionary effects on life and society, the affordable automobile was the decisive element in the age of high mass-consumption.

The United States was the first of the world's societies to move from technical maturity to the age of high mass-consumption. W.W. Rostow identifies the four phases of post-maturity development in American history over the first half the twentieth century: the progressive period, the 1920s period, the great depression of the 1930s, and the post-war boom of 1946-56. Americans' life style was transformed dramatically in what is known as the age of the mass-produced automobile of the 1920s. The widespread consumption of automobiles led to a vast inner migration into newly constructed single-family houses in the suburbs, which created the mass markets for household appliances and consumers' durables. The depression of 1929 interrupted the mass consumption process in the United States, while the post-war boom of 1946-56 is regarded as a resumption of the 1920s boom.

By the time diminishing returns inevitably appeared in the automobile and steel industries, the fourth Industrial Revolution was already on the horizon. Beginning in the mid-1970s with revolutionary innovations in semiconductors and industrial materials, computers, the laser, and genetic engineering, the fourth Industrial Revolution became self-sustained and rapidly expanded into the information technology revolution[40]. New Internet-related industries emerged from the horizon since the mid-1990s, showing their revo-

---

[40] W.W. Rostow, *2050: An Essay on the 21ˢᵗ Century*, January, 5, 1996.

lutionary effects on the business world as well as individuals' life style, as illustrated in Section 1-1. The fourth Industrial Revolution is initially identified as comprising four major component technologies: computers, genetic engineering, the laser, and new industrial materials. The explosion of new information technology has driven the fourth Industrial Revolution by creating new leading sectors that have extraordinary growth potential.

Bearing in mind the theory of the stages of economic growth in general and the stages of the U.S. economic growth in particular, we understand that economic transformation is an endless dynamic process that has moved the U.S. economy from one stage to the next for the last two centuries. Scientific breakthroughs and revolutionary engineering create numerous investment opportunities in machines and factories, methods of production and management, which result in improvements in efficiency, productivity and profitability, and finally in an improved standard of living for the majority of the U.S. population.

An economic system, however, is inevitably subject to diminishing returns on its input factors. This economic law states that initially increasing capital investment and labor input will increase output at an increasing pace until some point when further increases in input factors will yield decreasing marginal returns, and continuing the increases in input factors may even eventually reduce output. Exempting external shocks, when an economy reaches this stage of diminishing returns, it finds a temporary equilibrium.

New major breakthroughs in scientific research and technological innovations will emerge on the horizon to move the economy out of its temporary equilibrium by launching it into a new stage of growth. Because "the only factor of production not subject to diminishing returns is human creativity"[41], major emerging breakthroughs in scientific research and technological innovation always lead to a major economic transformation. This logic is demonstrated again and again by industrial revolutions and associated distinctive economic transformations in human history.

While the basic characteristics of the high mass-consumption stage identified by Rostow's theory still hold in the present economic development, the leading sectors have certainly shifted toward information- and knowledge-based industries, and consumer preferences have changed significantly compared with the 1950s and 1960s. We shall provide detailed analyses of these changes in the U.S. economy in the following chapters.

---

[42] W.W. Rostow, *2050: An Essay on the 21st Century*, January, 5, 1996.

Nevertheless, technology innovations remain the driving force for economic transformation in all sectors and industries. The stage theory of economic growth provides us with economists' perspectives on historical economic transformation, emphasizing issues related to economic theory such as the basic growth equation, population and working force, capital and technology, relative price, business cycle, stage and limit to growth, and noneconomic factors. These are common subjects and issues analyzed by many generations of economic-growth theorists from David Hume (1711-1776) to the present[43].

---

[43] W.W. Rostow, *Theorists of Economic Growth from David Hume to the Present, With a Perspective on the Next Century*, Oxford University Press, 1990.

# Chapter 2

## Theoretical Perspectives on Economic Transformation

As one may have observed in Rostow's growth theory and other publications in regards to social and economic development, economic growth has been a core issue in analyzing economic transformation and specifying the stages of social and economic development. In this section we will discuss how economists and business professionals recognize and measure economic growth. We will also discuss the limitation of the theoretical modeling of economic growth against the complexity of the real world.

## 2-1   Basic Growth Equation

It is astonishing that all the economic growth theories, from the eighteenth century to the present, have been based on one basic equation, the so-called production function. The most broadly expressed production function is formulated as[1]

$$Y_t = f(K_t, N_t, L_t, S_t, U_t).$$

---

[1] W.W. Rostow, *Theorists of Economic Growth from David Hume to the Present, With a Perspective on the Next Century*, Oxford University Press, 1990, p. 6.

$Y_t$ denotes output of an economy; $K_t$, the services flowing from the economy's capital stock; $N_t$, the services flowing from natural resources; $L_t$, the labor force; $S_t$, society's stock of applied knowledge; and $U_t$, the sociocultural setting within which the economy operates.

This basic equation is designed to depict a complex process of human economic actions as they respond to the challenges and opportunities offered by internal and external conditions and produce economic outcomes. Therefore, not only have the economic factors such as capital, labor, and natural resource entered the production function, a wide range of noneconomic factors relevant to science, technology, social settings and cultural traditions have also been included in the input factors that determine economic outcomes.

Only by taking such a broad view of the basic growth equation could economic growth theories analyze such economic issues as the demographic factors and productivity of labor force, the relationship between capital investment and productivity, the impact of technology innovation and diffusion, the phenomenon of the business cycle, and the linkage of noneconomic variables to the economic performance.

This basic equation, however, has encountered enormous mathematical difficulties on two fronts: defining and measuring the variables for all the input factors, and specifying the formulas for the production function that allow economists to put theoretical ideas into some kind of quantitative relationship of the defined variables. The results of this mathematical specification of all the variables and the production function should be consistent with actual historical and contemporary data.

A great deal of progress has been made by generations of economists, but these two basic difficulties remain a great challenge in the field of economics.

## 2-2   Growth Accounting Model

The latest development in economic growth theories is the method of growth accounting, which is viewed as an important step in the analysis of the fundamentals of economic growth. The growth accounting method breaks down observed economic growth into components associated with changes in factor inputs and a residual that reflects technological and sociocultural changes in an economy. As Nobel laureate Robert Solow, a professor in economics at MIT, initiated this approach in 1957[2], the residual is called the Solow residual. It is also called total factor productivity (TFP) growth or simply productivity growth.

Suppose a neoclassical production function is expressed by Y = f(A, K, L), where A denotes technology, K is the capital stock, and L is the quantity of labor. The growth rate of output $G_y$ = dY/dt /Y can be partitioned into components associated with growth rate of capital stock $G_k$ = dK/dt /K and growth rate of labor $G_1$ = dL/dt /L, and the technology progress, $G_A$ = dA/dt /A. That is

$$Gy = S_k * G_k + S_1 * G_1 + S_A * G_A,$$

where $S_k$, $S_1$, and $S_A$ are coefficients derived from production function.

If production function is in the form of Y = A*f(K, L), then $S_A$ is simplified to unity and the Solow residual or TFP growth rate can be estimated via the regression of the following simple equation,

$$G_A = Gy - S_k * G_k - S_1 * G_1 .$$

So far economists have not come up with a proper aggregate variable, A, to actually measure the level of technology of the economy and its growth rate. Solow's model provides an empirical approach to measuring the TFP growth rate, which represents gains in output not directly attributable to growth rates of capital and labor. TFP growth can occur with technology progress, improvement in quality of labor and capital, economy of scale, and changes in noneconomic factors.

In many theoretical and empirical studies on economic growth, the capital stock can be redefined as a vector with components of different vintages of capital goods, and the labor input can be treated as a vector of workers who vary in quality in terms of education and skill level. In recent years there have been many variations or improvements in the Solow model that introduce increasing returns and the spillover effects of technology progress, as well as modeling endogenous economic growth by adding human capital measured by years of education and number of patents[3]. These models try

---

[2] Robert M. Solow, Technical Change and the Aggregate Production Function, *Review of Economics and Statistics,* 39, August 1957.
[3] Paul M. Romer, Increasing Returns and Long-Run Growth, *Journal of Political Economy,* 94, 5 (October), 1986; and Paul M. Romer, Endogenous Technological Change, *Journal of Political Economy,* 98, 5 (October), 1990.

to give the Solow residuals clearer explanation in terms of R&D outlays, public policies, and other noneconomic factors, and as such, they are called the new neoclassical growth theories.

Using the growth-accounting procedure, Dale W. Jorgenson, a professor in economics at Harvard University, and his coauthors have estimated growth and productivity for fifty-one private and public sectors of the U.S. economy for the time period of 1948-79[4]. They also estimated the growth rate of value-added output and contributions of capital and labor inputs and the rate of TFP growth for the U.S. economy as a whole on an annual basis for the period of 1948-79 and for seven sub-periods.

According to their estimation, the average annual growth rate of the value-added output of the U.S. economy is 3.42% for the period 1948-79, the capital contribution is 1.56%, the labor contribution is 1.05%, and the growth rate of productivity is 0.81%. In other words, of the 3.42% annual growth rate of output, 45.6% comes from capital input growth, 30.7% is due to labor input growth, and 23.7% is from productivity growth. Capital input is the most significant source of growth for all the sub-periods except one, the period of 1960-66, in which of the 4.45% annual growth rate of output, 32.6% is from contribution of capital, 31.7% from labor, and 35.7% from productivity growth.

There are three consecutive sub-periods, 1953-57, 1957-60, and 1960-66, in which productivity growth accounts for more than 30% of output growth, greater than the contribution made by labor input growth. However, in the following sub-periods, 1966-69, 1969-73, and 1973-79, output growth slows down substantially, while contributions of capital and labor inputs decrease slightly. The largest decline in contribution occurs in productivity growth with only 0.6%, 18.8%, and 12.0% contributions to output growth in those sub-periods respectively[5].

The results for 1948-79 indicate that the growth of capital input is the most important source of economic growth of value-added output, and growth of labor input is the next most important factor. Productivity growth makes less of a contribution than growth of capital and labor input, but it causes the most fluctuation in output growth.

Recognizing that neoclassical growth theories deal with technology changes awkwardly at best, many economists are motivated to search for new ideas and methods of modeling the central elements of technology inno-

---

[4] Dale W. Jorgenson, Frank M. Gollop, and Barbara M. Fraumeni, *Productivity and U.S. Economic Growth,* Harvard University Press, Cambridge, Massachusetts, 1987.
[5] Ibid. These numbers are calculated from data in Table 1.2, p. 21.

vations and related activities and institutions for economic growth. The new neoclassical growth theories represent movement in that direction, but many economists do not believe that they have yet achieved consistency with empirical events and data[6]. Some economists, such as M. Scott, have suggested abandoning the use of production function[7]. The new neoclassical growth theories have recognized the primacy of the advance of technology as the key driving force behind economic growth, but their modeling far from achieves the goal of an explanation that matches historical facts.

We believe that any theories based upon the ideas of equilibrium and methodology of marginal analysis will fail to pass historical tests in their explanation of the causes of industrial revolutions or the timing of U.S. economic growth. As discussed in the previous sections, rapid technology advances are able to generate some discontinuous and sudden changes in the economy and in society. Technology-induced external and internal forces in the economic system can generate more than tenfold jumps[8] in some economic environment variables for an industry or for a company. That business would certainly lose its equilibrium. The effects of technology advances and innovations cannot be fully understood without considering those discontinuous changes. As economic historian W.W. Rostow points out,

.... From the 1780s, innovation altered in both character and scale. Smith's concept of mainly incremental technological change, brought about by inventive craftsmen in the workshop, could no longer suffice; although it was so convenient that some economists clung to it for two centuries. After the 1780s Smith's occasional major inventions became an uneven flow of changing composition; but this phenomenon, yielding endless disequilibrium, was so inconvenient for post-1870 mainstream economists that they have still not found a credible way to deal with it[9].

We believe that Rostow's assessment is still valid for present economic growth theories, which need to find solutions to cope with the radical and

[6] Richard R. Nelson, *The Source of Economic Growth.*
[7] Maurice F. Scott, *A New View of Economic Growth,* Oxford: Oxford University Press, 1989.
[8] Andrew S. Grove, *Only the Paranoid Survive*, Doubleday, 1996.
[9] W.W. Rostow, *Theorists of Economic Growth from David Hume to the Present, With a Perspective on the Next Century*, Oxford University Press, 1990, p. 35.

disruptive changes caused by technology innovations. It remains a great challenge in economics to present consistent growth theories that mirror reality at both macro and micro levels. In the following section, we shall discuss the economic growth phenomenon from perspectives of industries and corporations rather than from the viewpoint of the national economy as a whole.

## 2-3 Dynamics of Knowledge-Technology Innovation

The main difficulty in economic growth theories is to describe, qualitatively and quantitatively, technological innovations that generate both incremental and discontinuous changes in the economy. Neoclassical growth theories and growth accounting approaches are able to deal with incremental technology innovations through the component of total factor productivity (TFP) growth. They are, however, unable to accommodate discontinuous technology innovations and the chaotic behavior of economic agents as they react to significant and sudden changes in their industries or market conditions. Our focus in this section is to understand the dynamic process of growth from a business point of view rather than from the point of view of economic theory.

### 2-3-1 An S-Shaped Growth Curve

In the business world, the dynamics of an industry or a company can be described by the so-called S-shaped curve of the life cycle in creating or marketing a new technology. In the fermentation stage of a new technology, there are many applications and business models that can be developed, and chances for success or failure of any of these models are still unknown. The rate of progress in performance of a new technology, therefore, is relatively slow, which is depicted by the virtually flat initial portion of the S-shaped curve in Figure 2-1.

Numerous tests and experiences determine what will be successful and the company moves into the second stage of development. As the technology becomes better understood and disseminated, the rate of technological improvement accelerates over time and the company grows quickly, denoted by the middle portion of the S-shaped curve in Figure 2-1.

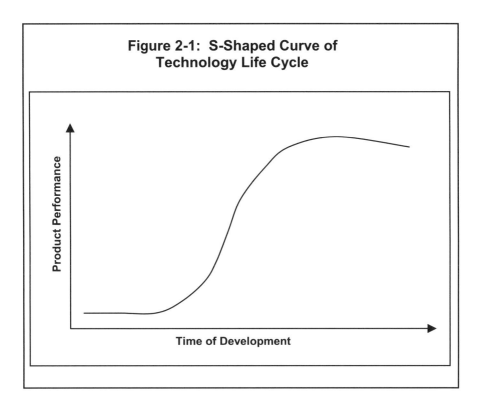

**Figure 2-1: S-Shaped Curve of Technology Life Cycle**

The top portion of the S-shaped curve represents the stage of maturity, in which the company becomes strong, acquires a large market share, and generates sizable profits. The technology becomes mature and approaches its natural limit. Any further development will require an increase in efforts with a diminishing benefit. Finally, the exhausted technology will reverse the company's competitive position and drives the S-shaped curve downwards. In order to continue the company's growth, the S-shaped curve that represents second-generation technology must be launched before the fall of first-generation technology (Figure 2-2). In this way, the company will continue its production, performance, and economic growth.

In general, the ability to generate or adopt the next generation of technology in order to capitalize on business opportunities that are created by threatening forces from dramatic and unexpected changes will result in enormous economic growth. Conversely, denying the emergence of technology innovations and being unwilling to make quick strategic adjustments will result in miserable business failures even for well-established companies.

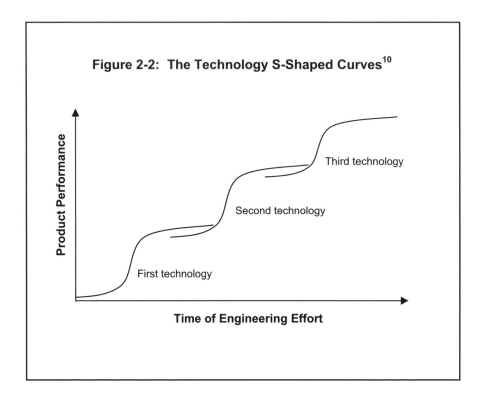

Figure 2-2:  The Technology S-Shaped Curves[10]

The intersecting part of an S-shaped curve with the next S-shaped curve represents a transitory period in which the business fundamentals of the industry begin to change, new players emerge to bring new rules of the game into the market, and old players decline or disappear along with their obsolete technologies.  People in the business world call this intersection period of two S-shaped curves the strategic inflection point, which is a crucial period that determines a business's success or failure, and which should be the focus of economic growth via technology innovations.

---

[10] Clayton M. Christensen, *The Innovator's Dilemma*, Harper Business, An Imprint of HarperCollins Publishers, 2000,  Figure 2-5, p. 45.

## 2-3-2   Strategic Inflection Points

Mathematically, an inflection point is defined as the point where the second derivative of a function changes signs. In other words, it occurs when the rate of change of slope of a curve alters sign, from negative to positive, or vice versa. It is worth noticing that the S-shaped curve of an industry or company's growth curve has an inflection point in the middle of the curve, where the rate of changing slope alters sign from positive to negative. However, that is not the inflection point of interest to most businesses.

The strategic inflection point is located in the area where an S-shaped curve approaches its end and the next S-shaped curve is about to start. If we imagine those two S-shaped curves touching together at some point, we can see the creation of a smooth growth curve. In that joining point the growth curve changes, in mathematical terms, from concave to convex, or in economic terms, from decreasing returns to scale to increasing returns to scale. This is the strategic inflection point that most concerns us.

In his book[11], the former CEO of Intel Corp, Andrew Grove, has illustrated many cases where both technology and non-technology companies have gone through strategic inflection points; some of them succeeded while others failed. The strategic inflection points are caused by sudden and unexpected changes that threaten the companies' core business. He calls these big changes in a company's competitive position 10X forces, emphasizing that the changes have become ten times what they were just recently. The 10X-force threat may come from changes in the power, vigor, and competence of existing competitors, complementors, customers, suppliers, potential competitors, and the possibility that what the firm is doing can be done in a different way. These six fronts comprise a company's competitive environment[12]. Any one of these competitive forces can become so strong that it alters the very essence of how business is conducted in an industry. It can also have the effect of transforming an entire industry into the period of the strategic inflection point, where turbulence and chaos is the temporary order of the industry, and where winners emerge and losers are wiped out.

---

[11] Andrew S. Grove, *Only the Paranoid Survive*, Doubleday, 1996.

[12] Andrew S. Grove, *Only the Paranoid Survive*, Doubleday, 1996, p. 30.

## • An Example — The U.S. Computer Industry

Let us recall a vivid example, the U.S. computer industry, which went through a dramatic transformation in the 1980s.

Before 1980, a typical computer company manufactured its own semi-conductor chips, built its own computer around its own hardware, developed its own operating system software and application software, and then sold its products as a proprietary package through its own salesmen.

In the early 1980s, technology innovations generated the 10X forces of the microprocessor and Windows operating system, which made the personal computer an enormously useful tool in both office and home. Many small companies entered the computer business and vigorously competed in a selected layer of the computer-related market, such as chip manufacturing, computer building, operating system development, application software generation, and sales and distribution of PCs.

Over time, the entire structure of the industry was transformed; the old style of the vertical industry structure was replaced by a new horizontal structure. Well-established computer companies, such as Wang Laboratories and Digital Equipment Corporation, who were innovators in the mainframe-dominated computer world, had become losers in the PC era. Wang Labs ended up in Chapter 11, and Digital Equipment Corp was acquired by Compaq, one of the emerging computer companies of the 1980s.

During the computer industry's transformation of the 1980s, the computer giant IBM could not afford its traditionally vertical way of doing business. The 10X force of the PC revolution had forced IBM to restructure itself, resulting in massive layoffs in the late 1980s and early 1990s. Even though IBM was the company to design and produce the original IBM PCs, it had to choose Intel Corp to provide 8088 microprocessors for its PCs. It was a painful process for IBM to adapt to the changing new industry order while witnessing those IBM-compatible PC makers, such as Compaq and Dell, surpass IBM as the world's largest PC producers. IBM's own PC business has been losing money for many years.

Going through the turbulence and chaos of the strategic inflection point period of the computer industry in the 1980s, Intel, Microsoft, Compaq and Dell emerged as the big winners and skyrocketed to become the new leaders of the horizontal PC industry. All of these four companies have already become the number one player in their business segments. Their sales revenues in comparison with the veteran company IBM can illustrate the magnificent growth of those four companies.

In 1982, the sales revenue was $34.4 billion for IBM, and $899 million for Intel, whose business was focused on manufacturing memory chips at that time. Microsoft was founded in 1975; it did not go public until 1986. Compaq was founded in 1982 and Dell was founded in 1984. Compaq's first record of sales revenue was $111 million in 1983. Microsoft's revenue was about $170 million in 1986 and Dell's revenue was $159 million in 1987. In 1992, however, sales revenues of all the four companies exceeded the $2 billion mark. Only eight years later, in 2000, sales revenue reached $42.383 billion for Compaq, $33.726 billion for Intel, $31.888 billion for Dell, and $22.956 billion for Microsoft.

It was the event of incorporation by Herman Hollerith of the Tabulating Machine Co., the part of C-T-R, on December 3, 1896 that led to the formation of IBM, and it was on February 14, 1924 that the name of C-T-R was changed to International Business Machines Corporation (IBM). It took nearly one hundred years for IBM to reach the scale of $30 billion business; it took only 18 years for Compaq and 14 years for Dell to move from zero revenue to exceeding $30 billion in sales revenue. This astonishing growth in the computer industry was a phenomenon observed after the period of the strategic inflection point of the 1980s.

From Figure 2-3, one can see that the explosive growth really occurred after 1991. We use 1991 as the base year to calculate indices of sale revenues for IBM and the four emerging computer companies. At base year, indices of sales revenues are assigned to be 100 for all the companies. Figure 2-4 depicts growth paths of sales indices for each company during this 9-year time period of take-off. Dell increased its sales revenue about 36 times during 1991 through 2000, Microsoft 14 times, Compaq 8.7 times, and Intel 7.1 times. IBM's sales revenue also increased from $64.766 billion in 1991 to $88.396 billion in 2000, a nearly 36% increase. Its big revenue number in year 2000, however, fell in short for IBM to reach its original projection of becoming a $100 billion company by the end of the 1980s[13].

It becomes very clear that the strategic inflection point triggers an explosive growth in the computer industry. Even though some well-managed large companies died during the turbulence and chaos of rapid industry transition, the emerging companies that replaced them generated more than 10 times greater economic growth. It is the emerging companies that embraced the new structural changes in the computer industry and took full advantage of

---

[13] Andrew S. Grove, *Only the Paranoid Survive*, Doubleday, 1996, p. 45.

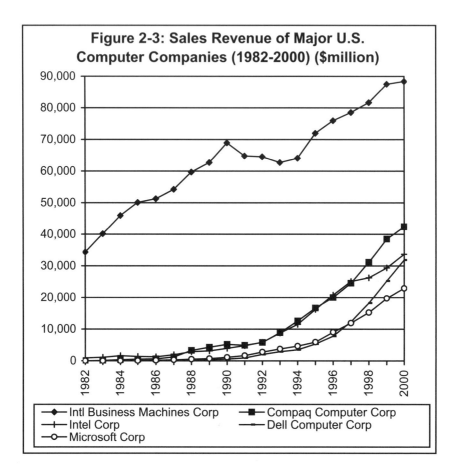

Figure 2-3: Sales Revenue of Major U.S. Computer Companies (1982-2000) ($million)

new technology innovations in the PC market. It is companies such as Digital Equipment and Wang Labs that ignored the arrival of the PC revolution at the zenith of their once innovative microcomputer business, which led to their decline and demise in the PC era.

Technology innovations always keep moving from one strategic inflection point to the next, with some emerging companies rising and some established companies falling. In the computer industry, IBM dominated the mainframe computer market but missed by years the emergence of minicomputers. In the minicomputer business the major players were not big manufacturers of mainframe computers but some aggressively managed companies such as Digital Equipment, Wang Labs, Hewlett-Packard, Data General, and others. Almost all of these minicomputer producers, however, missed the desktop PC market; none of them become the leader in the PC revolution.

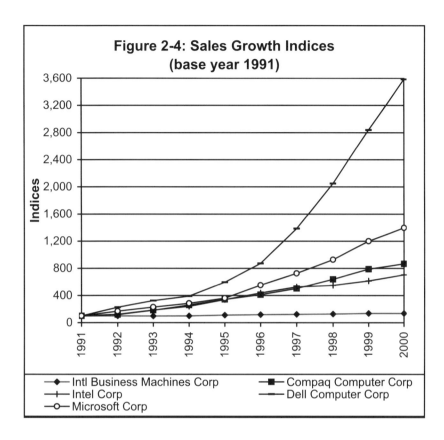

Figure 2-4: Sales Growth Indices (base year 1991)

The Internet revolution has offered extraordinary opportunities and posts unprecedented risks for all companies in the market. In the first two years of the new century, technology companies experienced a severe downturn that was triggered by the burst of the Internet dot-com bubble in early 2000. The Internet revolution and the hard economic times may serve as catalysts for strategic inflection points to occur again for many industries and corporations.

At present, the computer industry has entered a chaotic period in which the demand for PCs in the United States has fallen for the first time, and worldwide PC sales have also slowed substantially. Dell, however, has continued growing at a much faster pace than other computer companies. In the first quarter of 2001, Dell overtook Compaq as the worldwide leader in the PC market. Under its control of 13 percent of the global PC business, Dell has aimed to capture 40 percent of the global PC market over several years. The PC industry has been rocked by a price war that erupted among the biggest players, Dell, Compaq, IBM, Hewlett-Packard and Gateway. PCs have already become commodities with slim profit margins and not much differentiation power among products. The price war makes the PC industry's profit margin continue to decline and helps Dell achieve its ambitious goal for market share based largely on its cost advantages of a low-inventory, build-to-order, direct-sales business model.

The PC industry's consolidation has been going on for a few years; deteriorated economic and business conditions may accelerate it further. Already two companies have limited their exposure in the PC market. IBM pulled its desktop PCs out of retail stores in late 1999, while Micron Electronics, once the number 3 direct seller behind Dell and Gateway, sold its PC business in the early 2001. On June 25, 2001 Compaq announced its restructuring plan to transform the hardware giant to a company focusing more on software and services for large businesses in telecommunications, health care and financial services, more like IBM. As a part of the new strategy, Compaq is to switch its high-end server production to Intel Corp's Itanium microprocessors and to abandon its own proprietary Alpha chip by 2004. In the end, Compaq was acquired by the computer and printer maker Hewlett-Packard Company in May 2002[14].

Nevertheless, Compaq's strategic shift has changed the competitive landscape of the PC industry as well as the high-end network computer (commonly known as server) business. Compaq's plan of one microprocessor architecture for its entire server line has certainly strengthened the Win-Intel coalition to compete against Unix-based server producers like Sun Microsystems. And the server industry might undergo a similar process to what the PC industry went through in the 1980s, changing from vertical to horizontal industry structures. The rapid advances in the microprocessor technology and the Windows operating system will intensify competition in the computer industry and continue to generate turbulence and uncertainty. A new strategic inflection point might be already under way to create new winners and losers with a great probability of another astonishing economic growth period for the computer industry after the chaotic and turbulent economic and market situation straighten out.

As illustrated by the transformation of the computer industry, the strategic inflection point has been the crucial period for all companies in an industry in which the 10X forces are playing in full swing and industry's fundamentals begin to change. For established companies, the strategic inflection

---

[14] It was a roughly $19 billion buyout of Compaq after winning a court battle and gaining the official tally from the March 19 shareholder vote of the Hewlett Packard Co.

point will generate opportunities to rise to new heights as well as risks to fall to the ground. For emerged companies the strategic inflection point will offer opportunities for growing quickly as well as risks of being wiped out completely. Hence, the strategic inflection point represents a time period of confusion in a chaotic environment that swarms with opportunities of hyper growth as well as risks of business failure and extinction. Few top managers really know what's going on except for some observations and feelings of "things are different, and something has happened."

> When exactly does a strategic inflection point take place? It's hard to pinpoint, even in retrospect.... Timing is everything. If you undertake these changes while your company is still healthy, while your ongoing business forms a protective bubble in which you can experiment with the new ways of doing business, you can save much more of your company's strength, your employees and your strategic position. But that means acting when not everything is known, when the data aren't yet in. Even those who believe in a scientific approach to management will have to rely on instinct and personal judgment. When you're caught in the turbulence of a strategic inflection point, the sad fact is that instinct and judgment are all you've got to guide you through.[15]...

As even the veteran top manager of a company like Intel feels the urgency and difficulty of detecting a strategic inflection point, economists who study economic growth theory and are interested in real-world problems need to share business managers' observations and experiences in order to shift some of their research energy to the issues of strategic inflection points.

In the following section we shall study the conditions before the strategic inflection point takes place in the hope of shedding some light on how discontinuous technology innovations are developed and moved into the chaotic situation. Our basic ideas come from one of the authors who has spent his career managing technology companies, business schools, and university research institutes. He has also been dedicated to serious academic research on creative and innovative management, technology transfer and technology commercialization, at the same time practicing what have been discovered by establishing technology incubators and numerous entrepreneur

---

[15] Andrew S. Grove, *Only the Paranoid Survive*, Doubleday, 1996, p. 33.

projects that are oriented towards generating economic growth and prosperity for communities and societies around the globe.

## 2-3-3   The Kozmetsky Effect

Professor Ramamoorthy of the University of California-Berkeley, a renowned scientist in electrical engineering and computer science, was the first to give a brief description of the Kozmetsky Effect in discussing the knowledge-technology transfer process[16]:

> Prof. George Kozmetsky of the University of Texas, Austin, an internationally acclaimed business leader and a National Medal of Technology recipient, has shown the existence of a strong interaction between knowledge and technology growth.  According to him, the rapidity of knowledge growth exerts a strong synergistic attraction on the technology growth and pulls technology growth curve towards it…. Due to this convergence of knowledge-technology transfer curve the phase latencies shrink and may ultimately coalesce.  This implies that the technology has reached a saturation point and progress will be difficult, like trying to squeeze water out of a desert rock.  We shall call this convergence of knowledge-technology-transfer phases as the Kozmetsky Effect. This creates an inflection point in the technology growth curves similar to the Dr. Grove's inflection points in the growth curves of hi-tech enterprises....

We view the Kozmetsky Effect as a concept that defines a knowledge-technology innovation process. According to this concept, the knowledge-technology innovation process consists of four distinctive subprocesses, namely knowledge, technology, tools, and implementation. It is development in all these subprocesses and the interaction of multiple forces from knowledge, technology, engineering, business, economy and society that lead to the strategic inflection point period at the end of the knowledge-technology innovation process. We shall analyze major forces and their development patterns in order to understand their contributions to the

---

[16]  Chitoor V. Ramamoorthy, A Study of the Service Industry — Functions, Features and Control, *IEICE Transactions on Communications,* Vol.  E83-B, No. 5, May 2000, p. 891.

knowledge and technology innovations that produce the 10X forces and change the fundamentals of an industry.

In an attempt to describe the development process of new products in the engineering and business world, we divide all factors involved in the innovation process into four categories: knowledge, technology, tools, and implementation; each factor group has its own development phase. Knowledge generation is an instigator that initiates all the other factors' development paths and leads directly to technology innovations. Technology innovations are followed by the tool development phase, while the implementation phase completes the whole innovation process.

As depicted in Figure 2-5, we use four curves to denote the development processes for the four factor groups. A subprocess proceeds over time driven by its own dynamics and with some lags to its leading factor groups. The time lag can be measured by the so-called latency[17] that is defined as the time difference between two successive subprocesses during a specific instance of the innovations or at the certain level of development denoted by a horizontal line in Figure 2-5.

With a longer length on the right-hand side than on the left-hand side, three intervals on that horizontal line represent the different times required for development in one factor group to be transferred into development in another group. In the semiconductor industry, for example, the time to transfer knowledge into technology is shorter than the time it takes to develop support tools from technology. And the time required to develop support tools from technology is shorter than the time needed to use the tools to develop the new product.

The phenomenon of convergence of these four development paths is the focus of the Kozmetsky Effect. This convergence indicates that knowledge innovation has put forth a strong synergistic attraction on technology growth, leading to a diminishing latency between knowledge and technology development phases, and an ultimate coalescing of those two factor groups. The convergence also implies that knowledge and technology innovations accelerate the corresponding tools and implementation developments and that knowledge and technology have interacted directly and vigorously with designing, architecture, engineering, manufacturing, management, marketing, distribution, consumers' preference, community's needs, and society's attitude towards knowledge and technology innovations.

The above-described Kozmetsky Effect cannot occur until the specific knowledge and technology involved in a specific industry have reached a

---

[17] Chitoor V. Ramamoorthy, A Study of the Service Industry — Functions, Features and Control, *IEICE Transactions on Communications,* Vol. E83-B, No. 5, May 2000.

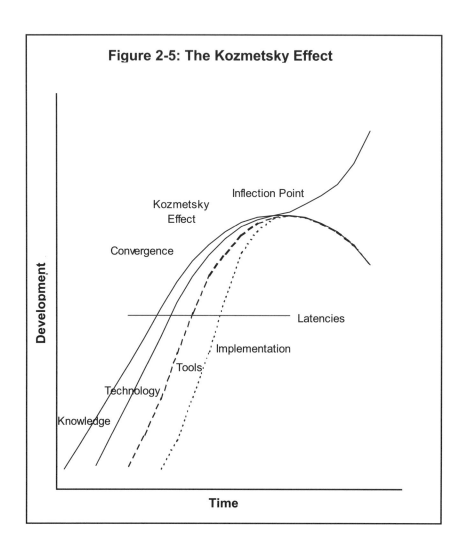

Figure 2-5: The Kozmetsky Effect

saturation state. This occurs when technology has reached its limits and it is difficult to achieve any incremental progress. Additionally, there will be few changes or little progress in the factor groups of tools and implementation. All factors affect the knowledge and technology innovations processes and converge into a state that intensifies interactions among all the factors.

Broad communications have been established by all the players: scientists, engineers, managers, workers, salespersons, consumers, the media, and the opinion leaders of community and society. Matured knowledge and technology have been fully understood in terms of their benefits and limitations; consumers' needs and community and society's attitude towards knowledge and technology innovations have been fully expressed and clearly understood by industries and corporations. It is understood that there is little hope from incremental technology improvement for further business growth, and new ideas, technology breakthroughs, and new market segments must be developed to serve new consumers.

The vigorous interaction of knowledge, technology, tools, and implementation provides valuable data and information that stimulates creativity and innovation. New ideas and technologies emerge, new product prototypes occur, and new market segments surface. At the initial phase, however, nobody knows which idea will work, which technology holds promise, which prototype addresses consumers' needs, which segment of the market offers room to grow, and which business model generates revenues and profits. This is the beginning of the strategic inflection-point period when all the new things are put on trial that create divergence, confusion, and chaotic situations.

To have a better understanding of the Kozmetsky Effect, particularly the conditions for creating the strategic inflection points, we shall study the development processes in the four factor groups—knowledge, technology, tools, and implementation.

## • Knowledge and Technology

The meaning of knowledge has radically evolved over time. In ancient Western philosophy, both Plato and Socrates held that the sole function of knowledge is self-knowledge: the intellectual, moral, and spiritual growth of the person. For Protagoras, knowledge meant logic, grammar, and rhetoric, the core of learning in the Middle Ages, and the core of today's "liberal education[18]." Similarly, in ancient Eastern philosophy knowledge, the road to enlightenment and wisdom, means knowing what to say and how to say it. In the ancient time of both West and East, knowledge meant learning, intelligence, wisdom — anything but utility and ability to do things.

---

[18] Peter F. Drucker, *Post-Capital Society*, Harper Business, Harper Collins Publishers, 1993, pp. 26-27.

After the First Industrial Revolution, skill became increasingly important in order to achieve economic goals. The word "technology" was invented as a combination of "techne," the mystery of a craft skill, with "logy," organized, systematic, purposeful knowledge[19]. During the industrial revolutions throughout human history, people have converted experience into knowledge, craft secrecy into methodology, simply doing tasks into applied knowledge, all under the name of technology. Finally, technology has meant a body of knowledge and know-how that can be used to produce certain specific types of physical effects. Technology, however, is not simply an engineering of things; it is a key economic resource or the means to obtain social and economic results. Therefore, technology can be treated as a type of wealth, one that we do not yet know how to measure for economic purposes. Wealth is a means of attaining economic, social, and cultural status for individuals, as well as a way of achieving institutional objectives and ensuring the general welfare of society[20].

In contemporary societies, knowledge has a broader scope, consisting of social science and the humanities as well as natural science and technology. In Western cultures the terms "science" and "knowledge" are often used interchangeably or are combined to form scientific knowledge.

The level of knowledge increases rapidly, and the process of generating knowledge or of knowledge production has also evolved over time. In the traditional production of knowledge, problems are set and solved largely by the academic or specific interest community. Traditional knowledge is discipline-based. There is a distinction between fundamental science and applied science, and a distinction between a theoretical core of knowledge and the areas of knowledge of applications. We shall present the current state of development of knowledge and technology.

## Trans-disciplinary Knowledge Generation

Presently, the production of knowledge is advancing into a new phase with far-reaching implications. In the knowledge generating process, there is a constant flow between fundamental and applied knowledge, between

---

[19] Peter F. Drucker, *Post-Capital Society*, Harper Business, Harper Collins Publishers, 1993.
[20] George Kozmetsky, *Technology Transfer in a Global Context,* the IC² Institute, the University of Texas, 1994.

theoretical and practical knowledge. Research interests have been shifting away from searching for fundamental principles toward problem solving, while interest originally developed in the industries increasingly guides the experimental process in knowledge production. Hence knowledge production is aiming toward utilities and actions, or toward application in the broad sense.

Difficult problems in the real world can never be isolated or fixed into disciplines established in the academic field. The knowledge generation movement toward problem solving and application, therefore, cannot be one, multiple or even interdisciplinary, it must be trans-disciplinary in its very nature. The authors of the book *The New Production of Knowledge* have summarized four distinct features for trans-disciplinary knowledge production[21].

At first, it develops an evolving framework to guide a group of participants in problem solving; solutions arise primarily from genuine intellectual creativity, rather than the application of existing knowledge; and the theories that result cannot be easily classified as a distinct discipline.

Secondly, trans-disciplinary knowledge develops its own theoretical structures, research methods and modes of practice, with both empirical and theoretical components that may not be located in the existing disciplines.

Thirdly, the diffusion of the results of trans-disciplinary research is accomplished initially in the process of knowledge generation and subsequently by original participants' moving to new problem solving after having gained trans-disciplinary knowledge. This is not similar to the conventional diffusion channels that report results in professional journals or conferences. Here a communication network becomes very important for acquiring the highly mobile and transient trans-disciplinary knowledge.

Finally, trans-disciplinary knowledge is dynamic, with the problem solving capabilities able to move with agility from one problem to the next. It is very difficult to predict where and how discoveries in trans-disciplinary research can be used for additional problem solving. Communications are crucial to link these discoveries with practitioners who are facing new challenges.

---

[21] Michael Gibbons, et al., *The New Production of Knowledge, The Dynamics of Science and Research in Contemporary Societies.*

## Knowledge-Based Businesses

These emerging trends in the knowledge generation process have set in motion the acceleration of human creativity through the closer linkage of theory and practice, and through the crucial communications network for knowledge creation and diffusion. No longer is knowledge generated solely by a society's elite, the academic circle, and then transferred or diffused into productive activities and services. The present information technology revolution has opened a new road toward knowledge creation and diffusion.

A new strategic map has emerged, starting with data, information, pattern recognizing, knowledge creation, diffusion, and application, and increasing productivity. The ultimate goal of this new strategic map is to raise the standard of living for the majority of Americans. Businesses that have adopted this new strategy for economic growth are called knowledge-based businesses[22].

According to this strategy, data forms the basic building block of the knowledge-based business and comes in four specific forms: numbers, words, sounds, and images. Advanced computer and telecommunications technologies provide many effective ways to collect, process, store, and manipulate various forms of data at affordable prices for corporations and individuals. People are overloaded with an enormous volume of raw data. This data can have misleading appearances and must be filtered, analyzed, and structured into meaningful patterns. The emerged patterns that are extracted from re-arranging the raw data is information. After the steps of collecting and analyzing data, both data and information become valuable economic resources that can be used for corporations to generate new revenues, profits, and economic growth.

The knowledge-based business, however, has to move to the next stage in order to figure out how to put information to productive use for creating and understanding new lines of business. Here knowledge means knowing how to use information productively and innovatively. This step converts information into knowledge in a process of simultaneously generating, diffusing, and applying knowledge, based on results of data and information. The ultimate goal of the knowledge-based business is to create "smart" products and services that use relevant information to offer additional value to

---

[22] Stan Davis and Jim Botkin, The Coming of Knowledge-Based Business, *Harvard Business Review,* September-October, 1994.

customers. These smart products and services promote productivity and economic growth for both corporations and their customers, which leads to a rise in the standard of living for the majority of people.

## Tacit Knowledge and Technology

The knowledge-based business strategy has far-reaching implications in the knowledge development phase depicted in Figure 2-5. People have to recognize the possibility of different kinds of human knowledge that are involved in their businesses. Not only scientific knowledge, but also other types of knowledge that are embedded in wider nonscientific frameworks of social conceptions and practices should be used to create new ideas and new ways of doing things more efficiently and more effectively.

Even though scientific knowledge need not be exclusively theoretical, it must be systematic enough to be written down and stored as codified knowledge. In every business segment and every unit of the corporation there are possibilities of identifying changing patterns and creating new ideas and then generating and applying that new knowledge. The knowledge created by businesses, however, is most likely to be tacit knowledge that is not available as a text but is embedded in the corporation and specifically resides in the minds of its workers. It is understandable that the business world focuses on transforming that knowledge into revenue and profit rather than turning that knowledge into publications in academic journals.

Technology as a form of knowledge has both codified and tacit components. Some technologies will be public; some are proprietary and protected by patents and trade secrecy.

Proprietary technology is still, however, subject to imitation, adaptation and replacement and may gradually lose its market value over time. The tacit components of technology are especially vulnerable, as workers might leave the company for a competitor and take the learned knowledge with them. In terms of the competitive advantage, tacit technologies are even more important than codified public and proprietary technologies to industries and corporations.

Tacit technologies, however, are created and held by industries and companies rather than by universities or national research laboratories. Not only are tacit technologies essential to business success but are also vitally important to any scientific research that is oriented toward problem solving. This is reflected in academia's increasing interest in collaborating with industries and companies in order to carry out transdisciplinary research projects. The trend has been set in motion in which science, technology, and industries are moving closer together. This trend speeds up the convergence of the four curves for knowledge, technology, tools and implementation depicted in Figure 1-10.

## Disruptive Technology and Sustaining Technology

Technology development is not confined to the applications of sophisticated scientific knowledge. As a matter of fact, the meaning of technology has been broadly extended far beyond scientific methodology, engineering, and manufacturing. According to Clayton Christensen, a professor at Harvard Business School, technology means "the processes by which an organization transforms labor, capital, materials, and information into products and services of greater value."[23] Under this definition, all companies in any business have their own technologies, no matter what business they are in. Technologies can be associated with technology and non-technology companies, manufacturers and services providers, as well as retail and wholesale businesses.

So far, two types of technology changes have been identified as bearing a great potential to generate the 10X revolutionary forces: technology breakthroughs and disruptive technologies. Technology breakthroughs are commonly recognized as such revolutionary forces; they are brought about by advances in scientific research and technology innovation. Various applications of these technology breakthroughs can generate discontinuous changes in engineering, manufacturing, management, and marketing, which in turn create opportunities for new and improved products and services with the potential to make existing products and technologies obsolete. Companies that capitalize on such opportunities can grow large in a very short time period, while companies that miss out may end up with business disasters or go out of business entirely.

Another kind of technology change that could generate the 10X force is disruptive technology, a term popularized by Clayton Christensen in his book *The Innovator's Dilemma*. Disruptive technologies are not necessarily

---

[23] Clayton Christensen, *The Innovator's Dilemma: When New Technologies Cause Great Firms to Fail,* Harvard Business School Press, 1997; HarperBusiness, 2000.

more advanced than existing technologies in terms of sophistication or technical merit, but they bring to the market a very different value proposition. Products based on disruptive technologies are typically cheaper, simpler, smaller, and more convenient to use. Examples can be found in many industries, such as minicomputers versus mainframes, and PCs versus minicomputers. All these disruptive computer technology changes have generated rapid industry transitions as well as fundamental shifts of customers' demand in the computer market.

Technology innovations based on discontinuous breakthroughs or incremental improvements are called sustaining technologies, because they upgrade the performance of existing products and services, and improve companies' profit margins. With competitive advantages in research and development as well as a deep pocket of financial resources, many well-established large companies have been at the front of sustaining technology innovations.

Faced with disruptive technology changes, however, many well-established and well-managed companies fall under attack by relatively unknown emerging companies. Christensen suggests a failure framework to explain why good management can still lead to failures; he proposes five principles to deal with disruptive technology innovations[24]. His findings reveal that, essentially, disruptive technology innovations are able to convert a great company's competitive advantages into disadvantages, which eventually lead to the great company's decline or demise in the increasingly intensified competitive environment.

For example, initially a disruptive technology produces smaller, simpler, and cheaper products that under-perform existing ones and target a small emerging market segment. This, of course, comes with great uncertainty and risk. In general, an established, successful company has already occupied a large market share in the matured mainstream market. There seems little demand for low-performance, cheaper products based on disruptive technology innovations, because big customers in the mainstream market do not want them. As large companies listen to their big-profit customers, the large company is not willing to be involved in the early stage of disruptive technology innovations. Hence, the advantage of their customer-driven operations becomes a great disadvantage when it keeps them away from emerging markets. In this way, they lose the significant first-mover advantage.

---

[24] Ibid.

A well-established company has often developed its own processes for evaluating technological innovations and for assessing its customers' needs. Those internal processes have guided the company's transformation of labor, capital, materials, and information into outputs of higher value, namely high-profit-margin products. Equipped with highly educated engineers and highly skilled professional workers as well as enormous financial assets, the well-established company has great capabilities to develop higher-performance, higher-margin products for the huge mainstream markets to maximize profits for its shareholders.

Facing with disruptive technology innovations, these capabilities interfere with the company's ability to address new problems in emerging markets, and to detect and respond quickly to the changing trend in the industries. It is against its value and economic rationale for the well-established company to shift its priority from developing high-margin products to developing low-margin products. Therefore, its failure to deal with disruptive technology innovations springs from the company's definition of value and its internal processes of allocating its human, financial, and knowledge resources.

Changing a company's value and internal process has proved very difficult, as there always exists a great resistance to the strategic adjustments required in dealing with disruptive technology innovations. Consequently, with all their priorities focusing on the high-end marketplace, well-established great companies create a vacuum at the low-end segment. This vacuum is filled by emerging competitors who use disruptive technology innovations to their advantage and eventually evolve to displace high-end competitors and their dominating technologies. That is why disruptive technology changes seem to be more dangerous than discontinuous technology breakthroughs to the well-established great company.

Nevertheless, it is important to identify both discontinuous technology breakthroughs and disruptive technology innovations to detect the potential 10X forces that trigger the strategic inflection points. Under the Kozmetsky Effect—namely the convergence and vigorous interaction of knowledge, technology, tools, and implementation—human creativity and ingenuity are able to produce technology breakthroughs at the high end as well as disruptive technology innovations at the low end of the marketplace. Both kinds of technology innovations have contributed to the rapid industry structure transformation and creation of big winners and losers, which has resulted in an enormous economic growth in the last a half of the twentieth century.

## • Tools and Implementation

The third and fourth development phases depicted in Figure 1-10 are "tools" and "implementation", representing two stages of science and technology commercialization. The first stage, "tools", denotes specification and design of a competitive product and the associated processes that manufacture and support the product; and the development of design methodologies and related computer-aided tools. The second stage, "implementation", includes a variety of product implementation activities such as manufacturing, testing, quality control, marketing, and customers' satisfaction and learning process, and society's acceptance and changing attitude toward the new product and technology innovation.

## Science and Technology Commercialization

Originally, science and technology commercialization has been understood largely in terms of the application and exploitation of existing knowledge, experience, and know-how. Now it is gradually recognized that commercialization is a complex process of multiple experiences in design, engineering, manufacturing, marketing and social experiences for generating economic returns and new knowledge.

The first stage of commercialization is the focus on the new product and process specification and design. The ultimate goal of knowledge and technology innovations toward problem-solving is to develop new product and service families that significantly add value to customers, meet the emerging demand of the market, and increase revenues and profits for both companies and their customers. As described in the above section, technology is a type of economic resource that can be employed in productive activities. Technology, however, is not a commodity available off the shelf, nor can it be guaranteed to work well through a technology transfer agreement or other intellectual property or loyalty arrangement. Technology needs to be developed and applied to meet the circumstances of a specific company in the process of technology commercialization.

The specification and design of a new product must address the changing market in order to meet shifting consumer preference. Importantly, there must be a skillful combination of technologies, both existing and newly developed. Equally important, the company must make the most of its specialist skills and management competence to keep abreast of its competition. There are many uncertainties and risks involved in the new product and process specification and design. Generally, new technologies come into practice in a very primitive setting; many technological details need to be worked out in order to apply them. Therefore, a vast amount of development work in the early stage has to be dedicated to expanding the invention for practical application.

The success of a company's product and process specification and design depends upon not only the application of new technology invention, but also the use of new or existing complementary technologies to support the products and services. New product specification and design are expensive endeavors undertaken by a company's engineers and designers, who have the knowledge about the company's capabilities to produce, but do not necessarily understand the management component or opportunities in future markets. It is difficult to appreciate the potential significance of new technology and associated new products and services at the time of their introduction.

Wisdom in the fundamental choices in product development is based on the right mixes of products, technical ability, management and targeted marketing. These choices will determine a company's future success. In particular, product and process design affects a company's production of a wide range of products, and determines appropriateness for different market segments. It allows companies to achieve cost-efficiency and substantial economies of scale on the production side as well as potential technical increment improvements on the product side.

Risks, however, arise once the design of product and process is chosen, as the company will be locked into those choices, imposing technological conditions and marketing constrains on the company's operation. If the market changes its direction, as when disruptive technologies take the mainstream market, the company can fail in those technology areas where it has no competence. Nearly 70-80% of the product's ultimate acquisition costs or life cycle costs is determined by decisions made from the conception in the product development cycle[25]. Once the product design has been

---

[25] Kenneth Crow, Achieving Design to Cost Objectives, Product Development Forum Home Page. According to Crow's definition, product acquisition costs include product costs plus selling, general & administrative costs, plus warranty costs and profit. Life cycle costs equal product acquisition costs plus other related capital costs, training costs, operating costs, support costs, and disposal costs.

completed, it will be too late for the company to take cost reduction and profit promotion measures, as most of its cost structure has been locked into place. Therefore, technology commercialization needs to be oriented in searching those new product and process specifications and designs that have the potential to be developed in a variety of ways to reduce locked-in technology risks.

## Concurrent Engineering

Currently, many new ideas and methodologies, such as integrated product development, concurrent engineering and computer-supported cooperative work, are employed to resolve the above-mentioned problems and to speed up the process of science and technology commercialization.

Integrated product development is a systematic approach to product development, and is based on the integrated design of products and their manufacturing and support processes. It involves a teaming of different functional disciplines to integrate and concurrently apply all necessary processes to in order to produce a competitive product that satisfies customers' needs.

Concurrent engineering is also known as simultaneous engineering. There are many perceptions about the nature of concurrent engineering, and it has presently not been well defined. Authors of an IDA report, *The Role of Concurrent Engineering in Weapons System Acquisition*, have initiated its framework as

.... a systematic approach to the integrated, concurrent design of products and their related processes, including manufacture and support. This approach is intended to cause the developers, from the outset, to consider all elements of the product life cycle from conception through disposal, including quality, cost, schedule, and user requirements[26].

Concurrent engineering has been understood as getting the right people together at the right time to identify and resolve design problems through

---

[26] Winner, R. I., J. P. Pennell, H. E. Bertrand, and M. M.G. Slusarezuk, *The Role of Concurrent Engineering in Weapons System Acquisition,* IDA Report R-338, Institute for Defense Analyses, 1988.

simultaneous designs. All attributes of products and processes are taken into consideration in the design phase, including manufacturing ability, assembly, operability, manageability, schedule or time to the market, cost, quality, safety, risk, performance, maintainability, customer satisfaction, social acceptability and others. Many potential problems that may arise during the entire life cycle of the product could be resolved in the early stage of product design.

The basic idea of integrated product development and concurrent engineering is the integration of methodologies, processes, human skills, and tools and methods to simultaneously design all desired downstream characteristics during the upstream phase in order to improve a product's quality and reduce developing time and costs. Integrated product development and concurrent engineering involve the interaction of a diverse group of individuals who may be located over a wide geographic area and have different professional information and knowledge. Therefore integrated product development and concurrent engineering must include an information and knowledge sharing system, or so-called computer-supported cooperative work. It consists of group decision support systems, sharable knowledge bases, intelligent systems, and expert systems for science and engineering. It also uses advanced communication tools such as the electronic meeting-room, video conferencing, calendar manager, and group authoring tools.

Advances in computer networking and telecommunications technology speed up the integration of the "tools" and "implementation" phases that leads to the overall convergence of the four subprocesses of "knowledge", "technology", "tools", and "implementation" depicted in Figure 2-5. To study and observe these four subprocesses in the knowledge and technology innovations for an industry is key to detect the potential 10X forces that generate the infraction points.

## 2-4   A Summary of Chapter 2

Summarizing what we have presented in this chapter, Theoretical Perspectives on Economic Transformation, one can find that there is apparently no one economic theory that explains how the U.S. economy has grown and transformed over time.

As shown in Figure 2-6, the neoclassical economic growth theory deals with a specific situation in which production function is defined as a concave growth curve with diminishing returns on labor and capital. It assumes that a company is aware of all the technological options available to it; therefore there exists a well-defined production possibility frontier. The company's goal is to maximize profits by choosing output and input factors in response to changing output price and factor input prices in the marketplace along the production frontier that is assumed to be given.

From the above analyses in Section 2-3, one can observe that companies cannot have complete information and knowledge about technology innovations, particularly the future direction of development of technologies. How to choose new technology and which products to develop are the strategic decisions that determine a company's fate. Unfortunately, none of the economic growth theories are able to answer that question.

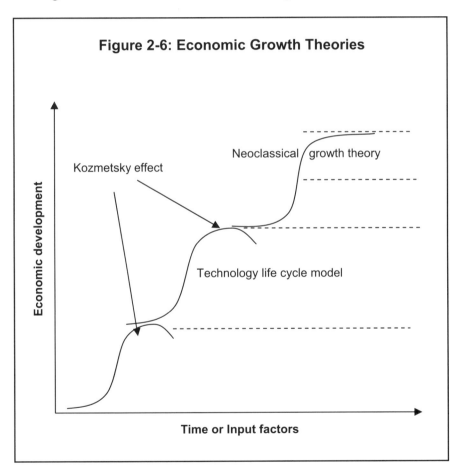

**Figure 2-6: Economic Growth Theories**

The technology and product life cycle theory in the business world has recognized a more complex growth process based on the S-shaped curve, with a phase of increasing returns to scale leading to a phase of decreasing return to scale, on which the neoclassical economic growth theory focuses. From our discussion in Section 2-3, it becomes clearer that it is the intersection of two S-shaped curves in which more important economic growth phenomena have been observed and felt by many top managers of American corporations. It offers interesting and exciting opportunities for hyper economic growth; at the same time truly miserable disasters are possible in this seemly chaotic and turbulent environment. Studying the Kozmetsky Effect is an endeavor that moves in the direction of searching for mechanism that leads to the creation of the strategic inflection points.

It should be recognized that economic transformation is a complicated and dynamic process in which economic growth has been a vitally important component. Unfortunately, economic theory has provided us with little knowledge about how scientific breakthroughs and disruptive technology innovations bring about economic growth. We have to continue to rely on empirical evidence to understand the real world phenomenon of economic transformation. That is our task in the following chapters of this book.

# PART TWO

# ECONOMIC GROWTH OF THE UNITED STATES

# Chapter 3

## Performance of the U.S. Economy

The preceding chapters covered the principal drivers of U.S. economic transformation as well as the demographic forces that influence the past, present, and future of this transformation. This chapter provides a quantitative presentation of U.S. economic transformation over the last fifty years from the standpoint of real economic activities.

Economic growth has been at the center of U.S. economic transformation for the last five decades. Rapidly growing amounts of goods and services are being produced in order to meet the escalating demands of consumers. This also serves to generate employment opportunities for the expanding U.S. population. Without economic growth, there would be no prosperity and no political and social stability for the majority of Americans. Faster economic growth results in a wealthy society, creating a large middle class that can afford to give individuals the opportunity to develop their careers and enjoy their lives.

The spectacular growth of the productive power of the U.S. economy has made America's standard of living the envy of the world. It has promoted the United States to superpower status in economic strength, military capacity, and political and cultural influences. This chapter will use macroeconomic variables to illustrate the growing power of the U.S. economy. A rising standard of living is accomplished through rapid economic growth, a relatively stable price level or moderation of inflation, and a high employment level. This chapter provides an analysis of how the U.S. economy has continued to grow in order to approach these economic goals.

This chapter is divided into three sections. Section 3-1 examines the potential growth of real GDP and the actual performance of the U.S. economy. Section 3-2 presents the changing picture of productivity in private business and the manufacturing sector over the last fifty years. Section 3-3 analyzes the relationship between the unemployment rate and price inflation in the U.S. economy.

## 3-1 Growth Potential and Actual Performance

As described in Part One of this book, U.S. economic transformation has been driven by revolutions in technology as well as America's ideology in the evolving capitalist system. The direct sources of economic growth are described by the basic growth equation and growth accounting model in Sections 2-1 and 2-2 of Chapter Two of Part One. In general, there are three main factors that allow an economy to grow: the quantity of labor input, the quantity of capital input, and productivity growth. Therefore, the speed by which an economy can grow is limited by various factors that determine both types of input and an improvement in productivity.

The desirability of further economic growth will be addressed in Part Three of this book, in which we will see that the U.S. population is expected to grow at 0.8-1.0% per year. In order to raise the standard of living for the majority of Americans, the real GDP must increase faster than the population rate. The growth rate of the working-age population rebounded from its low of 0.45% in 1990 to 0.9-1.2% in 2000. It is expected to decline to 0.2% by 2025 and to stabilize around 0.6-0.75% after exhausting the influence of baby boomers. There is no decline in U.S. working-age population in the official forecasts; therefore, the U.S. labor force will continue its growth at a moderate rate.

In order to secure the most benefit of economic growth to society, population growth must be moderate. Rapid economic growth, combined with a quickly expanding population, would create air pollution, proliferation of wastes, erosion of natural resources and landscape, excessive consumption of energy and energy crises, and destruction to the ecological system. Constrained by the capacity of the U.S. economic system, the potential growth rate is estimated to be about 3% per year for real GDP. Using data provided by the Congressional Budget Office and the actual real GDP in 1947–2000, Figure 3-1 depicts real potential GDP over the time period of 1949 through 2005, adjusted for inflation to 1996 dollars.

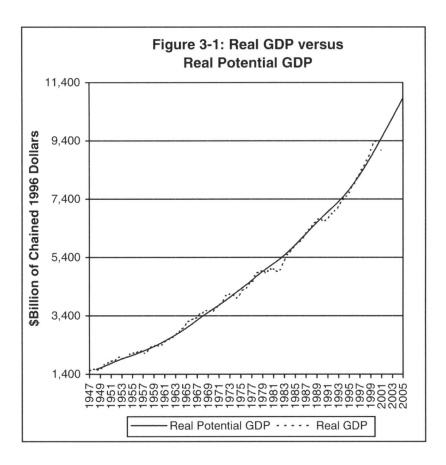

The potential GDP for a period T is defined as the level of real GDP at full employment. Full employment is defined as the amount of employment realized, given that existing incentives and fully flexible wages are responsive to supply and demand in the labor market. The unemployment rate that corresponds to full employment is called the natural rate of unemployment, or the "non-accelerating inflation rate of unemployment".

The growth rate of the potential GDP varies over time. A range of 4.9-4.78% during the years 1949-1953 declined to 3.10-3.98 in 1954-1961. During 1961-1969 the potential GDP rebounded, growing at an annual rate of 4.01-4.39%. In the 1970s the growth rate declined once more, falling into the range of 3.11-3.89%. It further declined to 2.54-2.98% in 1980-1984, and then grew to 3.0-3.34% in 1985-1989. The potential GDP grew 2.54-2.86% per year in the first half of the 1990s and 3.0-3.64% in the second half. As of 2000, the potential GDP grew at 3.72%, the highest rate since 1970.

Figure 3-1 shows that the real GDP has been quite close to the potential GDP. An up-shot period, in which actual real GDP rises above the potential GDP, is always followed by a down-shot period, in which the actual real GDP falls below the potential GDP, and vice versa. The percentage departure of actual real GDP from potential GDP is called the GDP gap. Table 3-1 provides the up-shot and down-shot periods and their duration in number of quarters and the ranges of their gaps.

Table 3-1: GDP Gaps (1949-2000)

| Time Period | Up-Shot | | Down-Shot | |
|---|---|---|---|---|
| | Duration quarter | Gap % | Duration quarter | Gap % |
| 1949.1-1950.1 | | | 5 | -(1.3-4.5) |
| **1950.2---1953.4** | 15 | 1.2-5.5 | | |
| 1954.1---1954.3 | | | 3 | -(0.2-0.8) |
| **1954.4---1957.3** | 12 | 0.7-4.2 | | |
| 1957.4---1959.1 | | | 6 | -(0.5-4.3) |
| **1959.2---1960.1** | 4 | 0.2-1.2 | | |
| 1960.2---1963.4 | | | 15 | -(0.1-3.8) |
| **1964.1---1970.1** | 25 | 0.5-6.4 | | |
| 1970.2---1972.1 | | | 8 | -(0.02-2.1) |
| **1972.2---1974.2** | 9 | 0.56-4.27 | | |
| 1974.3---1978.1 | | | 15 | -(0.05-4.85)% |
| **1978.2---1980.1** | 8 | 0.07-2.16% | | |
| 1980.2---1987.3 | | | 30 | -(0.31-7.63)% |
| **1987.4---1990.2** | 11 | 0.19-1.32% | | |
| 1990.3---1997.1 | | | 29 | -(0.20-3.46)% |
| **1997.2---2000.4** | 15 | 0.40-3.48% | | |

Table 3-1 indicates that as of 2000, the longest up-shot period (25 quarters), was from the first quarter of 1964 through the first quarter of 1970, with the largest gap (6.35%) occurring in the first quarter of 1966. There are two periods of 15 quarters each (1950 Q2 through 1953 Q4, and 1997 Q2 through 2000 Q4), ranked second in terms of duration, which have their largest GDP gap (5.52%) in Q1 of 1953 and 3.48% in the Q2 of 2000. Even though the latest up-shot (1997 Q2 through 2000 Q4) has not been the longest, the growth rate of the potential GDP has increased since 1993, and the real GDP has played catchup with the potential GDP, which postponed the up-shot until the second quarter of 1997.

The longest down-shot of 30 quarters appeared in 1980 Q2–1987 Q3, with real GDP falling below the potential by 7.63% in Q4 of 1982. The second longest down-shot period lasted 29 quarters in the 1990s, from Q3 of 1990 through Q1 of 1997, with the largest GDP gap 3.46% in Q1 of 1991.

Since the potential GDP expanded consistently for the past fifty years, the decrease of real GDP did not necessarily imply recession or depression. The actual performance of the U.S. economy can be observed from Figure 3-2, which provides the annualized growth rate of real GDP calculated from quarterly data. It is clear that the U.S. economy has grown quarter after quarter and year after year for the last fifty years with some brief exceptions. According to the commonly used definition of economic recession—two consecutive negative quarters of real GDP growth, there were eight recessions in the U.S. economy from 1947 through 2000. One can also observe that no recession lasted more than three quarters, and many expansions were longer than all of the recession periods combined. Table 3-2 provides more detailed data on the growth picture of the U.S. economy over 1947–2000.

Table 3-1 indicates the dominant nature of economic expansion over economic recession during the last fifty years. The most impressive expansion began in the middle of the 1950s and extended almost throughout the entire 1960s. During this expansion, there were three short periods of interruption to the growth of real GDP. The interruptions occurred in 1959 Q3 (the annualized growth rate of real GDP was -0.17%), 1960 Q1–1960 Q4 (-1.97%, 0.74%, and -5.15%), and 1967 Q2 (-0.26%). The expansion ended with the two-quarter recession of 1969 Q4–1970 Q1 when the real GDP declined at the annualized rate of 1.55% for two quarters. Economic growth in the 1970s and 1980s was more frequently interrupted by recessions, such as the ones in 1974 Q3–1975 Q1, 1980 Q2–1980 Q3, 1981 Q4–1982 Q1, and the latest recession of 1990 Q3–1991 Q1.

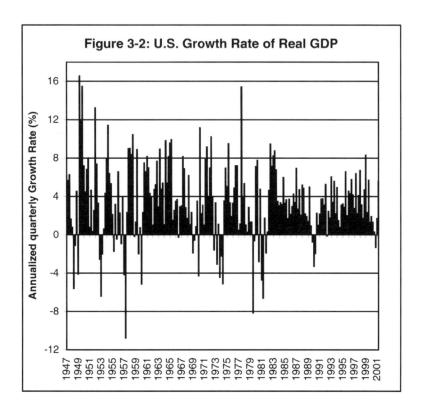

Figure 3-2: U.S. Growth Rate of Real GDP

The longest expansion period began in the second quarter of 1991 and paused in the first quarter of 1993, in which the real GDP declined by $1.9 billion, about 0.11% of the annual rate. The expansion resumed in the second quarter of 1993 and continued. After the beginning of the new century the U.S. economy decelerated its growth, with real GDP rising by 2.3%, 5.7%, 1.3% and 1.9% in the four quarters of 2000. The negative growth rate of real GDP occurred in the third quarter of 2001 (-1.3%), and followed by the positive growth rates 1.7% and 5.6% in the next two quarters. By the conventional definition of an economic recession as at least two consecutive declines in real GDP, the performance of the U.S. economy in the first two years of the new century could not be said to be an economic recession.

Ten years after the business-cycle trough of 1990-91, the U.S. economy has expanded with robust growth and moderate inflation. In 2000 the real GDP achieved a record high, $9.394 trillion of adjusted (1996) dollars, with the average annual rate of 3.76% over 32 quarters in a row. Even though the average growth rate of the 1990s was lower than that of previous expansions in the 1950s, 1960s, 1970s, and 1980s, the stability of economic growth significantly improved in the 1990s. As a result of economic expansion, the U.S. unemployment rate has been substantially reduced from 7.49% in 1992 to 4.50% in 1998, and further to 4.23% in 2000, the lowest unemployment rate since 1969 (U.S. unemployment rate was 3.49% in 1969).

Table 3-2: Expansion and Recession of the U.S. Economy
(1947-2001)

| Time Period | Expansion | | Recession | |
|---|---|---|---|---|
| | Duration (quarter) | Average Growth Rate (%) | Duration (quarter) | Average Growth Rate (%) |
| 1947.2-1948.4 | 7 | 3.38 | | |
| **1949.1-1949.2** | | | **2** | **-3.36** |
| 1950.1-1953.2 | 14 | 7.33 | | |
| **1953.3-1954.1** | | | **3** | **-3.65** |
| 1954.2-1955.4 | 7 | 5.45 | | |
| 1956.4-1957.1 | 2 | 4.42 | | |
| **1957.4-1958.1** | | | **2** | **-7.47** |
| 1958.2-1959.2 | 5 | 7.82 | | |
| 1959.4-1960.1 | 2 | 5.10 | | |
| 1961.1-1967.1 | 25 | 5.42 | | |
| 1967.3-1969.3 | 9 | 3.89 | | |
| **1969.4-1970.1** | | | **2** | **-1.55** |
| 1970.2-1970.3 | 2 | 2.17 | | |
| 1971.1-1973.2 | 10 | 5.96 | | |
| **1974.3-1975.1** | | | **3** | **-3.92** |
| 1975.2-1980.1 | 20 | 4.29 | | |
| **1980.2-1980.3** | | | **2** | **-4.39** |
| 1980.4-1981.1 | 2 | 7.44 | | |
| **1981.4-1982.1** | | | **2** | **-5.68** |
| 1982.4-1990.2 | 31 | 4.09 | | |
| **1990.3-1991.1** | | | **3** | **-2.00** |
| 1991.2-1992.4 | 7 | 3.03 | | |
| 1993.2-2001.1 | 32 | 3.76 | | |

Despite the high rate of resource utilization and the tightening labor market, inflation in the United States by some broad measures fell to its lowest level in three decades. The overall CPI (Consumer Price Index) inflation rate declined from 5.40% in 1990 to 1.56% in 1998, the lowest since 1965[1], and stayed at 2.21% in 1999, rebounding to 3.36% in 2000. The core inflation rate, measured by the price index of all consumer items less food and energy, has also declined, from 5.04% in 1990 to 2.08% in 1999. Economists use three key variables to gauge the general performance of an economy at a national aggregate level: real GDP growth rate, unemployment rate, and CPI inflation rate. The extraordinary performance of the U.S. economy in the 1990s was reflected in all those economic indicators.

Figure 3-3 provides a graphical view of those three variables over the time period of 1948 to 2000. Treating the brief recession of 1990-1991 as a short interruption, one can easily see that the economic expansion began shortly after 1982, when the real GDP growth rate jumped from -2.03% in 1982 to 4.33% in 1983, and then again to 7.27% in 1984. Economic growth brought the unemployment rate down from 9.71% in 1982 to 5.26% in 1989, and the CPI inflation rate also dropped from its peak of 13.50% in 1980 to 1.86% in 1986.

The three macroeconomic variables in Figure 3-3 indicate the dynamic evolution process of the U.S. economy at the national aggregate level. The exceptional performance of the U.S. economy in the last decade of the twentieth century is characterized by unprecedented economic growth in the leading emerging sectors. These sectors, including semiconductor and optical component manufacturing, computer manufacturing, software engineering, optical and wireless telecommunications network equipment, electronic commerce, and human genomic sectors, are all a direct result of scientific breakthroughs and revolutionary engineering.

As described in Section 2-3 of Part One, the dynamic process of technological innovation generates superior growth in emerging industries as well as turbulence and chaos. After ten years of exceptional growth, many U.S. technology industries have faced the challenges of new strategic inflection points that were brought about by technology maturity, changing market conditions, a drop in corporations' capital spending, and the plummeting stock market.

---

[1]The U.S. CPI inflation rate was 1.61% in 1965.

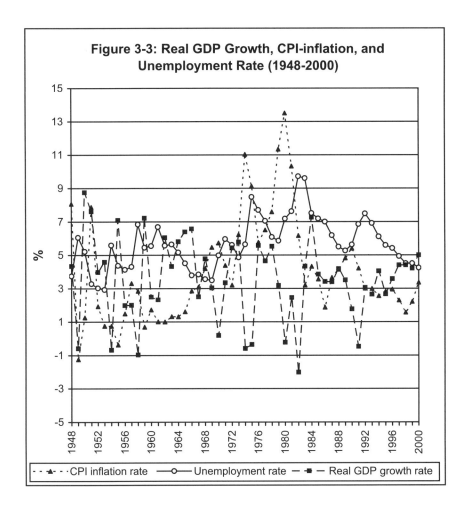

Figure 3-3: Real GDP Growth, CPI-inflation, and Unemployment Rate (1948-2000)

Beginning in the middle of 2000, sharp declines in the demand for computers, communications equipment, and software resulted in the toughest market for technology companies in ten years. Many companies found their revenues falling rapidly and profits in the red. The same industries that grew the U.S. economy so dramatically in the 1990s were now dragging it down. If history provides any guidance for the future, the companies, businesses and sectors that survive this transitional period will become even stronger and help pull the U.S. economy back to its sustainable growth trajectory. Historical data suggest that as the U.S. economy moves forward, both the potential and actual real GDP will continue to fluctuate around an overall trend toward long-term growth.

## 3-2    Increasing Productivity of the U.S. Economy

One of the main sources for economic growth is the rate of improvement in the production processes that convert input factors into the outputs of labor and capital. This improvement is expressed by the growth rate of productivity. One of the prominent characteristics of the prolonged economic expansion of the 1990s is the accelerating productivity of American industries.

On the national aggregate level, increasing productivity has become the key to solving the puzzle of continuous economic growth without inflation. The Chairman of the Federal Reserve Board has articulated his remarks on U.S. productivity changes:

> To illustrate with recent developments in the nonfinancial corporate sector, for about four years price inflation has remained subdued— with prices rising on average about 2 percent per year. During that period, growth in hourly compensation has stepped up, and profitability has been strong. How are these observations reconciled? In the framework of this income-side system, the answer is an acceleration of labor productivity; indeed, for the nonfinancial corporate sector, output per hour has accelerated from around a 1½ percent pace in the first half of the 1990s to more than a 4 percent pace over the past couple of years....
>
> Domestic operating profit margins, rising as they did from 1995 into 1997 in an environment of falling inflation, necessarily implied falling rates of total unit cost increase—most credibly the consequence of rising productivity growth[2].

The private business sector as a whole, the private nonfarm business sector, and the manufacturing sector can be used as examples of the improvements in U.S. productivity. The private business sector accounts for nearly 76% of the gross domestic product (GDP), excluding general government, government enterprises, and nonprofit institutions. The private nonfarm business sector excludes farms, but includes agricultural services. The output of the manufacturing sector is measured as the value of all production

---

[2] Remarks by Chairman Alan Greenspan, Before the New York Association for Business Economics, New York, June 13, 2000.

delivered to non-manufacturing industries as intermediary goods and delivered to consumers as final demand.

Four quantitative measures related to a sector's productivity have been widely used in both economic theory and the business world. They are: output per hour for all individuals in the sector, output per unit of capital, multifactor productivity, and unit labor costs. All of these measures are expressed by indices computed as chained superlative indices (Fisher Ideal indexes) of components of output as well as labor input and capital input. Output per hour represents labor productivity by all individuals, classified by education, work experience, and gender, and weighted by their share of labor compensation. Output per unit of capital denotes the productivity of capital as an input factor. Capital input measures the services derived from capital stock, which includes software and physical assets, such as business equipment, structures, inventories, and land.

The multifactor productivity index describes the relationship between output and all of the inputs involved in production. It is derived by dividing an output index by an input index of combined hours, capital services, energy, materials, and purchased business services. Rather than measuring a specific input factor's contribution to output, the multifactor productivity index is designed to measure the joint influences of a sector's output on technology changes, efficiency improvements, returns to scale, reallocation of resources due to shifts in factor inputs across industries, and other factors[3].

Figures 3-4 – 3-7 present the annual growth rates of output per hour, output per unit of capital, multifactor productivity, and unit labor costs. In each figure, there are three curves, representing the private business sector, private nonfarm business sector and manufacturing sector, and covering the time period of 1949-2000.

As all the curves in these figures represent the annual growth rates of productivity indices rather than the indices themselves, the curves fluctuate largely over time, reflecting the fact that the accelerating pace of productivity improvement is always followed by a decelerating pace of productivity growth or even a negative rate of productivity indexes.

Figure 3-4 shows clearly that since 1991 the fluctuation pattern has been broken by an ascending trend. Labor productivity in all three sectors, particularly in the manufacturing sector, has accelerated. In the past five decades, there was only one time period, from 1956 through 1962, that may be

---

[3] Detailed description of these measurements can be found in Bureau of Labor Statistics Bulletin 2178, September 1983.

comparable with the 1991-2000 period in terms of productivity improvement in the private business sector and in the private nonfarm business sector. In four additional time periods (1962-69, 1972-74, 1976-80, and 1983-91) there were evident trends of declining growth of productivity, each period ending with an economic recession, including the recessions of 1970, 1982, and 1991. After these recessions, the growth rate of productivity rebounded largely in 1971-72, 1975-76, 1983, 1986, and 1991. In the entire period of the 1970s and 1980s, however, the growth rate of labor productivity only fluctuated around 2.0%.

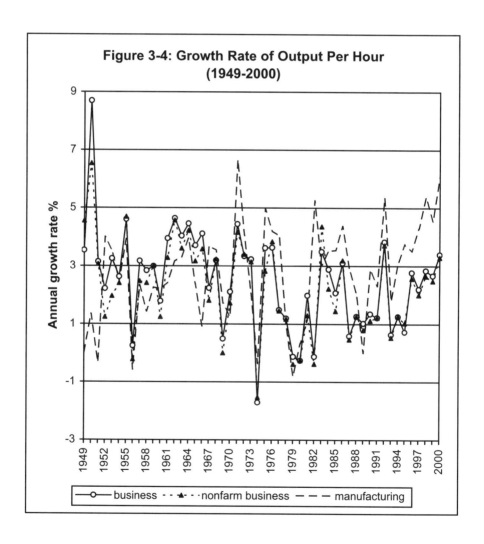

Figure 3-4: Growth Rate of Output Per Hour (1949-2000)

Figure 3-4 also shows that growth rates of labor productivity of the manu-facturing sector were lower than those of the private business sector and of the private nonfarm business sector in most years before 1967. Since 1967, however, productivity from the labor sector has improved more quickly in the manufacturing sector than in other private sectors of the U.S. economy. This is demonstrated in Figure 3-4, where the labor productivity growth curve of the manufacturing sector is the highest. Particularly during 1993-99, the labor productivity of U.S. manufacturing grew nearly two-times faster than private business.

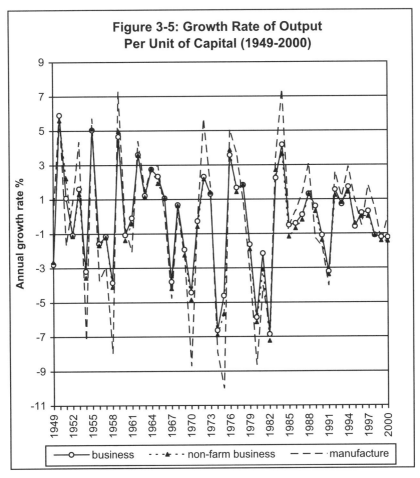

Figures 3-5 and 3-6 do not show significant gaps among the three sectors in terms of annual growth rates of productivity of capital input and multifactor productivity indexes. From 1991-1998, only the manufacturing sector showed increased productivity growth. Capital and multifactor productivity did not increase.

Therefore, during the last decade, the increasing pace of improvement in U.S. productivity for the last decade is primarily in labor productivity. The growth rates of capital productivity and multifactor productivity have not indicated an apparent break in recent decades from the previous years' pattern.

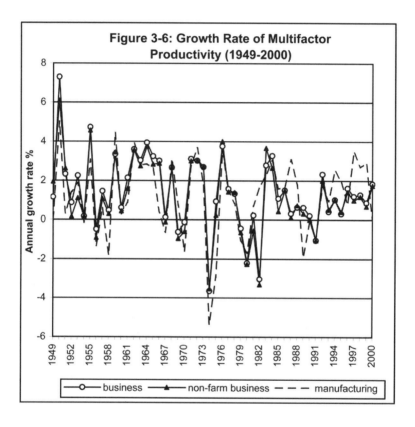

Figure 3-7 displays growth rates of unit labor costs for these three sectors. Since 1990, unit labor costs have increased at a declining pace. The manufacturing sector's unit labor costs have actually decreased since 1994. Theoretically, a strong consumer demand for goods and services, combined with the lowest unemployment rate in recent years, should have generated inflation pressure and pushed prices up. To date, that expected price inflation has not materialized in the U.S. economy, because the accelerating increases in labor productivity and the simultaneously decreasing rate of unit labor costs drive up corporate profits. Without raising output prices, American businesses were able to increase their profitability with continuously improving productivity and reduced costs.

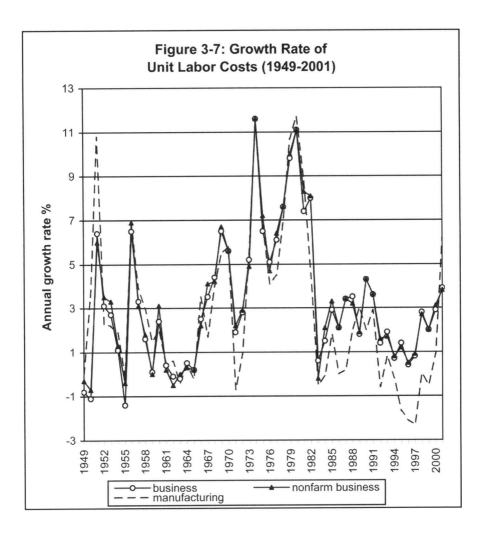

Figure 3-7: Growth Rate of
Unit Labor Costs (1949-2001)

Table 3-3 provides the average growth rates of the four measures of productivity for the three sectors over different time periods. As the table shows, in the first two time periods, 1949-55 and 1956-65, the four measures had increased at 0.9-3.9% per year except for output per unit of capital during 1956-1965, which increased less than 0.5% per year. The time period of 1966-70 was a prelude to the high inflation period of 1971-81. In 1966 the CPI inflation rate began to move out of the low inflation zone that kept the inflation rate below 2% in 1959–1965. The CPI inflation rate reached 5.72% in 1970, 11% in 1974, and 13.5% in 1980.

Increasingly high inflation is bad for productivity improvement in general and hurts capital productivity in particular. Higher inflation is usually associated with higher wages and compensation for workers, resulting in an increase in unit labor costs. Higher inflation also raises the nominal value of capital assets, which reduces the capital productivity even without increase in real capital assets. Higher inflation makes capital investment more expensive, which may cause businesses to cut back on their investments. Less investment in productive capital assets delays the process of innovation and slows the introduction of new technologies onto factory floors and design rooms. This in turn slows labor productivity. Dramatically increased unit labor costs, decreased capital productivity, and reduced labor and multifactor productivity can all be observed in the high-inflation time periods of 1966-70 and 1971-81 (Table 3-3).

Table 3-3: Average Annual Growth Rates of Productivity Indexes (1949-2000)

| | Output per hour for all persons (%) | | | | | | |
|---|---|---|---|---|---|---|---|
| | 1949-1955 | 1956-1965 | 1966-1970 | 1971-1981 | 1982-1990 | 1991-2000 | 1995-2000 |
| Private business | 3.95 | 3.24 | 2.38 | 1.87 | 1.68 | 2.03 | 2.27 |
| Private non-farm business | 3.26 | 2.80 | 2.01 | 1.72 | 1.55 | 1.96 | 2.17 |
| Manufacturing | 2.49 | 2.27 | 2.23 | 2.47 | 3.06 | 3.95 | 4.58 |
| | Output per unit capital (%) | | | | | | |
| Private business | 0.94 | 0.50 | -1.64 | -0.96 | 0.04 | -0.12 | -0.44 |
| Private non-farm business | 0.97 | 0.34 | -1.88 | -1.23 | -0.23 | -0.26 | -0.54 |
| Manufacturing | 1.33 | 0.14 | -3.06 | -1.52 | 0.61 | 0.42 | 0.26 |
| | Multifactor productivity index (%) | | | | | | |
| Private business | 2.68 | 2.08 | 1.02 | 0.95 | 0.84 | 0.93 | 1.08 |
| Private non-farm business | 2.38 | 1.81 | 0.78 | 0.81 | 0.69 | 0.83 | 0.98 |
| Manufacturing | 1.91 | 1.53 | 0.42 | 0.32 | 1.48 | 1.76 | 2.50 |
| | Unit labor costs (%) | | | | | | |
| Private business | 1.71 | 1.47 | 4.50 | 6.83 | 3.12 | 1.61 | 1.38 |
| Private non-farm business | 2.31 | 1.51 | 4.56 | 6.99 | 3.13 | 1.61 | 1.36 |
| Manufacturing | 3.43 | 1.82 | 4.10 | 6.44 | 1.43 | -0.46 | -1.38 |

   The time period of 1982-90 represents a transition from higher to lower inflation and from higher to lower unemployment in the U.S. economy. CPI inflation rates decreased from 6.16% in 1982 to nearly 4.8% in 1989, and unemployment rates declined from 9.7% in 1982 to 5.26% in 1989. Significant improvements in labor, capital productivity, and multifactor productivity were particularly evident in the manufacturing sector. In all three sectors, the pace of growth for the cost of labor was reduced.

   The time period of 1991-99 was characterized by lower inflation and unemployment rates. Since 1997, CPI inflation rates have remained below 5% per year while unemployment rates have been less than 3% per year. Correspondingly, the speed of productivity improvement has increased and the speed of increases in unit labor costs has declined. The manufacturing sector recorded an average increase of 3.95% per year in labor productivity over the last ten years. Simultaneously, the averaged reductions in unit labor costs were approximately 0.46% per year during 1991-99. The time period of 1995-99 witnessed a significant improvement in labor productivity, unit costs, and multifactor productivity. Beginning in 1994, the output per unit of capital continued to decrease annually.

   As discussed in Section 1-1 of Chapter 1, the information revolution is characterized by the explosive growth of semiconductors, PCs, communications equipment, and the Internet. Personal computers arrived on the market in the early 1980s and were quickly adopted by businesses and consumers. New computer technology has affected individual households, business firms, and government agencies and organizations, which should have made the U.S. economy more productive and efficient. In 1987, however, Robert Solow, a Nobel laureate in economics, observed that one could see the computer age everywhere except in the productivity statistics, because U.S. productivity began to slide in the 1970s and did not show any improvement as of the end of the 1980s. Solow's aphorism[4] is called the Solow productivity paradox and still continues to be debated.

   Labor productivity growth did decline significantly from an average of 3.95% in 1948-55 to 1.87% in 1971-81, and to 1.68% in 1982-90. A similar situation occurred in the multifactor productivity index in all three sectors shown in Table 3-3. In the 1990s, particularly in 1995-99, Solow's paradox appears to be reversed, as the average labor productivity and multifactor

---

[4] "You can see the computer age everywhere but in the productivity statistics." — Robert Solow, *New York Review of Books,* July 12, 1987, cited from "The Solow productivity paradox: What do computers do to productivity?" by Jack E. Triplett in *Canadian Journal of Economics,* Vol. 32, No. 2, April 1999.

productivity index increased at faster rates than in the 1980s and 1970s. The index of output per unit of capital, however, has continued to decline except in the manufacturing sector. The issues of how long the accelerating labor productivity can continue and how to explain the upswing in labor productivity after 1995 are still debated, though statistical data has begun to reveal the positive effects of information technology on the U.S. aggregate productivity measurements.

Taking the above observations into consideration, it is clear that the growth rates of productivity indexes are correlated with each other and that all of them are closely associated with economic growth and inflation within the U.S. economy. To explore these relationships we have calculated correlation coefficients of time series of growth rates of the four productivity indexes and the real GDP growth rate as well as CPI inflation rates. The results are presented in Table 3-4.

The growth rates of labor productivity, capital productivity, and multifactor productivity are all positively correlated, but are negatively correlated to the growth rate of the unit labor costs index. Growth rates of these three productivity indexes are positively correlated to the growth rate of real GDP, and negatively correlative to inflation rates. The growth rates of unit labor costs indexes, however, are negatively correlated to the growth rate of real GDP, while positively correlated to inflation rates. As Table 3-4 indicates, the private business sector, private nonfarm business sector, and manufacturing sector share a similar correlation coefficients pattern in each category. The correlation between labor productivity growth and real GDP growth is weaker for the manufacturing sector than for the other two sectors, which may be due to the declining share of the manufacturing sector in GDP. Nevertheless, the strong positive correlation between the growth rates of unit labor costs and inflation rates suggests that slower increases in unit labor costs have made a strong contribution to taming inflation in the recent decade.

## Table 3-4: Correlation Coefficients of Growth Rates of Productivity Indexes (1949-2000)

| Private Business Sector | | | | |
|---|---|---|---|---|
| Correlation coefficients | Output per hour | Output per unit capital | Multifactor productivity | Unit labor costs |
| Output per hour | 1 | 0.633 | 0.906 | -0.648 |
| Output per unit capital | | 1 | 0.876 | -0.587 |
| Multifactor productivity | | | 1 | -0.663 |
| Unit labor costs | | | | 1 |
| Real GDP growth rate | 0.588 | 0.911 | 0.813 | -0.381 |
| Inflation rate | -0.471 | -0.449 | -0.502 | 0.876 |
| Private Non-farm Business Sector | | | | |
| Correlation coefficients | Output per hour | Output per unit capital | Multifactor productivity | Unit labor costs |
| Output per hour | 1 | 0.654 | 0.909 | -0.701 |
| Output per unit capital | | 1 | 0.878 | -0.596 |
| Multifactor productivity | | | 1 | -0.681 |
| Unit labor costs | | | | 1 |
| Real GDP growth rate | 0.573 | 0.912 | 0.797 | -0.395 |
| Inflation rate | -0.529 | -0.446 | -0.503 | 0.877 |
| Manufacturing Sector | | | | |
| Correlation coefficients | Output per hour | Output per unit capital | Multifactor productivity | Unit labor costs |
| Output per hour | 1 | 0.312 | 0.521 | -0.681 |
| Output per unit capital | | 1 | 0.825 | -0.542 |
| Multifactor productivity | | | 1 | -0.609 |
| Unit labor costs | | | | 1 |
| Real GDP growth rate | 0.06 | 0.858 | 0.697 | -0.262 |
| Inflation rate | -0.408 | -0.508 | -0.554 | 0.812 |

## 3-3 Relationship Between Unemployment Rates and Inflation Rates—The Shifting Phillips Curve

The Phillips Curve is the statistical relationship of the rate of price inflation and the rate of unemployment in a national economy. This theory says that higher inflation rates are associated with lower unemployment rates, and vice-versa.

This relationship is based on an economic logic: When an economy's aggregate demand extends beyond its production capacity, the economy arrives at or goes below the "full-employment" unemployment rate. The tight labor market drives up wages and prices and generates a higher inflation rate. Therefore, excess aggregate demand creates an inflationary gap, which is closed by rising wages and prices. Facing high prices, consumers will usually reduce spending. The increased costs of labor and other input factors cause businesses to cut back on investment spending and reduce production. At this point the aggregate demand is brought back in line with the national production potential, resulting in lower unemployment rates and higher inflation rates. This process is referred to as an economy's self-correcting mechanism.

This self-correcting mechanism also works to close a recessionary gap. This gap is generated by the depressed aggregate demand and is characterized by higher unemployment rates and lower capacity utilization rates. In this situation, there are many workers willing to work for lower wages, which reduces costs and improves business profitability. Businesses add workers, produce more goods, and sell them at lower prices. These businesses continue to make money due to declining production costs. Falling prices and rising employment drive up aggregate demand and eliminate the recessionary gap. As this proceeds, unemployment rates decline and the economy moves towards its full employment state. In reality, however, the recessionary gap may not be closed so easily due to many factors, particularly rigid wage rates and prices.

The economy has not stayed in the specified combination of inflation rates and unemployment rates that people or policy makers may have desired or hope for. As the above economic logic shows, the self-correcting mechanism works to bring the economy back to the state of full employment in the long term. In the short term, however, many factors act on the economy simultaneously. This makes it difficult to feed U.S. data into the Phillips Curve.

Figure 3-8 provides a scatter diagram by plotting the U.S. unemployment rates and inflation rates over the years from 1955 through 2000. The data points are widely spread, with an inflation rate range of 0.4% (in 1955) to 13.5% (in 1980) and an unemployment rate range of 3.49% (in 1969) to 9.71% (in 1982). It is difficult to fit those points into one down-sloping Phillips Curve, but they can be fit into several down-sloping curves as shown in Figure 3-8.

Curve A-A in Figure 3-8 can be considered a Phillips Curve for the 1950s and 1960s, while the other three curves represent data for the 1970s and 1980s. These are the apparent shifts of the Phillips Curve for the past fifty years. In the 1950s and 1960s, the relationship between inflation rates and unemployment rates fits the down-sloping curve A-A well, with a few exceptions. One such exception occurred in 1958. The data for this year shows that given the unemployment rate, the inflation rate (2.8%) is too high to fit into the A-A curve—or given the inflation rate, the unemployment rate (6.84%) is too high.

The curve B-B in Figure 3-8 is surrounded by the data points of years from 1970–1996. The upward shift of curve B-B over curve A-A indicates that at a given unemployment rate, the corresponding inflation rate predicted by the new Phillips curve B-B will be greater than the corresponding inflation rate predicted by the Phillips curve A-A. When the aggregate demand changed in those years, the relationship between inflation rates and unemployment rates still held, that is, increasing inflation rates were associated with decreasing unemployment rates. Both rates, however, had ended at higher levels than was predicted by the Phillips curve A-A of the 1950s and 1960s. Curves C-C and D-D are generated by data from years during the 1970s and 1980s when the U.S. economy was in recession or in stagnation, characterized by both high inflation rates and high unemployment rates.

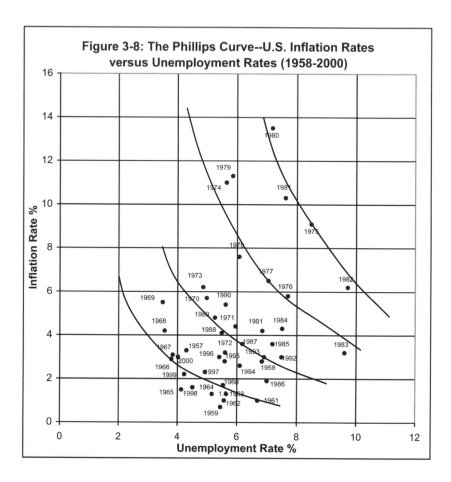

Figure 3-8: The Phillips Curve--U.S. Inflation Rates versus Unemployment Rates (1958-2000)

The Phillips Curve's shift was caused by external shocks to the U.S. economy. The Vietnam War had increased government spending and contributed to the expansion of aggregate demand. The data points in Figure 3-8 show that the inflation rate increased substantially, while unemployment fell below 4.0% during the years of 1966-1969.

In a situation of full employment and high inflation, supply side shocks such as poor harvests around the world in the early 1970s and the first oil crisis in 1973 sent prices for food, oil, and other raw materials skyrocketing. The increased costs of energy and other materials were soon reflected in the prices of manufactured goods and services. Businesses attempted to cut costs by laying off workers and by reducing production, which led the U.S. economy into a recession in 1974-1975. The real GDP fell 0.57% in 1974 and dropped another 0.36% in 1975; unemployment rates soared to

5.64% in 1974 and to 8.48% in 1975, while inflation rates continued to rise to 11% in 1974.

The second oil crisis attacked the world economy in 1979, when the price of oil more than doubled. The U.S. real GDP fell 0.23% in 1980 and nearly 2% in 1982. The unemployment rate rose to an extraordinary high of 9.71% in 1982, and the inflation rate hit 13.5% in 1980, the highest since the great depression of the early 1930s. These movements are reflected in the Phillips Curves that were shifting from curve B-B to curves C-C and D-D.

The reality of the past thirty years illustrates that whenever economic shocks appear in the supply side, the down-sloping curve predicting the movement of inflation rates and unemployment rates was altered. That is to say, increasing inflation was associated with rising unemployment when the economy responded to those inflationary shocks. Without further external shocks from the supply side, the economy would adjust aggregate demand to restore a new down-sloping curve at higher levels of both inflation rates and unemployment rates, which was reflected in the upward shifts of the Phillips Curve.

In the early 1980s, to fight against inflation and to bring the economy out of recession, the U.S. government adopted proactive policies, including a package of policies called "supply-side economics". When the recovery came, it was dramatic. Inflation rates were reduced to 3.2% in 1983 from 13.5% in 1980, and unemployment declined to 7% in 1986 from 9.71% in 1982. In the same time, the world oil price fell below $30.00 per barrel in 1983 from $38.00 per barrel in 1981.

The stabilization of oil prices and the expectation of a further price decrease released the major inflationary pressure from the economy. The policy changes and drop in energy prices in the global market actually reduced both inflation rates and unemployment rates in the U.S. This is reflected in the data points traveling from the D-D curve back to the B-B curve. During this time period, the relationship of inflation rates and unemployment rates predicted by the Phillips Curve did not hold, as the declining inflation rates were associated with reducing or flat unemployment rates.

In the early 1990s, the U.S. economy ran into a minor recession, with real GDP dropping by 0.47% in 1991 and unemployment increasing to 7.49% in 1992. The economy, however, quickly rebounded. Real GDP rose 3.1% in 1993, and unemployment gradually fell to 5.41% in 1996. Without sharp external shocks to the U.S. economy from the supply side, the changing aggregate demand and the economy's self-correcting mechanism had retained the data points for 1990 - 1996 around the Phillips Curve B-B, which was originally established by the data points for the 1950s and 1960s.

A world financial crisis was triggered by a sharp devaluation of local currency in Thailand in 1997, affecting many major economies around the globe, including South Korea, Japan, Russia, Mexico, and Brazil. The tumbling of global financial markets at that time indicated a looming worldwide economic recession. As a matter of fact, many economies fell into negative growth territories in 1998 and 1999. Rapidly declining outputs in Asia and other parts of the world reduced demand for oil and petroleum products, resulting in a sharp decline of the world oil price from $23.00 dollars per barrel in January 1997 to only $9.23 dollars in December 1998. Many economies in Asia and South America as well as Russia began to recover in 1999. They accelerated their exports of manufactured goods and materials in order to earn hard currency. This enabled them to support their economies, which did not have enough domestic consumption for growth. Huge amounts of inexpensive imported goods from those troubled nations flooded the U.S. and European markets.

Instead of being dragged into a recession, the U.S. economy remained on the track of sustainable expansion; its real GDP grew by 3-4% each year since 1993. Two kinds of favorable external forces affected the U.S. economy since the global financial crisis of 1997-1998: falling oil prices and increasing imports from the rest of the world with extremely low prices. These favorable supply side factors helped to keep the U.S. economy growing at 3-4% per year while keeping inflation rates below 3%.

Within the U.S. economy, the explosive development of information and telecommunications technology has accelerated the process of moving innovation from designing room and factory floor to distribution channels. Since 1990, a great deal of information technology capital has been installed in American businesses. The expanding application of e-commerce and computer networks has already changed the relationships of producers, suppliers, and customers. Using the Internet, businesses are able to acquire timely information from supply chains and customers, allowing them to reduce inventories and lead times for the delivery of products and services. Many established American companies engaged in conventional business have aggressively adopted new business models based on the Internet and e-commerce, and have greatly reduced their overall costs and improved their efficiency and profitability.

The resulting productivity gains in American corporations, industries, and sectors are widely recognized as a crucial part of the exceptional performance of the U.S. economy in the recent years. In fact, the increasing pace of productivity improvement works as a buffer to retain a stable price level by offsetting the pressure from increases in workers' wages and benefits under tightening labor market conditions. These favorable supply-side evolutions in the U.S. economy are dis-inflationary in nature. As a favorable productivity "shock" in supply side, information and telecommunications technology has driven the economy towards the best combination of lower inflation and lower unemployment.

Once again, we see the external shocks and internal evolutions in the supply side that have transformed the U.S. economy of the 1990s back into its Phillips Curve A-A, with both inflation and unemployment at lower levels than they had been for the 1970s and 1980s.

In Figure 3-8, the data points for years 1998, 1999, and 2000 approached the area of "full employment without inflation," the solution economists around the world dream about. Now the challenge arose: How long would the U.S. economy be able to maintain its current situation? Presently, no one has a clear answer. From the above analysis one recognizes that if there are no severe external shocks from supply side, the inflation rates and unemployment rates may move around the Phillips curve A-A. A large probability exists for the U.S economy to move towards the left end of the Phillips curve A-A. In this scenario, inflation rates may slowly pick up but still be able to remain below 4%, while unemployment rates may move up and down around 4%, which has been considered "full employment". This case seems to be the soft landing that was the goal of the U.S. monitary authorities in the year 2000. That goal can be achieved through adjusting interest rates in order to eliminate excess aggregate demand and release inflation pressure from the U.S. economy.

The soft landing policy does not guarantee that the best combination of low inflation rate and low unemployment rate will remain. This is indicated by historical data points for 1958-1964, when the inflation rate was well below 2.0%, but the unemployment rate was in the range of 5.0-7.0%, with the corresponding growth rate of real GDP of -1.0% in 1958 and below 2.5% in 1960 and 1961. The growth rate of real GDP went below 2.0% in the second half of 2000 and further decreased to 1.0% in the first half of 2001, while the inflation rate was below 3.0% and the unemployment rate increased to 4.5-5.0%.

The "full-employment" unemployment rate of 3.5-4.0% broke after the middle of 2000, and the growth of the U.S. economy slowed substantially in 2000. By the middle of 2001, the U.S. inflation-unemployment picture was clouded by the uncertainty of how far the U.S. economy would slow down.

Two possibilities seem to exist: a movement towards the right side of the Phillips Curve A-A, if the inflation rate drops below 2.0%, and a potential shift toward the B-B curve, if the inflation rate remains above 3.0% and the unemployment rate exceeds 5.0%, a scenario of an increase in both inflation rate and unemployment rate.

One can observe that the data points for 1999-2000 have approached the levels of 1966-1968, when external supply shocks raised the Phillips Curve, and resulted in a dramatic increase to inflation and unemployment. If the current data points follow this pattern, they may return to the Phillips Curve B-B, with both unemployment rates and inflation rates rising, which would be considered a hard landing for the economy.

If the U.S. economy has a soft landing, the inflation rate will remain moderate, the unemployment rate might pick up slightly and the data points will stay around the A-A curve. If the U.S. economy has a hard landing in response to external supply-side shocks, both rates will increase, and data points will jump to the Phillips Curve of B-B or C-C. How severely these shocks will damage the current picture of inflation and unemployment will depend upon the nature of those shocks, such as a future oil crisis, drastically changing weather, terrorist attack, a major policy mistake, and changes in global political and market conditions.

The U.S. economy has been in the process of transformation with efficiency and productivity gains brought about by the information revolution in American corporations, industries, and sectors. The changing structure and improving efficiency and productivity of the U.S. economy will play a crucial role from the supply side in fending off some unexpected shocks and limiting some unavoidable effects on the U.S. economy, should extraordinary external shocks occur. Currently, the major external shock is the changing price of oil in the global market. The next section examines the dependency of the U.S. economy on the world's oil market.

## Chapter 4

## *World Oil Price and Its Effect on the U.S. Economy*

The global market for crude oil has had a tremendous effect on the economies of the U.S. and many of the OECD nations. All of these countries depend heavily upon imported crude oil and petroleum products to produce goods and services.

The world's economy has been driven by an abundant supply of cheap oil-based energy for the last century. Decades of cheap oil led to the growth of heavily energy-dependent industries in the developed world. With gas-guzzling automobiles, expanding highways and mushrooming suburbs, the economic and social life of the United States and other advanced industrial nations has increasingly been fueled by oil. The world's oil supply, however, has been controlled mainly by the Organization of Petroleum Exporting Countries (OPEC). The OPEC is an international organization of eleven developing nations that are heavily reliant on oil-export revenues as their major source of income. The current OPEC members include seven Arab nations (Algeria, Iraq, Kuwait, Libya, Qatar, Saudi Arabia, and the United Arab Emirates), and four non-Arab nations (Iran, Indonesia, Nigeria, and Venezuela)[1]. OPEC

---

[1] The League of Arab States was founded in Cairo in 1945. Its current members include Algeria, Bahrain, Comoros, Djibouti, Egypt, Iraq, Jordan, Kuwait, Lebanon, Libya, Mauritania, Morocco, Oman, Palestine, Qatar, Saudi Arabia, Somalia, Sudan, Syria, Tunisia, United Arab Emirates, and Yemen.

nations collectively supply about 40% of the world's oil output, and possess more than 75% of the world's total proven crude oil reserves.

OPEC was formed in 1960, but its strength and impact were not felt until 1973, when it decided to raise oil prices dramatically by cutting back on the world's oil supply. This first big OPEC price rise was the main shock behind the deep recession of 1974-75 in all the industrial nations. In 1980, OPEC again pushed the oil price up to more than $30 a barrel with a tremendous effect on the world economy. The increase in oil prices led to stagflation, a combination of high inflation and high unemployment, in most industrial nations. The effect of the so-called second oil crisis spread around the globe, resulting in the deterioration of economic performance in all countries of the world.

The terrorist atrocities in New York, Washington, and Pennsylvania on September 11, 2001, raised important questions about the future of the world oil market and the risk that Muslim extremists may influence OPEC's Arab member nations to damage the West by cutting the output of crude oil. Past oil crises provide an important guide to predict and prevent future devastations that are caused by a sharp reduction in the world's oil supply and a resulting oil price hike. However, we will show that the picture of world oil supply and demand has changed noticeably since the first oil crisis in 1973. The enduring war on terrorism may some day bring stability to the oil producing nations in the Persian Gulf. Before that happens, the world's oil market is full of uncertainty and fragility, heavily influenced by geopolitical forces and changing supply-demand conditions in the world economy.

## 4-1    World's Production of Crude Oil

On the supply side, OPEC has dominated the production of crude oil of the world, and Iran and the Arab members of OPEC hold a lion's share of that production. Figures 4-1, 4-2.1, and 4-2.2 depict the evolution of crude oil production by Iran and Arab OPEC members (or Persian Gulf nations), other three Non-Arab OPEC members, and all the non-OPEC producers of the world (Data Source: Oil Production, *International Petroleum Monthly*).

In 1970, the world's total production of crude oil was 45.89 million barrels per day. The non-OPEC production of crude oil was about 22.59 million barrels per day. The OPEC production was 23.30 million barrels per day, of which the Persian Gulf nations' share was 17.65 million barrels per day and the three non-Arab members' was 5.65 million barrels per day. In terms of the percentage, in 1970 the Persian Gulf OPEC nations' production accounted for 38.5% of the world's total oil production and the three non-Arab OPEC members' production[2] accounted for 12.3%, and the non-OPEC producers' share was 49.2%.

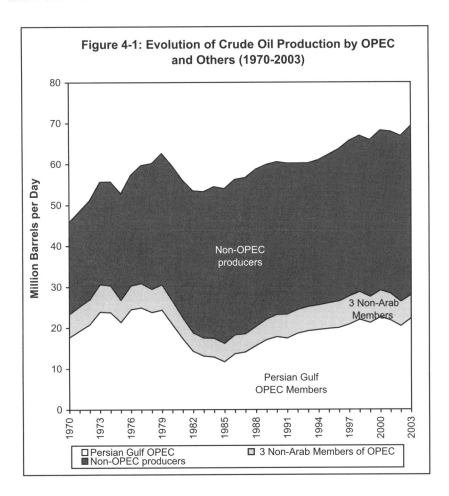

Figure 4-1: Evolution of Crude Oil Production by OPEC and Others (1970-2003)

During the global oil crisis of 1973, Arab oil producing nations announced major cuts in their production and an embargo of shipments to the United States and other nations that supported Israel in the Fourth Arab-Israeli War. The second oil crisis followed the overthrow of the Shah of Iran and the outbreak of war between two major OPEC oil producers, Iraq and Iran. As Figure 4-1 shows, the OPEC cartel reduced its oil production from 30.63 million barrels per day in 1973 to 16.18 million barrels per day in 1985. By

---

[2] The three include Indonesia, Nigeria and Venezuela.

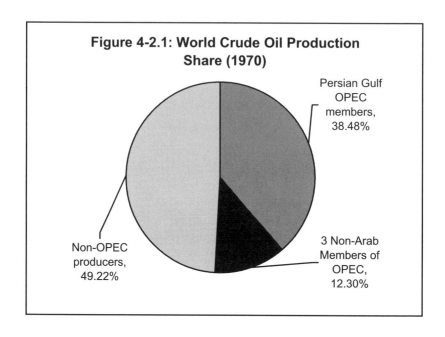

Figure 4-2.1: World Crude Oil Production Share (1970)

Persian Gulf OPEC members, 38.48%

3 Non-Arab Members of OPEC, 12.30%

Non-OPEC producers, 49.22%

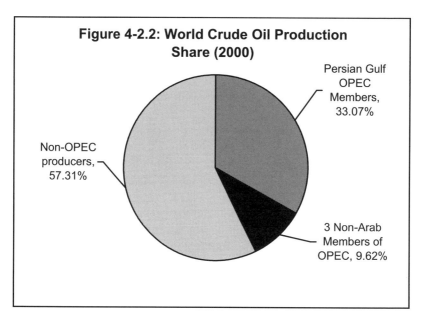

Figure 4-2.2: World Crude Oil Production Share (2000)

Persian Gulf OPEC Members, 33.07%

3 Non-Arab Members of OPEC, 9.62%

Non-OPEC producers, 57.31%

cutting output, OPEC quadrupled world oil prices from $3.0 per barrel to $12.0 per barrel during 1973-74. Oil prices rose significantly again in 1979 in the wake of the Iranian Revolution. Greatly increased oil prices encouraged endeavors to discover new oil reserves and develop new oil fields.

Consequently, the non-OPEC producers raised their production from 25.05 million barrels per day to 37.80 million barrels per day in the same time frame, and the total world's crude oil production was reduced merely by about 3% from 55.68 million barrels per day in 1973 to 53.98 million barrels per day in 1985. Although the two most disastrous economic recessions of the postwar period were associated with those global oil crises, the total output of oil production decreased only moderately, thanks to the new supply sources from the North Sea, Mexico, China, and elsewhere.

In 2000, the world's crude oil production reached 68.2 million barrels per day, of which Persian Gulf OPEC members' production accounted for 33.1% (22.55 million barrels per day), non-Arab OPEC members' for 9.6% (6.56 million barrels per day), and non-OPEC producers' for 57.3% (39.09 million barrels per day), as shown in Figures 4-2.2. These data clearly indicate that the OPEC members' share decreased significantly, while non-OPEC producers' share increased. Nevertheless, the OPEC nations, particularly the Persian Gulf OPEC nations, have still controlled nearly one third of the world's crude oil production. These nations' stability and reaction to world events will continue to affect the world's oil production and oil prices.

Figure 4-3 depicts the evolution of crude oil production by the top ten nations in the world. As a matter of fact, the United States was the number one crude oil producer in the world in 1970; its oil production was about 9.64 million barrels per day. In the same year, the Soviet Union was second with production of about 6.99 million barrels per day. Those two top producers were followed by Iran (3.83 million barrels per day), Saudi Arabia (3.80 million barrels per day), and Libya (3.32 million barrels per day).

In 2000, however, Saudi Arabia became the number one oil producer in the world, with 8.40 million barrels per day, and was followed by Russia (6.48 million barrels per day), North Sea[3] (6.01 million barrels per day), the United States (5.82 million barrels per day), and Iran (3.72 million barrels per day). It is worth noticing that besides those top five oil producers, China, Norway, and Mexico have become competitive oil producers, as their daily production exceeded 3.0 million barrels in 2000 (about 3.25, 3.18, and 3.01 million barrels respectively).

---

[3] North Sea includes the United Kingdom offshore, Norway, Denmark, Netherlands offshore and Germany offshore.

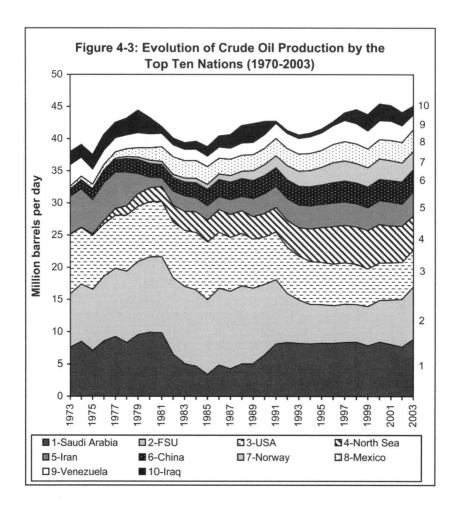

Figure 4-3: Evolution of Crude Oil Production by the Top Ten Nations (1970-2003)

Data Source: Oil Production, *International Petroleum Monthly.*
FSU = the Former Soviet Union.

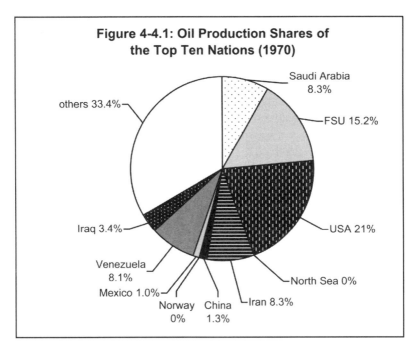

Figure 4-4.1: Oil Production Shares of the Top Ten Nations (1970)

others 33.4%

Saudi Arabia 8.3%

FSU 15.2%

USA 21%

Iraq 3.4%

Venezuela 8.1%

Mexico 1.0%

Norway 0%

China 1.3%

Iran 8.3%

North Sea 0%

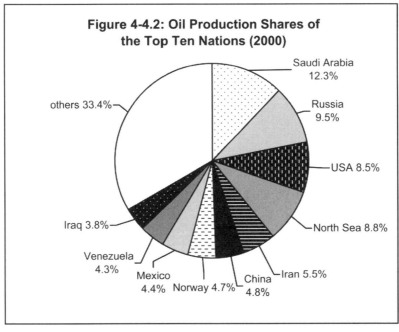

Figure 4-4.2: Oil Production Shares of the Top Ten Nations (2000)

others 33.4%

Saudi Arabia 12.3%

Russia 9.5%

USA 8.5%

North Sea 8.8%

Iraq 3.8%

Venezuela 4.3%

Mexico 4.4%

Norway 4.7%

China 4.8%

Iran 5.5%

Changes in oil production significantly altered the production share of nations, as shown in Figures 4-4.1 and 4-4.2. The United States' share of crude oil production dramatically declined from 21% in 1970 to 8.5% in 2000. The former Soviet Union's share also decreased significantly, from 15.2% to 9.5%. Similarly, Iran's share declined from 8.3% to 5.5%, and Venezuela's share decreased from 8.1% to 4.3% during the same time period. Those nations' share loss became the share gain for other oil producing nations such as Saudi Arabia, China, and Norway. Great share gains occurred in the North Sea region (from 0% to 8.8%), Saudi Arabia (from 8.3% to 12.3%), China (from 1.3% to 4.8%), Norway (from 0% to 4.7%), and Mexico (from 1.0% to 4.4%) during 1970 - 2000.

Iraq's oil production was 3.477 million barrels per day in 1979 and accounted for 5.6% of the world's oil production; it declined to 2.897 million barrels per day in 1989. In August 1990 Iraq invaded Kuwait and the UN Security Council immediately imposed comprehensive mandatory economic sanctions on Iraq in the hope of convincing Saddam Hussein to withdraw from Kuwait. The UN's attempt ended in vain and the use of military force was required. The United States led the successful Desert Storm operation against Iraq and liberated Kuwait. After the Gulf War, economic sanctions were imposed as an enforcement mechanism for the UN resolution, which required Iraq to disclose, destroy, and abandon all nuclear, chemical and biological weapons as well as long-range missiles.

Iraq had historically depended on imports for 75% of its food consumption, and 95% of Iraq's foreign revenues were derived from oil exports. Because of Iraq's very limited access to the sea, 90% of its oil was exported through two pipelines, one crossing into Turkey and the other into Saudi Arabia. The UN's economic sanction, known as the "oil-for-food" program, allowed Iraq to resume oil exports to fund the purchase of food and medicines, and required that the food and medicines purchased under this plan reach the people of Iraq rather than Saddam's armed forces.

Until November 1996 Iraq did not accept the implementation of the UN's program, and the Iraqi people suffered tremendously from the embargo. Despite U.S. increased efforts at a naval blockade, widespread illegal exports of Iraq oil, sold at heavily discounted prices, travelled through Iranian waters and across land borders with its neighboring countries. There has been widespread smuggling of goods and equipment into Iraq from Jordan, Turkey, and Iran, including sizable quantities of food, textiles, medicines, and other consumer goods as well as contraband military supplies for the Iraqi Army.

According to the *International Petroleum Monthly* data base of oil production, Iraq's oil output was 1.55 million barrel per day (3.4% of the world's total) in 1970; it dropped to 0.31 million barrels per day in 1991 and gradually recovered to 2.57 million barrels per day (about 3.8% of the world's total) in 2000. Even though Iraq's oil output was less than 4% of the world's total production, it still can stir the world's oil prices and creates uncertainty and fragility in the global market.

Since the first oil crisis, Saudi Arabia has seized the opportunity to increase its oil production. Saudi Arabia's output was 3.8 million barrels per day in 1970, slightly less than that of Iran. In the following four years, Saudi Arabia doubled its output to 8.48 million barrels per day. In 1980, during the second oil crisis, Saudi Arabia's output reached the historical record of 9.9 million barrels per day. Now Saudi Arabia has become the largest producer in the world with an oil output of 8.4 million barrels per day in 2000. Saudi Arabia also holds the leadership of the OPEC cartel and has its own capacity to increase or decrease oil production in order to keep world's oil prices in the desired range, between $25 and $30 per barrel.

Another important producer in the world oil market is Russia with its oil industry awakening from long hibernation. Russia was already the world's second largest producer and exporter of crude oil, with an output of 6.48 million barrels per day in 2000. OPEC still produces 40% of the world's oil, but Russia, with greater reserves than any other non-OPEC country, has been grabbing market share. In fact, in 1970, the Soviet Union was the world's second largest oil producer next to the United States. The total output of Russia and the former Soviet republics of Azerbaijan and Kazakhstan was 6.98 million barrels per day in 1970, accounting for 15.2% of the world's total output. In 2000, Russia's oil output alone exceeded that of the U.S. and accounted for 9.5% of the world's total. Still, Russia needs more help from foreign investors and oil firms to exploit frozen and remote oil fields. And Russia's uncertain laws, high taxes, stultifying bureaucracy, and corruption have become great obstacles to the development of its oil industry.

The oil production share of all other small producer nations remained nearly 33.4%, but their output increased from 15.39 million barrels per day in 1970 to 22.79 million barrels per day in 2000.

Production data indicate that the top ten oil producer nations have controlled nearly 67% of the total crude oil production for the last thirty years. In 1970 the top five producers included the United States, the Soviet Union, Saudi Arabia, Iran, and Venezuela; they controlled about 61% of the total oil production. In 2000, however, the top five producer nations were ranked as

Saudi Arabia, the countries of the former Soviet Union, the United States, the North Sea, and Iran, with a combined production share of only 44.6%. Although four of these producers (the United States, the former Soviet Union, Saudi Arabia, and Iran) were on the top-five list in 1970, their declining share indicates the reduced concentration of the world's crude oil production. Nevertheless, the former Soviet Union territory has become a major energy resource center in the world to compete with the Persian Gulf region for export revenues and investment dollars. The changed geography of the world oil supply will certainly influence oil prices and the stability of the global oil market.

## 4-2   World Demand for Crude Oil

On the demand side, the world's demand for crude oil increased rapidly from 46.81 million barrels per day in 1970 to 63.07 million barrels per day in 1980, and to 75.54 million barrels per day in 2000.

Figure 4-5.1 indicates that the OECD (Organization for Economic Cooperation and Development) nations have been the major consumers in the global oil market. The demand by the OECD nations increased from 34.50 million barrels per day in 1970 to 47.93 million barrels per day in 2000, an increase of about 39%. In the same time frame, non-OECD nations' demand for crude oil increased from 13.34 to 27.61 million barrels per day, an increase of about 107%.

Figure 4-5.2 depicts the annual growth rates of the world's crude oil demand by OECD and non-OECD nations for the last thirty years. The growth rate of demand for crude oil fluctuated markedly over time and declined from 8% in early 1970s to 2.1% in the 1990s. Except for the early 1990s, the oil demand growth rate of non-OECD nations stayed above the growth rate of OECD nations, reflecting the faster-growing demand for crude oil of developing nations than that of developed nations.

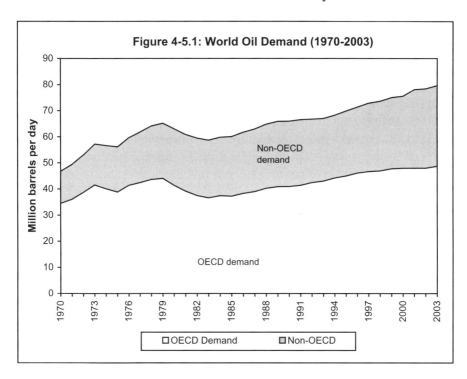

Figure 4-5.1: World Oil Demand (1970-2003)

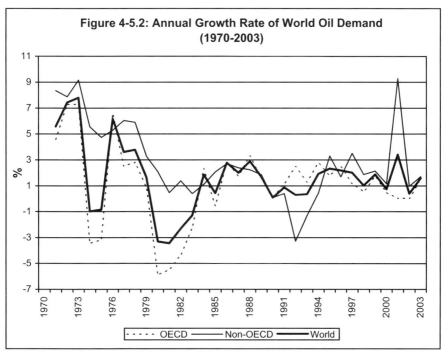

Figure 4-5.2: Annual Growth Rate of World Oil Demand (1970-2003)

Figure 4-6 presents the evolution of the world's demand for crude oil by nations.

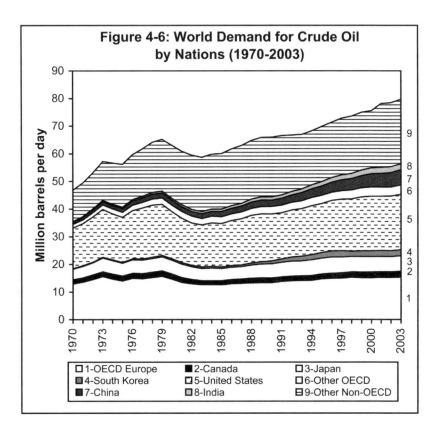

Figure 4-6: World Demand for Crude Oil by Nations (1970-2003)

Legend:
☐ 1-OECD Europe    ■ 2-Canada    ☐ 3-Japan
■ 4-South Korea    ☐ 5-United States    ☐ 6-Other OECD
■ 7-China    ☐ 8-India    ⊟ 9-Other Non-OECD

\* Other OECD nations include Australia, Mexico, and New Zealand.

The U.S. economy is the biggest consumer in the global oil market; its demand for crude oil rose from 14.70 million barrels per day in 1970 to 19.70 million barrels per day in 2000. "OECD Europe" consists of twenty-two European nations with their demand for crude oil increasing from 12.92 million barrels per day in 1970 to 15.15 million barrels per day in 2000. In the time period of 1970-2000, Japan's demand increased from 3.82 to 5.53 million barrels per day, South Korea's from 0.20 to 2.15 million barrels per day, China's from 0.62 to 4.8 million barrels per day, and India's from 0.40 to 2.13 million barrels per day. In 2003, China's demand, about 5.53 million barrels per day, approached Japan's demand, 5.58 million barrels per day.

Figures 4-7.1 and 4-7.2 depict oil demand shares of major consumer nations in 1970 and 2000.

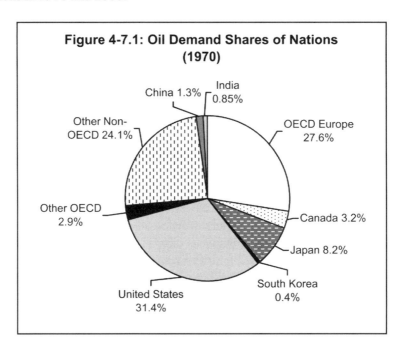

**Figure 4-7.1: Oil Demand Shares of Nations (1970)**

China 1.3%
India 0.85%
Other Non-OECD 24.1%
OECD Europe 27.6%
Other OECD 2.9%
Canada 3.2%
Japan 8.2%
United States 31.4%
South Korea 0.4%

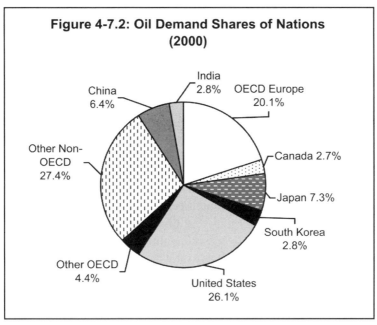

**Figure 4-7.2: Oil Demand Shares of Nations (2000)**

India 2.8%
OECD Europe 20.1%
China 6.4%
Other Non-OECD 27.4%
Canada 2.7%
Japan 7.3%
South Korea 2.8%
Other OECD 4.4%
United States 26.1%

A comparison of these two charts clearly shows that the developed nations, including OECD Europe, the United States, Canada, and Japan, have significantly reduced their demand shares. The newly industrialized nations and developing nations, including China, India and other non-OECD nations, South Korea, and other OECD nations (Australia, Mexico, and New Zealand), significantly increased their demand share in the global crude oil market during the last thirty years.

The changing shares of oil demand by nations reflect the changing reality of economic development across the globe. Many OECD nations have adopted energy efficiency policies that encourage reduction of energy intensity or energy use per unit of economic activity. These nations have also transformed their advanced economies towards service-oriented activities that require less energy to produce. Some manufacturing and industrial activities in the developed nations have been reallocated and moved to developing nations in Asia and South America. The rapid expansion of population and local economies, combined with global reallocation of production, causes the increasing demand for energy in the developing nations. The significantly increased oil demand share by China, India and other non-OECD nations indicates the future demand pressure in the world oil market from the developing nations.

## 4-3   Net Imports of Crude Oil

From the above analyses of supply and demand conditions of the global crude oil market, one can see that oil production capacity has been controlled by the OPEC nations, while the demand has mainly come from the OECD nations. Therefore, the majority of OECD nations are the net importers and the OPEC nations are the net exporters in the global crude oil market.

Figure 4-8.1 presents the evolution of net imports of crude oil by major importing nations over the last fourteen years. The total amount of net imported crude oil by the OECD nations increased from 20.57 million barrels per day in 1990 to 25.23 million barrels per day in 2003 with a 23% rise in fourteen years. The United States has been the largest net importer in the world. Its net imported crude oil rose from 7.16 million barrels per day in 1990 to 11.24 million barrels per day in 2003 for a 57% increase in fourteen years. China was a net oil exporting country in the 1970s and 1980s with its net oil export of 0.46 million barrels per day during the 1980s. Rapid economic growth has turned China into a net oil importer since 1993. During 2003

China imported about 2.13 million barrels of oil per day. India, an oil importing country, increased its oil import from 0.51 million barrels per day in 1990 to 1.52 million barrels per day in 2003.

Figure 4-8.2 indicates that the annual growth rate of U.S. net imports of crude oil exceeded the growth rate of total net imports by all the OECD nations and the growth rate of Japan except in 1991 and 1995.

Only four OECD nations (Norway, the United Kingdom, Mexico, and Canada) have been net exporters in the global oil market. In the time period from 1990 through 2003, Norway's net export of crude oil increased from 1.54 million barrels per day in 1990 to 3.07 million barrels per day; the United Kingdom's from 0.21 to 0.61 million barrels per day; Mexico's from 1.33 to 1.89 million barrels per day; and Canada's from 0.43 to 1.01 million barrels per day. As those limited exports of crude oil cannot meet the demand from the OECD group, many industrialized nations have to import crude oil from OPEC nations.

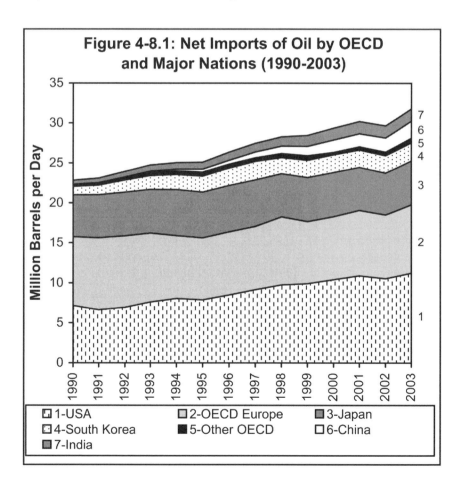

Figure 4-8.1: Net Imports of Oil by OECD and Major Nations (1990-2003)

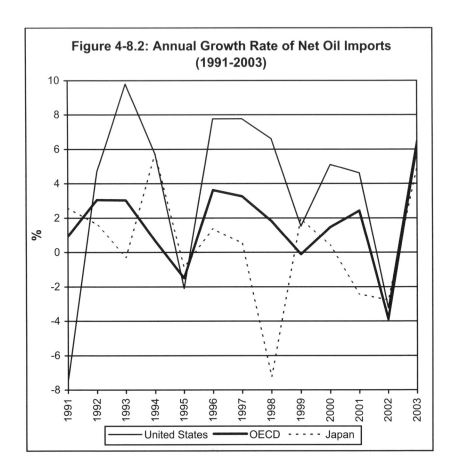

Figure 4-8.2: Annual Growth Rate of Net Oil Imports (1991-2003)

Even though the relative share of the U.S. demand in the total world demand has declined from 31.4% in 1970 to 26.1% in 2000, the declining U.S. production and increasing consumption of crude oil have raised the amount of crude oil imported from the rest of the world. U.S. net import of crude oil reached 10.42 million barrels per day in 2000, compared with OECD Europe's net oil import of 7.82 million barrels per day, Japan's 5.49 million, and South Korea's 2.22 million barrels per day during the same year. Recalling the U.S. demand for crude oil of 19.70 million barrels per day and the U.S. production of only 5.82 million barrels per day in 2000, one can see that the huge gap between demand and supply must be filled by imports and strategic reserves of crude oil. U.S. imports of oil were responsible for meeting 58% of U.S. demand in 1990, and 53% of U.S. demand in 2000, indicating the heavy dependence of the U.S. economy on the global oil market.

Figure 4-9 depicts the evolution of U.S. net imports from different nations during 1990–2003. Figures 4-10.1 and 4-10.2 show changes in U.S. oil import shares from these nations.

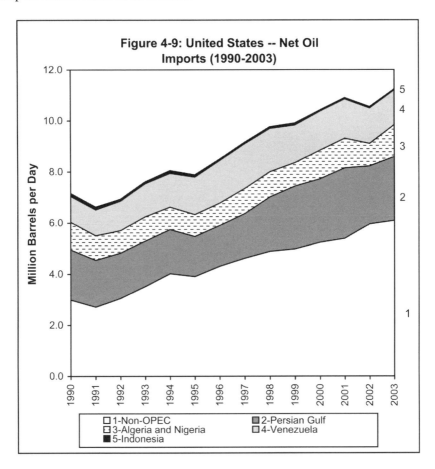

These charts show that non-OPEC producer nations, such as countries of the former Soviet Union, the North Sea producers, Norway, Mexico, the UK, and Canada, have become large suppliers to the U.S. demand for crude oil, with their share increasing from 41.7% in 1990 to 50.3% in 2000. The share of imported oil from the Persian Gulf declined from 27.4% to 25.6% and the share of Algeria and Nigeria declined from 15.1% to 10.6% in 1990–2000. Among all the OPEC nations, Saudi Arabia, Venezuela, and Nigeria hold large shares of imported oil to United States. In 1990–2000, Saudi Arabia's crude oil imported to United States increased from 1.34 to 1.57 million barrels per day, Venezuela's rose from 1.02 to 1.53 million barrels per day, and Nigeria's from 0.80 to 0.90 million barrels per day.

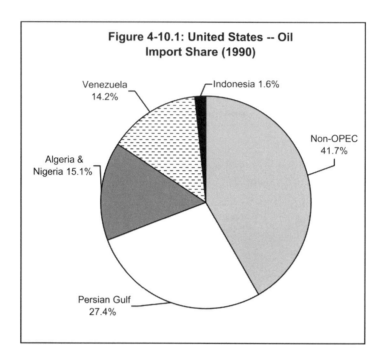

Figure 4-10.1: United States -- Oil Import Share (1990)

Venezuela 14.2%
Indonesia 1.6%
Non-OPEC 41.7%
Algeria & Nigeria 15.1%
Persian Gulf 27.4%

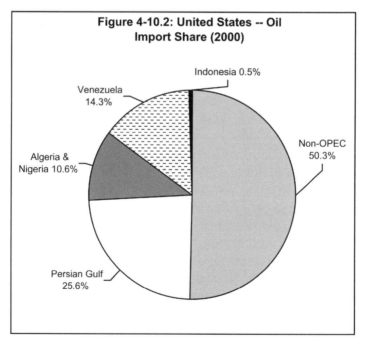

Figure 4-10.2: United States -- Oil Import Share (2000)

Indonesia 0.5%
Venezuela 14.3%
Non-OPEC 50.3%
Algeria & Nigeria 10.6%
Persian Gulf 25.6%

Even though Saudi Arabia and Venezuela are still the largest suppliers of crude oil to the United States, U.S. dependency on imported oil has clearly and gradually shifted toward some non-OPEC nations that enjoy more stable political and economic environments.

## 4-4    Oil Prices and the U.S. Economy

The above statistics of the global oil market illustrate that the U.S. economy depends heavily on the world oil market. Changes in oil prices have become significant external shocks to the U.S. economic system. The response of the U.S. economy to the oil crises of the 1970s and to the oil price hikes in the early 1990s and in 2003-2004 is shown in Figure 4-11. This figure depicts the quarterly average of the U.S. refiner acquisition cost of imported crude oil, along with the annualized quarterly growth rate of real GDP and the inflation rate of the United States from the first quarter Q1 of 1970 through the third quarter Q3 of 2004.

Economists usually provide two principal arguments to assess how changes in oil and energy prices affect the economy. The first argument focuses on the supply side of the market for goods and services. Since energy resources are used to produce goods and services, a change in their prices affects the quantity of the goods and determines which resources will be used to produce them. Higher energy costs raise the total output costs. This leads businesses to switch to less energy-intensive production methods, which could result in some productive capital becoming obsolete and a decline in output. Hence, high energy prices can reduce the aggregate supply of goods and services of an economy.

The second argument focuses on the demand side of the market. A rise in oil prices increases expenditures on imported petroleum products and thereby reduces net exports. The rise in the price of crude oil acts like a tax on domestic income, which reduces aggregate demand. Particularly for those nations that depend heavily on net oil imports, a rising oil price can substantially reduce a nation's output, aggregate demand, and employment. Even though some of these effects are not permanent, a rise in energy price can cause some transitory and reversionary declines in output and employment and generate high inflation.

According to these arguments, a rising oil price will reduce the growth rate of output and increase the unemployment and inflation rates. In other words, the growth rate of real GDP should be negatively correlated with the oil price, while the unemployment rate and the inflation rate should be positively correlated with the price of oil.

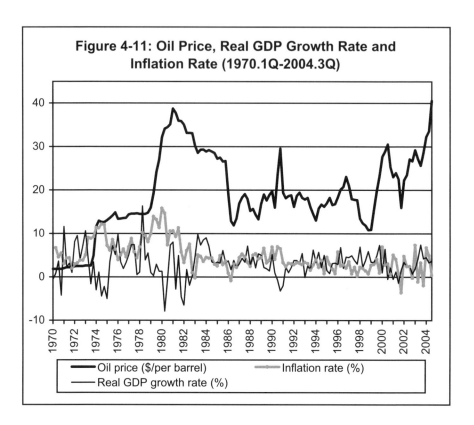

Figure 4-11: Oil Price, Real GDP Growth Rate and Inflation Rate (1970.1Q-2004.3Q)

Table 4-1 provides a summary of the performance of the U.S. economy during the six specific time periods in which oil prices rose significantly. Changes in oil price, growth rate of real GDP, inflation rate, and unemployment rate over each time period are displayed in corresponding columns. The correlation coefficients between oil prices and the growth rates of real GDP, inflation, and unemployment are displayed in the last three rows of Table 4-1.

The first world oil crisis started with OPEC's oil embargo in October 1973, which caused the price of oil to rise to $5.18 per barrel from $2.58 per barrel in the previous months. The oil embargo ended in March of 1974, and the oil price surged to $12.82 per barrel in January of 1975. During the time period of 1973 Q1–1975 Q1, the price of oil rose by $10.44 or 403%. At the same time, the real GDP growth rate of the U.S. economy declined from 10.2% in the first quarter of 1973 to -5.1% in the first quarter of 1975, with a net change of -(15.3)%.  In fact, in the three consecutive quarters of 1974 Q3, Q4, and 1975 Q1, the real GDP growth rate fell into negative territory, -4.4%, -2.2%, and -5.0% respectively. The CPI inflation rate increased from 5% in 1973 Q1 to 12.12% in 1974 Q3 and 7.22% in 1975 Q1, while the unemployment rate rose from 4.93% in 1973 Q1 to 8.26% in 1975 Q1. The correlation coefficients are significantly positive between oil prices and inflation rates, and between oil prices and unemployment rates. The coefficient is significantly negative between the oil price and real GDP growth rate for the time period of 1973 Q1–1975 Q1.

Table 4-1: U.S. Economic Performance versus Oil Price Changes

| Period | 73.1- 75.1 | 78.2- 80.2 | 80.2- 81.1 | 86.3- 90.4 | 94.1- 96.4 | 98.4- 2004.3 |
|---|---|---|---|---|---|---|
| Duration | 9Q | 9Q | 4Q | 18Q | 12Q | 24Q |
| Change in oil price ($/per barrel) | $10.44 | $19.65 | $4.60 | $17.66 | $10.05 | $29.70 |
| % Change in oil price | 403% | 136% | 13% | 149% | 77% | 274% |
| Net change in growth rate of real GDP (%) | -15.6 | -24.2 | 15.9 | -7.0 | 1.2 | -2.20 |
| Net change in inflation rate (%) | 2.22 | 4.53 | -4.08 | 3.54 | -1.90 | -0.31 |
| Net change in unemployment rate (%) | 3.33 | 1.33 | 0.10 | -0.83 | -1.10 | 1.00 |
| **Correlation Coefficients Between Oil Price and** | | | | | | |
| Growth rate of real GDP | -0.713 | -0.667 | 0.710 | -0.604 | 0.095 | -0.061 |
| Inflation rate | 0.611 | 0.835 | -0.120 | 0.662 | -0.070 | 0.196 |
| Unemployment rate | 0.619 | 0.692 | -0.110 | -0.118 | -0.779 | 0.314 |

A similar situation occurred during the second world oil crisis.  Starting in April 1979, OPEC raised the price of oil several times during 1979 and 1980. In early 1981, fighting escalated in the Iran-Iraq War, and the price of oil hit an all-time high of $39.00 per barrel.  The time frame surrounding the second world oil crisis can be divided into two sub-periods: 1978 Q2–1980 Q2 and 1980 Q2–1981 Q1. In the first sub-period, the U.S. economy moved from a business cycle's peak to a trough, with real GDP growth rate dropping from 16.3% in 1978 Q2 to -7.9% in 1980 Q2, for a net change of -(24.2%).

The inflation rate jumped from 6.85% in 1978 Q1 to 10.17% in 1978 Q2, and continued rising to 14.7% in 1980 Q2, with a net change of 4.53% in 1978 Q2–1980 Q2. The unemployment rate rose from 6.0% to 7.33% in the same time period, a net change of 1.33%. The rise in the price of oil during this sub-period reduced real output, engendered price inflation, and increased the unemployment rate of the U.S. economy. This was also reflected in the significantly negative and positive correlation coefficients between the oil price and the three macroeconomic variables.

In the second sub-period, 1980 Q2–1981 Q1, the price of oil reached a peak of $39.00 per barrel in February 1981. The change in oil price in this time period, however, was only $4.60 or a 13% rise. The U.S. economy rebounded from its trough, with the real GDP growth rate rising to 8% in the first quarter of 1981. In this sub-period, the conventional relationships of oil price, real GDP growth rate, inflation rate, and unemployment rate did not hold up, because the statistical test indicates a positive correlation between the oil price and real GDP growth rate, and negative correlation between oil price and inflation rate and unemployment rate.

During the next five years, the U.S. economy went through the swings of a business cycle, while oil prices declined from above $35.00 per barrel to $10.91 per barrel in July 1986. The conventional relationship of oil price and macroeconomic variables did not exist except for inflation rate, because oil prices and economic variables went through different cycles.

Iraq's invasion of Kuwait in August 1990 interrupted the global oil market, with the price of oil jumping from $16.54 per barrel to $24.26 per barrel in August 1990. Operation Desert Storm was launched by the United States and ended the Persian Gulf War in a short time period. The world oil price declined from $32.88 per barrel in October 1990 to $17.58 per barrel in March 1991. The spark in oil prices in 1990 was coincidental to the U.S. economic recession, the real GDP growth rate was recorded as -0.7%, -3.2%, and -2.0% for three consecutive quarters of 1990 Q3, Q4 and 1991 Q1. The inflation rate rose from 2.94% in 1986 Q3 to 6.48% in 1990 Q4. The unemployment rate, however, did not show any increase until 1991. Hence, the conventional relationship held up between the price of oil and real GDP growth rate and inflation rate, but not between oil prices and the unemployment rate.

From 1994 Q1 to 1996 Q4 oil prices went through another upswing, rising 77% to $23.05 per barrel from $13.00 per barrel. At the same time, the real GDP growth rate rose from 3.4% to 4.6%, and the unemployment rate declined from 6.56% to 5.33%, while the inflation rate rose slightly from 2.55% to 2.87%. It appeared that the 77% rise in the price of oil did not produce the expected results of decreasing output and increasing the inflation and unemployment rates. In 1998 Q4–2004 Q3, oil prices increased again, from $10.83 per barrel to $40.53 per barrel, a 274% rise. In this time period, the real GDP growth rate went down from 5.9% to 3.7%, the unemployment rate increased from 4.4% to 5.4%, and the inflation rate changed from 0.73% to 0.42%. Even though the correlation coefficients have the right signs, their values are statistically insignificant. Again, the conventional relationships did not hold well.

Table 4-1 indicates that responses of the U.S. economy to increases in oil prices have changed during the past three decades. The positive correlation between rising oil prices and increasing inflation has sustained, while the changes in real GDP growth and unemployment rate cannot simply be explained by increasing oil prices after the second world oil crisis in 1979.

The structure of the U.S. economy has substantially changed since 1970, with a declining share of conventional industries and an increasing share of information-based technology and services industries. This has reduced the effects of changing oil prices on the performance of the U.S. economy. The aggregate data of energy consumption has shown great improvement in efficiency of using energy to produce output by the U.S. economy.

Figure 4-12 depicts the energy consumption per unit of real GDP over the years of 1970 through 1999; it is calculated by using energy consumption data from the "State Energy Price and Expenditure Report 1999" of the Energy Information Administration (EIA).

The curves represent ratios of gross consumption and net consumption of energy divided by real GDP. The gross consumption of energy includes both residential and commercial usage of all forms of energy, and the net consumption of energy is the gross consumption adjusted for electrical system energy losses and process fuel and intermediate products. The measuring unit for energy consumption is the BTU (British Thermal Unit).[4]

---

[4] British thermal unit: the quantity of heat needed to raise the temperature of 1 pound of water by 1° F at or near 39.2° F.

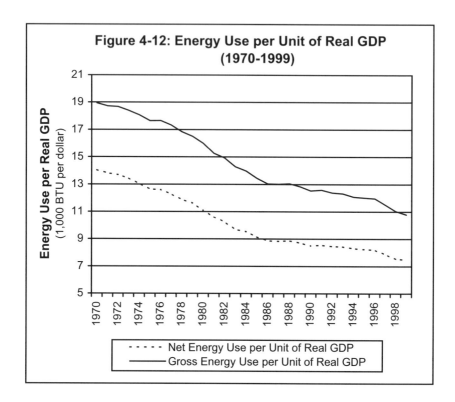

Figure 4-12 shows that the U.S. economy consumed approximately 18.94 thousand BTUs of gross energy to generate one dollar of real GDP in 1970, whereas in 1999, only 10.79 thousand BTUs were needed to do the job, which indicates a 43% decline in gross energy consumption per unit of real GDP over a 29-year period. The net energy consumption per unit of real GDP declined by 47% from 14.00 thousand BTUs in 1970 to 7.49 thousand BTUs in 1999. The U.S. economy has become much more energy-efficient and less dependent on energy consumption for producing goods and services.

Figure 4-13 shows that the growth rate of energy consumption has closely followed the growth rate of real GDP during the economic boom. When recessions hit the U.S. economy in 1974-75, 1980-82, and 1990-91, energy consumption declined more than the real GDP in terms of a percentage change. The historical pattern implies that the energy crisis that troubled California in 2001 could be a temporary and regional imbalance of energy demand and supply. At the national aggregate level, the growth rate of energy consumption should decrease substantially or fall into negative num-bers, as the growth rate of real GDP declined from 1.9% in 2000 Q4 to -1.3% in 2001 Q3.

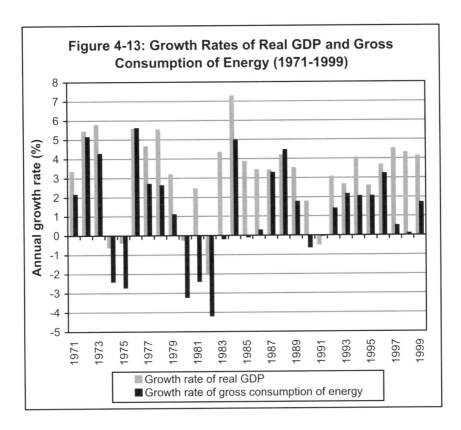

Figure 4-13: Growth Rates of Real GDP and Gross Consumption of Energy (1971-1999)

The changing effects of the price of oil and the improvement in the efficiency of energy consumption provide clear evidence of the transforming economic structure of the United States over the past three decades. The U.S. economy has become more efficient, more productive, and more resil-ient to external shocks in the price of crude oil. Although rising oil prices created unfavorable conditions during the last three decades of the twentieth century, the U.S. economy continued to grow, demonstrating the unusual strength of the economic system. Nevertheless, sustainable economic growth must entail the increase of energy consumption and therefore require sustainable growth in energy production. Even if the U.S. economy becomes more energy-efficient, the age of cheap oil is over, and the supply of crude oil remains a significant constraint to economic growth in the United States.

This chapter discussed economic transformation of the United States in the real economic activity part of macroeconomics, through variables such as the growth rate of real GDP, improvements in productivity, changing relationships between inflation and unemployment, the major external shocks to the U.S. economy, the global oil market, and the changing responses of the U.S. economy to oil price hikes. The real economic activities have made great contributions to the achievement of such economic goals as high employment, moderation of inflation, and sustainable economic growth.

# PART THREE

# DEMOGRAPHIC TRANSFORMATION
# OF THE UNITED STATES

# *Introduction*

Any economic transformation in a society is carried out by its people, when they produce and consume the goods and services that meet their needs. It is Americans' ability to be scientifically creative, technologically innovative, managerially adept, and entrepreneurially daring that has made the United States the power house of the world economy.

Demographic factors play important roles in both production and consumption for economic and social development. Economic transformation both influences and is influenced by population changes. Economic transformation, however, is a long-term process that requires careful investigation into the companion demographic transformation of the society in order to understand the underlying forces changing the economic system.

Unlike social, economic, and political events, a demographic transformation comes about very slowly. To observe any significant effect of external forces on the population size takes more than three generations, or about 80 years, and it is conceivable that many people ignore demographic factors when analyzing short-term economic issues and problems.

The United States has the world's largest economy and the world's third largest population. Its citizens have enjoyed a higher standard of living than people in most nations of the world. Achievements in scientific research, technology innovation, economic growth, political and social stability, and the increasingly leading role in world humanities and peacekeeping activities are hallmarks of America's contribution to human civilization. Labor, capital, and natural resources have been the input factors that determine the outputs of production. These factors, however, are subject to an economic law of diminishing returns. According to this law, at the present large scale of U.S. production, further increases in the three factors will bring in proportionally smaller output amounts.

J.M. Clark's famous dictum indicates: "Knowledge is the only instrument of production not subject to diminishing returns[1]." To further raise the standard of living for the majority of Americans requires sustainable economic growth and an increase in per capita consumption of goods and services. Future

---

[1] W.W. Rostow, *Theorists of Economic Growth From David Hume to the Present, with a Perspective on the Next Century,* Oxford University Press, 1990.

sustainable economic growth must rely on knowledge and technology innovations to promote the generation of productivity and wealth. It becomes
increasingly important for workers to be highly skilled.

In today's changing economic environment, the educational achievement
of the labor force and the quality of education and job training are decisive
factors both for the generation of knowledge and for the application of innovative technologies. Increases in production and consumption, combined with
a growing population, will inevitably put excessive pressures on the natural
resources of land, water, and energy. The consequences of an increasing
population will negatively affect the environment and threaten the sustainability
of economic growth. Therefore, the U.S. population's transformation shall
be considered a major continuous underlying force that transforms the U.S.
economy and society.

Part Three is divided into six chapters. Chapter 5 presents an analysis of
the U.S. population in the twentieth century and estimated projections for the
twenty-first century. We analyze demographic transformation in terms of
changes in racial and ethnic groups, international migration, and geographic
distribution. In Chapter 6 we discuss the demographic characteristics of the
U.S. population, including the changing patterns of fertility and mortality, and
their effects on the age structure. In Chapter 7, we focus our attention on
the U.S. labor market and the intellectual ability of the U.S. labor force,
including immigrant workers. Chapter 8 discusses personal income and income distribution as well as the poverty status of families, revealing the increasing inequality of income distribution during American demographic and
economic transformations. Chapter 9 analyzes the linkage of educational
attainment of American workers and their participation ratios, unemployment rates, and earnings. The final section provides a brief summary of Part
Three.

# Chapter 5

## *U.S. Population Estimates and Projections*

The United States conducted its first population census in 1790. Since then a regular population census has been required by the U.S. Constitution to provide accurate population data. This allows the government to allocate seats in the House of Representatives and to distribute federal funds. The Bureau of the Census, a division of the U.S. Commerce Department, conducts the census every ten years. These censuses are an invaluable source of data used for analyzing both past and present, and making projections for the future. Although the latest census was completed in April of 2000, official population projections based on the 2000 census will not be available for years. Hence, our analyses of the U.S. population transformation must rely on the 1990 census.

In the Census Bureau's database, there are three time series of the population projection, the high, middle, and low series that are results from different assumptions regarding births, deaths, and international migration, which are the major determinants of population changes. The middle series is considered as the most likely to occur. The low and high series are forecasts based upon some extreme assumptions about the three determinants for illustrating uncertainties around the central middle series rather than alternative scenarios of the future U.S. population. Hence, we shall concentrate on population estimates and the middle series of population projection, with the time span of two hundred years, from 1900 to 2100. In this chapter, the U.S. population is compared with the populations of seven developed nations.

The following sections discuss four specific topics by using U.S. population estimations and projections: population expansion, race, immigration and foreign-born population, and regional distribution of the U.S. population.

## 5-1   Population Expansion

According to population data recorded by the Bureau of Census, there were 76 million people in the United States in 1900. In 1950, that number grew to approximately 152 million people, and to 275 million by 2000. The middle series of the population projection indicates the U.S. population size will reach 404 million by the year 2050 and 571 million by 2100.

Figure 5-1 depicts the estimation and projection of the U.S. population over a 200-year time span. In the last 100 years the U.S. population increased 3.6 times, and in the last 50 years it increased 1.8 times. In the next 50 years, the U.S. population is projected to increase 1.5 times, and in the next 100 years it will increase 2.1 times. In this 200-year time span, 1900–2100, the U.S. population's expansion is projected to increase 7.5 times.

The United States has the third largest population in the world, behind China and India. In terms of population size, it is expected to keep its "top third" rank throughout the next century. Important characteristics of the U.S. population have been the moderate and persistent pace of its growth, its ethnic diversity, and its mobility. This growth has lasted for a full century and is expected to continue. Unlike China and India, which have suffered from large population swings, the United States has experienced a more stable population expansion.

Table 5-1 displays the average annual increment changes and the average annual growth rates of the U.S. population for ten decades in the last century. In the early 1900s, the U.S. population increased at a relatively stable pace, about 1.9-2.0% per year. Over the last century, there was only one year in which U.S. population declined; in 1918 the population decreased by nearly 60,000 people. In the time period from 1900 to 1946, annual population increases in the U.S. fluctuated between 1.3 million and 1.7 million, except for two years (1921 and 1924) in which the population increased by slightly over 2 million per year.

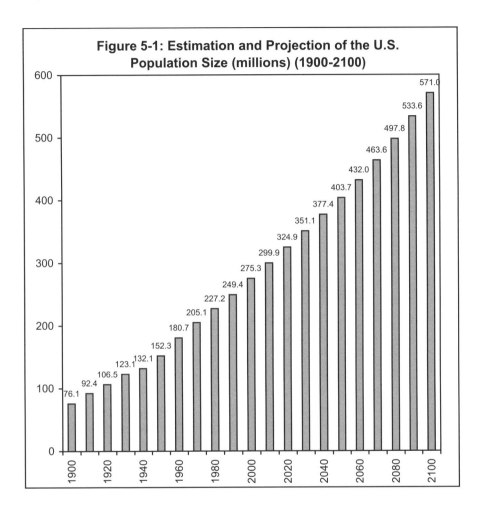

Figure 5-1: Estimation and Projection of the U.S. Population Size (millions) (1900-2100)

The end of the First World War allowed the U.S. population to resume its ascending path, and the annual growth rate increased gradually to 1.9% in 1924. The great depression in 1929–1933, which was the most severe in the nation's history, drastically slowed the population expansion, and the annual

Table 5-1: Annual Increments and Growth Rate of the U.S. Population

| Decades | Annual Increments (million) | Annual Growth Rate (%) |
|---------|------------------------------|------------------------|
| 1900s   | 1.600                        | 1.94                   |
| 1910s   | 1.402                        | 1.45                   |
| 1920s   | 1.725                        | 1.54                   |
| 1930s   | 0.911                        | 0.72                   |
| 1940s   | 1.831                        | 1.32                   |
| 1950s   | 2.864                        | 1.77                   |
| 1960s   | 2.485                        | 1.32                   |
| 1970s   | 2.238                        | 1.05                   |
| 1980s   | 2.176                        | 0.93                   |
| 1990s   | 2.600                        | 1.01                   |

population growth rate fell to 1.04% in 1929. The continuous hard economic times of the 1930s further slowed the population's expansion, and the annual growth rate fell as low as 0.59% in 1933. The Second World War did not cause a decline in the overall U.S. population, although it did cap the population's growth at approximately 0.8-1.0% per year.

At the end of the Second World War the U.S. entered a new era of peacetime expansion. The annual growth rate rose quickly to 2.07% in 1950 and stabilized at 1.6-1.8% in the 1950s. The huge jump in the population from 1946 to 1964 has given people born in this period the nickname "Baby Boomers." The net increase was estimated to be more than 2.6 million people per year, each year from 1946 to 1964. The Baby Boom generations and their children, called the echo generations, have profoundly altered the age structure of the U.S. population. The influence of these two generations will continue to be felt for the next 50 years. This will be discussed in more detail in Chapter Two.

The growth rate of the U.S. population declined gradually from 1.40% in 1964 to 0.98% in 1969. Since 1970, it has fluctuated in a narrow range of 0.87 - 1.14%. In only two years, 1984 and 1985, the population growth rate fell to its low boundary (0.87% and 0.89% respectively), and in only two time periods, 1977–1979 and 1990–1993, the population growth rate climbed slightly above 1.0%. This fact indicates that the U.S. population was steadily increasing with a moderate annual growth rate of nearly 1.0% over the last three decades.

Unlike some underdeveloped nations in which the probability of improving the standard of living is severely hampered by population expansion, the United States has experienced positive interactions between population expansion and economic growth. Figure 5-2 shows the annual growth rate of the population and the real GDP per capita for the United States. A rapid expansion of the U.S. population, which started in the middle of the 1940s and ended in the middle of the 1960s, corresponds to the moderate slope of the rising real GDP per capita. Stable and low population growth rates since 1970 are associated with steady increases in real GDP per capita.

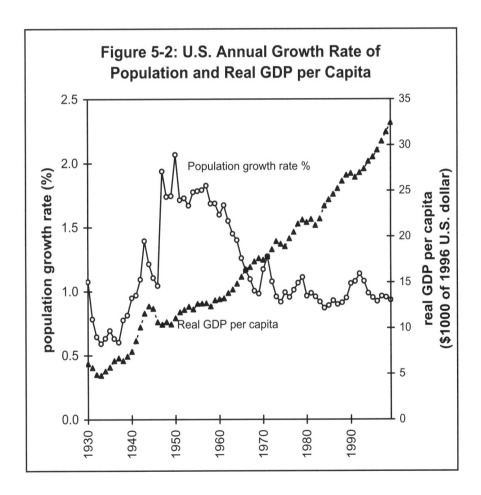

**Figure 5-2: U.S. Annual Growth Rate of Population and Real GDP per Capita**

By definition, real GDP per capita is the nation's real GDP divided by the total number of its people. In order for real GDP per capita to rise, real GDP produced by the nation must grow more rapidly than its population does. In the last thirty years U.S. real GDP increased faster than its population did, with only a few exceptions when the U.S. economy ran into some short-lived recessions in 1974–1975, 1980–1981, and 1991. Overall, the U.S. economy has shown its ability to accommodate persistent and moderate population expansion and to continuously raise the standard of living for the majority of Americans, even though population size has remained one of the top three in the world.

The rapid population expansion of the 1950s–1970s raised some general concerns over U.S. population growth and its effect on the U.S. economy[2]. Compared with many other nations, the United States is in a very privileged situation in terms of the per capita endowment of natural resources. For instance, according to world population statistics from 1989–1990, the availability of arable land at the world level was less than 0.27 ha. (hectare) per capita. In the U.S., the average is 0.76 ha. per capita. Japan and China, by contrast, have only 0.03 ha. and 0.08 ha. per capita respectively. Doubling the U.S. population in the twenty-first century, however, would reduce the arable land to less than 0.38 ha. per capita, not even taking into consideration the natural soil erosion and continuous losses of cropland due to urbanization, transportation networks, and industry takeover.

Population growth has a tremendous effect on U.S. agriculture, American food supply, and, as the U.S. has become the largest food exporter, the rest of the world as well.

U.S. energy consumption per capita is the highest in the world. In 1995, the total energy consumed in the United State was 90.6 quadrillion BTU[3], accounting for 25% of the total energy consumed by all the nations of the globe, while the U.S. population accounted for only 4.5% of the total world population. Fossil fuel is the main energy source powering industrial development, an advanced agricultural system, and a vast transportation network. The availability of fossil-fuel energy is also used to improve quality of life, to protect humans from numerous diseases, and to protect the environment from pollution and contamination via purification of water and waste

---

[2] *Food, Land, Population and the U.S. Economy,* by David Pimentel and Mario Giampietro, Carrying Capacity Network, Washington, D.C., 1994.
[3] *Annual Energy Outlook 1996,* by Energy Information Administration, Washington, DC, January 1996.

processing. Americans consume 20 to 30 times more fossil energy per capita than people in developing countries, with nearly 54% of the oil used in the United States imported from the Middle East and other areas of the world. Fossil fuels, of course, are subject to depletion and once gone cannot be replenished. A rapid increase of the U.S. population would accelerate the demand for oil and gas, which will intensify the dependence of the U.S. economy upon imported fossil fuels, and these will be depleted sooner than expected.

Judging from historical records and current fertility patterns, however, the U.S. population seems unlikely to experience the population explosions that occurred in the two most populated nations of the world, China and India, from 1960 through 1980[4]. As we shall see in Section 5-3, a unique characteristic of the U.S. population is that one third of its growth comes from net international migration, which provides a special way of balancing population expansion, economic growth, and environmental protection.

Projections from the Census Bureau indicate that the U.S. population is expected to remain on its ascending trajectory with a gradually declining slope. These forecasts should relieve Americans from fears triggered by warning signs from Japan and some Western European nations, which are facing the threat of shrinking population in the next several decades. To make a comparison, we provide estimates and projections of population growth rates for eight developed nations, including Russia, in Table 5-2. These rates represent annual percentage changes of the populations, averaged by decades.

As Table 5-2 shows, in the 1950s, Canada, the United States, Russia, and Japan experienced a relatively rapid population expansion, with annual growth rates in the range of 1.22% - 2.84%. The population growth rates of Germany, Britain, Italy, and France in the 1950s were lower, in the range of 0.34% - 0.90%. Since 1960, Canada and the U.S. have gradually reduced the pace of their population expansion. Their annual population growth rates fell to nearly 1.0% per year in the 1990s. In the 1970s and 1980s, a rapid deceleration in population growth can be observed for Japan, Germany, Britain, Italy, France, and Russia. In the 1990s, Italy's growth rate declined to 0.09% per year, Britain's to 0.24% per year, Germany's to 0.32% per year, and Japan's to 0.46% per year.

---

[4] George Kozmetsky and Piyu Yue, *Embracing the Global Demographic Transformation, 1950-2050,* an IC2 Monograph, Austin, Texas, 2000.

Table 5-2: Population Annual Growth Rates of Eight Nations
(%) (1950-2050)

| Decade | U.S.A. | Japan | Germany | Britain |
|--------|--------|-------|---------|---------|
| 1950s | 1.77 | 1.22 | 0.62 | 0.34 |
| 1960s | 1.32 | 1.02 | 0.80 | 0.61 |
| 1970s | 1.05 | 1.15 | 0.52 | 0.48 |
| 1980s | 0.93 | 0.99 | -0.03 | 0.10 |
| 1990s | 1.01 | 0.46 | 0.32 | 0.24 |
| 2000s | 0.84 | 0.20 | 0.27 | 0.11 |
| 2010s | 0.78 | **-0.03** | **-0.05** | 0.08 |
| 2020s | 0.68 | **-0.31** | **-0.14** | 0.09 |
| 2030s | 0.35 | **-0.43** | **-0.39** | **-0.01** |
| 2040s | 0.15 | **-0.39** | **-0.61** | **-0.07** |
| 2050s | 0.13 | **-0.39** | **-0.70** | **-0.08** |
| **Decade** | **Italy** | **France** | **Russia** | **Canada** |
| 1950s | 0.65 | 0.90 | 1.66 | 2.84 |
| 1960s | 0.70 | 1.05 | 1.49 | 2.37 |
| 1970s | 0.67 | 0.94 | 0.77 | 1.77 |
| 1980s | 0.36 | 0.53 | 0.64 | 1.31 |
| 1990s | 0.09 | 0.52 | 0.52 | 1.27 |
| 2000s | **-0.03** | 0.33 | **-0.24** | 0.92 |
| 2010s | **-0.30** | 0.12 | **-0.37** | 0.73 |
| 2020s | **-0.51** | 0.05 | **-0.47** | 0.66 |
| 2030s | **-0.63** | **-0.06** | **-0.53** | 0.22 |
| 2040s | **-0.81** | **-0.14** | **-0.57** | **-0.04** |
| 2050s | **-0.95** | **-0.17** | **-0.53** | **-0.07** |

   An actual population reduction is expected to occur in the first decade of this century in Russia and Italy. Russia's declining population rate is projected to be 0.24% per year in the next ten years and its population reduction is expected to speed up to 0.57% per year in the 2040s. Italy and Germany are expected to see their populations shrink at 0.95% and 0.70% per year in the 2050s. Japan's population is projected to decline by about 0.4% per year in 2030-2050. Even Canada's population is expected to see a small negative rate in the 2040s and 2050s. The United States is the only nation in this group whose population will continue to expand in the next fifty years.

Figure 5-3 shows populations' evolving paths over a 100-year time span, 1950–2050, for these eight nations. One can easily observe that the U.S. population will stay on its ascending path with a gradually declining slope, while other populations have transferred or soon will transfer from an ascending path into a descending path. In the rich and developed nations of the world, the current decelerating population growth and expected declining population size are the inescapable consequences of dropping fertility rates below the replacement rate since 1970.

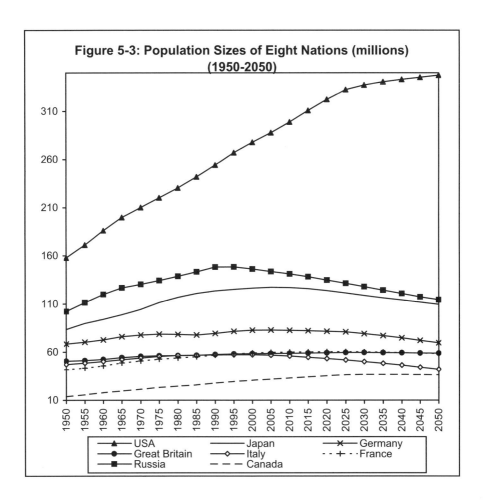

**Figure 5-3: Population Sizes of Eight Nations (millions) (1950-2050)**

For the last three decades, developed nations' death rates have reduced to the minimum, thanks to advances in medical science and health care services as well as general improvements in the standard of living. The birth rates in those nations, however, have decreased much faster than the death rates, resulting in an increasing number of elderly and decreasing number of youths. Therefore, serious population problems encountered by Japan, Russia, and Western European nations are not only declines in population size, but also declines in population's physical strength, due to unfavorable changes in population's age structure. Peter Drucker offered a serious warning in 1997:

> The developed world is in the process of committing collective suicide. Its citizens are not having enough babies to reproduce themselves, and the cause is quite clear: its younger people are no longer able to bear the increasing burden of supporting a growing population of older nonworking people. They can offset that rising burden only by cutting back at the other end of the dependence, which means having fewer or no children[5].

Fortunately, the U.S. population is expected to follow a quite different trajectory that will keep the population size rising and the population's aging process moving much more slowly than other rich developed nations of the world. This unique demographic nature provides the U.S. economy with a strong base for a sustainable long-term growth in the 21st century. The growing U.S. population is able to prevent any long-term shortages in working-age people and to keep the pool of labor force growing. The growing U.S. population is able to generate an increasing number of American consumers who are buying goods and services that keep the U.S. economy growing. From both the supply and demand sides, the U.S. population is expected to provide a solid base for a sustainable economic growth in the next fifty years. Compared with Japan and Western European nations, the United States has a significant advantage in the demographic nature, which prophesies a great probability that the United States will maintain its dominant position in the world.

---

[5] Peter Drucker, "Looking Ahead: Implications of the Present," *Harvard Business Review,* September-October 1997,  pp. 18-24.

## 5-2   Ethnic Distribution

The United States has had an increasingly diversified population in terms of races and ethnicity. The first population census in 1790 revealed that the number of the white people living in this country was 3.172 million and the number of blacks, the only minority recorded, was 0.757 million. In subsequent censuses conducted in 1890, 1900, 1970, and 2000, additional races were added as separate categories, such as American Indian, Japanese, Chinese, Filipino, Korean, Vietnamese, Mexican, Cuban, Spanish/Hispanic/Latino, and others. The number of racial categories has grown rapidly, reflecting the increasing diversification of the U.S. population due to immigration.

U.S. demographic statistics are now reported in four major racial groups: white, black, American Indians and Eskimos, and Asians and Pacific Islanders. There is also an ethnic group of Hispanic origin. Because many Hispanics do not identify with a particular racial group, a separate category of Hispanic origin has been added to the population censuses since 1970. Figure 5-4 presents estimates and projections of the changing racial composition of the U.S. population over the time period from 1850 to 2050. Except for the black group, the other minority groups have only had their population statistics available since 1980.

Census data presented in Figure 5-4 indicates that Caucasians have dominated the U.S. population since 1850. The number of whites living in the U.S. territory increased from 19.6 million in 1850 to 178.1 million in 1970 and further to 209.2 million in 1990. It is estimated that that figure will be 225.5 million in 2000, and will grow to 294.6 million by 2050. The white group's share in the total population also increased in the time period of 1850 – 1930, from 84.3% in 1850 to 89.8% in 1930.  Since then the share has declined, from its top of 89.8% in 1930 to 76.9% in 1990 and is expected to continue declining in the next fifty years to around 60% in 2050.

The black group has been the largest minority of the U.S. population. The size of this group increased from about 3.6 million people in 1850 to 22.6 million in 1970, and 30.6 million in 1990. It is expected to be 35.5 million in 2000 and nearly 60.6 million in 2050.  The black people accounted for 15.7% of the total population in 1850 and 9.7% in 1930, the lowest share for this group in the records. Since 1930, the black population has expanded faster than the majority group of the white population due to a high birth rate. Consequently, the population share of the black people increased to 11.25% in 1990 and 11.59% in 2000. It is forecasted to reach 12.35% in 2050.

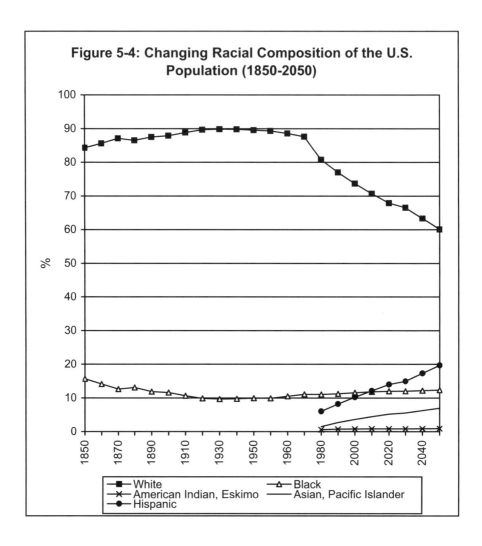

The Hispanic population in the United States has been the fastest-growing minority group. Its population size was 14.6 million in 1980, accounting for 6.1% of the total U.S. population and slightly greater than half of the black population. In 1995 the Hispanic population reached 27.1 million, nearly doubling its size in this 15-year period. It is projected that in the year 2010, the Hispanic group will become the largest minority in the United States. The number of Hispanic Americans will reach 41 million in 2010, accounting for 12% of the total U.S. population and exceeding the number of African Americans, about 40 million (11.8% of the total) in that year. The large number of immigrants entering this country in the 1980s and 1990s from Mexico and Southern America has contributed to the rapidly increasing Hispanic population. Higher fertility rates among Hispanic families have also been an important factor for the rapid growth of the U.S. Hispanic population.

The third largest minority group in the United States consists of Asians and Pacific Islanders. Population numbers for this group increased from 3.73 million in 1980 to 11.25 million in 2000, accounting for 1.6% of the total U.S. population in 1980 and for about 3.7% in 2000, and they are projected to be 34.4 million in 2050, corresponding to a population share 7.0%. The substantially increased population share of this group reflects the fact that the number of the Asian Americans has increased at a faster pace than the total U.S. population.

The number of American Indians and Eskimos rose gradually from 2.06 million in 1990 to 2.37 million in 2000. The population projection for the year 2050 for this group is about 4.37 million, twice the population of 1990. It remains the smallest minority group, even with an increasing population share from 0.76% in 1990 to 0.78% in 2000, and 0.89% in 2050.

The rapid population growth of American minorities has been the result of a disproportionately high share of births by minority women. The increasing immigration from various parts of the world into the United States has also contributed to the increasing diversification of the U.S. population.

## 5-3   Immigration

The United States is a nation of immigrants, and immigration has played a vital role in shaping the American population since 1607 when the first English settlers arrived in Jamestown, Virginia. The scale of immigration and originated regions and countries, however, has changed drastically according to records for the last one hundred and fifty years. Table 5-3 presents a dynamic picture of the foreign-born population in the United States over the time frame of 1850–1990[6].

---

[6] Source: U.S. Bureau of the Census, Internet Release Date: March 9, 1999. It is the latest data available as of our present analysis.

Table 5-3: Birth Regions and Countries of U.S. Foreign-Born Population (1850–1990)

| Year | Foreign-born population (million) | % of the Total U.S. Population |
|---|---|---|
| 1850 | 2.244 | 9.70% |
| 1900 | 10.341 | 13.60% |
| 1930 | 14.204 | 11.60% |
| 1960 | 9.738 | 5.40% |
| 1970 | 9.619 | 4.70% |
| 1980 | 14.080 | 6.20% |
| 1990 | 19.767 | 7.90% |

**Distribution of Originated Regions (million and % of the total foreign-born people)**

| Year | Europe | | Asia | | Africa | | Latin America | |
|---|---|---|---|---|---|---|---|---|
| 1850 | 2.03 | 90.5% | 0.001 | 0.05% | 0.0005 | 0.02% | 0.021 | 0.9% |
| 1900 | 8.88 | 85.9% | 0.12 | 1.2% | 0.0025 | 0.02% | 0.14 | 1.3% |
| 1930 | 11.78 | 83.0% | 0.28 | 1.9% | 0.018 | 0.13% | 0.79 | 5.6% |
| 1960 | 7.25 | 74.5% | 0.49 | 5.0% | 0.035 | 0.36% | 0.91 | 9.3% |
| 1970 | 5.74 | 59.7% | 0.82 | 8.6% | 0.08 | 0.83% | 1.80 | 18.8% |
| 1980 | 5.15 | 36.5% | 2.54 | 18.0% | 0.199 | 1.42% | 4.37 | 31.1% |
| 1990 | 2.35 | 22.0% | 4.98 | 25.2% | 0.38 | 1.84% | 8.41 | 42.5% |

**Distribution of Originated Countries (million and % of the total foreign-born people)**

| Year | Canada | | Great Britain | | Ireland | | Germany | |
|---|---|---|---|---|---|---|---|---|
| 1850 | 0.148 | 6.6% | 0.38 | 16.9% | 0.96 | 42.9% | 0.58 | 26.0% |
| 1900 | 1.18 | 11.4% | 1.17 | 11.3% | 1.62 | 15.6% | 2.66 | 25.8% |
| 1930 | 1.31 | 9.3% | 1.22 | 8.6% | 0.74 | 5.3% | 1.61 | 11.3% |
| 1960 | 0.95 | 9.8% | 0.76 | 7.9% | 0.34 | 3.5% | 0.99 | 10.2% |
| 1970 | 0.81 | 8.5% | 0.65 | 6.7% | 0.25 | 2.6% | 0.83 | 8.7% |
| 1980 | 0.84 | 6.0% | 0.65 | 4.6% | 0.20 | 1.4% | 0.85 | 6.0% |
| 1990 | 0.74 | 3.8% | 0.62 | 3.2% | 0.17 | 0.9% | 0.71 | 3.6% |

| Year | Italy | | Poland | | Soviet Union | | China | |
|---|---|---|---|---|---|---|---|---|
| 1850 | 0.0036 | 0.16% | 0.007 | 0.18%* | 0.0014 | 0.06% | 0.0007 | 0.03% |
| 1900 | 0.48 | 4.68% | 0.38 | 3.7% | 0.42 | 4.1% | 0.081 | 0.8% |
| 1930 | 1.79 | 12.6% | 1.27 | 8.9% | 1.15 | 8.1% | 0.046 | 0.3% |
| 1960 | 1.26 | 12.9% | 0.75 | 7.7% | 0.69 | 7.1% | 0.099 | 1.0% |
| 1970 | 1 | 10.5% | 0.55 | 5.7% | 0.46 | 4.8% | 0.17 | 1.8% |
| 1980 | 0.83 | 5.9% | 0.42 | 3.0% | 0.41 | 2.9% | 0.29 | 2.0% |
| 1990 | 0.58 | 2.9% | 0.39 | 2.0% | 0.33 | 1.7% | 0.53 | 2.7% |

| Year | India | | Japan | | Mexico | |
|---|---|---|---|---|---|---|
| 1850 | 0.0006 | 0.01%# | .0004 | 0.01%@ | 0.013 | 0.59% |
| 1900 | 0.002 | 0.02% | 0.025 | 0.24% | 0.103 | 1.00% |
| 1930 | 0.0058 | 0.04% | 0.07 | 0.50% | 0.64 | 4.52% |
| 1960 | 0.012 | 0.13% | 0.11 | 1.12% | 0.57 | 5.91% |
| 1970 | 0.051 | 0.53% | 0.12 | 1.25% | 0.76 | 7.90% |
| 1980 | 0.21 | 1.46% | 0.22 | 1.58% | 2.2 | 15.62% |
| 1990 | 0.45 | 2.28% | 0.29 | 1.47% | 4.3 | 21.74% |

*It is for the year of 1860, # is for the year of 1870, and @ is for the year of 1880.

In 1850, 2.24 million Americans who had been born in foreign countries, accounting for 9.7% of the total U.S. population. In that year, 90.5% of the foreign-born Americans came from Europe; immigrants from Great Britain, Ireland and Germany accounted for major portion of this number. Only 20,773 Americans were born in South and Latin America and only 1,135 Americans were born in Asia.

At the turn of the twentieth century, the U.S. Industrial Revolution attracted many people from different parts of the world. Europe was still the major source of immigrants. In 1900, about 10.34 million Americans, nearly 13.6% of the total U.S. population, were foreign-born, with 86% of them originating in European nations, such as Germany, Great Britain, Ireland, Italy, and the Soviet Union.

The number of Canadian-born Americans increased from 0.147 million in 1850 to 1.18 million in 1900. The number of South and Latin American-born Americans were about 0.137 million and Asia-born Americans were 0.12 million in 1900.

In 1910, the foreign-born population increased to 14.7% of the total U.S. population, the largest share ever. The increased share of the foreign-born population was associated with a decreasing share of the native population, indicating not only the number of new immigrants exceeding the number of deaths among the foreign-born people, but also the net new immigrants increasing even faster than the total U.S. population. Indeed, immigration played a crucial role in the expansion of the U.S. population over the time period of 1850–1910.

In 1921, however, the U.S. Congress imposed restrictive immigration legislations that dampened the immigration momentum. The population share of foreign-born Americans was reduced to 11.6% in 1930, and further to 4.7% in 1970, the lowest share to date. Not only did its population share decrease steadily after 1930, the actual number of foreign-born Americans also declined, from 14.2 million in 1930 to 9.6 million in 1970. This fact indicates that the deaths of foreign-born Americans outnumbered the new immigrants during the time period of 1930–1970.

In 1965 the Congress passed a piece of legislation to relax immigration barriers in the United States, which changed the U.S. immigration system from a skill-based system to a family preference-based system resulted in a large increase of foreign-born population in the United States. In 1980, the number of foreign-born Americans jumped to 14.08 million, accounting for 6.2% of the total U.S. population. In 1990, it was 19.77 million or 7.9% of the total population. The increasing share of foreign-born population since

1970 indicates that the number of new immigrants has grown much faster than does the U.S. population.

In this recent wave of immigration, newcomers were originated with diversified regions and nations, which has greatly altered the ethnic composition of foreign-born population in the United States. The number of European-born Americans has markedly declined, while the number of Asian-born and Latin-American-born people living in the United States has rapidly increased. As Table 5-3 shows, the British-born people living in the United States were 1.17 million, accounting for 11.29% of the total foreign-born population in 1900, 1.22 million (8.62%) in 1930, 0.76 million (7.85%) in 1960, and 0.62 million (3.15%) in 1990. The Irish-born Americans were 1.62 million (15.62%) in 1900, 0.74 million (5.24%) in 1930, 0.34 million (3.48%) in 1960 and only 0.17 million (0.86%) in 1990. Similar changes took place in population size and composition shares of the other European-nation-born people living in the United States. Both measures of size and share of people who are originated with Europe have declined since 1930.

Immigrants from Asia and Latin America into this country have increased rapidly since 1970. The sizes and composition shares of Asian-born and Latin-American-born people in the United States have risen correspondingly. The number of Asian-born Americans was only 0.49 million or 5.04% of the total foreign-born population in 1960, it rose to 2.54 million (18.04%) in 1980, and to 4.98 million (25.19%) in 1990. The number of Latin-America-born people in the United States was 0.91 million or 9.33% of the total foreign-born population in 1960, it increased to 4.37 million (31.05%) in 1980 and to 8.41 million (42.53%) in 1990. Millions of Mexicans have immigrated into the United States since 1970, which boosted the number of Mexican-born Americans from 0.76 million (7.90% of the total foreign-born population) in 1970 to 4.30 million (21.74%) in 1990.

As of 1990, Latin America was the largest immigrating region to the United States; for every one hundred foreign-born people living in this country, 43 people came from Latin America, 25 people from Asia, 22 people from Europe, 3 or 4 people from North America (Canada), and 1 or 2 persons from Africa. Asia has now surpassed Europe as the second largest immigrating region to the United States.

In terms of composition share of the foreign-born population, in 1990 Mexico was number one (21.74%), followed by Canada (3.77%), Germany (3.60%), and Britain (3.15%). From Table 5-3, one can clearly observe the declining trend in population size and composition share of immigrants from Canada, Germany, and Britain, indicating that the deaths within these population groups outnumber new immigrants from these nations.

As of 1990, China and India had composition share of 2.68% and 2.28% respectively. Since 1970, the number of new immigrants from the two most populous nations of the world has increased rapidly. In 1960 the United States had less than 0.1 million people who originated from China and only 0.012 million people from India. In 1990, these numbers grew to 0.53 million and 0.45 million respectively.

Clearly, the increasing immigration from Latin America and Asia and the decreasing immigration from Europe was one of important factors that have generated the rapidly rising population share of Hispanic and Asian groups and the declining population share of the white group. Indeed, the changing pattern of international immigration into this country has played a crucial role in America's racial and ethnic diversification.

The above analysis is based upon census data for the foreign-born population in the United Sates rather than some direct measures of tracing international migration. According to the U.S. Census Bureau, international migration data is now available for the years from 1991 through 1999. The net international migration into the United States is defined as the number of people who immigrated into this country in a given time period minus the number of people who emigrated from this country to the rest of the world in the same time period. The United States had the total number 7.306 million of net international migration over the time span from 1991 to 1999, and about 0.939 million in 1997, which was the largest net international migration in a single year into this country in the 1990s.

The net international migration accounted for 0.26% of the total U.S. population in 1991; it increased to 0.35% in 1997 and 0.31% in 1999. Even though the number of net immigrants into the United States every year accounted for a very small portion of the total U.S. population, it has accounted for a large portion of the annual increases of the U.S. population. Table 5-4 presents a comparison of the number of net immigrants and the number of annual population increases over the years from 1991 to 1999.

Since 1996 the number of net immigrants has accounted for more than one third of all the increases in the total U.S. population. That is to say, unlike most nations of the world, the United States has transformed its population through not only the changing pattern of birth rate and death rate, but also international immigration.

Table 5-4: Net International Immigrants Into the United States

| Year | (1) Net Immigrants (million) | (2) Annual Increase of US Population (million) | % of (1) in (2) |
|---|---|---|---|
| 1991 | 0.649 | 2.688 | 24.1% |
| 1992 | 0.773 | 2.868 | 27.0% |
| 1993 | 0.826 | 2.751 | 30.0% |
| 1994 | 0.764 | 2.543 | 30.0% |
| 1995 | 0.785 | 2.476 | 31.7% |
| 1996 | 0.864 | 2.425 | 35.6% |
| 1997 | 0.939 | 2.554 | 36.8% |
| 1998 | 0.854 | 2.555 | 33.4% |
| 1999 | 0.852 | 2.521 | 33.8% |

Because the net international migration accounts for one-third of the total U.S. population growth, policy makers must take immigration into consideration for its overall effect on the U.S. population, economy, and society. Immigrants are usually in the youth or the working-age groups and become an important part of the U.S. labor force, particularly for many unskilled jobs in the construction and agricultural sectors. Immigrants have higher birth rates and lower educational levels, which contributes to the national birth rate positively and to the average educational attainment rate negatively. More efforts from national and local communities are needed to help these immigrants receive educations, find jobs, and establish themselves in the new environment.

From the above analysis one can observe that the number of immigrants into the United States has varied greatly according to federal regulations and immigration policies. The size and intellectual quality of the net international migration into this country can be adjusted by imposing special regulations that aim at bringing in skilled people from the rest of the world. If the population expansion became excessive and threatened the natural environment or if the economy ran into a severe recession, rigid policies would be imposed on immigration that would immediately reduce the population growth. Taking advantages of international migration, the United States does not really need to worry about its declining birth rate, as Japan or Western European nations do, nor does it need to worry about the possibility of a population explosion, as China, India and many less developed nations do. Indeed, immigration has provided the United States with a special buffer to balance its population expansion, economic growth, and social development.

## 5-4  Regional Distribution

In 1990, there were 249.4 million people residing in the United States in the 50 states and the District of Columbia. The U.S. population grew at nearly 1.0% per year in the 1990s, reaching about 275.3 million in 2000. The U.S. population, however, is not evenly distributed over regions and states; the population growth rate also varies significantly across the country.

The Census Bureau divides the United States into four regions, and each region into two or three divisions. The population distribution over these regions and divisions is displayed in the first column of Table 5-5.

As of 1999, about 96.47 million Americans lived in the South Region, accounting for 35.4% of the total U.S. population, with 49.56 million in the South Atlantic Division, 16.58 million in the East South Central Division, and 30.33 million in the West South Central Division. 63.24 million, or 23.2% of the total U.S. population, lived in the Midwest Region, accounting for 23.2% of the total U.S. population (44.44 million in the East North Central Division and 18.80 million in the West North Division). There were 61.15 million Americans in the West Region, accounting for 22.4% of the total U.S. population (17.13 million in the Mountain Division and 44.02 million in the Pacific Division), and 51.83 million Americans in the Northeast Region, accounting for 19.0% of the total U.S. population (13.50 million in the New England Division and 38.33 million in the Middle Atlantic Division).

There are three major demographic components that determine population changes within a region or division. The first component is the natural increase of population, which is the number of births minus the number of deaths in a region (or division) during a given time period. The second component is net domestic migration, which is the difference between immigration to a region and emigration from the region during a given time period. This calculation is for origins and destinations within the United States.

Table 5-5:  Demographic Components by Regions and Divisions

| Region & Division | In 1999 Number of People | In 1990 - 1999 Population Increase | | Natural Increase | | Net Domestic Migration | | Net International migration | |
|---|---|---|---|---|---|---|---|---|---|
| | million | million | % | million | % | million | % | million | % |
| **USA** | 272.69 | 23.900 | 9.6 | 15.886 | 6.4 | 0 | 0 | 7.478 | 3.0 |
| **South** | 96.468 35.4% | 11.013 | 12.9 | 5.271 | 6.2 | 3.598 | 4.2 | 1.990 | 2.3 |
| South Atlantic | 49.560 | 5.989 | 13.7 | 2.305 | 5.3 | 2.403 | 5.5 | 1.143 | 2.6 |
| East South Central | 16.583 | 1.403 | 9.2 | 0.703 | 4.6 | 0.611 | 4.0 | 0.067 | 0.4 |
| West South Central | 30.326 | 3.621 | 13.6 | 2.263 | 8.5 | 0.584 | 2.2 | 0.780 | 2.9 |
| **Midwest** | 63.242 23.2% | 3.573 | 6.0 | 3.140 | 5.3 | -0.641 | -1.1 | 0.759 | 1.3 |
| East North Central | 44.442 | 2.433 | 5.8 | 2.307 | 5.5 | -0.753 | -1.8 | 0.591 | 1.4 |
| West North Central | 18.800 | 1.140 | 6.5 | 0.833 | 4.7 | 0.112 | 0.6 | 0.168 | 1.0 |
| **West** | 61.150 22.4% | 8.313 | 15.7 | 5.194 | 9.8 | 0.067 | 0.1 | 2.875 | 5.4 |
| Mountain | 17.127 | 3.469 | 25.4 | 1.323 | 9.7 | 1.709 | 12.5 | 0.319 | 2.3 |
| Pacific | 44.023 | 4.844 | 12.4 | 3.871 | 9.9 | -1.642 | -4.2 | 2.556 | 6.5 |
| **Northeast** | 51.830 19.0% | 1.002 | 2.0 | 2.280 | 4.5 | -3.025 | -6.0 | 1.854 | 3.6 |
| New England | 13.496 | 0.289 | 2.2 | 0.574 | 4.3 | 0.506 | -3.8 | 0.253 | 1.9 |
| Middle Atlantic | 38.334 | 0.713 | 1.9 | 1.706 | 4.5 | -2.518 | -6.7 | 1.601 | 4.3 |

The third component is net international migration, which is the difference between immigration to a region from outside the United States and emigration from the region to other countries during the given time period. Immigration includes both legal and estimated undocumented immigration. The rate of the component change is defined as a percentage of the component change in terms of the region's population size at the beginning of the given time period. Table 5-5 provides population increases in the three components and their rates in the time period from 1990 through 1999 for the United States, its four regions and nine divisions.

In the time period of 1990–1999, the U.S. population increased by 9.6% or added 23.9 million people, in which the natural increase was about 15.9 million and net international migration was 7.5 million. The natural increase rate was 6.4% and the net international migration rate was 3.0%[7]. During this time period, net international migration accounted for nearly one third and the natural increase accounted for two thirds of the population increase in the United States. The population changes in this time period varied across regions and divisions.

The West Region had the fastest population growth. Its population increased by 15.7%; the natural increase was 5.2 million, net international migration was 2.9 million, and the net domestic migration was only 67,000. Within the West Region, the Mountain Division showed a 25.4% increase in its population. It added about 3.5 million people in this time period, including 1.3 million of natural increase, 1.7 million of net domestic migration, and only 0.3 million of net international migration. The Pacific Division added about 4.8 million people; nearly 3.9 million came from natural increase, and 2.5 million came from net international migration. The net domestic migration was negative: the number of people who moved out from the Pacific Division minus the number of people who moved in was 1.6 million.

The South Region recorded the second fastest population growth, with a 12.9% rise or about 11 million additional people. Nearly half of this increase came from the natural increase component, three tenths of it from domestic migration and the remaining two tenths from international immigration. Among its three divisions, the West South Central Division had the fastest growth in natural increase and net international migration, because it contains a large state, Texas, which held the fastest growing components.

The Midwest Region recorded a 6.0% population increase or a 3.6-million-people increase during 1990-1999. The natural increase component was the major part, about 3.1 million people, while the other two components almost offset each other, as the net domestic migration decreased by 0.64 million and the net international migration increased by 0.76 million.

---

[7] It is worth noticing that from the original data the sum of natural increase and net international migration does not equal the population increase for some unexplained reason. As a result, the sum of the rate of natural increase and the rate of net international migration does not equal the rate of population increase in the time period.

The Northeast Region increased its population by only 2.0%, compared with a national 9.6% increase in the same time period. Its natural increase was 2.28 million people, but its net domestic migration was negative. About 3.0 million people had moved out from this region after subtracting the number of people who moved in.

From Table 5-5 one can see that all the regions and divisions recorded positive natural population increases and positive net international migration in the time period of 1990–1999, even though the rates of change in those two components varied substantially across regions and divisions. In terms of the net domestic migration, the Northeast and Midwest Regions and the East North Central, Pacific, New England and Middle Atlantic Divisions were the places from which Americans had moved out into the rest of the country. People who move long distances are prompted by many practical considerations, such as education, job opportunity and career, marriage and family building. Those regions and divisions that attract net domestic migration must provide better education and job opportunities as well as better living conditions for individuals and families.

A similar analysis has been done for the distribution of population and its component changes over the fifty states in the time period of 1990–1999. We do not present the detailed analysis at the state level, but highlight the results in Tables 5-6 and 5-7.

The upper panel of Table 5-6 displays the top ten states ranked by population size in 1999; and the lower panel presents the top ten states ranked by the rate of population changes in the time period of 1990–1999.

In 1999, California had the largest population, 33.145 million people, followed by Texas (20.044 million), New York (18.197 million), and Florida (15.111 million). Those four states had their population each accounting for more than 5.0% of the total U.S. population. The sum of all the populations in the top ten states was 147.671 million in 1999, accounting for 54.16% of the total U.S. population; it increased by 9.1% or 12.264 million people during 1990–1999, which was below the national rate of 9.6% in the same time period.

The lower panel of Table 5-6 indicates that in terms of population growth rates during 1990–1999, the top five states are all located in the Mountain Division of the West Region. Nevada's population increased by 0.66 million people, which was a 50.6% rise, the greatest rate of population change in the United States. Arizona, Idaho, Utah, and Colorado increased their populations by more than 23% during 1990–1999. Three states in the South Region— Georgia, Texas, and Florida—are included in the top-ten list; their rates of population changes exceeded 16% during 1990–1999, compared with the national rate of 9.6% during the same time period. The remaining two states in the top-ten list are Washington and Oregon in the Pacific Division of the West Region. The total population of the top-ten states ranked by the population change rate was 66.04 million in 1999, accounting for 24.22% of the U.S. population; their populations increased by about 11.04 million, a 20.1% rise in 1990–1999.

Table 5-6: The Top Ten States by Population

| Top Ten States by Population Size | | | | |
|---|---|---|---|---|
| States | Population size in 1999 (million) | % of the total U.S. population | Population changes in 1990-1999 | |
| | | | (million) | Rate (%) |
| California | 33.145 | 12.15 | 3.334 | 11.2 |
| Texas | 20.044 | 7.35 | 3.058 | 18.0 |
| New York | 18.197 | 6.67 | 0.206 | 1.1 |
| Florida | 15.111 | 5.54 | 2.173 | 16.8 |
| Illinois | 12.128 | 4.45 | 0.698 | 6.1 |
| Pennsylvania | 11.994 | 4.40 | 0.111 | 0.9 |
| Ohio | 11.257 | 4.13 | 0.410 | 3.8 |
| Michigan | 9.864 | 3.62 | 0.568 | 6.1 |
| New Jersey | 8.143 | 2.99 | 0.396 | 5.1 |
| Georgia | 7.788 | 2.86 | 1.310 | 20.2 |
| **Sum of ten states** | 147.671 | 54.16 | 12.264 | 9.1 |
| Top Ten States by Population Change Rate | | | | |
| Nevada | 1.809 | 0.66 | 0.608 | 50.6 |
| Arizona | 4.778 | 1.75 | 1.113 | 30.4 |
| Idaho | 1.252 | 0.46 | 0.245 | 24.3 |
| Utah | 2.130 | 0.78 | 0.407 | 23.6 |
| Colorado | 4.056 | 1.49 | 0.762 | 23.1 |
| Georgia | 7.788 | 2.86 | 1.310 | 20.2 |
| Washington | 5.756 | 2.11 | 0.890 | 18.3 |
| Texas | 20.044 | 7.35 | 3.058 | 18.0 |
| Florida | 15.111 | 5.54 | 2.173 | 16.8 |
| Oregon | 3.316 | 1.22 | 0.474 | 16.7 |
| **Sum of ten states** | 66.040 | 24.22 | 11.040 | 20.1 |

Table 5-7 presents three top-ten lists of states in terms of component change rates of natural increase, net domestic migration, and net international migration.

Table 5-7: The Top Ten States by Demographic Components

| Top ten states by natural increases of population | | | | |
|---|---|---|---|---|
| States | Population size in 1999 (million) | Natural increase in 1990-1999 | | Population changes in 1990-1999 | |
| | | (Million) | Rate (%) | (million) | Rate (%) |
| Utah | 2.130 | 0.271 | 15.7 | 0.407 | 23.6 |
| Alaska | 0.619 | 0.077 | 13.9 | 0.069 | 12.6 |
| California | 33.145 | 3.188 | 10.7 | 3.334 | 11.2 |
| Texas | 20.044 | 1.772 | 10.4 | 3.058 | 18.0 |
| Nevada | 1.809 | 0.117 | 9.8 | 0.608 | 50.6 |
| Arizona | 4.778 | 0.353 | 9.6 | 1.113 | 30.4 |
| Hawaii | 1.185 | 0.106 | 9.5 | 0.077 | 7.0 |
| New Mexico | 1.740 | 0.143 | 9.4 | 0.225 | 14.8 |
| Idaho | 1.252 | 0.088 | 8.8 | 0.245 | 24.3 |
| Colorado | 4.056 | 0.288 | 8.8 | 0.762 | 23.1 |
| Sum of ten states | 70.758 | 6.403 | 10.5 | 9.898 | 16.3 |
| **Top ten states by net domestic migration** | | | | | |
| States | Population size in 1999 (million) | Net domestic migration in 1990-1999 | | Population changes in 1990-1999 | |
| | | (Million) | Rate (%) | (million) | Rate (%) |
| Nevada | 1.809 | 0.434 | 36.1 | 0.608 | 50.6 |
| Arizona | 4.778 | 0.577 | 15.7 | 1.113 | 30.4 |
| Idaho | 1.252 | 0.136 | 13.5 | 0.245 | 24.3 |
| Colorado | 4.056 | 0.403 | 12.2 | 0.762 | 23.1 |
| Georgia | 7.788 | 0.665 | 10.3 | 1.310 | 20.2 |
| Oregon | 3.316 | 0.271 | 9.5 | 0.474 | 16.7 |
| Florida | 15.111 | 1.109 | 8.6 | 2.173 | 16.8 |
| North Carolina | 7.651 | 0.554 | 8.4 | 1.018 | 15.4 |
| Washington | 5.756 | 0.382 | 7.8 | 0.890 | 18.3 |
| Tennessee | 5.484 | 0.357 | 7.3 | 0.606 | 12.4 |
| Sum of ten states | 57.001 | 4.888 | 10.2 | 9.199 | 19.2 |

Table 5-7 continued

| Top ten states by net international migration | | | | | |
|---|---|---|---|---|---|
| States | Population size in 1999 (million) | Net international migration in 1990-1999 | | Population changes in 1990-1999 | |
| | | (Million) | Rate (%) | (million) | Rate (%) |
| California | 33.145 | 2.280 | 7.6 | 3.334 | 11.2 |
| New York | 18.197 | 1.108 | 6.2 | 0.206 | 1.1 |
| Florida | 15.111 | 0.640 | 4.9 | 2.173 | 16.8 |
| District of Columbia | 0.519 | 0.300 | 4.9 | -0.088 | -14.5 |
| Hawaii | 1.185 | 0.540 | 4.9 | 0.077 | 7.0 |
| New Jersey | 8.143 | 0.378 | 4.9 | 0.396 | 5.1 |
| Nevada | 1.809 | 0.056 | 4.6 | 0.608 | 50.6 |
| Texas | 20.044 | 0.715 | 4.2 | 3.058 | 18.0 |
| Illinois | 12.128 | 0.384 | 3.4 | 0.698 | 6.1 |
| Washington | 5.756 | 0.147 | 3.0 | 0.890 | 18.3 |
| Sum of ten states | 116.037 | 6.549 | 6.3 | 11.352 | 10.8 |

The upper panel of Table 5-7 shows that Utah, Alaska, California, and Texas held their rates of natural increases above 10.0% during 1990–1999, which well exceeded the national level of 6.4% (in Table 5-5). The total population of these top-ten states was 70.758 million in 1999, and their population increase was 9.898 million during 1990–1999, with 6.403 million coming from a natural increase.

The middle panel of Table 5-7 indicates four states in the Mountain Division—Nevada, Arizona, Idaho, and Colorado—with rates of natural increase and domestic migration ranked in the top ten and rates of domestic migration above 12.0%. Comparing their rates of population change and rates of domestic migration, one can observe that the net domestic migration accounted for more than a half of their population increases during 1990–1999. The total population of these top-ten states was about 57 million, and their population increase was 9.2 million in 1990–1999, in which about 4.9 million came from the net domestic migration.

The lower panel of Table 5-7 displays the top-ten states ranked by international migration during 1990–1999. California was number one, with nearly 2.28 million of the net international migration occurring during 1990–1999, accounting for 68.4% of its population increase. New York had the second largest rate of net international migration, followed by Florida, the District of Columbia, and Hawaii. Recalling Table 5-5, one can see that the rate of net international migration is 3.0% for the United States, and the top nine states had all exceeded that national rate. As Table 5-5 showed, the net international migration of the United States was 7.478 million during 1990–1999, in which 6.549 million, or 87.6%, of the total net international migration had belonged to the top-ten states. Hence, those states on the coasts and borders of the West, East, and South had absorbed a major portion of immigrants into the United States from the rest of the world.

In this chapter we have discussed the U.S. population transformation in terms of population size, demographic components, and racial and ethnic diversification as well as geographic distribution. In the next chapter we shall analyze the sources of population's natural changes and their impacts on the age structure and laboring force.

# Chapter 6

## The U.S. Population in the Post-Transitional Period

The dynamic process of a population's transformation is determined by three variables: births, deaths, and immigrants. Not only do these variables determine current states of the population, they also explain past population changes and predict the future course of population transformation. The following population identity describes a simple relationship of those variables:

$$N(t) = N(t-1) + B(t) - D(t) + I(t) - E(t),$$

where t denotes year t, N(t) represents total population of year t, N(t-1) represents total population of previous year t-1. B(t) denotes births, D(t) denotes deaths, I(t) represents immigration and E(t) represents emigration—all in year t.

The identity clearly shows that the number of people of a nation's population in a given year, N(t), is a continuation of the previous year's population N(t-1), with births and immigration adding to N(t-1) and deaths and emigration reducing it. The combined (I(t)- E(t)) represents net international migration into the nation during year t. In Section 5-3, we presented the evolution of the foreign-born population in the United States and its impact on U.S. population growth.

Now we shall focus on the demographic component of natural increases of the population, namely the major portion of N(t-1) + B(t) - D(t) in the above basic population equation. We analyze the changing patterns of vital parameters of the U.S. population in Section 6-1 and their effects on the age structure in Sections 6-2 and 6-3. Section 6-4 provides a comparison of the total fertility rate as well as its impacts on the demographic transformation for some developed nations.

## 6-1  Vital Parameters

A population's vital parameters include birth rate, total fertility rate, death rate, and life expectancy at birth. Changes in these parameters explain the population's transformation in the past and present, and predict its future.

The process of movement for a population from the state of high birth rate and high death rate but low population growth rate to move towards the state of low birth rate, low death rate and low population growth rate is called the "demographic transition." We have made some observations regarding to the current state of demographic transition in our book *Embracing the Global Demographic Transformation, 1950-2050*:

> What makes the current emerging demographic transition significant and challenging, beyond its complexity, is that it is a trend that has never been seen before in human history. According to the conventional view, population transition ends with a stabilized population with low birth and death rates. Now, if this view is accurate, many developed nations in the world have now completed their population transition. What is the next for them? Many evidences have indicated that the developed world is about to enter a post transitional era that is characterized by aging population and stagnating or declining population size, a condition never before experienced by our ancestors[1].

Indeed, as an advanced nation in the developed world, the United States has completed its demographic transition and entered a post-transitional era.

---

[1] George Kozmetsky and Piyu Yue, *Embracing the Global Demographic Transformation, 1950-2050,* IC² Institute, The University of Texas at Austin, 2000, p. 33.

In Section 1-1, we observed that unlike Japan and other developed nations in Europe, the United States is not expected to see a stagnating or declining population size in the next one hundred years. Instead, the U.S. population has been on an ascending trajectory and its moderate expansion is expected to continue throughout this century. The post-transitional process in the United States is unique, because it does not fit the identified pattern in other post-transitional populations of the developed world. Nevertheless, the continuous evolutionary process of the U.S. population is determined by the dynamics of the population's vital parameters. We will take a close look at the birth rate and total fertility rate (TFR) as well as the death rate and life expectancy in order to have a better understanding of the demographic transformation in the United States.

There are two commonly used measures of a population's births: the crude birth rate and the total fertility rate. The crude birth rate represents the number of births in a given year per 1000 people of the total population; it is useful as a general measure. The total fertility rate is defined as the average number of children a woman would have, assuming that current age-specific birth rates remain constant throughout her reproductive years, usually considered age 15 to 49. The total fertility rate is preferred by demographers, as it takes into account the age structure of the population, and it is comparable across populations with different age profiles.

Figure 6-1 presents crude birth rates of the U.S. population from 1910 to 1999 with the crude birth rates of racial groups for the later years of that period. Figure 6-2 displays the total fertility rates for the U.S. population and its racial groups. The crude birth rate for the entire population of all races fell steadily in the 1910s and 1920s when the conventional demographic transition sped up. Industrialization and urbanization during those years had helped reduce family size and change Americans' preference from large numbers of children to the much smaller family prevalent today. This demographic transition was characterized by the shift of the nation's previously high levels of fertility and mortality to lower levels of both, which resulted in the slow down of the population's expansion. In the 1930s, the crude birth rate bottomed out at around 18.5 births per 1000 people. In the early 1940s, the crude birth rate began to rebound after the Great Depression. Similarly, the total fertility rate declined from 3.2 children per woman in the early 1920s to 2.2 children per woman in the 1930s and started to increase in 1941.

The postwar era from 1946 to 1964 is identified by demographers as a baby boom period for the United States, in which the crude birth rate reached a plateau of approximately 25 births per 1000 people. Since 1964 the crude

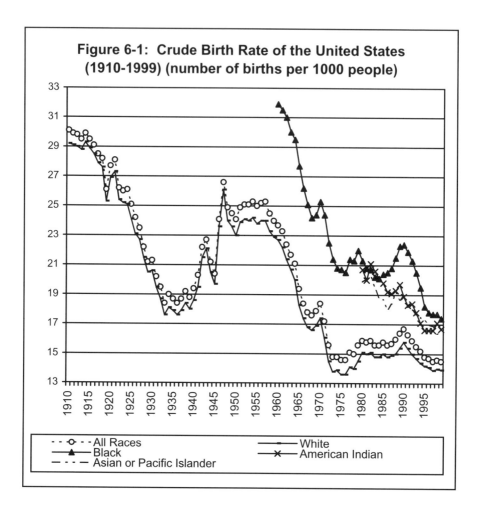

Figure 6-1:  Crude Birth Rate of the United States (1910-1999) (number of births per 1000 people)

birth rate has fallen; it reached 14.5 births per 1000 people in the year 1999. Prior to World War II, the total fertility rate followed a similar pattern, declining in the 1920s and rising in the 1930s. After World War II, however, the total fertility rate climbed faster than did the crude birth rate; because the total fertility rate reached 2.86 children per woman in 1946, exceeding the 1920s' high level, 2.26 children per woman, while the crude birth rate did not reach the previous high. During the 6-year period from 1956 to 1961, the total fertility rate stayed high, more than 3.6 children per woman.

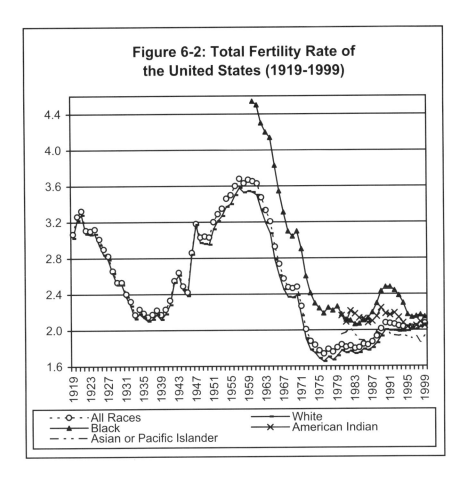

Figure 6-2: Total Fertility Rate of the United States (1919-1999)

Since 1964, the total fertility rate has declined rapidly, reaching 2.48 in 1968, and 1.74 in 1976. The number of 1.74 has been the lowest total fertility rate in American demographic statistics. In the late 1980s, the total fertility rate reassumed its upwards movement and reached 2.08 in 1990 and 1999. Even though it remained above 2.0 during the 1990s, the total fertility rate in the United States was still less than the replacement rate commonly recognized as an average of 2.1 children per woman on the average.

American women born in the 1930s and 1940s were in their 20s at the height of the baby boom; they were the most prolific recent generation of American women with the highest fertility over the last century, and averaged

3.2 children per woman. American baby boomers are defined as those people who were born between 1946 and 1964, years when the number of births was substantially higher than in years before or after. The baby boom generation has dominated the transformation of U.S population for the last five decades and will continue its great influence as they grow older.

As Figures 6-1 and 6-2 show, the crude birth rates and total fertility rates vary markedly among the population's racial groups. The white group has the lowest fertility rate and the black group has the highest fertility rate, with the American Indian and Asian/Pacific Islanders groups between them. All birth rates and total fertility rates have declined—since 1960, the initial reporting year, for the black group, and since 1980 for the other two racial groups. It is apparent that the birth rate gaps among the racial groups have been narrowed substantially since 1990. In 1990, the total fertility rate was 2.00 for the white group, 2.48 for the black group, 2.18 for the Native American group, and 2.00 for the Asian/Pacific Islanders group, while in 1999, the total fertility rates became 2.06, 2.15, 2.05, and 1.93 for these groups respectively. It seems that the total fertility rates of major racial groups are converging to the replacement rate of 2.1 children per woman on the average.

The declining fertility in the United States reflects many social changes and preference shifts in American personal life. Over the past 30 years, the percentage of persons who have never been married has increased from about 22% to 28%. Particularly for the black group, the never-married rate increased from 32% in 1975 to 44% in 1999, and the percentage of blacks who are married declined from 42% to 32% in the same time frame.The percentage of divorced people was in the range 9.3%–11.0% for different racial groups. The declining percentage of people who stay married and increasing percentage of people who have never been married certainly contributed to reducing America's fertility.

The changing life style of Americans is also reflected in the shrinking American household. The U.S. Census Bureau's data indicates that the average household size has declined over the past thirty years, from 3.1 to 2.6 persons per household, namely for every two households one person has been lost. The shrinking size of the household was mainly due to people's changing preference from having many children to having a few, reflected in the decrease of fertility. In the Asian group, however, the number of persons per household has remained steady at about 3.2 since 1990. And among Hispanics, the average household size has actually increased, from 3.0 in 1975 to 3.5 in 1999. The different household pattern in racial groups has affected their fertility rates.

Although the total fertility rate of the U.S. population has been below the replacement rate since 1972, the size of the U.S. population continues increasing steadily. The reason for this phenomena is not just the population dynamics built up by the high fertility rate during the baby-boom period; increases in net international immigrants since 1965 have also made a great contribution to the recent population growth. As we discussed in Section 5-3, net international migration accounted for nearly one third of the population's growth in the 1990s and is expected to further increase in this century. The effects of international immigration on U.S. population can be viewed as actually boosting the "equivalent" total fertility rate well above the 2.1 replacement level and resulting in a continuous population expansion.

There are three variables that measure a population's mortality, the crude death rate, infant mortality rate, and life expectancy at birth. The first two measures represent numbers of deaths per 1000 people or per 1000 infants. Life expectancy at birth is defined as the average number of years a newborn infant can expect to live given the current age-distributed mortality pattern of the population. These variables of the U.S. population are depicted in Figure 6-3 for the time period of 1950 through 1999.

The crude death rate in the United States declined from 9.54 in 1950 to 8.52 in 1982, the lowest number during the last five decades. Since then the crude death rate has increased slightly and reached 8.70 in 1999 due to the population's growing cohort of old people, which has a higher death rate than other cohorts. There was also a rapid decline in the infant mortality rate, from 29.2 deaths per 1000 newborn babies in 1950 to the 1999 level of only 6.89 deaths per 1000 babies. The United States is among the nations with the lowest infant mortality rates in the world, which reflects the relatively high standard of living in general, and its continuously improved health care and medical conditions in particular.

The life expectancy of Americans has steadily risen over the last fifty years, from 68.2 years in 1950 to 76.98 years in 1999. It was 65.60 years for men and 71.10 years for women in 1950; both numbers increased substantially to 74.24 and 79.90 in 1999 respectively. According to projections by the U.S. Bureau of the Census, the infant mortality rate is expected to be 5.50 by 2020 and 3.30 by 2050. And life expectancy will reach 79.90 years (76.85 for males and 82.93 for females) in 2020 and 83.94 years (81.23 for males and 86.62 for females) in 2050.

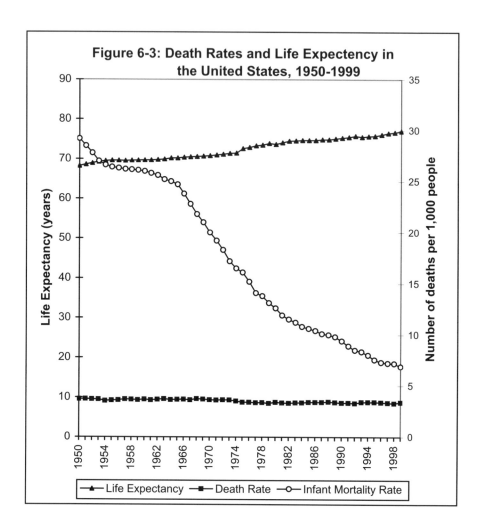

Figure 6-3: Death Rates and Life Expectency in the United States, 1950-1999

The increasing life expectancy means that more Americans are expected to live much longer than their parents, and their children are expected to live even longer. Combined with declining fertility, which reduces the proportion of children and youth in the population, the increasing life expectancy leads to an aging population. This has been recognized as a big demographic threat to the developed world. How serious could the U.S. population's aging become? This is the issue for the next section.

## 6-2   The Age Structure

The age structure of a population is defined as the proportions of different age groups, such as children, youngsters, adults, and the elderly, relative to the total population. Changes in the age structure are inevitable and part of a natural process as members of a society age. Although all the vital parameters discussed in the previous section affect population's age structure, the total fertility rate has the heaviest influence on the long-term age pattern of the population.

Age-gender pyramids are used to show the general shape of a population's age structure. A population with a broad base of younger people and with a few people surviving to old age has an age structure resembling a pyramid; this is the case for younger populations in the developing world. A population with a declining fertility rate and increasing life expectancy has a relatively narrow base of younger people and a broad base of elderly people; some examples of this are found in the populations of Japan and some Western European nations.

The age-gender pyramids of the U.S. population are displayed in Figure 6-4 for six distinct years. On those age-gender pyramids the bars on the left represent males by five-year age categories.  On the bottom are males ages 0 through 4, then 5 through 9, 10 through 14, etc. Female age distribution is shown to the right in the same manner.

On the pyramid for 1950, three cohort bars for the age groups of 10-14, 15-19, and 20-24 form an inward dent, which corresponds to the low total fertility rates during the 1930s when the economic depression reduced the birth rate substantially. The bars above this dimple reflect high fertility rates in the 1920s and earlier, and a natural pattern of increasing death rates of older cohorts. The bars on the bottom represent those people who were born between 1946-1950. They were the first batch of the post-war baby boomers. There were also some visible differences in age distribution between female and male.  For instance, in the 0-4 grouping, there were 8.425 million girls versus 8.812 million boys, whereas 1.026 million American women survived past 85 years in 1950 versus only 0.774 million American men.

## Figure 6-4: U.S.
## Population Pyramids

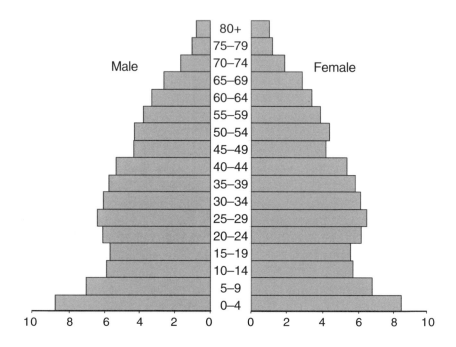

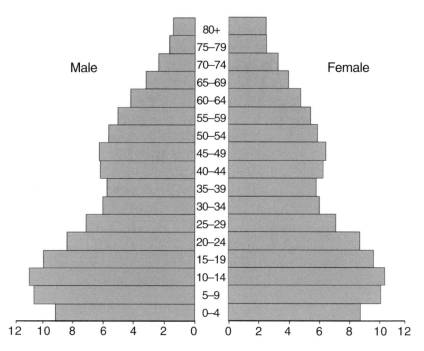

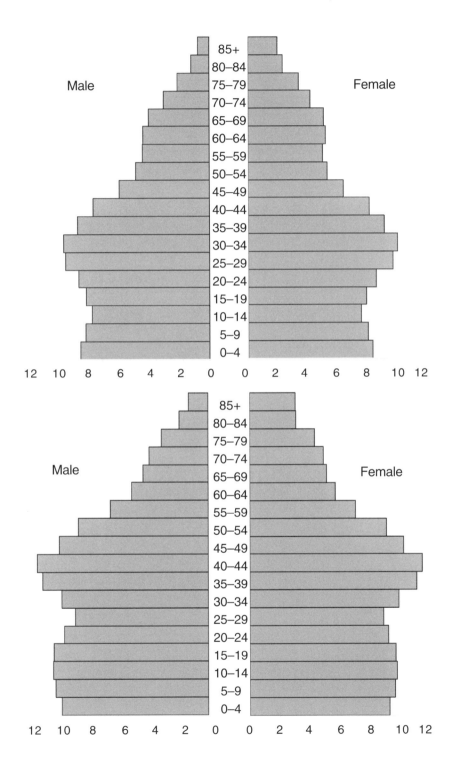

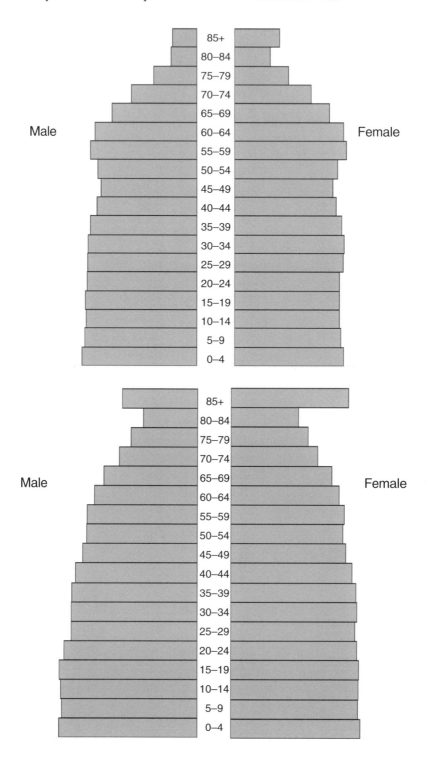

Baby boomers born, from 1946 through 1964, all came into the age-gender pyramid for 1970 and occupied four bars from the second bottom bar up for the cohorts 5-9, 10-14, 15-19, and 20-24. Those four protruding bars on the age-gender pyramid reflect the high fertility rates in the post-war baby boom period. The shortened bottom bars for the cohort group 0-4 in the 1970 pyramid reflect the sudden decline of the birth rate after 1964. On the age-gender pyramid of 1990, baby boomers moved into the 25-44 group, and their children, who were born in 1971–1989, moved into this pyramid. The bottom bar of the 0-4 group represents children of baby boomers aged between 25 and 29, and the second bottom bar represents children of baby boomers aged 30-34, and so forth. As a matter of fact, the four bars from the bottom up on the 1990 pyramid represent the "echo generation", consisting of children of the post-war baby boomers.

Using the middle series of projections from the U.S. Census Bureau we have drawn the pyramids for 2020 and 2050. On the 2020 pyramid, the baby boomers have moved into the 55-74 age group, and the echo generation has moved up to 30-49. The bottom grouping of 0-29 is expected to consist of those who were born between 1990 and 2020. Those baby boomers who are able to survive until 2050 will reach 85 and over. Most of them will fall off the population ladder after 2050. In 2020, there are expected to be 2.326 million men and 4.436 million women aged 85 and over. Incredibly, those numbers are projected to be 7.431 million for men and 11.921 million for women by the year 2050. The number of those Americans aged 90 years and over is expected to be 3.527 million for men and 6.361 million for women by 2050. The predicted changes in the shape of pyramids for 2020 and 2050 indicate that the U.S. population's aging might be in its full swing around the middle of this century.

Observing the movement of cohort bars in the age-gender pyramids from 1950 to 2050 in Figure 6-4, one can recognize that the baby boomers and their echo generation are truly the major determinant of the U.S. population's age structure over the 100-year period from 1950 through 2050. Their enormous effect on the U.S. economy and society should be taken into serious consideration by governments and the private business sector as well.

## 6-3  The Three Cohorts

Age-gender pyramids are able to provide detailed information about the population's distribution over age and gender for a given year, but they are not convenient for tracking the continuously changing age compositions over a long time frame. Three aggregated age groups are used to describe the general evolution of the population's changing age structure—the children aged 0-14, the working-age population, aged 15-64, and the elderly aged 65 and over. Population shares of those three cohorts are displayed in Figure 6-5 for the time span from 1950 through 2100.

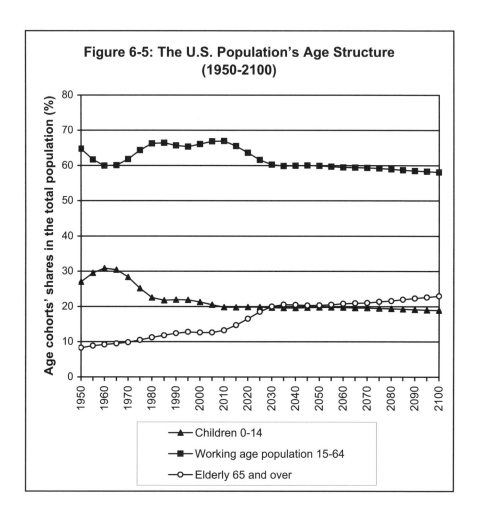

In 1950, the United States had approximately 42.6 million children under the age of 15, accounting for 27% of the total U.S. population. In 1960, the size of the child group increased to 57.4 million, accounting for 30.8% of the population, the highest percentage of children over the entire time period. This is a result of the entire baby boom generation being under 15 years old in this time period. After 1964, the U.S. total fertility rates (FTR) declined substantially, resulting in a decline in the number of American children and the declining population share. The size of the child group was about 58.6 million (or 21.3% of the total population) in 2000; it is expected to increase to 64.5 million (19.9% of the total population) in 2020, 79.8 million (19.8%) in 2050, and 107.8 million (19.0%) in 2100. Even though their share of the overall total is gradually declining, the number of American children is projected to increase throughout this century.

The elderly population has substantially increased in both size and share for the last fifty years. The United States had about 13 million people aged 65 and over in 1950, accounting for 8.2% of the total population; the number of elderly grew to 25.8 million (or 11.2% of the total population) in 1980, and 34.7 million (12.6%) in 2000. In the next thirty years, this number is expected to grow with increasing speed, reaching 70.237 million (20.0% of the total population) by 2030. This dramatic increase is due to the fact that the majority of baby boomers are expected to enter the 65-and-plus group during 2010-2030. After 2030, the share of elderly population is projected to level off at 20% for thirty years and then rise slowly. According to the population projection by the Bureau of Census, the number of American elderly will reach 82 million, accounting for 20.2% of the total population by 2050, and 131 million (or 23% of the total population) by 2100.

The share of the American working-age population slowly climbed to 60-66% over the last fifty years, while the number of working-age Americans rose from 102.2 million in 1950 to 111.6 million in 1960, 152.7 million in 1980, and 181.9 million in 2000. The share of working-age Americans will decrease from 66.1% in 2000 to 60.0% in 2030, while the number of working-age people will continue to increase, to 211.6 million in 2030. The share of working-age people is projected to stay at 60.0% in 2030-2050 and then to decline gradually to 58.0% in 2100. The number of working-age Americans, however, is expected to rise from 241.9 million in 2050 to 332 million in 2100, which exceeds the *total* U.S. population of the year 2000 (275.3 million).

Based on the United Nations' estimates and projections of the world population for 2000, the population shares are 30%, 63%, and 7%, for groups of children, working age people, and the elderly respectively on a global average. For less-developed regions, these shares become 33%, 62%, and 5% and for the more-developed regions, these shares are 18%, 68%, and 14%[2]. For the same year, the U.S. cohort shares are 21.3%, 66.1%, and 12.6%.

---

[2] *Embracing the Global Demographic Transformation 1950-2050,* by George Kozmetsky and Piyu Yue, IC2 Institute, The University of Texas at Austin, 2000.

Comparing these shares, one can observe that the U.S. population is younger than many populations in the developed world. By 2050, the elderly group's share is expected to be 20.2% in the United States, compared with 30% in Japan, 29% in Germany, 36% in Italy, and 23% in the United Kingdom. The children's share is projected to be 19% in the United States, 14% in Japan and Germany, 12% in Italy, and 18% in the United Kingdom by 2050. In terms of the above comparison, therefore the aging process is projected to move slowly in the United States. Even if all of the baby boomers and the echo generation enter the elderly cohort by 2050, the U.S. population in 2050 will be younger than the populations of Japan, France, and Italy in the year 2020.

Nevertheless, the U.S. population is getting older year by year. In 2000, on average, every 67 persons at working age were supporting 21 children and 12 elderly. By 2050, every 60 working-age people must support 20 children and 20 elderly. The increasing number of elderly people has demanded that the economy and society provide special services and public support, including health care, recreation, housing, and nutrition for this group. In the United States, the percentage of people living by themselves is increasing, with older Americans the most likely to live alone. In 1999, about 30% of those people 65 years old or older lived alone, and required some special living arrangement of home care or nursing home care. The demographic trend of an increasingly aged population also indicates a large increase in the members participating in various entitlement programs such as Social Security and Medicare. Indeed, many social and economic arrangements in American society need to be changed or adjusted in order to balance the underlying demographic force.

Japan and the Western European nations will shortly face population-aging problems. It will probably be 20–30 years before the population's aging is running at its full swing in the United States. Learning from the experiences of other developed nations and taking advantage of timing, the United States has opportunities to prepare better solutions for its aging population problems. The working-age population includes people aged 15–64, who possess working abilities and are able to conduct various economic activities. Based on the latest estimates and projections from the U.S. Bureau of Census, the size of the working-age population increased nearly 80% in the last fifty years, from 102 million in 1950 to 182 million in 2000 (Figure 6-6). It is projected to stabilize around 200–210 million in the next thirty years and then climb again, from 211 million in 2030 to 332 million by 2100.

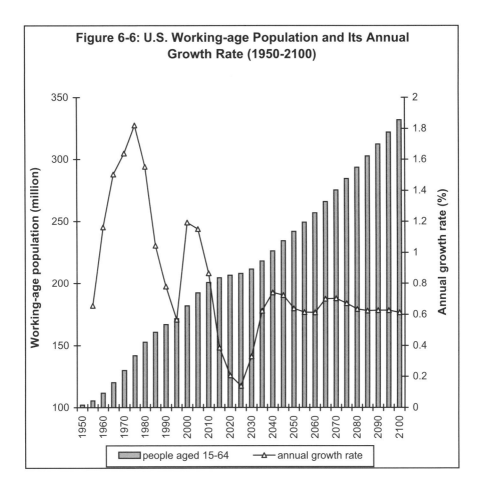

Figure 6-6: U.S. Working-age Population and Its Annual Growth Rate (1950-2100)

The annual growth rate of the working-age population displayed in Figure 6-6 reflects the changing age structure of the U.S. population. Particularly, the baby boomers' movements along the time and age dimensions have created the oscillatory growth rate of the working-age population.

In 1965, the first batch of baby boomers entered the working-age category, and by 1980 all the baby boomers were over 15 years old. That is why an increase in the growth rate of the working-age population occurred during 1965–1980. The growth rate reached 1.83% in 1975; it was the highest in the last fifty years. In 1990, the growth rate dropped substantially to 0.45%, because those who were born during the high fertility period before 1929 were no longer in the working-age group. After 1995, those who were born during the low fertility period of the 1930s turned 65 years or older and left the working-age group. Meanwhile, all baby boomers and some of their children entered the working-age group in the last 15 years. Both factors caused a rebound in the growth rate of the working-age population to 0.9-1.2% per year around year 2000.

In the next 25–30 years, the baby boomers will gradually withdraw from the working-age group and their children and grandchildren will replace them as the main body of the working-age population. Since the boomers and their children—the echo generation—have much lower total fertility rates than their parents, 1.7–2.4 versus 2.8–3.6, when their children make up the bulk of working-age Americans, that group's growth rate will drop significantly.

After 2025, the baby boomers' influence on the working-age population will be exhausted; the number of working-age Americans is projected to grow at a steady pace of 0.6-0.75% per year. This projection is based on the gradually changing total fertility rates during the last thirty years and the assumption of its converging to the replacement rate, 2.1 children per woman on average, in the next fifty years. Had there been no such sudden movements in total fertility rates as in the 1930s' decline and the postwar booming, the U.S. population and its working-age group would have remained on a steady and gradually ascending path. It is clear that the swing of fertility in 1920s–1960s has dominated U.S. population dynamics for the last fifty years; it will continue to do so until the demise of the baby boomers.

## 6-4    A Comparison of Total Fertility Rates of Developed Nations

This section serves as a summary of Chapter Two. We have pointed out that the U.S. population has completed the conventional demographic transition that converts the high levels of fertility and mortality into low levels of fertility and mortality, resulting in a slow pace of population growth and a changing age structure. The U.S. population is now in the post-transitional era; its current state and future path are quite different from other post-transitional populations in the developed world.

As Table 5-2 and Figure 5-3 above indicate, seven post-transitional populations of the developed world are expected to reduce their population size in 20–50 years. The U.S. population, however, is projected to continue its expansion throughout the twenty-first century. This dramatically different path of the U.S. population from the others in the developed world is a consequence of the great disparity in the total fertility rates shown in Table 6-1.

Table 6-1: Estimates and Projections of Total Fertility Rates for Eight Developed Nations

| Year | U.S.A. | Japan | Germany | Britain |
|------|--------|-------|---------|---------|
| 1975 | 1.774 | 1.940 | NA | NA |
| 1985 | 1.844 | 1.743 | NA | NA |
| 1990 | 2.081 | 1.503 | 1.453 | 1.821 |
| 1995 | 2.019 | 1.397 | 1.236 | 1.711 |
| 2000 | 2.000 | 1.408 | 1.375 | 1.730 |
| 2010 | 2.123 | 1.466 | 1.440 | 1.724 |
| 2020 | 2.180 | 1.525 | 1.505 | 1.718 |
| 2030 | 2.212 | 1.583 | 1.570 | 1.712 |
| 2040 | 2.215 | 1.642 | 1.635 | 1.706 |
| 2050 | 2.219 | 1.700 | 1.700 | 1.700 |
| Year | Italy | France | Russia | Canada |
| 1975 | 2.180 | 1.930 | NA | 1.850 |
| 1985 | 1.542 | 1.807 | 2.07 | 1.669 |
| 1990 | 1.306 | 1.777 | 1.955 | 1.794 |
| 1995 | 1.171 | 1.701 | 1.385 | 1.665 |
| 2000 | 1.180 | 1.747 | 1.246 | 1.600 |
| 2010 | 1.215 | 1.737 | 1.562 | 1.620 |
| 2020 | 1.250 | 1.728 | 1.699 | 1.640 |
| 2030 | 1.400 | 1.719 | 1.615 | 1.660 |
| 2040 | 1.550 | 1.709 | 1.566 | 1.680 |
| 2050 | 1.700 | 1.700 | 1.548 | 1.700 |

The U.S. total fertility rate in the 1990s was significantly higher than that of the seven nations listed in Table 6-1. The U.S. rate is projected to rise from 2.0 in the year 2000 to 2.2 by 2050, while the rates of Great Britain and France are expected to decline to 1.7 in 2050. The other five nations' rates will probably continue to slide, bottom out in ten years, and gradually climb back to 1.7 by 2050, except for Russia, whose rate is projected to be 1.548 by year 2050. With their total fertility rates having stayed well below the replacement rate of 2.1 for nearly thirty years, the populations of Japan, Russia, and the Western European nations are doomed to decline in the near future.

A declining population implies a declining labor pool and a shrinking consumer base. Soon nations will face a serious problem when their shrinking and aging populations generate shortages of young workers and they are overloaded with retirees and elderly who need increasing special services and public support from their economies and societies.

Fortunately, the United States is the only advanced nation that is able to avoid the falling population destiny, which is about to challenge so many nations in the developed world. Although the U.S population is expected to increase steadily in this century, the speed of growth will decline over time, from 0.78% per year in the 2010s to 0.68% per year in the 2020s, and to 0.13% in the 2050s. Compared with the forecast of over 1.3% per year for the global population in the next three decades, the projected U.S. population growth is modest and will bear small risk of running into a population explosion and thus creating an ecological disaster. The modest increases in the U.S. population provide a solid foundation for a sustainable economic growth and for better environmental protection.

Net international migration accounts for nearly one third of U.S. population growth, and immigrants usually have higher fertility rates than the average members of the U.S. population. It is important to monitor immigration situations and to adjust immigration policies according to the U.S. economy's changing demand for labor and a comprehensive assessment of the carrying capacity[3] of the United States. We observe that the current total fertility rate of U.S. residents is below the replacement rate 2.10, and the projected future fertility rate is not far from 2.10.

Therefore the conventional source of a population's potential explosion—a total fertility rate well above 3.0—does not exist in the current U.S. population system now or in the projected future. Rapidly increasing immigration, however, could be the major source of a potential excessive population growth that might threaten the sustainability of economic growth and cause environmental degradation. National policymakers need to pay special attention to immigration issues and view immigration as a buffer to balance U.S. population expansion, economic growth, and environmental protection.

---

[3] "Carrying capacity refers to the number of individuals who can be supported without degrading the natural, cultural, and social environment, i.e. without reducing the ability of the environment to sustain the desired quality of life over the long term". See *Food, Land, Population and the U.S. Economy*, by David Pimentel and Mario Giampietro, Carrying Capacity Network, Washington, D.C., 1994.

Chapters 5 and 6 have focused on quantitative measures of demographic transformation, such as changes in population size, vital parameters, age structure, racial and ethnic composition, geographic distribution and international migrations. In Chapter 7 we will analyze the changing quality of the U.S. population.

# Chapter 7

## *The Intellectual Quality of the U.S. Population*

A large number of working-age people provide the economy with a large labor pool. Not every working-age person in the labor force is employed; and not every employee is in the age range of 15-64 years old. Hence, the size of the working-age population is closely related, but not identical, to the labor force. Section 7-1 will examine the situation of labor participation and employment of the U.S. economy.

As discussed previously in Chapters 1 and 2, U.S. economic growth has become increasingly dependent upon knowledge and technology innovations in order to introduce products and services, promote productivity, increase corporations' profits and workers' real income, and generate wealth and prosperity. As knowledge and technology innovations are products of human creativity and ingenuity, the intellectual quality of the population becomes crucial for the present economic transformation in the United States. In Sections 7-2, 7-3, and 7-4, educational attainment is used as a quantitative measure to make assessments about the intellectual abilities of the U.S. population and its racial and ethnic groups, as well as geographic distribution of the population in terms of its education levels.

## 7-1    Labor Participation and Employment

Statistics about the U.S. labor market come from two major surveys, the Current Household Survey and the Current Establishment Survey. The household survey provides information on the labor force, employment, and unemployment. It is a sample survey of about 50,000 households conducted by the U.S. Census Bureau for the Bureau of Labor Statistics (BLS). The establishment survey provides information on employment, hours, and earnings of workers on nonfarm payrolls, which are collected from payroll records by the BLS.

In the household survey, each person aged 16 and over in a sample household is classified as belonging to one of three categories: employed, unemployed, and not in the labor force. People are classified as employed if they are paid employees or work in their own business. People are classified as unemployed if they do not have paying jobs while they are available for work and are making specific efforts to find employment. Those not classified as employed or unemployed are classified as not in the labor force. The civilian labor force is defined as the sum of employed and unemployed people. The labor force participation rate is defined as a ratio of the labor force to the total civilian noninstitutional population. The civilian noninstitutional population includes persons 16 years of age and older residing in the United States who are not inmates of institutions (e.g., penal and mental facilities, homes for the aged), and who are not on active duty in the armed forces. The unemployment rate is the number of unemployed persons as a percent of the labor force.

The size of the U.S. labor force and the level of employment and unemployment fluctuate due to such seasonal events as changes in weather, reduced or expanded production, harvests, major holidays, and the opening and closing of schools. Because these seasonal events follow some regular pattern each year, adjusting the statistics from month to month can eliminate their influence on statistical trends. This chapter will use seasonally adjusted data to analyze changes in the labor market and in economic activities. The annual labor statistics presented in this section are calculated as the averages of seasonally adjusted monthly statistical data from the Bureau of Labor Statistics.

Figure 7-1 shows the level of the U.S. civilian labor force and the labor force participation rate; and Figure 7-2 illustrates the level of civilian employment and the unemployment rate over the time period of 1948 to 2000.

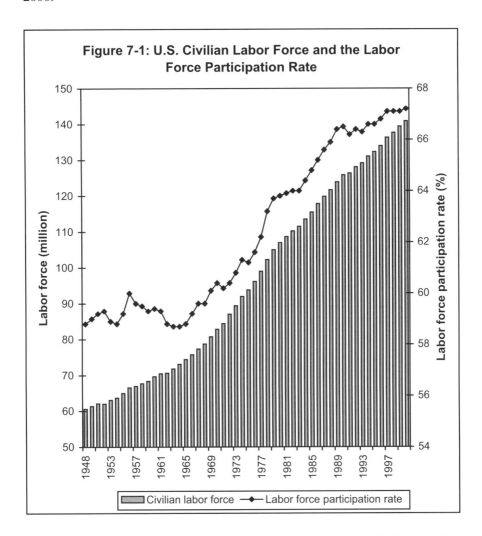

Figure 7-1: U.S. Civilian Labor Force and the Labor Force Participation Rate

The U.S. labor force steadily increased in this time period, from 62.1 million in 1950 to 82.8 million in 1980, 125.8 million in 1990, and 140.9 million in 2000. It has increased 2.27 times, while the number of working-age Americans has grown 1.78 times for the same time period. It is apparent that, on the average, the growth rate of the labor force has been greater than the growth rate of the American working-age population over the past fifty years, as a result of the substantial increases in the labor participation rate, from 59.2% in 1950 to 67.2% by 2000.

It is worthwhile to notice that the population share of working-age people is not comparable with the labor force participation rate. By definition, the labor force participation rate is a ratio of labor force to the total civilian noninstitutional population (age 16 and above). The share of the working-age population is the ratio of the number of people who are 15-64 years of age to the total U.S. population. According to labor statistics, the U.S. civilian non-institutional population was about 104.995 million in 1950, and 209.699 million in 2000; the U.S. working-age population was 102.2 million in 1950, and 181.9 million in 2000.

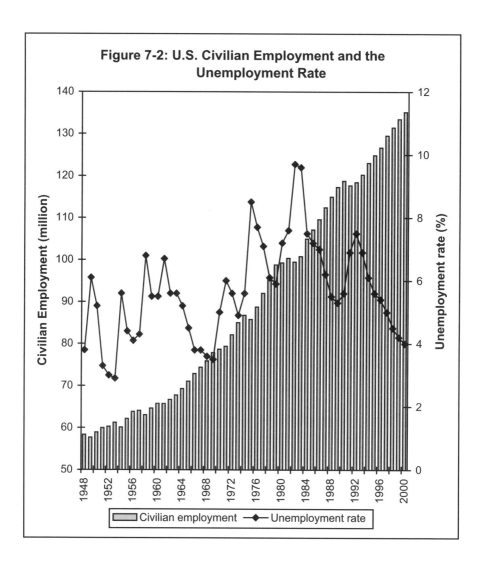

Figure 7-2: U.S. Civilian Employment and the Unemployment Rate

The level of civilian employment has also increased, from 58.8 million in 1950 to 78.6 million in 1970, to 99.3 million in 1980, to 118.8 million in 1990, and to 135.2 million in 2000. Net job creation was 6.893 million in the 1950s, 12.884 million in the 1960s, 20.634 million in the 1970s, 19.493 million in the 1980s, and 16.419 million in the 1990s. As Figures 7-1 and 7-2 indicate, the labor force has steadily increased, while the level of employment fluctuated around a generally ascending trend.

During the time period of 1961–1969, the number of employed people increased from 65.744 million in 1961 to 77.875 million in 1969, driving the unemployment rate down from 6.7% to 3.5%. The longest economic expansion in U.S. history occurred in the 1980s and 1990s, and was characterized by the information technology revolution and the creation of new jobs. The number of employed people increased from 99.529 million in 1982 to 135.215 million in 2000, representing a 35.8% rise. About 35.686 million net job positions were created in this 18-year period. Even though the number of working-age Americans increased substantially, economic expansion created many job opportunities and pushed the unemployment rate down from 9.7% in 1982 to 4% in 2000.

Gaps exist in labor force participation and employment among different races and genders in the U.S. population. As Table 7-1 shows, the labor participation rates of all three major ethnic groups have increased steadily, except for 1983 and 1992 when the U.S. economy was in a recession.

Table 7-1: Labor Participation Rate and
Unemployment Rate of Ethnic Groups

| Year | Labor Force Participation Rate (%) | | | Unemployment Rates (%) | | |
|---|---|---|---|---|---|---|
| | White | Black | Hispanic | White | Black | Hispanic |
| 1955 | 58.7 | NA | NA | 5.1 | NA | NA |
| 1973 | 60.8 | 60.2 | 59.8 | 4.3 | 9.4 | 7.7 |
| 1975 | 61.5 | 58.8 | 60.8 | 7.8 | 14.8 | 12.2 |
| 1980 | 64.1 | 61.0 | 64.1 | 6.3 | 14.3 | 10.1 |
| 1983 | 64.3 | 61.5 | 63.7 | 8.4 | 19.5 | 13.7 |
| 1990 | 66.9 | 64.0 | 67.4 | 4.8 | 11.4 | 8.2 |
| 1992 | 66.8 | 64.0 | 66.8 | 6.6 | 14.2 | 11.6 |
| 1995 | 67.1 | 63.7 | 65.9 | 4.9 | 10.4 | 9.3 |
| 2000 | 67.4 | 65.8 | 68.6 | 3.4 | 7.6 | 5.7 |

As of 2000, the Hispanic group's participation rate exceeded that of the white group, 68.6% versus 67.4%, while the black group still had the lowest participation rate, 65.8%. The white group has always had the lowest unemployment rate. In 1983, when the U.S. economy was still in the early 1980s recession, the unemployment rates were 8.4% for the white group, 13.7% for the Hispanic group, and 19.5% for the black group. In the 1990s, however, unemployment rates decreased significantly for all racial groups. As of 2000, the unemployment rate reached 3.4% for the white group and 5.7% for the Hispanic group, and stayed at 7.6% for the black group.

Table 7-2 illustrates differences of labor participation rates and unemployment rates among gender groups of whites and blacks. A common trend in both ethnic groups is that the labor force participation rates for men have decreased steadily, while the same rates for women have increased. The gap of participation and unemployment between men and women still exists, but it has diminished substantially.

Table 7-2: Labor Participation Rate and
Unemployment Rate of Gender Groups

| Year | Labor Force Participation Rate (%) | | | |
| | White | | Black | |
| | Male | Female | Male | Female |
|---|---|---|---|---|
| 1955 | 87.5 | 34.0 | NA | NA |
| 1973 | 81.6 | 43.5 | 78.4 | 51.6 |
| 1975 | 80.7 | 45.3 | 76.1 | 51.1 |
| 1980 | 79.9 | 50.7 | 75.2 | 55.7 |
| 1983 | 78.8 | 52.5 | 75.1 | 56.8 |
| 1990 | 78.6 | 57.6 | 75.0 | 60.5 |
| 1992 | 78.0 | 58.1 | 74.3 | 60.8 |
| 1995 | 77.1 | 59.2 | 72.5 | 61.4 |
| 2000 | 77.0 | 60.2 | 72.7 | 65.6 |
| Year | Unemployment Rate (%) | | | |
| | White | | Black | |
| | Male | Female | Male | Female |
| 1955 | 3.2 | 3.9 | NA | NA |
| 1973 | 3.0 | 4.3 | 6.0 | 8.6 |
| 1975 | 6.2 | 7.5 | 12.5 | 12.2 |
| 1980 | 5.3 | 5.6 | 12.4 | 11.8 |
| 1983 | 7.9 | 7.0 | 18.1 | 16.6 |
| 1990 | 4.3 | 4.2 | 10.5 | 9.7 |
| 1992 | 6.4 | 5.5 | 13.5 | 11.8 |
| 1995 | 4.3 | 4.3 | 8.8 | 8.6 |
| 2000 | 2.9 | 3.1 | 7.0 | 6.2 |

In 1955, 87.5% of white American men aged 16 and over were in the labor force, compared to 34.0% white American women in the same age group. In 2000, however, the participation rates became 77.0% for white men and 60.2% for white women. A similar situation took place for the black group. Although the participation rate for black males dropped from 78.4% in 1973 to 72.7% in 2000, the participation rate for black females grew from 51.6% to 65.6% in the same time frame. The difference in the unemployment rates between white males and white females has been small; there is a slight advantage for males over females. It has been an opposite situation for the black group; black females had a lower unemployment rate than black males after 1980.

Even though the unemployment rate declined markedly across races and genders during the last twenty years of economic expansion, the benefits of abundant job opportunities were not evenly distributed. Inequality in the employment of different population groups seems more closely related to their educational levels rather than their differences in ethnicity, gender, and age status. In the next sections we will discuss educational attainment of U.S. adults across race and gender, as well as across geographic regions.

## 7-2  Educational Attainment by Ethnic Group and Gender

The educational achievement of its adults is commonly used as a measure of the intellectual quality of a population's labor force. We use historical data to illustrate the great improvement in the educational attainment of the U.S. population and the uneven distribution of educated people among ethnic and gender groups. As people aged 25 and over have usually completed their full-time formal school education and are considered to form the main body of the labor force, their educational attainment becomes more important than any other factors in determining American workers' income. Records exist for the educational attainment of three ethnic categories—white, black, and Hispanic. The Hispanic group incorporates different races, including white Hispanic and black Hispanic or other Hispanic races.

People who are aged 25 and over are divided into three educational categories. The first category consists of those people who have completed at least four years of college education and received a bachelor's degree or advanced degrees (master's degree, doctoral degree, or other professional degree). The second category contains people who graduated from high school or had some college (non-degree) education or an associate's degree. People who have not completed their high school education are put in the third category.

In Table 7-3, we present the educational attainment of three ethnic groups by gender at the three levels of educational achievement in percentages. In 1940, there were 74.776 million Americans aged 25 and over; only 4.6% of them held bachelor's or advanced degrees, 19.9% of them were high school graduates, and 75.5% of them did not complete high school. Sixty years later, there were 175.23 million Americans aged 25 and over, and 25.6% of them completed college or hold master's or doctor's degrees; 58.5% of them graduated from high school; and only 15.9% of them did not finish high school. The second column of Table 7-3 clearly indicates a general trend of rapid improvement in U.S. educational achievement

This significant improvement in the educational level of the U.S. population appears across all ethnic and gender groups within the same time frame. The white group had the highest percentage of college graduates in 2000, which increased from 5.9% and 4.0% in 1940 to 28.5% and 23.9% in 2000 for white males and white females respectively. The white group also had the lowest percentage of non-high-school graduates in 2000, which decreased from 75.8% and 71.9% in 1940 to 15.2% and 15.0% in 2000 respectively.

Both black male and female cohorts increased their percentages of college graduates, from 1.4% and 1.2% in 1940 to 16.3% and 16.7% in 2000; they also reduced their percentages of non-high-school graduates, from 93.1% and 91.6% in 1940 to 21.3% and 21.7% in 2000. The Hispanic group still contains the lowest percentage of college graduates and highest percentage of non-high-school graduates, although they have followed the common trend of improvement in educational attainment.

From Table 7-3, one can easily observe that the difference in educational attainment between males and females has diminished over time. It is still a factor at the college and high school graduate level, but not a significant one at the non-high school level. It seems that white males still held an advantage in 2000 over the white female group at the level of college graduates, 28.5% versus 23.9%, while the difference is not significant for the black and Hispanic groups.

Table 7-3: Education Attainment of Americans 25 Years Old and Over

| Year | All Races | White | | Black | | Hispanic | |
|------|-----------|-------|-------|-------|-------|----------|--------|
| **Percentage of people who have completed 4 years of college (%)** | | | | | | | |
| | | Male | Female | Male | Female | Male | Female |
| 1940 | 4.6 | 5.9 | 4.0 | 1.4 | 1.2 | NA | NA |
| 1947 | 5.4 | 6.6 | 4.7 | 2.4 | 2.6 | NA | NA |
| 1959 | 8.1 | 11.0 | 6.2 | 3.8 | 2.9 | NA | NA |
| 1965 | 9.4 | 12.7 | 7.3 | 4.9 | 4.5 | NA | NA |
| 1970 | 11.0 | 15.0 | 8.9 | 4.7 | 4.3 | NA | NA |
| 1975 | 13.9 | 18.4 | 11.0 | 6.7 | 6.2 | 8.3 | 4.6 |
| 1980 | 17.0 | 22.1 | 14.0 | 7.7 | 8.1 | 9.7 | 6.2 |
| 1985 | 19.4 | 24.0 | 16.3 | 11.2 | 11.0 | 9.7 | 7.3 |
| 1990 | 21.3 | 25.3 | 19.0 | 11.9 | 10.8 | 9.8 | 8.7 |
| 1995 | 23.0 | 27.2 | 21.0 | 13.6 | 12.9 | 10.1 | 8.4 |
| 1999 | 25.2 | 28.5 | 23.5 | 14.2 | 16.4 | 10.7 | 11.0 |
| 2000 | 25.6 | 28.5 | 23.9 | 16.3 | 16.7 | 10.7 | 10.6 |
| **Percentage of people who have completed high school but not college (%)** | | | | | | | |
| Year | All Races | White | | Black | | Hispanic | |
| | | Male | Female | Male | Female | Male | Female |
| 1940 | 19.9 | 18.3 | 24.1 | 5.5 | 7.2 | NA | NA |
| 1947 | 27.7 | 26.6 | 31.8 | 10.3 | 11.9 | NA | NA |
| 1959 | 35.6 | 33.5 | 41.5 | 15.8 | 18.7 | NA | NA |
| 1965 | 39.6 | 37.5 | 44.9 | 20.9 | 23.9 | NA | NA |
| 1970 | 44.2 | 42.2 | 49.0 | 27.8 | 30.4 | NA | NA |
| 1975 | 48.6 | 46.6 | 53.1 | 34.9 | 37.1 | 31.2 | 32.1 |
| 1980 | 51.6 | 48.9 | 56.1 | 43.4 | 43.2 | 36.7 | 37.9 |
| 1985 | 54.5 | 52.0 | 58.8 | 47.2 | 49.8 | 38.8 | 40.1 |
| 1990 | 56.3 | 53.8 | 60.0 | 53.9 | 55.7 | 40.5 | 42.6 |
| 1995 | 58.7 | 55.8 | 62.0 | 59.8 | 61.2 | 42.8 | 45.4 |
| 1999 | 58.2 | 55.7 | 60.8 | 62.5 | 60.8 | 45.3 | 45.3 |
| 2000 | 58.5 | 56.3 | 61.1 | 62.4 | 61.6 | 45.9 | 46.9 |
| **Percentage of people who have not completed high school (%)** | | | | | | | |
| Year | All Races | White | | Black | | Hispanic | |
| | | Male | Female | Male | Female | Male | Female |
| 1940 | 75.5 | 75.8 | 71.9 | 93.1 | 91.6 | NA | NA |
| 1947 | 66.9 | 66.8 | 63.3 | 87.3 | 85.5 | NA | NA |
| 1959 | 56.3 | 55.5 | 52.3 | 80.4 | 78.4 | NA | NA |
| 1965 | 51.0 | 49.8 | 47.8 | 74.2 | 71.6 | NA | NA |
| 1970 | 44.8 | 42.8 | 42.4 | 67.6 | 65.2 | NA | NA |
| 1975 | 37.5 | 35.0 | 35.9 | 58.4 | 56.7 | 60.5 | 63.3 |
| 1980 | 31.4 | 29.0 | 29.9 | 48.9 | 48.7 | 53.6 | 55.9 |
| 1985 | 26.1 | 24.0 | 24.9 | 41.6 | 39.2 | 51.5 | 52.6 |
| 1990 | 22.4 | 20.9 | 21.0 | 34.2 | 33.5 | 49.7 | 48.7 |
| 1995 | 18.3 | 17.0 | 17.0 | 26.6 | 25.9 | 47.1 | 46.2 |
| 1999 | 16.6 | 15.8 | 15.7 | 23.3 | 22.8 | 44.0 | 43.7 |
| 2000 | 15.9 | 15.2 | 15.0 | 21.3 | 21.7 | 43.4 | 42.5 |

Data source: U.S. Census Bureau, Educational Attainment, Historical Tables, Table A-2.

There is no historical data available for the ethnic group of Asian and Pacific Islanders except for 1999 and 2000, displayed in Table 7-4. The data for these two years clearly indicates that the level of educational attainment of this group is substantially higher than all other ethnic groups in the U.S. population, particularly at the college graduate level. In 2000, about 47.6% of all male adults and 40.7% of all female adults in this ethnic group held at least a bachelor's degree, compared with the national average of 25.6%. Only 11.8% of males and 16.6% of females in the Asian and Pacific Islander group did not completed their high school education, compared with the national average of 15.9% in 2000.

Table 7-4: Education Attainment of Asians and Pacific Islanders

| Year | College graduate and plus | | High school graduate | | Non high school graduate | |
|------|------|--------|------|--------|------|--------|
|      | Male | Female | Male | Female | Male | Female |
| 1999 | 46.3 | 39.0   | 40.6 | 43.8   | 13.1 | 17.2   |
| 2000 | 47.6 | 40.7   | 40.6 | 42.7   | 11.8 | 16.6   |

In conclusion, the intellectual achievement of the U.S. population has dramatically improved over the last sixty years. This increase includes all major race groups, as well as both genders. The Hispanic group, however, has not advanced as quickly as other minority populations. This group continues to contain a lower percentage of college graduates and high school graduates, and a higher percentage of people who have not completed high school, as compared with the national averages.

## 7-3  Regional Distribution of Educational Attainment

To see the pattern of education attainment of ethnic groups over different regions in the United States, we have calculated percentages of regional educational attainment for people aged 25 and above by sex, race, and Hispanic origin. The original data come from the U.S. Census Bureau reports for 1999 and the results are presented in Table 7-5.

The Northeast Region has the highest percentage of college and advanced degree graduates of people aged 25 and over in all races. In 1999, this percentage was 30.0% for males and 25.4% for females. The Western Region is ranked second in terms of the college level of educational attainment and is followed by the Midwest Region. Even though the Midwest's percentage of college graduates is not the highest, its percentage of high school graduates is the highest, and its percent of non-high-school graduates is the lowest in the nation. The Southern Region falls behind with its lower percentage of college graduates and higher percentage of non-high-school graduates. Overall, the Northeast and Midwest Regions have achieved higher educational attainment than the West and South Regions have.

Table 7-5: Education Attainment over Regions by Gender (%) (1999)

| | Northeast | | Midwest | | South | | West | |
|---|---|---|---|---|---|---|---|---|
| **All Races** | M | F | M | F | M | F | M | F |
| College & advanced degree | 30.0 | 25.4 | 25.9 | 22.2 | 25.6 | 21.4 | 29.8 | 24.9 |
| High school graduate | 54.8 | 58.9 | 60.1 | 64.2 | 55.1 | 59.3 | 54.1 | 58.7 |
| Non-high school graduate | 15.2 | 15.7 | 14.0 | 13.6 | 19.3 | 19.3 | 16.1 | 16.4 |
| **White** | M | F | M | F | M | F | M | F |
| College & advanced degree | 31.0 | 26.0 | 26.4 | 22.5 | 27.8 | 22.3 | 29.4 | 23.9 |
| High school graduate | 54.9 | 59.2 | 60.2 | 64.8 | 54.1 | 59.8 | 54.1 | 59.7 |
| Non-high school graduate | 14.1 | 14.8 | 13.4 | 12.7 | 18.1 | 17.9 | 16.5 | 16.4 |
| **Black** | M | F | M | F | M | F | M | F |
| College & advanced degree | 15.6 | 16.9 | 14.6 | 15.5 | 12.2 | 15.6 | 22.5 | 23.1 |
| High school graduate | 60.3 | 62.3 | 64.3 | 62.8 | 61.9 | 58.9 | 66.9 | 64.7 |
| Non-high school graduate | 24.1 | 20.8 | 21.1 | 21.7 | 25.9 | 25.5 | 10.6 | 12.2 |
| **Hispanic** | M | F | M | F | M | F | M | F |
| College & advanced degree | 10.7 | 11.7 | 9.5 | 13.4 | 13.1 | 13.9 | 9.1 | 8.0 |
| High school graduate | 48.8 | 48.1 | 47.8 | 49.2 | 44.9 | 45.9 | 43.9 | 42.9 |
| Non-high school graduate | 40.5 | 40.2 | 42.7 | 37.4 | 42.0 | 40.2 | 47.0 | 49.1 |
| **Asian & Pacific Islander** | M | F | M | F | M | F | M | F |
| College & advanced degree | 48.7 | 41.8 | 62.9 | 58.0 | 55.8 | 38.3 | 39.7 | 35.6 |
| High school graduate | 35.7 | 38.3 | 31.9 | 28.7 | 32.3 | 47.0 | 46.3 | 46.6 |
| Non-high school graduate | 15.6 | 19.9 | 5.2 | 13.3 | 11.9 | 14.7 | 14.0 | 17.8 |

The white group has a high level of educational attainment in the North-east and Midwest Regions and a relatively low level in the West and South Regions. This pattern is similar to the national pattern.

The regional distribution of educational achievement for black people aged 25 and over is different from the national pattern. The West Region has shown the highest percentage of college and advanced degree graduates, 22.5% for black males and 23.1% for black females. It also has the highest percentage of high school graduates, 66.9% for black males and 64.7% for black females and the lowest percentage of non-high-school graduates, 10.6% for black males and 12.2% for black females. Again, among all the regions, the South Region has shown the lowest percentage of college and advanced degree graduates, 12.2% for black males and 15.6% for black females, and the highest percent of non-high-school graduates, 25.9% for black males and 25.5% for black females.

In the Southern Region, however, the Hispanic group has held a rela-tively high percentage of college graduates, 13.1% for males and 13.9% for females. In the West Region, the Hispanic group has the lowest percentage of college and high school graduates and the highest percentage of non-high school graduates. This data tells us that Hispanic people in the South Region seem to have been better educated than Hispanic people in the West Region and in the rest of the United States.

The Asian and Pacific Islander group in the Midwest Region had the highest percentage of people with college and advanced degrees, 62.9% for males and 58.0% for females. Their percentage of non-high-school graduates was the lowest, 5.2% for male and 13.3% for female. In the West Region, however, the Asian and Pacific Islander group had the lowest percentage of college graduates, 39.7% for males and 35.6% for females, but the highest percentage of high school graduates, 46.3% for males and 46.6% for females. In the South Region, about 55.8% of the Asian-American men held at least a bachelor's degree, and only 11.9% of them did not complete a high school education. The Asian-American women in the South were less educated than the Asian American men; only 38.3% of them completed college or advanced education, while 14.0% of them did not finish their high school education.

Comparing the regional distribution of educational achievements across racial and ethnic groups, one can clearly observe that the differences in educational attainment among different ethnic groups are more substantial and significant than that over different regions. The Asian and Pacific Is-lander group has reached a relatively high level of education across all re-gions, followed by the white group. The black and Hispanic groups had a significant disadvantage in their education achievement in all regions, except for the West Region, in which the black group achieved higher educational attainment than the national levels in 1999.

## 7-4  Educational Attainment of Immigrants

In Section 5-3, we discussed how the U.S. population has been shaped by immigrants from the rest of the world. As the increasing net international migration accounts for nearly one third of the U.S. population increase each year, the educational level of immigrants should affect the overall educational attainment of the American population as well. We illustrate the differences of educational attainment between Native Americans and foreign-born people living in the United States, including those of noncitizens and naturalized citizens. Foreign-born people can be divided into four ethnic groups: White, Black, Hispanic, and Asian and Pacific Islanders. In each ethnic group, foreign-born people are further divided into four categories according to their entry time periods: the 1990s, 1980s, 1970s, and before 1970. We can compare the educational attainment of foreign-born people in each category with that of Americans born in the U.S. in the same racial group.

Table 7-6 shows the percentage of educated people aged 25 and over at different achievement levels for native-born Americans and foreign-born immigrants in the United States for a single year, 1999. The category of all races and both sexes represents the national level, which can be used for comparisons with race groups. In 1999 there were 173.8 million Americans aged 25 and over, 16.6% of them had not completed high school; 58.2% of them were high school graduates; and 25.2% of them had completed college or advanced degree programs, of which 17.0% held bachelor's degrees, 7.0% held master's or professional degrees, and 1.2% held a doctoral degree (see the first row of data in Table 7-6).

The second and third rows of Table 7-6 show the educational attainment of native-born Americans and of all foreign-born people aged 25 and over in the United States. In general, foreign-born people were less educated than native-born Americans. Foreign-born people had a higher percentage of non-high-school graduates and a lower percentage of high school graduates. At the bachelor's level, foreign-born people made up a smaller percentage of the total than the native-born, but at both the master's and doctor's levels they held a higher percentage.

Table 7-6: Education Attainment of Native- and Foreign-born People 25 Years Old and Over by Entry Period (1999)

| | Number of people | Non-high school | High school grads | College & adv-degrees | BS degree | Master/profes degree | Doctor degree |
|---|---|---|---|---|---|---|---|
| All races & both sexes | 173.75 million | 16.6% | 58.2% | 25.2% | 17.0% | 7.0% | 1.2% |
| Native | 152.56 | 14.1 | 60.7 | 25.2 | 17.1 | 7.0 | 1.1 |
| F - born | 21.19 | 34.3 | 40.3 | 25.4 | 15.8 | 7.6 | 2.0 |
| 1990s | 5.77 | 32.6 | 36.7 | 30.7 | 19.3 | 9.2 | 2.2 |
| 1980s | 6.40 | 38.1 | 38.8 | 23.1 | 14.1 | 6.7 | 2.3 |
| 1970s | 4.39 | 33.7 | 41.3 | 25.0 | 16.8 | 6.7 | 1.5 |
| Before 1970 | 4.63 | 31.7 | 45.7 | 22.6 | 12.9 | 8.0 | 1.7 |
| **White** | | | | | | | |
| Native | 131.77 | 13.0 | 60.5 | 26.5 | 18.0 | 7.4 | 1.1 |
| F - born | 14.31 | 41.1 | 39.4 | 19.5 | 11.8 | 6.1 | 1.6 |
| 1990s | 3.52 | 39.0 | 35.7 | 25.3 | 16.0 | 7.3 | 2.0 |
| 1980s | 3.94 | 47.3 | 36.5 | 16.2 | 9.7 | 4.7 | 1.8 |
| 1970s | 2.87 | 45.1 | 38.7 | 16.2 | 10.1 | 5.0 | 1.1 |
| Before 1970 | 3.97 | 33.9 | 46.1 | 20.0 | 11.3 | 7.1 | 1.6 |
| **Black** | | | | | | | |
| Native | 18.15 | 22.6 | 62.3 | 15.1 | 10.8 | 4.0 | 0.3 |
| F - born | 1.59 | 27.6 | 53.5 | 19.9 | 11.3 | 6.9 | 0.7 |
| 1990s | 0.48 | 31.1 | 47.5 | 21.4 | 10.0 | 10.3 | 1.1 |
| 1980s | 0.54 | 29.7 | 57.9 | 12.4 | 10.7 | 1.7 | 0.0 |
| 1970s | 0.35 | 19.1 | 54.5 | 26.4 | 15.2 | 10.3 | 0.9 |
| Before 1970 | 0.22 | 28.0 | 53.7 | 18.3 | 9.2 | 7.8 | 1.3 |
| **Hispanic** | | | | | | | |
| Native | 7.477 | 29.5 | 58.0 | 12.5 | 9.3 | 2.8 | 0.4 |
| F - born | 8.949 | 55.9 | 34.6 | 9.5 | 6.6 | 2.3 | 0.6 |
| 1990s | 2.319 | 55.0 | 34.0 | 11.0 | 7.9 | 2.7 | 0.4 |
| 1980s | 3.086 | 57.6 | 34.5 | 7.9 | 5.3 | 2.0 | 0.6 |
| 1970s | 2.002 | 59.4 | 33.1 | 7.5 | 5.7 | 1.3 | 0.5 |
| Before 1970 | 1.542 | 49.3 | 37.9 | 12.8 | 8.2 | 3.9 | 0.7 |
| **Asian & Pacific Islander** | | | | | | | |
| Native | 1.349 | 7.1 | 55.8 | 37.1 | 26.6 | 9.8 | 0.7 |
| F - born | 5.138 | 17.4 | 38.8 | 43.8 | 28.0 | 12.5 | 3.3 |
| 1990s | 1.706 | 19.2 | 35.9 | 44.9 | 28.7 | 12.9 | 3.3 |
| 1980s | 1.867 | 21.5 | 38.4 | 40.1 | 24.0 | 12.4 | 3.7 |
| 1970s | 1.123 | 9.7 | 43.9 | 46.4 | 33.4 | 10.3 | 2.7 |
| Before 1970 | 0.442 | 12.6 | 37.9 | 49.5 | 29.4 | 17.0 | 3.1 |

Of those immigrants who entered this country before 1970, 45.7% had completed high school, only 22.6% held bachelor's or advanced degrees, and 31.7% had not completed high school. Of new immigrants in the 1990s, however, 30.7% had received bachelor's or advanced degrees, including 9.2% holding master's or professional degrees and 2.2% holding doctoral degrees, which was significantly higher than the national levels. New immigrants' percentage of non-high-school graduates remains high—more than double the native-borns' level, 32.6% versus 14.1%.

In 1999, a large number of immigrants were still less educated than the average native-born American. However, those people who did hold master's or doctoral degrees were greater in terms of percentage within their cohort group than the counterparts of the native-born populations, particularly at the level of doctoral degrees.

Comparing the educational attainment of those immigrants who entered the United States at different time periods, one can observe that recent immigrants had a significant improvement in college and advanced level of education. But little change took place at the level of non-high-school education; therefore there was a substantial fall in the percentage of high school graduates of immigrants.

The four ethnic immigrant groups have followed the general pattern as described in the above paragraph: a higher percentage of doctoral degree holders and higher percentage of non-high-school graduates than the corresponding native-born population. Hispanic immigrants have a much lower education attainment than native Hispanic Americans at all the levels except the doctoral degree level. Those Hispanic immigrants who came to the United States before 1970 now have a high percentage at the levels of high school, college, and advanced education and a lower percentage of non-high-school graduates. This fact indicates that Hispanic immigrants before 1970 are better educated now than those Hispanic immigrants who arrived after 1970, which could be a result of continuous education after entering the United States. From Table 7-6, one can also observe that the 1990s Hispanic immigrants seem to be better educated than the 1980s and 1970s Hispanic immigrants. In general, Hispanic immigrants' education levels are not only lower than the national average, but also lower than that of native-born Hispanic Americans.

Native-born Asian Americans have a higher level of educational achievement than the national average at all the levels except the doctoral level. Only 7.1% of all the native-born Asian Americans aged 25 and over have not completed high school versus 16.6% for all Americans aged 25 and over. Asian immigrants have a higher percentage of college graduates or advanced education programs than the native-born Asian Americans, particularly at the doctoral and master's degrees levels. In 1999, 28.0% of adult Asian immigrants held bachelor's degrees, 12.5% of them had master's degrees, and 3.3% doctoral degrees, compared with the native-born Asian Americans' 26.6%, 9.8%, and 0.7% respectively, and compared with the national average of 17.0%, 7.0%, and 1.2% respectively. At the lower level of educational attainment, however, the Asian immigrants have a slightly greater percentage of people who have not completed high school than the national average, 17.4% versus 16.6%.

Similar to the situation of Hispanic immigrants, Asian immigrants who entered the United States before 1970 now have higher educational attainment than those Asian immigrants who entered after 1970. Nevertheless, those new Asian immigrants have been better educated not only than all other ethnic immigrants, but also than the average of Americans. In the following two sections, we see that in general the attainment of a higher educational level leads to a higher income, and intellectual quality may have become an important factor in the increasing inequality of personal income in the United States.

*Chapter 8*

*Increasing Personal Income and Increasing Inequality*

The ultimate goal of U.S. economic growth is to promote the standard of living for the majority of Americans. A commonly used measure of the standard of living is per capita personal income, by which international comparisons are made to evaluate the standard of living for nations around the globe. This chapter analyzes the statistics on U.S. per capita personal income over the time period of 1948-2000, the income distribution of U.S. households, and the poverty status of U.S. families over the time period of 1967-1999.

## 8-1  Personal Income Per Capita and Hourly Earnings of American Workers

Personal income is the income received by all residents of the United States from participation in production, from government and business transfer payments, and from interest income. The greatest portion of personal income comes from net earnings, which is the sum of wage and salary disbursements, other labor income, and proprietors' income minus personal contributions for Social Security. Personal income is measured before the deduction of personal income taxes and other personal taxes and reported in current dollars. No adjustment is made for inflation.

Figure 8-1 displays per capita personal income and its real growth rate over the time period of 1948–2000. Per capita personal income is defined as the annual personal income of residents divided by the annual resident population. In 1948 the U.S. per capita personal income was $1,435 dollars; it nearly doubled in 1965 to $2,859 dollars, and continued rising to $4,095 dollars by 1970. In 1980, the U.S. per capita personal income reached $10,183 dollars, the first time it passed the $10,000 mark. By 2000, it increased to $29,676 dollars, almost tripling in three decades.

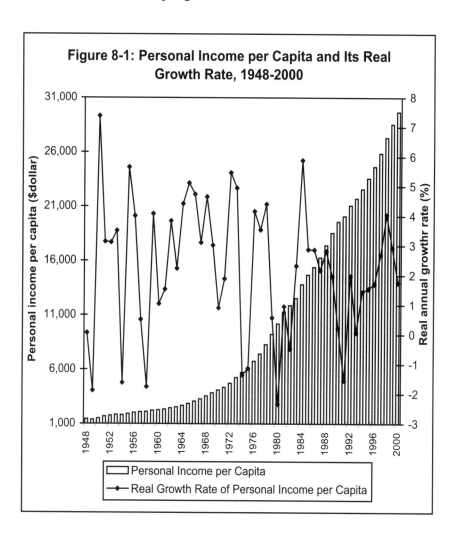

Figure 8-1: Personal Income per Capita and Its Real Growth Rate, 1948-2000

As personal income is measured in current dollars, the inflation rate is subtracted from the growth rate of per capita income in order to measure the real growth rate of per capita personal income. The resulting real growth rate is depicted in Figure 8-1. The real growth rate of per capita income fluctuated between 7% and -2.5% in the last fifty years, remaining positive much of time and only dipping into negative territory for a few years. The years 1959 to 1973 saw consistent increases in personal income in real terms, while the 1970s and the early 1980s witnessed damages to personal income with skyrocketing price inflation. For instance, in 1974, 1975, and 1980, the growth rate of per capita income was 9.1%, 7.6% and 10.3% respectively, but the inflation rate was 10.5%, 8.7%, and 12.7%, which resulted in a declining per capita income in real terms. In the 1990s, the inflation rate declined gradually from 4.5% to 2.5%, while the growth rate of per capita income inched up from 2.5% to 5.0%. Consequently, per capita personal income has increased in real terms since 1992. The economic recession of the early 1990s caused personal income per capita to decline by 1.5% in 1991 and increase by only 0.07% in 1993 in real terms.

We use average hourly earnings of production workers in all the private industries as a general measure of American workers' earnings. As the hourly earnings are measured in current dollars, subtracting the inflation rate of the consumer price index from the annual growth rate of hourly earnings yields the real growth rate of average hourly earnings of production workers in the private sector. The real rate of earning growth represents a percentage increase or a decrease in purchasing power that wage earners actually received from their paychecks. In Figure 8-2 there are four curves representing hourly earnings in current dollars, CPI inflation rate, nominal earning growth rate, and real earning growth rate.

In terms of current dollars, the average hourly earnings of production workers increased more than tenfold in the last five decades of the twentieth century, from $1.23 in 1948 to $2.09 in 1960, $3.23 in 1980, $6.66 in 1980, $10.01 in 1990, and $13.74 in 2000. Nominal earnings have steadily increased over time though the growth rate of nominal earnings has fluctuated. It declined from 7.9% in 1951 to 2.4% in 1961, and then steadily climbed to 8.5% in 1981. In the following five years, however, it declined again from 8.5% to 2.2%. Since 1986, the nominal earning growth rate has fluctuated within a narrow range of 2.4–4.0%. The real earning growth rate has been largely affected by the U.S. inflation rate. Even though the nominal earning growth rate showed an upward trend for the time period of 1948–1981, the real earning growth rate was declining because the inflation rate was moving up rapidly and reached 10.5% in 1974 and 12.7% in 1980.

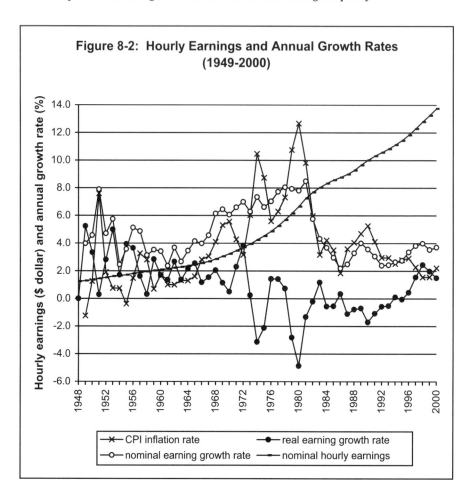

Figure 8-2: Hourly Earnings and Annual Growth Rates (1949-2000)

High inflation in the 1970s and early 1980s cancelled the purchasing power of the largely increased nominal earnings, leaving the real earning growth rate in the negative territory. Particularly in 1974 and 1980, the real earning growth rate was negative and as low as -3.1% and -4.9% respectively. Figure 8-2 shows that the declining trend probably ended in 1990, when the real earning growth rate reached -1.7%. Since 1990, an increase in the real earning growth was established, thanks to the increasing nominal earning rate and the decreasing inflation rate. The inflation rate declined from 5.26% in 1990 to 1.56% in 1999, and 2.21% in 2000, while the nominal earning growth rate increased from 2.4% in 1992 to 4.0% in 1998.

During the time period of 1948-1973 American workers did enjoy a consistent increase in purchasing power from their salaries and wages, because their real earning growth rate had improved. However, in the 21 years from 1974 through 1995, American workers' real earnings decreased except during six years, 1976–1978, 1983, 1986 and 1994, in which the real earning growth rates were small positive numbers. Starting in 1995, real earnings grew steadily, with the annual growth rate rising from -0.05% in 1995 to 2.4% in 1998, which was the highest rate since 1972. In 1999 and 2000, the real earning growth rate pulled back to 2.0% and 1.5% due to slightly reduced nominal earning growth and a minor pick up of inflation. It is clear that in the 1990s nominal earnings and inflation behaved in a favorable way to benefit the majority of American workers.

## 8-2   Income Distribution of Households and Poverty Status of Families

Increased earnings and personal income has not been distributed evenly among U.S. households and families. Income inequality can be measured in different ways; two commonly used measures are income shares and Gini ratios. This section will also examine the improving economic status and reduced poverty rate of American families.

### • Income Distribution Share of American Households

By the income share approach, households are ranked from lowest to highest in terms of their personal income, and then divided into groups, such as quintiles, with equal population size. The aggregate income of each group is divided by the total aggregate income to yield income share for each household group. Table 8-1 displays income shares and the upper limits of income for U.S. household quintiles over the time period from 1967 through 1999, based on the historical records from the U.S. Census Bureau.

As the upper panel of Table 8-1 shows, in 1967 the bottom 20% of the U.S. population received 4.0% of total personal income, and its income share rose to 4.4% in 1975–1977. Since 1978, the bottom group's income share declined steadily to its lowest share, 3.6% in 1999. The income share of the second 20% of the U.S. population was 10.8% in 1967, and 11.1% in 1968, which was the highest income share this group held as of 1999. Similar to the bottom group, the second 20% of the U.S. population saw their income share shrink gradually, to 8.9% in 1999.

Table 8-1: U.S. Income Distribution by Household Quintiles

| Year | Share of Aggregate Income | | | | | |
|---|---|---|---|---|---|---|
| | Bottom 20% | Second 20% | Middle 20% | Fourth 20% | Top 20% | Top 5% |
| 1967 | 4.0 | 10.8 | 17.3 | 24.2 | 43.8 | 17.5 |
| 1970 | 4.1 | 10.8 | 17.4 | 24.5 | 43.3 | 16.6 |
| 1975 | 4.4 | 10.5 | 17.1 | 24.8 | 43.2 | 15.9 |
| 1980 | 4.3 | 10.3 | 16.9 | 24.9 | 43.7 | 15.8 |
| 1985 | 4.0 | 9.7 | 16.3 | 24.6 | 45.3 | 17.0 |
| 1990 | 3.9 | 9.6 | 15.9 | 24.0 | 46.6 | 18.6 |
| 1991 | 3.8 | 9.6 | 15.9 | 24.2 | 46.5 | 18.1 |
| 1992 | 3.8 | 9.4 | 15.8 | 24.2 | 46.9 | 18.6 |
| 1993 | 3.6 | 9.0 | 15.1 | 23.5 | 48.9 | 21.0 |
| 1994 | 3.6 | 8.9 | 15.0 | 23.4 | 49.1 | 21.2 |
| 1995 | 3.7 | 9.1 | 15.2 | 23.3 | 48.7 | 21.0 |
| 1996 | 3.7 | 9.0 | 15.1 | 23.3 | 49.0 | 21.4 |
| 1997 | 3.6 | 8.9 | 15.0 | 23.2 | 49.4 | 21.7 |
| 1998 | 3.6 | 9.0 | 15.0 | 23.2 | 49.2 | 21.4 |
| 1999 | 3.6 | 8.9 | 14.9 | 23.2 | 49.4 | 21.5 |
| **Income Upper Limit of Each Quintile and Lower Limit of Top 5% (in 1999 dollars)** | | | | | | |
| Year | Bottom 20% | Second 20% | Middle 20% | Fourth 20% | Top 5% | Number of Households |
| 1967 | $13,769 | $26,849 | $38,121 | $54,345 | $87,201 | 60,446 thous. |
| 1970 | 14,873 | 28,495 | 41,452 | 59,141 | 93,498 | 64,374 |
| 1975 | 14,896 | 28,014 | 42,231 | 60,759 | 96,880 | 72,867 |
| 1980 | 15,296 | 28,543 | 43,745 | 64,170 | 104,252 | 82,368 |
| 1985 | 15,483 | 29,189 | 44,936 | 67,831 | 113,435 | 88,458 |
| 1990 | 15,933 | 30,161 | 46,143 | 70,368 | 120,773 | 94,312 |
| 1991 | 15,398 | 29,357 | 45,344 | 69,429 | 117,917 | 95,669 |
| 1992 | 14,962 | 28,665 | 45,005 | 68,881 | 117,582 | 96,426 |
| 1993 | 14,950 | 28,453 | 44,726 | 69,522 | 120,643 | 97,107 |
| 1994 | 15,093 | 28,329 | 45,079 | 70,643 | 123,456 | 98,990 |
| 1995 | 15,742 | 29,422 | 45,916 | 71,192 | 123,529 | 99,627 |
| 1996 | 15,681 | 29,476 | 46,727 | 72,220 | 126,930 | 101,018 |
| 1997 | 15,985 | 30,310 | 47,748 | 74,217 | 131,360 | 102,528 |
| 1998 | 16,472 | 31,080 | 49,405 | 76,656 | 135,119 | 103,874 |
| 1999 | 17,196 | 32,000 | 50,520 | 79,375 | 142,021 | 104,705 |
| **% Change in 1967-1999** | | | | | | |
| | 24.9% | 19.2% | 32.5% | 46.1% | 62.9% | |

The income share of the middle 20% of the U.S. population was 17.3% in 1967, and 17.5% in 1968 and 1969, the highest income share that this group attained. This group's income share stepped down from 17.5% to 17.0% in the 1970s, from 16.9% to 16.0% in the 1980s, then from 15.9% to 14.9% in the 1990s, and arrived at 14.9% in 1999. The income share of the fourth 20% of the U.S. population was 24.2% in 1967, and rose to 25.0% in 1981. After that it declined and reached its lowest share, 23.2%, in 1999.

All of these four quintiles of the U.S. population lost their income share in the time period from 1967 through 1999 by 0.4%, 1.9%, 2.4%, and 1.0% from bottom up respectively. The top 20% of the U.S. population is the only quintile that showed a rising income share, from 43.8% in 1967 to 49.4% in 1999 with an income share gain of 5.6%, in which a 4.0% income share gain belonged to the top 5% of the U.S. population. The top 5% of the U.S. population received 17.5% of total personal income in 1967, which was greater than the combined income shares of the bottom and the second quintile. In 1999, the income share of the top 5% was 21.5%, a 4.0% share gain from its 17.5% income share of 1967.

A decreasing (or increasing) income share of a group indicates that the aggregate income received by the group has grown relatively slowly (or quickly) compared with the total U.S. personal income. A decreasing income share does not necessarily imply a declining aggregate income; but it is certainly an indicator of slower increases in the group's income. The lower panel of Table 8-1 displays the upper limit of income for each quintile and the lower limit of income of the top 5%. Measured by constant 1999 dollars, the highest household income for the bottom 20% was $13,769 in 1967, and rose to $17,196 in 1999, which was a 24.9% increase. Similarly, all groups showed significant increases in the upper limits of income in the last row of Table 8-1.

From Table 8-1 one can see evidence of the increasing U.S. household income and the increasing income inequality. Not only do the top 20% of Americans enjoy more than 45% of total U.S. personal income on the average, they have also seen their aggregate income rise faster than the income of the other 80% of Americans. In particular, the top 5% richest Americans have controlled 17-21% of total U.S. income, and the annual income benchmark for being qualified as the top 5% richest has increased by 62.9%, from $87,201 in 1967 to $142,02 in 1999.

## • The Gini Ratio of Racial Groups

The second measure of income inequality is called the Gini ratio or the Gini coefficient, which is a statistical measure of income equality from zero to one. The Gini ratio of one indicates perfect inequality: that is, one person (or household) has all the income and the rest have none. The Gini ration zero represents perfect equality: namely, all people have equal shares of income. Of course, those two extremes do not exist in reality in the U.S. economy. Figure 8-3 depicts U.S. income distribution for four years, 1968, 1980, 1990, and 1999. The horizontal axis shows the population quintiles, and the vertical axis represents the cumulative share of income earned by the plotted quintile and the others on the left side.

The income distribution curve is called the Lorenz curve, and the diagonal line represents perfectly equal income distribution. The Gini ratio measures the gap between the actual Lorenz curve and the diagonal line; and the gap is a

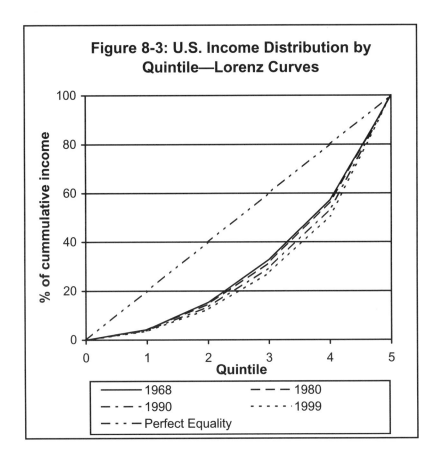

function of the degree of income inequality. In an egalitarian society, the Gini ratio should be zero, and the Lorenz curve would be the diagonal line. Therefore, the higher the Gini ratio, the greater the distance between the Lorenz curve and the diagonal line, and the more unequal the distribution of income. In a perfectly unequal society, in which one household has all the income, the Lorenz curve would be zero for all the quintiles except for one household on the right, whose income share would be 100%, and then the Gini ratio would be one. Figure 8-3 clearly shows the increasing degree of inequality in U.S. income distribution, because the Lorenz curve moved further away from the diagonal line as the years progressed from 1968 to 1999, which indicates an increasing Gini ratio of the U.S. income.

Based on the historical data of the Gini ratio published by the U.S. Census Bureau, Figure 8-4 depicts the ascending paths of the Gini ratios for U.S. households by all races.

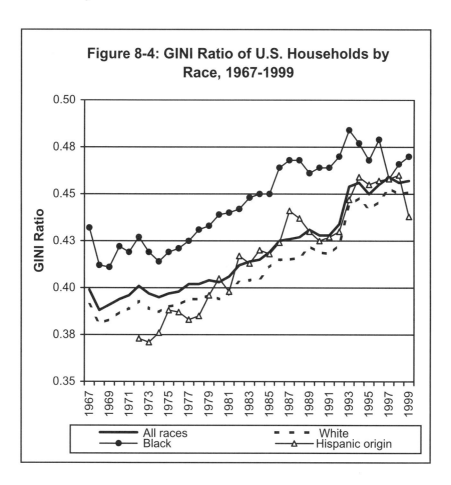

Figure 8-4: GINI Ratio of U.S. Households by Race, 1967-1999

An upward trend occurs in all of the four Gini ratio curves, indicating the increasing inequality of income distribution for all racial groups of the U.S. population. The Gini ratios indicate that the lower the income of the racial group, the higher the degree of inequality of income distribution among the group. The White group had a lower Gini ratio than the U.S. population as a whole, while the Black group had the highest Gini ratio of all.People of Hispanic origin had the lowest Gini ratio in the 1970s. The increasing inequality in their income has moved their Gini ratio up to between the White and Black groups.

In 1967–1974, three Gini ratios fluctuated with no significant trend. After 1974 all four Gini ratios increased considerably, particularly during the time period of 1991–1993, when the U.S. economy was in recession and the unemployment rate spiked up, resulting in more people in the bottom quintile losing their jobs than people above. After 1993, however, the Gini ratios of the Black and Hispanic groups tended to fall, while the Gini ratios of the White group and all races as a whole still trended up with a declining slope. This indicates an improvement in income distribution for all races in generally, and for the Black and Hispanic groups in particular.


## • The Poverty Status of American Families

The U.S. Census Bureau has an official definition for establishing poverty. In this definition there is a set of income thresholds that vary by family size and composition. If a family's total income is less than that family's threshold, then that family and each individual member of the family is considered poor. The family's income is defined as money income before taxes, which does not include capital gains and non-cash benefits, such as public housing, Medicaid, and food stamps. The poverty thresholds are updated annually, taking price inflation into consideration. For example, the average poverty threshold for a family of four was $8,414 dollars in 1980, $13,359 dollars in 1990, and $17,029 dollars in 1999. If this four-person family has one child under 18 years old, the poverty threshold increases a little, to $17,465 dollars in 1999. Similarly, the threshold increases or decreases little by little according to different compositions of families.

In Figure 8-5, we display the percentage of families under the poverty thresholds in terms of the total number of families for all racial groups. In 1959 there were 45.054 million families in the United States, and 8.32 million of them were under the poverty threshold. In short, 18.5% of American families were considered poor. In 1973 and 1974, there were a total of 55-55.7 million American families, of which about 4.8-4.9 million were poor, accounting for 8.8% of the total number of American families. After 1975, the percentage of poor families of all races increased and fluctuated around 10%. This number reached 12.3% in 1993, and declined after that point. In 1999 there were 72.031 million American families, and 6.676 million of them were poor, showing that the number of poor families decreased by 1.644 million compared with 1959 (8.32 million poor families). In a relative sense, nearly one out of every five American families was poor in 1959, but only one out of every eleven American families was poor in 1999, indicating a significant improvement in the economic status of the American families of all races.

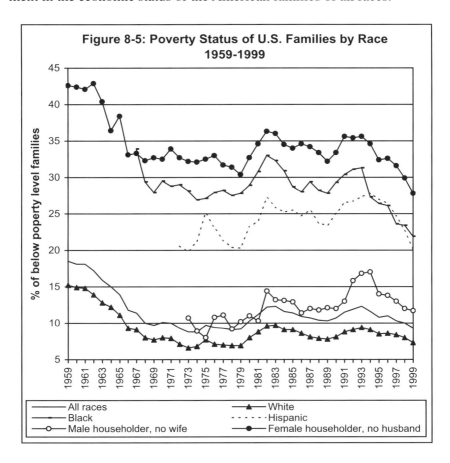

Figure 8-5: Poverty Status of U.S. Families by Race 1959-1999

The number of White families increased from 40.820 million in 1959 to 60.256 million in 1999, while the number of poor White families decreased from 6.185 million to 4.377 million in the same time period. The percentage of poor families in the White group declined from 15.2% in 1959 to 7.3% in 1999, which was lower than the average for all races in 1959–1999.

As Figure 8-5 indicates, the percentages of poor families in the Black and Hispanic racial groups were twice or three times of the average level for all racial groups. One of every three Black families was poor in 1967, while only one of every five Black families was poor in 1999. However, the number of poor Black families increased from 1.555 million in 1967 to 1.898 million in 1999, because the total number of the Black families almost doubled in that time period. The percentage of poor Hispanic families was 20.6% in 1972 and 20.2% in 1999, and the highest was 27.8% in 1994. The number of Hispanic families in the United States increased dramatically from 2.312 million in 1972 to 7.561 million in 1999, while the number of Hispanic poor families increased almost proportionally, from 0.477 million in 1972 to 1.525 million in 1999. As a result the ratio of poor families showed no significant trend for the Hispanic group.

Not only does the racial factor reflect the different poverty status of American families; the family composition also plays an important role in determining which families are poor. Two polarized family compositions are displayed in Figure 8-5: families with a male householder and no wife present, and families with a female householder and no husband present, both for all racial families. The poverty status of families with no wife present is slightly worse than the average level of all families; it becomes much worse for the families with no husband present. The percentage of poor families with a single female as head of household was 42.6% in 1959 and 36.3% in 1982. It declined to 27.8% in 1999, but was still higher than that of poor families with a single male as the head of household (11.7% in 1999), and also higher than the percentage of poor minority families.

We have used three quantitative measures to illustrate the increasing per capita income and the increasing inequality of American households' income distribution. Consistent with the increasing per capita income, the number of American families under the poverty threshold has decreased over time. Particularly in the time period 1993 through 1999, all six curves in Figure 8-5 show substantial declines, and the poor family percentages of those racial and different composition families reached their historically lowest level in 1999. In Chapter 9, we will demonstrate that educational attainment has been the major contributor to the inequality of income distribution in the United States.

# Chapter 9

## The Creative and Innovative Class

It has been widely recognized that in the late twentieth century, revolutionary changes in technology transformed the U.S. economy from traditionally modern industries that were based on mechanical and electrical technologies into innovative industries and services based on new information technology. Consequently, the minimum requirements for performing a job were continuously raised in order to operate innovative tools and machines, and to constantly manage increasing information flow for business success. More importantly, the information technology revolution and the structure shift of the U.S. economy induced a fundamental change: the decline of the working class and the emergence of the creative and innovative class in the U.S. workforce. This chapter explains what the new class is and how workers in the new class benefit from this economic transformation.

## 9-1   The Emerging Creative and Innovative Class

In later chapters of this book we provide a large amount of evidence to illustrate the great economic transition that has been occurring in the U.S. for some time. This economic transformation is characterized by the systematic decline of the manufacturing sector and the rapidly rising services-producing sector. Our analyses, which are based on the time series from U.S. National Income and Product Account (NIPA), indicate that the whole U.S. manufacturing sector experienced a dramatic shift. Its highest GDP- and labor-shares (contributions to GDP and employment), 29.62% and 27.50%, occurred in 1953. Those shares, however, were almost halved in 2000, dropping to 15.88% and 13.68%. The number of manufacturing workers decreased from 20.175 million in 1980 to 18.511 million in 2000, but its nominal value-added more than doubled, from $587 billion in 1980 to $1.567 trillion, thanks to the extraordinary productivity gain in manufacturing. The U.S. manufacturing sector stopped creating new jobs after 1980. As a matter of fact, a net of 1.5 million U.S. manufacturing jobs were eliminated in the last two decades of the twentieth century.

Finance, insurance and real estate were the fastest-growing industries in the U.S. during the second half of the century; their contribution to GDP rose from 9.8% in 1948 to 19.6% in 2000, which surpassed the GDP-share of the entire manufacturing sector, 15.9%, in 2000. The subindustry of banking and credit agency alone made a greater contribution to GDP than the combined industries of metal, motor vehicle and transportation equipment all together. The great creators of job and wealth in the U.S. economy also include business services, health services, education, legal and social services, as well as other professional services. Nearly 20 million Americans engaged in the business services and health services in 2000, accounting for 14.8% of the total U.S. employment, compared with the 18.5 million Americans who were employed by the manufacturing sector in 2000.

Although many features and consequences of this on-going dynamic transition are waiting to be identified and comprehended, one of them is clear: the emergence of the creative and innovative class in U.S. society. We shall explain why these two adjectives are used to describe this new social group.

During the process of the sector structure change, the dominance of manufacturing workers is replaced by the dominance of service workers. A typical manufacturing worker performs essentially a manual job with his/her hands that requires simple skills on the assembly lines and factory floors. Many services workers, however, are usually not called "workers" but "professionals" or "specialists", who provide specific services with professional knowledge. They act as doctors, nurses, medical technologists, lawyers, teachers, researchers, scientists, accountants, financial analysts, investment advisors, engineers, computer technicians, software designers, data processing staff members, project managers, technologists, and consultants and so on. Manufacturing workers and professionals constitute two very different classes in U.S. society: the working class and the creative and innovative class, with different educational backgrounds, values, attitudes, preferences, and lifestyles.

The traditional working class consists of employees who work in the sectors of manufacturing, construction, transportation, mining and agriculture. Many jobs in those sectors require only limited education and simple technical skills that can be acquired through practices on the job or skill training programs. Those technical skills can suffice for a long time, some even a lifetime, in manual work. As goods-producing jobs decline steadily, the working class fell substantially after 1950. At the end of the century, more Americans were delivering services rather than producing goods. The simple technical skills and the low level of education became obstacles for unemployed manual workers to find jobs in the rapidly growing services industries, which require different kinds of knowledge and professional skills.

The term "knowledge worker", which was originally used by Peter Drucker[1], has become popular to characterize professionals who are working for the services and manufacturing industries, as well as for the public sector. In Drucker's opinion, the next society will be a knowledge society, in which knowledge will be its key economic resource or the means of production, and knowledge workers will be the dominating group in its workforce, with three main characteristics[2]:

---

[1] "Peter Drucker is a writer, teacher and consultant who has published 32 books, mostly on various aspects of society, economics, politics and management. Born in 1909 in Vienna, Mr. Drucker was educated in Austria and England, and holds a doctorate from Frankfurt University. Since 1971 he has been Professor of Social Science and Management at Claremont Graduate University, California," cited from *The Economist*, November 3, 2001.

[2] Peter Drucker, "The Next Society: A Survey of the Near Future," *The Economist,* November 3, 2001.

- Borderlessness, because knowledge travels even more effortlessly than money.
- Upward mobility, available to everyone through easily acquired formal education.
- The potential for failure as well as success. Anyone can acquire the "means of production", i.e. the knowledge required for the job, but not everyone can win.

What identifies knowledge workers are their jobs, which involve putting formal knowledge to work. The knowledge is acquired in formal education rather than through apprenticeship. Unlike traditional skills, which change very slowly, knowledge in this rapidly changing area becomes obsolete. Therefore, knowledge workers have to go back to school regularly in order to update their specialties. Continuing education throughout their working lives becomes crucial for knowledge workers to keep their knowledge up to date and to retain their jobs.

Peter Drucker also emphasizes a unique nature of knowledge workers. He observes that low-skilled workers in manufacturing plants are employees who take orders from their supervisors and carry out routine procedures. Knowledge workers, however, are regarded by themselves and in the public's mind as professionals, specialists, and experts rather than subordinates or workers managed by their bosses or someone else. This change in the workplace becomes so deep that " it is no accident that yesterday's "secretary" is rapidly turning into an "assistant", having become the manager of the boss's office and of his work[3]."

Knowledge workers by and large are self-managed or loosely controlled by corporations and organizations they work with. They favor the flexibility and the no-collar workplace of a more casual, relaxing and stimulating environment over the homogeneity and conformity under the traditional hierarchical management system of control.

Instead of using the term "knowledge workers," Richard Florida[4] has defined a similar group of people as the "creative class." In his opinion[5],

---

[3] Peter Drucker, "The Next Society: A Survey of the Near Future," *The Economist,* November 3, 2001.

[4] Richard Florida is a professor of regional economic development at Carnegie Mellon University and a columnist for *Information Week.*

[5] Richard Florida, *The Rise of The Creative Class and How It's Transforming Work, Leisure, Community and Everyday Life* (Basic Books, 2002).

... A class is a cluster of people, who have common interests and tend to think, feel and behave similarly, but these similarities are fundamentally determined by economic function—by the kind of work they do for living. All the other dimensions follow from that. And a key factor of our age is that more of us than ever are doing creative work for living...

By his definition, the core of the creative class includes people in science and engineering, architecture and design, education, arts, music and entertainment whose economic function is to create new ideas, new technology and new creative contents. This creative core is surrounded by a large number of members in the creative class, including professionals in business, finance, law, health care and related fields. These people are engaged in complex problem solving that requires high levels of education, independent judgment, and creativity in technological, cultural, and economic dimensions. In Peter Drucker's terminology, those same people are called knowledge workers, who hold up-to-date professional knowledge and know how to apply their knowledge to work.

Like Peter Drucker, who puts a great emphasis on knowledge as a major economic resource for the next society, Richard Florida focuses his attention on human creativity. He believes that the rise of human creativity is the key factor in our economy and society, and the winners in the long run are those who can create and keep creating. Human creativity is assigned a central role in production activities and wealth generation. Creativity stimulates new ideas, and a good idea can be used over and over again. Human creativity is the only economic resource that offers increasing returns rather than diminishing returns, which is an inescapable economic law of production for all other resources such as labor, land, and capital. Creativity has been a driving force for all the economic transformations in human history. In this on-going U.S. economic transition, not just the fruits of creativity— namely scientific inventions and technology innovations—are harnessed, but human creativity itself is being widely harnessed on a truly massive scale, as never before.

Both Drucker and Florida have captured the profound features of this emerging class. We think the dividing line between the group of knowledge workers (or the creative class) and the traditional working class depends on their capability of management. Manual workers are traditionally managed by their supervisors and conduct planned work procedures with clearly defined and limited responsibilities. Knowledge workers and creative people, however, are essentially self-managed, with a large degree of autonomy, which allows them to build up their own visions for work, leisure, and life, to choose their course of career, to be engaged in education and continuous education, to decide which corporation or organization to work with, and when, where and how to work, and finally to choose their own life-styles rather than fit into one predetermined by others.

The management theory and practice, therefore, are applied by the rapidly growing number of knowledge workers, who are conceived as creative and innovative decision makers for their work, leisure, time, and life, as well as for corporations, organizations and communities. They manage their work by themselves creatively and innovatively; they create new ideas and methods, new technologies and products; they collectively organize new workplaces and communities for nurturing individuality, self-expression and openness to difference, which stimulate, harness and promulgate creativity and innovation for economic growth and wealth creation. Hence, the new class of workers reaps the great benefits of the economic transformation through their creative and innovative management capability, which we will see in the following two sections. They will also continue to play an important role in shaping the U.S. economy and society for the 21st century. Therefore we think it might be more accurate to name this rapidly growing social group of knowledge workers as the "creative and innovative class."

Creative and innovative management, which has been recognized as a new framework of management science, includes different dimensions. As defined by George Kozmetsky[6],

> Creative management consists of new concepts, new ideas, new methods, new directions, and new modes of operation. The operative word is "new." Innovative management consists of the ability to implement creative ideas and/or move successfully in such new directions. The operative words are "to implement" and "to move successfully." Creative and innovative management focuses on coupling, that is, linking creative and innovative management. The operative notion here is an "act of management" rather than the act of an individual....
>
> The acts of management link together organizational form, motivations and incentives, culture and environment, and strategy....

---

[6] George Kozmetsky, *Economic Growth Through Technology: A New Framework for Creative and Innovative Managers.* The IC2 Institute, The University of Texas at Austin, 1986.

Unlike the traditional management decision making centered on efficiency and effectiveness, creative and innovative management focuses on flexibility and adaptability to deal with process of managing change, including the required public/private infrastructures....

Creative and innovative management covers the nature of creative and innovative activities, organizational design for improving creativity and innovation, organizational creativity and individual personality, creative and innovative management in public sector structures, joint public/private organizations and activities, strategies for academic research and curriculum, and implications for public policy.

With the emergence of human creativity and knowledge as the economy's new resources and the creative and innovative class as society's representative class, U.S. corporations have experienced fundamental changes in their workforce, technology, markets, and organizational strategy and structure. As the means of production, professional knowledge becomes as important as capital to corporations' businesses. The knowledge needed for a successful business has become highly specialized, expensive to upgrade, and increasingly difficult to maintain within a corporation. Professionals, specialists, and experts collectively own knowledge that is acquired through formal higher education and continuous education. Those people can easily move within their fields among very different companies, taking knowledge with them.

Facing such a high mobility of the expensive economic resource, professional knowledge, U.S. corporations begin to decentralize their activities through outsourcing contractors. Now the outsourcing has been extended rapidly into not only manufacturing work, but also management of information technology, data processing, computer systems, as well as the entire human resource management, such as hiring, firing, and training. U.S. corporations have created new sources and forms for business development and economic growth, including partnerships, joint ventures, alliances, and know-how agreements with a variety of organizations. It can be corporations in different industries, universities, not-for-profit institutions, communities, as well as government agencies.

All these activities in the newer institutional developments require a good management of professional knowledge and its carriers, the creative and innovative class. We believe that the framework of creative and innovative management, with its emphasis on creativity and innovation, flexibility and adaptability, competition and cooperation, provides a foundation for this growing new area of management science, which, despite all the present talk of "knowledge management", no one yet really knows how to implement[7].

The creative and innovative class consists of all the professionals and specialists in all sectors and industries with a concentration on the services-producing activities. However, the lowest-end services, such as personal care and food delivery, involve mainly low-skilled manual work, and those workers in the low-end services will not be included in the new class. On the other hand, many professionals are engaged in goods-producing activities, such as R&D scientists, researchers, engineers, designers, project managers and so on, and they certainly belong to the new class. It seems incorrect to identify the new class through the industry classification, as both kinds of workers are employed in all the industries and sectors, though in quite different proportions.

People in this new class are widely separated from people in the working class by occupation and education, which allow researchers to estimate the size of the new class. It has been found that professional, technical, and managerial occupations increased from 10% of the workforce in 1900 to 30% by 1991[8]. An estimate that measures U.S. industries that have at least 5% of the workforce with graduate degrees indicates that the new class accounted for nearly 36% of all U.S. employment in 1999[9]. Based on the standard occupational classifications collected by the U.S. Census and available in its historical statistics from 1900 to the present, Richard Florida estimated that the new class included some 38.3 million Americans, roughly 30% of the entire workforce, in 1999, increasing more than tenfold, compared with 3 million in 1900[10]. The estimate also indicates that the rapid growth of the new class began in 1950. It took fifty years for its numbers to rise from 10% in 1990 to 15% in 1950, while another fifty years doubled the number to 30% in 1999.

---

[7] Peter Drucker, "The Next Society: A Survey of the Near Future," *The Economist,* November 3, 2001.

[8] Steven Barley, *The New World of Work* (London: British North American Committee, 1996).

[9] Steven Brint, Professionals and the Knowledge Economy: Rethinking the Theory of the Postindustrial Society, *Current Sociology,* 49 (1), July 2001.

[10] Richard Florida, *The Rise of The Creative Class and How It's Transforming Work, Leisure, Community and Everyday Life* (Basic Books, 2002).

In the following section we use the educational attainment of the U.S. adult population to measure the rapid growth of this new class, which is prompted by the increasing demand for employees with high levels of education. Special skills in computer operating and networking and in computer software engineering and programming have become core competencies for the manufacturing industries and information technology industries, and for many services industries. High school education and training do not prepare students with the core technical knowledge and competence to do creative and innovative jobs in today's workplace. Hence, college and advanced degrees have become necessary to enter the high-end services industries, such as research and development, software developing, financial, health care, business services and consultants. Less educated people in the working class, therefore, are facing a great challenge to participate in rapidly transforming industries.

This changing situation in the job market is clearly reflected in the unevenly distributed unemployment rates among workers who have different levels of educational attainment. We will examine this evidence in the next section.

## 9-2    The Increasing Demand for Well-Educated Workers

In Table 9-1 we illustrate labor force participation rates and unemployment rates of Americans aged 25 and over by four levels of educational attainment. The original data is extracted from the database of the Bureau of Labor Statistics (LSB) and aggregated from monthly records, which are available for the time period from 1992 through 2000.

Comparing the labor participation rates and unemployment rates of the groups characterized by different educational levels with the national averages, one can clearly see that those workers who have not completed high school have not received much benefit from economic growth and industrial transformation. Even though their participation rate increased slightly and their unemployment rate declined substantially, those rates are still unfavorable to them in the U.S. job market, compared with the national average level. This group's participation rate was 43.0% and their unemployment rate was 6.4% in 2000 versus 67.2% and 4.0% respectively for the national average in the same year.

Table 9-1: Labor Participation Rates and Unemployment Rates by
Educational Attainment

| Labor force participation rates (%) | | | | | |
|---|---|---|---|---|---|
| Year | Non high school graduate | High school graduate | Some college less than bachelor's degree | College and advanced degree graduates | National average |
| 1992 | 41.2 | 66.4 | 75.3 | 81.3 | 66.4 |
| 1993 | 40.2 | 65.6 | 75.1 | 81.1 | 66.3 |
| 1994 | 40.0 | 65.5 | 75.2 | 81.1 | 66.6 |
| 1995 | 40.0 | 65.5 | 74.5 | 81.0 | 66.6 |
| 1996 | 41.1 | 65.7 | 74.7 | 80.5 | 66.8 |
| 1997 | 42.2 | 65.8 | 74.7 | 80.5 | 67.1 |
| 1998 | 42.8 | 65.1 | 74.3 | 80.2 | 67.1 |
| 1999 | 42.7 | 64.9 | 74.1 | 79.9 | 67.1 |
| 2000 | 43.0 | 65.1 | 74.1 | 80.4 | 67.2 |
| Unemployment rates (%) | | | | | |
| 1992 | 11.5 | 6.8 | 5.7 | 3.2 | 7.5 |
| 1993 | 10.8 | 6.3 | 5.2 | 3.0 | 6.9 |
| 1994 | 9.8 | 5.3 | 4.4 | 2.6 | 6.1 |
| 1995 | 9.0 | 4.7 | 4.0 | 2.5 | 5.6 |
| 1996 | 8.7 | 4.7 | 3.7 | 2.3 | 5.4 |
| 1997 | 8.1 | 4.2 | 3.2 | 2.0 | 5.0 |
| 1998 | 7.0 | 4.0 | 3.0 | 1.8 | 4.5 |
| 1999 | 6.8 | 3.5 | 2.8 | 1.8 | 4.2 |
| 2000 | 6.4 | 3.5 | 2.7 | 1.6 | 4.0 |

Those people with a high school diploma have done better than those without it. The high school graduates' participation rate was slightly lower than the average, and their unemployment rate was also lower than the national average, which means there were still plenty of job opportunities in the U.S. economy for those with only a high school education.

Most of the job opportunities from the economic expansion at the end of the twentieth century were for those people with a bachelor's or advanced degree. Their education and technological skills were most suitable for the innovative new industries and for the conventional industries that were transforming themselves by using new technologies. Those people were in the most demand in the U.S. labor market, with their labor participation rate around 80% in the last nine years of the century and unemployment rate declining from 3.2% in 1992 to 1.6% in 2000. In the same time frame, however, the national unemployment rate only decreased from 7.5% to 4.0%. This group's consistent high participation rate and low unemployment rate indicate that opportunities in the U.S. economy for people with at least a college degree are strong, robust, and more certain in all economic conditions.

People who have some non-degree college education or received associate's degrees also did quite well, with their participation rates above the national average and their unemployment rates below the national average in the time frame of 1992–2000.

In 2000, the civilian noninstitutional population aged 25 and over reached 174.6 million in the United States. Among them there were 27.7 million people who had not finished their high school education. With their participation rate of 43%, there were nearly 15.8 million people in this group who remained out of the labor force. Had this group of Americans completed their high school education and thus increased their participation rate to 65.1%, with other high school graduates, the U.S. labor pool would have enlarged by 6.12 million, nearly a 5.2% rise from the labor force of 118.3 million in 2000.

In 2000, the number of high school graduates aged 25 and over was 57.8 million. With their participation rate of 65.1%, there were about 20.2 million high school graduates out of the labor force. To promote their educational attainment to the next level of some college or an associate degree would raise their participation rate to 74.1%, implying an increase of nearly 5.2 million people in the U.S. labor pool. Therefore, there are at least 11.3 million people who could be added into the U.S. labor force, had the two low levels of educational attainment been upgraded into the next level of education. This potential increase in working people represents a 10% rise in the U.S. labor force, which would significantly relieve the tightness of labor supply in the U.S. economy.

In the 1990s' economic expansion, U.S. economic policy makers were constantly worried about the tightening of the U.S. labor market, and they watched the unemployment rate approaching the lowest level for three decades. According to conventional economic logic, a low unemployment rate indicates a labor shortage. In that situation, corporations would have to offer higher salaries and better employment benefits to attract needed workers, which would result in higher costs of production. To maintain their profit margin, corporations have to raise the prices of their products and pass along the high labor costs to consumers. Higher salaries will be transferred into higher consumer income and higher purchasing power, which increases market pressures from the demand side.

Those factors from both supply and demand sides would work together to push up the general price index and create inflation in the economy. As fighting against inflation has been considered a primary goal of monetary policies, the tightness of the labor market becomes the most important barometer for policy makers. Indications from the labor market can help policy makers decide how fast or how slow the economy should be allowed to grow. Besides a limited energy supply, the shortage of working people is viewed as a major constraint on the economic growth in the United States, and it was the dominating factor behind the six interest rates hike by the Fed during 1999-2000.

In our analysis, there are nearly 11 million people who could be added to the U.S. labor force to relieve tensions in the labor market. Economic policy makers need to take a close look at the possibilities of improving education proactively as a fundamental measure to relax the bottleneck constraint from the labor market on economic growth. Improving Americans' education is a better solution to the tightening labor market than simply raising interest rates to pull the expanding economy back in order to produce a higher unemployment rate against inflation.

## 9-3   Educational Attainment Generates Income Gaps

The real economic benefit from creative and innovative jobs that require a high level of educational attainment is reflected not only in great job opportunities and better choices of working conditions, but also in the wages and benefits received by professionals for their operations and services. A general picture of American workers' increasing earnings was covered in Section 8-1. This section takes a close look at the gaps or discrepancies of earnings among workers with different levels of education.

Although the average nominal earnings have increased steadily, the pace of this growth for American workers with different educational levels is substantially different. In Table 9-2 we present the national average of annual earnings of American workers who were aged 18 years old and above by educational attainment over the time period of 1975 though 1999.

Table 9-2: Annual Earnings of American Workers (U.S. dollars)
(1975-1999)

| Year | Non high school graduate | High school graduate | Some college less than bachelor's degree | Bachelor's degree | Advanced degrees |
|---|---|---|---|---|---|
| 1975 | 6,198 | 7,843 | 8,388 | 12,332 | 16,725 |
| 1980 | 8,845 | 11,314 | 12,409 | 18,075 | 23,308 |
| 1985 | 10,726 | 14,457 | 16,349 | 24,877 | 32,909 |
| 1990 | 12,582 | 17,820 | 20,694 | 31,112 | 41,458 |
| 1995 | 14,013 | 21,431 | 23,862 | 36,980 | 56,667 |
| 1996 | 15,011 | 22,154 | 25,181 | 38,112 | 61,317 |
| 1997 | 16,124 | 22,895 | 26,235 | 40,478 | 63,229 |
| 1998 | 16,053 | 23,594 | 27,566 | 43,782 | 63,473 |
| 1999 | 16,121 | 24,572 | 28,403 | 45,678 | 67,687 |
| Increased by | 260% | 313% | 339% | 370% | 405% |

In these years the annual earnings of American workers increased in every category of educational attainment. In terms of the percentage change from 1975 to 1999, the largest rise was for those professionals with advanced degrees (405% in 1975–1999), while those workers who had not completed their high school education and low-skilled manual workers received the smallest increase, as shown in the bottom row of Table 9-2.

In order to make an easier comparison we have normalized annual earnings by dividing them by the corresponding numbers in 1975 and multiplying the result by 100. This procedure generates earning index numbers for the five categories of workers over the time period of 1975 to 1999. Earning discrepancies can be easily observed from Figure 9-1, in which we draw earning index curves for the five categories of educational attainment. The slope of each curve represents the growth rate of annual nominal earnings.

From Figure 9-1 one can see that there was little difference in the growth of earnings among all of the five categories during years of 1975–1981. The index curve of the non-high school graduate group has moved away from the other four index curves since 1982 and was always below the other groups. One can also observe that a similar situation occurred in 1985 to the index curve of high school graduates, which has moved away from the other three curves since 1985. In 1991 the top three index curves began to separate; the index curve of the advanced-degree group sped up with a steeper slope, and the other two fell behind. During two time periods, 1989–1993 and 1997–1999, the index curve of the non-high-school group was flat, which indicates that the annual earnings of this group were most likely unchanged.

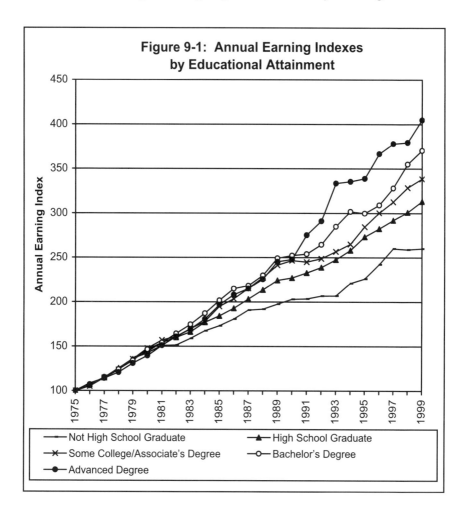

If one views the change in earnings as an indicator of an economy's demand for human capital, Figure 9-1 clearly shows that after 1981 U.S. industries began to differentiate their salary increases to workers by their educational levels. Workers with less than a high school degree received a lower proportional increase or no increase at all in their salaries, while workers with high levels of education saw their salaries and wages growing faster than the national average. Discrepancies in earnings of American workers continued to grow after 1981 and accelerated in 1995, which indicates an increasing demand for well-educated professionals in the creative and innovative class and less of a demand for non-high school graduates or low-skilled people in the working class by the U.S. economy and society.

Revolutionary technology innovations have upgraded American corporations' production procedures and operational processes, and the sector structure change has reduced U.S. manufacturing and increased the groups that develop and deliver services. This economic transition requires a well-educated workforce with professional knowledge, a high level of technical skill and competence that cannot be acquired through high school or even a college education.

Many labor-intensive factories, which traditionally produce consumer staple goods, have been relocated to third world countries, where wages of low-skilled workers are only a small fraction of American workers' at the same skill level. In fact, American corporations' strategy of building and integrating their global production system accelerated the U.S. economic transformation by further reducing the domestic goods-producing sector. Facing the intensified competitive pressure in U.S. job markets, labor unions of the working class have vigorously protested U.S. multinational companies' practice of exporting U.S. workers' jobs to foreign countries.

## A Summary of Part Three

Part Three of this volume has examined the transformation of the U.S. population by emphasizing some demographic issues related to the U.S. economy. The main conclusions from this analysis follow.

The U.S. population has been in a post-transitional process, characterized by both a low fertility rate and low mortality rate, as well as prolonged life expectancy. Unlike Japan and Western European nations, the United States is not expected to have a population decline in this century. Instead, the U.S. population is projected to continue to grow at a moderate and declining pace from 275 million people in 2000 to 404 million by 2050 and to 571 million by 2100.

The steadily increasing U.S. population provides the U.S. economy with a growing pool of labor to ensure sustainable economic growth. In order to raise the standard of living for that increasing number of Americans, the U.S. economy must grow faster than the population does. This requires a sustainable growth for the U.S. economy in order to produce increasing amounts of goods and services as well as to generate new job opportunities.

Under the condition of proper political and economic policies, the U.S. economy and U.S. population could support each other and reach the common goal of raising the standard of living for the majority of Americans for many years to come. Because of its demographic strength and economic power, the United States is expected to continue playing the most important role in global affairs and to maintain its leadership of the world in the future.

Diversity and mobility have been trademarks of the U.S. population, which are associated with changing political power and the economic strength of racial and ethnic groups as well as geographic regions in the United States. The White group saw its population share decline from about 90% of the total U.S. population in 1930 to 74% in 2000, and it will probably fall to 60% in 2050. The Black group, however, saw its population share rise, from 9.7% in 1930 to 11.6% in 2000, and it will probably grow to 12.4% by 2050. The Hispanic population in the United States has become the fastest growing minority group, with its population share increasing from 6.1% in 1980 to 10.1% in 2000, and will probably reach 12% by 2050. The Asian and Pacific Islanders group also saw its population share rise, from 1.6% in 1980 to 3.7% in 2000, and it will probably reach 7.0% by 2050.

The rising population shares of all the minority groups indicate that the minority populations have expanded at a faster pace than the total U.S. population. In the near future more and more workers, consumers, and voters are expected to be in racial groups other than the White group. The increasing minority population in the United States has created diversification in traditions and cultures and increased the probability of sharing economic wealth and political power by Whites, Blacks, Hispanics, and other minorities.

During the course of development in the last two hundred years, immigrants have made great contributions to the United States. Currently the net international migration accounts for nearly one third of yearly increases in the total U.S. population. Immigrants have brought into this country some special skills and competence at the high end of intellectual quality as well as unskilled physical labor at the low end. Policies of dealing with broad immigration issues become more important than ever before, and international migration should be viewed as a special buffer, an additional advantage to the United States, to balance population expansion, economic growth and environmental protection.

The educational attainment of the American adult population has improved significantly over time. In 2000, of 175.23 million American adults, 25.6% had completed four years of college or held advanced degrees, 58.5% were high school graduates, and 15.9% had not completed high school. The educational attainment varies among racial and ethnic groups as well as geographic regions and divisions.

The labor participation rates, unemployment rates, and personal income are unevenly distributed over different levels of educational attainment. In 2000, the labor participation rate was 80.4% for those people with college or advanced degrees, and 43.0% for those people who did not complete a high school education. The unemployment rate was only 1.6% for college graduates and advanced degree holders, but was 6.4% for non-high-school graduates. Our analysis has shown that improving educational levels could enlarge the U.S. labor force by nearly 10%, representing a significant relief to the tightness of the U.S. labor market. Raising the educational attainment of American workers would reduce inequality of income distribution and improve the economic status of American families.

The sector structure change in the U.S. economy has caused the decline of the working class and the rise of the creative and innovative class, which is expected to have far-reaching effects on the U.S. economy and society in the 21st century. Now, Americans have a great opportunity to promote themselves to high-paid jobs in the growing services industries through formal education and continuing education. They also face a great risk of being left behind in the on-going economic transition due to increasingly intensified domestic and international competition in the labor market. Low-skilled workers will be the losers, and highly specialized professionals or knowledge workers will be the winners in the next economy and society. Americans will not win the global economic competition by bringing back the manual jobs that have been shipped to the less-developed nations, but will win by turning low-skilled U.S. workers and the young into professionals and specialists through education and continuing education and training. This is an astonishing challenge to individuals, corporations, institutions, organizations, communities and governments in the United States for the 21st century.

All in all, we have shown a positive correlation between economic growth and the population expansion in the United States. The continuously moderate total fertility rate, combined with net international migration, allows America to avoid a diminishing population size and to postpone the aging process of the U.S. population. These underlying demographic characteristics provide a solid foundation for a sustainable economic growth for many years to come, as long as policy makers recognize the unique nature of the U.S. demographic transformation and take advantage of it.

# THE TRANSFORMATION OF THE SECTOR STRUCTURE OF THE U.S. ECONOMY

## PART FOUR

## THE TRANSFORMATION OF THE SECTOR STRUCTURE OF THE U.S. ECONOMY

# Chapter 10

## The Changing Aggregate Demand of the U.S. Economy

The first side of the U.S. economy to be examined is the side of aggregate demand, which is defined as the total amount that all consumers, businesses, government agencies, and foreigners want to spend on all U.S. final goods and services. The aggregate demand includes four components: consumer expenditure, investment, government expenditure, and net exports. The sum of these four components is equal to Gross Domestic Products, GDP. Hence, when aggregate demand grows rapidly, the economy booms; when aggregate demand stagnates, a recession is likely to follow.

Figure 10-1 presents percentage shares of four components of aggregate demand accounting of the U.S. GDP from 1946 through 2000. Consumption clearly took a lion's share in the U.S. nominal GDP. There is an obvious ascending trend in the consumption share over the time period from 1967 through 2000, with the share rising from 61.0% to 68.2%. The growth rate of the GDP is a weighted sum of the four component-growth rates, and the GDP share of each component determines the contribution of that component's growth to the economy's growth rate. As the consumption share has grown as high as 67% on average from 1990 through 2000, one can roughly say that about 67% of GDP growth of the U.S. economy has come from the increasing consumers' expenditure.

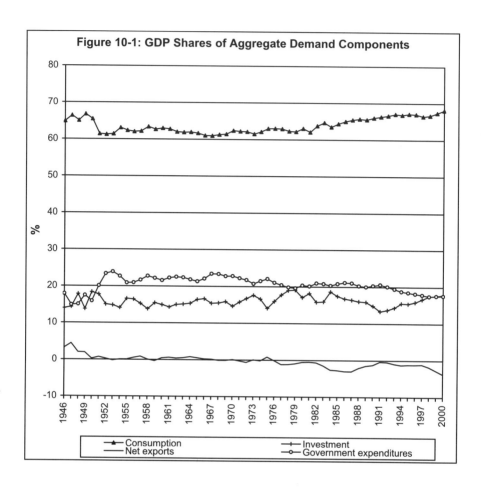

Figure 10-1: GDP Shares of Aggregate Demand Components

## 10-1  Consumption and Saving

Consumer expenditure, symbolized by the letter C, is the total amount spent by consumers on goods and services, excluding purchases of new homes (included in the investment component). Consumption is a function of total disposable income (defined as GDP minus taxes and plus transfer payment from government) and other variables of the economy.

Statistics indicate that for each dollar increase in consumers' disposable income an additional $0.9 consumer spending is stimulated. One important factor affecting consumption is consumers' wealth, which is an additional source of purchasing power added to their disposable income. A good deal of consumer wealth is held in the forms of savings accounts, government bonds, corporate bonds, mutual funds, and equity shares in stock markets. As we will discuss in Part Five of this book, the dramatic growth of mutual funds has helped to spread the ownership of equities across the country. The stock markets' unprecedented surge in the 1990s had greatly raised the wealth of ordinary Americans, while the bear stock market of 2000–2001 wiped out trillions of dollars worth of capital assets.

Increasing income and surging wealth resulted in higher consumer confidence and the rapid growth of consumption, the chief source of a strong demand that powered the prolonged expansion of the U.S. economy in the 1990s. Conversely, the massive layoffs by U.S. technology companies and financial firms in 2000 and 2001 reduced American workers' income and their expectations of future income. Combined with capital losses in U.S. stock markets, the income effect began to erode American consumers' confidence and reduce the growth rate of consumption component of aggregate demand, which contributed to the declining growth rate of GDP in 2000 and 2001. The value of personal consumption measured by current dollars and the real growth rate of personal consumption (growth rate of personal consumption minus CPI inflation rate) are depicted in Figure 10-2.

Personal consumption was about $1.763 trillion in 1980, $3.832 trillion in 1990 and $6.738 trillion in 2000, increasing 3.8 fold in the last twenty years. The average annual growth rate of real consumption was about 3.3% during the time period of 1948–2000. In the 1960s, the average real consumption growth rate was 4.3% per year, compared with 3.9% in the 1950s, 3.1%, 2.9%, and 2.7% in the 1970s, 1980s, and 1990s respectively. In the three-year period, 1998–2000, personal consumption grew even faster, at 4.4% per year. Figure 10-2 indicates an ascending trend in the growth rate of real consumption during the 1990s, and large fluctuations in the previous decades.

Continuously increasing personal consumption has resulted in decreasing personal savings for the 1990s as shown in Figure 10-3.

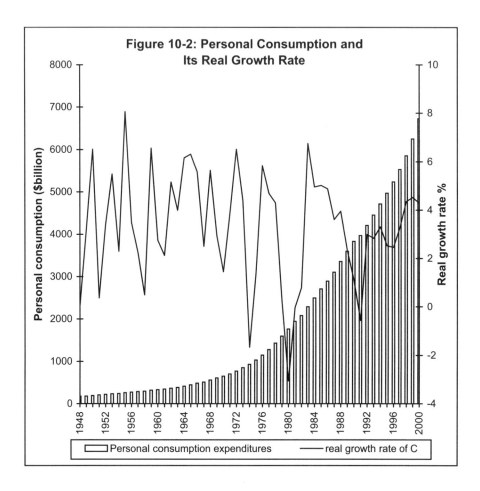

Figure 10-2: Personal Consumption and Its Real Growth Rate

The most useful measure of the personal saving rate is defined as the ratio of personal saving to disposable personal income based on the National Income and Product Accounts (NIPA). Personal income includes wage and salary income, net proprietors' income, transfer payments less social insurance, income from interest and dividends, and net rental income. Disposable income is defined as personal income less tax and non-tax payment to governments. Personal saving is the difference between personal disposable income and personal outlays, 97% of which consists of personal consumption expenditures. Hence, increases in personal consumption lead to decreases in the personal saving rate.

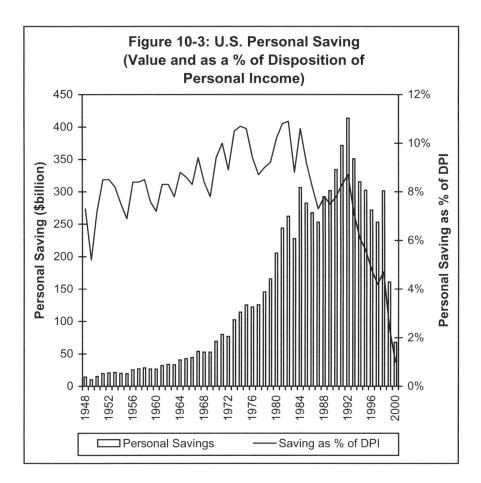

Figure 10-3: U.S. Personal Saving (Value and as a % of Disposition of Personal Income)

In constructing the NIPA, however, capital gains and losses from financial assets are excluded from personal income such that the volatility in the stock market would not show up as changes in personal income as well as the personal saving rate. The NIPA also treats personal expenditures on education and training as consumption, which may overstate the consumption component of the national GDP and understate the personal saving rate.

From Figure 10-3 one can see a gradually ascending trend in the personal saving rate before 1984 and a sharply declining trend afterwards. During the time period of 1948–1984, the personal saving rate increased from 5.2% in 1949 to 10.6% in 1984, and its high level occurred in 1973–1975 (10.5%–

10.7%) and 1981–1982 (10.8% and 10.9%), when the U.S. economy was in the short-lived recessions, people spent less and saved more for an uncertain future. The personal saving rate reduced to 7.3% in 1987 and rebounded to 8.7% in 1992 when personal savings in the United States reached a record high of $413.7 billion. Since 1992, both the value and the rate of personal savings have declined dramatically, reaching $67.7 billion and only 1% of disposable income in 2000.

The exceptionally low personal saving rate in recent years is associated with the consumption boom in the 1990s. Economists provide three reasons to explain American households' changing consumption behavior. One involves the "wealth effect," in which increases in the value of assets stimulate consumption. The soaring stock market in the 1990s boosted consumers' spending and resulted in a steep fall of the personal saving rate. Even though the measures of personal income and saving do not include capital gains and losses, increasing households' net wealth from rising prices of financial assets and real estate raised consumers' confidence and contributed to the boom of consumption and the fall of personal saving.

The second reason for the sharp decline in the saving rate is related to rises in labor productivity, which we examined in Chapter 3 of this book. In general, higher labor productivity always results in higher real wage and salary for employees. With continuously increasing labor productivity, workers could expect their future permanent income to rise that may reduce the need for additional savings out of present income.

The third explanation is that financial innovations, which we will discuss later in Chapter 12, has relaxed liquidity constraints to Americans' access to the credit markets. The large increase in consumer credit has stimulated the consumption boom for the 1990s.

Many people worry about the very low level of the personal saving rate, compared either to U.S. historical experience or to many other industrialized countries. But some economists argue that

> It may also be the case that a lower personal saving rate will be a feature of the U.S. economy for the foreseeable future. This persistence could be attributed to a relaxation of financing constraints due to financial innovation. To the extent that these factors are important, the current low personal saving rate would not represent a problem that is overhanging the U.S. economy, but it instead a manifestation of more efficient deployment of the economy's resources[1].

A great concern is that a very low personal saving rate may cause national savings to be insufficient to support the level of investment necessary to sustain the long-run economic growth. National savings (or gross savings) consist of three components: personal saving, corporate saving, and governments' saving. National savings increased from $45.6 billion in 1948 to $1.016 trillion in 1990 and $1.786 trillion in 2000. The average growth rate over the last fifty years was 7.2% per year (Figure 10-4).

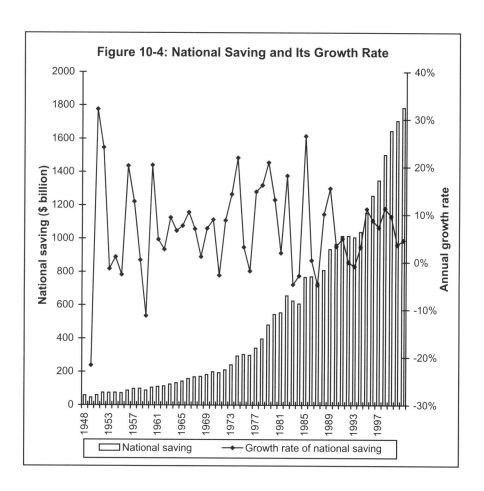

Figure 10-4: National Saving and Its Growth Rate

---

[1] Milt Marquis, What's Behind the Low U.S. Personal Saving Rate? Economic Letter, the Federal Reserve Bank of San Francisco, March 29, 2002.

In percentage terms, the national saving was about 17.0% of U.S. GDP in 1948; it increased to 22.4% in 1956, the highest share in the last five decades (Figure 10-5).

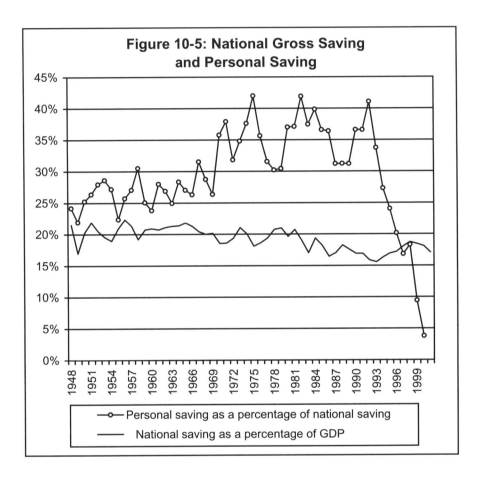

Figure 10-5: National Gross Saving and Personal Saving

—○— Personal saving as a percentage of national saving

—— National saving as a percentage of GDP

Figure 10-5 depicts the evolution of U.S. national saving as a percentage of GDP over time. A declining trend in this percentage has been observed since the early 1980s. The percentage of national saving fell to the lowest level 15.9% in 1992 and 15.6% in 1993, and rebounded to 18.8% in 1998. In 2000, national saving was about $1.786 trillion, while gross private domestic investment was $1.768 trillion and gross government investment was $318 billion (or total gross domestic investment $2.086 trillion). There was at least a $300-billion shortage of funds needed for domestic investment that was provided by foreigners. We will address this issue later in analyses of the external sector of the U.S. economy.

Figure 10-5 also displays personal savings as a percentage of the gross national savings. U.S. personal savings accounted for 22.0% of gross national savings in 1948, and increased to 42.0% in 1975 and 1982, and 41.1% in 1992. Since 1993 the share of personal saving has declined dramatically, falling from 33.8% in 1993 to 9.4% in 1999 and 3.8% in 2000. Figure 10-5 clearly indicates a radical shift in the aggregate demand of the U.S. economy in the 1990s: Americans' disposable personal income has literally gone for paying consumption expenditures, while corporations and governments as well as foreigners have to be responsible for the domestic investment in the United States.

Changes have taken place not only in the GDP share of consumption but also in the composition of consumers' spending as well. Consumers' expenditure is divided into three categories: spending on durable goods, spending on non-durable goods, and spending on services. The corresponding GDP shares for those categories are displayed in Figure 10-6.

Historical data indicates that the GDP share of durable goods consumed in the United States remained fairly stable over the last 50 years at about 8.5%. When the GDP grows, a person's disposable income rises, and spending on durable goods increases proportionally, resulting in the nearly constant GDP share. Because a family or an individual can only have so many cars, washing machines, and other durable goods, the demand for those big-ticket items seems to be contained, even if people's income and wealth rises substantially.

The GDP share of consumers' expenditure on non-durable goods, such as food and clothing, has been steadily declining, from 37.2% in 1946 to 19.5% in 1998 and 20.2% in 2000. The large reduction in the GDP share of non-durable goods consumed in the United States could be related to the increasing GDP per capita and the slower population growth in the United States. Considering the affluence of average Americans with GDP per capita exceeding $11 thousand in the 1980s and $22 thousand in the 1990s, one can imagine that consumers' demand for food and clothing could be easily satisfied.

The effects that income has on consumer demand have been studied in microeconomics via the Engle curve. This is a function that relates income to the demand for each commodity at fixed prices. Several possibilities arise. One is the demand curve with unit income elasticity. This means that people will consume the same proportion of each commodity in their consumption bundle when income changes but prices are fixed. The second is that as people get more income they wish to consume more of all commodities in their consumption bundle but proportionally more of the luxury goods than of the necessary goods. Finally, as income increases people may consume fewer of certain types of goods such as necessary goods of cheap food stuff, whose consumption is increased when the income level is low. Those goods are called inferior goods, for which more income means less demand.

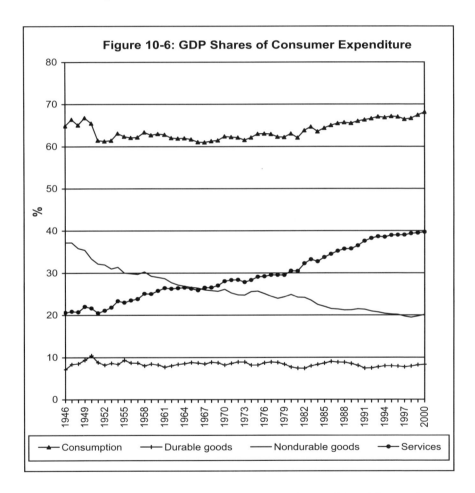

In Figure 10-6 the almost constant GDP share of durable goods consumed by Americans over the time period from 1946 through 2000 indicates that the consumption of durable goods has increased proportionally with GDP growth. The changing consumption pattern, however, indicates a shift between the share of non-durable goods and the share of services.

The three scenarios studied for individual consumer's behaviors in the theory of microeconomics may have actually happened at the aggregate level of the U.S. economy for the last fifty years. As the standard of living has risen to a high level, the aggregate demand for non-durable goods is determined primarily by the nation's population growth. The annual growth rate of the U.S. population has slowed for the last five decades, reducing from 1.8% in the 1950s to 0.93% in the 1990s. The nominal GDP, however, has grown at the annual rate of 6.7% in the 1950s and 5.6% in the 1990s, much greater rates than those of population growth. Therefore the aggregate demand for non-durable goods has grown at a slower pace than the growth rate of nominal GDP, which resulted in the gradual decline of the GDP share of non-durable goods consumed in the United States.

The GDP share of consumers' expenditure on services, such as health care, education, entertainment, and financial services, was steadily increasing from 20.6% in 1946 to 39.7% by 2000, the highest share over the last five decades. In 1946, nominal U.S. GDP reached $222 billion dollars, with $144 billion dollars in personal consumption, in which only $45.8 billion dollars spent on service consumption. In 2000, Americans created about $9.872-trillion of nominal GDP, and spent about $6.728 trillion on personal consumption, in which $3.919 trillion went to various kinds of services. This disproportionally-increased demand for services could be explained by income effects on consumers' demand (the preceding second case) and by the demographic changes in the United States.

According to the population census the number of children aged 0-14 was 42.6 million in 1950, it rose to 59.6 million in 1970. The baby boom after World War II fueled the increasing demand for medical services, education, and other social services in the 1960's and 1970's. Another significant demographic factor that raised the demand for services was the aging population. The number of people aged 65 and over in the United States was about 13 million in 1950. This number was rapidly rising to 20.7 million in 1970, 25.8 million in 1980, and 31.5 million in 1990. The estimate for 2000 is 34.5 million and the percentage of aging Americans is expected to increase continuously. In relative terms, the group of Americans aged 65 and over accounted for 8% of the total U.S. population in 1950 and for 12% in 1990-2000. Certainly the increasing proportion of aging people has created a huge demand for health care services, travel and entertainment services, financial and personal services, and the like.

The combination of increased incomes and an aging population have significantly changed consumption patterns in the United States. The largest portion of disposable income has shifted from purchasing non-durable goods to consuming services.

As discussed in Part One of this book, according to the economic growth theory elaborated by W.W. Rostow, there are five distinctive stages of economic growth in a human society: traditional society, preconditions, takeoff, drive to technological maturity, and age of high mass consumption. Similar to industrialized nations in Western Europe, the United States has already entered the fifth stage of economic growth, the age of high mass consumption.

The U.S. economy is able to produce an amount of goods that is more than enough to satisfy its whole population's demand for necessities with excess outputs spent on improving the quality of life. Income and wealth have been raised to such a high level that consumers' demand could be easily satiated for both non-durable and durable goods in the sense that more consumption on them may actually reduce consumers' satisfaction. A family can have a limited number of cars and washing machines, and can consume limited amount of food and beverage no matter how much income increases. The changing tastes of American consumers lead to the increasing demand for intangible products of the service industries.

We believe that the shifting consumption pattern from non-durable and durable goods to services in the United States represents a driving force that has transformed the sector structure of the U.S. economy. To achieve the sustainable GDP growth, demand must be balanced with supply not only at the aggregate level, but at the sectional level as well. Producers or corporations have to respond to consumers' needs and tastes accordingly in order to keep their business profitable. We will analyze the induced structure changes from the production side of the U.S. economy in Chapter 11.

## 10-2 Gross Private Investment

Gross private domestic investment includes business expenditures on new plants, machinery, and equipment plus the expenditures of households on new homes. As a component of aggregate demand, investment does not include financial investment in stock markets or in bank accounts.

Figure 10-1 showed that the GDP share of investment fluctuated in a range between 13.4% and 19.1% during the last five decades. Large fluctuations appeared in 1947–1950 and in 1973–1984. In the 1960s, the GDP share of investment stayed relatively stable at the level of 15-16%. It declined significantly from 18.7% in 1984 to 13.4% in 1991, the lowest GDP share over the last five decades. When the investment share began to rise in 1992, the U.S. economy pulled itself out of the brief recession of 1990-91. In 1994 gross private domestic investment accounted for about 15.6% of the nation's GDP; it continued rising to 17.9% in 2000.

Gross private domestic investment is divided into four categories, residential, structures, equipment, and software, and the change in business inventories (CBI). The sum of the first three categories is called fixed investment. Figure 10-7 presents GDP shares of gross investment and its four components for the years 1946 through 2000. Since 1952, changes of business inventories have been under 1.2% of the GDP, mostly with a positive sign for this fifty-year period, except for two years of 1966 and 1984 in which changes in private inventories accounted for 1.7% of GDP. This indicates that the change in business inventories accounts for a small and fairly stable share of GDP.

Residential investment, representing consumers' expenditures on new existing homes, shows large fluctuations and a declining trend in terms of its GDP share. Residential investment accounted for more than 5% of U.S. GDP almost every year before 1965. Since 1980, residential investment has accounted for less than 5% of GDP. In the recession years of 1970, 1975, 1982, and 1991, the residential investment share of the GDP dropped into the range of (3.2–3.9)%. In 1991 the residential investment share was 3.2%, the lowest in five decades. U.S. residential investment decreased from $234 billion in 1988 to $192 billion in 1991. Since 1991 residential investment has increased quickly, from $226 billion in 1992 to $425 billion in 2000, with the corresponding GDP share rising from 3.6% to 4.3%. Even though the residential investment in the United States has not increased to its historical level of above 5% of the GDP, its rapid growth during 1992-2000 has made a significant contribution to the economic expansion of the 1990s.

Nonresidential investment represents the amounts of money private firms spend on new plants (structures), machinery, equipment (PDE – producers' durable equipment), and software. One portion of nonresidential investment is business expenditure on the structure of new plants. In terms of GDP share, this portion of investment remained fairly stable around 3.7% with a minor rising trend during 1947-76. In 1976 it began to increase dramatically and hit 5.4% in 1982, the highest share in the last five decades. Since 1982, this share has consistently declined, to 4.4% in 1983-85, 3.5% in 1987-90, and 2.7% in 1994.

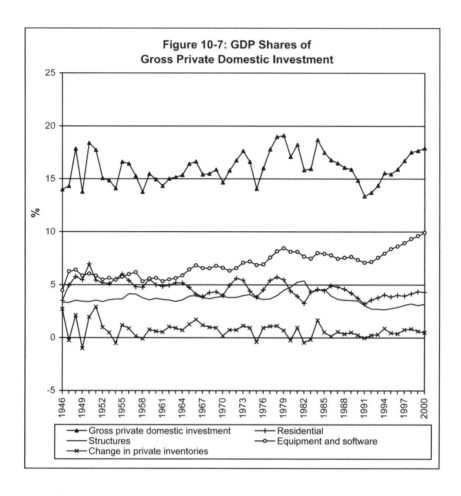

In 1982 American corporations spent about $175 billion on structure investment, which was recorded as the largest GDP share (5.4%) for the last five decades. In 1994, structure investment was approximately $187.5 billion, accounting for only 2.7% of the year's GDP. This rose to $331 billion in 2000, nearly 3.2% of year 2000's GDP. The declining share of business structure investment indicates that American corporations have built their new plants at a slower pace than the GDP growth, even in the recent remarkable economic expansion.

American corporations' investment in producers' durable equipment and software held the largest share among the four investment components over the entire five decades. Its GDP share increased from 4.5% in 1946 to 8.4%

in 1979, and then declined to 7.5% in 1983 and 7.1% in1991. The 1980s will be remembered as an era when U.S. corporations downsized and restructured, and when both the GDP shares of structure investment and equipment/ software investment slid substantially.

Pulling out from the 1991 business-cycle trough, the U.S. economy has rapidly increased its business investment. In particular, the investment in equipment and software has increased steadily since 1991, rising from $425 billion in 1991 to $980 billion in 2000. During the economic expansion of the 1990s, the producers' durable equipment/software investment share increased markedly and completed a straight nine-year increase to 9.9% in 2000.

From Figure 10-7 one can observe that in the 1990s, the GDP shares of the other three components of U.S. gross private investment were virtually flat, while the GDP share of the investment in equipment and software increased significantly, which was reflected in the steep incline in the GDP share of the gross private investment in the United States. The increased share of the investment in producers' durable equipment and software indicates that the growth rate of this investment has substantially exceeded the growth rate of GDP. In fact, the investment in producers' durable equipment and software was an important driving force for the 1990s expansion and a dragging force behind the 2001 economic slide.

To see how American corporations allocated their capital in the last three decades, we calculate the shares for four components of investment in PDE: information processing equipment and software, industrial equipment, transportation equipment, and other equipment, using total spending on producers' durable goods as a common denominator. Figure 10-8 depicts the changing paths of these shares for the four investment components.

In 1959, American corporations spent about $28.36 billion on producers' durable equipment, of which only $4.02 billion belonged to expenditures of information processing equipment such as computers and peripheral equipment, software, communication equipment, office and accounting equipment, photocopy, and related equipment. The spending on industrial equipment (fabricated metal products, engines and turbines, metalworking machinery, electrical transmission, distribution etc.) was about $8.45 billion, transportation equipment (trucks, buses, autos, aircrafts, ships and boats, and railroad equipment) accounted for about $8.27 billion, and other equipment (furniture and fixtures, tractors and agriculture machinery, construction machinery, mining and oilfield machinery, and household appliances etc.) accounting for $7.74 billion. The spending on information processing equipment and software accounted for only 14.1% of total expenditure of PDE in 1959, while the other

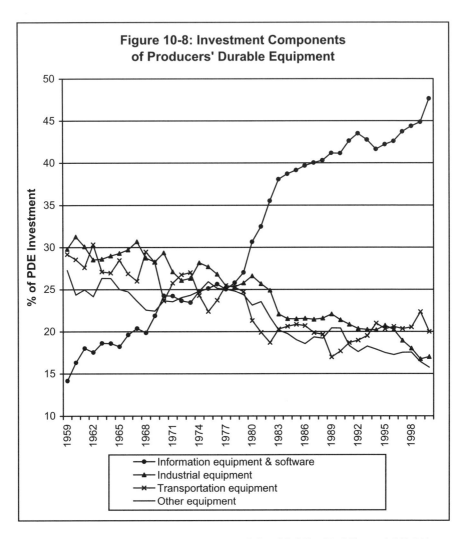

Figure 10-8: Investment Components of Producers' Durable Equipment

three investment components accounted for 29.8%, 29.2%, and 27.3% respectively in the same year.

American corporations' spending on information technology has dramatically increased, from $4.02 billion in 1959 to $466.5 billion in 2000, boosting its PDE share from 14.1% in 1959 to 47.6% in 2000. The other three investment components of the PDE rose (in terms of current dollars) to $166.7 billion, $195.9 billion and $154.3 billion respectively in 2000. Their growth paces, however, were much slower than that of investment in information technology, which resulted in the considerably declined shares, 17.0%, 20.0%, and 15.7% respectively in 2000. Figure 10-8 shows that since 1978 the share of information equipment purchase has grown beyond the other three shares of investment, indicating the great shift of American corporations' capital investment towards information technology.

Figure 10-9 depicts the PDE shares of four major investment components of information technology: computers and peripheral equipment, software, communication equipment, and instruments; all of which have shown significant share gains from 1959 through 2000.

During 1959–1989, American corporations' investment in communication equipment held the largest share in the purchases of information technology; its share had declined in the 1990s and rebounded to 12% in 2000, the highest level since 1990. The share of computers and peripheral equipment purchases showed a rapid rise during 1978–1984 from 4% to 10%. Since then it has hovered around the 10% level. Following the rise of corporations' spending on computer hardware, the investment in software has also moved forward quickly. In 1990, the PDE share of software began to exceed the other three shares; it reached 13.8% in 1993 and continued rising to 18.6% in 2000. American corporations' spending on instruments also increased, but its the pace of growth was slower than that of other three investment components in information technology, resulting in a decline of its PDE share from 5.9% in 1992 to 4.0% in 2000.

To show changes in the composition of America's private investment, we provide more detailed data for years 1978 and 2000 in Table 10-1.

In 1978, the U.S. private sector invested a total of $436 billion dollars, of which the fixed investment accounted for 94.1%, the remaining 5.9% was the change in private inventories. In 2000, gross private investments in the United States soared to $1,767.5 billion and 97.2% of them went to fixed investments. The fixed investment is divided into two categories, residential and nonresidential. Although the residential investment increased to $425.1 billion in 2000 from $131.6 billion in 1978, the percentage of residential investment in the gross private investment reduced to 24.1% from 30.2% in 1978, while the percentage of nonresidential investment increased from 63.9% of 1978 to 73.2% of 2000. The changing percentages of these two components reveal that the nonresidential investment has grown at a greater pace than that of residential investment since 1978.

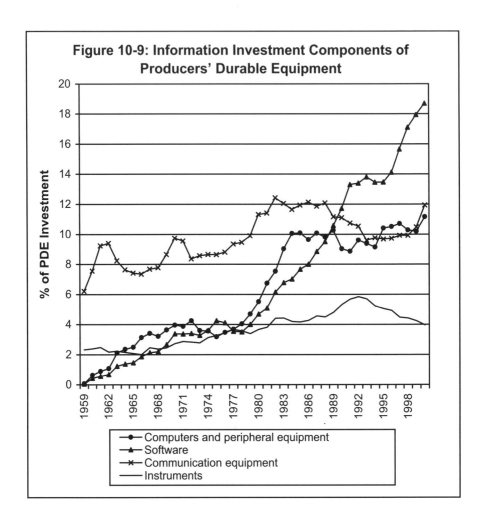

Figure 10-9: Information Investment Components of Producers' Durable Equipment

Nonresidential investment includes two components, the spending on new buildings, utilities, mining exploration, and other structures, and the purchase of producers' durable equipment (PDE). The investment on structures was about $91.4 billion in 1978 and increased to $313.6 billion in 2000. Its percentage in the gross private investment, however, reduced from 21.0% in 1978 to 17.7% in 2000. Hence the great growth in U.S. private investment has been taking place in the form of purchasing producers' durable equipment, which rose from $187.2 billion in 1978 to $979.5 billion in 2000, with the corresponding percentage rising from 42.9% to 55.4%.

| Type of Investment | 1978 | | 2000 | |
|---|---|---|---|---|
| | Amount $billion | % of Gross Private Investment | Amount $billion | % of Gross Private Investment |
| Gross Private Investment | 436.00 | 100% | 1767.50 | 100% |
| Changes in inventories | 25.80 | 5.9 | 49.40 | 2.8 |
| Fixed Investment | 410.20 | 94.1 | 1718.10 | 97.2 |
| Residential | 131.60 | 30.2 | 425.10 | 24.1 |
| Nonresidential | 278.60 | 63.9 | 1293.10 | 73.2 |
| Structures | 91.40 | 21.0 | 313.60 | 17.7 |
| **Producers' Durable Equipment (PDE)** | **187.20** | **42.9** | **979.50** | **55.4** |
| Industrial equipment | 47.43 | 10.9 | 166.72 | 9.4 |
| Transportation equipment | 47.32 | 10.9 | 195.90 | 11.1 |
| Other PDE | 46.48 | 10.7 | 154.32 | 8.7 |
| **Information Processing & software** | **48.33** | **11.1** | **466.54** | **26.4** |
| Computers & Peripheral | 7.56 | 1.7 | 109.29 | 6.2 |
| Software | 6.57 | 1.5 | 183.10 | 10.4 |
| Communication equipment | 17.71 | 4.1 | 116.84 | 6.6 |
| Instruments | 6.71 | 1.5 | 38.82 | 2.2 |
| Photocopy & related | 5.23 | 1.2 | 11.05 | 0.6 |
| Office & Accounting | 4.54 | 1.0 | 7.44 | 0.4 |

Table 10-1: Private Domestic Investment (1978 and 2000)

From Table 10-1 one can observe that the distribution of expenditures on the PDE was almost distributed evenly in 1978 among its four categories: industrial equipment, transportation equipment, other PDE, and information processing and software. Each category accounted for about $46 - $48 billion. In 2000, however, American corporations' expenditures on information processing and software reached $466.5 billion, which was close to the sum of expenditures for the other three categories of the PDE investment. This clearly indicates American corporations' enthusiasm for investing in information technologies.

We provide distribution of the investment on information processing and software over its six components in Table 10-1: computers and peripheral equipment, software, communication equipment, instruments, photocopy and related equipment, and office and accounting equipment. American corporations' spending on communication equipment was about $17.71 billion in

1978; it increased to $116.8 billion in 2000 and its percentage also increased from 4.1% in 1978 to 6.6% in 2000.

However, the largest amount of investment in information technology went to expenditures on software in 2000, about $183.1 billion, which increased from only $6.57 billion in 1978. The corresponding percentage of software spending surged from 1.5% of gross private investment in 1978 to 10.4% in 2000. American corporations' spending on computer hardware also increased greatly from $7.56 billion (or 1.7% of gross private investment) in 1978 to $109.3 billion (or 6.2%) in 2000. The spending on photocopy, office, and accounting equipment grew at a relatively slow pace and their percentages declined substantially.

From the shifting investment pattern expressed in Figures 10-6, 10-7, 10-8, 10-9, and Table 10-1 one can recognize that smart American corporations have rapidly developed new kinds of assets through investment in the information technology. Companies begin to understand that in the information age and in the on-line world, the structure of corporations' assets must be changed accordingly. The conventional tangible assets that can be accumulated through investment in new building, utility, equipment, and machinery may have partially lost their value in the innovative e-commerce environment, while a new breed of competitive and knowledge-based assets has emerged.

The concept of knowledge as a type of asset needs to be understood. In a broad sense an asset is a stock from which a number of services are expected to flow. Knowledge assets are stocks of knowledge from which various services and benefits can be drawn and can be passed from one person to another, and from one generation to another. Many challenges lie ahead in the so-called information age of economic growth. How to create knowledge assets through investment? How to educate people with existing knowledge and how to train workers with the proper skills and competences? How to embed knowledge assets into tangible and physical assets in order to enhance productivity, efficiency, and competitiveness in the global market? We expect many industries and corporations will make smart investments in knowledge creating and knowledge embedding in order to secure their competitive advantages in the changing global market.

In the 1990s, American corporations dramatically increased their investment in information technologies to improve productivity and efficiency. The enormous private investment in computer hardware and software and in telecommunications equipment fueled the unprecedented economic expansion in the 1990s. However, the record sales of PCs, servers, routers, storage equipment, cell phones, etc. that repeated year after year in the 1990s disappeared suddenly in 2000 and 2001. Instead, revenues of American high tech companies have declined at a double-digit rate quarter after quarter in 2000 and 2001. A lot of Internet companies, which used to be the buyers of hardware, software, and Internet equipment, have gone out of business; and hundreds of thousands of jobs and billions of dollars in capital spending went with them.

Corporate spending on IT rapidly declined, due to massive layoffs and bankruptcies of many Internet companies. Staggering 415,000 jobs were lost in October 2001, the largest amount for any single month since May 1980. It is unlikely that those companies firing workers and staff members will be spending as much on new computers, software, and telecommunications equipment before their business and profits pick up significantly. U.S. technology companies' excess capacity and weak end-market demand continued after the bust of the Internet industry, simply because they have too many products but not enough market to absorb them. Corporations' investment in information technologies continues to decline as never before, and the negative economic consequences are believed to be a major source leading to the economic recession of 2001. Information technologies' effect on economic fluctuations through business cycles is viewed as an emerging challenge to the U.S. economy at the new stage of economic growth.

## 10-3 Government Spending and National Debt

The third component of aggregate demand is government spending, symbolized by the letter G in economics books, which represents the amount of goods and services purchased by all levels of government for purposes of consumption and investment. To pay its employees and to pay for armies, science and research, education, national infrastructure, etc., government uses a part of national product that is included in the aggregate demand. Government also spends a lot of money on transfer payments either to individuals or to other levels of government. But that kind of government spending is not included in the aggregate demand, because transfer payments represent the shuffling of purchasing power rather than creating real economic resources for the whole economy.

As Figure 10-10 shows, government consumption and investment accounted for only 15-17% of GDP in 1946-50. This GDP share popped up above 23% after 1951 due to the Korean War. In the cold-war period, the U.S. government's spending remained around 22% of the GDP. In 1975 the GDP share of the government's consumption and investment began to drop below the 22% mark. This share remained at about 20% during the 1980s, declining in the 1990s, and remained at 17.6% in 1999 and 2000. Government consumption and investment has grown more slowly than the economy as a whole since 1967, particularly after 1991, resulting in the decline of the governments' share in the aggregate demand.

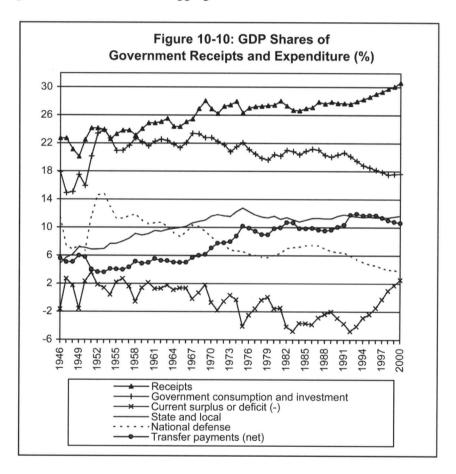

Figure 10-10: GDP Shares of Government Receipts and Expenditure (%)

Government consumption and investment is divided into federal spending and state and local government spending. The main portion of federal spending is for national defense, which jumped to 14.7% of GDP in 1952 and

1953, and since then decreased continuously in terms of GDP share. Federal spending on national defense accounted for 3.8% of the GDP in 2000, about $375.4 billion dollars. This was still less than the record defense spending of $384.5 billion in 1991. The GDP share of spending by state and local governments increased from 4.9% in 1946 to 12.8% in 1975, decreased slightly in the second half of the 1970s, and flattened out around 11.5% in the 1980s and 1990s. The spending by state and local governments reached $1,150.8 billion in 2000, or 11.7% of GDP. This was nearly as twice as much as the consumption and investment made by the Federal government, about $590.2 billion in the same year.

Balance of government outlays and receipts bears important economic consequences for growth and price stability. Outlays include government consumption and investment (G), and transfer payments. Receipts include individual income taxes, corporation's income taxes, Social Security contributions, excise taxes, and customs duties and fees. Using GDP as a common denominator, we compute shares of government receipts, federal surplus or deficit, and transfer payments, and display them in Figure 10-10. The GDP share of receipts rose from 22.70% in 1946 to 28.0% in 1969, stayed around 27.5% during the 1970s and 1980s, and increased to 30.6% in 2000.

It is noteworthy from Figure 10-10 that during 1946 - 1969, there were only four years, 1946, 1949, 1958, and 1967, in which the federal government was running a deficit; it was less than $4 billion of current dollars each year. Since 1970, however, the federal deficit has become overwhelming; it increased from $7.3 billion in 1970 to $169.1 billion (or 4.8% of GDP) in 1983, and declined to $110.7 billion (or 2% of GDP) in 1989, and then resurged to $302.5 billion (or 4.8% of GDP) in 1992. Since 1992 the federal deficit has decreased continuously due to the prolonged economic growth in the 1990s that raised the governments' receipts substantially.

The government receipts reached $3,024 billion of current dollars in 2000, about 30.6% of GDP. Combined with slowly growing government spending and transfer payments in the last decade of the twentieth century, the increasing receipts helped to reduce government deficits and to turn deficits into surpluses. In 1997 the federal deficit was reduced to $22.3 billion (or 0.27% of GDP). In the following year, 1998, there was a federal surplus of $84.5 billion for the first time in 19 years (1979 was the last year in which a $1.7 billion surplus was recorded). In the years 1999 and 2000, the federal surplus rose to $161.3 billion and $251.4 billion, or 1.7% and 2.6% of GDP respectively.

A declining federal deficit has some favorable economic consequences to private industries and to consumers in general. For example, a reduction in the federal government's deficit implies less borrowing from the public sector via the issuance of securities, which decreases supplies in the bond market and supports higher prices for bonds. Higher bond prices induce lower interest rates and lower borrowing costs for corporations that raise capital in financial markets.

In the meantime, lower interest rates lead to higher corporation profits and higher stock prices, which boost the value of Americans' financial assets. The increasing wealth of average Americans fortifies consumers' confidence and increases their spending on consumer goods and services, which generates robust economic growth. In both economic theory and real life, those economic variables, such as interest rates, stock prices, consumer spending, and economic growth, are always correlated. In terms of lowing federal deficit, the U.S. government was quite cooperative with the private sector and made its contributions to the excellent performance of the U.S. economy in the 1990s.

After ten years of extraordinary growth, the U.S. economy eventually began to slow down in 2000 and declined in 2001 Q3. This time, the cumulated federal surpluses in previous three years led a great confidence in the Bush Administration. This administration promoted its economic stimulus package of $60-$75 billion at the early beginning of the pending recession. Compared with the economic recession of 1990–1991 when the federal deficit was running as high as $170 billion and $223 billion, the expected economic recession of 2001 will receive favorable treatments from fiscal and monetary policies. This will help to alleviate the pains caused by the plunging economy and rising unemployment as well as to expedite an economic recovery in the United States and the world.

A few years of improvement in government deficit, however, do not change much the picture of U.S. national debt. The national debt is the total amount of money owed by the government, while the federal budget deficit is the yearly amount by which federal government's spending exceeds its revenue. Adding up all the deficits and surpluses for the past nearly two hundred years yields the current national debt of the United States as depicted in Figure 10-11[2].

The U.S. national debt was about $257 billion in 1950, which significantly increased from its level in 1940 due to the government deficits during World

---

[2] The original data of U.S. national debt come from *The Public Debt on Line*, of U.S. Department of the Treasury: www.publicdebt.treas.gov.

War II. Since 1945 the U.S. national debt had remained nearly constant for three decades and began to increase slowly in the middle of the 1970s because of high inflation in the 1970s and early 1980s. From 1983 on, however, the national debt has been rocketing upwards, continuing to grow year to year. The debt was $1.028 trillion in 1981; it was the first time in U.S. history the national debt surpassed the $1 trillion mark. It doubled in the next five years and reached $2.125 trillion in 1986. The debt doubled again and became $4.411 trillion in 1993. In 1996, U.S. national debt exceeded $5 trillion mark the first time in the U.S. history and reached $5.674 trillion in 2000. The rapid increases in U.S. national debt in the 1980s and 1990s reflects the growing government deficits that added to the cumulated national debt year after year. The federal surpluses in 1999 and 2000 did slow the pace of rising national debt, but had not yet reduced the national debt. The debt was recorded as $5.526 trillion in 1998, $5.656 trillion in 1999, and $5.674 trillion in 2000, still increasing slowly.

The increasing national debt is a heavy burden to the U.S. economy and American people. The government budget deficits require the Treasury to borrow money to raise cash needed to keep the government operating. It borrows money by selling Treasury securities such as T-bills, notes, bonds, and saving bonds to the public. It is American individuals and foreigners, corporations, state or local governments, foreign governments, and other entities outside of the United States that hold U.S. national debts. The U.S. federal government has to pay interests on all the outstanding debts. The U.S. Treasury Department spent $360 billion on interest payments for national debts in 2001, compared to expenditures of $14 billion on NASA, of $32 billion on education, and of $51 billion on the Department of Transportation in the same year[3]. A huge amount of taxpayers' money has to be spent on interest payment for serving the national debts. Figure 10-12 depicts U.S. national debts in terms of the GDP share and U.S. national debts per capita.

Measured by U.S. GDP, the U.S. national debt was 87.5% of GDP in 1950, and reduced to 32.8% in 1974. This decrease in its GDP share was due to the expansion of the U.S. economy that increased GDP fivefold in the time period of 1950–1974 when the national debt increased only 92%. The GDP share of national debt rose rapidly in the 1980s, from 32.9% in 1981 to 61% in 1991, and reached a recent high level of 67.2% in 1995. The expeditious growth of the U.S. economy in the second half of the 1990s, combined with the declined federal deficits, reduced the GDP share of national debt to 57.5% in 2000.

---

[3] National Debt Awareness Center, July 2002, or at www.federalbudget.com.

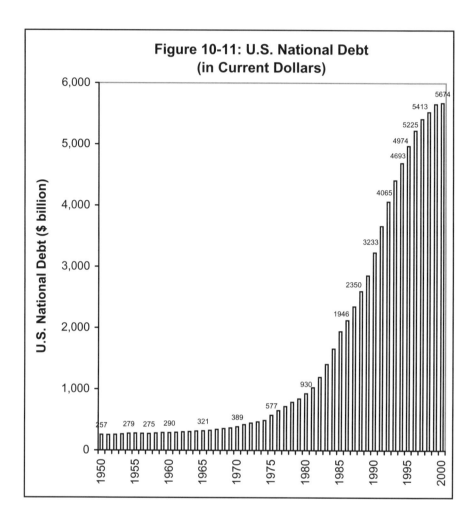

Figure 10-11: U.S. National Debt (in Current Dollars)

Eventually the U.S. national debt has to be paid off by American taxpayers. In terms of each citizen's share, the U.S. national debt was $1,690 per capita in 1950 and remained nearly flat in the 1950s and 1960s. It rose to $1,897 in 1970 and doubled to $4,094 in 1980. Since 1980 the growth of national debt per capita has sped up. It increased to $8,178 in 1985, $10,644 in 1988, $20,733 in 1999, and then declined slightly to $20,610 in 2000.

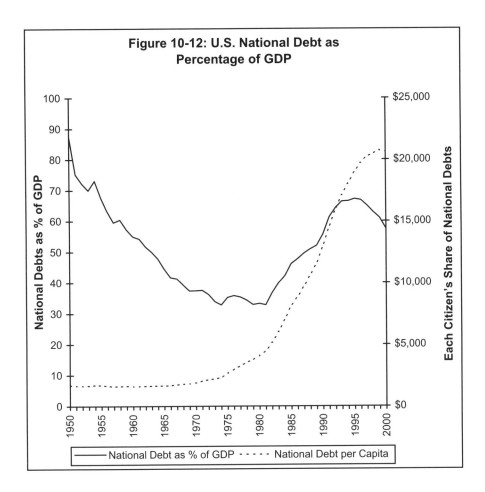

Figure 10-12: U.S. National Debt as Percentage of GDP

The budget deficit was a major concern in the U.S. economic transformation over the 1980s and 1990s. A hope of overturning the government deficit into a surplus through economic growth and constrained government expenditure emerged shortly in 1999 and 2000. However, the slowing U.S. economy and increasing government spending on national defense and homeland security after the tragedy of September 11, 2001, certainly diminishes any near-term expectation of gaining budget surpluses. Even if the government's budget is balanced or surpluses occur, to reduce the existing huge amount of national debt remains a great challenge to the U.S. economy for many years to come.

## 10-4  Exports and Imports

The final component of aggregate demand is net exports, symbolized by EX-IM. This component measures the difference between exports (EX) and imports (IM), which represent the external sector of the U.S. economy.

Foreigners beyond U.S. borders purchase American goods and services, such as aircraft, cars, computers, wheat, apple, and banking services. These purchases must be added into the aggregate demand for U.S. products and services. At the same time, American consumers spend their money on Japanese cars, Malaysian TV sets, Korean memory chips, Chinese textiles, and so on. Those goods are produced outside of U.S. borders, but the amounts of purchases are already included in three components of aggregate demand —consumption, gross private investment, and government spending. Therefore, U.S. imports from abroad must be subtracted from aggregate demand. Hence, the final component EX-IM is introduced into aggregate demand to take care of these international transactions.

Figure 10-13 presents the GDP shares of U.S. total imports, exports and net exports, and GDP shares of exports of services and imports of services over the time period from 1946 through 2000. In 1947 total exports accounted for 7.7% of U.S. GDP of the year, which was the highest share in the following twenty-seven years (1947–1973), while the GDP share of total imports was only 3.2% in 1947. The net exports were about $10.8 billion in surplus in 1947, accounting for 4.5% of GDP. Since then there has not been a single year that U.S. trade surplus exceeded the $10.8 billion mark that was established more than fifty years ago.

Nevertheless, international trade developed rapidly and was essentially balanced in 1950–1976 with a small surplus in some years and a small deficit in other years. Figure 10-13 indicates that U.S. trade with foreign countries really picked up after 1973 with shares of both exports and imports climbing above 8% in 1974 and 10% in 1980. A temporary setback pushed the export share down to 7.2% in 1985–1986, while the import share still remained around 10%. This created serious deficits in U.S. foreign trade, $132 billion in 1986, and $142 billion in 1987, about 3% of the GDP. The export share bounced from its low of 1984–1985 to above 10% in 1991, and both export and import shares have continued to rise since then. Meanwhile, the U.S. trade-deficit decreased to $20.7 billion in 1991, about 0.35% of the GDP.

Figure 10-13: GDP Shares of Imports and Exports (%)

In the 1990s, expanded economic growth and unprecedented prosperity in the United States created an enormous demand for imported goods and services, while the less impressive performance of European economies and the sluggish economy of Japan slowed the demand for American goods and services abroad. In 1997 and 1998 in particular, many economies in Asia, South America, and Russia were plagued with financial disasters that caused a wave of currency devaluation in many U.S. trading partner countries around the world. The strong dollar has made American goods more expensive and harder to sell in foreign markets, whereas imported foreign goods have become cheaper and flood U.S. markets.

U.S. imports from abroad surged from $664.6 billion in 1992 to $1,467 billion in 2000, about 14.9% of the GDP. The momentum of the rising export share in 1987–1997 was disrupted in 1998 and 1999, with the share dropping from 11.6% in 1997 to 10.7% in 1999. U.S. exports increased from $636.8 billion in 1992 to $1,103 billion in 2000, about 11.2% of GDP. Consequently, the trade deficit resurged from $27.9 billion in 1992 to $364 billion in 2000, about 3.7% of GDP, which was the all-time high trade deficit in terms of both the dollar value and the GDP share.

A favorable development in U.S. international trade has taken place in the service sector. U.S. exports of services accounted for only 1.0% of GDP in 1946; this rose to 3.2% of the GDP in 2000. U.S. imports of services increased in tandem with service exports from 0.9% to 2.3% of GDP in the same time period. The type of services for U.S. foreign trade has changed considerably.

In 1965 the dollar-amount of U.S. service exports was $8.8 billion, of which about 2.5 billion (or 28% of the total service exports) fell into the category of transfers under U.S. military agency sales contracts. Similarly, of the $9.1-billion U.S. imports of services in 1965 $2.95 billion (or 32%) fit into the category of direct defense expenditure. In 1984, however, military-related service exports reduced to 14% of the total U.S. service exports, and the counterpart of imports declined to 18%. In 1997, the total U.S. service-exports rose to $258 billion, of which only 7% (about $18 billion) was military-related, and total U.S. service imports rose to $170 billion, of which only 6.7% (about $11 billion) was direct defense purchasing.

These evidences reveal that U.S. international trade of services has surged in terms of not only the total value, but also the value of civilian services, which reflects a significant shift of contents from the military to civilians. The changing pattern of U.S. international trade on services is illustrated in Table 10-2, where S-EX and S-IM denote the total U.S. exports and imports of services respectively, and EX and IM denote the total U.S. exports and imports of goods and services.

It is worth noticing that U.S. export value declined to $959.0 billion in 1998 from its $965.4 billion one year early, while imports rose to $1,110.2 billion from $1,058.8 billion of 1997. Consequently the trade balance was worsening with $151.2 billion in the red. Both U.S. exports and imports of services, however, continued to rise in 1998, and U.S. international trade for services reached a record $100.4 billion in surplus. At the same time, U.S. good-trade created a new record $251.6 billion deficit. Table 10-3 provides a comparison of U.S. trade balances for goods and services.

## Table 10-2: U.S. Exports and Imports of Services

| Year | S-EX Service Exports | | Military Service Exports | |
|------|---------------------|----------|-------------------------|-----------|
| | Value ($billion) | % of EX | Value ($billion) | % of S-EX |
| 1965 | 8.824 | 24.9 | 2.465 | 27.9 |
| 1975 | 25.497 | 18.7 | 6.256 | 24.5 |
| 1985 | 73.155 | 24.1 | 8.718 | 11.9 |
| 1995 | 219.802 | 26.8 | 14.755 | 6.7 |
| 1997 | 258.268 | 26.8 | 18.269 | 7.1 |
| 1998 | 278.200 | 29.0 | NA | NA |

| Year | S-IM Service Exports | | Military Service Imports | |
|------|---------------------|----------|-------------------------|-----------|
| | Value ($billion) | % of S-IM | Value ($billion) | % of S-EX |
| 1965 | 9.111 | 28.9 | 2.952 | 32.4 |
| 1975 | 21.996 | 17.9 | 4.795 | 21.8 |
| 1985 | 72.862 | 17.5 | 13.108 | 18.0 |
| 1995 | 145.964 | 16.2 | 9.986 | 6.8 |
| 1997 | 170.520 | 16.1 | 11.488 | 6.7 |
| 1998 | 177.800 | 16.0 | NA | NA |

## Table 10-3: U.S. International Trade Balances

| Year | Total Trade Balance($billion) | Goods Trade Balance ($billion) | Service Trade Balance ($billion) |
|------|-------------------------------|--------------------------------|----------------------------------|
| 1985 | -114.2 | -114.493 | 0.293 |
| 1986 | -131.5 | -131.915 | 4.515 |
| 1987 | -142.2 | -139.444 | -2.756 |
| 1988 | -106.0 | -117.103 | 11.103 |
| 1989 | -80.4 | -103.448 | 23.048 |
| 1990 | -71.3 | -99.201 | 27.901 |
| 1991 | -20.5 | -63.637 | 43.137 |
| 1992 | -29.6 | -87.021 | 57.421 |
| 1993 | -60.7 | -121.370 | 60.670 |
| 1994 | -90.9 | -156.179 | 65.279 |
| 1995 | -83.9 | -157.736 | 73.836 |
| 1996 | -91.2 | -173.963 | 82.763 |
| 1997 | -93.4 | -181.148 | 87.748 |
| 1998 | -151.2 | -251.600 | 100.400 |
| 1999 | -250.9 | -348.6 | 97.7 |
| 2000 | -364.0 | -459.4 | 95.4 |

Since 1988, U.S. international trade on services has developed rapidly, and the service-trade surplus has continued to rise year after year except for 1999 and 2000. This excellent performance also reflects a structure change in the U.S. economy. The services-producing industries provide great value not only to Americans but also to consumers abroad. Thanks to the advanced information technology of telecommunications and computer networks, many services performed by local professionals are no longer restricted to local and national markets. Now, digital technology can translate music, picture, text, and software products into the 0-1-computer language that can be easily sent through the Internet and retrieved wherever consumers are and whenever they need. Hence, the digital revolution has created brand new ways of distributing and delivering services to markets around the globe.

A conventional approach in economics that treats services as non-tradable goods no longer applies to the new realities of the world of international trade. As a matter of fact, the services-producing sector has consistently outperformed the goods-producing sector in terms of creating international trade surpluses for the U.S. economy. U.S. international trade data indicates that the service sector has played a growing role not only in American domestic markets but in foreign markets around the globe as well.

## 10-5  The Current Account Deficit and International Debt

International transactions in the external sector of the U.S. economy are measured not only by the changes in exports and imports, but also by the balance of payments accounts. The balance of payments consists of two main accounts: the current account and the financial account (what was previously called the capital account).

The current account has three components: the trade account, the income account, and the transfer account. The trade account measures the values of exports and imports and their difference as a trade surplus or deficit. The income account measures the income payments made to foreigners and received from foreigners as well as their difference. The income account mainly reflects interest payments from international investments in the United States by foreigners and in foreign countries by Americans. The transfer account measures values of private and official transfer payments to and from other countries. The largest entry in the transfer account is foreign-aid payments by the U. S. government.

The trade deficit is by far the largest component of the U.S. current account deficit as depicted in Figure 10-14. In the time period of 1960–1976, both balances in the trade account and the current account showed surpluses except for 1971 and 1972. Since 1976, the U.S. trade deficit has enduringly hung on and fluctuated greatly over business cycles. In 1987, the trade deficit increased to $142 billion and the current account deficit rose to $160 billion, which were their historical highs. In 1991 the trade deficit reduced to $20 billion while the current account recorded a surplus of $3.7 billion, primarily due to the economic recession in the early 1990s that reduced American consumers' demand for imported goods and services. Since 1992, both the trade deficit and current account deficit have increased dramatically from $27.9 billion and $48.5 billion in 1992 to $364 billion and $410 billion in 2000 respectively.

Measured by the GDP ratio, the current account deficit rose to 3.4% of GDP in 1987 from merely 0.7% of GDP in 1977. The GDP ratio of current account deficit surpassed its historical record of 3.4% and reached 4.2% in 2000, primarily due to the surge of the trade deficit.

The current account deficit is financed by net capital inflows from abroad. The financial account measures changes over time in the U.S. international borrowing and lending. When U.S. governments, corporations and individuals sell domestic assets to foreign governments, corporations and individuals, the U.S. borrows in the international market with financial capital flowing into the country. When the U.S. lends in the international market, it buys foreign assets with financial capital flowing out of the country. A surplus in the financial account indicates that the U.S. borrows more than it lends, or more financial capital flows into than out of the country. Hence, a financial account surplus is a net capital inflow, while a financial account deficit is a net capital outflow.

As the balance of payment accounts must be zero by definition, these two component balances (the current account balance and the financial account balance) must be cancelled out by themselves. Therefore, the deficit on the current account is the surplus on the financial account. The U.S. experienced a $410-billion deficit on its current account in 2000, which means its net borrowing from foreigners was as much as $410 billion in a single year in order to finance its aggregate spending.

Accumulated balances on the financial account over time become the international debt (if positive) or credit (if negative) for the United States. The international debt (or credit) can also be measured by the foreign-owned assets in the United States net of U.S.-owned assets abroad. Figure 10-15 displays the changing position of U.S. international debt and credit.

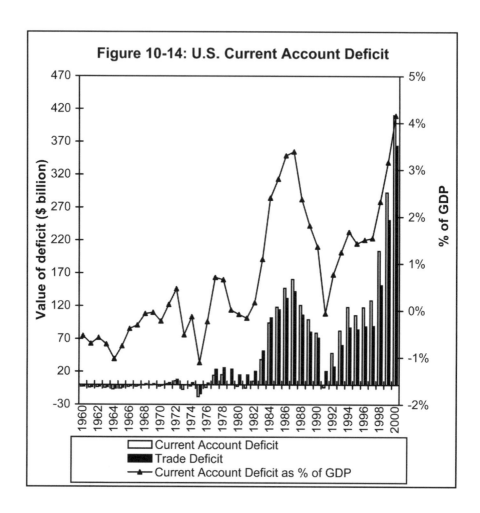

Figure 10-14: U.S. Current Account Deficit

In 1980, the U.S. owned $361-billion more foreign assets than foreigners' assets in the United States. That credit situation changed in 1986 when foreigners owned $36 billion more U.S. assets than U.S.-owned assets abroad. Since 1986, U.S. international debt has increased rapidly, reaching $246 billion in 1990, $496 billion in 1995, and $1.35 trillion in 2000. In terms of the ratio to GDP, U.S. international debt increased from 4.2% of GDP in 1990 to 13.7 % of GDP in 2000.

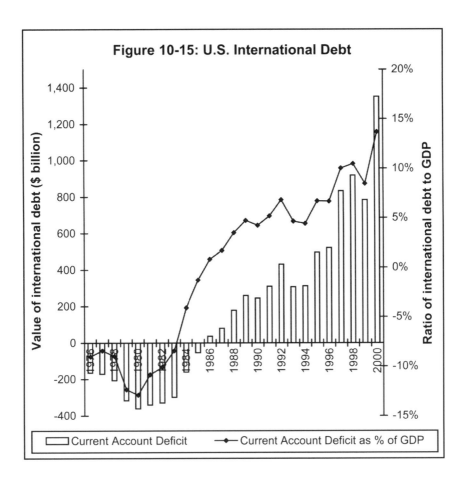

Figure 10-15: U.S. International Debt

Two major component assets of the international investment are securities and direct investment abroad. Figure 10-16 depicts U.S. investment in foreign securities abroad and foreigners' investment in U.S. securities.

U.S. investment in foreign securities was about $44 billion in 1976; it increased to $342 billion in 1990 and $2.583 trillion (a record high) in 1999, and then reduced to $2.389 trillion in 2000.

U.S. securities are divided into two categories: U.S. treasury securities and other securities, including corporate stocks and bonds, other bonds and derivatives. Foreigners' investment in U.S. treasury securities was $77.6 billion in 1976, in which foreign governments' holding was $70.5 billion.

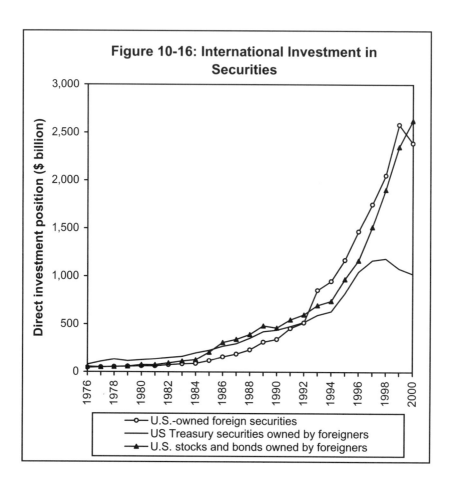

In 1990, U.S. treasury securities held by foreign governments increased to $286 billion and $152 billion by other foreign entities. The record high foreign holding of U.S. securities occurred in 1998, at $1.185 trillion.  In 2000, foreign investment in U.S. treasuries reduced to $1.026 trillion, of which 60% belonged to foreign governments and 40% to the foreign private sector.

Foreign investment in U.S. corporate stocks and bonds has increased dramatically since 1986, when it surpassed foreign investment in U.S. treasuries for the first time. The continuously growing U.S. economy combined with the explosive U.S. stock market attracted many foreign investors during the 1990's, which fueled the surge of foreign holdings of U.S. equities and bonds.

Adding two categories of U.S. securities, one can see that foreigners held $132 billion in U.S. securities in 1976, $1.022 trillion in 1991, and $3.639 trillion in 2000. In a comparison, U.S.-owned foreign securities were $44 billion in 1976, $456 billion in 1991, and $2.386 billion in 2000. Therefore the U.S. international debt was held largely in the form of U.S. securities.

Foreign direct investment (FDI) is another important instrument for international investment. According to an official definition[1], foreign direct investment refers to ownership and control of 10% or more of an enterprise's voting securities, or in other words, the lasting interest and degree of influence over management by a foreign person. The foreign person in this definition is broadly defined to include any individual, branch, partnership, associated group, association, trust, corporation, or other organization and any government. Therefore, FDI involves activities that are controlled and organized by firms outside of the nation in which their headquarters and principal decision makers are located. The foreign country received FDI is called the host and the country where decision-making control resides is called the donor.

Portfolio investment consists of short-term investment in U.S. Treasury securities, corporate stocks, bonds, and derivatives. It gains its returns through interest payments, dividends, and capital gains or losses via buying and selling securities and stocks. Direct investment, on the other hand, looks for returns through the running of a successful enterprise. Compared with portfolio investment, FDI not only provides capital from a lender to a borrower in order to gain returns on investment, but also involves issues of direct control of enterprises' business and operation, such as management strategy, technology transfer, marketing, human resources and so on.

FDI is thought to bring certain benefits to host countries, including improvements in capital formation and balance of payments, stimulation of export markets, and transfer of advanced technologies and management skills. FDI also provides benefits and opportunities to multinational corporations in donor countries, such as stimulating product and geography diversification through investments into new products for various indigenous markets, reallocating financial and human resources on the global base of production, promoting cost efficiency and profitability, enhancing competitiveness, and gaining new opportunities for economic expansion.

Figure 10-17 displays positions of U.S. direct investment abroad and

---

[1] OECD, Detailed Benchmark Definition of Foreign Direct Investment, 2nd ed. 1992.

foreign direct investment in the U.S. over the time period of 1976–2000, both measured at current cost[2].

Over the entire time period of 1976–2000, direct investments in both directions rapidly increased. U.S. overseas direct investment was greater than the total foreign direct investment in the United States. In 1976, U.S. direct investment overseas was $222 billion versus $175 billion of foreign direct investment in the U.S. Those numbers became $617 billion versus $505 billion in 1990, and $1.515 trillion versus $1.374 trillion in 2000. The surplus of U.S. overseas direct investment over foreign direct investment in the U.S., about $276 billion in 1999 and $141 billion in 2000, represents a net capital outflow from the U.S. to the rest of the world. In fact, the United States is the largest investor abroad and the largest recipient of direct investment in the world.

The increasing foreign direct investment in the U.S. indicates the great attraction of American corporations to foreign firms and investors. The accelerating productivity of U.S. workers and the increasing cost efficiency and profitability of American corporations, compared with workers and firms in other countries[3], have led to an investment boom. As Section 10-2 indicated, since 1991 U.S. gross private domestic investment as a share of GDP has increased steady, rising from 13% in 1991 to 17.9% in 2000. The increasing investment speeds up technology innovations and raises productivity, which translate into actual increases in outputs of goods and services. Expectations on future high productivity and profitability of American corporations induce further investment from domestic and foreign resources, which would explain the accelerating FDI in the U.S. as illustrated in Figure 10-17.

The rising productivity and the speculation for future returns on investment in American corporations also fueled the U.S. stock market. The booming U.S. stock market enhanced household wealth, increased consumer spending, enlarged the U.S. domestic market, and sustained economic growth in the 1990s. Economic prosperity in the United States became a magnet to investors around the globe, drawing financial capital into U.S. markets. Other important factors that attracted foreign direct investment include America's higher standard of living, the still-increasing size of the largest domestic market in

---

[2] International Investment Position of the United States at Year End 1976-2001, Bureau of Economic Analysis.

[3] George Kozmetsky and Piyu Yue: Global Economic Competition, Today's Warfare in Global Electronics Industries and Companies, KAP, 1997.

the world, advanced U.S. technology, skilled U.S. workers, deregulation of the U.S. capital market, and openness of the U.S.economy.

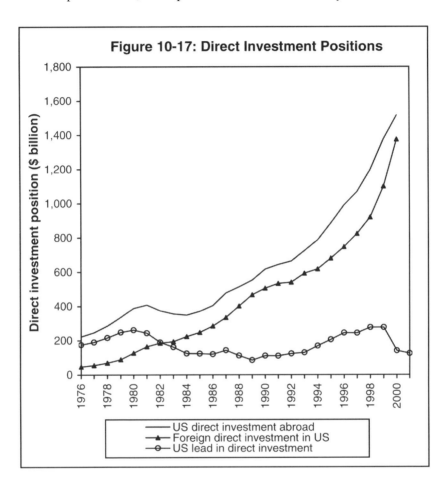

The increasing U.S. overseas direct investment reflects the changing environment of the global financial market. Before 1982, the net capital flows from developed to developing nations consisted mostly of loans; net direct investment was merely one third of those loans. The debt payment crises in developing nations in the 1980s and 1990s caused the International Monetary Funds (IMF) to refinance loans with structural adjustment requirements that greatly reduced regulations on foreign direct investment in developing nations.

The restrictions to foreign direct investment include requirements of local content, manufacturing, trade balance, exports performance, domestic sales, technology transfer, licensing, and employment restrictions. These measures have impeded foreign direct investment capital flowing around the world. The reduction or elimination of capital controls and the national deregulation in many developing nations has led to the sharply growing U.S. overseas direct investment. Multinational corporations have now established their subsidiaries and foreign affiliates around the globe in order to rationally allocate resources and efficiently produce and sell goods and services based on changing supply and demand conditions of the world markets.

The increasing U.S. overseas direct investment in the 1990's was accompanied by the rapidly increasing trade deficit, which raised concerns by some Americans. The major concern is that multinational corporations have sent technologies and jobs overseas, particularly in the manufacturing sector, which may reduce economic growth and lead to higher unemployment or underemployment in the United States. They argue that national benefits received from U.S. overseas direct investment may not compensate the local losses of jobs and reduced economic prosperity. In our opinion, it seems doubtful that this argument could explain the concurrent phenomena of sustained economic growth, the sharply rising U.S. direct investment abroad, and the record low level of unemployment rate in the U.S. during the 1990's. In the following chapter we will study the transformation of the sector structure of the U.S. economy, from which one can see that the job loss in the manufacturing sector was due to economic structure changes rather than American corporations' disappointment of sending jobs overseas.

## 10-6  Summary

In this section we have analyzed the structural changes of the U.S. economy by looking at evolutions of aggregate demand and its components. Two striking facts are emerging and are expected to continue: the increasing demand for American services by U.S. consumers and by the rest of the world, and the rapidly increasing investment by American corporations for producers' durable equipment, particularly in information technology related applications.

As the four components of aggregate demand make up the Gross Domestic Product (GDP), their growth rates directly contribute to the growth rate of GDP, which is a weighted sum of components' growth rates with the weights equal to their GDP shares. Therefore, GDP shares and growth rates of aggregate demand components can measure economic growth. In practice, however, economic growth is denoted by the growth rate of real GDP and the real GDP is measured by chained dollars. The components of real GDP are also measured by chained dollars and do not carry the additive property; hence they cannot be used to calculate GDP shares for these components. For the purpose of illustrating the contribution of aggregate demand to GDP, we use GDP shares, which are calculated from nominal GDP and its components measured by current dollars, and the growth rates, which are calculated from real GDP and its components measured by the chained dollars.

Table 10-4 displays average GDP shares for aggregate demand, the mean and standard deviation of real growth rates of GDP and the components over the time period of 1990-2000. We have also calculated correlation coefficients between the real growth rate of GDP and the real growth rate of each component, displayed in Table 10-4.

In order to show how differently GDP and its components grow in an economic boom and in a recession, we provide, in Table 10-5, the actual growth rates in three specific time periods: the fourth quarter 1990, the fourth quarter 1998, and the second quarter 2001. 1990 Q4 was the middle of the 1990-91 recession; 1998 Q4 was the heyday of an economic boom; and 2001 Q2 was the prelude to the economic slide of 2001. All the numbers in Tables 10-4 and 10-5 are calculated by using quarterly data and all the growth rates are the annualized rates of growth.

Private consumption accounted for nearly 70% of nominal GDP over the time period of 1990-2000, and consumptions of services and non-durable goods accounted for a large share of total private consumption. It is worth noticing from Table 10-4 that consumption of durable goods accounted for a smaller GDP share than other two consumption components (7.9% versus 20.4% and 38.6%), its average real growth rate 5.8% was nearly as twice large growth rate of GDP (3.0%) and growth rate of total private consumption (3.3%). However, the standard deviation of durable goods consumption was greater than its mean, indicating the large volatility of consumers' spending on durable goods. This fact can be verified by the actual number of the growth rate of (-12.2%) in the recession and 22.1% in the boom, which are displayed in the three columns of Table 10-5.

Table 10-4: GDP and Components of Aggregate Demand

| GDP & Components | Share Mean % 1990-2000 | Real Growth Rate 1990-2000 | | Growth Rate Correlation Coefficient 1990-2000 |
|---|---|---|---|---|
| | | Mean | Standard deviation | |
| GDP | 100% | 2.99% | 2.30% | 1.00 |
| Consumption | 66.9 | 3.26 | 2.01 | 0.62 |
| Durable goods | 7.9 | 5.84 | 8.34 | 0.53 |
| Non-durable goods | 20.4 | 2.79 | 2.46 | 0.59 |
| Services | 38.6 | 3.00 | 1.34 | 0.34 |
| Gross Private Investment | 15.7 | 5.36 | 12.54 | 0.76 |
| Changes in Inventories | 0.48 | -150.9 | 1614.7 | 0.18 |
| Residential | 3.91 | 3.12 | 11.88 | 0.61 |
| Structure | 2.98 | 1.71 | 9.71 | 0.41 |
| PDE | 8.36 | 8.16 | 8.78 | 0.57 |
| Industrial equip. | 1.61 | 3.38 | 9.73 | 0.40 |
| Transportation equip. | 1.67 | 7.48 | 22.94 | 0.34 |
| Other PDE | 1.45 | 3.19 | 10.08 | 0.47 |
| Information technology | 3.64 | 13.03 | 10.31 | 0.38 |
| Computers | 0.84 | 27.12 | 22.68 | 0.32 |
| Software | 1.26 | 13.13 | 6.87 | 0.26 |
| Communication | 0.86 | 8.55 | 18.52 | 0.36 |
| Instruments | 0.41 | 4.37 | 7.46 | -0.08 |
| Photocopy | 0.18 | -2.52 | 15.67 | -0.07 |
| Office machine | 0.09 | 1.69 | 18.50 | -0.09 |
| Government Spending | 18.8 | 1.55 | 3.30 | 0.22 |
| Federal | 7.26 | -0.59 | 7.64 | 0.21 |
| State & Local govt. | 11.54 | 2.94 | 2.01 | 0.09 |
| Net Exports | -1.42 | 42.11 | 184.5 | 0.08 |
| Exports | 10.60 | 6.29 | 8.14 | 0.45 |
| Imports | 12.02 | 7.91 | 7.24 | 0.62 |

From the first five rows of Table 10-4 one can see that the growth rate of GDP closely followed the growth rate of private consumption, with a correlation coefficient of 0.62 over the 1990s. Consumption of non-durable goods and services grew slowly but steadily, and was less sensitive to economic fluctuation, while the growth rate of durable goods consumption largely reflected economic fluctuations over time. By the second quarter of 2001, the consumption of durable goods and services continued to grow, and counterbalanced the decline in private investment, keeping the growth rate

Table 10-5: Growth Rate of GDP and Components
of Aggregate Demand

| GDP & Components | Annualized Real Growth Rate (%) | | |
|---|---|---|---|
| | 1990 Q4 | 1998 Q4 | 2001 Q2 |
| GDP | -3.3% | 6.5% | 0.3% |
| Consumption | -3.4 | 4.9 | 2.5 |
| Durable goods | -12.2 | 22.1 | 6.8 |
| Non-durable goods | -4.7 | 5.1 | 0.3 |
| Services | -0.7 | 1.5 | 2.7 |
| Gross Private Investment | -27.6 | 13.4 | -12.7 |
| Changes in Inventories | -564.3 | 45.7 | 165.3 |
| Residential | -29.1 | 9.0 | 5.8 |
| Structure | -18.3 | 3.2 | -12.9 |
| PDE | -3.4 | 17.3 | -16.4 |
| Industrial equip. | -14.3 | 4.0 | -22.3 |
| Transportation equipment | -11.9 | 41.1 | -6.8 |
| Other PDE | -8.4 | -4.8 | -6.4 |
| Information technology | 8.7 | 20.9 | -21.1 |
| Computers | 27.0 | 54.1 | -34.5 |
| Software | 12.1 | 13.4 | -3.7 |
| Communication | -6.3 | 26.9 | -49.7 |
| Instruments | 1.8 | 5.1 | 2.7 |
| Photocopy | 15.6 | -53.9 | -21.2 |
| Office machine | -2.3 | -28.4 | -11.6 |
| Government Spending | 4.0 | 4.0 | 4.9 |
| Federal | 3.1 | 5.2 | 1.8 |
| State & Local govt. | 4.7 | 3.4 | 6.4 |
| Net Exports | 195.3 | 3.3 | -2.2 |
| Exports | 9.6 | 15.4 | -12.5 |
| Imports | -12.1 | 11.7 | -8.7 |

of GDP in the positive territory. If the consumption of services declines, the economy will surely run into a recession, simply due to its large GDP share of 38.6%. The strength of American consumers was the main reason why some economists had hoped before the national disaster of terrorist attacks on September 11, 2001 that the U.S. economy might not run into a recession.

Even through gross private investment accounted for 15.7% of GDP on the average over 1990–2000, its real growth rate of 5.36% was much higher than the growth rate of real GDP, 2.99%. Its standard deviation of 12.54% was more than twice as large as that of its mean, indicating a great volatility in private investment. Compared with durable goods consumption, gross private investment holds a larger GDP share and has a larger standard deviation but a similar mean. Therefore, the gross private investment makes a greater contribution to economic fluctuation than the consumption of durable goods. This fact is also verified by the largest correlation coefficient, 0.76, between growth rate of GDP and growth rate of investment in Table 10-4.

Among the four components of private investment, American corporations' spending on producers' durable equipment (PDE) held the largest share, 8.36%, and the largest average growth rate of 8.16%. In the economic boom, investment in PDE grew faster than other investment components except for the change in private inventories. This is the most volatile economic variable but it bears a small weight due to its tiny share of 0.48%. In the fourth quarter of 1990, a time of economic recession, 18-29% declines occurred in residential and structure investment, only 3.35% reduction appeared in the PDE spending. In 2001 Q2, however, residential investment continued to rise at an annual rate of 5.8%, while structure spending declined at a rate 12.9%, and the PDE spending declined at a rate 16.4%. In the fourth quarter 1998, a time of economic boom, investment in PDE increased at an annual rate of 17.3%, and the consumption of durable goods grew at 22.1%, which reflect the nature of the 1990s economic expansion fueled by growing consumption and investment.

In prelude to the 2001 recession, three components of consumers' spending continued to grow; residential investment increased at an annual rate of 5.8% in 2001 Q2, which was only slightly lower than the rate of 9.0% during the economic boom of 1998 Q4. This data shows that American consumers were still buying homes, cars, and other durable goods, taking advantage of declining interest rates and mortgage rates. These declining rates were induced by U.S. monetary authority's aggressive policy of cutting the federal funds rate and discount rate ten times during 2001.

Gross private investment, however, declined in 2001 Q2 at an annualized rate of 12.7%, in which corporations' spending on PDE reduced at an annual rate of 16.4% and all of the four components of PDE investment suffered large declines. American corporations' investment in information processing equipment and software reduced at an annual rate of 21.1% in 2001 Q2, compared with the rate of increase 20.9% in the economic boom of 1998 Q4, and the 8.7% increase in the recession of 1990 Q4. Large declines in corporations' investment in 2001 Q2 occurred in communication equipment

(-49.7%), computers and peripheral equipment (-34.5%), and photocopy and related equipment (-21.2%).

In the economic boom of 1998 Q4, investments in communication equipment and computer hardware increased at annual rates of 26.9% and 54.1% respectively. Even in the recession of 1990 Q4, American corporations' investment in computer hardware and software rose at annual rates of 27.0% and 12.1% respectively. Hence, declining consumer spending, the significant decrease in residential investment and corporate investment in structure, industrial equipment and transportation equipment had created the economic recession of 1990-1991. However, American corporations' investment in information technologies continued to increase, particularly for computer hardware and software, during those same years.

The stock market burst of the Internet bubble in 2000 has led to the bankruptcy of many dot-com companies and e-commerce software companies as well as many local Internet access telecommunications services companies. As those companies were the major customers of high technology products in the late 1990s, disappearance of those firms dramatically reduced American corporations' demand for computer hardware and communications equipment. This effect is clearly reflected in the declining rates of American corporate investment in information processing equipment in 2001 Q2 (21.1%). At the same time, however, American consumers' spending on durable goods and housing remained at 6.8% and 5.8% respectively.

This data explains the difference between the 2001 economic recession and the 1990-91 recession. The 1990-91 recession was induced by the decrease of consumer spending on durable goods and homes, and by the reduction of corporate investment in structures and inventories. The 2001 recession seems to be the result of the bust of the Internet industry and the tumbling corporate investment in information technologies. This investment-led plunge of the U.S. economy began to be observed first in the manufacturing sector, and then in the services sector. The unemployment rate soared and consumers' confidence and spending began to decline in the second half of 2001.

The federal government's spending accounted for 7.26% of GDP on average over 1990-2000; it declined by 0.6% annually and its fluctuation was positively correlated to the GDP growth, with a correlation coefficient of 0.21. Local governments' spending accounted for a large share of the GDP (11.54%), and was rising. Its growth rate, however, showed a weak correlation coefficient (0.09) to the growth rate of GDP.

Net exports accounted for a negative -1.42% of GDP. Because the U.S. economy imported more foreign goods and services than exported U.S.

goods and services to foreign countries, the negative net exports represent the amount that has been subtracted from GDP. The net exports fluctuated largely over time and its growth rate showed a weak correlation coefficient (0.08) to the growth rate of GDP. The increasing GDP shares of both exports and imports indicate escalating activities in U.S. international trade. Exports and imports grew at the annual rates of 6.29% and 7.91% respectively on the average over 1990-2000; their fluctuations showed strong positive correlations to the growth rate of real GDP.

The analyses in this chapter indicate that private consumption and investment have become the major source of economic growth in the United States. American consumers' expenditures on housing and durable goods, such as cars, and American corporations' spending on information technologies, such as computer hardware, software, and communications equipment, have provided the U.S. economy with not only the tremendous force for growth but also the large volatility for economic fluctuation and business cycle. Among all the components of aggregate demand, consumption of services has accounted for the largest share of GDP and has grown steadily at 3.0% per year in 1990-2000. The long-term prosperity of the U.S. economy seems to depend on how well and how fast the services sector develops in the future.

Responding to the changing demand domestically and globally, U.S. corporations have quickly reoriented themselves to become integrated and able to deliver around the world. They are providing customers not only with manufactured goods, but also with various kinds of related services. Some technology companies have begun to call themselves service organizations, as they recognize that the most important thing to customers is not only the equipment they produce and put on the market but also the degree of value that can be actualized by using the equipment. To create great value for their customers and for themselves, U.S. corporations must develop relevant service-business and integrate their manufacturing capacity with services such as distribution, delivering, maintenance, on-site training, continuously upgrading, and so on.

The shifting emphasis towards services by American corporations should be reflected in the structure change of U.S. industries. In the following chapter, we present a sectional analysis from the production side of the U.S. economy.

# Chapter 11

# The Evolution of Sectors in the U.S. Economy

## 11-1  Introduction to an Analysis of Sectors' Evolution

We analyze a sector's evolution by using the framework advocated by
W.W. Rostow. As a historian as well as an economist, Rostow consistently
emphasizes the important role of a sector's evolution in an economy's growth
process. He suggests that

> ... the overall rate of growth of an economy must be regarded in
> the first instance as the consequence of differing growth rates in
> particular sectors of the economy, such sectoral growth-rates being
> in part derived from certain overall demand factors (for example
> population, consumers' income, tastes etc.); in part, from the primary
> and secondary effects of changing supply factors, when these are
> effectively exploited.[1]

We believe that any structure changes in an economy are subordinate
to the big picture of the economy's stages of growth. To understand the
meaning of the structure changes that have taken place over the last half

---

[1] W.W. Rostow, *The Stages of Economic Growth,* second edition, Cambridge University
Press, 1971, p. 52.

of the twentieth century in the U.S. economy, we need to recall the theory of the stages of economic growth we discussed in Part One of this book. This theory explains an economy's era and place in the unfolding process of economic growth. It also explains the stages of economic growth with the leading sectors and associated structure changes taking place in the process of economic growth.

In a traditional society, the level of productivity is limited by the inaccessibility of modern science and technology; it has to devote a very high proportion of resources to the leading sector of agriculture. In the stage of preconditions for take-off, modern science begins to be translated into the production of agriculture and industry in order to develop predominance for transportation, communications, and trade. Agriculture and transportation are the leading industries in the preconditions for take-off. The first Industrial Revolution opens the stage of take-off, in which technologies spread quickly. A group of new industries such as machinery-manufactured cotton textile industry, coke-manufactured iron, and the railroad becomes the leading sector. After the take-off comes the stage of driving to maturity, in which the second Industrial Revolution generates the new leading industries of steel, shipbuilding, chemicals, electricity and machine tools industries to replace the industries of coal, iron, and textile.

The next stage is called the era for high mass-consumption in which presently developed nations around the globe are now staged. At this stage of growth, increasing real income per capita allows the majority of citizens to consume not just necessaries but also modern durable goods such as cars, PCs, cell phones, and electronic gadgetry. The Third and Fourth Industrial Revolutions have played crucial roles in shifting the leading industries from the automobile and steel industries into the revolutionary and innovative industries of semiconductors, advanced materials, computers, the laser, and genetic engineering. These industries produce modern consumer durable goods and various kinds of services in finance, medical and health care, education, entertainment and so on.

The United States was the first society in the world to move from technical maturity to the age of high mass-consumption. W.W. Rostow has identified four phases of post-maturity development in American history over the first half of the twentieth century: the progressive period, the 1920s, the great depression of the 1930s, and the post-war boom of 1946-56. In the 1920s, the age of the mass-produced automobile, Americans' life style was transformed dramatically. Automobiles led to a vast inner migration to newly constructed single-family houses in the suburbs, which created the mass markets for household appliances and consumers' durables. The depression of 1929 interrupted the mass consumption process in the United States, while the post-war boom of 1946-56 is regarded as a resumption of the 1920's boom. Development of the mass consumption stage in the United States was illustrated by the following impressive statistics.

> ... In 1948 54% of American families owned their own cars; a decade later, 73%. In 1946, 69% of houses wired for electricity had electric refrigerators; a decade later the figure was 96%; and the figures for other electric gadgets—for example, the vacuum cleaner and electric washer—are similar. Television was installed in 86% of such homes by 1956.[2]

The new statistics show that more than 50% of U.S. households have PCs. The home PC penetration rate has exceeded 70% in some cities and many families have multiple PCs at home. About 37% of U.S. households have connections to the Internet, and about 134.6 million Americans were Internet users at the end of 2000. It is projected that this number will be 214 million by the end of 2005[3]. The mass consumption era has continued to run its course in the United States, with new information technology products and services added into American consumers and corporations' purchasing lists.

Our study covers the post-war boom period of 1946-56 and the subsequent forty years, in which the U.S. economy staged its maturity phase of the age of high mass-consumption. Bearing in mind the theory of the stages of economic growth in general and the stages of the U.S. economic growth in particular, we examine the sectors' evolution in the U.S. economy over the last fifty years of the twentieth century. The analysis of these sectors is the main subject of the rest of this section.

---

[2] W.W. Rostow, *The Stages of Economic Growth,* second edition, Cambridge University Press, 1971, p. 79.

[3] See Section 10-1-1 of Chapter 10.

- ## Measurement of Value-Added and Data Source for the Analysis

A sector's evolution is reflected in the changing relative strength of sectors, which can be measured through comparisons of a sectors' contribution to the U.S. economy. As a sector's evolution is a dynamic process, we have to look over a lengthy time period to properly observe and identify shifting patterns. To conduct this kind of analyses as well as economic policy-evaluation, real-world data is necessary. The National Income Accounting is a system of measurement devised for this purpose and has been adopted by all nations around the world. The approach of dividing GDP into components of aggregate demand is one way to count up national output, which was applied in Chapter 10. Another way to count GDP is to add up all the outputs in the economy from the side of production.

A corporation's revenues from sales must be equal to the sum of all factor payments, such as wages paid to workers, interest paid for capital, rentals paid for land, purchases from other firms, plus profits/losses earned in production. Applying this accounting identity to all the businesses in the economy discloses that total purchases from other firms represent payments for intermediate goods rather than final products of the economy. As GDP is the sum of the money values of all the final goods and services produced during a specified period, the payments for intermediate goods and services must be subtracted from the total revenue of all the firms in order to arrive at the GDP measure. This is an important concept in businesses and economic affairs, what is called "value added". Revenues from selling products minus the amount paid for goods and services purchased from other businesses define the value added by the business. Taking a total sum of values added by all businesses in the economy results in the total value of the entire final products and services. Hence GDP can be measured as the sum of the values added by all businesses in the nation.

In this measurement system of national income and product accounts (NIPA), the value-added approach is applied to all private industries and governments in order to count up GDP. The value added by an industry is called "Gross Product Origination" (abbreviated as GPO). An industry's GPO is equal to its gross output (sales and other operating income plus inventory change) minus its intermediate inputs (consumption of goods and services purchased from other industries). This is often referred to as the industry's value added. The U.S. Department of Commerce now makes the annual estimates of industries' GPO available to the public via its Internet site. In this section we present an analysis of U.S. sectors' evolution by using this GPO data.

All of the GPO estimates are reported according to the Standard Industrial Classification, or SIC code. This defines industries in terms of the U.S. economy's structure more than sixty years ago, when the SIC system was first introduced. Despite modifications in the 1970s and 1980s, the SIC code did not change drastically until 1999. In March 1999, the U.S. Commerce Department's Census Bureau released the "1997 Economic Census," which marked the premiere of a new industrial classification system to measure the U.S. economy in the 21st century. Under the new system, the 1997 economic census contains only four economic variables—establishments, sales and receipts or shipments, annual payroll, and paid employees—for the single year of 1997. We have to rely on the original NIPA (National Income and Product Accounts) time series data that was reported according to the old SIC (Standard Industrial Classification) system. An analysis based on the new measurement system will be made in the final part of this section.

A sector's evolution is studied by using a time series of value added, employment, and productivity of industries and sectors for the past fifty years. Comparing these three variables among sectors over time gives a clearer picture of changing relative strengths and contributions to the U.S. economy by industries and sectors. We shall proceed from aggregate sectors to groups of industries, and to individual industries classified by the SIC code.

## 11-2  Sectors' Contribution to the U.S. Economy

In our study a sector's contribution to the U.S. economy is measured by its share of value-added in the GDP and its share of workers in the total employment of the U.S. economy.  We use current-dollar NIPA (National Income and Product Accounts) time series to compute sectors' value-added shares (or GDP share) with respect to nominal GDP as a common denominator. The labor share of a sector is calculated by the number of persons engaged in the sector divided by the total employment of the U.S. domestic economy. We also calculate a proxy measure of productivity, namely a sector's output of value-added divided by the number of persons engaged in the sector, to indicate the strength of the sector. The time series of GDP-share, employment share, and productivity measure, illustrate a sector's evolution over time in terms of its weight and strength in the U.S. economy. The time period covered by this study is from 1948 through 2000, for which the NIPA data of value-added and employment are available. The results are presented in both graphical and tabulated forms for related sectors and industries.

Figure 11-1.1 presents four GDP-share time series for the private sector (including all private industries), the public sector (including federal and all local governments), and two separated private industry groups, the goods-producing sector and the services-producing sector.

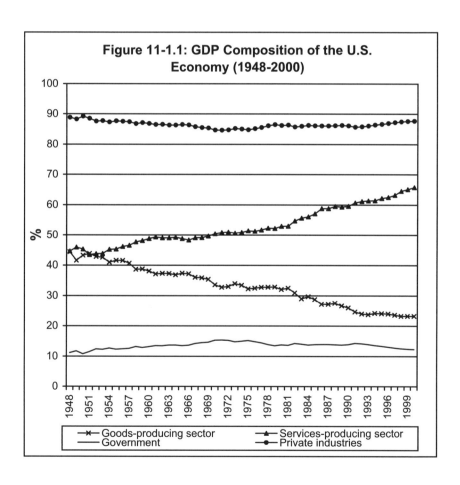

The public sector's GDP share varied in the range of 11-15% over the entire time period, with the minimum share of 10.8% in 1950 and the maximum share of 15.3% in 1971. Since 1991, the GDP share of governments has been declining, from 14.3% in 1991 to 12.3% in 2000. Moving in the opposite direction, the private sector's GDP share reduced from 89.2% in 1950 to 84.7% in 1971, and then gradually increased to 85.7% in 1991, and 87.7% in 2000.

Following the method of classifying economic activities that is frequently employed in the publication of *Survey of Current Business* by the U.S. Commerce Department, we divide all private industries into two groups. The goods-producing group consists of agriculture, forestry and fishing, mining, construction, and manufacturing. The services-producing group includes transportation and public utilities, wholesale trade, retail trade, finance, insurance, real estate, and services. It is worth noticing that the services industry defined by the SIC (Standard Industrial Classification) system is narrowly oriented. It consists of hotels, personal and business services, repair services, motion pictures and recreation services, health service, and legal, educational and social services. Given this restrictive definition of services, the SIC-defined service industry has excluded many important services-producing activities, such as transportation, trade, and finance. Therefore, the service industry in the SIC system is just a component industry of the complex services-producing sector.

The services-producing sector has significantly increased its weight in the U.S. economy, with its GDP share increasing from 44.7% in 1948 to 50.8% in 1971, 60.7% in 1991, and 65.8% in 2000. The goods-producing sector, however, reduced its GDP-share from 44.7% in 1948 to 32.8% in 1971, 24.7% in 1991, and 23.2% in 2000. The changing GDP share indicates that the total amount of value-added generated each year by service producing activities has grown much faster than the GDP grows. On the opposite, the goods-producing sector has grown more slowly than the economy has. Consequently, the relative economic strength has shifted from the goods-producing sector to the services-producing sector. Services-producing activities generated about $6.494 trillion dollars of value added in 2000, which overwhelmed the $2.293 trillion dollars of value added from the goods-producing activities in the same year.

The changing relative strengths of economic sectors are also reflected in changing employment shares. Figure 11-1.2 presents a time series of shares of workers engaged in the public and private sectors, and in the goods- and services-producing sectors with respect to the number of persons engaged in the U.S. domestic production as a common denominator. The labor share of the public sector increased from 11.6% in 1948 to 18.8% in 1971 and then gradually reduced to 16.2 in 1991, and 14.1% in 2000. Conversely, the labor share of the private sector declined from 88.4% to 81.2% and then rose to 83.8% and 85.9% in the same time frame. A major shift of employment took place not between the private and public sectors, but within the private sector. The labor share of the services-producing sector rose from 42.2% in 1948 to 63.2% in 2000, whereas the labor share of the goods-producing sector reduced from 46.2% to 22.7% during the same time period.

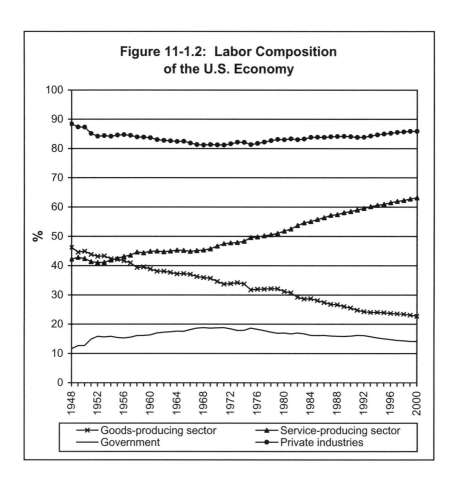

As a tabulate presentation, Table 11-1.1 displays the amounts of value added and the GDP shares, Table 11-1.2 presents the numbers of employees and the labor shares; and Table 11-1.3 denotes the proxy measurement of productivity in the lower panel for the U.S. economy and the four sectors. In Table 11-1.3 we also provide a comparison of each sector's productivity with the productivity of the entire economy via a ratio, which is calculated by dividing a sector's productivity measure by the economy's productivity measure.

Tables 11-1.1 indicates that the total amount of value-added of the U.S. economy, namely the nominal GDP, increased from $270 billion in 1948 to $9.873 trillion in 2000, which increased nearly 36 times in fifty years. The number of persons engaged in the domestic economy increased from 58 million to 135 million, a 2.3-time rise in the same time frame (Table 11-1.2). The productivity measure of the U.S. economy as a whole increased from $4,629 per person in 1948 to $72,941 per person in 2000, 15.7 times over the fifty-two-year period (Table 11-1.3).

Table 11-1.1: Contributions to GDP

| | GDP | Government | | Private Industries |
|---|---|---|---|---|
| Year | $ billion | $ billion | % of GDP | $ billion |
| 1948 | 269.573 | 30.122 | 11.17 | 239.451 |
| 1955 | 415.209 | 51.029 | 12.29 | 364.176 |
| 1960 | 527.38 | 69.488 | 13.18 | 457.892 |
| 1965 | 720.108 | 97.121 | 13.49 | 622.987 |
| 1970 | 1039.674 | 158.935 | 15.29 | 880.739 |
| 1975 | 1635.165 | 248.676 | 15.21 | 1,386.489 |
| 1980 | 2,795.561 | 384.753 | 13.76 | 2,410.808 |
| 1985 | 4,213.016 | 585.104 | 13.89 | 3,627.912 |
| 1990 | 5,803.246 | 806.535 | 13.9 | 4,996.711 |
| 1995 | 7,400.534 | 989.451 | 13.37 | 6,411.083 |
| 2000 | 9,872.938 | 1,216.346 | 12.32 | 8,656.493 |
| | **Goods-producing Sector** | | **Services-producing Sector** | |
| Year | $ billion | % of GDP | $ billion | % of GDP |
| 1948 | 119.747 | 44.42 | 120.448 | 44.68 |
| 1955 | 172.885 | 41.64 | 188.235 | 45.34 |
| 1960 | 200.953 | 38.1 | 257.493 | 48.83 |
| 1965 | 269.45 | 37.42 | 351.622 | 48.83 |
| 1970 | 349.486 | 33.62 | 524.38 | 50.44 |
| 1975 | 527.995 | 32.29 | 840.818 | 51.42 |
| 1980 | 897.096 | 32.09 | 1,479.774 | 52.93 |
| 1985 | 1,210.737 | 28.74 | 2,405.464 | 57.1 |
| 1990 | 1,509.424 | 26.01 | 3,456.703 | 59.57 |
| 1995 | 1,784.861 | 24.12 | 4,599.728 | 62.15 |
| 2000 | 2,292.990 | 23.23 | 6,493.826 | 65.77 |

Table 11-1.2: Contributions to Employment

| Year | Total Employment for Domestic Production Million | Government Employment Million | % of total | Private Industry Employment Million |
|------|------|------|------|------|
| 1948 | 58.233 | 6.744 | 11.58 | 51.489 |
| 1955 | 63.275 | 9.745 | 15.40 | 53.530 |
| 1960 | 65.029 | 10.621 | 16.33 | 54.408 |
| 1965 | 70.180 | 12.316 | 17.55 | 57.864 |
| 1970 | 78.342 | 14.691 | 18.75 | 63.651 |
| 1975 | 82.907 | 15.464 | 18.65 | 67.443 |
| 1980 | 95.913 | 16.288 | 16.98 | 79.625 |
| 1985 | 103.099 | 16.617 | 16.12 | 86.482 |
| 1990 | 115.122 | 18.340 | 15.93 | 96.782 |
| 1995 | 121.982 | 18.335 | 15.03 | 103.647 |
| 2000 | 135.355 | 19.103 | 14.11 | 116.252 |

| Year | Goods-producing Sector Million | % of total | Services-producing Sector Million | % of total |
|------|------|------|------|------|
| 1948 | 26.919 | 46.23 | 24.570 | 42.19 |
| 1955 | 26.675 | 42.16 | 26.855 | 42.44 |
| 1960 | 25.241 | 38.82 | 29.167 | 44.85 |
| 1965 | 26.162 | 37.28 | 31.702 | 45.17 |
| 1970 | 27.103 | 34.60 | 36.547 | 46.65 |
| 1975 | 26.305 | 31.73 | 41.139 | 49.62 |
| 1980 | 29.916 | 31.19 | 49.709 | 51.83 |
| 1985 | 28.945 | 28.08 | 57.536 | 55.81 |
| 1990 | 29.404 | 25.54 | 67.377 | 58.53 |
| 1995 | 29.246 | 23.98 | 74.402 | 60.99 |
| 2000 | 30.762 | 22.73 | 85.490 | 63.16 |

The private sector not only dominates the value added activities in the United States, but also shows a higher productivity than that of the public sector, whose productivity measure was nearly 20% lower than the private sector during 1955-1980 and was still 13% lower in 2000.

The amount of value added by the goods producing sector rose from $119.75 billion of the 1948-dollar to $2.293 trillion of the 2000-dollar, a 19-fold rise in fifty-two years. The number of people engaged in this sector increased by about 3.8 million, from 26.92 million in 1948 to 30.76 million in 2000. In the same time frame the amount of value-added by the services-producing sector surged from $120 billion to $6.494 trillion, a 54-fold rise in fifty-two years. The number of people working for the services-producing sector more than tripled, soaring from 24.57 million to 85.49 million, a net 60.9-million increase. Clearly, the services-producing sector in the United States grew more rapidly than the goods-producing sector. As of 2000, about 85.49 million Americans who were engaged in the services-producing activities generated $6.494 trillion dollars out of the $9.873 trillion dollars of U.S. GDP.

Conventional wisdom believes that the services sector has lower productivity than the goods-producing sector. The statistics presented in Tables 11-1.1, 11-1.2, and 11-1.3 reveal that the services-producing sector outperformed the goods-producing sector before 1980 and slightly fell behind for a couple of years in the 1980's and outperformed the goods-producing sector again in the 1990's. Therefore, the services-producing sector must contain some industries that have played a leading role in economic growth for the last fifty years.

Table 11-1.3: Productivity

| Year | Domestic Production $1000 per person (1) | Government $1000 per person (2) | Ratio (2)/(1) (3) | Private Industries $1000 per person (1) |
|------|------|------|------|------|
| 1948 | 4.629 | 4.466 | 0.96 | 4.651 |
| 1955 | 6.562 | 5.236 | 0.80 | 6.803 |
| 1960 | 8.110 | 6.543 | 0.81 | 8.416 |
| 1965 | 10.261 | 7.886 | 0.77 | 10.766 |
| 1970 | 13.271 | 10.819 | 0.82 | 13.837 |
| 1975 | 19.723 | 16.081 | 0.82 | 20.558 |
| 1980 | 29.147 | 23.622 | 0.81 | 30.277 |
| 1985 | 40.864 | 35.211 | 0.86 | 41.950 |
| 1990 | 50.410 | 43.977 | 0.87 | 51.629 |
| 1995 | 60.669 | 53.965 | 0.89 | 61.855 |
| 2000 | 72.941 | 63.674 | 0.87 | 74.463 |

| Year | Goods-producing Sector $1000 per person (5) | Ratio (5)/(1) (6) | Services-producing Sector $1000 per person (7) | Ratio (7)/(1) (8) |
|------|------|------|------|------|
| 1948 | 4.448 | 0.96 | 4.902 | 1.06 |
| 1955 | 6.481 | 0.99 | 7.009 | 1.07 |
| 1960 | 7.961 | 0.98 | 8.828 | 1.09 |
| 1965 | 10.299 | 1.00 | 11.091 | 1.08 |
| 1970 | 12.895 | 0.97 | 14.348 | 1.08 |
| 1975 | 20.072 | 1.02 | 20.438 | 1.04 |
| 1980 | 29.987 | 1.03 | 29.769 | 1.02 |
| 1985 | 41.829 | 1.02 | 41.808 | 1.02 |
| 1990 | 51.333 | 1.02 | 51.304 | 1.02 |
| 1995 | 61.028 | 1.01 | 61.823 | 1.02 |
| 2000 | 74.539 | 1.02 | 75.960 | 1.04 |

As both goods- and services-producing sectors consist of many different industries, we need to proceed into less aggregated industries for a better understanding structure changes in the U.S. economy. The following sections focus primarily on the detailed analyses of the goods- and services-producing sectors.

## 11-3 The Goods-Producing Sector

The goods-producing sector consists of four major industry groups: (1) agriculture, forestry and fishing, (2) mining, (3) construction, and (4) manufacturing. The manufacturing industry is divided into two categories, durable goods and non-durable goods. We use nominal GDP as a common denominator to compute an industry's value-added contribution to the U.S. economy, and use the number of all the working people engaged in domestic productive activities as a common denominator to calculate the labor share for each industry. A time series of GDP shares and labor shares are displayed in Figures 11-2.1 and 11-2.2 for those industries that make up the goods-producing sector.

Figure 11-2.1 indicates that three component industries in the goods producing sector followed a declining trend in their GDP shares in the last fifty years. Agriculture's value-added accounted for 8.89% of U.S. GDP in 1948, but only 1.38% of GDP in 2000. The mining industry's GDP share reduced from 3.50% in 1948 to 1.29% in 2000. During the second half of the 1970s and the early 1980s, the mining industry experienced a boom that was triggered by the oil crises of 1973 and 1979. The mining industry's value added soared from 1.62% of GDP in 1972 to 2.62% in 1975 and to 4.05% in 1980 and 4.87% in 1981. This surge lasted another five years before the industry's GDP share began once again to decline in 1986.

The construction industry raised its GDP share from 4.27% in 1948 to 4.90% in 1970. Since 1972 this share has fluctuated, chasing the business cycle. For example, the construction share reduced to 3.96% in the 1982 business trough and recovered to 4.6% in 1986. It decreased to 3.71% in 1992 and rose to 4.70% in 2000. In the time frame of 1948-2000, the GDP share of the construction industry rose by merely 0.43%, while the net share drop of the combined agriculture and mining was about 9.73%, of which agriculture claimed 7.52%.

In the goods-producing sector, the manufacturing industry is the largest among the four industry groups. Its value-added accounted for 27.76% of the GDP in 1948 and rose to 29.25% of the GDP in 1953. Since then the

GDP share of manufacturing has declined substantially. It was approximately 28% in the 1950s, 26.5% in the 1960s, 22.5% in the 1970s, 19% in the 1980s and 17.4% in the 1990s, and further reduced to 15.88% in 2000, which represents a net 11.9%-share drop over a 52-year period.

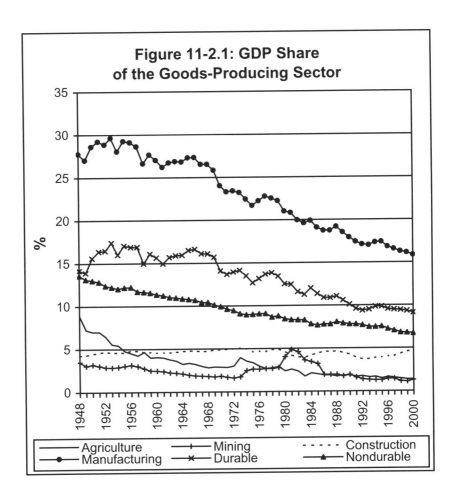

Figure 11-2.1: GDP Share of the Goods-Producing Sector

Both durable- and non-durable-goods manufacturing industry groups have contributed to the GDP-share decline of the manufacturing sector. The GDP share of non-durable-goods manufacturing decreased continuously from 13.59% in 1948 to 6.73% in 2000. The GDP share of durable-goods manufacturing, however, had a surge from 14.17% to 17.4% in the economic boom of 1948-53. In the following two decades this share fluctuated in the range of 15-17%. Since 1969 a declining trend has occurred in the GDP share of durable-goods production, which caused the share to drop farther in the business cycle's down swings than it could recover in the following upswings. During 1994-2000 the GDP share of durable goods seemed to stabilize around 9.7%. Nevertheless, production of durable goods is sensitive to business cycles and apparently fluctuates more than that of non-durable goods, construction, mining, and agriculture.

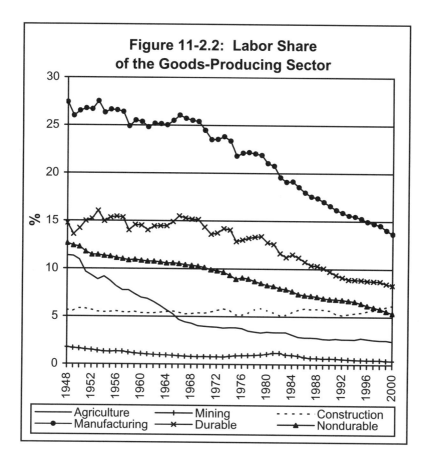

Figure 11-2.2: Labor Share of the Goods-Producing Sector

Parallel observations can be made from Figure 11-2.2 in regards to employment contributions made by the goods-producing sector. Three industry groups of goods production reduced their labor shares in the U.S. economy over the last fifty-two years: agriculture from 11.38% to 2.47%, mining from 1.77% to 0.41%, and manufacturing from 27.41% to 13.68%, while the labor share of construction remained in the range of 5-6%. The labor share of durable-goods manufacturing was above 14.5% in the 1950s and 1960s, and began to decline in 1970. This trend leveled off in 1993 and has since stabilized around 8.75%. The labor share of non-durable-goods manufacturing reduced continuously from 12.66% in 1948 to 5.4% in 2000.

Tables 11-2.1, 11-2.2, and 11-2.3 provide the GDP- and labor-shares and productivity measures for the major industry groups of goods-production.

Table 11-2.1: Contributions to GDP by the Goods-Producing Sector

| | Manufacturing | | Durable-goods Manufacturing | | Non-durable-goods Manufacturing | |
|---|---|---|---|---|---|---|
| Year | $ billion | % of GDP | $ billion | $ billion | % of GDP | $ billion |
| 1948 | 74.823 | 27.76 | 38.201 | 14.17 | 36.621 | 13.59 |
| 1955 | 121.432 | 29.25 | 70.876 | 17.07 | 50.556 | 12.18 |
| 1960 | 142.54 | 27.03 | 82.662 | 15.67 | 59.879 | 11.35 |
| 1965 | 196.568 | 27.3 | 118.89 | 16.51 | 77.678 | 10.79 |
| 1970 | 249.792 | 24.03 | 146.604 | 14.1 | 103.188 | 9.93 |
| 1975 | 354.765 | 21.7 | 207.502 | 12.69 | 147.263 | 9.01 |
| 1980 | 587.487 | 21.02 | 350.815 | 12.55 | 236.672 | 8.47 |
| 1985 | 804.391 | 19.09 | 479.273 | 11.38 | 325.118 | 7.72 |
| 1990 | 1040.58 | 17.93 | 586.534 | 10.11 | 454.046 | 7.82 |
| 1995 | 1289.099 | 17.42 | 729.841 | 9.86 | 559.258 | 7.56 |
| 2000 | 1567.428 | 15.88 | 902.584 | 9.14 | 664.844 | 6.73 |
| | Construction | | Mining | | Agriculture | |
| Year | $ billion | % of GDP | $ billion | % of GDP | $ billion | % of GDP |
| 1948 | 11.511 | 4.27 | 9.438 | 3.50 | 23.976 | 8.89 |
| 1955 | 18.992 | 4.57 | 12.627 | 3.04 | 19.835 | 4.78 |
| 1960 | 24.107 | 4.57 | 12.958 | 2.46 | 21.348 | 4.05 |
| 1965 | 34.479 | 4.79 | 14.165 | 1.97 | 24.239 | 3.37 |
| 1970 | 50.944 | 4.9 | 18.912 | 1.82 | 29.839 | 2.87 |
| 1975 | 75.528 | 4.62 | 42.809 | 2.62 | 54.892 | 3.36 |
| 1980 | 129.826 | 4.64 | 113.08 | 4.05 | 66.702 | 2.39 |
| 1985 | 186.3 | 4.42 | 135.322 | 3.21 | 84.724 | 2.01 |
| 1990 | 248.727 | 4.29 | 111.887 | 1.93 | 108.231 | 1.87 |
| 1995 | 290.323 | 3.92 | 95.615 | 1.29 | 109.824 | 1.48 |
| 2000 | 463.633 | 4.70 | 127.065 | 1.29 | 135.753 | 1.38 |

Table 11-2.2: Contributions to Employment by
the Goods-Producing Sector

| Year | Manufacturing | | Durable-goods Manufacturing | | Non-durable-goods Manufacturing | |
|---|---|---|---|---|---|---|
| | Persons million | % of total* | Persons million | Persons million | % of total* | Persons million |
| 1948 | 15.961 | 27.41 | 8.591 | 14.75 | 7.37 | 12.66 |
| 1955 | 16.852 | 26.63 | 9.709 | 15.34 | 7.143 | 11.29 |
| 1960 | 16.498 | 25.37 | 9.436 | 14.51 | 7.062 | 10.86 |
| 1965 | 17.902 | 25.51 | 10.458 | 14.9 | 7.444 | 10.61 |
| 1970 | 19.177 | 24.48 | 11.236 | 14.34 | 7.941 | 10.14 |
| 1975 | 18.062 | 21.79 | 10.665 | 12.86 | 7.397 | 8.92 |
| 1980 | 20.175 | 21.04 | 12.236 | 12.76 | 7.939 | 8.28 |
| 1985 | 19.132 | 18.56 | 11.539 | 11.19 | 7.593 | 7.37 |
| 1990 | 19.111 | 16.6 | 11.217 | 9.74 | 7.894 | 6.86 |
| 1995 | 18.625 | 15.27 | 10.816 | 8.87 | 7.811 | 6.40 |
| 2000 | 18.511 | 13.68 | 11.220 | 8.29 | 7.292 | 5.39 |
| Year | Construction | | Mining | | Agriculture | |
| | Persons million | % of total* | Persons million | Persons million | % of total* | Persons million |
| 1948 | 3.305 | 5.68 | 1.028 | 1.77 | 6.625 | 11.38 |
| 1955 | 3.463 | 5.47 | 0.835 | 1.32 | 5.525 | 8.73 |
| 1960 | 3.491 | 5.37 | 0.721 | 1.11 | 4.531 | 6.97 |
| 1965 | 3.903 | 5.56 | 0.644 | 0.92 | 3.713 | 5.29 |
| 1970 | 4.179 | 5.33 | 0.629 | 0.80 | 3.118 | 3.98 |
| 1975 | 4.296 | 5.18 | 0.755 | 0.91 | 3.191 | 3.85 |
| 1980 | 5.417 | 5.65 | 1.048 | 1.09 | 3.275 | 3.42 |
| 1985 | 5.904 | 5.73 | 0.93 | 0.90 | 2.979 | 2.89 |
| 1990 | 6.512 | 5.66 | 0.725 | 0.63 | 3.055 | 2.65 |
| 1995 | 6.650 | 5.45 | 0.590 | 0.48 | 3.38 | 2.77 |
| 2000 | 8.368 | 6.18 | 0.555 | 0.41 | 3.338 | 2.47 |

*The total represents the number of persons engaged in the U.S. domestic production.

These tables reveal that, albeit with differing degrees, productivity has greatly improved in each industry group. The productivity ratio of manufacturing was around 1.0 before 1985 and increased to 1.16 in 2000. In the 1970s and 1980s, both durable and non-durable goods manufacturing sectors showed smaller productivity ratios than for previous years. Particularly in the durable-goods manufacturing group, the productivity ratio fell below 1.0 in those years, indicating its productivity under the average productivity of the U.S. economy. American corporations went through a restructuring process during the 1980s, which was signified by corporations' downsizing, layoffs, and adoption of advanced information technology. Those efforts had greatly boosted manufacturing productivity and brought the ratio back above 1.0 after 1985. It is worth noticing that since 1975 non-durable-goods manufacturing has had higher productivity than durable-goods manufacturing.

Table 11-2.3: Productivity of the Goods-Producing Sector

| Year | Manufacturing | | Durable-goods Manufacturing | | Non-durable-goods Manufacturing | |
|---|---|---|---|---|---|---|
| | $1000 per person | Ratio* | $1000 per person | Ratio | $1000 per person | Ratio |
| 1948 | 4.688 | 1.01 | 4.447 | 0.96 | 4.969 | 1.07 |
| 1955 | 7.206 | 1.10 | 7.300 | 1.11 | 7.078 | 1.08 |
| 1960 | 8.64 | 1.07 | 8.761 | 1.08 | 8.479 | 1.05 |
| 1965 | 10.98 | 1.07 | 11.368 | 1.11 | 10.435 | 1.02 |
| 1970 | 13.025 | 0.98 | 13.048 | 0.98 | 12.995 | 0.98 |
| 1975 | 19.641 | 1.00 | 19.456 | 0.99 | 19.909 | 1.01 |
| 1980 | 29.119 | 1.00 | 28.672 | 0.98 | 29.812 | 1.02 |
| 1985 | 42.044 | 1.03 | 41.536 | 1.02 | 42.817 | 1.05 |
| 1990 | 54.448 | 1.08 | 52.287 | 1.04 | 57.518 | 1.14 |
| 1995 | 69.212 | 1.14 | 67.477 | 1.11 | 71.603 | 1.18 |
| 2000 | 84.675 | 1.16 | 80.447 | 1.10 | 91.180 | 1.25 |
| Year | Construction | | Mining | | Agriculture | |
| | $1000 per person | Ratio | $1000 per person | Ratio | $1000 per person | Ratio |
| 1948 | 3.483 | 0.75 | 9.182 | 1.98 | 3.619 | 0.78 |
| 1955 | 5.484 | 0.84 | 15.117 | 2.30 | 3.590 | 0.55 |
| 1960 | 6.906 | 0.85 | 17.968 | 2.22 | 4.711 | 0.58 |
| 1965 | 8.835 | 0.86 | 21.986 | 2.14 | 6.528 | 0.64 |
| 1970 | 12.191 | 0.92 | 30.062 | 2.27 | 9.570 | 0.72 |
| 1975 | 17.580 | 0.89 | 56.679 | 2.87 | 17.202 | 0.87 |
| 1980 | 23.966 | 0.82 | 107.867 | 3.70 | 20.364 | 0.70 |
| 1985 | 31.552 | 0.77 | 145.515 | 3.56 | 28.445 | 0.70 |
| 1990 | 38.193 | 0.76 | 154.269 | 3.06 | 35.423 | 0.70 |
| 1995 | 43.655 | 0.72 | 161.951 | 2.67 | 32.491 | 0.54 |
| 2000 | 55.408 | 0.76 | 228.964 | 3.14 | 40.671 | 0.56 |

* Ratios denote sector's productivity measure divided by the productivity measure of the entire domestic production.

The mining industry experienced the highest productivity among the goods-producing industry groups, while construction and agriculture fell behind with their productivity lower than the average productivity of the U.S. economy. The mining industry's growth rate of value-added was slower than the growth rate of GDP, which is indicated by its declining trend of GDP share. Its employment, however, actually declined from 1.03 million in 1948 to 0.555 million in 2000, which resulted in the high productivity measure. A similar situation occurred in U.S. agriculture, slowly growing its value-added and decreasing its working force. The construction industry experienced average growth in terms of both value-added and employment, which was evidenced by the little changes in its GDP- and labor-shares over this fifty-two-year period.

The facts revealed by GDP- and labor-shares indicate that in the last five decades, the agriculture, mining, and construction industries were no longer the leading sector for economic growth in the United as they were in the stage of pre-condition for take-off during 1815 - 1840. In the current stage of high mass-consumption, these industries' economic weight has diminished over time.

The GDP- and labor-share of the manufacturing sector, particularly the durable-goods manufacturing, rose substantially in the 1950s, due to its faster expansion in both value-added and the work force. In that decade manufacturing productivity was also higher than the average of the U.S. economy. The entire manufacturing sector played a leading role in U.S. economic growth during the 1950s. Since 1970, however, its leadership has deteriorated, which is reflected in a slowing growth rate, diminishing GDP- and labor-shares, and a reduction in the relative productivity ratio.

As an aggregated group, the manufacturing sector seemed no longer to be a leading sector for the 1990s U.S. economy. This observation, however, does not imply that all the less aggregated manufacturing industries did not provide leadership for extraordinary economic expansion in the 1990s. Quite the contrary, information technology-related manufacturing industries such as semiconductor, computer, and telecommunications equipment manufacturing have played a crucial role in creating advanced technologies and in accelerating their applications and adoptions in American corporations, governments, universities, communities and society. To identify those leading industries within the manufacturing sector one has to rely on less aggregated industry data.

As both durable- and non-durable-goods manufacturing sectors consist of different less-aggregated industries, we need to know how those component industries have changed their relative strength in the national economy. That is the purpose of the next two sub-sections.

## 11-3-1 Durable-Goods Manufacturing

In the SIC (Standard Industrial Classification) code system there are ten 2-digit industries recorded under the head of durable goods manufacturing. We consolidate those component industries into five groups in order to facilitate graphic and tabulate presentations. The durable-goods manufacturing groups include:

Metal            (primary metal industries SIC33 and fabricated metal products SIC34)

Machinery        (industrial machinery and equipment, except electric equipment, SIC35)

Electric & Electronic Equipment & Instruments
                 (electric and electronic equipment SIC36, and instruments and related products SIC38)

Motor            (motor vehicles and equipment, and other transportation equipment SIC37)

Wood & Stone (lumber and wood products SIC24, furniture and fixtures SIC25, and stone, clay, and glass SIC32, and miscellaneous manufacturing industries SIC39)

The metal industry, particularly the steel industry, was a leading sector during the Second Industrial Revolution. In the late 1860s a break-through occurred in the metal industry. At this time several methods of producing cheap steel were invented and the industry expanded rapidly in response to a huge demand from the railroad industry. The steel industry was a driving force for economic growth in the United States and many Western nations when they were in the third stage of economic growth – "drive to technological maturity." In the United States the third stage of economic growth took place during the time period from 1830 to 1920.

The important role of the metal industry extended into the third industrial revolution, in which many modern industries, such as internal combustion engine, electricity, and modern chemicals, joined the leading sector to drive economic growth. The metal industry is the major supplier to the automobile, shipbuilding, and airplane manufacturing industries as well as the construction industry. At the beginning of the twentieth century, the United States entered the fifth stage of economic growth, called "high mass-consumption." In this stage, established leading industries continued to play an important role, but the driving force for economic growth was provided by new industries, which shall be observed via a detailed industry analysis.

For the above five industry groups of durable-goods manufacturing, we compute their value-added contributions (GDP shares) and employment contributions (labor shares) to the U.S. economy, as well as their proxy productivity measures and relative productivity ratios to the average productivity of the U.S. economy as a whole. The results are presented in Figures 11-3.1 and 11-3.2, and Tables 11-3.1, 11-3.2, and 11-3.3 ( Ele & Ele & Ins denotes the electrical and electronic equipment and instruments group).

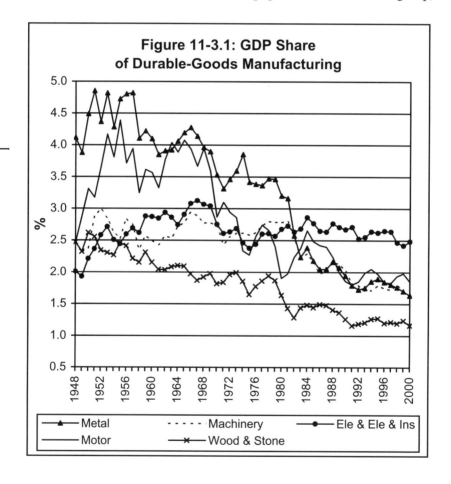

Among the five groups of durable-goods manufacturing, the metal industry held the largest position until 1980 in terms of both the GDP- and labor-shares. The metal industry's important role in economic growth for the 1950s, 60s and 70s can be observed through the fact that when its share increased there was an economic boom, such as in 1948-51, 1961-66, and 1972-74, and when its share declined, there was an economic recession, such as in 1957-58, 1969-71, and 1982-83. The metal industry's relative strength, however, has declined since 1957, with its GDP-share dropping from 4.80% in 1957 to 2.18% in 1985, and to 1.64% in 2000. At the same time its labor-share reduced from 4.03% to 2.19% and to 1.65%. The continuous decline in its GDP- and labor-share shows that the metal industry has grown at a slower pace than the average growth rate of the U.S. economy.

**Figure 11-3.2: Labor Share of Durable-Goods Manufacturing**

Starting with a 2.49% GDP share in 1948, the industry group of motor vehicles and other transportation equipment surged during the early 1950s. Its GDP-share reached 4.39% in 1955, the largest share over the last fifty years. Even though its GDP share dropped below 3.5% in 1958 and 1961, this group remained second only to the metal industry during the 1960s.

Since 1969, however, the relative strength of the auto and other transportation equipment industry group has declined substantially. Its value-added dropped from $35.418 billion in 1969 to $29.818 billion in 1970, and its GDP share from 3.59% to 2.87%.

Table 11-3.1: Contribution to GDP by Durable-Goods Manufacturing

| | Metal | | Motor Vehicle & Transportation | | Wood-products & Others | |
|---|---|---|---|---|---|---|
| Year | $ billion | % of GDP | $ billion | $ billion | % of GDP | $ billion |
| 1948 | 11.093 | 4.12 | 6.642 | 2.46 | 6.661 | 2.47 |
| 1955 | 19.619 | 4.73 | 18.232 | 4.39 | 10.206 | 2.46 |
| 1960 | 21.607 | 4.10 | 18.812 | 3.57 | 11.370 | 2.16 |
| 1965 | 30.201 | 4.19 | 29.352 | 4.08 | 15.093 | 2.10 |
| 1970 | 36.700 | 3.53 | 29.818 | 2.87 | 18.901 | 1.82 |
| 1975 | 55.890 | 3.42 | 37.151 | 2.27 | 26.948 | 1.65 |
| 1980 | 89.570 | 3.20 | 53.200 | 1.90 | 45.763 | 1.64 |
| 1985 | 91.886 | 2.18 | 104.651 | 2.48 | 60.878 | 1.45 |
| 1990 | 112.641 | 1.94 | 107.824 | 1.86 | 73.121 | 1.26 |
| 1995 | 140.166 | 1.89 | 145.865 | 1.97 | 94.209 | 1.27 |
| 2000 | 161.620 | 1.64 | 182.946 | 1.85 | 114.921 | 1.16 |

| Year | Industrial Machinery | | Electric & Electro & Instruments | |
|---|---|---|---|---|
| | $billion | % of GDP | $billion | % of GDP |
| 1948 | 6.702 | 2.49 | 5.418 | 2.01 |
| 1955 | 10.472 | 2.52 | 10.144 | 2.44 |
| 1960 | 13.185 | 2.50 | 15.146 | 2.87 |
| 1965 | 20.077 | 2.79 | 20.934 | 2.91 |
| 1970 | 28.425 | 2.73 | 28.612 | 2.75 |
| 1975 | 42.236 | 2.58 | 38.852 | 2.38 |
| 1980 | 77.773 | 2.78 | 74.837 | 2.68 |
| 1985 | 90.790 | 2.16 | 116.574 | 2.77 |
| 1990 | 118.212 | 2.04 | 155.005 | 2.67 |
| 1995 | 132.840 | 1.80 | 194.042 | 2.62 |
| 2000 | 167.642 | 1.70 | 245.441 | 2.65 |

The global oil market has also exercised its great influence on the auto industry of the U.S. economy. The first oil crisis caused the value-added of the U.S. motor vehicle and equipment industry to drop from $29.303 billion in 1973 to $19.358 billion in 1974. The second oil crisis reduced the U.S. auto industry's value added from $37.644 billion in 1979 to $27.109 billion in 1980. Those large output drops of the auto industry were reflected in the GDP share decline from 2.86% in 1973 to 2.34% in

1974 and from 2.41% in 1979 to 1.90% in 1980 for the broad transportation equipment industry group.

Table 11-3-2: Contribution to Employment by Durable-Goods Manufacturing

| Year | Metal | | Motor Vehicle & Transportation | | Wood-products & Others | |
|------|-------------------|------------------|-------------------|-------------------|------------------|-------------------|
| | Persons million | % of total* | Persons million | Persons million | % of total* | Persons million |
| 1948 | 2.338 | 4.02 | 1.231 | 2.11 | 1.898 | 3.26 |
| 1955 | 2.550 | 4.03 | 1.867 | 2.95 | 1.804 | 2.85 |
| 1960 | 2.389 | 3.67 | 1.643 | 2.53 | 1.696 | 2.61 |
| 1965 | 2.630 | 3.75 | 1.836 | 2.62 | 1.769 | 2.52 |
| 1970 | 2.797 | 3.57 | 1.836 | 2.34 | 1.807 | 2.31 |
| 1975 | 2.564 | 3.09 | 1.685 | 2.03 | 1.697 | 2.05 |
| 1980 | 2.734 | 2.85 | 1.895 | 1.98 | 1.897 | 1.98 |
| 1985 | 2.257 | 2.19 | 1.978 | 1.92 | 1.830 | 1.78 |
| 1990 | 2.169 | 1.88 | 2.002 | 1.74 | 1.883 | 1.64 |
| 1995 | 2.142 | 1.76 | 1.778 | 1.46 | 1.933 | 1.59 |
| 2000 | 2.233 | 1.65 | 1.853 | 1.37 | 2.049 | 1.51 |

| Year | Industrial Machinery | | Electric & Electro & Instruments | |
|------|-------------------|------------|-------|-------------------|
| | Persons million | % of total | Year | Persons million |
| 1948 | 1.432 | 2.46 | 1.250 | 2.15 |
| 1955 | 1.480 | 2.34 | 1.586 | 2.51 |
| 1960 | 1.481 | 2.28 | 1.829 | 2.81 |
| 1965 | 1.760 | 2.51 | 2.035 | 2.90 |
| 1970 | 1.985 | 2.53 | 2.378 | 3.04 |
| 1975 | 2.061 | 2.49 | 2.224 | 2.68 |
| 1980 | 2.490 | 2.60 | 2.782 | 2.90 |
| 1985 | 2.189 | 2.12 | 2.887 | 2.80 |
| 1990 | 2.091 | 1.82 | 2.656 | 2.31 |
| 1995 | 2.083 | 1.71 | 2.452 | 2.01 |
| 2000 | 2.109 | 1.56 | 2.543 | 1.88 |

*The total represents the number of persons engaged in the U.S. domestic production.

Besides the trend of decline that prevailed in the 1970's and 1980's, the business cycle caused large fluctuations in the GDP share of the transportation equipment industry group. Its recent top of GDP-share appeared in 1994 with $144.614 billion of value added, accounting for only 2.05% of GDP. As of 2000, the value-added by the transportation equipment industry group reached $182.95 billion, accounting for only 1.85% of the 9-trillion U.S economy, which was close to the smallest share (1.80% in 1991) this industry group has had during the last five decades. The labor share of the auto and transportation equipment industry group rose from 2.11% in 1948 to 3.24% in 1953 and decreased to 1.37% in 2000.

Table 11-3.3: Productivity of Durable-Goods Manufacturing

| Year | Metal | | Motor Vehicle & Transportation | | Wood-products & Others | |
|---|---|---|---|---|---|---|
| | $1000 per person | Ratio* | $1000 per person | Ratio | $1000 per person | Ratio |
| 1948 | 4.745 | 1.02 | 5.396 | 1.17 | 3.509 | 0.76 |
| 1955 | 7.694 | 1.17 | 9.767 | 1.49 | 5.657 | 0.86 |
| 1960 | 9.046 | 1.12 | 11.448 | 1.41 | 6.704 | 0.83 |
| 1965 | 11.485 | 1.12 | 15.988 | 1.56 | 8.534 | 0.83 |
| 1970 | 13.122 | 0.99 | 16.245 | 1.22 | 10.463 | 0.79 |
| 1975 | 21.795 | 1.11 | 22.042 | 1.12 | 15.879 | 0.81 |
| 1980 | 32.756 | 1.12 | 28.070 | 0.96 | 24.122 | 0.83 |
| 1985 | 40.714 | 1.00 | 52.895 | 1.29 | 33.267 | 0.81 |
| 1990 | 51.935 | 1.03 | 53.859 | 1.07 | 38.824 | 0.77 |
| 1995 | 65.437 | 1.08 | 82.016 | 1.35 | 48.727 | 0.80 |
| 2000 | 72.366 | 0.99 | 98.729 | 1.35 | 56.079 | 0.77 |

| Year | Industrial Machinery | | Electric & Electro & Instruments | |
|---|---|---|---|---|
| | $1000 per person | Ratio | $1000 per person | Ratio |
| 1948 | 4.680 | 1.01 | 4.334 | 0.94 |
| 1955 | 7.075 | 1.08 | 6.394 | 0.97 |
| 1960 | 8.904 | 1.10 | 8.283 | 1.02 |
| 1965 | 11.406 | 1.11 | 10.286 | 1.00 |
| 1970 | 14.318 | 1.08 | 12.030 | 0.91 |
| 1975 | 20.492 | 1.04 | 17.473 | 0.89 |
| 1980 | 31.235 | 1.07 | 26.896 | 0.92 |
| 1985 | 41.480 | 1.02 | 40.382 | 0.99 |
| 1990 | 56.544 | 1.12 | 58.363 | 1.16 |
| 1995 | 63.759 | 1.05 | 79.141 | 1.30 |
| 2000 | 79.495 | 1.09 | 96.504 | 1.32 |

* Ratios denote sector's productivity measure divided by the productivity measure of the entire domestic production.

The wood-product group's GDP share declined until 1982, and then held steady at 1.5% for about five years. This decline, however, reassumed in 1988, which pushed its GDP share down to 1.26 % in 1990 and 1.16% in 2000. Its labor-share also reduced from 3.26% in 1948 to 1.51% in 2000.

The group of industrial machinery had a significant rise in its GDP share during 1948-52, and reached its highest share of 3.03% in 1952. This group managed a sustainable value-added contribution to the U.S.

economy in the range of 2.5-2.9% of GDP during 1952-1981. Since the beginning of the 1980's its GDP share has rapidly diminished, from 2.78% in 1980 to 1.70% in 2000. Its labor share has followed a pattern similar to its GDP share, reducing from the average level of 2.5% over the three decades of 1950-1980 to 1.56% in 2000.

Among the five industry groups of durable-goods manufacturing, the electrical and electronic equipment and instruments group had the smallest GDP share in 1948, 2.01%. This group grew much faster than the economy during 1948-69, which resulted in a substantial rise in its GDP-share, above 3% in 1966-69. The economic recession caused its GDP-share to drop to 2.63% in 1971 and to 2.38% in 1975. Since 1975 this group has restored its growth momentum and raised its GDP-share up to 2.87% in 1984. The economic recession of 1991 had a minor effect on this group as its GDP-share hit the low 2.51% in 1992 and rose back to 2.65% in 1997, and fell to 2.49% in 2000. Its labor-share increased from 2.15% in 1948 to 3.04% in 1970, and the declining trend pushed the labor share to 1.88% in 2000.

The proxy measures of an industry group's productivity in Table 11-3.3 indicate that even though all the groups have raised their productivity over time, the relative productivity ratios have changed by different amounts. The wood-product group's productivity was the lowest among the five groups; it was 15-20% below the economy's average before 1985 and 23% below the average in 2000. The transportation equipment group had the highest productivity in the 1950s and 60s; it was 56% above the average in 1965 and 35% above the average in 2000. Only in 1980 did its productivity measure drop below the average by 4%. This was due to a big output shortfall of the motor vehicle and equipment industry caused by the second oil crisis.

The metal group's productivity was nearly 17% higher than the average in 1955; its relative strength was reduced and ended at the economy's average in 2000. The productivity of the industrial machinery group remained higher than the average of the economy over the entire fifty-two-year period, and it was about 9% higher than the average in 2000. The productivity of the electric and electronic equipment and instrument group was lower than the average before 1987, except for a few years in the 1960s. Since 1990, this group has consistently demonstrated the highest productivity among the five groups of durable-goods manufacturing. Its productivity was nearly 32% higher than the average of the U.S. economy in 2000.

The above analysis of productivity and contributions made by the durable-goods manufacturing industries indicates a changing picture of the leading sectors in the U.S. economy. With the rapid growth of value added and employment as well as the highest productivity, both the metal group and the motor vehicle and transportation equipment industry group were the leading sectors for the U.S. economy in the 1950s and 60s. Their leading role reduced substantially in the 1970's and 80's due to their slowing growth in value added and working force. Not only did these two industry groups fail to keep up their superior growth of the 1950s and 60s, but also their growth rate actually went below the economy's average in most years during the 1990's. Consequently, the metal and transportation equipment industries were not qualified as a leading sector of the U.S. economy for the 1990s.

The industrial machinery group also provided a leading role to economic growth in the 1950s, 60s, and 70s. Its leading position, however, deteriorated in the 1980s by the apparently slow growth and declining contributions to the economy. In the 1980s and 90s this group's growth and contributions were following the business cycle closely and it is hard to see a decisive up-trend in its GDP- and labor-shares that was badly needed to restore its leading position. The electric and electronic equipment and instruments group was a leading sector due to its faster growth and increasing contributions to the economy in the time period from 1950 through 1985. In the 1990s its GDP-share increased slightly, while the labor share reduced substantially, which resulted in the improvement of productivity. In terms of value added, it has still provided a favorable role in driving economic growth, but in terms of job creation its leadership was lost for the 1990s.

The wood-product group was never a leading sector in the U.S. economy during the last half of the twentieth century. Its declining contributions to GDP and employment along with its low productivity have continued for more than fifty years and may well extend in the future.

## 11-3-2 Non-durable-Goods Manufacturing

We divide non-durable-goods manufacturing into four industry groups as the following:

| | |
|---|---|
| Food & tobacco: | Food and kindred products (SIC20) |
| | Tobacco products (SIC21) |
| Textile & others: | Textile mill products (SIC22) |
| | Apparel and other textile products (SIC23) |

Paper & publishing:        Paper and allied products (SIC26)
                           Printing and publishing (SIC27).
Chemicals & petroleum:  Chemicals and allied products (SIC28)
                           Petroleum and coal products (SIC29)
                           Rubber and miscellaneous plastics products
                           (SIC30)
                           Leather and leather products (SIC31)

The GDP- and labor-shares of these industry groups are displayed in Figures 11-4.1 and 11-4.2, and the numerical results of both shares and productivity measures are provided in Tables 11-4.1, 11-4.2, and 11-4.3.

The paper and publishing group's GDP-share increased from 2.29% in 1948 to 2.49% in 1956, which was its largest share in the last fifty years. After 1956, this group grew at a slower pace than the average growth rate of the economy, resulting in a gradually decreasing GDP-share to 1.68% in 2000. The number of people working for this industry group increased from 1.28 million in 1948 to 2.19 million in 2000. But after 1970 its speed of job creation was slower than the average rate of the economy, which caused a decline in its labor-share from 2.25% in 1970 to 1.62% in 2000. Except for a few years in the 1970s, this group's productivity was about 2-3% higher than the economy's average productivity. Because the declining trend in both GDP- and labor-shares has well extended into the 1990s, the paper and publishing group has not been a leading sector in the contemporary U.S. economy.

The food & tobacco group reduced its GDP-share from 4.45% to 1.61% and its labor-share from 3.33% to 1.26% in the time period from 1948 through 2000. Its productivity, however, remained 20-30% higher than the average productivity of the U.S. economy. A large share drop also appeared in the textile group. Its GDP-share declined from 3.31% to 0.49%, and its labor share declined from 4.41% to 0.85% in 1948 - 2000. The textile group's productivity was the lowest in the non-durable-goods sector; it was only 57% of the economy's average productivity in 2000. Declining GDP- and labor-shares of these two groups reflect the slower than the average growth rates in both value added and employment. This fact clearly says that with continuously diminishing relative strength, the food and tobacco industry along with the textile industry has been a laggard sector in the U.S economy for a long time.

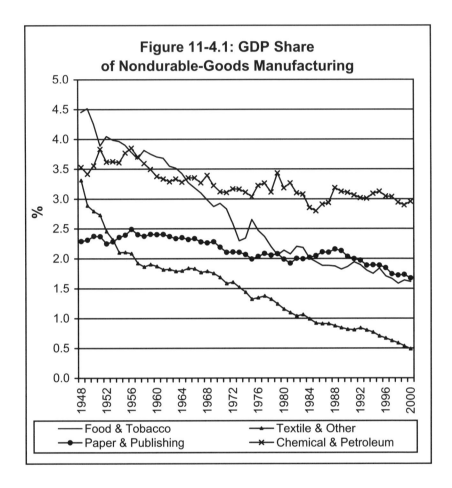

The chemical and petroleum group raised its GDP-share from 3.53% in 1948 to 3.85% in 1956 and maintained its labor-share steady at approximately 2.7% in 1948 - 56, with its productivity 28-39% higher than the economy's average productivity. These facts indicate that the chemical and petroleum group grew faster than the economy as a whole during 1950s. An apparent declining trend, however, depressed its GDP share from the historic high 3.85% in 1956 to 3.04% in 1975, while the labor-share had a minor deduction, and its relative productivity also reduced to 16-25% above the economy's average.

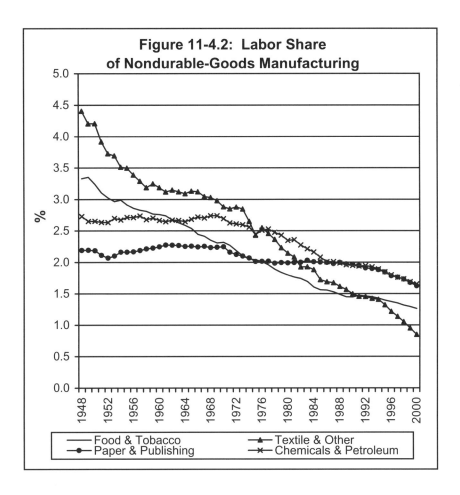

The changes in its relative strength indicate the deterioration of its leading role that was displayed during 1948 - 75. Since 1975, its GDP-share has been in flux, closely following business cycles, and its labor share has declined continuously. As a result, its productivity increased from 29% above the average in 1948 to 79% above the average in 2000.

Table 11-4.1: Contribution to GDP by Non-Durable-Goods
Manufacturing

| | Food & Tobacco | | Textile & Others | |
|---|---|---|---|---|
| Year | $ billion | % of GDP | $ billion | % of GDP |
| 1948 | 12.001 | 4.45 | 8.928 | 3.31 |
| 1955 | 16.197 | 3.90 | 8.753 | 2.11 |
| 1960 | 19.539 | 3.71 | 9.867 | 1.87 |
| 1965 | 23.569 | 3.27 | 13.257 | 1.84 |
| 1970 | 30.431 | 2.93 | 17.539 | 1.69 |
| 1975 | 43.463 | 2.66 | 21.568 | 1.32 |
| 1980 | 59.825 | 2.14 | 32.261 | 1.15 |
| 1985 | 82.027 | 1.95 | 38.802 | 0.92 |
| 1990 | 108.347 | 1.87 | 47.354 | 0.82 |
| 1995 | 136.244 | 1.84 | 52.026 | 0.70 |
| 2000 | 159.349 | 1.61 | 48.279 | 0.49 |
| | Paper & Publishing | | Chemical & Petroleum | |
| Year | $ billion | % of GDP | $ billion | % of GDP |
| 1948 | 6.176 | 2.29 | 9.519 | 3.53 |
| 1955 | 9.944 | 2.40 | 15.658 | 3.77 |
| 1960 | 12.673 | 2.40 | 17.81 | 3.38 |
| 1965 | 16.699 | 2.32 | 24.145 | 3.35 |
| 1970 | 22.79 | 2.19 | 32.427 | 3.12 |
| 1975 | 32.589 | 1.99 | 49.644 | 3.04 |
| 1980 | 55.604 | 1.99 | 88.983 | 3.18 |
| 1985 | 86.283 | 2.05 | 118.049 | 2.80 |
| 1990 | 118.096 | 2.04 | 180.307 | 3.11 |
| 1995 | 139.722 | 1.89 | 231.193 | 3.12 |
| 2000 | 165.372 | 1.68 | 291.943 | 2.96 |

Nevertheless, declines in the relative strength of the chemical and petroleum industry over the last five decades were fairly moderate, compared with many industries in the goods-producing sector. Particularly, in the cyclic upswings, such as in 1987-88, this group generated a strong momentum for economic growth. The opportunity to create new jobs seems quite limited due to the declining trend in its labor-share and the increasing pressure of raising productivity.

## Table 11-4.2: Contribution to Employment by
## Non-Durable-Goods Manufacturing

| Year | Food & Tobacco | | Textile & Others | |
|---|---|---|---|---|
| | Persons million | % of total | Persons million | % of total |
| 1948 | 1.940 | 3.33 | 2.566 | 4.41 |
| 1955 | 1.844 | 2.91 | 2.214 | 3.50 |
| 1960 | 1.795 | 2.76 | 2.073 | 3.19 |
| 1965 | 1.780 | 2.54 | 2.199 | 3.13 |
| 1970 | 1.815 | 2.32 | 2.258 | 2.88 |
| 1975 | 1.690 | 2.04 | 2.013 | 2.43 |
| 1980 | 1.723 | 1.80 | 2.057 | 2.15 |
| 1985 | 1.607 | 1.56 | 1.774 | 1.72 |
| 1990 | 1.665 | 1.45 | 1.722 | 1.50 |
| 1995 | 1.700 | 1.39 | 1.611 | 1.32 |
| 2000 | 1.708 | 1.26 | 1.152 | 0.85 |
| | Paper & Publishing | | Chemical & Petroleum | |
| Year | Persons million | % of total | Persons million | % of total |
| 1948 | 1.275 | 2.19 | 1.589 | 2.73 |
| 1955 | 1.368 | 2.16 | 1.717 | 2.71 |
| 1960 | 1.461 | 2.25 | 1.734 | 2.67 |
| 1965 | 1.583 | 2.26 | 1.882 | 2.68 |
| 1970 | 1.759 | 2.25 | 2.110 | 2.69 |
| 1975 | 1.669 | 2.01 | 2.025 | 2.44 |
| 1980 | 1.909 | 1.99 | 2.249 | 2.35 |
| 1985 | 2.065 | 2.00 | 2.147 | 2.08 |
| 1990 | 2.264 | 1.97 | 2.244 | 1.95 |
| 1995 | 2.247 | 1.84 | 2.252 | 1.85 |
| 2000 | 2.194 | 1.62 | 2.236 | 1.65 |

* The total represents the number of persons engaged in the U.S. domestic production.

Table 11-4.3: Productivity of Non-Durable-Goods Manufacturing

| | Food & Tobacco | | Textile & Others | |
|---|---|---|---|---|
| Year | $1000 per person | Ratio* | $1000 per person | Ratio |
| 1948 | 6.185 | 1.34 | 3.480 | 0.75 |
| 1955 | 8.785 | 1.34 | 3.953 | 0.60 |
| 1960 | 10.887 | 1.34 | 4.760 | 0.59 |
| 1965 | 13.238 | 1.29 | 6.029 | 0.59 |
| 1970 | 16.765 | 1.26 | 7.768 | 0.59 |
| 1975 | 25.710 | 1.30 | 10.714 | 0.54 |
| 1980 | 34.730 | 1.19 | 15.681 | 0.54 |
| 1985 | 51.034 | 1.25 | 21.868 | 0.54 |
| 1990 | 65.086 | 1.29 | 27.496 | 0.55 |
| 1995 | 80.123 | 1.32 | 32.286 | 0.53 |
| 2000 | 93.286 | 1.28 | 41.913 | 0.57 |
| | Paper & Publishing | | Chemical & Petroleum | |
| Year | $1000 per person | Ratio | $1000 per person | Ratio |
| 1948 | 4.843 | 1.05 | 5.990 | 1.29 |
| 1955 | 7.269 | 1.11 | 9.118 | 1.39 |
| 1960 | 8.677 | 1.07 | 10.273 | 1.27 |
| 1965 | 10.552 | 1.03 | 12.828 | 1.25 |
| 1970 | 12.958 | 0.98 | 15.370 | 1.16 |
| 1975 | 19.527 | 0.99 | 24.520 | 1.24 |
| 1980 | 29.132 | 1.00 | 39.563 | 1.36 |
| 1985 | 41.782 | 1.02 | 54.995 | 1.35 |
| 1990 | 52.152 | 1.03 | 80.360 | 1.59 |
| 1995 | 62.184 | 1.02 | 102.671 | 1.69 |
| 2000 | 75.371 | 1.03 | 130.561 | 1.79 |

\* Ratios denote sector's productivity measure divided by the productivity measure of the entire domestic production.

## 11-4  The Services-Producing Sector

Adopting a convention in the "Current Business Survey" by U.S. Department of Commerce, we include a broader set of industries into the services-producing sector, which are

> Transportation, communications, and utilities (SIC40-42 and SIC44-49)

Wholesale trade (SIC50-51)
Retail trade (SIC52-59)
Finance, insurance, and real estate (SIC60-67)
Services (SIC70-89)

First we present contributions to the U.S. economy made by these five industry groups of the services-producing sector. Then we take a look at the less aggregated-industry groups for the transportation, communications, and utilities group, the finance, insurance, and real estate group, and the services group in the following three subsections. The five industry groups' contributions to the U.S. economy are presented in Figures 11-5.1 and 11-5.2, and Tables 11-5.1, 11-5.2, and 11-5.3.

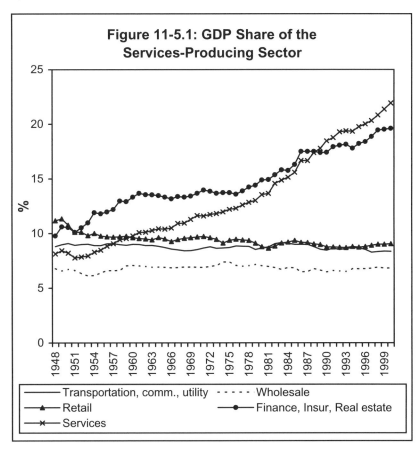

Figure 11-5.1: GDP Share of the Services-Producing Sector

The GDP-share of transportation, communications, and utility group remained flat, around 8.3-9.0% over the last fifty-two years, while its labor share reduced gradually from 7.42% in 1948 to 5.18% in 2000. Consequently, its productivity was improved from 19% above the economy's average in 1948 to a 61% above the average in 2000. The flat GDP share indicates that its growth rate of value added was closely following the growth rate of GDP over the entire time period.

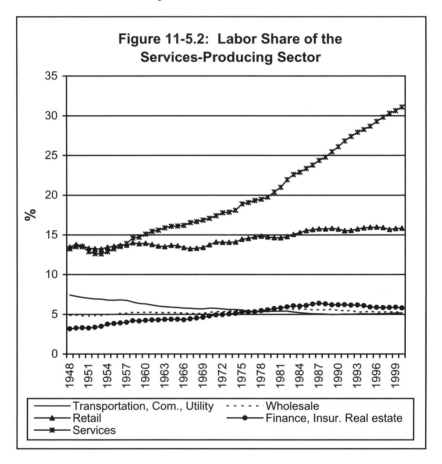

The wholesale trade group's GDP-share fluctuated in a narrow range of 6.4-7.4%, with a small upswing in 1953-59 and a small downswing in 1975-93. Similarly, its labor-share increased slightly from 4.88% in 1948 to 5.64% in 1985 and declined to 5.25% in 2000. Its productivity was 18-30% higher than the economy's average. The retail trade group reduced its GDP-share from 11.16% in 1948 to 9.05% in 2000, but raised its labor-share from 13.48% to 15.83% in the same time frame. Consequently, its relative productivity decreased from about 83% of the economy's average in 1948 to just 57% of the average in 2000. Although the retail trade group's labor force increased faster than the economy's growth rate of employment, its value added grew much more slowly than U.S. GDP. Lacking superior growth in both values added and employment, the wholesale trade and retail trade have not been a leading sector of the U.S. economy in the last fifty years.

Table 11-5.1: Contribution to GDP by the Services-Producing Sector

| Year | Transportation, Communication and Utilities | | Wholesale Trade | | Retail Trade | |
|---|---|---|---|---|---|---|
| | $ billion | % of GDP | $billion | % of GDP | $ billion | % of GDP |
| 1948 | 23.755 | 8.81 | 18.331 | 6.8 | 30.087 | 11.16 |
| 1955 | 36.929 | 8.89 | 26.557 | 6.4 | 40.537 | 9.76 |
| 1960 | 47.517 | 9.01 | 37.370 | 7.09 | 50.718 | 9.62 |
| 1965 | 62.700 | 8.71 | 49.702 | 6.90 | 68.367 | 9.49 |
| 1970 | 88.684 | 8.53 | 71.977 | 6.92 | 100.682 | 9.68 |
| 1975 | 142.439 | 8.71 | 121.084 | 7.41 | 153.182 | 9.37 |
| 1980 | 242.375 | 8.67 | 196.863 | 7.04 | 245.394 | 8.78 |
| 1985 | 379.045 | 9.00 | 289.097 | 6.86 | 394.338 | 9.36 |
| 1990 | 490.897 | 8.46 | 376.166 | 6.48 | 507.784 | 8.75 |
| 1995 | 642.588 | 8.68 | 500.646 | 6.77 | 646.807 | 8.74 |
| 2000 | 824.983 | 8.36 | 674.124 | 6.83 | 893.896 | 9.05 |

| Year | Finance, Insurance and Real estate | | Services | |
|---|---|---|---|---|
| | $ billion | % of GDP | $ billion | % of GDP |
| 1948 | 26.359 | 9.78 | 21.916 | 8.13 |
| 1955 | 49.007 | 11.80 | 35.206 | 8.48 |
| 1960 | 70.305 | 13.33 | 51.583 | 9.78 |
| 1965 | 96.012 | 13.33 | 74.841 | 10.39 |
| 1970 | 142.144 | 13.67 | 120.893 | 11.63 |
| 1975 | 224.59 | 13.74 | 199.523 | 12.20 |
| 1980 | 416.259 | 14.89 | 378.882 | 13.55 |
| 1985 | 686.511 | 16.30 | 656.472 | 15.58 |
| 1990 | 1010.345 | 17.41 | 1071.511 | 18.46 |
| 1995 | 1347.267 | 18.21 | 1462.42 | 19.76 |
| 2000 | 1936.182 | 19.61 | 2164.642 | 21.93 |

The group of finance, insurance, and real estate experienced a surge in 1948-60, with its value added increasing from $26.4 billion in 1948 to $1.936 trillion in 2000 and its GDP-share rising from 9.78% to 19.61%

correspondingly. In the meantime, its labor-share increased from 3.19% to 5.80%, and productivity ratio rose from 3.07 to 3.38.

These evidences indicate that during 1948-60 the finance group grew much faster than did the U.S. economy as a whole in terms of value-added, working force, and productivity improvement. Therefore, it played a leading role in economic growth during 1948-60. Its growth rate of value-added reduced to nearly the growth rate of the GDP in 1961-77, which was reflected in the flat GDP-share of about 13.6% in that time period. Its working force, however, continued to rise at the same speed as before, resulting in the increasing labor share and decreasing relative productivity ratio.

Table 11-5.2: Contribution to Employment by
the Services-Producing Sector

| Year | Transportation, Communication and Utilities | | Wholesale Trade | | Retail Trade | |
|---|---|---|---|---|---|---|
| | Persons million | % of Total* | Persons million | % of Total* | Persons million | % of Total* |
| 1948 | 4.318 | 7.42 | 2.839 | 4.88 | 7.851 | 13.48 |
| 1955 | 4.283 | 6.77 | 3.164 | 5.00 | 8.593 | 13.58 |
| 1960 | 4.100 | 6.31 | 3.421 | 5.26 | 9.075 | 13.96 |
| 1965 | 4.108 | 5.85 | 3.648 | 5.2 | 9.565 | 13.63 |
| 1970 | 4.53 | 5.78 | 4.123 | 5.26 | 10.766 | 13.74 |
| 1975 | 4.584 | 5.53 | 4.521 | 5.45 | 11.979 | 14.45 |
| 1980 | 5.173 | 5.39 | 5.406 | 5.64 | 14.053 | 14.65 |
| 1985 | 5.300 | 5.14 | 5.816 | 5.64 | 16.026 | 15.54 |
| 1990 | 5.754 | 5.00 | 6.347 | 5.51 | 18.099 | 15.72 |
| 1995 | 6.172 | 5.06 | 6.555 | 5.37 | 19.462 | 15.96 |
| 2000 | 7.015 | 5.18 | 7.107 | 5.25 | 21.432 | 15.83 |

| Year | Finance, Insurance and Real estate | | Services | |
|---|---|---|---|---|
| | Persons million | % of Total* | Persons million | % of Total* |
| 1948 | 1.855 | 3.19 | 7.707 | 13.24 |
| 1955 | 2.433 | 3.85 | 8.382 | 13.25 |
| 1960 | 2.754 | 4.24 | 9.817 | 15.1 |
| 1965 | 3.075 | 4.38 | 11.306 | 16.11 |
| 1970 | 3.749 | 4.79 | 13.38 | 17.08 |
| 1975 | 4.405 | 5.31 | 15.65 | 18.88 |
| 1980 | 5.497 | 5.73 | 19.581 | 20.42 |
| 1985 | 6.305 | 6.12 | 24.09 | 23.37 |
| 1990 | 7.13 | 6.19 | 30.048 | 26.10 |
| 1995 | 7.212 | 5.91 | 35.000 | 28.69 |
| 2000 | 7.855 | 5.80 | 42.081 | 31.09 |

Since 1980 this group has re-energized itself to get back on the track of high-speed growth. Its GDP-share broke through the 14% mark and quickly climbed up to 19.61% in 2000. Since 1990, its growth rate of employment has reduced, and its relative productivity ratio has been enhanced significantly. In 2000, this group's productivity was about 3.38 times of the economy's average, the all time record high. Clearly, the industry group of finance, insurance and real estate was a leading sector in 1948-60; its leading role deteriorated in 1961-79, but resumed in 1990.

Table 11-5.3: Productivity of the Services-Producing Sector

| Year | Transportation, Communication and Utilities | | Wholesale Trade | | Retail Trade | |
|---|---|---|---|---|---|---|
| | $1000 per person | Ratio* | $1000 per person | Ratio | $1000 per person | Ratio |
| 1948 | 5.501 | 1.19 | 6.457 | 1.39 | 3.832 | 0.83 |
| 1955 | 8.622 | 1.31 | 8.394 | 1.28 | 4.718 | 0.72 |
| 1960 | 11.589 | 1.43 | 10.923 | 1.35 | 5.589 | 0.69 |
| 1965 | 15.262 | 1.49 | 13.625 | 1.33 | 7.148 | 0.70 |
| 1970 | 19.578 | 1.48 | 17.457 | 1.32 | 9.352 | 0.70 |
| 1975 | 31.074 | 1.58 | 26.783 | 1.36 | 12.787 | 0.65 |
| 1980 | 46.858 | 1.61 | 36.418 | 1.25 | 17.462 | 0.60 |
| 1985 | 71.514 | 1.75 | 49.709 | 1.22 | 24.607 | 0.60 |
| 1990 | 85.317 | 1.69 | 59.27 | 1.18 | 28.055 | 0.56 |
| 1995 | 104.109 | 1.72 | 76.373 | 1.26 | 33.234 | 0.55 |
| 2000 | 117.595 | 1.61 | 94.847 | 1.30 | 41.708 | 0.57 |

| Year | Finance, Insurance and Real estate | | Services | |
|---|---|---|---|---|
| | $1000 per person | Ratio | $1000 per person | Ratio |
| 1948 | 14.212 | 3.07 | 2.844 | 0.61 |
| 1955 | 20.143 | 3.07 | 4.200 | 0.64 |
| 1960 | 25.529 | 3.15 | 5.255 | 0.65 |
| 1965 | 31.220 | 3.04 | 6.620 | 0.65 |
| 1970 | 37.919 | 2.86 | 9.035 | 0.68 |
| 1975 | 50.987 | 2.59 | 12.749 | 0.65 |
| 1980 | 75.728 | 2.60 | 19.350 | 0.66 |
| 1985 | 108.892 | 2.66 | 27.251 | 0.67 |
| 1990 | 141.713 | 2.81 | 35.660 | 0.71 |
| 1995 | 186.820 | 3.08 | 41.783 | 0.69 |
| 2000 | 246.501 | 3.38 | 51.440 | 0.71 |

* Ratios denote sector's productivity measure divided by the productivity measure of the entire domestic production.

The services group includes all the conventional services, such as personal services, business services, health, legal, and educational services, and so on. As an aggregate group, it has demonstrated remarkable growth momentum in both value-added and working force for the entire time period. Its GDP-share increased from 8.13% in 1948 to 21.93% in 2000, and its labor-share rose from 13.24% to 31.09% during the same time frame. The services group has employed more working force than proportionally required by the economy on the average. Traditionally its productivity was low, only 61% of the economy's average in 1948, which was behind the group of retail trade, whose productivity was about 83% of the economy's average in 1948. Unlike the retail trade that has shown the deterioration of its relative productivity over time, the services group has gradually improved its relative productivity ratio, from 0.61 in 1948 to 0.71 in 2000.

Despite the low relative productivity, the services group has provided sustainable and powerful momentum to U.S. economic growth with consistently increasing GDP- and labor-shares that have not been seen in other sectors. Its value-added increased from $21.9 billion in 1948 to $2.165 trillion in 2000, rising more than 90 times; its employment increased from 7.707 million people in 1948 to 42.081 million people in 2000, rising more than 5 fold. Recalling the analysis in previous sections, one can recognize that the services group has exceeded the manufacturing sector in terms of value-added since 1990, and in terms of employment since 1985. As of 2000, the manufacturing sector generated $1.567 trillion of value added and created 18.511 million jobs, while the services group generated $2.165 trillion of value added and created 42.081 million jobs. The services group's superior growth of value-added and job creation has made this group a real leading sector in the mass high-consumption stage of economic growth.

In the following subsections we shall analyze contributions to the U.S. economy made by three less-aggregated industry groups of the services-producing sector.

## 11-4-1  Transportation, Communications, and Utilities

The group of transportation, communications, and utilities includes three component industries as indicated by the group's title. We select two separated sub-industries, railroad and air-transportation, from the transportation industry to illustrate the changing structure. Therefore there are five groups of industries presented in Figures 11-6.1 and 11-6.2 along with Tables 11-6.1, 11-6.2, and 11-6.3.

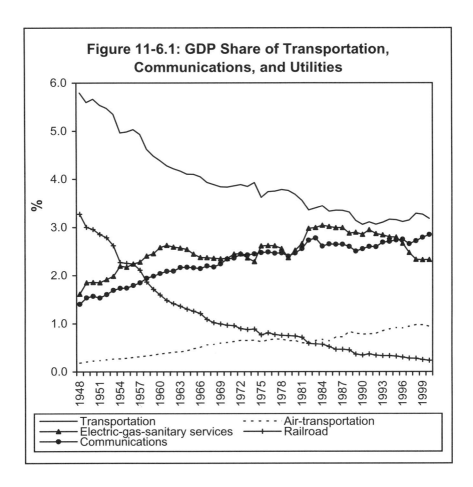

As illustrated in Figure 11-5.1 of the previous section, the GDP-share of the aggregated group of transportation, communications, and utilities was flat, around 8.7%. The three industries of this group, however, had experienced significant changes in their GDP-shares. The transportation industry's GDP share declined from 5.79% in 1948 to 3.06% in 1990 and rebounded to 3.18% in 2000.

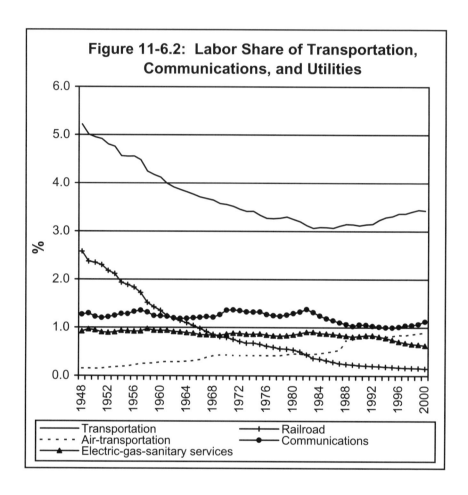

The communications industry raised its GDP share from 1.4% in 1948 to 2.85% in 2000; so did the utilities industry (or electric, gas, and sanitary services) from 1.61% to 2.33%. However, all three of the industries reduced their labor shares by different degrees even though the actual number of people engaged in those industries has increased substantially. The increasing GDP share and decreasing labor share has brought increases in the relative productivity ratio for the communications and utilities industries. As of 2000, productivity was 2.5 times that of the economy's average for the communications industry and 3.58 times for the utilities industry. For the transportation industry, however, its declining GDP- and labor-shares depressed its performance of relative productivity, with the ratio dropping from 1.11 in 1948 to 0.93 in 2000.

The transportation industry's decline over the last five decades was caused mainly by the railroad industry, whose GDP-share reduced from 3.27% in 1948 to only 0.23% in 2000 and its labor-share reduced from 2.58% to 0.15%. The actual number of people engaged in the railroad transportation industry declined from 1.5 million in 1948 to 202 thousand in 2000, declining by 86% over the last fifty-two years.

Table 11-6.1: Contribution to DGP by Transportation, Communications, and Utilities

| Year | Communications | | Electric, Gas and Sanitary Services | | Transportation | |
|---|---|---|---|---|---|---|
| | $ billion | % of GDP | $billion | % of GDP | $ billion | % of GDP |
| 1948 | 3.785 | 1.40 | 4.351 | 1.61 | 15.616 | 5.79 |
| 1955 | 7.212 | 1.74 | 9.018 | 2.17 | 20.698 | 4.99 |
| 1960 | 10.764 | 2.04 | 13.617 | 2.58 | 23.136 | 4.39 |
| 1965 | 15.554 | 2.16 | 17.614 | 2.45 | 29.532 | 4.10 |
| 1970 | 24.36 | 2.34 | 24.443 | 2.35 | 39.882 | 3.84 |
| 1975 | 40.487 | 2.48 | 42.711 | 2.61 | 59.242 | 3.62 |
| 1980 | 68.939 | 2.47 | 70.504 | 2.52 | 102.961 | 3.68 |
| 1985 | 111.687 | 2.65 | 126.938 | 3.01 | 140.420 | 3.33 |
| 1990 | 148.041 | 2.55 | 165.451 | 2.85 | 177.405 | 3.06 |
| 1995 | 202.331 | 2.73 | 206.845 | 2.8 | 233.413 | 3.15 |
| 2000 | 281.083 | 2.85 | 230.039 | 2.33 | 313.861 | 3.18 |

| Year | Railroad | | Air-transportation | |
|---|---|---|---|---|
| | $ billion | % of GDP | $ billion | % of GDP |
| 1948 | 8.826 | 3.27 | 0.488 | 0.18 |
| 1955 | 9.367 | 2.26 | 1.171 | 0.28 |
| 1960 | 8.401 | 1.59 | 1.957 | 0.37 |
| 1965 | 9.066 | 1.26 | 3.421 | 0.48 |
| 1970 | 10.054 | 0.97 | 6.363 | 0.61 |
| 1975 | 12.558 | 0.77 | 10.187 | 0.62 |
| 1980 | 20.743 | 0.74 | 18.199 | 0.65 |
| 1985 | 21.992 | 0.52 | 27.048 | 0.64 |
| 1990 | 19.847 | 0.34 | 45.323 | 0.78 |
| 1995 | 23.608 | 0.32 | 67.641 | 0.91 |
| 2000 | 22.905 | 0.23 | 93.003 | 0.94 |

Even though air-transportation has developed rapidly, with its GDP-share rising from 0.18% to 1.02% and the labor-share climbing from 0.16% to 0.88%, air-transportation's gain could not make up the railroad's loss. The rest of the industries in transportation, such as local and interurban passenger transit, trucking and warehousing, water transportation, etc., held a flat share over time. The railway transportation was the leading force for the Second Industrial Revolution in the drive to technological maturity stage of economic growth. In the mass high-consumption stage of economic growth, automobile and air-transportation have replaced the railway industry as a leading sector. Consequently, the railway transportation industry has become a laggard in the U.S. economy over the last five decades.

Table 11-6.2: Contribution to Employment by Transportation, Communications, and Utilities

| Year | Communications | | Electric, Gas and Sanitary Services | | Transportation | |
|------|-----------|------|-----------|------|-----------|------|
| | $ billion | % of GDP | $billion | % of GDP | $ billion | % of GDP |
| 1948 | 3.785 | 1.40 | 4.351 | 1.61 | 15.616 | 5.79 |
| 1955 | 7.212 | 1.74 | 9.018 | 2.17 | 20.698 | 4.99 |
| 1960 | 10.764 | 2.04 | 13.617 | 2.58 | 23.136 | 4.39 |
| 1965 | 15.554 | 2.16 | 17.614 | 2.45 | 29.532 | 4.10 |
| 1970 | 24.36 | 2.34 | 24.443 | 2.35 | 39.882 | 3.84 |
| 1975 | 40.487 | 2.48 | 42.711 | 2.61 | 59.242 | 3.62 |
| 1980 | 68.939 | 2.47 | 70.504 | 2.52 | 102.961 | 3.68 |
| 1985 | 111.687 | 2.65 | 126.938 | 3.01 | 140.420 | 3.33 |
| 1990 | 148.041 | 2.55 | 165.451 | 2.85 | 177.405 | 3.06 |
| 1995 | 202.331 | 2.73 | 206.845 | 2.8 | 233.413 | 3.15 |
| 2000 | 281.083 | 2.85 | 230.039 | 2.33 | 313.861 | 3.18 |

| Year | Railroad | | Air-transportation | |
|------|-----------|------|-----------|------|
| | $ billion | % of GDP | $ billion | % of GDP |
| 1948 | 8.826 | 3.27 | 0.488 | 0.18 |
| 1955 | 9.367 | 2.26 | 1.171 | 0.28 |
| 1960 | 8.401 | 1.59 | 1.957 | 0.37 |
| 1965 | 9.066 | 1.26 | 3.421 | 0.48 |
| 1970 | 10.054 | 0.97 | 6.363 | 0.61 |
| 1975 | 12.558 | 0.77 | 10.187 | 0.62 |
| 1980 | 20.743 | 0.74 | 18.199 | 0.65 |
| 1985 | 21.992 | 0.52 | 27.048 | 0.64 |
| 1990 | 19.847 | 0.34 | 45.323 | 0.78 |
| 1995 | 23.608 | 0.32 | 67.641 | 0.91 |
| 2000 | 22.905 | 0.23 | 93.003 | 0.94 |

Table 11-6.3: Productivity of Transportation,
Communications and Utilities

| Year | Communications $1000 per person | Ratio | Electric, Gas and Sanitary Services $1000 per person | Ratio | Transportation $1000 per person | Ratio |
|------|------|------|------|------|------|------|
| 1948 | 5.102 | 1.10 | 8.104 | 1.75 | 5.138 | 1.11 |
| 1955 | 8.863 | 1.35 | 15.358 | 2.34 | 7.181 | 1.09 |
| 1960 | 13.306 | 1.64 | 22.348 | 2.76 | 8.627 | 1.06 |
| 1965 | 18.393 | 1.79 | 28.456 | 2.77 | 11.174 | 1.09 |
| 1970 | 22.813 | 1.72 | 36.111 | 2.72 | 14.320 | 1.08 |
| 1975 | 36.772 | 1.86 | 59.419 | 3.01 | 21.433 | 1.09 |
| 1980 | 55.375 | 1.90 | 86.684 | 2.97 | 33.050 | 1.13 |
| 1985 | 91.187 | 2.23 | 141.520 | 3.46 | 44.192 | 1.08 |
| 1990 | 121.430 | 2.41 | 175.265 | 3.48 | 49.407 | 0.98 |
| 1995 | 165.704 | 2.73 | 227.306 | 3.75 | 57.757 | 0.95 |
| 2000 | 184.426 | 2.53 | 270.195 | 3.70 | 67.623 | 0.93 |

| Year | Railroad $1000 per person | Ratio | Air-transportation $1000 per person | Ratio |
|------|------|------|------|------|
| 1948 | 5.872 | 1.27 | 5.371 | 1.16 |
| 1955 | 7.833 | 1.19 | 9.161 | 1.40 |
| 1960 | 9.534 | 1.18 | 10.520 | 1.30 |
| 1965 | 12.422 | 1.21 | 15.473 | 1.51 |
| 1970 | 16.224 | 1.22 | 18.757 | 1.41 |
| 1975 | 23.196 | 1.18 | 29.048 | 1.47 |
| 1980 | 40.424 | 1.39 | 41.611 | 1.43 |
| 1985 | 67.933 | 1.66 | 54.316 | 1.33 |
| 1990 | 80.561 | 1.60 | 49.962 | 0.99 |
| 1995 | 107.519 | 1.77 | 67.541 | 1.11 |
| 2000 | 113.573 | 1.56 | 76.515 | 1.05 |

\* Ratios denote sector's productivity measure divided by the productivity measure of the entire domestic production.

## 11-4-2  Finance, Insurance, and Real Estate

There are four major less-aggregated industries in the finance, insurance, and real estate group: banking and credit agency (SIC60-61); security and commodity brokers (SIC62); insurance carrier and insurance agents, brokers, and service (SIC63-64); and real estate (SIC65-66).   The contributions to GDP and employment by these four industries are presented in Figures 11-7.1 and 11-7.2, and Tables 11-7.1 and 11-7.2; productivity measures and relative productivity ratios are also provided in Table 11-7.3.

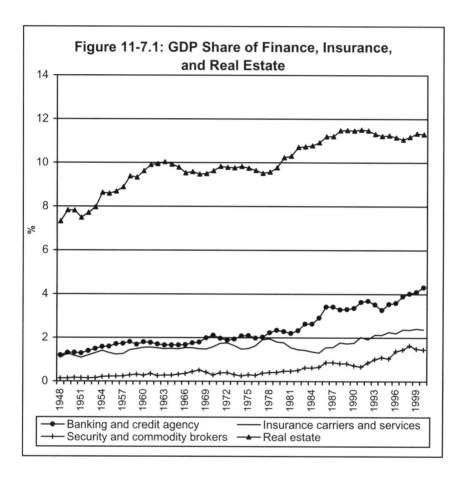

The real estate industry consists of real estate operators and lessors, real estate agents and managers, title abstract offices, and subdividers and developers. The real estate industry has gained a lion's share in this group; its GDP-share showed two big rises from 7.33% in 1948 to 10.04% in 1963 and from 9.52% in 1977 to 11.48% in 1988. These surges leveled off in subsequent time periods and ended at 11.31% in 2000. Its labor share, however, declined slightly from 1.04% in 1948 to 0.92% in 1966, rose to

1.43% in 1988 and slid to 1.31% in 2000. The proxy measure of productivity was extremely high for the real estate industry, more than 10 times that of the economy's average in the 1960s and more than 8 times that of the average in the 1990s. The real estate industry grew faster than the U.S. GDP during 1948 - 1963 and 1977 - 1988, which was indicated by its surging GDP share in those time periods. The flat GDP share in 1964 - 1976 and 1989 - 2000 implies that its value-added grew at nearly the average rate of the economy. Therefore, the real estate industry's leading role in economic growth was reduced somewhat in the 1990s.

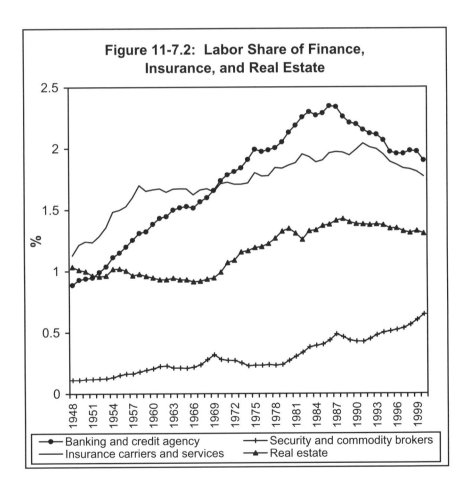

Figure 11-7.2: Labor Share of Finance, Insurance, and Real Estate

The other three industries in this group raised their GDP-shares, particularly in the 1980s and 90s. The industry of banking and credit agencies experienced the strongest growth in this group, with its GDP-share rising from 1.20% in 1948 to 4.31% in 2000, and its labor-share from 0.89% in 1948 to 2.35% in 1986 and back to 1.90% in 2000. In the late 1980s, the U.S. banking industry went through the saving-and-loan crisis in which a large number of commercial banks went bankrupt, which may contribute to the declining employment and labor share of the banking industry.

Table 11-7.1: Contribution to GDP by Finance, Insurance, and Real Estate

| Year | Real Estate | | Banking and Credit Agency | |
|---|---|---|---|---|
| | $billion | % of GDP | $billion | % of GDP |
| 1948 | 19.746 | 7.33 | 3.229 | 1.20 |
| 1955 | 35.679 | 8.59 | 6.647 | 1.60 |
| 1960 | 50.739 | 9.62 | 9.519 | 1.81 |
| 1965 | 70.520 | 9.79 | 11.990 | 1.67 |
| 1970 | 100.121 | 9.63 | 21.927 | 2.11 |
| 1975 | 159.412 | 9.75 | 34.338 | 2.10 |
| 1980 | 286.265 | 10.24 | 63.962 | 2.29 |
| 1985 | 460.441 | 10.93 | 122.262 | 2.90 |
| 1990 | 665.690 | 11.47 | 194.641 | 3.35 |
| 1995 | 832.560 | 11.25 | 261.461 | 3.53 |
| 2000 | 1116.234 | 11.31 | 425.425 | 4.31 |
| | Insurance Carriers and Services | | Security and Commodity Brokers | |
| Year | $billion | % of GDP | $billion | % of GDP |
| 1948 | 2.933 | 1.09 | 0.353 | 0.13 |
| 1955 | 5.435 | 1.31 | 0.943 | 0.23 |
| 1960 | 8.169 | 1.55 | 1.440 | 0.27 |
| 1965 | 10.722 | 1.49 | 2.304 | 0.32 |
| 1970 | 16.489 | 1.59 | 3.098 | 0.30 |
| 1975 | 24.642 | 1.51 | 4.955 | 0.30 |
| 1980 | 49.621 | 1.78 | 13.055 | 0.47 |
| 1985 | 55.401 | 1.32 | 27.764 | 0.66 |
| 1990 | 102.253 | 1.76 | 42.306 | 0.73 |
| 1995 | 167.400 | 2.26 | 77.780 | 1.05 |
| 2000 | 234.877 | 2.38 | 144.145 | 1.46 |

The creation of many innovative financial intermediates and the changing government regulations for finance has helped the banking industry to return to its growth track with significantly enhanced productivity. Even in 1997 and 1998 when the global financial crisis broke out in Asia and spread around the globe, the U.S. banking industry remained strong and kept improving its productivity. The productivity measure of the banking industry was 2.3 times that of the economy's average in 2000.

Table 11-7.2: Contribution to Employment by Finance, Insurance, and Real Estate

| Year | Real Estate | | Banking and Credit Agency | |
|---|---|---|---|---|
| | Persons million | % of Total* | Persons million | % of Total* |
| 1948 | 0.603 | 1.04 | 0.517 | 0.89 |
| 1955 | 0.645 | 1.02 | 0.727 | 1.15 |
| 1960 | 0.615 | 0.95 | 0.900 | 1.38 |
| 1965 | 0.652 | 0.93 | 1.072 | 1.53 |
| 1970 | 0.777 | 0.99 | 1.36 | 1.74 |
| 1975 | 0.987 | 1.19 | 1.652 | 1.99 |
| 1980 | 1.292 | 1.35 | 2.043 | 2.13 |
| 1985 | 1.411 | 1.37 | 2.357 | 2.29 |
| 1990 | 1.593 | 1.38 | 2.528 | 2.20 |
| 1995 | 1.643 | 1.35 | 2.405 | 1.97 |
| 2000 | 1.766 | 1.31 | 2.573 | 1.90 |
| | Insurance Carriers and Services | | Security and Commodity Brokers | |
| Year | Persons million | % of Total | Persons million | % of Total* |
| 1948 | 0.657 | 1.13 | 0.066 | 0.11 |
| 1955 | 0.948 | 1.50 | 0.096 | 0.15 |
| 1960 | 1.082 | 1.66 | 0.133 | 0.21 |
| 1965 | 1.173 | 1.67 | 0.147 | 0.21 |
| 1970 | 1.341 | 1.71 | 0.219 | 0.28 |
| 1975 | 1.493 | 1.80 | 0.192 | 0.23 |
| 1980 | 1.787 | 1.86 | 0.260 | 0.27 |
| 1985 | 1.962 | 1.90 | 0.414 | 0.40 |
| 1990 | 2.290 | 1.99 | 0.489 | 0.43 |
| 1995 | 2.305 | 1.89 | 0.620 | 0.51 |
| 2000 | 2.394 | 1.77 | 0.873 | 0.65 |

\* The total represents the number of persons engaged in the U.S. domestic production

The other two industries, insurance services and security and commodity broker services, have demonstrated a similar performance to the banking industry on smaller scales. Compared with the real estate industry, the insurance industry hired more people but generated less value-added, therefore, had a lower productivity. Nevertheless, its relative productivity has improved significantly from 16% below the economy's average in 1975 to 34% above the average in 2000. The brokerage industry was the smallest but the fastest growing industry among the four groups. Its value-added was only $353 million in 1948 and increased to $144 billion in 2000, a 408-fold rise in the last fifty-two years. It provided jobs for 66 thousand people in 1948, and for 873 thousand people in 2000, a 13-fold rise. Productivity of the brokerage industry was 16% above the economy's average in 1948 and increased to 2.3 times of the economy's average in 2000.

Table 11-7.3: Productivity of Finance, Insurance, and Real Estate

| Year | Real Estate | | Banking and Credit Agency | |
|------|-------------|--------|---------------------------|-------|
|      | $1000 per person | Ratio* | $1000 per person | Ratio |
| 1948 | 32.762  | 7.08  | 6.245   | 1.35 |
| 1955 | 55.336  | 8.43  | 9.143   | 1.39 |
| 1960 | 82.479  | 10.17 | 10.577  | 1.30 |
| 1965 | 108.164 | 10.54 | 11.188  | 1.09 |
| 1970 | 128.830 | 9.71  | 16.122  | 1.21 |
| 1975 | 161.578 | 8.19  | 20.792  | 1.05 |
| 1980 | 221.577 | 7.60  | 31.309  | 1.07 |
| 1985 | 326.224 | 7.98  | 51.875  | 1.27 |
| 1990 | 417.809 | 8.29  | 76.992  | 1.53 |
| 1995 | 506.702 | 8.35  | 108.694 | 1.79 |
| 2000 | 631.932 | 9.02  | 165.336 | 2.36 |
|      | Insurance Carriers and Services | | Security and Commodity Brokers | |
| Year | $1000 per person | Ratio | $1000 per person | Ratio |
| 1948 | 4.465  | 0.96 | 5.367   | 1.16 |
| 1955 | 5.734  | 0.87 | 9.800   | 1.49 |
| 1960 | 7.549  | 0.93 | 10.800  | 1.33 |
| 1965 | 9.143  | 0.89 | 15.710  | 1.53 |
| 1970 | 12.294 | 0.93 | 14.124  | 1.06 |
| 1975 | 16.503 | 0.84 | 25.759  | 1.31 |
| 1980 | 27.770 | 0.95 | 50.227  | 1.72 |
| 1985 | 28.237 | 0.69 | 66.988  | 1.64 |
| 1990 | 44.656 | 0.89 | 86.467  | 1.72 |
| 1995 | 72.610 | 1.20 | 125.518 | 2.07 |
| 2000 | 98.093 | 1.40 | 165.107 | 2.36 |

* Ratios denote sector's productivity measure divided by the productivity measure of the entire domestic production.

Clearly, all of the four industry groups in the finance sector have been growing faster than the U.S. economy. Particularly, during the 1980's and 1990s, these industry groups were the leading forces to generate fast growing value added and to create new jobs for Americans while continuing to improve their productivity over time.

## 11-4-3 The Services Industry

The narrowly defined services industry includes fourteen small industries in the services-producing sector. To facilitate the comparison and presentation we consolidate them into five major groups: business services (SIC73); amusement and motion picture (SIC76, 78); health services (SIC80); education, legal and social services (SIC81, 82, 83); and miscellaneous professional services (SIC84, 89). Some service businesses, such as hotel, auto repair, miscellaneous repair, membership organization and so on, are excluded from this analysis due to their very small shares in the U.S. economy. Contributions to the U.S. economy made by these five service groups along with their productivity measures are presented in Figures 11-8.1, 11-8.2, and Tables 11-8.1, 11-8.2, and 11-8.3.

Each group significantly raised their GDP- and labor-shares over the time frame of 1948-2000. The business services and health services groups demonstrated the most rapid economic growth, with their GDP-shares rising from 0.61% to 5.79% and from 1.54% to 5.54% respectively in 1948-2000. The labor-share of business services increased even faster than its GDP-share, from 0.66% in 1948 to 7.55% in 2000, which resulted in a declining relative productivity ratio from 1.03 in 1955 to 0.77 in 2000[1]. Since 1992, the growth of health services slowed down in both fronts of value-added and of work force, which resulted in a declining GDP-share and a flat labor-share in 1992-2000. Productivity of the health services remained 20-30% below the economy's average productivity over the last five decades.

---

[1] A remark: the sudden drop in both GDP- and labor-shares of business services in 1987 was caused by original data recorded according to the 1972-SIC system for 1947-87 and shifted to the 1987-SIC system for 1987-99. The shift of the SIC code does not change the 1987-data for the majority of industries, but does affect a few, including business services and miscellaneous services. Both groups showed a sudden rise or drop in their GDP- and labor-shares that reflect the shifting data records rather than the changing performance of those industries.

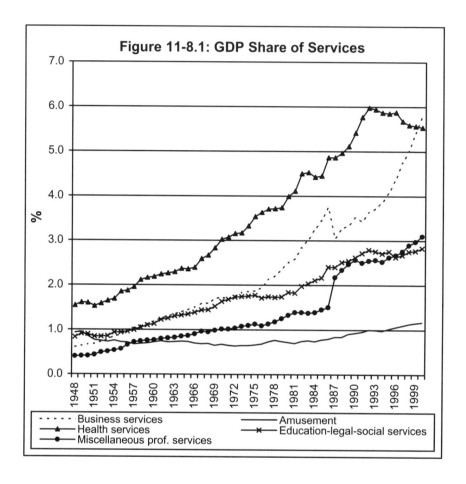

Figure 11-8.1: GDP Share of Services

The other three groups were relatively small, but their GDP- and labor-shares increased rapidly and consistently over time. Their productivity, however, was fairly lower, compared with industries in other sectors, except for miscellaneous professional services, whose productivity ratio was in the range of 0.96-1.15 over the last fifty years.

Figure 11-8.2:  Labor Share of Services

Table 11-8.1: Contribution to GDP by the Services Industry

| Year | Business Services | | Health Services | | Amusement and Motion Picture | |
|---|---|---|---|---|---|---|
| | $ billion | % of GDP | $ billion | % of GDP | $ billion | % of GDP |
| 1948 | 1.639 | 0.61 | 4.162 | 1.54 | 1.084 | 0.40 |
| 1955 | 3.679 | 0.89 | 7.690 | 1.85 | 1.785 | 0.43 |
| 1960 | 6.271 | 1.19 | 11.544 | 2.19 | 2.669 | 0.51 |
| 1965 | 10.398 | 1.44 | 17.016 | 2.36 | 3.637 | 0.51 |
| 1970 | 17.986 | 1.73 | 31.440 | 3.02 | 4.762 | 0.46 |
| 1975 | 30.561 | 1.87 | 57.819 | 3.54 | 7.718 | 0.47 |
| 1980 | 70.057 | 2.51 | 111.627 | 3.99 | 14.201 | 0.51 |
| 1985 | 145.391 | 3.45 | 187.606 | 4.45 | 22.624 | 0.54 |
| 1990 | 203.926 | 3.51 | 314.362 | 5.42 | 36.444 | 0.63 |
| 1995 | 301.942 | 4.08 | 433.079 | 5.85 | 53.507 | 0.72 |
| 2000 | 571.742 | 5.79 | 546.763 | 5.54 | 80.761 | 0.82 |

| Year | Education, Legal Social Services | | Miscellaneous Professional Services | |
|---|---|---|---|---|
| | $ billion | % of GDP | $ billion | % of GDP |
| 1948 | 2.256 | 0.84 | 1.084 | 0.40 |
| 1955 | 3.907 | 0.94 | 2.367 | 0.57 |
| 1960 | 5.980 | 1.13 | 4.061 | 0.77 |
| 1965 | 9.736 | 1.35 | 6.258 | 0.87 |
| 1970 | 16.988 | 1.63 | 10.594 | 1.02 |
| 1975 | 29.008 | 1.77 | 18.477 | 1.13 |
| 1980 | 51.382 | 1.84 | 37.237 | 1.33 |
| 1985 | 91.338 | 2.17 | 61.215 | 1.45 |
| 1990 | 152.277 | 2.62 | 149.259 | 2.57 |
| 1995 | 204.181 | 2.76 | 194.412 | 2.63 |
| 2000 | 279.700 | 2.83 | 306.259 | 3.10 |

In general, the services industry has grown faster than the economy as a whole for the last five decades, and its work force has grown even faster than the values-added. Therefore, the services industry continues to be a great source of new job creation and its productivity may remain below the average of the economy for some time.

Table 11-8.2: Contribution to Employment by the Services Industry

| Year | Business Services | | Health Services | | Amusement and Motion Picture | |
|---|---|---|---|---|---|---|
| | Persons million | % of Total* | Persons million | % of Total* | Persons million | % of Total* |
| 1948 | 0.382 | 0.66 | 1.132 | 1.94 | 0.522 | 0.90 |
| 1955 | 0.542 | 0.86 | 1.455 | 2.30 | 0.464 | 0.73 |
| 1960 | 0.819 | 1.26 | 1.777 | 2.73 | 0.472 | 0.73 |
| 1965 | 1.162 | 1.66 | 2.123 | 3.03 | 0.503 | 0.72 |
| 1970 | 1.666 | 2.13 | 2.905 | 3.71 | 0.583 | 0.74 |
| 1975 | 2.054 | 2.48 | 4.114 | 4.96 | 0.737 | 0.89 |
| 1980 | 3.083 | 3.21 | 5.233 | 5.46 | 0.935 | 0.98 |
| 1985 | 4.652 | 4.51 | 6.189 | 6.00 | 1.042 | 1.01 |
| 1990 | 5.679 | 4.93 | 7.507 | 6.52 | 1.469 | 1.28 |
| 1995 | 7.096 | 5.82 | 8.902 | 7.30 | 1.865 | 1.53 |
| 2000 | 10.222 | 7.55 | 9.773 | 7.22 | 2.289 | 1.69 |

| | Year | Education, Legal Social Services | | Miscellaneous Professional Services | |
|---|---|---|---|---|---|
| | | Persons million | % of Total* | Persons million | % of Total* |
| | 1948 | 1.357 | 2.33 | 0.257 | 0.44 |
| | 1955 | 1.644 | 2.60 | 0.362 | 0.57 |
| | 1960 | 2.143 | 3.30 | 0.439 | 0.68 |
| | 1965 | 2.614 | 3.73 | 0.53 | 0.76 |
| | 1970 | 3.158 | 4.03 | 0.746 | 0.95 |
| | 1975 | 3.676 | 4.43 | 0.939 | 1.13 |
| | 1980 | 4.282 | 4.46 | 1.361 | 1.42 |
| | 1985 | 5.017 | 4.87 | 1.657 | 1.61 |
| | 1990 | 6.301 | 5.47 | 3.001 | 2.61 |
| | 1995 | 7.567 | 6.20 | 3.434 | 2.82 |
| | 2000 | 8.848 | 6.54 | 4.291 | 3.17 |

* The total represents the number of persons engaged in the U.S. domestic production

In Sections 11-2, 11-3, and 11-4 we have analyzed the evolution of sectors and industry groups in the U.S. economy via the changing GDP- and labor-shares as well as the proxy measures of productivity. Although these sector's analyses have revealed the U.S. economy's structure changes, such as the diminishment of previously leading sectors and the characteristics of new sectors, many newly developed industries are still grouped in some mixed old sectors. This makes it difficult to analyze the emerging industries with great growth performance and potential. The limitation of the Standard Industrial Classification system has been recognized and the new system for industrial classification has been developed and put into use. In the next section we shall use economic census data recorded under the new system to take a close look at recent changes in the structure of the U.S. economy.

Table 11-8.3: Productivity of the Services Industry

| Year | Business Services $1000 a person | Ratio | Health Services $1000 a person | Ratio | Amusement and Motion Picture $1000 a person | Ratio |
|------|------|------|------|------|------|------|
| 1948 | 4.290 | 0.93 | 3.677 | 0.79 | 2.077 | 0.45 |
| 1955 | 6.784 | 1.03 | 5.286 | 0.81 | 3.844 | 0.59 |
| 1960 | 7.659 | 0.94 | 6.496 | 0.80 | 5.652 | 0.70 |
| 1965 | 8.947 | 0.87 | 8.015 | 0.78 | 7.227 | 0.70 |
| 1970 | 10.794 | 0.81 | 10.823 | 0.82 | 8.169 | 0.62 |
| 1975 | 14.882 | 0.75 | 14.055 | 0.71 | 10.472 | 0.53 |
| 1980 | 22.726 | 0.78 | 21.331 | 0.73 | 15.186 | 0.52 |
| 1985 | 31.255 | 0.76 | 30.313 | 0.74 | 21.705 | 0.53 |
| 1990 | 35.909 | 0.71 | 41.875 | 0.83 | 24.810 | 0.49 |
| 1995 | 42.553 | 0.70 | 48.648 | 0.80 | 28.688 | 0.47 |
| 2000 | 55.932 | 0.77 | 55.948 | 0.77 | 35.284 | 0.48 |

| Year | Education, Legal Social Services $1000 a person | Ratio | Miscellaneous Professional Services $1000 a person | Ratio |
|------|------|------|------|------|
| 1948 | 1.663 | 0.36 | 4.220 | 0.91 |
| 1955 | 2.377 | 0.36 | 6.539 | 1.00 |
| 1960 | 2.790 | 0.34 | 9.251 | 1.14 |
| 1965 | 3.724 | 0.36 | 11.810 | 1.15 |
| 1970 | 5.379 | 0.41 | 14.205 | 1.07 |
| 1975 | 7.891 | 0.40 | 19.671 | 1.00 |
| 1980 | 12.001 | 0.41 | 27.360 | 0.94 |
| 1985 | 18.206 | 0.45 | 36.948 | 0.90 |
| 1990 | 24.169 | 0.48 | 49.733 | 0.99 |
| 1995 | 26.985 | 0.44 | 56.617 | 0.93 |
| 2000 | 31.611 | 0.43 | 71.376 | 0.98 |

* Ratios denote sector's productivity measure divided by the productivity measure of the entire domestic production.

## 11-5  New NAICS Sectors and Their Contributions
    to the U.S. Economy

In March 1999 the U.S. Department of Commerce published all-new industry classifications data from the 1997 economic census. It was the first time the North American Industry Classification System (NAICS) was used for recording economic census data in order to provide essential information for government, industry, and general public use.

There are 20 NAICS sectors with two-digit codes. These 20 sectors are divided into 96 sub-sectors with three-digit codes. These sub-sectors are further divided into 313 industry groups with four-digit codes. As implemented in the 1997 economic census in the United States, the NAICS has identified 1170 industries with five- or six-digit codes. Compared with the Standard Industry Classification (SIC), the new system has shown most of the major changes in the higher level groupings, while many of the individual NAICS industries correspond directly to industries as defined under the SIC system. We provide a list of the 2-digit NAICS sectors that have been covered by the 1997 economic census as the following:

| NAICS Code | Industries |
|---|---|
| 21 | Mining |
| 22 | Utility (new) |
| 23 | Construction |
| 33-33 | Manufacturing |
| 42 | Wholesale Trade |
| 45-45 | Retail trade |
| 49-49 | Transportation and Warehousing (new) |
| 51 | Information (new) |
| 52 | Finance and Insurance (new) |
| 53 | Real Estate and Rental and leasing (new) |
| 54 | Professional, Scientific, and Technical Services (new) |
| 55 | Management of Companies and Enterprises (new) |
| 56 | Administrative Support and Waste Management and Remediation Services (new) |
| 61 | Educational Services (new) |

| 62 | Health Care and Social Assistance (new) |
| 71 | Arts, Entertainment, and Recreation (new) |
| 72 | Accommodation and Foodservices (new) |
| 81 | Other services (except Public Administration) |

It is noticed that two sectors not listed in the above are the Agriculture, Forestry, Fishing, and Hunting sector (NAICS 11) and the Public Administration sector (NAICS 92). The NAICS 11 sector was covered by the census of agriculture conducted by the U.S. Department of Agriculture and the NAICS 92 sector was covered by the census of governments conducted by the Census Bureau. Out of the above-listed 18 NAICS sectors (2-digit codes) there are 12 sectors that are newly created from regrouping industries in the old SIC system, while other sectors bearing the same name as in the SIC system have also had some changes in their component industries. For example, within the mining sector, some industries that are now in the SIC system are moved from the mining sector into the services sector, such as geophysical surveying and mapping services for metal mining and oil and gas extraction.

The Information sector is newly created with a 2-digit code, which includes three types of establishments that are selected from SIC Divisions:

(1)   Publishing establishments classified in SIC Division D (Manufacturing),
(2)   Telecommunications and broadcasting establishments classified in SIC Division E (Transportation, Communications, and Utilities) and
(3)   Various kinds of information-related establishments classified in SIC Division I (Services). These information-related business establishments include software publishing, motion picture production, data processing, on-line information services, and libraries.

The sector of management of companies and enterprises includes holding companies that are classified in SIC Division H (Finance, Insurance, and Real Estate). It also includes corporate subsidiaries and regional managing offices that are considered to be "auxiliary" establishments in the old SIC system.

It is clear that the new system has created more sectors to classify services-producing activities in the U.S. economy. As previous sections of this chapter demonstrate, the demand and supply of services have grown very quickly and diversified into many different dimensions of the U.S economy. It seems impossible to use a single SIC Division I (Services) to properly measure and record actual productive-activities in the service domain of the U.S. economy. Creation of so many new service-related sectors at higher-level groupings of the NAICS indicates that authorities of data collection and process have recognized significant structural changes brought about by the increasing share of services in the U.S. economy. Indeed, the new measurement system of economic activities is organized by how the U.S. economy actually worked in the 1990s. It also reserves a great deal of room to accommodate future structural changes in the U.S. economy.

The 1997 economic census data are preliminary and include only four variables: the number of establishments; employment; payroll; and value of sales, receipts, revenue, or shipments. The data are reported in the two- and three-digit NAICS groups. We have used this data to calculate sales, employment, and payroll for some consolidated sectors and industry groups. Their percentage shares are accounted for in the corresponding measures of the entire private sector of the U.S. economy. We have also calculated some proxy measures of average productivity as sales divided by employment; labor cost or wage as payroll divided by employment; and labor-cost productivity as sales divided by payroll. For the purpose of comparison, we have defined the wage ratio as a sector's wage divided by average wage of the entire private sector, and the labor productivity ratio as a sector's productivity divided by productivity of the private sector.

When computing shares for the NAICS sectors and industry groups, we use measurements of the private sector (excluding the agriculture sector) as corresponding denominators rather than the whole U.S. economy (private and public sectors combined) for lack of data. Therefore, bases for computing all of the shares are reduced from the national level to the private-sector level, which has resulted in a greater number of shares than the analytical counterparts of previous sections. We present the results in Tables 11-9.1 and 11-9.2 for the new industry classification sectors and groups.

Table 11-9.1: NAICS Sectors and Their Relative Strength (1997)

| Industry | Sales $billion | Sales % of total | Employment million | Employment % of total | Payroll $billion | Payroll % of total |
|---|---|---|---|---|---|---|
| **Goods-producing Sector** | **4878.93** | **27.97** | **23.280** | **26.07** | **770.81** | **29.16** |
| Mining | 158.09 | 0.91 | 0.547 | 0.61 | 22.05 | 0.83 |
| Construction | 865.31 | 4.96 | 5.732 | 6.42 | 174.68 | 6.61 |
| Manufacturing | 3855.53 | 22.11 | 16.999 | 19.04 | 574.08 | 21.72 |
| Transp equipment | 577.92 | 3.31 | 1.887 | 2.11 | 80.24 | 3.04 |
| Computer & electronic product | 431.38 | 2.47 | 1.690 | 1.89 | 71.45 | 2.70 |
| Metal mfg | 419.76 | 2.41 | 2.389 | 2.68 | 81.33 | 3.08 |
| Chemical mfg | 417.69 | 2.39 | 0.903 | 1.01 | 40.81 | 1.54 |
| Machinery mfg | 271.54 | 1.56 | 1.434 | 1.61 | 53.41 | 2.02 |
| Electric equipment | 112.39 | 0.64 | 0.595 | 0.67 | 18.99 | 0.72 |
| **Services-Producing Sector** | **12562.5** | **72.03** | **66.019** | **73.93** | **1872.36** | **70.84** |
| Wholesale | 4055.02 | 23.25 | 5.820 | 6.52 | 215.74 | 8.16 |
| Retail | 2456.57 | 14.08 | 14.116 | 15.81 | 238.79 | 9.03 |
| Finance, insurance | 2254.49 | 12.93 | 5.768 | 6.46 | 263.34 | 9.96 |
| Health care | 889.60 | 5.10 | 13.617 | 15.25 | 379.31 | 14.35 |
| Information | 641.65 | 3.68 | 3.221 | 3.61 | 135.23 | 5.12 |
| Professional | 608.63 | 3.49 | 5.416 | 6.07 | 233.32 | 8.83 |
| Transportation | 318.54 | 1.83 | 2.927 | 3.28 | 82.41 | 3.12 |
| Administrative | 302.76 | 1.74 | 7.439 | 8.33 | 137.70 | 5.21 |
| Real estate | 249.52 | 1.43 | 1.761 | 1.97 | 43.56 | 1.65 |
| Arts, entertainment | 103.11 | 0.59 | 1.572 | 1.76 | 32.33 | 1.22 |
| Educational | 20.93 | 0.12 | 0.332 | 0.37 | 6.63 | 0.25 |

In 1997, the private sector (excluding agriculture) generated about $17.441 trillion in sales revenue, and employed 89.3 million people, who were paid $2.643 trillion in total. On the average, each worker created $195,300 in sales revenue, and each dollar paid for labor generated $6.60 sales revenue. The average wage in the private sector was $29,598. These numbers are used as the economy's benchmark to compare relative strength of sectors and industries.

The goods-producing sector, as defined in Section 11-3, generated $4.879 trillion sales (28% of the total sales of the private sector), and employed 23.28 million people (26% of the total employment), and its payroll cost $770.8 billion (29% of the total payroll). As its labor share was lower than its sales share and its payroll share greater than the sales share, this sector experienced higher wages, higher labor productivity, but smaller sales-dollars per each payroll-dollar than the corresponding averages of the private sector. The services-producing sector created $12.562 trillion in sales (72% of the total sales), and hired 66 million people (74% of the total employment), and paid $1.872 trillion for labor force (71% of the total payroll). As opposed to the goods-producing sector, the services-producing sector experienced lower wages, lower labor productivity, but greater sales-dollars per each payroll dollar than the benchmark of the private sector.

Table 11-9.2: NAICS Sectors and Their Relative Strength (1997)

| Industries | Average Wage | | Sales/ employment | | Sales/ payroll |
|---|---|---|---|---|---|
| | $1000 | Ratio | $1000 | Ratio | Ratio |
| **Private sector** | **29.598** | **1.00** | **195.3** | **1.00** | **6.60** |
| **Goods-producing Sector** | **33.111** | **1.12** | **209.6** | **1.07** | **6.33** |
| Mining | 40.276 | 1.36 | 288.7 | 1.48 | 7.17 |
| Construction | 30.471 | 1.03 | 150.9 | 0.77 | 4.95 |
| Manufacturing | 33.770 | 1.14 | 226.8 | 1.16 | 6.72 |
| Transp equipment mfg | 42.531 | 1.44 | 306.3 | 1.57 | 7.20 |
| Computer, & electronic product mfg | 42.281 | 1.43 | 255.3 | 1.31 | 6.04 |
| Metal mfg | 34.040 | 1.15 | 175.7 | 0.90 | 5.16 |
| Chemical mfg | 45.187 | 1.53 | 462.4 | 2.37 | 10.23 |
| Machinery mfg | 37.220 | 1.26 | 189.2 | 0.97 | 5.08 |
| Electric equipment mfg | 31.906 | 1.08 | 188.8 | 0.97 | 5.92 |
| **Services-producing Sector** | **28.361** | **0.96** | **190.3** | **0.97** | **6.71** |
| Wholesale | 37.066 | 1.25 | 696.7 | 3.57 | 18.80 |
| Retail | 16.917 | 0.57 | 174.0 | 0.89 | 10.29 |
| Finance, insurance | 45.656 | 1.54 | 390.9 | 2.00 | 8.56 |
| Health care | 27.856 | 0.94 | 65.3 | 0.33 | 2.35 |
| Information | 41.972 | 1.42 | 199.1 | 1.02 | 4.74 |
| Professional | 43.080 | 1.46 | 112.4 | 0.58 | 2.61 |
| Transportation | 28.155 | 0.95 | 108.8 | 0.56 | 3.87 |
| Administrative | 18.511 | 0.63 | 40.7 | 0.21 | 2.20 |
| Real estate | 24.733 | 0.84 | 141.7 | 0.73 | 5.73 |
| Arts, entertainment | 20.567 | 0.67 | 65.6 | 0.34 | 3.19 |
| Educational | 19.937 | 0.67 | 63.0 | 0.32 | 3.16 |

In the goods-producing sector, the manufacturing sector took the lion's share, 22% of the total sales revenue, 19% of the total working force, and 22% of the total payroll. Within the manufacturing sector, large shares went to transportation equipment manufacturing (3.31%, 2.11%, and 3.04% of the total sales, employment, and payroll respectively), computer and electronic product manufacturing (2.47%, 1.89%, and 2.70%), metal manufacturing (2.41%, 2.68%, and 3.08%), and chemical manufacturing (2.39%, 1.01%, and 1.54%).

Combining the computer and electronic product-manufacturing group with the electrical equipment, appliance, and component-manufacturing group, one comes up with the sales revenue of $543.77 trillion, employment of 2.285 million, and payroll of $90.44 billion. This combined group's employment and payroll was greater than the counterparts of transportation equipment manufacturing, and its sales revenue was slightly lower. This comparison shows that the computer manufacturing and the related electrical equipment and component sector has grown very fast in the United States. In terms of job creation, computer and related electric equipment and component manufacturing already exceeded transportation equipment manufacturing (2.285 million versus 1.887 million) in 1997. It is worth noticing that transportation equipment manufacturing consists of a whole array of modern manufacturing industries, such as the automobile industry, aircraft and parts manufacturing, the ship and boat building industry, motorcycle, bicycle and parts manufacturing, railroad equipment, guided missiles, space vehicles and parts manufacturing.

In terms of labor productivity defined by sales revenue per worker, the chemical industry, the transportation equipment industry, and the computer manufacturing were the top three in the manufacturing sector in 1997. Consequently, the average wage in those industries was 43-53% higher than the private sector's average wage. They also held large sales revenue per each labor cost dollar.

In the services-producing sector, a large share of sales revenue went to wholesale trade (23%), retail trade (14%), and finance and insurance (13%), while a large share of employment belonged to retail trade (16%) and health care & social assistance (15%) in 1997. Only one NAICS service sector, health care & social assistance, had a 2-digit payroll-share (14%), which was the second largest in the 20 NAICS sectors next to the manufacturing sector (22%). Only three service sectors experienced higher productivity than the average of the private sector: wholesale trade (3.57 times of the average), finance & insurance (2.0 times), and information (1.02 times).

The average wage of the private sector was about $29,598 dollars in 1997. Four services sectors paid higher than the average wage to their employees. The finance & insurance sector paid $45,656 dollars per worker, 54% higher than the average wage, the professional, scientific & technical services sector paid 46% higher than the average, the information sector 42% higher, and wholesale trade 25% higher.

All of the other services sectors paid less than the average wage. Lower-pay sectors include retail trade (only 57% of the average wage), administrative & support & waste management & remediation services (63% of the average), educational services (67% of the average), and arts, entertainment, & recreation (67% of the average).

For every dollar spent on payroll, the wholesale-trade sector generated $18.80 dollar of sales revenue, which was the greatest ratio among the 20 NAICS sectors listed in Table 11-9.2. The retail-trade sector and chemical manufacturing also held a high sales/payroll ratio, 10.29 and 10.23 respectively. Most of the low-productivity sectors were in the services producing sector, with low wages and low sales/payroll ratios. These sectors include transportation and warehousing, professional, scientific, and technical services, administrative support, waste management, remediation services, educational services, health care, social assistance, arts, entertainment, and recreation. The health care and social assistance had the second lowest productivity and sales/payroll ratio. The worst performer was the sector of administrative support, waste management , and remediation services.

In terms of job creation, the health care sector was the third largest in the private sector, next to the manufacturing sector and retail-trade. In the United States, there were 13.617 million people working in the health case & social assistance sector in 1997 and were paid $27,856 dollars on average, which was lower than the private sector's average wage ($29,598 dollars) in the year. The sales revenue per worker of the health care & social assistance sector was $65,300 dollars, only 33% of the private sector's average ($195,000 dollars). These statistics have clearly pointed out that it is extremely important to improve the productivity and efficiency of the whole services-producing sector in general, and the health case & social assistance sector in particular.

## 11-6  The IT-producing Industry and the IT-using Industry

In Sections 11-2, 11-3, and 11-4 we presented an analysis of the evolution of sectors based upon conventional SIC codes for dividing industries into groups and sectors. Lacking detailed less-aggregated-industry data, we could not identify leading industries in some specific areas such as electric and electronic equipment, instruments and related products of electronic components, electric industrial apparatus, household appliances, audio and video equipment, and communications equipment. In the meantime, the computer and office equipment industry has been classified as a component industry in the broad group of industrial machinery and equipment (SIC code 35), along with engine and turbines, construction and related machinery, metalworking machinery, and special industrial machinery. At the high level of industrial aggregation, the SIC grouping contains a mix of rapidly growing leading industries as well as some declining industries in the manufacturing sector.

In Section 11-5 we employed the latest industrial survey data that are based upon the newly introduced NAICS industry grouping. Because the survey only covers 1997, no time series data have been made available to permit comparisons of growth rates and changing shares of industries and sectors, which are crucial for identifying leading sectors of the U.S. economy. As a compromise between data availability and options of industrial grouping, we adopt a mid-way approach towards a time series analysis of two specific industry groups: the information technology (IT) producing industry and the IT using industry.

Researchers in the U.S. Department of Commerce have identified the IT-producing industry and the IT-using industry in a 1999 published report, *The Emerging Digital Economy II*[2]. The IT producing industry includes producers of computer hardware and software, communications equipment and services, and instruments. Member industries of the IT using industry are selected as extensive users of information technology.

As Table 10-1 in Section 10-2 of Chapter 10 indicates, American industries' spending on information processing equipment rose from $142 billion in 1993[3] to $466.5 billion in 2000 and has consistently accounted for about (1/3 - 1/2) of spending on all types of capital equipment, namely the producers' durable equipment (PDE). IT equipment includes office computing and accounting machinery, communications equipment, photocopy and related equipment, and instruments. The U.S. Department of Commerce has used two measurements for identifying industries that are intensive users of IT equipment.

---

[2] The Emerging Digital Economy II, Economic and Statistics and Administration, U.S. Department of Commerce, July 1999.
[3] The Emerging Digital Economy II, Economic and Statistics and Administration, U.S. Department of Commerce, July 1999, Figure 2.5.

The first measurement is the current dollar value of an industry's IT capital stock relative to its total equipment stock in four categories: information processing, industrial equipment, transportation equipment, and other PDE (see Table 10-1). Net capital stock is the cumulative value of past gross investment minus capital depreciation. The telephone and telegraph, radio and television, and security and commodity brokers were the top-three industries ranked by this measurement in 1996. The IT net capital stock of those three industries accounted for 84.4%, 78.8%, and 56.3% of total equipment capital stock respectively. The bottom three industries were construction, motor vehicles and equipment, and auto repair, services and parking, with their IT net capital only 1.6%, 3.3%, and 4.5% of total equipment capital respectively in 1996[4].

The second measurement is IT investment expenditures per worker, namely annual purchases of IT equipment divided by the number of workers in each industry. In terms of the second measurement, the top three industries were telephone and telegraph, non-depository institutions, and pipeline, except natural gas. Their IT investment per worker reached $29,236, $18,129, and $18,069 respectively in 1996. The bottom three industries were construction, educational services, and amusement and recreation services, with their IT investment per worker of $35, $51, and $218 respectively in 1996[5]. U.S. Commerce Department has selected nineteen consolidated IT-using industries according to both measures as the extensive users of information technology. We have aggregated these nineteen industries into twelve categories and will analyze their contributions to the U.S. economy in Section 11-6-2.

We use the value-added and employment data provided by Table A-2-2 and Table A-4.1 of the report from U.S. Department of Commerce to calculate the IT-producing industry's GDP- and labor-shares, and a similar analysis is applied to the twelve categories of the IT-using industry. We present these results in the following two sections.

---

[4] The Emerging Digital Economy II, Economic and Statistics and Administration, U.S. Department of Commerce, July 1999, Table A-3.1.

[5] The Emerging Digital Economy II, Economic and Statistics and Administration, U.S. Department of Commerce, July 1999, Table A-3.2.

## 11-6-1 Contributions by the IT-producing Industry

According to U.S. Commerce Department's classification, the IT-producing industry consists of industries that produce, process, or transmit information goods and services either as intermediate inputs for other industries or as final demand by consumers, investors and governments, or for the purpose of exporting. It also includes industries that provide the infrastructure necessary to operate the Internet and electronic commerce. There are four industry categories included in the IT-producing industry:

(1) Hardware industries (computers and equipment manufacture, computer and equipment wholesale, computer and equipment retail, electron tubes, printed circuit board and passive electronic components, semiconductors, industrial instruments for measurement, instruments for measuring electricity, and laboratory analytical instruments);

(2) Software and services (computer programming services, prepackaged software, computer integrated system design, computer processing and data preparation, information retrieval services, computer services management and rental and leasing, computer maintenance and repair, prepackaged software wholesale, prepackaged software retail);

(3) Communications equipment (household audio and video equipment, telephone and telegraph equipment, radio and TV communications equipment, magnetic and optical recording media);

(4) Communications services (telephone and telegraph communications, radio broadcasting, television broadcasting, cable and other PAY-TV services).

Contributions made by the IT-producing industry to the U.S economy are denoted by their value-added to GDP, employment, GDP- and labor-shares, growth rate of value-added, and productivity measured by value-added divided by number of employees. The time frame covered by this analysis is from 1990 through 1997, for which the detailed IT industrial data have been made available by the Commerce Department's report. Table 11-10 displays these results for the four groups of the IT-producing industry.

Table 11-10: Contribution by the IT-producing Industries

| | GDP | Hardware | Software | Commun. equipment | Commun services | Total IT producing |
|---|---|---|---|---|---|---|
| | | | **Value-added ($ million)** | | | |
| 1990 | 5,743,837 | 102,677 | 59,661 | 21,038 | 146,700 | **330,076** |
| 1991 | 5,916,668 | 103,635 | 64,027 | 20,054 | 154,200 | **341,916** |
| 1992 | 6,244,445 | 109,416 | 73,435 | 23,800 | 161,200 | **367,851** |
| 1993 | 6,558,092 | 117,766 | 79,475 | 23,952 | 175,600 | **396,793** |
| 1994 | 6,946,974 | 133,012 | 90,834 | 27,813 | 184,600 | **436,258** |
| 1995 | 7,269,599 | 154,517 | 104,466 | 30,549 | 193,300 | **482,832** |
| 1996 | 7,661,578 | 171,852 | 132,032 | 32,210 | 207,400 | **543,494** |
| 1997 | 8,110,897 | 197,375 | 150,034 | 34,367 | 214,869 | **596,645** |
| | | | **GDP Share (%)** | | | |
| 1990 | 100 | 1.79 | 1.04 | 0.37 | 2.56 | **5.75** |
| 1991 | 100 | 1.75 | 1.08 | 0.34 | 2.61 | **5.78** |
| 1992 | 100 | 1.75 | 1.18 | 0.38 | 2.58 | **5.89** |
| 1993 | 100 | 1.8 | 1.21 | 0.37 | 2.68 | **6.05** |
| 1994 | 100 | 1.92 | 1.31 | 0.4 | 2.66 | **6.28** |
| 1995 | 100 | 2.13 | 1.44 | 0.42 | 2.66 | **6.64** |
| 1996 | 100 | 2.24 | 1.72 | 0.42 | 2.71 | **7.09** |
| 1997 | 100 | 2.43 | 1.85 | 0.42 | 2.65 | **7.36** |
| | | | **Employment (thousand)** | | | |
| 1990 | 114,608 | 1,574 | 790 | 345 | 1,309 | **4,018** |
| 1991 | 113,814 | 1,513 | 816 | 332 | 1,299 | **3,960** |
| 1992 | 113,671 | 1,437 | 853 | 317 | 1,269 | **3,876** |
| 1993 | 116,046 | 1,402 | 911 | 317 | 1,269 | **3,899** |
| 1994 | 119,042 | 1,415 | 977 | 327 | 1,295 | **4,014** |
| 1995 | 122,148 | 1,476 | 1,109 | 337 | 1,318 | **4,240** |
| 1996 | 124,390 | 1,556 | 1,248 | 342 | 1,351 | **4,497** |
| 1997 | 127,254 | 1,643 | 1,433 | 347 | 1,424 | **4,847** |
| | | | **Labor Share (%)** | | | |
| 1990 | 100 | 1.37 | 0.69 | 0.3 | 1.14 | **3.51** |
| 1991 | 100 | 1.33 | 0.72 | 0.29 | 1.14 | **3.48** |
| 1992 | 100 | 1.26 | 0.75 | 0.28 | 1.12 | **3.41** |
| 1993 | 100 | 1.21 | 0.79 | 0.27 | 1.09 | **3.36** |
| 1994 | 100 | 1.19 | 0.82 | 0.27 | 1.09 | **3.37** |
| 1995 | 100 | 1.21 | 0.91 | 0.28 | 1.08 | **3.47** |
| 1996 | 100 | 1.25 | 1 | 0.28 | 1.09 | **3.62** |
| 1997 | 100 | 1.29 | 1.13 | 0.27 | 1.12 | **3.81** |
| | | | **Productivity ($ thousand/per worker)** | | | |
| 1990 | 50.117 | 65.246 | 75.482 | 61.015 | 112.079 | **82.155** |
| 1991 | 51.985 | 68.492 | 78.512 | 60.348 | 118.725 | **86.349** |
| 1992 | 54.934 | 76.163 | 86.06 | 75.174 | 127.039 | **94.919** |
| 1993 | 56.513 | 84.022 | 87.287 | 75.631 | 138.366 | **101.797** |
| 1994 | 58.357 | 94.015 | 93.01 | 85.184 | 142.57 | **108.717** |
| 1995 | 59.515 | 104.694 | 94.199 | 90.568 | 146.706 | **113.878** |
| 1996 | 61.593 | 110.424 | 105.769 | 94.21 | 153.561 | **120.857** |
| 1997 | 63.738 | 120.131 | 104.692 | 99.127 | 150.944 | **123.113** |

Table 11-10 continued

|  | GDP | Hardware | Software | Commun. equipment | Commun services | Total IT producing |
|---|---|---|---|---|---|---|
| **Annual Growth Rate of Value-added (%)** | | | | | | |
| 1991 | 3.01 | 0.93 | 7.32 | -4.68 | 5.11 | **3.59** |
| 1992 | 5.54 | 5.58 | 14.69 | 18.68 | 4.54 | **7.59** |
| 1993 | 5.02 | 7.63 | 8.23 | 0.64 | 8.93 | **7.87** |
| 1994 | 5.93 | 12.95 | 14.29 | 16.12 | 5.13 | **9.95** |
| 1995 | 4.64 | 16.17 | 15.01 | 9.84 | 4.71 | **10.68** |
| 1996 | 5.39 | 11.22 | 26.39 | 5.44 | 7.29 | **12.56** |
| 1997 | 5.86 | 14.85 | 13.63 | 6.7 | 3.6 | **9.78** |
| **Annual Growth Rate of Productivity (%)** | | | | | | |
| 1991 | 3.73 | 4.98 | 4.02 | -1.09 | 5.93 | **5.1** |
| 1992 | 5.67 | 11.2 | 9.61 | 24.57 | 7 | **9.93** |
| 1993 | 2.87 | 10.32 | 1.43 | 0.61 | 8.92 | **7.25** |
| 1994 | 3.26 | 11.89 | 6.56 | 12.63 | 3.04 | **6.8** |
| 1995 | 1.98 | 11.36 | 1.28 | 6.32 | 2.9 | **4.75** |
| 1996 | 3.49 | 5.47 | 12.28 | 4.02 | 4.67 | **6.13** |
| 1997 | 3.48 | 8.79 | -1.02 | 5.22 | -1.71 | **1.87** |

Data source: The Emerging Digital Economy II, Economic and Statistics and Administration, U.S. Department of Commerce, July 1999.

The IT-producing industry's GDP-share rose from 5.75% in 1990 to 7.36% in 1997. The major GDP-share gain occurred in both hardware and software categories. The GDP-share increased from 1.79% to 2.43% for the hardware group and from 1.04% to 1.85% for the software group over the time period of 1990-97. The GDP-share remained less than 0.5% for the entire time period for the communications equipment industry; for the communications services industry, it rose from 2.56% in 1990 to 2.65% in 1997. In particular, the semiconductor industry raised its value added from $15.733 billion in 1990 to $54.602 billion in 1997, and the estimate for 1999 was $63.861 billion. Consequently, the semiconductor industry's GDP-share increased from 0.27% in 1990 to 0.67% in 1997. The second largest share gain in the hardware group appeared in computer and equipment wholesale, with its GDP-share rising from 0.58% in 1990 to 0.86% in 1997. The computer and equipment manufacturing industry's GDP-share fluctuated in a narrow range of 0.36-0.47%, and the GDP-shares of other industries in the hardware category were either flat or slightly raised.

Every industry in the software group raised GDP-share considerably in the 1990s. GDP-shares of the top three software industries rose from

0.26% to 0.39% for computer programming services, from 0.19% to 0.36% for prepackaged software, and from 0.18% to 0.37% for computer processing and data preparation. Other software industries' GDP-shares were all relatively small. For example, value-added by the prepackaged software wholesale accounted for 0.04% of the GDP in 1997. Similarly, prepackaged software retail only accounted for about 0.02%.

Significant increases in GDP-share occurred in the telecommunications services industries. The GDP-share rose from 0.18% to 0.33% for cable and other pay-TV services, from 0.09% to 0.12% for radio broadcasting, and from 0.21% to 0.25% for television broadcasting. The share of telephone and telegraph communications fluctuated slightly around 2.0%, which was the largest share in the communications equipment and services industries as a whole.

The increasing GDP-share has reflected the rapid growth of the IT-producing industry for the 1990s. As the second panel from the bottom of Table 11-10 indicates, the annual growth rate of the total value added of the IT-producing industry was substantially higher than the growth rate of nominal GDP. Both the hardware and software groups registered a double-digit annual growth rate in 1994-97. The estimated growth rate was 6.81% in 1998 and 8.73% in 1999 for the hardware group, and 15.28% and 15.22% for the software group. The communications equipment industry has been steadily growing since 1994: its estimated growth rate was 6.92% and 6.11% in 1998 and 1999. Compared with the other three categories of the IT-producing industry, communications services grew relatively slowly, but its speed picked up in the late 1990s. The estimated growth rate was 13.1% for 1998 and 7.6% for 1999. The extraordinary growth of the IT-producing industry has clearly demonstrated its leading role in the U.S. economic expansion over the 1990s.

Job creation by the IT-producing industry was less extraordinary than its value-added creation. In fact, 829,000 net new positions were added into the IT producing industry during 1990-97, among them 643,000 jobs created by the software industry. Only the software industry's labor-share increased from 0.69% in 1990 to 1.13% in 1997, while the other three groups reduced their labor-share slightly.

Rapidly growing output and a slowly increasing working force has resulted in a great enhancement in productivity for the IT-producing industry. As the bottom panel of Table 11-10 shows, the annual rate of productivity change was in the range of 1.98% – 5.67% over the years 1990-97 for the U.S. economy, while it was in the range of 1.87% - 9.93% for the IT-producing industry.

Compared with the goods-producing industries analyzed in Section 11-3, the IT-producing industry has shown an extraordinary performance of rapid growth and increasing productivity. Table 11-11 presents some highlights of this comparison in terms of GDP- and labor-shares and productivity measures over 1990 - 97.

Table 11-11: Comparison of Major Industries
in the Goods-Producing Sectors

| | IT producing industry | Construction | Motor & transportation equipment | Metal | Chemical, petroleum & rubber, leather product |
|---|---|---|---|---|---|
| **GDP Share (%)** | | | | | |
| 1990 | **5.75** | 4.27 | 1.86 | 1.95 | 3.17 |
| 1991 | **5.78** | 3.87 | 1.76 | 1.81 | 3.11 |
| 1992 | **5.89** | 3.68 | 1.75 | 1.75 | 3.07 |
| 1993 | **6.05** | 3.7 | 1.91 | 1.76 | 3.08 |
| 1994 | **6.28** | 3.87 | 1.97 | 1.88 | 3.17 |
| 1995 | **6.64** | 3.94 | 1.81 | 1.92 | 3.23 |
| 1996 | **7.09** | 4.07 | 1.72 | 1.89 | 3.11 |
| 1997 | **7.36** | 4.05 | 1.68 | 1.88 | 3.09 |
| **Labor Share (%)** | | | | | |
| 1990 | **3.51** | 5.69 | 1.73 | 1.88 | 1.95 |
| 1991 | **3.48** | 5.3 | 1.66 | 1.81 | 1.94 |
| 1992 | **3.41** | 5.17 | 1.61 | 1.76 | 1.95 |
| 1993 | **3.36** | 5.28 | 1.51 | 1.73 | 1.93 |
| 1994 | **3.37** | 5.38 | 1.47 | 1.75 | 1.89 |
| 1995 | **3.47** | 5.45 | 1.46 | 1.75 | 1.85 |
| 1996 | **3.62** | 5.59 | 1.43 | 1.73 | 1.8 |
| 1997 | **3.81** | 5.7 | 1.44 | 1.72 | 1.76 |
| **Productivity (thousand/per worker)** | | | | | |
| 1990 | **82.155** | 37.612 | 35.823 | 51.861 | 81.201 |
| 1991 | **86.349** | 37.907 | 55.391 | 51.944 | 83.263 |
| 1992 | **94.919** | 39.091 | 59.674 | 54.418 | 86.517 |
| 1993 | **101.797** | 39.55 | 71.314 | 57.564 | 90.301 |
| 1994 | **108.717** | 41.944 | 78.403 | 62.643 | 97.683 |
| 1995 | **113.878** | 43.002 | 73.77 | 65.103 | 103.788 |
| 1996 | **120.857** | 44.837 | 73.808 | 67.176 | 106.531 |
| 1997 | **123.113** | 45.353 | 74.35 | 69.616 | 111.929 |
| **Annual Growth Rate of Value Added (%)** | | | | | |
| 1990 | | 1.24 | -3.74 | -1.15 | 5.88 |
| 1991 | **3.59** | -6.71 | -2.08 | -4.34 | 1.12 |
| 1992 | **7.59** | 0.39 | 4.82 | 1.77 | 4.14 |
| 1993 | **7.87** | 5.55 | 14.29 | 6.1 | 5.36 |
| 1994 | **9.95** | 10.84 | 9.44 | 12.78 | 9.05 |
| 1995 | **10.68** | 6.59 | -4.03 | 6.77 | 6.58 |
| 1996 | **12.56** | 8.9 | 0.05 | 3.81 | 1.64 |
| 1997 | **9.78** | 5.43 | 3.56 | 5.41 | 5.16 |

There are four major industries in the goods producing sector displayed in Table 11-11: construction, transportation equipment manufacturing, all metal production, and chemical, petroleum, rubber and leather production. None of them showed an increasing GDP-share in the time period of 1990-97. Their annual growth rates of value-added were substantially lower than that of the IT-producing industry. The IT-producing industry's excellent performance has been demonstrated not only by its largest GDP-share and consistency of increasing GDP-share but also by its highest productivity measure, which made the IT-producing industry a true leading sector in the U.S economy of the 1990s.

In particular, the hardware and communications equipment industries registered double-digit growth rates of productivity during 1992-95, but the productivity improvement was less smooth over time in the software and communications services industries. In terms of value-added per worker, the communications services industry remained at the top, its productivity measure was $150,944 per worker in 1997. The communications equipment industry, however, showed the lowest productivity in the IT-producing industry, only $99,127 per worker in 1997, which was still 55% higher than the average productivity, $63,738 per worker, of the U.S. economy as a whole.

## 11-6-2 Contributions by the IT-using Industry

The IT-using industry consists of twelve industrial groups that have been identified as extensive users of information technology in the U.S. economy. Most of the IT-using industries belong to the services producing sector; only two groups are in the goods producing sector. These are the industries of electronic and electric equipment and instruments, and of chemical and petroleum products. The former is a producer as well as an extensive user of information technology, the latter consists of manufacturing chemicals and allied products and petroleum and coal products, but does not include rubber and leather products in SIC30 and SIC31[6]. The IT-using industry's contributions to the U.S. economy are presented in Tables 11-12 and 11-13 in terms of value added, GDP-share, employment, labor-share, proxy measure of

---

[6] It is worth noticing that the industries in SIC30 and SIC31 are included in the chemicals & petroleum group of Section 11-3-2 above, but they are excluded from this group in this section.

productivity, growth rate of value added and growth rate of productivity for the time period from 1990 through 1997.

As Table 11-12 shows, the total value added of the IT-using industry was about $2.67 trillion in 1990, accounting for 46.49% of the year's GDP, and it rose to $4.07 trillion in 1997, or 50.18% of GDP. Employment of the IT-using industry was less proportional to its value added. It was 39.373 million in 1990, accounting for 34.36% of the total work force in the U.S. economy, and rose to 46.810 million in 1997, 36.79% of the economy's work force. These GDP- and labor-shares reveal an important fact in the U.S economy of the 1990s, that is more than 50% of GDP has been generated by industries that are intensively using information technologies. And more than 36% of the total U.S. work force is engaged in goods or services production that requires a heavy usage of information technologies. These results indicate that information technologies are no longer confined within the electronic industry of its origin, IT applications have reached various services industries as well as many industries in the goods-producing sector.

The increasing GDP- and labor-shares reflect the rapid growth of value added and job creation by the IT-using industry. Growth rates indicate that the IT-using industry raised its value added more rapidly than the nominal GDP growth for each year from 1990 through 1997. Some industries, such as business services, banking and credit agencies, insurance, security and commodity brokers, have registered double-digit annual growth rates in several years. Consequently their GDP-share increased remarkably. Over 1990-97, the GDP-share rose from 3.47% to 4.50% for business services, from 1.85% to 2.42% for insurance, and from 0.69% to 1.31% for security and commodity brokers. Recalling the declining GDP-shares of the four major goods producing industries presented in Table 11-11, one can clearly see that the contributions to GDP by the business services industry in 1997 was even greater than that from each the four major industries of the U.S. economy.

Extensive usage of information technology has been a main factor in productivity enhancement. The productivity panel of Table 11-13 shows that the average productivity measure for the IT-using industry rose from $67,812 in 1990 to $86,934 in 1997. This was significantly higher than the U.S. economy's average productivity measure ($50,117 and $63,738) for the corresponding years. Three groups (real estate, railroad and pipeline and utility, and chemicals and petroleum products) were on top in 1990 and retained their positions over 1990-97. Their productivity measures were $553,272, $219,773, and $167,102 in 1997 respectively.

## Table 11-12:  Contribution by the IT-using Industries

| Categories | 1990 | 1992 | 1995 | 1997 |
|---|---|---|---|---|
| | **Value Added ($ million)** | | | |
| **U.S. economy (GDP)** | **5,743,837** | **6,244,445** | **7,269,599** | **8,110,897** |
| Real estate | 671,891 | 734,858 | 843,807 | 935,032 |
| Wholesale trade | 367,206 | 406,414 | 491,399 | 562,755 |
| Health services | 307,909 | 369,052 | 428,853 | 460,105 |
| Legal, social, other services | 293,110 | 328,127 | 388,808 | 444,307 |
| Business services | 198,986 | 218,911 | 284,920 | 364,722 |
| Banking & credit | 190,622 | 228,455 | 268,882 | 322,697 |
| Railroad, pipeline, utilities | 183,688 | 201,671 | 224,887 | 238,893 |
| Elec. equipment, instruments | 147,138 | 152,847 | 185,757 | 213,188 |
| Insurance | 106,399 | 122,802 | 165,155 | 196,641 |
| Chemicals & petroleum | 143,333 | 148,682 | 184,432 | 194,005 |
| Security, commodity brokers | 39,671 | 49,504 | 73,424 | 106,568 |
| Motion picture | 20,363 | 19,968 | 26,343 | 30,472 |
| **IT using industry** | **2,670,316** | **2,981,291** | **3,566,667** | **4,069,385** |
| | **GDP Share of Value-Added (%)** | | | |
| Real estate | 11.70 | 11.77 | 11.61 | 11.53 |
| Wholesale trade | 6.39 | 6.51 | 6.76 | 6.94 |
| Health services | 5.36 | 5.91 | 5.90 | 5.67 |
| Legal, social, other services | 5.10 | 5.26 | 5.35 | 5.48 |
| Business services | 3.46 | 3.51 | 3.92 | 4.50 |
| Banking & credit | 3.32 | 3.66 | 3.70 | 3.98 |
| Railroad, pipeline, utilities | 3.20 | 3.23 | 3.10 | 2.95 |
| Elec. equipment, instruments | 2.56 | 2.45 | 2.56 | 2.63 |
| Insurance | 1.85 | 1.97 | 2.27 | 2.42 |
| Chemicals & petroleum | 2.50 | 2.38 | 2.54 | 2.39 |
| Security, commodity brokers | 0.69 | 0.79 | 1.01 | 1.31 |
| Motion picture | 0.36 | 0.32 | 0.36 | 0.38 |
| **IT using industry** | **46.49** | **47.76** | **49.08** | **50.18** |
| | **Annual Growth Rate of Value-Added (%)** | | | |
| **Nominal GDP growth rate** | **5.61** | **5.54** | **4.64** | **5.86** |
| Real estate | 5.75 | 5.79 | 5.09 | 4.80 |
| Wholesale trade | 3.06 | 4.72 | 4.99 | 8.27 |
| Health services | 11.44 | 9.28 | 4.54 | 3.27 |
| Legal, social, other services | 9.63 | 8.03 | 6.63 | 7.45 |
| Business services | 11.17 | 10.71 | 11.29 | 13.22 |
| Banking & credit | 10.13 | 5.62 | 10.45 | 13.29 |
| Railroad, pipeline, utilities | 2.82 | 1.63 | 0.86 | 2.31 |
| Elec. equipment, instruments | 2.65 | 0.02 | 2.26 | 8.20 |
| Insurance | 4.84 | 0.88 | 7.38 | 15.67 |
| Chemicals & petroleum | 7.17 | 3.36 | 7.86 | 4.62 |
| Security, commodity brokers | -5.72 | 32.74 | -6.52 | 10.41 |
| Motion picture | 1.25 | -0.47 | 14.55 | 7.37 |
| **IT using industry** | **6.52** | **6.00** | **5.64** | **7.40** |

## Table 11-13:  Contribution by the IT-using Industries

| Categories | 1990 | 1992 | 1995 | 1997 |
|---|---|---|---|---|
| | **Employment (thousand)** | | | |
| **U.S. economy** | **114,608** | **113,671** | **122,148** | **127,254** |
| Real estate | 1,596 | 1,564 | 1,648 | 1,689 |
| Wholesale trade | 6,291 | 6,207 | 6,563 | 6,735 |
| Health services | 7,507 | 8,205 | 8,909 | 9,404 |
| Legal, social, other services | 7,600 | 8,193 | 9,103 | 9,808 |
| Business services | 5,551 | 5,552 | 7,116 | 8,293 |
| Banking & credit | 2,518 | 2,409 | 2,403 | 2,484 |
| Railroad, pipeline, utilities | 1,209 | 1,197 | 1,144 | 1,087 |
| Elec. equipment, instruments | 2,651 | 2,436 | 2,450 | 2,539 |
| Insurance | 2,278 | 2,283 | 2,307 | 2,336 |
| Chemicals & petroleum | 1,235 | 1,224 | 1,178 | 1,161 |
| Security, commodity brokers | 489 | 510 | 621 | 680 |
| Motion picture | 448 | 461 | 544 | 594 |
| **IT using industry** | **39,373** | **40,241** | **43,986** | **46,810** |
| | **Labor Share (%)** | | | |
| Real estate | 1.39 | 1.38 | 1.35 | 1.33 |
| Wholesale trade | 5.49 | 5.46 | 5.37 | 5.30 |
| Health services | 6.55 | 7.22 | 7.29 | 7.39 |
| Legal, social, other service | 6.63 | 7.21 | 7.45 | 7.71 |
| Business services | 4.84 | 4.88 | 5.83 | 6.51 |
| Banking & credit | 2.20 | 2.12 | 1.96 | 1.95 |
| Railroad, pipeline, utilities | 1.06 | 1.05 | 0.94 | 0.85 |
| Elec. equipment, instruments | 2.31 | 2.14 | 2.01 | 2.00 |
| Insurance | 1.99 | 2.01 | 1.89 | 1.84 |
| Chemicals & petroleum | 1.08 | 1.08 | 0.96 | 0.91 |
| Security, commodity brokers | 0.43 | 0.45 | 0.51 | 0.53 |
| Motion picture | 0.39 | 0.41 | 0.45 | 0.47 |
| **IT using industry** | **34.36** | **35.41** | **36.01** | **36.79** |
| | **Productivity ($thousand per worker)** | | | |
| **U.S. economy** | **50.117** | **54.934** | **59.515** | **63.738** |
| Real estate | 422.572 | 469.858 | 511.400 | 553.272 |
| Wholesale trade | 58.380 | 65.477 | 74.909 | 83.496 |
| Health services | 41.000 | 44.979 | 48.131 | 48.948 |
| Legal, social, other services | 38.567 | 40.050 | 42.712 | 45.300 |
| Business services | 35.854 | 39.429 | 40.017 | 43.995 |
| Banking & credit | 75.643 | 94.834 | 112.033 | 130.117 |
| Railroad, pipeline, utilities | 151.934 | 168.480 | 196.580 | 219.773 |
| Elec. equipment, instruments | 55.529 | 62.745 | 75.820 | 83.933 |
| Insurance | 46.667 | 53.790 | 71.498 | 84.179 |
| Chemicals & petroleum | 116.059 | 121.472 | 156.564 | 167.102 |
| Security, commodity brokers | 81.127 | 97.067 | 118.235 | 156.718 |
| Motion picture | 45.453 | 43.315 | 48.425 | 51.300 |
| **IT using industry** | **67.812** | **74.086** | **81.086** | **86.934** |

Table 11-13 (continued)

| Categories | 1990 | 1992 | 1995 | 1997 |
|---|---|---|---|---|
| | Annual Growth Rate of Productivity (%) | | | |
| **U.S. economy** | **4.97** | **5.67** | **1.98** | **3.48** |
| Real estate | 5.42 | 6.33 | 4.26 | 4.31 |
| Wholesale trade | 5.09 | 4.62 | 1.17 | 6.02 |
| Health services | 6.73 | 4.27 | 1.81 | 0.74 |
| Legal, social, other services | 6.30 | 4.48 | 2.96 | 2.44 |
| Business services | 7.27 | 10.55 | 2.25 | 4.72 |
| Banking & credit | 10.13 | 7.28 | 12.98 | 10.78 |
| Railroad, pipeline, utilities | 2.23 | 2.48 | 2.98 | 3.91 |
| Elec. equipment, instruments | 6.48 | 4.37 | 1.26 | 6.70 |
| Insurance | 1.89 | 2.60 | 8.03 | 14.97 |
| Chemicals & petroleum | 5.52 | 4.04 | 8.41 | 4.98 |
| Security, commodity brokers | -4.56 | 25.98 | -10.88 | 5.05 |
| Motion picture | -0.33 | -2.42 | 4.86 | 3.38 |
| **IT using industry** | **4.65** | **4.73** | **2.34** | **3.74** |

There are two categories that have significantly increased their productivity in this time period: the industry of banking and credit (from $75,643 to $130,117) and the industry of security and commodity brokers (from $81,127 to $156,718).

In the IT-using industry there are four categories with productivity measures lower than the average productivity of the U.S. economy. These categories include health services; legal, social, and other services; business services; and motion pictures. The increasing labor shares of those industries, however, indicate that more new jobs have been created in those categories than in any other IT-using industries. Productivity growth in the health services was very slow, with less than a 1% annual increase in 1996-97, which was substantially lower than the average productivity growth of 3.48% for those two years. Boosting productivity in the services industries still remains a great challenge.

## 11-7  Summary

To highlight the structure changes of the U.S. economy over the last five decades, we put together the GDP-shares for the sectors, the aggregated and less-aggregated industry groups in Table 11-14, and the employment-shares in Table 11-15, and their relative productivity ratios in Table 11-16 for three years, 1948, 1975, and 2000.

Tables 11-14, 11-15, and 11-16 summarize the results produced in Sections 11-2, 11-3, and 11-4 in the order of the Standard Industrial Classification (SIC) that divides the U.S. economy into sectors and aggregated industry groups, and less aggregated industries. From these Tables, one can observe that the relative strength of economic sectors has decisively shifted from the goods-producing sector to the services-producing sector. This transformation is caused by the changing consumption pattern of Americans from mass material consumption to mass services consumption, as was discussed in Section 10-1 of Chapter 10.

Table 11-14: Changing Structure of the U.S. Economy
— GDP Shares of Sectors and Industries

| | GDP Share % | | |
|---|---|---|---|
| | **1948** | **1975** | **2000** |
| **Governments** | 11.17 | 15.21 | 12.32 |
| **Goods-producing** | **44.42** | **32.29** | **23.23** |
| Agriculture | 8.89 | 3.36 | 1.38 |
| Mining | 3.50 | 2.62 | 1.29 |
| Construction | 4.27 | 4.62 | 4.70 |
| Manufacturing | 27.76 | 21.70 | 15.88 |
| Durable-goods | 14.17 | 12.69 | 9.14 |
| Transportation Equipments | 4.39* | 2.27 | 1.85 |
| Metal | 4.73* | 3.42 | 1.64 |
| Wood & Stone Products | 2.47 | 1.65 | 1.16 |
| Industrial Machinery | 2.49 | 2.58 | 1.70 |
| Electric & Electronic | 2.01 | 2.38 | 2.49 |
| Non-durable-goods | 13.59 | 9.01 | 6.73 |
| Food & Tobacco | 4.45 | 2.66 | 1.61 |
| Textile & Others | 3.31 | 1.32 | 0.49 |
| Paper & Publishing | 2.29 | 1.99 | 1.68 |
| Chemical & Petroleum | 3.53 | 3.04 | 2.96 |
| **Services-producing** | **44.68** | **51.42** | **65.77** |
| Wholesale Trade | 6.80 | 7.41 | 6.83 |
| Retail Trade | 11.16 | 9.37 | 9.05 |
| Transportation, Communications, and Utilities | 8.81 | 8.71 | 8.36 |
| Transportation | 5.78 | 3.62 | 3.18 |
| Railroad | 3.27 | 0.77 | 0.23 |
| Air- transportation | 0.18 | 0.62 | 0.94 |
| Communications | 1.40 | 2.48 | 2.85 |
| Electric Gas Sanitary | 1.61 | 2.61 | 2.33 |
| Finance, Insurance, Real Estate | 9.78 | 13.74 | 19.61 |
| Banking & Credit | 1.20 | 2.10 | 4.31 |
| Security, Brokers | 0.13 | 0.30 | 1.46 |
| Insurance | 1.09 | 1.51 | 2.38 |
| Real Estate | 7.33 | 9.75 | 11.31 |
| Services Industry | 8.13 | 12.20 | 21.93 |
| Business Services | 0.61 | 1.87 | 5.79 |
| Health services | 1.54 | 3.54 | 5.54 |
| Education, Legal, & Social Services | 0.84 | 1.77 | 2.83 |
| Amusement | 0.40 | 0.47 | 0.82 |
| Miscellaneous Professional Services | 0.40 | 1.13 | 3.10 |

*It indicates the record high share occurring in 1955.

Table 11-15: Changing Structure of the U.S. Economy
— Employment Shares of Sectors and Industries

| | Employment Share % | | |
|---|---|---|---|
| | **1948** | **1975** | **2000** |
| **Governments** | 11.58 | 18.65 | 14.11 |
| **Goods-producing** | **46.23** | **31.73** | **22.73** |
| Agriculture | 11.38 | 3.85 | 2.47 |
| Mining | 1.77 | 0.91 | 0.41 |
| Construction | 5.68 | 5.18 | 6.18 |
| Manufacturing | 27.41 | 21.79 | 13.68 |
| **Durable-goods** | **14.75** | **12.86** | **8.29** |
| Transportation Equipments | 2.95* | 2.03 | 1.37 |
| Metal | 4.03* | 3.09 | 1.65 |
| Wood & Stone Products | 3.26 | 2.05 | 1.51 |
| Industrial Machinery | 2.46 | 2.49 | 1.56 |
| Electric & Electronic | 2.15 | 2.68 | 1.88 |
| **Non-durable-goods** | **12.66** | **8.92** | **5.39** |
| Food & Tobacco | 3.33 | 2.04 | 1.26 |
| Textile & Others | 4.41 | 2.43 | 0.85 |
| Paper & Publishing | 2.19 | 2.01 | 1.62 |
| Chemical & Petroleum | 2.73 | 2.44 | 1.65 |
| **Services-producing** | **42.19** | **49.62** | **63.16** |
| Wholesale Trade | 4.88 | 5.45 | 5.25 |
| Retail Trade | 13.48 | 14.45 | 15.83 |
| Transportation, Communications, and Utilities | 7.42 | 5.53 | 5.18 |
| Transportation | 5.22 | 3.33 | 3.43 |
| Railroad | 2.58 | 0.65 | 0.15 |
| Air- transportation | 0.16 | 0.42 | 0.90 |
| Communications | 1.27 | 1.33 | 1.13 |
| Electric Gas Sanitary | 0.92 | 0.87 | 0.63 |
| **Finance, Insurance, Real Estate** | **3.19** | **5.31** | **5.80** |
| Banking & Credit | 0.89 | 1.99 | 1.90 |
| Security, Brokers | 0.11 | 0.23 | 0.65 |
| Insurance | 1.13 | 1.80 | 1.77 |
| Real Estate | 1.04 | 1.19 | 1.31 |
| **Services Industry** | **13.24** | **18.88** | **31.09** |
| Business Services | 0.66 | 2.48 | 7.55 |
| Health services | 1.94 | 4.96 | 7.22 |
| Education, Legal, & Social Services | 2.33 | 4.43 | 6.54 |
| Amusement | 0.90 | 0.89 | 1.69 |
| Miscellaneous Professional Services | 0.44 | 1.13 | 3.17 |

*It indicates the record high share occurring in 1955.

## Table 11-16: Changing Structure of the U.S. Economy
## — Relative Productivity of Sectors and Industries

| | Relative Productivity** | | |
|---|---|---|---|
| | 1948 | 1975 | 2000 |
| **Governments** | 0.96 | 0.82 | 0.87 |
| **Goods-producing** | **0.96** | **1.02** | **1.02** |
| Agriculture | 0.78 | 0.87 | 0.56 |
| Mining | 1.98 | 2.87 | 3.14 |
| Construction | 0.75 | 0.89 | 0.76 |
| Manufacturing | 1.01 | 1.00 | 1.16 |
| **Durable-goods** | **0.96** | **0.99** | **1.10** |
| Transportation Equipments | 1.49* | 1.12 | 1.35 |
| Metal | 1.17* | 1.11 | 0.99 |
| Wood & Stone Products | 0.76 | 0.81 | 0.77 |
| Industrial Machinery | 1.01 | 1.04 | 1.09 |
| Electric & Electronic | 0.94 | 0.89 | 1.32 |
| **Non-durable-goods** | **1.07** | **1.01** | **1.25** |
| Food & Tobacco | 1.34 | 1.30 | 1.28 |
| Textile & Others | 0.75 | 0.54 | 0.57 |
| Paper & Publishing | 1.05 | 0.99 | 1.03 |
| Chemical & Petroleum | 1.29 | 1.24 | 1.79 |
| **Services-producing** | **1.06** | **1.04** | **1.04** |
| Wholesale Trade | 1.39 | 1.36 | 1.30 |
| Retail Trade | 0.83 | 0.65 | 0.57 |
| Transportation, Communications, and Utilities | 1.19 | 1.58 | 1.61 |
| Transportation | 1.11 | 1.09 | 0.93 |
| Railroad | 1.27 | 1.18 | 1.56 |
| Air- transportation | 1.16 | 1.47 | 1.05 |
| Communications | 1.10 | 1.86 | 2.53 |
| Electric Gas Sanitary | 1.75 | 3.01 | 3.70 |
| **Finance, Insurance, Real Estate** | **3.07** | **2.59** | **3.38** |
| Banking & Credit | 1.35 | 1.05 | 2.27 |
| Security, Brokers | 1.16 | 1.31 | 2.26 |
| Insurance | 0.96 | 0.84 | 1.34 |
| Real Estate | 7.08 | 8.19 | 8.66 |
| **Services Industry** | **0.61** | **0.65** | **0.71** |
| Business Services | 0.93 | 0.75 | 0.77 |
| Health services | 0.79 | 0.71 | 0.77 |
| Education, Legal, & Social Services | 0.36 | 0.40 | 0.43 |
| Amusement | 0.45 | 0.53 | 0.48 |
| Miscellaneous Professional Services | 0.91 | 1.00 | 0.98 |

* It indicates the record high share occurring in 1955.
** Relative productivity represents the ratio of industry's productivity to the economy's average productivity, measured by value-added per employee.

To rank the growth performance of sectors and industries, we use the percentage change of GDP-shares over the time period from 1975 through 2000. Sectors and industries can be regrouped into three categories: the leading sector with GDP-share increasing more than 15%, the follower sector with GDP-share between -15% and 15%, and the laggard sector with GDP-share declining more than 15%. The dividing lines of 15% and -15% that identify the leader, follower, and laggard sectors and industries are quite arbitrary, as we do not have a rigid definition for them and the regrouping is primarily based on the relative strength of the growth rate of value added. Nevertheless, these categories provide a clear comparison of all sectors and industries in terms of economic growth in the last twenty-five years. These results are presented in Table 11-17 for the sectors and industry groups with 2-digit SIC codes and in Table 11-18 for the less-aggregated industries.

Table 11-17: Leader, Follower, and Laggard
(Sectors and Industry Groups)

| Status | Sector | %-change of GDP Share over 1975-2000 | %-change of labor Share over 1975-2000 |
|---|---|---|---|
| **Leader** | Services-producing Sector | 27.9% | 27.3% |
| Growth Rate of GDP Share > 15% | Services industry | 79.8% | 64.7% |
| | Finance, insurance, and Real estate | 42.7% | 9.2% |
| **Follower** | Construction | 1.7% | 19.3% |
| Growth Rate of GDP Share -15%--15% | Retail trade | -3.4% | 9.6% |
| | Transportation, Communications, Utilities | -4.0% | -6.3% |
| | Wholesale Trade | -7.8% | -3.7% |
| **Laggard** | Goods-producing Sector | -28.1% | -28.4% |
| Growth Rate of GDP Share <-15% | Manufacturing | -26.8% | -37.2% |
| | Non-durable Goods Manufacturing | -25.3% | -39.6% |
| | Durable Goods Manufacturing | -28.0% | -35.5% |
| | Mining | -50.8% | -54.9% |
| | Agriculture | -58.9% | -35.8% |

Table 11-18:  Leader, Follower, and Laggard (Industries)

| Status | Industry | %-change of GDP Share Over 1975-2000 | %-change of Labor Share Over 1975-2000 |
|---|---|---|---|
| **Leader**<br><br>Growth Rate of GDP Share > 15% | Security, commodity, brokers | 386.7% | 182.6% |
| | Business services | 209.6% | 204.4% |
| | Professional services | 174.3% | 180.5% |
| | Banking & credit agency | 105.2% | -4.5% |
| | Amusement & motion picture | 74.5% | 89.9% |
| | Education, legal, social services | 59.9% | 47.6% |
| | Insurance | 57.6% | -1.7% |
| | Health services | 56.5% | 45.6% |
| | Air-transportation | 51.6% | 114.3% |
| | Real estate | 16.0% | 10.1% |
| **Follower**<br><br>Growth rate of GDP-share -15%--15% | Communications | 14.9% | -15.0% |
| | Electric & electronic equipment | 4.6% | -29.9% |
| | Chemical & petroleum | -2.6% | -32.4% |
| | Retail trade | -3.4% | 9.6% |
| | Wholesale trade | -7.8% | -3.7% |
| | Electric, gas, sanitary | -10.7% | -27.6% |
| | Transportation | -12.2% | 3.0% |
| **Laggard**<br><br>Growth rate of GDP-share <-15% | Paper & publishing | -15.6% | -19.4% |
| | Transportation equipment manufacturing | -18.5% | -32.5% |
| | Wood, stone products | -29.7% | -26.3% |
| | Industrial machinery | -34.1% | -37.3% |
| | Food & tobacco | -39.5% | -38.2% |
| | Metal | -52.0% | -46.6% |
| | Textile | -62.7% | -65.0% |
| | Railroad | -70.1% | -76.9% |

The services-producing sector has been the leading sector with its large gains in both GDP- and labor-shares for this 25-year period. Two aggregated industry groups in the services-producing sector, the services industry group and the finance, insurance and real estate group, have received the greatest percentage gains in their GDP-shares, making them the leader for economic growth in the last twenty-five years. There are four industry groups that fall into the follower status category, including the industry group of construction in the goods-producing sector and three industry groups in the services-producing sector: retail trade, wholesale trade, and transportation, communications and utilities. Three industry groups in this category have reduced their relative strength in the U.S. economy, which is indicated by the declining GDP-shares. The labor-share, however, has increased for retail trade and construction groups.

The goods-producing sector as a whole has been the laggard sector along with its aggregated component industry groups of manufacturing (both durable and non-durable goods manufacturing), mining, and agriculture. The GDP- and labor-shares for the good-producing sector and its industry groups have reduced by 25-58% for the last twenty five years, indicating their significantly slower pace of growth than the average growth rate of the U.S. economy. In Table 11-16, there are ten less-aggregated industries in the leader category; all of them belong to the services-producing sector. The top three industries (security, commodity, and brokers; business services; and professional services) raised their GDP- and labor-shares by 174-386% in the last twenty-five years, indicating extraordinary economic growth in those industries. The other seven industries in the leader category raised their GDP-share by 16-105%, and labor-share by 10-114%, except for two industries with declining labor shares. The banking and insurance industry's labor-share reduced by 4.5% and the insurance industry's by 1.7% in 1975-2000.

In the follower category, there are seven industries, two industries in the goods-producing sector (electric and electronic equipment manufacturing and the chemical and petroleum industry) and five industries in the services-producing sector. The electric and electronic equipment and instruments industry consists of many less-aggregated high technology industries such as manufacture of semiconductor and electronic component, communications equipment, computer, consumer electronic equipment, industrial instrument, medical equipment, and measuring and controlling device. Even though some of these industries have shown extraordinary growth in the last five decades, they have been mixed with some slow-growing industries in this group, which resulted in the less impressive growth of the group's GDP-share by only 4.6% and a labor-share decline by nearly 30% in 1975-2000.

All of the eight industries in the laggard category belong to the goods-producing sector except for the railroad industry, which is in the services-producing sector. The bottom three are railroad, textile, and metal, with their GDP-share decreasing by (52-70)% and labor share declining by (46-77)% in 1975-2000. The textile industry was a leading sector in the First Industrial Revolution for the stage of take-off, and the metal and railroad industries were leading sectors in the Second Industrial Revolution for the stage of drive to technological maturity. In the current stage of high mass-consumption, all three of these used-to-be leading sectors have become laggard, with their GDP- and labor-shares shrinking year after year.

From the services-producing sector of the U.S. economy have emerged many new industries that provide sustainable economic growth and create many new jobs for American workers. In the goods-producing sector, however, many formerly leading industries from the previous stages of economic growth have become followers or laggards in the present stage of high mass-consumption; their relative strength in the U.S. economy has been continuously diminishing over time. In particular, the cyclical industries that produce staple commodities such as steel, iron, paper, wood-product, chemicals, industrial capital goods, etc. have dramatically reduced their GDP- and labor-shares and transformed them from the leaders of the 1950s –1970s to the laggards of the 1990s.

# PART FIVE

# THE TRANSFORMATION OF THE FINANCIAL SERVICES SECTOR OF THE U.S. ECONOMY

# Chapter 12

## *Transformation from Financial Turbulence to Financial Engineering*

The financial services sector in the United States consists of two kinds of firms: financial intermediaries and financial facilitators. The financial intermediaries include commercial banks and depository institutions (such as savings banks, savings and loan associations, and credit unions), insurance companies, pension funds, mutual funds, and mortgage companies. These firms stand between lenders and borrowers by issuing liabilities (deposits, insurance policies, pension obligations, etc.) and holding financial assets (loans, mortgages, bonds, equity shares, etc.). The financial facilitators include stockbrokers, securities underwriters, market makers, dealers, investment bankers, financial advisers and analysts, accountants, rating agencies and the financial press. These firms facilitate the financial transactions between the primary issuers of financial liabilities and investors who purchase financial assets. Many financial firms in the United States operate a wide variety of businesses, acting as both intermediaries and facilitators.

Monetary policy is considered the most important component of economic policymaking for the nation's economic well-being. Congress has entrusted the Federal Reserve with the responsibility of conducting monetary policy. The process of formulating and implementing monetary policy involves continuing interactions among the Federal Reserve, financial institutions, the financial markets, non-financial enterprises, and the public. All firms in the financial services sector play a role in transmitting the Federal Reserve's policy impulses into the U.S. economy. Changes in monetary policy directly influence short-term and long-term interest rates as well as reserve requirements that will immediately alter financial firms' costs of liabilities and the returns on capital the financial assets should generate. The Federal Reserve also acts as a regulator to supervise and regulate the nation's financial services sector to ensure financial firms' soundness and compliance with banking, consumer, and other applicable laws.

## 12-1  The Federal Reserve and Monetary Policy

The Federal Reserve, often called the Fed, is the central bank of the United States, managing the nation's supply of money and credit and operating at the center of the U.S. financial sector. It also serves as the banker for the federal government by providing financial services for the U.S. Department of the Treasury, and regulates and supervises the nation's banking and financial system.

The United States did not have a central bank until 1913 when Congress passed the Federal Reserve Act establishing the Federal Reserve in order to balance the financial needs of the nation. The Federal Reserve System has been an independent agency of the U.S. government with unique autonomy and authority to formulate and implement monetary policy free from short-term partisan political pressures. As the nation's money manager, the Fed controls the flow of money and credit in the economy. Money comprises currency and coin issued by the Fed or U.S. Treasury and various kinds of deposits at commercial banks and other depository institutions. Credit consists of loans and debt instruments such as notes or bonds made by depository institutions and other financial and non-financial entities.

Money and credit are the lifeblood of the economy, facilitating business operations and transactions, creating jobs, fueling economic growth, and generating wealth. On the one hand, if money and credit expand too rapidly, the nation's capacity of production may reach its limit, and corporations cannot produce enough goods and services to keep up with increased spending. Prices have to rise and inflation may accelerate quickly. On the other hand, if the flow of money and credit is constricted too greatly, consumers' spending and businesses' investment may dwindle, resulting in declines in sales revenues and profits. As factories close down and workers lose their jobs, an economic recession begins. The Fed's ultimate goal is to sustain economic growth with price stability, or in other words, to avoid those two extremes in order to keep prices steady, workers employed, and businesses productive and profitable. To reach its ultimate goal, the Fed formulates and conducts monetary policy in a way that promotes sustainable economic expansion and price stability.

Because there is no way for the Fed to directly control its ultimate goal, a monetary aggregate has been used to serve as an intermediate target or indicator, standing between the Fed's ultimate goal and the Fed's operational policy tools. A great difficulty arises in the monetary policy process: to determine the appropriate behavior of money that will produce both desirable economic expansion and price stability. As a result of financial innovations in the last three decades, many new instruments have been created and widely used to facilitate financial transactions between the primary issuers of financial liabilities and the depositors and investors who purchase these instruments, such as money market mutual funds at commercial banks and thrifts. As all the financial instruments that exist in the U.S. economy have varying degrees of "moneyness", the Fed has set forth several definitions of monetary aggregates.

M1 is a monetary aggregate narrowly defined and often used as money in most economic analyses. M1 consists of currency in circulation, traveler's checks, demand deposits at commercial banks, and other checkable deposits. M2 is a broadly defined monetary aggregate, consisting of M1 plus overnight and continuing contract repurchase agreements (RPs) issued by all commercial banks, overnight Eurodollars, money market deposit accounts, and savings and small denomination time deposits. The broader measure of M3 consists of M2 plus large-denomination time deposits, term PR liabilities, term Eurodollars and all balances in institution-only money market mutual funds. The broadest measure of L consists of M3 plus the non-bank public holdings of U.S. savings bonds, short-term Treasury securities, commercial paper and banker acceptances.

The Fed has an ability to imprecisely control M1, but not other monetary aggregates. The M1 measure of money used to be an important indicator for conducting monetary policy. It was closely related to economic activities via the income velocity of money. The velocity of money is defined as the number of times per year the average dollar is spent on final goods and services. If the velocity remains nearly stable, the money supply will become a more important determinate of the level of output, employment, and prices, with its direct and predictable effects on the economy. As a matter of fact, the Fed employed M1 as its intermediate target tied to reserve operating objectives for reducing money supply that had successfully reversed the surge of inflation during the 1970s.

Indeed, in the 1950s, 60s, and 70s M1 showed a steady upward velocity of 3.2% per year from 1953 Q1 to 1979 Q4[1]. Since the early 1980's, however, the steady upward trend of the velocity of M1 has reversed due to the spread of interest-bearing NOW accounts, reduced inflation and interest rates, and the increased interest-rate-sensitivity of components of M1. As the changed trend of the velocity of M1 reduced its reliability as an indicator for monetary policy, the Fed has shifted its focus on the broad measure of M2 that has demonstrated a long-term trend in its velocity. By the early 1990's, however, the velocity of M2 surged unexpectedly because of the increased attractiveness and availability of alternative financial instruments for saving and investment, such as bonds and stock mutual funds. The irregular behavior of the velocity of M2 has forced the Fed to reduce its reliance on M2 for conducting the monetary policy.

As the behavior of all the monetary aggregates does not guarantee a steady long-term trend of velocities of money, the adoption of certain monetary rules, as advocated by Milton Friedman, recipient of the 1976 Nobel Memorial Prize for economic science[2], becomes very difficult in conducting monetary policy. The long-lasting debate between two camps in economics, Keynesian versus Monetarist, has demonstrated their different views on the mechanism through which monetary policy impulses are transmitted to economic activities.

In the Keynesian view, monetary policy involves a rather lengthy transmission, traveling from changes in monetary policy to changes in commercial bank reserves, to changes in money supply, to changes in the interest rates, to changes in business investment and consumer spending, and finally to changes in the level of output, employment, and prices. Compared with fiscal policy (changes in government spending and taxation), the monetary policy is weak and should be used discretionally as a stabilization tool to modify the ups and downs of the business cycle.

---

[1] U.S. Monetary Policy and Financial Markets, by Ann-Marie Meulendyke, Federal Reserve Bank of New York, 1989.

[2] Friedman advocates legislating the monetary rule that the money supply be expanded each year at the same annual rate as the potential growth rate of real GDP. According to this rule, the supply of money should be increased steadily at 3-5% per year regardless any other changes in the economy.

The monetarists believe that the cause-effect chain between the supply of money and the level of economic activity is short, direct and tight. In the monetarist view, changes in money supply will be simply and directly transmitted into changes in nominal GDP, and, therefore, the quantity of money and monetary policy are the critical determinants of the level of economic activity and the level of general prices. They argue that the discretionary changes in the money supply made by the Fed have in fact been a destabilizing factor since the establishment of the Federal Reserve System in 1913.

The monetarists have particularly attributed the Great Depression of 1929 - 1933 to faulty decisions by the Fed that reduced the money supply by 30% in a few years following the stock market crash in 1929. The Fed's action turned an economic recession into the Great Depression. They have also blamed the Fed for mismanaging the money supply in the 1970s by fostering excessive monetary creation and contributed to the surging inflation. No wonder Milton Friedman has still insisted: "we don't need a Fed. ... I have, for many years, been in favor of replacing the Fed with a computer. ...., for most of its history, the Fed has been a loose cannon on the deck, and not a source of stability."[3] Nevertheless, he has admitted: "the Fed has learned from experience. ..., and performance of the Fed under Mr. Greenspan has been better than any prior chairman[4]."

In the real world, formulating and implementing monetary policy are much more difficult than developing arguments in any academic and intellectual debates. The prudent monetary policy under the leadership of Alan Greenspan has involved degrees of rule- and discretionary-based modes of monetary operation over time[5].

The rule-based part is reflected in the Fed's exploiting past patterns and regularities in order to operate in a systematic way, and its inferring as much as possible from the past in order to make judgment based on historical regularities in behavior of monetary aggregates and economic activity.

The discretionary-based part includes recognizing the often-disrupted historical regularities by unanticipated changes, especially in technologies and financial innovations. In an ever-changing world, the performance of

---

[3] Milton and Rose Friedman Offer Radical Ideas for the 21st Century, by Deroy Murdock, December 8, 1999, GATO, Today's Commentary.

[4] Uncommon Knowledge: The New Economy, by Peter Robinson, March 10, 2000.

[5] Remarks by Chairman Alan Greenspan, at the 15th Anniversary Conference of the Center for Economic Research at Stanford University, September 5, 1997.

the economy under rule-based monetary policy would deviate from the past patterns of behavior. The Fed frequently has attempted to judge to what extent its monetary policy would cause deviation from the past regular behavior of the economy.

Since the monetary aggregates have become unreliable as the intermediate targets for monetary policy, the Fed has been setting the federal funds rate directly, in response to a wide variety of changes in the economy. The nominal short-term interest rates that are directly linked with the funds rate have also become Fed's operating targets, with their indirect and complex linkages to spending, output, employment, and prices. In a compromise of the lack of reliable information on the balance of money supply and demand, the Fed routinely investigates a variety of financial variables from foreign exchange, bond, and equity markets, along with credit supply conditions at financial intermediaries and other financial institutions in order to judge the stance of its monetary policy[6].

The nature of the Fed's discretionary monetary policy can be observed via Figure 12-1, which depicts the federal funds rate from July 1954 to July 2002. From Figure 12-1 one can see that the Fed aggressively and quickly reduced the federal funds rate from 9.53% in June 1989 to 3.09% in November 1992 in order to fend off the 1990-1991 recession. The Fed allowed the low rate to stay nearly one year before raising it to 5.85% in July 1995. During 1995 - 2000, the federal funds rate drifted around 5.5% and reached 6.40% in December 2000, reflecting the Fed's worry about the tightening U.S. labor market and a potential inflation rise, which has not materialized so far. Since January 2001, however, the Fed has shifted its focus on the weakness of the U.S. economy and aggressively cut the federal funds rate eleven times, pushing the rate down from 6.40% in December 2000 to 1.75% in July 2002, when the federal funds rate reached a 40-year low, 1.75%.

Since the Fed's first cut of interest rate in January 2001 during this easing phase of the monetary policy cycle, more than twenty months have passed. Many people expected the U.S. economy to resume its sustainable growth path, but the economy has recovered very slowly, reflecting the long delay from the policy action to changes in economic performance.

Nevertheless, the Fed has been guided by a firm commitment to contain any forces that would undermine economic expansion and efficiency by raising inflation. Since 1982, the Fed's monetary policy has been successful

---

[6] Remarks by Chairman Alan Greenspan, at the 15th Anniversary Conference of the Center for Economic Research at Stanford University, September 5, 1997.

in focusing firmly on the ultimate goal of the sustained economic expansion with reasonable price stability. The exceptional performance of the U.S. economy in the last twenty years, that is, the continuous economic expansion interrupted by only minor recessions of 1990 and 2001, and the tamed inflation rate of general prices combined with the relatively low unemployment rate, has manifested a triumph of the Fed's monetary policy.

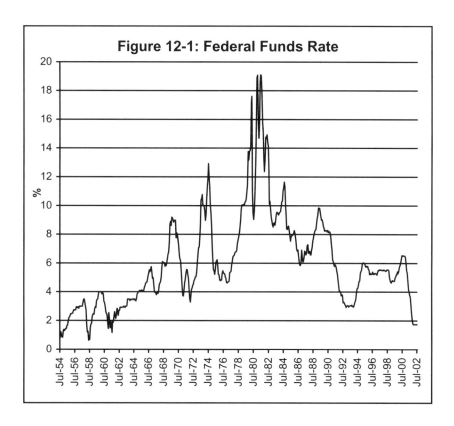

## 12-2     The S&L Insurance Mess

The U.S. economy went through a series of financial crises during the last fifty years. The experiences of dealing with the financial turbulence of those years led to the adoption of prudent banking policies and regulations to improve the safety and soundness of the financial services sector for the U.S. economy, one of the crucial factors that supported the sustainable economic growth of the 1990s.

The stock market crash on October 29, 1929 started the Great Depression in the United States and the consequent banking crisis of the early 1930s, and led to the development of federal insurance for deposits. After the establishment of the Federal Deposit Insurance Corporation (FDIC) in 1933, the United States enjoyed a stable banking system for many years. The total number of bank failures between 1943 and 1974 was only 121[7].

Bank failures, however, began escalating in the 1970s and developed into what has been called the "S & L Insurance Mess" of the 1980s[8]. Between 1985 and 1990, an average of 169 banks failed per year. The number of insolvency resolutions by the Federal Savings and Loan Insurance Corporation (FSLIC) reached 1,092 and the number of GAAP (Generally Accepted Accounting Principles) insolvent institutions was about 3,594[9] over the time period of 1975 through 1988.

The traditional role of savings and loan associations was to accept savings deposits and lend out money in the form of long-term mortgages. Savings and loan associations and commercial banks financed the real estate booms of the 1970s and 1980s that resulted in sharp increases in property prices and the over-building of commercial properties. Slumps in the construction and real estate markets in the mid-1970s and in the late 1980s caused the price of commercial and residential properties in many parts of the United States to plunge. Banks that had extended credit to real estate developers found the value of their assets and collateral value decrease and the delinquency rate increase.

The U.S. banking industry also encountered unfavorable external shocks in those decades. In addition to the international financial crisis involving many developing debtor nations, such as Mexico, Brazil, and Argentina, which did not meet their debt obligations, the oil crises had a great effect

---

[7] Sangkyun Park, Explanations for the Increased Riskiness of Banks in the 1980s, *Review,* Vol. 76, No 4, July/August 1994.

[8] Edward J. Kane, *The S & L Insurance Mess: How Did It Happen?* The Urban Institute Press, Washington, D.C.

[9] Calculated from data in Table 2-1, p. 26 of *The S & L Insurance Mess: How Did It Happen?* An insolvency resolution is defined as a regulator-induced operation cessation, such as liquidation, merge or acquisition. GAAP-insolvent institution is defined as the one whose net wealth is less than or equal to zero under Generally Accepted Accounting Principles (GAAP).

on the overall conditions of the U.S. economy. The first oil crisis generated a high inflation rate and caused a sudden rise in the short-term interest rate. The three-month Treasury bill rate jumped above 8% in 1973 from less than 4% in 1972. The second oil crisis pushed the U.S. inflation rate over 13% in 1980 and the short-term interest rate rose as high as 15.66% in December 1980. The long-term interest rate, represented by the ten-year Treasury Constant Maturity rate, followed suit by surging to 15.32% in September 1981 (see Figure 12-2).

When interest rates skyrocketed, commercial banks and S & Ls found themselves losing money because the interest rates they were paying on deposits rose above the rates they were earning on loans and mortgages. As the average maturity of bank liabilities is generally shorter than that of their assets, banks' lending rates adjust more slowly than funding rates. The sudden interest rises in the 1970s and 1980s reduced bank profits and placed many banks in financial troubles. This was particularly serious for the savings and loan associations. Abusing the protection by the Federal Deposit Insurance Corporation (FDIC), the management at many S & Ls had become aggressively involved in risky investments and speculative ventures with new deposits with above-market interest rates. In the end, many of them lost money in a big way and went bankrupt. The U.S. government, however, had the obligation of the federal deposit insurance to pay off the depositors up to $100,000 per account for any insured banks that went into insolvency. Cleaning up the mess left by years of mismanagement of the savings and loan industry cost the nation's taxpayers nearly $200 billion[10].

Since 1990, major changes have been made in the supervision and regulation of depository institutions. Stiff penalties for fraud and higher premiums for deposit insurance have also been imposed in order to make the banking industry safe and sound. Although the S & L crisis was an expensive lesson for the U.S. government and its taxpayers, it has not stopped the process of financial innovation and deregulation in the U.S. banking industry.

The U.S. banking system had been highly protected since 1933, when the Glass-Steagall Act was passed, which banned any connection between commercial banks and investment banking to insure that the tragedy of the 4,000-bank failure during the stock market crash of 1929 would never be repeated. Banks were also prohibited from interstate branching and from

---

[10] Mark D. Flood, The Great Deposit Insurance Debate, *Review*, The Federal Reserve Bank of St. Louis, Vol. 74, No. 4, July/August 1992.

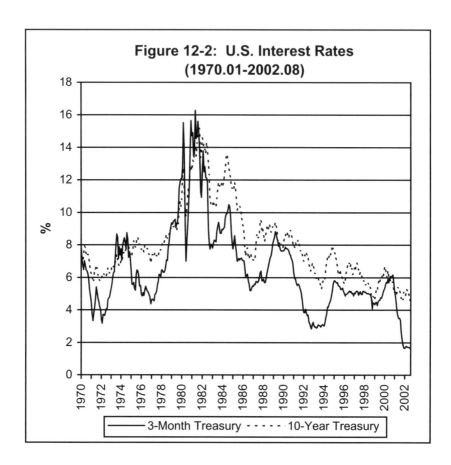

**Figure 12-2:  U.S. Interest Rates (1970.01-2002.08)**

engaging in other businesses.  The payment of interests on demand deposits was prohibited, and the interests on time and savings deposits were limited. Not only did these measures enhance the safety and soundness of the banking industry, they also granted a kind of monopoly power that relieved banks from competition pressure.

The deregulation process of the U.S. banking industry started in the 1970s.  Banks now could be owned by an out-of-state holding company, which lowered geographic barriers for competing banks.  In the 1980s, allowing greater competition for deposits among commercial banks and S & Ls gradually lifted restrictions on interest rates. Many new financial products, such as money market mutual funds and NOW (negotiable order of withdrawal) accounts, were created that could substitute for conventional banking products in lending and funding markets. At the same time, many large corporations found it attractive to borrow directly by issuing commercial papers. Increasingly, banks have to compete with non-bank financial intermediaries for funds and loan customers.

## 3-3   Financial Engineering

In recent years significant developments in technology and in the pricing of assets have sped up financial innovations and improved risk management systems for financial intermediates. Two dramatic financial innovations have taken place recently in the U.S. financial services sector. They are the growing use of financial derivatives and the increasing presence of banks in the private equity market.

Financial derivatives, including options, swaps, futures, and forwards, are instruments whose value is linked to or derived from some other underlying financial instrument or index. These new financial instruments facilitate risk-taking and generate complexities that have never been seen before. Complex financial instruments combined with complex new activities in derivatives have increased market risk, which was illustrated by the Orange County's derivatives debacle in 1996 and the failure of the Long Term Capital Management (LTCM) in October 1998. However, appraising the risks of financial derivatives in the U.S. banking industry, the Chairman of the Federal Reserve, Alan Greenspan, has judged that "derivatives credit exposure, as you all know, are quite small relative to credit exposures in traditional assets, such as banks' loans"[11]. In fact the Chairman and many other authorities have viewed the remarkable expansion of finance in recent years as a significant net benefit for the large majority of the American people.

The Banking Act of 1933 (the Glass-Steagall Act) prohibits the affiliation of a bank with a company that is engaged principally in underwriting or dealing in securities. In 1987, the Federal Reserve Board of Governors approved proposals to underwrite and deal on a limited basis in specified classes of securities, such as commercial paper, certain municipal bonds, conventional mortgage-related securities and consumer loans. Signed into

---

[11] Remarks by Chairman Alan Greenspan, at the 36th Annual Conference on Bank Structure and Competition of the Federal Reserve Bank of Chicago, Illinois, May 4, 2000.

law by President Clinton on November 12, 1999, the Gramm-Leach Bliley Act represents the most sweeping reform of financial service regulation. The Gramm-Leach Bliley Act permits the creation of new financial service holding companies that can offer a full range of financial products, eliminating legal barriers to affiliation among banks and securities firms, insurance companies, and other financial services companies. Under this law, some large financial intermediates are able to conduct what has been called financial engineering by structuring new financial affiliations through a holding company that can offer one-stop shopping for financial services with banking, insurance, and securities activities.

More significantly, the Gramm-Leach Bliley Act has granted very large U.S. banking organizations "merchant banking power", namely financial equity investment in non-financial firms. To enhance safety and soundness, only those banks that are well capitalized and well managed are granted the generalized broad authority to make merchant banking investments. Previously, only extremely limited types of merchant banking investment were allowed. Presently, there are about 155 domestic and more than 10 foreign financial holding companies that can undertake merchant banking. Private equity investments by banks have become one of the substantial variations in banks' profits, as a significant share of large banking organizations' business has already been in equity investment.

For instance, the merger of Citicorp and Travelers Group in October 1998 produced the largest financial service company in the world, Citigroup Inc. Its controlled depository institutions are "well capitalized" and "well managed" as defined in the Federal Reserve Regulation, hence Citigroup is qualified to be a financial holding company. Not only is Citigroup permitted to continue all the operations previously in the Citicorp and Travelers Groups, but also it has ability to engage in a broader spectrum of activities, including insurance underwriting and dealing in securities without a revenue limit. New merchant banking rules permit Citigroup to make investments in companies that engaged in activities that are not financial in nature without regard to the previously existing 5% limit for domestic investments and 20% limit for overseas investments[12].

Indeed, financial innovation and deregulation in recent years has provided unprecedented opportunities for large U.S. banks to become global leaders in financial services. According to its annual report to shareholders, Citigroup had assets of $716.9 billion, total revenues of $82 billion, net income

---

[12] Citigroup Annual Report, 1999.

of $9.867 billion, and equity of $49.7 billion at the end of year 1999; its capitalization reached $237.9 billion, ranked number one among the world's financial service companies. Its businesses provide a broad range of financial services to consumers and corporate customers in 101 countries through three major lines of business: global consumer business, global asset management, and global corporate business. In recent years, financial engineering, innovation and deregulation have represented a great evolution in the history of the U.S. financial system. The contribution of the financial services sector to the nation's GDP has significantly increased. The value added of the financial services sector was about $6.515 billion in 1948, accounting for 2.4% of U.S. GDP in that year. In the year 2000, the value added of the financial services sector reached $804.447 billion, accounting for 8.2% of GDP[13].

## 12-4  Information Technology Speeds Up Financial Innovations

One of the crucial components that made possible what has happened in the U.S. financial system is the broad application of information and communications technology for providing financial services.

The financial services sector relies upon the flow of information, which has made all financial institutions critically dependent on advanced technologies in order to reach customers, deliver services, and make strategic planning, smarter investments, and more effective executions. The banking information system uses the integration of individual components and different operation environments in order to ensure the reliability, accuracy, and completeness of information, delivered to the end-users on a timely basis in support of business and decision-making processes. This same system also makes use of effective security in order to prevent unauthorized access, modification, destruction, or disclosure of information assets. It is not coincidental that financial innovations and deregulations have followed breakthroughs in information and communications technology, such as PCs, broadband technology, and the Internet. New communications channels and devices allow financial service providers and their customers to transact an expanding range of business at virtually any time and any place. Many financial service companies are involved in electronic commerce by providing websites that can be used to conduct transactions conveniently and safely.

---

[13] See Section 11-4-2 of Chapter 11.

Even though bank failure has been rare in the United States in recent years, uncertainties and risks remain major concerns, and result in stringent functional regulations in the U.S. financial services sector. The Securities and Exchange Commission closely examines securities activities; the banking regulators examine banking activities; and the Federal Reserve has enhanced powers to look at financial holding companies and other major financial institutions. These authorities want to ensure that strong risk-management systems are in place and manage those risks accordingly. The recent innovative financial instruments, particularly derivatives and merchant banking investments, must be submitted to market tests not only under the conditions of economic expansion but also economic recession. Economic growth has been proceeding for a record-long period, while the economic recession has only been seen for one quarter in 2001 in the United States, but may occur in the unknown future.

The recent years of strong performance in the U.S. banking industry have not relieved the monetary authorities from worrying about the safety and soundness of the U.S. financial services sector. The Chairman of the Federal Reserve, Alan Greenspan, asks: "Has the financial system become more stable, or has it simply not been tested?"[14] As of yet, no one has had the answer. Nevertheless, information and communications technologies, combined with financial innovation and deregulation, have transformed the U.S. banking industry into a highly efficient and sophisticated financial services sector. Many institutions that are not necessarily financial in nature—such as Sears and GE—have engaged in financial activities through subsidiaries, and deal with securities, engage in mortgage banking, and provide savings and loan facilities as well as insurance. Fundamental changes in financial instruments, financial institutions, and financial markets have taken place, and have contributed to America's continuous economic growth, high employment rate, and low inflation.

---

[14] Remarks by Chairman Alan Greenspan, at the 36th Annual Conference on Bank Structure and Competition of the Federal Reserve Bank of Chicago, Illinois, May 4, 2000.

# Chapter 13

# *Changing Portfolio of American Households' Assets*

In American households, rapidly increasing amounts of personal income, net wealth, and total assets manifest the achievement of U.S. economic transformation over the last fifty years. This transformation has led directly to increasing consumption, sustaining economic growth, and raising the standard of living for the majority of Americans.

## 13-1 Disposable Income and Net Wealth of American Households

Disposable income is defined as the sum of the incomes of all individuals in an economy after all taxes have been deducted and all transfer payments have been added. Disposable income represents how many dollars consumers actually have available to spend or to save. This makes it an important macroeconomic variable in the determination of the level of aggregate demand for consumption and investment. Net wealth is the value of all assets minus the value of all liabilities owned by U.S. households and nonprofit organizations.

Figure 13-1 depicts disposable income in current dollars and net wealth as a percentage of disposable income for U.S. households and nonprofit organizations over the years of 1946-2000.

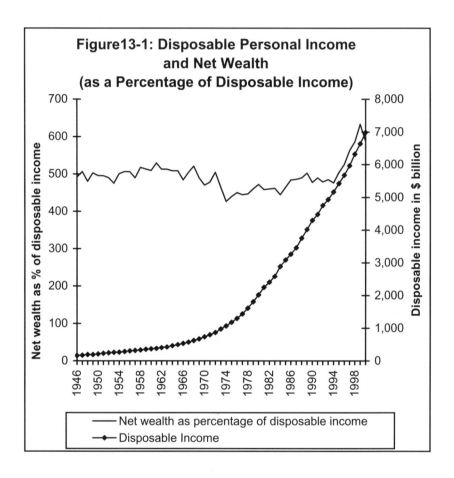

During 1946-1972, a households' net wealth was about five fold that of disposable income, and that ratio was fairly stable for that time period. Disposable income increased from $162 billion in 1946 to $366 billion in 1960 and $869 billion in 1972, while the net wealth increased proportionally from $796 billion in 1946 to $1.866 trillion in 1960, and $4.382 trillion in 1972. The ratio of net wealth to disposable income decreased to 4.27 in

1974, the lowest ratio in the entire period of 1946-2000. During the time period of 1975-1994, the ratio increased slightly and averaged at 4.69. After 1994, net wealth rose much faster than disposable income, pushing the ratio to an unprecedented 6.33 in 1999. Although the ratio of net wealth to disposable income fell to 5.87 in 2000, it was still very high compared with its historical pattern.

In terms of dollar value, disposable income reached $4.293 trillion in 1990, rose to $6.638 trillion in 1999, and continued rising to $6.989 trillion in 2000. Net wealth of American households and nonprofit organizations more than doubled in the 1990s, rising from $20.508 trillion in 1990 to $42.031 trillion in 1999, and declining to $41.025 trillion in 2000.

Dramatically rising disposable income and the net wealth of American households and nonprofit organizations fueled the tremendous economic growth of the 1990s. This was accomplished through large increases in aggregate demand for consumption and investments that have directly contributed to the growth of real GDP. Both the disposable income and net wealth are sources of consumers' purchasing power. Not only does current income support consumers' spending on goods and services, withdrawals from their bank accounts and cashing in various forms of capital assets can finance expenditures. The current unprecedented high level of net wealth to disposable income implies a greater effect of net wealth on aggregate consumption. When net wealth rises, consumers' spending may increase more in the 1990s than would have been possible if the ratio of net wealth to disposable income were at the level of the 1970s or 1980s. Certainly the accelerating net wealth of U.S. households raised the confidence and purchasing power of American consumers in the 1990s.

In 2000, however, the net wealth of U.S. households and nonprofit organizations reduced by more than 5%, and the ratio of net wealth to disposable income fell from its unprecedented high of 1999. Consequently, the decline in net wealth has reduced American consumers' purchasing power and confidence, which could induce a cutback on aggregate consumption on goods and services. Since the middle of 2000, the aggregate investment by U.S. corporations has decreased dramatically, which dragged U.S. real GDP growth rate close to -1.3% in the third quarter of 2001. The aggregate consumption rate is now the only major factor supporting the U.S. economy that has not fallen into officially defined recession (two consecutive quarters of real GDP decline). The declining net wealth of U.S. households and nonprofit organizations could exercise its reverse wealth effects on the aggregate demand through reducing consumptions on goods and services, which would depress the economy into a recession. How to evaluate and project the wealth effects on the U.S. economy has concerned the monetary authorities of the United States1.  Unfortunately, the quantitative answers to that question have not been developed in contemporary economics.

## 13-2  Assets Portfolio of U.S. Households and Nonprofit Organizations

Financial innovations in the 1980s and 1990s created many new forms of investments and services.  An individual's assets can be held in a diversified portfolio in order to gain yields as high as possible with limited risks.  Total assets of households and nonprofit organizations are divided into two categories: tangible assets and financial assets.  Tangible assets include non-liquid assets, such as real estate, consumer durable goods, and equipment and software owned by nonprofit organizations.  Tangible assets are capital directly owned by households to provide utilities such as shelter, transportation, security, convenience and rent income.  Financial assets include currency and various forms of financial claims against governments, corporations, or someone's money holdings at a future date.  These financial claims are called securities and provide an expected return in the form of interest or dividends.

Figure 13-2 presents the growing paths of total assets and its two components, tangible assets and financial assets, of U.S. households and nonprofit organizations over the years from 1945 through 2000.  In 1946, the market value of total assets was $833.5 billion, of which $231.5 billion was in the form of tangible assets and $602.0 billion was in financial assets. Total assets and its two components have increased dramatically for the last fifty years, particularly during the 1990's.  In order to compare historical experiences of increasing Americans' wealth, we provide market values and average growth rates of total assets, tangible assets, and financial assets of U.S. households and nonprofit organizations in the previous five decades and in the recent six years in Table 13-1.

---

[1] Remarks by Chairman Alan Greenspan, at a symposium sponsored by the Federal Reserve Bank of Kansas City, Jackson Hole, Wyoming, August 31, 2001.

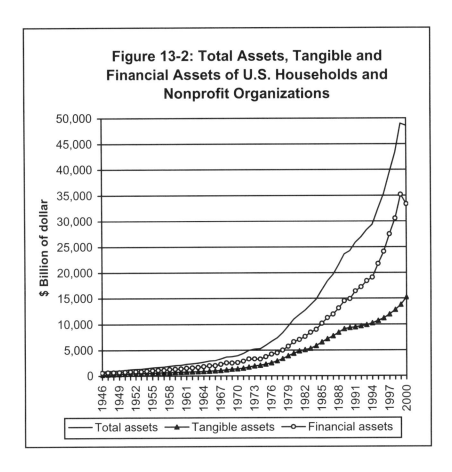

Figure 13-2: Total Assets, Tangible and Financial Assets of U.S. Households and Nonprofit Organizations

The market value of total assets owned by U.S. households and nonprofit organizations was approximately $833.5 billion in 1946, of which $231.5 billion were tangible assets and $602.0 billion were financial assets. In 1970, total assets reached $3.942 trillion, with $1.375 trillion in tangible assets and $2.567 trillion in financial assets. In 2000, the market value of total assets was $48.566 trillion, or 12.32 times the market value of total assets of 1970. In the last three decades the market value of tangible assets increased by 11.06 times to $15.215 trillion, and financial assets rose 12.99 times to $33.352 trillion in 2000.

Table 13-1:  Market Values of Assets and Their Growth Rates

| Time period | Total assets | | Tangible assets | | Financial assets | |
|---|---|---|---|---|---|---|
| | Market value $billion* | Annual growth rate | Market value $billion* | Annual growth rate | Market value $billion* | Annual growth rate |
| 1946-49 | 833.5 | 8.0% | 231.5 | 14.9% | 602.0 | 5.2% |
| 1950-59 | 1,120.0 | 6.9% | 381.7 | 7.3% | 738.3 | 6.7% |
| 1960-69 | 2,089.0 | 6.5% | 729.6 | 6.4% | 1,359.4 | 6.7% |
| 1970-79 | 3,942.2 | 9.9% | 1,375.2 | 11.7% | 2,567.0 | 8.9% |
| 1980-89 | 10,988.5 | 9.4% | 4,381.3 | 8.9% | 6,607.2 | 9.7% |
| 1990-99 | 24,255.6 | 7.6% | 9,326.1 | 4.3% | 14,929.5 | 9.4% |
| 1995 | 32,438.7 | 10.6% | 10,696.8 | 4.6% | 21,741.9 | 13.8% |
| 1996 | 35,297.5 | 8.8% | 11,190.3 | 4.6% | 24,107.2 | 10.9% |
| 1997 | 39,416.4 | 11.7% | 11,928.1 | 6.6% | 27,488.4 | 14.0% |
| 1998 | 43,346.7 | 9.9% | 12,809.3 | 7.4% | 30,537.4 | 11.1% |
| 1999 | 48,976.0 | 13.0% | 13,800.7 | 7.7% | 35,175.3 | 15.2% |
| 2000 | 48,566.4 | -0.8% | 15,214.8 | 10.3% | 33,351.6 | -5.2% |
| Ratio of 2000 to 1970 | 12.32 | | 11.06 | | 12.99 | |

* The market value at the beginning year of each time period

(U.S. Households and Nonprofit Organizations)

The average growth rates in Table 13-1 indicate that tangible assets grew faster than financial assets in the three time periods of 1946-49, 1950-59, and 1970-79. Financial assets have grown much faster than tangible assets since 1980 with the exception of 2000, in which the stock market fell into a bear trap and the market value of equity shares declined substantially. In 1999 the stock market soured with the NASDAQ index rising more than 80%, which inflated the market value of equity assets and resulted in a 15.19% increase in households' financial assets. In 2000, however, the NASDAQ index declined by nearly 40%, and the market value of households' financial assets was reduced by 5.18%. The performance of the U.S. stock market has greatly influenced the market value of households' financial assets through some dramatic capital gains and losses in equity markets in recent years.

When the market value of financial assets declined by 5.18% in 2000, the market value of tangible assets increased by 10.25% within the same year (Table 13-1), indicating the shifting allocation of a households' asset portfolio. Households' decisions on the level of spending on goods and services and the levels and kinds of assets to hold are determined by marginal utilities yield by consumptions and asset holdings. An individual's decisions on how to allocate assets can be quite complicated, and depends on personal preference, income, consumption, interest rates, inflation rate, unemployment rate, economic growth, and market conditions at home and abroad. Total assets owned by U.S. households and nonprofit organizations are aggregated over all individuals and nonprofit organizations, which are more complex than any simple sum of individual decisions. Trying to estimate and project households' consumption and allocation of assets remains a great challenge to economists who must take into consideration these crucial variables in determining aggregate demand for goods and services as well as aggregate investment in businesses.

Figure 13-3 depicts tangible assets and its two components, real estate and consumer durable goods, equipment and software in terms of percentages of total assets owned by U.S. households and nonprofit organizations. In 1946, tangible assets accounted for 27.8% of total assets; real estate accounted for 21.0%, and consumer durable goods and equipment and software accounted for only 6.7%. The asset shares of both components of tangible assets increased in the 1940s and the early 1950s and declined slightly in the 1960s. In the 1970s, real estate grew faster than other forms of assets, resulting in greatly increased asset shares of real estate and tangible assets, from 24.2% and 32.2% in 1968 to 32.1% and 40.8% in 1981.

In the 1980s, the asset share of real estate remained around 31% and the share of tangible assets around 39%, while the share of consumer durable goods and equipment and software has declined since 1974. In the time period of 1990 - 1999, the share of real estate assets reduced from 30.6% to 22.7%, and the share of consumer durables decreased from 7.9% to 5.4%, which resulted in the decline of the tangible asset share from 38.5% in 1990 to 28.2% in 1999. The large share reduction of tangible assets in the 1990s was due to a large increase in U.S. households' financial assets in that decade. The rebound of the real estate share in 2000 was due to the meltdown of the stock markets that dramatically reduced the market value of households' financial assets.

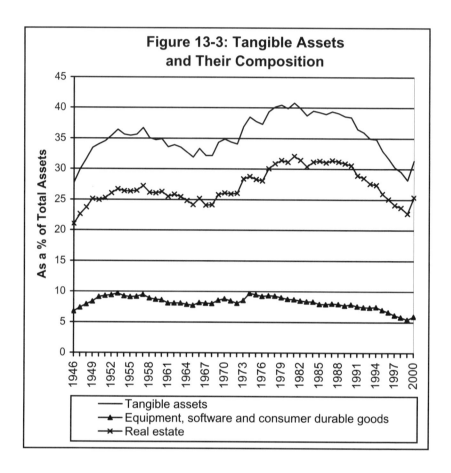

Figure 13-3: Tangible Assets and Their Composition

— Tangible assets
—▲— Equipment, software and consumer durable goods
—✕— Real estate

As Figure 13-2 indicates, the market value of financial assets held by U.S. households and nonprofit organizations increased rapidly in the time period of 1946-2000, from $602.0 billion in 1946 to $14.930 trillion in 1990, $35.175 trillion in 1999, and $33.352 trillion in 2000. Financial assets accounted for 72.2% of total assets owned by U.S. households and nonprofit organizations in 1946. The share of financial assets declined to 59.2% in 1981 and rose to 71.8% in 1999 and 68.7% in 2000. Financial assets are various forms of financial instruments that bear different degrees of risks and yield different returns on holdings. Large components of financial assets include deposits in banks, credit market instruments, corporate equities, mutual funds, pension funds, investment in bank personal trusts, and equity in non-corporate business.

Deposits include currency and checkable deposits, time and savings deposits, money market fund shares, and foreign deposits. Currency and checkable deposits are held for their convenience and liquidity but they do not earn interest and are subject to purchasing power risk. This is risk due to an unexpectedly high inflation rate, which will reduce the purchasing power of interest payments and principals. Savings and time deposits are held because of their high liquidity and safety, as well as their interest yield. The money market is used for short-term funds borrowing and lending, in which many types of short-term financial assets are traded. Short-term interest rates are determined in the money market and influenced directly by the Fed's monetary policy. Individuals did not participate in the money market until the end of the 1970s when very high returns on money market instruments were available with a high degree of safety. In the 1980s most of the instruments in the money market have been accessible to small investors through the purchase of shares in money market mutual funds.

In 1946, total deposits of U.S. households and nonprofit organizations were $115.5 billion, divided fairly evenly between checkable deposits and currency, and time and savings deposits. In 1974, money market fund shares were only $2.4 billion, compared with $670 billion of time and savings deposits. Money market shares rose to $62.2 billion in 1980, $364.9 billion in 1990, and $864.6 billion in 1999. As of the end of 2000, the market value of all deposits reached $4.526 trillion with $3.226 trillion in time and savings deposits, $994.6 billion in money market funds, $255.5 billion in checkable deposits, and only $50.6 billion in foreign deposits.

Credit market instruments include open market paper, U.S. government securities, such as treasury bills, notes and savings bonds, municipal securities, corporate and foreign bonds and mortgages. These credit market instruments pay interests and are relatively liquid. Government securities, in particularly, are risk-free, in the sense that even if businesses and banks fail, the government can always redeem its securities for cash. In 1946, credit market instruments were valued at $90.3 billion, of which U.S. government securities were $65.2 billion, municipal securities $3.8 billion, corporate and foreign bonds $7.5 billion, and mortgages $13.7 billion. In 1990, credit market instruments reached $1,556.3 billion, with $555.0 billion in U.S. government securities, $575.0 billion in municipal securities, $219.0 billion in corporate and foreign bonds, and $144.2 billion in mortgages.

The upper panel of Table 13-2 provides data on the market values of seven large components of financial assets owned by U.S. households and nonprofit organizations: deposits, credit market instruments, corporate equities, mutual funds, pension funds, bank trusts, and equities in non-corporate businesses. The lower panel of Table 13-2 shows the corresponding average annual growth rates of these components.

Table 13-2: Market Values of Financial Component Assets
and Their Growth Rates

| Time Period | Market Value ($billion) | | | | | | |
|---|---|---|---|---|---|---|---|
| | Depos. | Credit market | Corp. equities | Mutu. funds | Pens. funds | Bank trusts | Equity in non- |
| 1946 | 116 | 90 | 101 | 1.3 | 13.5 | 0.0 | 229 |
| 1950 | 124 | 96 | 129 | 3.3 | 24.3 | 0.0 | 297 |
| 1960 | 238 | 151 | 360 | 17 | 93.9 | 0.0 | 401 |
| 1970 | 532 | 216 | 573 | 40 | 254 | 137 | 653 |
| 1980 | 1,517 | 425 | 875 | 46 | 970 | 265 | 2,198 |
| 1990 | 3,253 | 1,556 | 1,781 | 457 | 3,376 | 552 | 3,275 |
| 1995 | 3,310 | 1,947 | 4,183 | 1,159 | 5,671 | 803 | 3,684 |
| 1996 | 3,457 | 2,122 | 4,872 | 1,495 | 6,325 | 871 | 3,889 |
| 1997 | 3,642 | 2,076 | 6,209 | 1,941 | 7,323 | 943 | 4,163 |
| 1998 | 4,006 | 2,035 | 7,177 | 2,375 | 8,194 | 1,001 | 4,428 |
| 1999 | 4,180 | 2,295 | 9,240 | 3,106 | 9,042 | 1,130 | 4,736 |
| 2000 | 4,526 | 2,153 | 7,003 | 3,058 | 9,054 | 1,039 | 4,945 |
| Ratio of 2000 to 1970 | 8.51 | 9.95 | 12.23 | 75.69 | 35.67 | 7.53 | 7.58 |
| Time Period | Average Annual Growth Rate (%) | | | | | | |
| | Depos. | Credit market | Corp. equities | Mutu. funds | Pens. funds | Bank trusts | Equity in non- |
| 1946-49 | 3.55 | 0.98 | -0.89 | 32.46 | 14.48 | 0 | 9.60 |
| 1950-59 | 6.49 | 4.25 | 13.98 | 18.92 | 14.98 | 0 | 3.26 |
| 1960-69 | 8.05 | 4.31 | 6.41 | 11.22 | 10.55 | 0 | 4.82 |
| 1970-79 | 10.91 | 6.67 | 4.27 | 0.70 | 13.47 | 6.05 | 12.16 |
| 1980-89 | 8.97 | 12.84 | 12.08 | 30.59 | 15.05 | 9.02 | 5.12 |
| 1990-99 | 2.78 | 5.98 | 17.90 | 21.55 | 10.93 | 7.76 | 4.05 |
| 1995 | 6.19 | -0.63 | 35.05 | 16.27 | 16.16 | 14.81 | 6.94 |
| 1996 | 4.46 | 8.97 | 16.48 | 29.04 | 11.53 | 8.51 | 5.58 |
| 1997 | 5.35 | -2.18 | 27.43 | 29.81 | 15.78 | 8.17 | 7.03 |
| 1998 | 9.99 | -1.96 | 15.59 | 22.33 | 11.88 | 6.21 | 6.39 |
| 1999 | 4.33 | 12.75 | 28.75 | 30.80 | 10.35 | 12.93 | 6.96 |
| 2000 | 8.29 | -6.18 | -24.21 | -1.56 | 0.14 | -8.08 | 4.40 |

Table 13-2 indicates that mutual fund shares had a spectacular growth in the last five decades. The only exception to this growth occurred in the

1970s, when the annual growth rate averaged 0.70%. This was due to the dramatic decline in the market value of mutual funds from $50.6 billion in 1972 to $28.2 billion in 1974. The market value of mutual fund shares resumed its astonishing growth in the 1980s and 1990s, rising from $104.6 billion in 1984 to $381.7 billion in 1986, and from $1.941 trillion in 1997 to $3.058 trillion in 2000, increasing by nearly 76 times in the last three decades.

Pension funds have been the largest component of financial assets owned by U.S. households and nonprofit organizations. The market value of pension funds grew at double-digit annual rates on the average over the last five decades. For every year from 1946-2000 pension funds showed positive growth. The market value of pension funds increased approximately 36 times over the last three decades. U.S. households' holdings on corporate equities and credit market instruments also showed impressive growth, with their market values rising nearly 12 and 10 times respectively in the last three decades. The other three components of financial assets increased at different growth rates, resulting in changes in the portfolio of U.S. households and non-profit organizations.

Table 13-3 provides the percentage of financial assets relative to the total assets, and the percentages of component financial assets relative to the total financial assets. All the assets are measured by their market value and held by American households and non-profit organizations.

Table 13-3:  Shares of Financial Assets (%)
(U.S. Households and Nonprofit Organizations)

| Year | Total financial assets* | Deposit | Credit market | Corp. equity | Mutual funds | Pension funds | Bank trusts | Equity in non- |
|------|------|------|------|------|------|------|------|------|
| 1946 | 72.23 | 19.19 | 15.00 | 16.83 | 0.22 | 2.24 | 0 | 27.46 |
| 1950 | 65.92 | 16.84 | 13.03 | 17.43 | 0.45 | 3.29 | 0 | 26.50 |
| 1960 | 65.07 | 17.48 | 11.10 | 26.47 | 1.25 | 6.91 | 0 | 19.18 |
| 1970 | 65.12 | 20.72 | 8.43 | 22.30 | 1.57 | 9.89 | 5.37 | 16.56 |
| 1980 | 60.13 | 22.96 | 6.44 | 13.25 | 0.69 | 14.69 | 4.02 | 20.00 |
| 1990 | 61.55 | 21.79 | 10.42 | 11.93 | 3.06 | 22.61 | 3.70 | 13.50 |
| 1995 | 67.02 | 15.22 | 8.96 | 19.24 | 5.33 | 26.08 | 3.69 | 11.36 |
| 1996 | 68.30 | 14.34 | 8.80 | 20.21 | 6.20 | 26.24 | 3.61 | 11.02 |
| 1997 | 69.74 | 13.25 | 7.55 | 22.59 | 7.06 | 26.64 | 3.43 | 10.56 |
| 1998 | 70.45 | 13.12 | 6.66 | 23.50 | 7.78 | 26.83 | 3.28 | 10.22 |
| 1999 | 71.82 | 11.88 | 6.52 | 26.27 | 8.83 | 25.70 | 3.21 | 9.67 |
| 2000 | 68.67 | 13.57 | 6.46 | 21.00 | 9.17 | 27.15 | 3.12 | 10.18 |

* Percentage of total assets

The market value of financial assets accounted for 72% of the total assets in 1946, with 27% of financial assets in equities of non-corporate business, 19% in deposits, 17% in corporate equities, and 15% in credit market instruments. In 1980 the share of financial assets dropped to nearly 60% of total assets. Large declines in shares occurred in credit market instruments, corporate equities, equities in non-corporate business, while the share of deposits and pension funds increased substantially. In the 1990s, the asset shares of pension funds, corporate equities, and mutual funds rose dramatically, while the shares of deposits, credit market instruments, and equities in non-corporate business were significantly reduced.

It is clear that prolonged economic growth and the lasting bull market of the 1990's encouraged U.S. households and nonprofit organizations to change their preference from risk-averse to risk-taking by reallocating their assets into riskier categories of corporate equities and mutual fund that bear higher returns. This is reflected by the declined asset share of credit market instruments from 10.4% in 1990 to 6.5% in 2000, and the declined share of deposits from 21.8% in 1990 to 13.6% in 2000. Those changes in component shares of financial assets are provided in Figures 13-4.1 and 13-4.2 for 1970 and 2000.

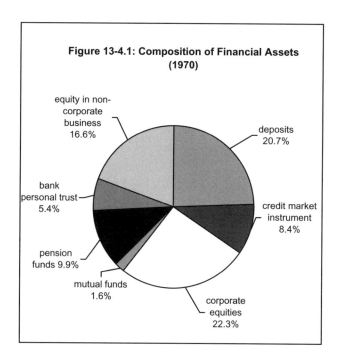

**Figure 13-4.1: Composition of Financial Assets (1970)**

equity in non-corporate business 16.6%

deposits 20.7%

bank personal trust 5.4%

credit market instrument 8.4%

pension funds 9.9%

mutual funds 1.6%

corporate equities 22.3%

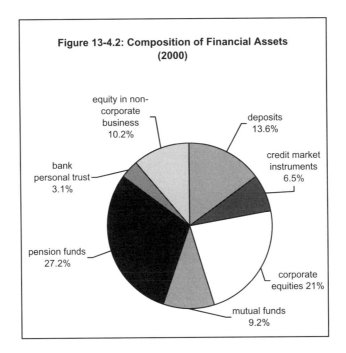

Figure 13-4.2: Composition of Financial Assets (2000)

## 13-3 Liabilities of U.S. Households and Nonprofit Organizations

In the balance sheet of U.S. households and nonprofit organizations, liability includes credit market instruments, security credits, trade payables, and deferred and unpaid life insurance premiums. Credit market instruments hold the lion's share of all liabilities, and the largest two component debts are home mortgages and consumer credit.

Figure 13-5 depicts the growing paths of total liabilities, debts on home mortgages, and debts on consumer credits for U.S. households and nonprofit organizations. Total liabilities were valued at $37.1 billion in 1946, and increased to $478.7 billion in 1970, $3.747 trillion in 1990, and $7.542 trillion in 2000. The annual growth rate of total liabilities reduced from the double digital rate in the 1950s, 1970s, and 1980s to a high single digital rate in the 1990s. Total liabilities accounted for only 4.46% of total assets held by U.S. households and nonprofit organizations in 1946, but for 15.53% of those total assets in 2000.

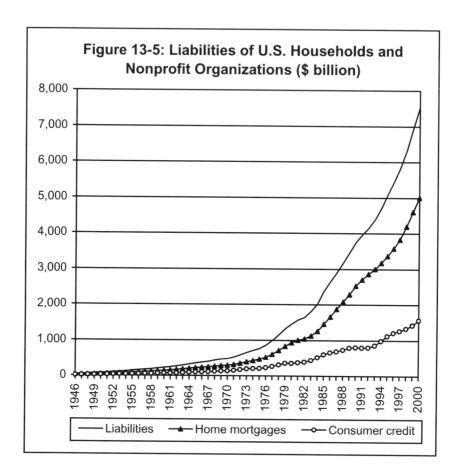

Figure 13-5: Liabilities of U.S. Households and Nonprofit Organizations ($ billion)

Home mortgages are credits secured by home mortgages on real estate. Most houses and a large amount of nonresidential construction, including those undertaken by nonprofit organizations, make use of mortgage credit. Thus mortgage credit demand comes from consumers, nonprofit organizations, and to some extent from business firms for subsidization through low interest rates and tax benefits. Mortgage credit is used to finance the construction of new houses and new buildings as well as to finance purchases of existing houses, offices, and buildings.

Table 13-4 provides market values, average annual growth rates, and shares for total liabilities, home mortgages, and consumer credits in the time period from 1946 through 2000.

## Table 13-4: Liabilities of U.S. Households and Nonprofit Organizations

| Time periods | Market value* ($billion) | Average growth rate (%) | Share in total assets* (%) |
|---|---|---|---|
| **Total Liability** | | | |
| 1946-49 | 37.1 | 24.71 | 4.46 |
| 1950-59 | 76.3 | 10.97 | 6.81 |
| 1960-69 | 223.3 | 8.46 | 10.69 |
| 1970-79 | 478.7 | 11.15 | 12.14 |
| 1980-89 | 1,455.5 | 10.13 | 13.25 |
| 1990-99 | 3,747.4 | 7.21 | 15.45 |
| 1995 | 5,095.6 | 7.96 | 15.71 |
| 1996 | 5,444.3 | 6.84 | 15.42 |
| 1997 | 5,827.7 | 7.04 | 14.78 |
| 1998 | 6,327.6 | 8.58 | 14.60 |
| 1999 | 6,944.7 | 9.75 | 14.18 |
| 2000 | 7,541.7 | 8.60 | 15.53 |
| **Home mortgages** | | | |
| 1946-49 | 22.9 | 19.15 | 61.56 |
| 1950-59 | 44.9 | 13.28 | 58.85 |
| 1960-69 | 140.8 | 8.02 | 63.03 |
| 1970-79 | 289.0 | 11.59 | 60.37 |
| 1980-89 | 934.5 | 10.68 | 64.20 |
| 1990-99 | 2,532.3 | 7.27 | 67.57 |
| 1995 | 3,367.6 | 5.96 | 66.09 |
| 1996 | 3,578.7 | 6.27 | 65.73 |
| 1997 | 3,828.5 | 6.98 | 65.69 |
| 1998 | 4,197.3 | 9.63 | 66.33 |
| 1999 | 4,607.1 | 9.76 | 66.34 |
| 2000 | 5,004.9 | 8.63 | 66.36 |
| **Consumer credits** | | | |
| 1946-49 | 9.7 | 30.31 | 26.08 |
| 1950-59 | 23.9 | 11.66 | 31.32 |
| 1960-69 | 61.2 | 8.53 | 27.39 |
| 1970-79 | 133.7 | 10.69 | 27.93 |
| 1980-89 | 355.4 | 8.56 | 24.42 |
| 1990-99 | 805.1 | 6.16 | 21.48 |
| 1995 | 1,122.8 | 14.12 | 22.03 |
| 1996 | 1,211.6 | 7.91 | 22.25 |
| 1997 | 1,264.1 | 4.33 | 21.69 |
| 1998 | 1,331.7 | 5.35 | 21.05 |
| 1999 | 1,426.2 | 7.10 | 20.54 |
| 2000 | 1,566.5 | 9.84 | 20.77 |

Table 13-4 shows that home mortgages were approximately $22.9 billion in 1946, accounting for 61.56% of total liabilities. Home mortgages increased to $2.532 trillion in 1990, accounting for 67.57% of total liabilities for that year. Home mortgages rose to about $5 trillion in 2000, accounting for 66.36% of the total liabilities of U.S. households and nonprofit organizations. Hence, home mortgages have been the major form of U.S. households' debts, which grew at double digital rate annually in the 1950s, 1970s, and 1990s, and at a high single digital rate in the 1960s and 1990s. In the late 1940s and early 1950s, home mortgages rose rapidly with the annual growth rate in the range of 15-20%. Growing mortgage credit reflected the increases in new homes due to increased number of marriages and new family formation after World War II, which also resulted in the baby boom and the subsequent demand for houses and mortgage credit. The growth rate of home mortgages and long-term interest rate, ten-year treasury rate, are provided in Figure 13-6.

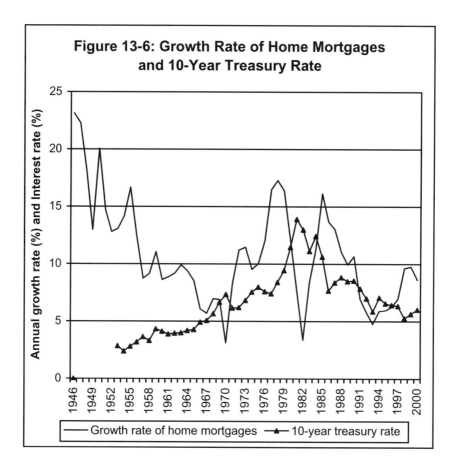

Figure 13-6: Growth Rate of Home Mortgages and 10-Year Treasury Rate

Economic growth is the driving force for the home mortgage market. When an economy is booming, the housing sector is the first to flourish, with a large number of new homes and many nonresidential constructions. Most of these new houses, offices, and buildings are financed by mortgage loans, which increases the demand for home mortgage credit. In an economic recession, however, the high unemployment rate reduces personal income and cuts into consumers' expenditures on housing and durable goods, resulting in a declining demand for new homes and home mortgage loans. As Figure 13-6 indicates, in 1970, 1982 and 1991 the growth rate of home mortgages dropped below 5%, corresponding to economic declines in the early years of each of these three decades.

In general, when the long-term interest rate rises above a certain interest level, demand for mortgage credit becomes responsive to changes in interest rates, as borrowers find higher monthly payments may not be payable without a sufficient increases in their income. Home mortgage credit is closely related to the housing industry, which has been a volatile industry with severe cyclical fluctuations. As interest rate costs are a large part of the total costs of construction financing, a rise in interest rates during an economy's growth period tends to hamper the housing industry before the economy reaches its peak. However, in the late part of an economy's slow down or recession, construction begins to rise first because of declining interest rates. The housing industry continues to grow and help the economy get out of its recession. Therefore construction activity exhibits a pro-cyclic pattern different from that of general business cycle. The fluctuation of construction activity certainly affects the home mortgage market.

The major source of mortgage funds is from savings and loan associations and mutual savings banks. The heavy concentration of assets in these two financial institutions has made the mortgage credit supply reliant on the flows of funds into these institutions and on their operation and performance. High inflation and high interest rates in the 1970s and 1980s put serious pressure on the savings and loan associations and mutual savings banks. The majority of their assets of home mortgage loans were long-term fixed-rate mortgages at relatively low interest rates, while they had to pay very high interest rates on deposit liabilities, which resulted in huge losses and many bankruptcies of these institutions in the 1980s and a large swing in the home mortgage credit market as is shown in Figure 13-6. Continuous economic growth and favorable macroeconomic conditions of low inflation and low interest rates increased the demand for home mortgage loans during the 1990s, when the annual growth rate of home mortgage credit rebounded from 4.7% in 1993 to 9.76% in 1999.

Consumer credit has grown rapidly for the last five decades. It was valued at $9.7 billion in 1946, and increased to $805 billion in 1990 and $1.567 trillion in 2000. American consumers have been borrowing money to purchase automobile, appliances, and other consumer durable goods for years. These borrowers pay their loans in interest and principal over a period of time. The increasing consumer credit has a double-edge effect on the U.S. economy. On the one hand, the growth of consumer debt permits increased consumer spending and thus an increased demand for goods and services. This stimulates production and economic activities, creates jobs, and increases GDP. On the other hand, growing consumer credit creates a large liability for U.S. households that will compete with home mortgage credits and other liabilities and may cause interest rate to rise higher and reduce investment spending on productive assets. This will have a negative impact on economic growth.

The percentage of consumer credit in the total liability of U.S. households and nonprofit organizations was 26.8% in 1946, 21.48% in 1990, and 21.77% in 2000. On average, consumer credit grew at a slower pace than that of home mortgage loans, which resulted in the declining share of consumer credits in the total liability, from 31.32% in the 1950s to 21.48% in the 1990s, and 20.77% in 2000 (Table 13-4).

Figure 13-7 depicts the annual growth rate of consumer credit, and short-term interest rate (3-month treasury bill rate). The annual growth rate of consumer credit was more than 20% in the post-war period before 1950; it has declined and fluctuated around 8.0% since then. When the U.S. economy was in a temporary recession (1958, 1975, 1980, and 1991), the growth rate of consumer credit approached zero. When the economy was in a growth period, the rate of consumer credit rose above 10%, as in 1963, 1972, 1978, 1984, 1994, and 1995. Figure 13-7 also indicates the influence of changes in the short-term interest rate on the demand for consumer loans. Particularly, the interest hike in the 1970s and 1980s caused the growth rate of consumer credit to be more volatile and to bounce back and forth between its upper and lower levels.

Figure 13-7 shows the growth path of consumer credit as a percentage of disposable income. The percentage of consumers' credit increased rapidly in the 1950s and 1960s, from 6.0% in 1946 to 11.4% in 1950, and to 19.2% in 1965. In the 1970s and 1980s, consumer credit stayed in the high level of the range of 16.5—20.0% of disposable income, with the long-term trend almost flat. The percentage has risen quickly in the 1990s, from 16.8% in 1992 to 22.4% in 2000, the highest in the last fifty years, and appears to be increasing substantially.

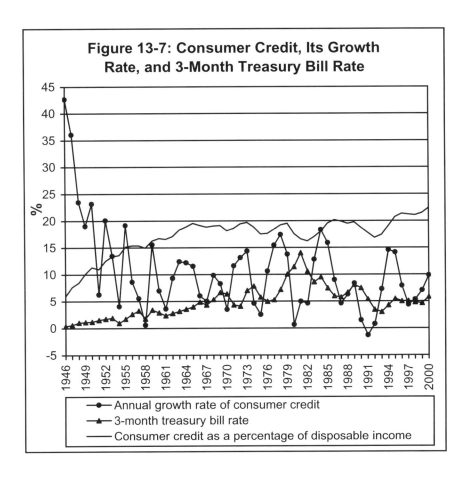

**Figure 13-7: Consumer Credit, Its Growth Rate, and 3-Month Treasury Bill Rate**

The high level of consumer debt has concerned many analysts and observers who are worrying that the possibility of delinquencies on those debts will reduce aggregate consumption, which could make the economy slow down further and unemployment rate quickly pick up. Particularly in the first two years of the twenty first century, the growth rate of U.S. real GDP has declined dramatically, from 8.0% of 1999 Q4 to –1.3% of 2001 Q3. Consumer spending has been robust, preventing the economy from sliding into an officially defined recession. However, American consumers' confidence measures began to show signs of weakening in the second half of 2001. At a historical high level of consumers' expenditure and a high level of consumers' debts, the future course of the U.S. economy is very much dependent on American consumers' reactions to monetary and fiscal policies and to the changing financial market conditions at home and abroad.

# Chapter 14

## Transformation of U.S. Stock Markets

The role of the stock market in economic activities has become increasingly important in both an economic expansion and contraction. As a leading indicator, the startling performance of the U.S. stock market in the 1990s had boded well the continuation of the longest economic expansion in the history of the United States. The waning stock market in the beginning of the twenty first century put the prolonged economic growth in the United States on hold and may be a prophesy of a short-term economic hard time ahead.

In any modern economy, income is partly spent on consumption and partly saved; much of that savings is channeled into investments via financial markets, namely money markets and capital markets. The market in which the short-term instruments are issued and traded is referred to as the money market. The market dealing in instruments with maturities that exceed one year is often referred to as capital market, since credit to finance investments in capital would generally be needed for more than one year. These financial markets provide borrowers with the funds they need, and, at the same time, allow lenders to grow their assets in order to gain future purchasing power.

This function is more significant in terms of the viewpoint of economic development. Financial markets facilitate the transfer of real economic resources from savers and lenders to developers and investors, who put those resources into productive use, such as investing in land, purchasing plant and equipment, and hiring labor and so on, in order to increase production of goods and services. Hence, financial markets transfer the command over real economic resources from lenders to entrepreneurs and producers, who generate large incomes with increasing investments in productive assets, which will raise the real standard of living not only for borrowers, but also for lenders and workers in the economy.

In the free-market and free-enterprise economic system, financial markets are essential for allocating resources into most productive and profitable users in an effective and efficient way. Performance of financial markets, therefore, affect directly changes in investments, and fluctuations in output and employment of the economy.

## 14-1  A Brief Overview of U.S. Financial Markets

In the United States there are highly diversified financial markets. Two categories of financial markets are generally classified: money markets and capital markets. Money markets include short-term loans and short-term securities, such as Treasury bills, federal funds, and other money market instruments, which provide liquidity for various economic activities. Capital markets include those for long-term marketable government securities (Treasury notes and Treasury bonds), corporate bonds, municipal bonds issued by state and local government units, mortgages, and stocks. In the process of converting savings into investments, capital markets are more important than money markets because they channel funds into long-term investment projects.

Both stocks and bonds are called securities, as they represent claims against someone's money holdings at a future date, and they provide an expected return in the form of interest or dividends. The stock market, however, is quite different from the markets for bonds and other debt securities. On the balance sheet, a business firm's total assets equal shareholders' equities plus its liabilities. Stocks are shareholders' equities, representing ownership of business firms, while bonds belong to liabilities, representing creditor claims by bondholders. In times of financial difficulties and bankruptcies, although bondholders may suffer some losses, shareholders always experience greater losses than creditors. Bonds normally have a maturity date with a fixed value attached to the securities, while stocks have no maturity date. Stocks may be outstanding as long as the business continues to operate, or they may be converted into other equities if firms are acquired or merged.

In the United States there are two kinds of security markets, the organized exchange and over-the-counter markets. The New York Stock Exchange (NYSE) and the American Stock Exchange (AMEX) are the two largest organized markets. They provide a meeting place for the demand and supply of securities rather than for the buyers and sellers themselves. Investors who want to purchase or to sell stocks must use a broker or specialist as an agent to buy or sell for them. The New York Stock Exchange is the oldest security market in the United States, as well as the biggest and the most important organized security exchange in the world.

The National Association of Security Dealers is a self-regulated organization charged by law with overseeing the over-the-counter market, in which brokerage houses and other participates create a market, selling securities at the asked price and buying securities at the bid price. The spread between the bid and asked prices provides the brokers' return on the transaction. The automated over-the-counter securities system was constructed in the late 1960s and celebrated its first official trading day on February 8th, 1971. It is known as the National Association of Securities Dealers Automated Quotation System, or "NASDAQ". The NASDAQ stock market is the world's first electronic stock market and ranks second to the NYSE in the world's security markets in terms of dollar volume. Unlike traditional floor-based stock markets, NASDAQ does not have specialists to facilitate transactions. Multiple-market participates directly trade through a sophisticated computer and telecommunications network that links buyers and sellers around the world. Because competing offers to buy and sell stocks are displayed on computer screens, the NASDAQ is called the screen-based market.

## 14-2 The Stock Market Helps the Investment-led Economic Expansion

Markets for stocks and bonds channel savings into capital formations that significantly affects allocation of capital resources into sectors, industries, and companies of the economy. The rapidly increasing investments of

American corporations have been an engine of the sustainable economic expansion of the 1990s. It is the primary market, however, for the newly issued securities that provides the funds to finance companies' capital investment and operation. Through initial public offerings (IPOs) and the issue of additional shares of existing stocks (secondary public offerings), companies acquire hundreds of millions of dollars from individual and institutional investors who buy the newly issued shares of equities.

Most stocks, however, belong to the secondary market, in which securities are traded after they have been issued. Although transactions in the secondary market do not provide additional funds to businesses for financing their capital investments, they provide significant liquidity for investors to gain returns and to manage risks by selling and buying existing shares. The trade in the secondary market allows investors to easily switch ownership of business firms, should their investment goals and preferences changes over time.

Great liquidity of the secondary market promotes investors' willingness to acquire new issues in the IPO market and additional shares of existing equities in secondary public offerings (SPO), which directly generate capital funds for businesses. As a matter of fact, the well-developed secondary market provides businesses with long-term fixed investments that have been financed perpetually by shareholders who are constantly changing groups of individual and institutional investors. Without a highly efficient and liquid secondary market, few investors would make their commitment in the initial public offerings; companies and other borrowers would hardly acquire any capital funds for their business development and long-term projects.

In Table 14-1, we present two quantitative measures, the number of public offerings and the dollar value of public offerings. The upper panel is for initial public offerings (IPOs) and the lower panel is for secondary public offerings (SPOs) in three major U.S. markets (NYSE, NASDAQ, and AMEX) over the time period from 1991 through 2000.

As the table shows, in 1991 the total amount of $45.976 billion was channeled into businesses for capital formation via public offerings in stock markets, including $16.350 billion in IPOs and $32.203 billion in SPOs. The total value of all public offerings in 2000 reached $233.557 billion, with a 5-fold rise in their dollar value over this 10-year time period. In particular, the extraordinary boom of the U.S. stock markets in 1998 and 1999 provided great opportunities for private companies to go to public by issuing equity shares, namely exchanging private ownership for acquiring cash from investors. The IPO market was the hottest in those years. IPO companies collected nearly $50 billion in 1998, $105 billion in 1999, and

$112.5 billion in 2000 representing a 30%, 110% and 7.2% respective annual growth rate.

Table 14-1: Initial and Secondary Public Offerings (1991-2000)

| Initial Public Offerings (IPOs) | | | | | | | | |
|---|---|---|---|---|---|---|---|---|
| Year | NYSE | | NASDAQ | | AMEX | | Total | |
| | N* | Value $billion | N | Value $billion | N | Value $billion | N | Value $billion |
| 1991 | 49 | 8.351 | 320 | 7.730 | 11 | 0.269 | 380 | 16.350 |
| 1992 | 80 | 15.661 | 442 | 13.586 | 6 | 0.112 | 528 | 29.359 |
| 1993 | 97 | 22.308 | 520 | 16.070 | 11 | 0.147 | 628 | 38.525 |
| 1994 | 82 | 18.164 | 444 | 13.187 | 13 | 0.269 | 539 | 31.620 |
| 1995 | 72 | 14.753 | 476 | 16.734 | 9 | 0.283 | 557 | 31.770 |
| 1996 | 88 | 11.948 | 680 | 24.498 | 18 | 0.510 | 786 | 36.956 |
| 1997 | 87 | 18.202 | 494 | 19.367 | 22 | 0.880 | 603 | 38.449 |
| 1998 | 68 | 35.848 | 273 | 13.757 | 21 | 0.387 | 362 | 49.992 |
| 1999 | 49 | 54.419 | 485 | 50.425 | 11 | 0.138 | 545 | 104.98 |
| 2000 | 48 | 59.700 | 397 | 52.585 | 6 | 0.230 | 451 | 112.52 |
| Secondary Public Offerings (SPOs) | | | | | | | | |
| Year | NYSE | | NASDAQ | | AMEX | | Total | |
| | N | Value $billion | N | Value $billion | N | Value $billion | N | Value $billion |
| 1991 | 155 | 19.635 | 241 | 8.140 | 40 | 1.851 | 436 | 29.626 |
| 1992 | 172 | 23.725 | 223 | 7.019 | 47 | 1.459 | 442 | 32.203 |
| 1993 | 195 | 32.738 | 343 | 13.526 | 45 | 1.875 | 583 | 48.139 |
| 1994 | 140 | 24.074 | 222 | 8.851 | 24 | 0.721 | 386 | 33.646 |
| 1995 | 142 | 29.862 | 372 | 24.641 | 21 | 0.561 | 535 | 55.064 |
| 1996 | 169 | 28.548 | 428 | 27.751 | 19 | 0.714 | 616 | 57.013 |
| 1997 | 158 | 31.712 | 355 | 25.649 | 31 | 1.563 | 544 | 58.924 |
| 1998 | 257 | 47.838 | 215 | 19.652 | 23 | 1.333 | 495 | 68.823 |
| 1999 | 108 | 47.230 | 281 | 53.455 | 11 | 0.794 | 400 | 101.48 |
| 2000 | 90 | 39.379 | 306 | 80.775 | 11 | 0.887 | 407 | 121.04 |

N denotes the number of offerings
Data source: Market Data, http://www.marketdata.NASDAQ.com

Rising share prices in the secondary market helped companies with existing shares to raise additional cash via the SPOs. Even when the number of SPOs declined to 400 in 1999 from 495 in 1998, the dollar value of those SPOs increased to $101.479 billion in 1999 from $68.823 billion in 1998. Thanks to the accelerating rise of equity prices in 1999, corporations issued many shares at higher prices, which were backed by the very strong secondary market. In terms of dollar value, the annual growth rate of the SPOs was 16.8% in 1998, 47.4% in 1999, and 19.3% in 2000.

In the recent decade, the prolonged economic expansion in the U.S. has been powered by increasing aggregate demand, in which private investment is one of the components besides consumption, government spending, and net exports. As the capital raised in stock markets is an important part of private investment, stock markets have certainly made a great contribution to the investment surge in the recent years of the U.S. economy. Funds from public offerings are used for financing research and development, purchasing new computers and telecommunications equipment, and nurturing inventions and innovations of information technology. This was evident in the IPO market that was particularly hospitable to many dot-com offerings in 1998 and 1999.

Wall Street financed almost 600 Internet-related IPOs from 1998 to 2000. American bankers raised more than $240 billion via those IPOs, secondary stock offerings, and venture capital backing[1]. Many technology start-ups have received funding to build up Internet infrastructures, such as optical networks and broadband applications, and to promote widely applicable computer- and communications-technology. The productivity gains flowing from improved information technology are apparent and material in almost every sectors of the U.S. economy. The increase in productivity has generated a higher growth of output, lower unemployment rate, lower wage growth, and therefore relatively stable prices in the United States.

## 14-3  The Broadening Base of Equity Shareholders

Many economists suggest that changes in the size and composition of wealth held by the public are expected to generate a wealth effect on the national economy.

An increase in public wealth will boost consumers' confidence in the expectation of future income and produce an increase in spending and a decrease in saving. Conversely, a decline in the public's wealth will reduce consumers' expectations, resulting in less spending and an increase in saving. Thus, changes in wealth are expected to alter consumers' spending-saving decisions with a consequent affects on output, employment, price level, and other economic indications of the national economy. If the largest portion

---

[1] Analyst Sees Panic Selling Ahead, by Thom Calandra, FT MarketWatch.com, Oct. 9, 2000.

of public wealth were controlled by a small number of individuals in the nation, there would have been a very limited affect on the national economy. This section shows that a great many Americans have been involved in processes of wealth creation and accumulation through stock markets, which broadens the base of ownership of financial assets and enlarges the wealth affect on the U.S. economy.

Although the public's wealth is held in various forms of assets that make up a portfolio, financial assets represent a great chunk of public wealth (illustrated in Chapter 11). As Tables 13-2 and 13-3 in Section 13-2 of Chapter 13 indicate, the market value of corporate equities has increased by 12 times in the last fifty years. Corporate equities accounted for 26.3% of the total assets of U.S. households and nonprofit organizations in 1999. In a single year, however, the market value of corporate equities held by U.S. households dropped by 24.2%, from $9.24 trillion in 1999 to $7 trillion in 2000. Such a dramatic rise and fall in U.S. households' equity shares reflects the fluctuation of the stock markets and is expected to generate the most influential wealth affects on the U.S. economy.

Individuals and institutions owning corporate stocks are looking for higher returns than they can realize by investing in fixed return assets (such as money market funds and debt securities). Historical records show that between 1926 and 1997, the arithmetic average return on large company stocks in the United States was 13.0% per year, on small company stocks 17.7%, compared with the average return on short-term Treasury bills of 3.8%, and 5.6% on long-term treasury bonds[2]. Returns on investments in corporate stocks come from dividends issued regularly by some companies and capital gains or losses when equity shares are traded over time. The U.S. stock market has experienced a spectacular bull run in recent years, with an extraordinary rise in stock prices that rewarded investors with huge capital gains. Consequently, a large number of Americans have been motivated to participate in the U.S. capital market.

Individuals can own corporate stocks directly, either through a conventional brokerage account or similar vehicle. They also can own corporate stocks indirectly, either through a mutual fund, or through participation in supplemental retirement accounts, such as 401(k)s, and defined contribution pension accounts. According to the 2000 Share Ownership Report, published by the New York Stock Exchange, the level of public participation in capital markets grew rapidly in the 1990s. The report is based on evidence from the 1998 Survey of Consumer Finances, which is the latest available

---

[2] Summary of 1998 Share Ownership Report, NYSE, 1998.

household survey of asset ownership in the United States. The distribution data on equity shareowners in Table 14-2 comes from the 2000 Share Ownership Report for four years of 1989, 1992, 1995, and 1998.

Table 14-2: The Number of Shareowners, 1989-1998

| Stock Ownership | 1989 million | 1992 million | 1995 million | 1998 million |
|---|---|---|---|---|
| Total number of shareholders | 52.3 | 61.4 (17.4%) | 69.3 (12.9%) | 84.0 (21.2%) |
| Directly owning stocks | 27.0 | 29.2 (8.1%) | 27.4 (-6.2%) | 33.8 (23.3%) |
| Indirectly owning stocks | 25.3 | 32.2 (27.3%) | 41.9 (30.1%) | 50.2 (19.8%) |
| Mutual funds Owners | 4.5 | 6.1 (35.6%) | 11.2 (83.6%) | 14.7 (31.2%) |
| Self-directed retirement account | 10.6 | 16.2 (52.8%) | 21.0 (29.6%) | 27.3 (30%) |
| Contribution pension plans | 10.2 | 9.9 (-2.9%) | 9.7 (-2.0%) | 8.2 (-15%) |
| Percent of total population | 21.2% | 24.1% | 26.4% | 31.1% |

Data source: Share Ownership 2000, NYSE,
www.nyse.com/marketinfo/shareownersurvey.html
(%) denotes the growth rate over the time  period of previous three years.

As Table 14-2 indicates, the total number of Americans owning corporate stocks, directly and indirectly, increased from 52.3 million in 1989 to 61.4 million in 1992 (a 17.4% rise), and further to 69.3 million in 1995 (a 12.9% rise from the 1992 level), and 84.0 million in 1998 (a 21.2% rise from the 1995 level). Those shareowners accounted for 21.2% of the total U.S. population in 1989, 26.4% in 1995, and 31.1% in 1998, which indicates impressively increased public participation in the stock markets. At the end of 1998, there were about 84 million individual investors in the United States. These individuals provided a huge pool of capital and created the most liquid and dynamic stock markets in the world.

In 1989, 27 million Americans directly owned equity shares, this number increased to 29.2 million in 1992, 27.4 million in 1995, and again to 33.8 million in 1998. This reflects a substantial rise of 23.3% by 1998 from the level of 1995. More Americans have participated in wealth creation through purchasing mutual fund shares, owning retirement saving accounts, or through contribution pension plans. Mutual funds and pension funds have become the major players in stock markets with a large amount of capital collected from workers and other individuals. The number of Americans owning mutual fund shares increased rapidly from 4.5 million in 1989 to 14.7 million in 1998, a 3.3-fold rise in nine years.

In the second half of the 1990s, a growing number of workers participated in various retirements saving plans, particularly through employer-sponsored retirement 401(K) plans. This has also indirectly contributed to stock ownership. The number of Americans owning stock through self-directed retirement accounts rose by 52.8% from 10.6 million in 1989 to 16.2 million in 1992, and continued rising rapidly to 27.3 million in 1998. However, the number of Americans owning stock through defined contribution pension plans has reduced gradually, from 10.2 million in 1989 to 8.2 million in 1998. Nevertheless, the total number of Americans owning stock through indirect methods was nearly doubled in nine years from 25.3 million in 1989 to 50.2 million in 1998.

Table 14-2 also indicates that in 1995–1998 direct stock ownership increased faster than indirect ownership, growing by 23.3% versus 19.8%. In the same time period, however, stock ownership through mutual funds grew faster than direct stock ownership, growing by 31.2% versus 23.3%. The soaring stock market in 1999 attracted many more people into the markets. Investor's Business Daily reported[3] that 49% of American owned equity shares by the end of 2000. Similarly, a Paine Webber survey shows that 50% of Americans are equity shareholders. A sharply increasing number of accounts in equity mutual funds suggests that the ongoing trend of growing indirect methods of equity ownership is expected to continue in the future.

Table 14-3 presents shareowners' age distribution and household income distribution in 1998. Shareowners' age composition is denoted both by the number of shareowners in different age groups and by the percentage of stock shares owned by those groups. There were about 18.2 million shareholders under the age of 35 in 1998, accounting for nearly 22% of all shareholders. These investors, however, owned only 5.6% of total shares overall. About 23.9 million or 28.4% of all shareowners were between ages of 35 and 44 in 1998, with their shares accounting for 17.4% of the total. Investors between the ages of 45-65 accounted for 37.3% of all shareowners in 1998, but they owned 53% of all shares outstanding. The number of shareholders aged 65 years and over in 1998 was about 10.6

---

[3] Bush Widens Lead Among Investors: Can This New Bloc Make a Difference?, *Investor's Business Daily,* October 11, 2000.

million, accounting for 12.6% of all shareholders. The equity shares held by this age group accounted for 24% of all shares outstanding.

Table 14-3: Shareowners' Age and Income Distribution (1998)

| Age cohort | Number of shareowners (million) | Percent of shareowners % | Percent of shares owned % |
|---|---|---|---|
| Under 35 | 18.2 | 21.7 | 5.6 |
| 35-44 | 23.9 | 28.4 | 17.4 |
| 45-65 | 31.3 | 37.3 | 53.0 |
| 65 and Over | 10.6 | 12.6 | 24.0 |
| Total | 84.0 | 100 | 100 |
| **Household income of shareholders** | **Number of shareowners (million)** | **Percent of shareowners** | **Percent of shares owned** |
| Under $15,000 | 3.0 | 3.5% | 0.8% |
| $15-25,000 | 6.6 | 7.9 | 2.7 |
| $25-50,000 | 24.7 | 29.4 | 8.9 |
| $50-75,000 | 22.8 | 27.2 | 13.7 |
| $75-100,000 | 12.1 | 14.3 | 10.9 |
| $100-250,000 | 11.9 | 14.2 | 27.7 |
| Over $250,000 | 2.9 | 3.5 | 35.3 |
| Total | 84.0 | 100 | 100 |

Data source: Shareownership 2000, NYSE.

Shareholders under the age of 44 accounted for 50.1% of all shareholders, while they owned only 23% of all equity shares in 1998. The group of investors aged 45 and over accounted for 49.9% of all shareholders; their equity shares were about 77% of all shares outstanding in 1998. The differences between the fraction of shareowners and the fraction of shares held by those cohorts reflect the fact that on the average younger adults have smaller portfolios and hold fewer stocks than older workers and retired investors do.

The household income distribution of shareowners in 1998 is presented in the lower section of Table 14-3, which reveals that a large percentage of shareowners fell into the low and middle-income groups, while a large percentage of shares belonged to high-income groups. 24.7 million or nearly 30% of all shareowners had household income between $25,000 and $50,000, but their shares accounted for only 8.9% of all shares held in 1998. About 27.2% of all shareowners had a household income between $50,000 and

$75,000, while their shares accounted for 13.7% of all shares held. The high-income group ($75,000-$100,000) accounted for 14.3% of the total number of shareholders and for 10.9% of the total number of equity shares. The super-high-income group ($100,000-$250,000) accounted for only 11.9% of all shareowners, but owned 27.7% of all equity shares held. The highest income (over $250,000) group of 2.9 million investors accounted for only 3.5% of all shareholders. However, they held 35.3% of all equity shares outstanding in 1998.

In general, shareholders with household income under $75,000 per year accounted for 68% of all shareholders and owned 26.1% of all shares outstanding. Shareholders with household income above $75,000 per year accounted for 32% of all shareholders and held 73.9% of the total outstanding shares. This evidence shows that U.S. equity shares are concentrated in the hands of high-income households.

Interestingly enough, there were 9.6 million people, about 11% of all shareowners, who held equity shares and whose household income was under $25,000 in 1998. About 0.8% of all shares were owned by 3 million Americans whose household income was less than $15,000 in 1998. This fact indicates that owning equity shares is no longer the privilege of rich people; ordinary Americans, even low-income households, have participated in this process of creating wealth through stock markets. Therefore economic policy makers should pay special attention to the changes in the stock markets that have been closely related to more than a half population's earnings and retirement across an entire income-spectrum of American families.

Investing in corporate stocks provides a powerful means of long-term wealth accumulation for the middle- and high-income families in the United States. The ongoing trend of rapidly increasing indirect methods of owning equity shares has opened the door of stock markets to low-income Americans. It has also greatly enhanced the development of financial institutions and promoted the activities of institutional investors in stock markets. Growing public wealth is reflected in the dollar value of holdings of corporate equities by different ownership categories.

Table 14-4 presents market value, percentage of equity value of different ownership groups in the total market value of all corporate equity shares outstanding, and the arithmetic average annual growth rate of equity values.

As Table 14-4 shows, total market value of U.S. equities increased from $142.7 billion in 1950 to $3.54 trillion in 1990, $8.49 trillion in 1995, and $19.05 trillion at the end of the third quarter of 2000. The average growth rate was 24.5% per year in 1950–1970, 16.1% per year in 1970–1990, 28.0% per year in 1990–1995, and 24.8% per year in 1995–2000.

Table 14-4: Market Value of Holdings of Corporate Equities (in $billion)

| Owning sector | 1950 | 1970 | 1990 | 1995 | 3Q2000 |
|---|---|---|---|---|---|
| **Total U.S. equities** | **142.7** | **841.4** | **3,542.6** | **8,495.7** | **19,047.1** |
| **Equity by U.S. institutions** | **10.3** | **236.9** | **1,478.2** | **3,807.1** | **9,680.5** |
| Pension funds | 1.1 | 77.2 | 876.9 | 2,069.7 | 4,404.9 |
| Insurance companies | 4.7 | 27.8 | 161.8 | 449.6 | 1,231.7 |
| Mutual funds | 4.5 | 44.0 | 249.4 | 1,062.9 | 3,686.1 |
| Bank personal trusts | 0.0 | 87.9 | 190.1 | 224.9 | 357.8 |
| **Households & nonprofit organizations** | **128.7** | **572.5** | **1,795.3** | **4,081.5** | **7,447.6** |
| Foreign sector | 2.9 | 27.2 | 243.8 | 527.6 | 1,691.4 |
| Other | 0.8 | 4.8 | 25.3 | 79.5 | 227.6 |
| Foreign equity By U.S .residents | 1.2 | 6.6 | 197.6 | 776.8 | 1,830.4 |
| **Percent of U.S. Equity Held by** | | | | | |
| **Equity by U.S. institutions** | **7.2%** | **28.2%** | **41.7%** | **44.8%** | **50.9%** |
| Pension funds | 0.8 | 9.2 | 24.8 | 24.4 | 23.1 |
| Insurance companies | 3.2 | 3.4 | 4.5 | 5.3 | 6.5 |
| Mutual funds | 3.2 | 5.2 | 7.0 | 12.5 | 19.4 |
| Bank personal trusts | 0 | 10.4 | 5.4 | 2.6 | 1.9 |
| **Households & nonprofit organizations** | **90.2** | **68.0** | **50.7** | **48.0** | **39.1** |
| Foreign sector | 2.0 | 3.2 | 6.9 | 6.2 | 8.9 |
| Other | 0.6 | 0.6 | 0.7 | 0.9 | 1.2 |
| **Arithmetic Average Annual Growth Rate (%) of Equity Value** | | | | | |
| | 1950-70 | 1970-90 | | 1990-95 | 1995-99 |
| **Total U.S. equities** | **24.5%** | **16.1%** | | **28.0%** | **24.8%** |
| **Equity by U.S. institutions** | **110.0** | **26.2** | | **31.5** | **30.9** |
| Pension funds | 345.9 | 51.8 | | 27.2 | 22.6 |
| Insurance companies | 24.6 | 24.1 | | 35.6 | 34.8 |
| Mutual funds | 43.9 | 23.3 | | 65.2 | 49.4 |
| Bank personal trusts | - | 5.8 | | 3.7 | 11.8 |
| **Households & nonprofit organizations** | **17.2** | **10.7** | | **25.5** | **16.5** |
| Foreign sector | 41.9 | 39.8 | | 23.3 | 44.1 |
| Other | 25.0 | 21.4 | | 42.8 | 37.3 |
| U.S. institutions | 110.0 | 26.2 | | 31.5 | 30.9 |
| Holdings of foreign equity by U.S. residents | 22.5 | 144.7 | | 58.6 | 27.1 |

The annual growth rate was substantially higher in the 1990s than in the 1970s and 1980s.

The dollar value of all the equities held by U.S. institution investors, including pension funds, insurance companies, mutual funds, and bank personal trusts, increased rapidly, from 10.3 billion in 1950 to $239.9 billion in 1970, $1.478 trillion in 1990, and $9.68 trillion at the end of third quarter of 2000.

The percentage of market value of equities owned by U.S. institutions rose from 7.2% in 1950 to 28.2% in 1970, 41.7% in 1990, and 50.8% at the end of 2000, reflecting the dramatic surge in the indirect methods of owning equity shares. As shown in the bottom of Table 14-4, the market value of institutions' equity holdings grew at a triple-digital rate in 1950 - 1970, and at double-digit rates in the 1970s, 1980s and 1990s.

Among all the categories of U.S. equity holdings by institutions, pension funds grew at the fastest rate in 1950 - 1990, with market value rising from $1.1 billion in 1950 to $877 billion in 1990 and the percentage of market value rising from 0.8% in 1950 to 24.8% in 1990. After 1990 the market value of equity shares owned by pension funds continued to grow, but at a slightly slower pace than the total U.S. equity shares outstanding, resulting in the slightly decreased percentage, from 24.8% in 1990 to 23.1% in 2000.

Since 1990 mutual funds have become the fastest-moving sector with their market value surging from $249 billion in 1990 to $3.686 trillion in 2000. Their share of market value rose from 7.0% in 1990 to 19.4% in 2000. Their annual growth rate was 65.2% in 1990 - 1995, and 49.4% in 1995 - 2000, which was the highest growth rate across all categories of equity ownerships. The market value of equity shares owned by insurance companies also increased rapidly in the 1990s, from $161.8 billion in 1990 to $1.232 trillion in 2000; their percentage of market value rose from 4.6% in 1990 to 6.5% in 2000. The market value of equity shares held by bank personal trusts increased from $87.9 billion in 1970 to $357.8 billion in 2000. Its growth rate, however, was the slowest among all categories of equity owners. Consequently, the percentage of market value of bank personal trusts declined from 10.4% in 1970 to merely 1.9% in 2000.

Households and nonprofit organizations held $128.7 billion in equity shares in 1950, or 90.2% of the total value of all U.S. equity shares outstanding. The market value of their equities rose to $7.448 trillion at the end of the third quarter of 2000, but accounted for only 39.1% of the total value of all outstanding U.S. equity shares in 2000.

The lower panel of Table 14-4 shows that the market value of directly owned equities by U.S. households and nonprofit organizations grew at a slower rate than the indirect methods of owning corporate equities through institution investors. This resulted in the largely increased percentage of market value of indirectly owned equities and the largely decreased percentage of market value of directly owned equities by U.S. households and nonprofit organizations. This data clearly reflects the fact that indirectly investing in corporate stocks through institutions has become an important channel for Americans to create and accumulate wealth on the capital market.

The foreign sector consists of foreign governments, institutions and individuals, who held $1.691-trillion worth of U.S. equities or 8.9% of U.S. equities outstanding in 2000, increasing from $2.9 billion or 2.0% in 1950, and $243.8 billion or 6.9% in 1990. U.S. investors also owned $1.830 trillion-worth of foreign equities in 2000, increasing from $1.2 billion in 1950 and $197.6 billion in 1990.

The sharply increased public wealth through investing in corporate equities can be illustrated clearly in Table 14-5 by the changing ratio of the dollar value of all U.S. equities to the nominal GDP of the United States over the past five decades.

Table 14-5: Ratio of U.S. Equity Value to Nominal GDP

|  | 1950 | 1970 | 1990 | 1995 | 2000 |
|---|---|---|---|---|---|
| Total U.S equity outstanding ($billion) | 142.7 | 841.4 | 3,542.6 | 8,495.7 | 19,047.1 |
| Nominal GDP ($billion) | 294.6 | 1,039.7 | 5,803.2 | 7,400.5 | 9,963.1 |
| Equity value/GDP | 0.48 | 0.81 | 0.61 | 1.15 | 1.91 |

The ratio of U.S. equity value to GDP was 0.48 in 1950. It rose to 1.15 in 1995 and reached 1.91 in 2000. That is, the dollar value of all U.S. equities in 1950 was less than a half of U.S. GDP of that year, now it became about 1.91-fold of nominal U.S. GDP in 2000. Measured by either absolute magnitude or relative term to GDP, such a huge amount of accumulated wealth by American public in the form of corporate equities must have an unprecedented wealth effect on the U.S. economy.

## 14-4  The Long-Term Trend of U.S. Stock Markets

At the end of 2000, 4,734 companies with 5,053 issues were listed on the NASDAQ, and 2,862 companies with 3,522 issues were listed on the NYSE, and 765 companies with 894 issues were listed in the AMEX. Those companies listed on U.S. stock markets include U.S. and non-U.S. corporations across the globe. The volume of shares traded on the NASDAQ reached a record of 442.7 billion during 2000, up 437% compared with trading volume of 101.2 billion in 1995[4]. The NYSE also set its ninth consecutive trading-volume record in 2000, with a total of 262.5 billion shares traded during 2000, up 29% from 203.9 billion shares in 1999, and up 300% from 87.5 billion shares in 1995[5]. The extraordinarily increased activities in U.S. stock markets are due to the remarkable appreciation of stock prices and exceptional returns on equity investment in the long run, which are illustrated in Table 14-6.

Table 14-6: Annual Rate of Returns on Investments

| Investments in | 1926 - 1996 | 1978 - 1998 |
|---|---|---|
| Small stocks | 12.5% | 18.5% |
| Large stocks | - | 14.2% |
| Intermediate-term bonds | 5.2% | 9.8% |
| Treasury bills | 3.7% | 7.3% |
| Business real estates | 11.1% | 8.4% |
| Commodities | - | 10.7% |
| Gold | - | 5.8% |
| **Average inflation rate** | 3.1% | 5.2% |

Data source: "How to Make $61 Million, Slowly" Dow Diaries, Sep. 2001, http://www.mdleasing.com/ddmillio.htm

According to historical records, the long-term investment in equity shares did outperform significantly over investments in long-term and short-term government debts, real estates, commodities, and gold. Returns on equities come from dividends and capital gains. In recent years, dividends have accounted for only 10% of stock-market investors' total returns, and capital gains become the focus of investors' interests due to faster growing returns and better tax treatment[6]. The capital gain or loss is directly derived from rising or declining stock prices.

The general trend of stock price movement is described by various indexes currently employed by the investment circle to provide averages of individual stock prices in the course of the market. Among them the Dow Jones

---

[4] From data source of http://www.marketdata.nasdaq.com.

[5] 1999 NYSE Fact Book, http://www.NYSE.com

[6] "The Power of Dow Dividends" Dow Diaries, http://averages.dowjones.com/ddpower.html.

industrials index, NYSE composite index, and NASDAQ composite index are the most popular in the world.

The Dow Jones industrial average was first published in 1896 with twelve original stocks. The number of stocks in this average expanded to 20 in 1916 and to 30 in 1928. Over a hundred-year period, the U.S. economy has expanded and changed from an economy producing mainly agricultural products and basic materials into the most advanced modern economy in the world. Consequently, the component stocks in the Dow Jones industrial average have adjusted accordingly.

At present, General Electric is the only stock from the original twelve that remains in the average. Other component stocks had been removed from or added into the industrial average. The Dow Jones industrial average has included all major factors in their industries with their stocks widely held and frequently traded by individual and institutional investors. The average contains major technology companies, such as Microsoft and Intel (even though they are listed on the NASDAQ), IBM and Hewlett-Packard. It also includes financial service providers, such as Citigroup Inc., J.P. Morgan & Co., and American Express Co., and major industrial companies, such as Boeing, DuPont Co. and General Motor, as well as the Entertainment Company, Walt Disney, and giant retailer Wal-Mart Stores Inc.

Another popular index is the NYSE Composite Index, which was initiated in 1966 to provide a comprehensive measure of the market trend. The NYSE Composite Index consists of all common stocks listed on the NYSE and it is expressed by the aggregate market value, which is the sum of market values of individual stocks, as a relative of the base period market value. The market value of each stock is obtained by multiplying its price per share by the number of outstanding shares. The base date is December 31, 1965, and the base value was set at $50.00, because this figure was very close to the actual average price of all common stocks on the base date.

On the NASDAQ market, a similar composite index has been published since 1971, the first official trading year of the NASDAQ electronic trading system. This composite index is comprised of all domestic and non-U.S. companies' common stocks listed on NASDAQ, about 5,053 issues at the end of 2000[7]. Each stock's weight in the index is proportional to its market capitalization. Figure 14-1 presents these three indexes over the time period of 1981–2001, and Figure 14-2 depicts the annual growth rates of the two indexes.

---

[7] The NASDAQ Stock Market Five-Year Statistical Review, Market Data, http://www.marketdata.nasdaq.com.

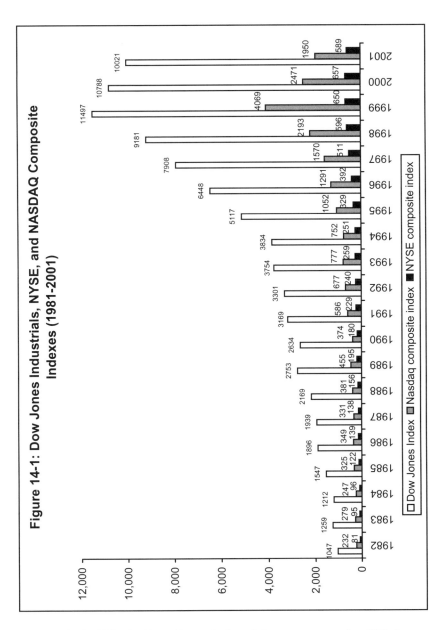

Figure 14-1: Dow Jones Industrials, NYSE, and NASDAQ Composite Indexes (1981-2001)

At the end of 1928, the Dow Jones industrial average stood at 300, it went down as low as 59.9 in 1932 and moved back to 200 in the end of 1949. After that, it took nine years for the average to cross the 500-mark in 1958, and another fourteen years to cross the 1,000 mark for the first time in 1972. In the 1970s, the Dow Jones industrial average drifted between 600 and 900, and finally reached 1,047 at the end of 1982. After the Dow Jones industrial average reached the 1,000 mark, it took six years to cross the 2000-mark in 1988, and another three years to cross the 3,000 mark in 1991.

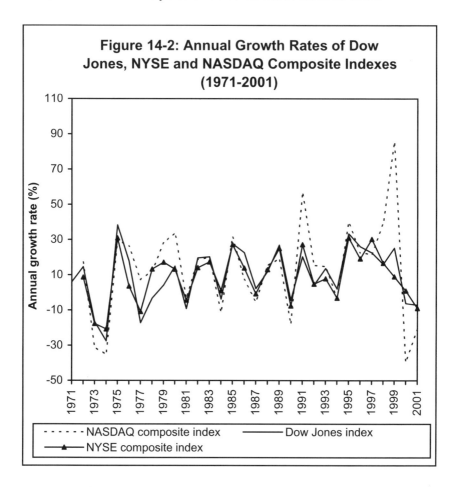

Figure 14-2: Annual Growth Rates of Dow Jones, NYSE and NASDAQ Composite Indexes (1971-2001)

Since entering the decade of the 1990s, the Dow Jones industrial average has rapidly moved forward. It reached 5,117 in 1995, 6,448 in 1996, 7,908 in 1997, 9181 in 1998, and 11,497 at the end of 1999. In 1982-2000, there were only three years, 1984, 1990, and 2000 in which the Dow Jones industrial average declined by 3.7%, 4.3%, and 6.2% respectively when compared with the prior year's index. After 1991, the Dow Jones industrial average increased year after year, all with double-digit annual growth rate except for 1992 (4%), 1994 (2%), and 2000 (-6.2%). Its annual growth rate was about 24.6% on the average from 1995 through 1999, and reduced to -6.2% in 2000. That is the reason why the index has quickly jumped over all the major marks from 3,000 all the way to 11,000. Up until the end of 1999, the Dow Jones industrial average has manifested the longest bull market in the history of U.S. stock markets. On the last day of 2000, the Dow Jones industrial average closed at 10,788 with a 6.6% drop, which was the largest daily percentage drop since 1981.

In the time period from 1975 through 1980, the NASDAQ composite index showed a consecutive rise year after year, with growth rate averaged at 22.9% per year. That bull-run had raised the index from about 60 at the end of 1974 to 202 by the end of 1980. In the same time frame, however, the Dow Jones industrial average had shown a consecutive two-year decline, -17.3% in 1977 and -3% in 1978. Although the rising market of 1991–1999 created the longest expansion for the Dow Jones Industrial average, it had not broken the record set in 1975-1980 for the NASDAQ composite index, as the NASDAQ showed a negative growth of -3.2% in 1994. Since 1995, the NASDAQ index has increased sharply, with the average annual growth rate of nearly 42% in 1995–1999. The NASDAQ composite index jumped over the 500-mark in 1991, the 1,000-mark in 1995, the 1,500-mark in 1997, and the 2,000-mark in 1998, and stood at 4,069 at the end of 1999.

The growth rates over different time frames for the three indexes are summarized in Table 14-7 for the purpose of comparisons. In terms of one-year returns, the performance of three indexes is volatile. The Dow Jones industrial average registered a 25.2% gain in 1999, but a loss of 6.1% in 2000. Similarly, the broad NYSE composite index had a 9.1% gain in 1999 and a small gain of 1.1% in 2000. In particular, the NASDAQ composite index showed a huge 85.6% gain in 1999, but a great loss of 39.3% in 2000. In terms of 3-year returns, all losses of indexes in 2000 have been offset by previous two years' gains. In terms of 10-year returns, the one bad year of 2000 does not make a big difference for the Dow Jones industrial index and the NYSE composite index, but it has made a substantial difference for the NASDAQ composite index, as the 10-year return from 1989-1999 was 794.7% versus the 10-year return from 1990–2000 declined to 561.0%. This reflects the more volatile nature of the NASDAQ market than that of the NYSE market.

It has been widely recognized that the fundamental determinants of the long-term level of stock market prices include the growth rate of nominal GDP, the rate of increase in corporate profits, and the inflation rate of the national economy.

## Table 14-7: Growth Rate of Stock Market Indexes

| Benchmark | 1 year | 3 years | 5 years | 10 years |
|---|---|---|---|---|
| | As of December 31, 1999 | | | |
| Dow Jones industrial average | 25.2% | 78.3% | 199.8% | 317.6% |
| NYSE composite | 9.1% | 65.8% | 159.0% | 233.3% |
| NASDAQ composite | 85.6% | 215.2% | 441.2% | 794.7% |
| | As of December 31, 2000 | | | |
| Dow Jones industrial average | -6.1% | 36.4% | 110.8% | 309.6% |
| NYSE composite | 1.1% | 28.7% | 99.7% | 265.0% |
| NASDAQ composite | -39.3% | 57.4% | 134.9% | 561.0% |

In the 1970s, the U.S. nominal GDP grew at the annual rate of between 8.3% and 13.0%, and the profits of non-financial corporate business grew at a rate of between 2.4% and 29%. The inflation rate, however, increased rapidly from 4.38% in 1971 to 11% in 1974 and 13.5% in 1980. The Dow Jones industrial average was 838.9 at the end of 1970, and 838.7 at the end of 1979. In that decade, the Dow Jones industrial average rose in some years and fell in other years, and ended with nearly no net rise at all. In the decade of 1980s, the annual growth rate of nominal GDP stayed at around 7.5%, and inflation rate declined from 10% in 1981 to 4.8% in 1989, but corporate profits showed large declines in 1982 (-24%), 1985 (-16%) and 1986 (-29%), which limited the appreciation of stock prices. Nevertheless, the Dow Jones industrial average had managed to rise from 964.0 in the end of 1980 to 2753.2 in the end of 1989; and the NASDAQ composite index increased from 202.3 to 454.8 in the same time period.

Since 1991 the three fundamental determinants of stock prices have been in a favorite combination. The growth rate of nominal GDP moved between 4.9% and 6.5%; inflation rate retained less than 3.0%; and corporate profits grew 20-25% per year in 1992–1994, and 13%, 8.7% and 8.9% in 1995–1997. In 1998, however, the global financial crisis generated many problems for multinational corporations, which reduced U.S. corporate profits by 2.1% from the level of 1997. The strong U.S. economy quickly brought corporate profits back to an ascending trajectory; a 12.9% rise in corporate profits has recorded in 1999. It is the excellent performance of the U.S. economy during the 1990s that fueled the longest bull market in U.S. history to date, and pushed the Dow Jones industrial average from 2,634 to 11,497, and the NASDAQ composite index from 374 to 4,069 in the time period of the end of 1990 to the end of 1999.

Although all three indexes have demonstrated exceptional performance on the U.S. stock markets, the NASDAQ composite index has greatly exceeded the other two in terms of longer-term stock price appreciation, which has been illustrated in Table 14-7. The different paces of stock price changes on the NYSE and NASDAQ reflect the different appearance of industries and companies listed on these markets. Table 14-8 displays the numbers of the industries and companies listed in the NYSE and NASDAQ stock markets.

The upper panel of Table 14-8 shows that at the end of 1999, there were 4,829 companies listed on the NASDAQ and 2,764 companies listed on the NYSE. A large percentage of the NASDAQ companies belong to the manufacturing industry, with 1,242 manufacturing companies accounting for 25.5% of the total. The largest percentage of the NYSE companies is in the industries of finance, insurance, and real estate. These companies added with companies in the manufacturing industry account for nearly 65% of all companies listed on the NYSE. Computer hardware and software companies account for only 2.57% of all the NYSE companies, however, they account for 16.58% of all the NASDAQ companies. The fractions of drug companies and retail/wholesale trade and services companies are also greater on the NASDAQ than on the NYSE.

The lower panel of Table 14-8 displays the number of IPO companies by industry on both markets in 1999. The number of IPOs on the NASDAQ is as nearly ten times large as the number of IPOs on the NYSE, 485 versus 49. Nearly 40% of all the IPOs on the NASDAQ are computer software companies that develop various kinds of application software for Internet infrastructure and implementation, while only two IPOs on the NYSE, accounting for 4%, are computer software companies. More than a half of the IPOs on the NYSE belong to the manufacturing industry (28.5%) and the industry of finance, insurance and real estate. It clearly shows that information technology companies, particularly Internet infrastructure companies, or so-called new economy companies fueled the spectacular bull-run of the NASDAQ composite index in 1995–1999.

Table 14-8: Listed Companies on the NYSE and NASDAQ
by Industry (1999)

| Industry | NASDAQ Companies | | NYSE Companies | |
|---|---|---|---|---|
| | Number | % | Number | % |
| Transportation & communications | 365 | 7.5% | 300 | 10.9% |
| Computer hardware &office equipment | 165 | 3.4 | 27 | 1.0 |
| Computer software | 642 | 13.2 | 44 | 1.6 |
| Manufacturing | 1242 | 25.5 | 850 | 30.8 |
| Drugs | 269 | 5.5 | 41 | 1.5 |
| Finance, insurance & real estate | 938 | 19.3 | 941 | 34.0 |
| Retail/wholesale trade | 525 | 10.8 | 223 | 8.1 |
| Services | 507 | 10.4 | 171 | 6.2 |
| Other* | 176 | 3.6 | 167 | 6.0 |
| All | 4829 | 100% | 2764 | 100% |
| Industry | NASDAQ IPO Companies | | NYSE IPO Companies | |
| | Number | % | Number | % |
| Transportation & communications | 65 | 13.4% | 9 | 18.4% |
| Computer hardware &office equipment | 14 | 2.9 | - | - |
| Computer software | 191 | 39.4 | 2 | 4.1 |
| Manufacturing | 61 | 12.6 | 14 | 28.6 |
| Drugs | 8 | 1.7 | 1 | 2.0 |
| Finance, insurance & real estate | 22 | 4.5 | 12 | 24.5 |
| Retail/wholesale trade | 38 | 7.8 | 4 | 8.2 |
| Services | 82 | 16.9 | 3 | 6.1 |
| Other* | 4 | 0.8 | 4 | 8.2 |
| All | 485 | 100% | 49 | 100% |

## 14-5  Volatility of the U.S. Stock Market

In terms of the short-term behavior of equity share prices, stock markets bear the notorious name of "random walk" in academic circle, as many financial economists believe that past stock prices have no effect on future stock prices, namely future stock prices are expected to fluctuate randomly from past levels.  On Wall Street, however, many traders and analysts have devoted a great deal of energy identifying patterns of stock price movements that they believe can be used to predict future trends and specific shifts of stock prices. Still, it is very difficult to correctly predict the day-to-day drift of an individual stock price; even through the long-term changes in general market trends are guided by the fundamental determinants of the economy.

The graphics of the Dow Jones industrial average and NASDAQ composite index illustrated in Figure 14-1 tell little about fluctuations of stock prices, because they display the index values at the last day of each year and ignore changes over the entire year. The real volatility of the stock market should be observed daily, or preferably, the intra-day movements of individual stocks. Our purpose is to investigate the changing nature of volatility over time in the general market situation rather than fluctuations of specific individual stocks. We will still use monthly and daily Dow Jones industrial average and NASDAQ composite indexes. The available daily record of the Dow Jones industrial average is from October 1,1928, through September 29, 2000 and the record of the NASDAQ composite index is from February 5, 1971 through September of 2000. Let us first take a look at the extreme situation of volatility, the so-called the market crash, and then examine daily percent changes in stock price indexes.

## • **Stock Market Crashes**

In the history of the U.S. stock markets there are two famous market crashes, the 1929 crash and the 1987 crash, both occurring in the month of October. In the 1990s the U.S. stock markets advanced more rapidly than ever before. Instead of a big crash on a single trading day, U.S. stock markets experienced several large-scale market devaluations over short-time periods of several days or weeks, comprising the mini-crashes of the 1990s.

### *The 1929 Stock Market Crash*

Figure 14-3 depicts the evolution of the Dow Jones industrial average over the time period of 1928–1959, which illustrates the market volatility, the first stock market crash, the slow recovery, and the bounce-back to its previous high.

On October 28, 1929, the Dow Jones industrial average dropped by 13.5% and was followed by another sharp drop of 11.7% on October 29, 1929. Within the first few hours the stock market was open, prices fell so far as to wipe out all the gains that had been made in the previous years, and the October 29, 1929, was remembered as the Black Tuesday.

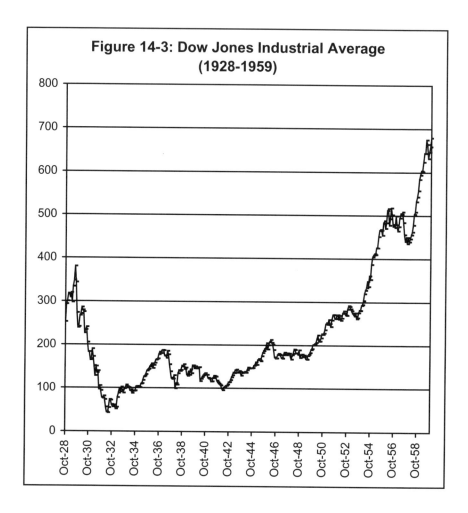

Before this two-day crash, there were ten days in September and October of 1929 that the index plunged more than 2.0% each day, with an one-day rebound of 6.3%. After the two-day crash, the index jumped back 12.3% and 5.8% in the following two days before reassuming the continuous volatility of more than 5% changes in both directions. The declining trend, however, pushed the index as low as 41.2 on July 8, 1932. Until July 18, 1950, the index did not move above 200, and until November 23 , 1954, the index did not exceed its previous maximum, 381, which was set in September of 1929.

As Figure 14-3 shows, the 1929 market crash took nearly three years to move the Dow Jones industrial average from its peak (09/03/1929) to its trough (07/08/1932). However, it took nearly twenty-five years for the index to recover (09/03/1929–11/23/54); that is to say, people who bought stock at the Dow Jones industrial average index at the peak in September 1929 had to wait for more than twenty-five years to sell at the same index market value. This fact illustrates how severe the bear market was at the end of 1920s and the early 1930s.

In fact, after the stock market crash, U.S. production fell by nearly 50% from the business cycle peak in August 1929 to the trough in March 1933, which was coincident with the sharp three-year decline in the stock market. Since the Great Depression occurred after the 1929 stock market crash, many people blamed it for the economic collapse, though both phenomena were interdependent. It seems unlikely that we can declare one as the cause and the other as the outcome.

## The 1987 Stock Market Crash

The second well-known stock market crash happened in October 1987, which is displayed by market indexes on the left side of Figure 14-4. On August 25, 1987, the Dow Jones industrial average reached a maximum, 2,722, and the NASDAQ composite index came to its cyclic peak, 456, two days later, on August 27, 1987. Since then, both indexes had declined and bounced back at a percentage-change rate of less than 2% daily before entering the month of October.

Preceding the market crash of October 19, there was a three-day market plunge with a consecutive daily decline of 3.8%, 2.4%, and 4.6% respectively. On October 19, 1987, the stock market crashed, the Dow Jones industrial average plunged by 508 points to 1739, a 22.6% decline In one day, the entire seven-month gain was wiped out. On October 19, the NASDAQ composite index plunged 46 points, representing an 11.4% decline, and another 32 points or 9% decline on October 20, when the Dow Jones industrial average already rebounded by more than 100 points or a 5.9% rise on the day.

After the crash, the stock market was extremely volatile for three months with many large swings in both directions. The upward trend in the stock markets, however, resumed and brought the Dow Jones industrial average back to its pre-crash high on August 24, 1989, while the NASDAQ composite index exceeded its previous high on August 3, 1989.

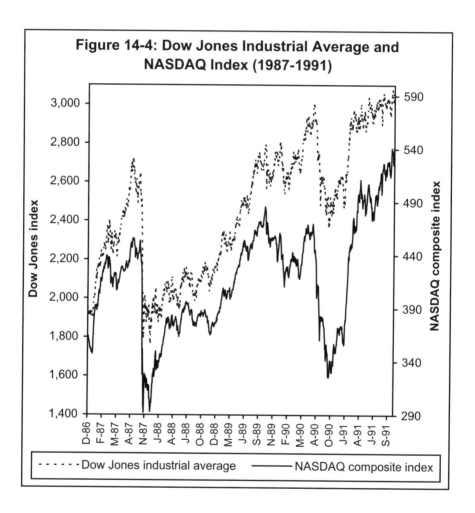

Compared with the 1929 market crash, the 1987 crash is quite severe in terms of big percentage drops for consecutive two days, 4.6% and 22.6% in 1987 versus 13.5% and 11.7% in 1929. The market recovered from the

1987 crash in two years, while it had taken nearly twenty-five years to come back from its 1929 crash. The stock market has been the most important barometer of the overall confidence of society in terms of future business and economic conditions of the nation. A rising bull market reflects public confidence in the economic future whereas a falling bear market indicates a lack of confidence in future business conditions. Hence, public confidence was reassumed better and more quickly from the 1987 market crash than from the 1929 crash, indicating some fundamental changes of the U.S. economy that have substantially improved public confidence in the overall business conditions.

## *The 1990s' Stock Market Mini-Crashes*

In the 1990s the U.S. stock markets experienced tremendous growth. The Dow Jones industrial average rose more than four times from 2,753 in 1989 to 11,497 in 1999, and the NASDAQ composite index increased nearly nine times from 455 to 4,069 in the same time frame. On their way up hill, the U.S. stock markets more frequently pulled back than in previous decades; some severe market corrections developed into markets crashes, specifically large rapid drops in equity share prices across all categories of stocks.

The right side of 14-4 displays a market crash in October 1990. This time the falling of market indexes occurred over three months instead of several days. The market's fall began in the middle of July 1990 when both indexes reached their high. In the middle of October 1990, the stock market found its bottom and reversed the declining trend. During this three-month period, Dow Jones industrial average moved from 3000 to 2381, dropping nearly 21%, and the NASDAQ composite index from 470 to 325, declining 31%.

During this fall, there were five days when the Dow Jones index plunged 2-3% per day and eleven days when the NASDAQ index dropped 2-4% per day. Many declines of less than 2%, interrupted by a few small bounce backs, pushed indexes to their bottom. On March 5, 1991, however, the NASDAQ composite index came back to its previous high, and the Dow Jones industrial average exceeded its previous high of April 17, 1991. Moreover, the strong ascending trend established during the time period from October 1988 to October 1989 was restored after the 1990 market crash and extended well into the rest of 1991. Although this time the market crash had taken three month to reach the market bottom, it only took fewer than five months for the indexes to recover completely.

Figure 14-5 depicts the Dow Jones industrial average and NASDAQ composite index with close prices for each trading day since January 1, 1997 until the last trading day of the twentieth century, December 31.

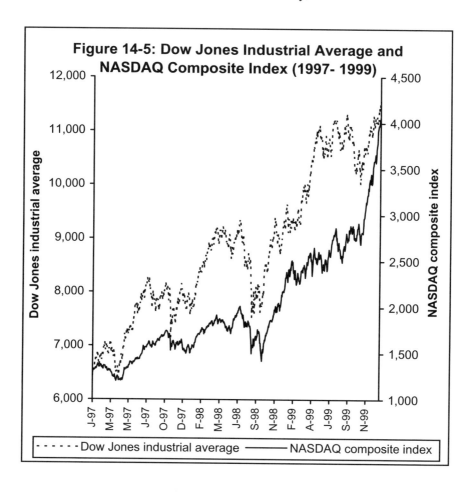

Figure 14-5: Dow Jones Industrial Average and NASDAQ Composite Index (1997- 1999)

It clearly shows that whenever the Dow Jones industrial average closed above a major landmark, such as 7,000, 8,000, 9,000, and 11,000, there has been some major pull back. Sometimes the pull back has developed into a severe market crash.

On March 11, 1997, the Dow Jones index closed at 7,085. In the following month U.S. stock markets declined substantially and pulled the Dow Jones index back to 4,391 on April 11, 1997, which was a 38% drop in one month. Similarly, the NASDAQ composite index declined from its peak 1,388 on January 22, 1997 to 1,201 on April 2, 1997, which was a 13.5% decline.

On October 22, 1997, both indexes reached their high values, 8,034 and 1,708 respectively. In the next three days, however, the Dow Jones index plunged 187 (2.3%), 132 (1.7%), and 554 points (7.2%), and reached its bottom, 7,381, on October 30, 1997. It was an 8.1% drop from the high 8,034 to the low 7381. The NASDAQ composite index followed the Dow's suit by falling 37 (2.2%), 20 (1.2%), and 118 points (7.2%) in the first three days and continued declining to find its bottom 1,503 on January 9, 1998. It was a 12% drop from the high 1,708 to the low 1,503.

Stock markets rebounded quickly; both indexes moved above the previous highs in February 1998. Very soon, the Dow Jones industrial average crossed the 9,000-mark and arrived at 9,337 on July 17, 1998, and the NASDAQ index reached 2,014 on July 20. However, an even more severe pull back followed and was played out in two stages. First, between the middle of July and middle of August 1998, the Dow Jones index fell nearly 740 points and the NASDAQ index reduced by 216 points. Secondly, on the last three trading days of August 1998, the Dow Jones index plunged 357 (4.2%), 114 (1.4%), and 513 points (6.4%), while the NASDAQ dropped 82 (4.6%), 47 (2.8%), and 140 point (8.6%). This time the Dow Jones industrial average plunged by 18.4% from a high of 9,337 to a low of 7,615, and the NASDAQ composite index declined by 29.5% from a high of 2,014 to a low of 1,419; and the NASDAQ market suffered more damages than the NYSE market. Like the previous mini-crashes in April and October 1997, the U.S. stock markets rebounded quickly and strongly. Both indexes reached an all-time high on May 3, 1999: 11,014 and 2,535 respectively.

When the Dow Jones index went through the 10,000-mark, instead of pulling back, it continued charging ahead to the 11,000-mark. Soon enough, on May 3, 1999, the Dow Jones industrial average closed at 11,014, the first time in history it hit above the 11,000-mark. The NASDAQ composite index also stood at 2,536. During the time period from August 25, 1999, through October 15, 1999, the Dow Jones industrial average had pulled back by 11.5%

from 11,326 to 10,019, while the NASDAQ composite index did not suffer such a major setback. In the last two and a half months of 1999, both indexes had vigorously charged ahead and closed at the high ground, with the Dow Jones industrial average 11,497, and the NASDAQ composite index at an all-time high of 4, 069.

## The First Bear Market of the New Century

Entering the twenty-first century, U.S. stock markets continued their extended ascendancy from the huge 1990s bull market. The Dow Jones industrial average reached a new record high of 11,723 on January 14, 2000, and the NASDAQ composite index arrived at its new record high of 5,048 on March 10, 2000 (Figure 14-6). Since then a major pull-back has occurred in the Dow Jones index, a 16.4% decline from 11,723 to 9,796 on March 7, 2000; and the NASDAQ composite index plunged by 36.5% from 5,048 to 3,205 on May 26, 2000. In three months, the U.S. stock markets recovered nicely, the Dow Jones index rose to 11,310 on September 6, 2000, and the NASDAQ composite index rose to 4,234 on September 1, 2000. It would have been a normal stock market correction as we have seen in the 1990s, had the NASDAQ market prevented the implosion of the Internet related stocks.

It turns out that this time the NASDAQ market had been turning into a large bear market with four stages of cascading declines so far. The NASDAQ composite index plunged from 4,234 on September 1, 2000, to 3,074 on October 12, 2000 (a 27.4% drop), and from 3,415 on November 7, 2000, to 2,470 at the end of 1999 (a 27.7% drop), which was a 51% decline from its peak 5,048. The NASDAQ composite index continued decreasing in 2001, plunging from 2,859 on January 24, 2001, to 1,639 on April 4, 2001, (a 42.7% drop) and from 2,282 on May 24, 2001, to 1,423 on September 21, 2001 (a 37.6% drop).

On September 10, 2001, one day before the most horrible and unprecedented terrorist attacks in human history, the Dow Jones industrial average and the NASDAQ composite index had both closed near their previous lows of early April 2001. On September 11 the terrorist hit caused the U.S. stock markets to close for four days and the global stock markets to drop more than 10-20% in a couple of days.

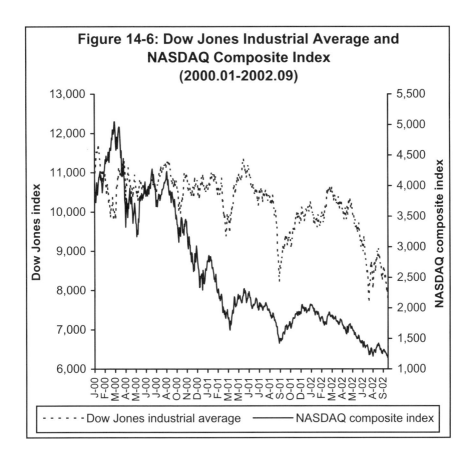

Figure 14-6: Dow Jones Industrial Average and NASDAQ Composite Index (2000.01-2002.09)

When the U.S. stock market reopened on September 17, 2001, both indexes declined by nearly 7% on that day and continued to plunge for another four days, which pushed the Dow Jones index to its new low of 8,236 and the NASDAQ index to 1,423 on September 21, 2001. In five trading days, the terrorist attacks knocked down the Dow Jones industrial average by 14.3% and the NASDAQ composite index by 16.0%. The terrorist attacks have generated a storm of political, economic, and market uncertainties, which came together to knock down consumers' confidence, to create deeper fears for investors, and to hammer U.S. stock markets and the global markets as well.

Following the three-month rebound from oversold conditions, the U.S. stock market resumed its declining trend in the early 2002. In July and September of 2002, the Dow Jones Industrial Average reached its five-year low of 7,600, and the NASDAQ Composite Index was at its six-year low of 1,180. Many risks and worries were reflected in the stock market, including slower than expected recovery of the U.S. economy, corporate accounting and business scandals signified by Enron and WorldCom debacles, disappointment of corporate earnings, increasing layoffs, decreasing confidence of consumers and investors, as well as potential terrorist attacks and the pending war against Iraq. All these economic, psychological, and geopolitical forces were factored into the U.S. stock market, which was in a deep bear mood during 2002.

## • Inter Day Changes of the Dow Jones Industrial Average and NASDAQ Composite Index

Uncertainties in the economic fundamentals, namely GDP growth, corporate profits and inflation rate, will continue to alter the long-term and short-term market trends. Upward or downward revisions to companies' earnings estimates, concerns about end demand in the face of a fast-growing or slowing economy, and an increase or a decrease in capital spending will all weigh on the sentiments of investors and markets. Many other factors also come together to influence the stock market's performance such as political uncertainty, eruption of unexpected national or global events, terrorist attacks, and so forth.

After all, the stock market is a highly speculative market participated in by millions of individuals and institutional investors who are human beings with both greed and fear deeply embedded in their blood. A piece of over-hyped information could drive some equity prices up or drag them down abruptly. Many traders who jump on the bandwagon to buy when stock prices begin to rise and to sell when stock prices begin to fall could seriously intensify the initially modest changes in stock prices. This is particularly true in today's information age.

Millions of investors participate in stock markets across the globe via the Internet and online trading. Even taxi drivers in New York City can check their stock orders through a palm pilot wireless device, and travelers can issue their stock orders and monitor executions by using a laptop computer while they are waiting for flight at the airport. Day trading has become a kind of professional career for some youth, housewives, and retirees. Broadly participating and instantly accessing stock markets, combined with the increasing number of day traders (including individuals and institutional investors) whose holding period of stocks is measured by seconds and minutes rather than days, weeks and months, have made the stock markets more variable than ever before.

The increasing volatility of the stock markets over the past seventy years can be observed by the changing patterns of the daily percentage rise or fall summarized in Tables 14-9.1 and 14-9.2 for the Dow Jones Industrial Average.

### Table 14-9.1: Summary of Daily Changes in Dow Jones Industrial Average

| Number of up-days with change | 1928-29* | 1930-39 | 1940-49 | 1950-59 | 1960-69 |
|---|---|---|---|---|---|
| 2.00% - 2.99% | 19 | 141 | 14 | 8 | 6 |
| 3.00% - 3.99% | 7 | 64 | 5 | 0 | 2 |
| 4.00% - 4.99% | 0 | 25 | 4 | 1 | 2 |
| 5.00% - 5.99% | 2 | 20 | 0 | 0 | 0 |
| 6.00% - 6.99% | 1 | 8 | 0 | 0 | 0 |
| >= 7.00% | 2 | 16 | 0 | 0 | 0 |
| Second largest % | 9.36% | 14.8% | 4.39% | 2.8% | 4.5% |
| Change in the index | +18.6 | +12.8 | +5.8 | +6.3 | +32 |
| Date | 11/14/29 | **10/6/31** | 11/7/40 | 12/18/50 | 11/26/63 |
| The largest % | 12.34% | 15.43% | 4.74% | 4.12% | 4.7% |
| Change in the index | +28.4 | +8.3 | +5.5 | 17.3 | +27.1 |
| Date | **10/30/29** | 3/15/33 | 6/12/40 | 10/23/57 | **5/29/62** |
| **Number of down-days with change** | **1928-29** | **1930-39** | **1940-49** | **1950-59** | **1960-69** |
| (-2.99%) - (-2.00%) | 15 | 142 | 31 | 20 | 7 |
| (-3.99%) - (-3.00%) | 9 | 79 | 8 | 1 | 0 |
| (-4.99%) - (-4.00%) | 5 | 35 | 4 | 1 | 0 |
| (-5.99%) - (-5.00%) | 3 | 29 | 1 | 0 | 1 |
| (-6.99%) - (-6.00%) | 2 | 6 | 2 | 1 | 0 |
| <= (-7.00%) | 3 | 9 | 0 | 0 | 0 |
| Second largest % | -11.70% | -8.42% | -6.76% | -4.68% | -2.89% |
| Change in the index | -30.5 | -5.8 | -9.3 | -10.5 | -21.2 |
| Date | **10/29/29** | 8/12/32 | 5/14/40 | 6/26/50 | 11/22/63 |
| The largest % | -13.48% | -10.73% | -6.78% | -6.54% | -5.72% |
| Change in the index | -40.6 | -10.4 | -8.3 | -31.9 | -35 |
| Date | **10/28/29** | **10/5/31** | 5/21/40 | 9/26/55 | **5/28/62** |

Table 14-9.2: Summary of Daily Changes in Dow Jones
Industrial Average

| Number of up-days with change | 1970-79 | 1980-89 | 1990-99 | 1/1/00-9/29/01 |
|---|---|---|---|---|
| 2.00% - 2.99% | 44 | 71 | 38 | 14 |
| 3.00% - 3.99% | 11 | 12 | 7 | 4 |
| 4.00% - 4.99% | 3 | 5 | 4 | 3 |
| 5.00% - 5.99% | 1 | 1 | 0 | 0 |
| 6.00% - 6.99% | 0 | 0 | 0 | 0 |
| >= 7.00% | 0 | 1 | 0 | 0 |
| Second largest % | 4.71% | 5.88% | 4.71% | 4.47% |
| Change in the index | +28.4 | +102 | +337 | +368 |
| Date | 10/9/74 | **10/20/87** | **10/28/97** | 9/24/01 |
| The largest % | 5.07% | 10.15% | 4.98% | 4.93% |
| Change in the index | +32 | 187 | 381 | +499 |
| Date | 5/27/70 | **10/21/87** | 9/8/98 | 3/16/00 |
| Number of down-days with change | 1970-79 | 1980-89 | 1990-99 | 1/1/00-9/29/01 |
| (-2.99%) - (-2.00%) | 40 | 40 | 35 | 21 |
| (-3.99%) - (-3.00%) | 5 | 7 | 8 | 4 |
| (-4.99%) - (-4.00%) | 0 | 4 | 1 | 2 |
| (-5.99%) - (-5.00%) | 0 | 0 | 0 | 1 |
| (-6.99%) - (-6.00%) | 0 | 2 | 1 | 0 |
| <= (-7.00%) | 0 | 2 | 1 | 0 |
| Second largest % | -3.4% | -8.04% | -6.37% | -5.66% |
| Change in the index | -29 | -157 | -513 | -618 |
| Date | 11/26/73 | 10/26/87 | 8/31/98 | 4/14/00 |
| The largest % | -3.51% | -22.61% | -7.18% | -7.13% |
| Change in the index | -22.7 | -508 | -554 | -685 |
| Date | 11/18/74 | **10/19/87** | **10/27/97** | 9/17/01 |

In these tables, each decade is adopted as a time frame in which the large daily percent movements of the stock market indexes in both directions are depicted in each column. The column of 1928 - 29 covers the days from October 1, 1928 (the beginning of available historical daily data for the Dow Jones Industrial average) through December 31, 1929. The last column denotes large percentage changes for the time period of January 1, 2000 to September 28, 2001. The other columns consist of entire decades, except for the NASDAQ market that celebrated its inauguration in February of 1971. The NASDAQ composite index started on February 5, 1971, with an initial value of 100.

Tables 14-9.1 and 14-9.2 list the largest and second largest percentage changes in the Dow Jones industrial average index, representing big drops and rebounds during the market crashes and mini crashes of the decade. The number of trading days with different daily percent changes is displayed in each column. The greater the number of big-change days, the more volatile the stock markets.

The decade of 1930-1939 had the most volatile stock markets as the greatest numbers of big-change trading days in all percentage ranges occurred up in both directions. The 1980s had the second most volatile market, which is indicated by the great market crash of 1987 and the large number of trading days in each range and in both directions. The 1950s and 1960s decades had relatively tranquil stock markets, as a small number of trading days showed the more than 2% daily changes in the both directions and the largest percent daily change was (-6.54%) over the 10-year period. In terms of the Dow Jones industrial average, the 1990s was more volatile than the 1970s in the downward changes due to the mini crashes in 1990, 1997, and 1998.

Table 14-10 provides inter-day changes in the NASDAQ composite index over the last thirty years. It shows that a similar pattern to the Dow Jones industrial average existed in the NASDAQ composite index. That is, the NASDAQ stock market became more volatile in the 1990s than in the 1970s and 1980s.

Comparing corresponding columns in Tables 14-9.2 and 14-10, one can see that the NASDAQ market was less variable than the NYSE market during the 1970s and 1980s, because a small number of trading days with large percentage changes occurred in the NASDAQ stock market, while a large number of trading days with large percentage changes occurred in the NYSE market. The NASDAQ market, however, became much more volatile than the NYSE market during the 1990s and for 2000 and 2001, which was indicated by large percentage changes in the mini-crashes of 1990, 1997, 1998, and 2000, as well as a large number of trading days with large percentage changes.

In Table 14-10, the column 1/1/00-9/29/01 displays the extremely volatile situation of the NASDAQ stock market. In a mere 21 months during 2000-2001, the NASDAQ composite index showed a large number of trading days with more than 3% index changes in both up- and down-directions, which was greater than the counterpart of the trading days in 120 months during the 1990s. The abnormal inter day changes in the NASDAQ composite index reflect the struggles of U.S. technology companies in the severe bear market of the new century.

Table 14-10: Summary of Daily Changes in the NASDAQ
Composite Index

| Number of up-days with change | 1971-79* | 1980-89 | 1990-99 | 1/1/00-9/29/01 |
|---|---|---|---|---|
| 2.00% — 2.99% | 15 | 11 | 78 | 45 |
| 3.00% - 3.99% | 1 | 1 | 18 | 22 |
| 4.00% - 4.99% | 0 | 1 | 4 | 8 |
| 5.00% - 5.99% | 0 | 2 | 5 | 7 |
| 6.00% - 6.99% | 0 | 0 | 1 | 4 |
| >= 7.00% | 0 | 1 | 0 | 9 |
| Second largest % | 2.71% | 5.28% | 5.17% | 10.48% |
| Change in the index | +1.56 | +16.2 | +73 | +274 |
| Date | 10/10/74 | 10/30/87 | 10/9/98 | 12/5/00 |
| The largest % | 3.18% | 7.35% | 6.02% | 14.17% |
| Change in the index | +3.53 | +24.1 | +94 | +325 |
| Date | 11/1/78 | **10/21/87** | 9/8/98 | 1/3/01 |
| **Number of down-days with change** | 1971-79* | 1980-89 | 1990-99 | 1/1/00-9/29/01 |
| (-2.99%) - (-2.00%) | 32 | 26 | 74 | 57 |
| (-3.99%) - (-3.00%) | 5 | 9 | 17 | 36 |
| (-4.99%) - (-4.00%) | 0 | 1 | 5 | 16 |
| (-5.99%) - (-5.00%) | 1 | 0 | 1 | 12 |
| (-6.99%) - (-6.00%) | 0 | 1 | 0 | 4 |
| <=(-7.00%) | 0 | 3 | 2 | 4 |
| Second largest % | -3.83% | -9.01% | -7.16% | -7.64% |
| Change in the index | -5.78 | -29.6 | -118 | -349 |
| Date | 10/9/79 | 10/26/87 | 10/27/97 | 4/3/00 |
| The largest % | -4.06% | -11.35% | -8.56% | -9.67% |
| Change in the index | -5.89 | -360 | -140 | -356 |
| Date | 10/10/79 | **10/19/87** | 8/31/98 | 4/14/00 |

Table 14-11 provides a concise summary of daily changes in the Dow Jones industrial average and in the NASDAQ composite index. We list the number of trading days with a 2% or greater gain and the number of trading days with a 2% or greater loss in both Dow Jones industrial average and the NASDAQ composite index for each decade and specified time period. The percentage in parentheses represents the ratio of those trading days to the total number of trading days in the specified time period.

In 1928-29 and 1930-39, the number of trading days with a 2% and greater gain accounted for 10-11% of total number of trading days, and the number of trading days with a 2% and greater loss accounted for 12% of total trading days. Those fractions reduced to less than 1% in the 1950s and 1960s, and increased back to 2.2-3.6% for the Dow Jones index in the 1980s. In the 1970s and 1980s, the fractions for the NASDAQ composite index were between 0.6% and 1.7%, less than the counterpart of the Dow Jones index. In the 1990s, however, the fractions of the NASDAQ index increased substantially to nearly 4%, greater than the fractions of Dow Jones index, which had declined to less than 2%.

These simple statistics clearly indicate that since 1990 the NASDAQ market has become more volatile than ever before and more volatile than the NYSE market. In particular, the 436 trading days' data in 2000 and 2001 illustrate an extreme situation, in which the NASDAQ composite index looked unstable, that 21.8% of trading days showed a 2% plus gain and 29.6% of trading days suffered a 2% plus loss. That is to say in every ten trading days there were at least two days with a more than 2% gain and another 3 days with a more than 2% loss.

Table 14-11: Summary of Daily Changes in the Dow Jones Industrial Average and the NASDAQ Composite Index

| Time period | Number of trading days | Dow Jones industrial average | | NASDAQ Composite index | |
|---|---|---|---|---|---|
| | | Number of days with >= 2% gain | Number of days with >= 2% loss | Number of days with >= 2% gain | Number of days with >= 2% loss |
| 1928-29 | 310 | 31 (10%) | 37 (12%) | - | - |
| 1930-39 | 2524 | 274 (11%) | 300 (12%) | - | - |
| 1940-49 | 2520 | 21 (0.8%) | 46 (1.8%) | - | - |
| 1950-59 | 2516 | 9 (0.4%) | 23 (0.9%) | - | - |
| 1960-69 | 2488 | 10 (0.4%) | 8 (0.3%) | - | - |
| 1970-79 | 2523 (2252)* | 59 (2.3%) | 45 (1.8%) | 16 (0.7%) | 38 (1.7%) |
| 1980-89 | 2525 | 90 (3.6%) | 55 (2.2%) | 16 (0.6) | 40 (1.6%) |
| 1990-99 | 2528 | 49 (1.9%) | 46 (1.8%) | 106 (4.2%) | 99 (3.9%) |
| 2000# | 436 | 21 (4.8%) | 29 (6.7%) | 95 (21.8%) | 129 (29.6%) |

* Number of trading days for the NASDAQ stock market; # Number of trading days during 1/1/00-9/28/01

In the same time period, however, 4.8% of the trading days on the Dow Jones had a gain of more than 2%, and 6.7% of trading days that lost more than 2%, which was significantly volatile compared with the Dow Jones index itself in all previous time periods except for 1929–1939, but much less volatile than the NASDAQ composite index in 2000–2001. In recent years, technology companies whose earnings miss Wall Street's expectation by as little as a penny a share found their stock prices hammered by more than 20-30%. The extremely volatile stock markets reflect sentiment shifting from bullish to bearish or vice versa daily, if not hourly.

Tech stocks have dominated the NASDAQ market. They sent the NASDAQ index on a moon-shot surge of 85.6% in 1999, the biggest gain ever for the U.S. stock exchange, while they suffered a severe plunge of 39.3% in 2000 and still wandered in bear territory at the end of September 2001. The extremely volatile tech stocks reflect the Internet hype and the bust of the Internet bubble in U.S. stock markets. It may also reflect a growing pain for many emerging technology companies.

Demands for emerging technological products and services are very strong in years of economic booming but hold a higher degree of uncertainty than traditional technologies and businesses, which could easily spook investors' confidence and cause big sell-offs in the market. Since the pioneer Internet stock Netscape hit the market in 1995, investors have been charged up with a high level of emotions as they embraced the emerging tech stocks of the 'New Economy', willing to pay sky-high prices and ignoring evaluation issues. Those so-called "zero gravity" Internet stocks with or without earnings fell under scrutiny when investors were expecting a slow down or recession ahead in the U.S. economy. Many Internet stocks have lost their market value by 90-95% and many high tech stocks suffered a more than 70% reduction of their stock prices. However, as we have illustrated in Figures 14-8 and 14-9, after the market crash and mini-crashes the stock markets have always come back strongly and decisively; the only problem is when.

The stock market's wealth effect on the economy works in two ways. The wealth generated from the stock market raises confidence and purchasing power for nearly a half of the total U.S. population, which increases consumers' and corporations' spending. The increasing aggregate demand generates the economic expansion and may add inflationary pressures on the economy. The stock market's mini-crashes, however, wipes out wealth as quickly as it is produced, which makes many people worry about their money and financial future. Consequently, consumers will likely tighten their spending and corporations may cut back their expansion budget, which may induce an economic recession. The effect of wealth generation and wealth destruction in the stock market on the U.S. economy has become more significant than ever before due to the largely increasing involvement in stock markets of the hundred million Americans who make up half of the U.S. population.

- ### Technology Industries and Companies in the Stock Markets of 1997–2002

A few analysts and observers of the U.S. economy and stock markets expected such a long-lasting and painful market plunge after the euphoria brought by the longest bull market of the 1990s. The U.S. technology industries and companies have been taking the worst hit in the recent bear market, although they were the ones enjoying a huge appreciation in their capitalization during the 1990's bull market. People have blamed the recent bear market on the failures of many dot com companies and the burst of the Internet bubble in the stock markets. We shall show that not only has the Internet industry generated the huge run-up in stock markets and suffered the worst attack, many technology industries have shared the doom with the Internet industry.

Wall Street has invented numerous industry indexes to capture different patterns of equity price movements for more than 197 individual industry groups that have been classified and tracked by the well-known newspaper, Investor's Business Daily. We have selected four technology industry indexes that have at least five years of daily trading data to show how the technology industry has performed in periods of rise and fall in the U.S. stock markets. Figures 14-7 and 14-8 depict four industry indexes versus the NASDAQ composite index for the time frame from 1997 to the end of Q3 of 2001. All the indexes are normalized at 100 on the first trading day, January 2, 1997, in order to make easy comparisons.

The high technology index (TXX) is a price-weighted index for 30 high technology stocks traded on the New York Stock Exchange and NASDAQ. It includes most of the prestigious U.S. high technology companies such as telecommunications equipment companies Cisco Systems, Lucent Technologies, Qualcomm, and Motorola; computer makers Dell, Apple Computer, Compaq, Gateway and Sun Microsystems; software developers Microsoft, Computer Associates, Computer Sciences Corp, Oracle, and Adobe Systems; semiconductor manufacturers Intel, Applied Materials, Micron Technology, and Texas Instruments; Internet companies Yahoo and

America Online; as well as technology giant companies IBM and Hewlett Packard.

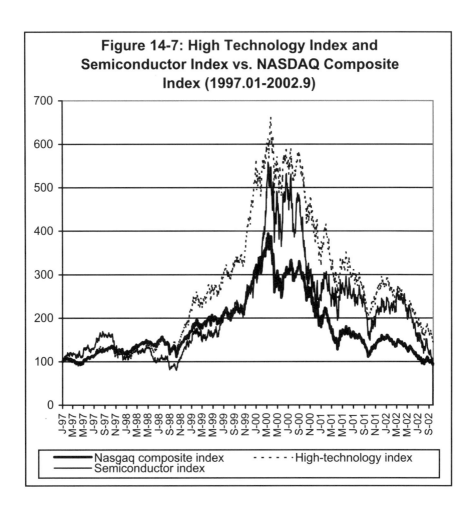

**Figure 14-7: High Technology Index and Semiconductor Index vs. NASDAQ Composite Index (1997.01-2002.9)**

The semiconductor index (SOXX) is a price-weighted index composed of 16 U.S. companies primarily involved in the design, manufacture, distribution, and sale of semiconductors. These companies include Intel, Texas Instruments, Motorola, Advanced Micro Devices, Applied Materials, LSI Logic, National Semiconductor, Rambus, and others. The Internet (IIX) is designed to measure a cross section of companies involved in providing Internet infrastructure and access, developing and marketing Internet content and software, and conducting business over the Internet.

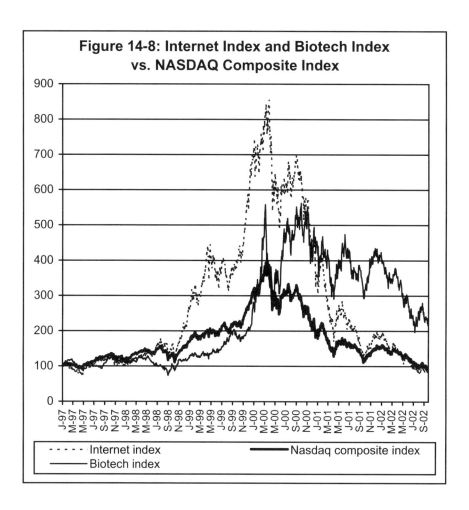

Figure 14-8: Internet Index and Biotech Index vs. NASDAQ Composite Index

The Internet Index was developed by The American Stock Exchange; it is a market-capitalization weighted index for 50 U.S. companies, including Cisco Systems, Juniper Networks, America Online, Amazon, Ebay,

Doubleclick, At Home, Broadvision, Exdous, Vignette, Verisign, Checkpoint, CMGI, Internet Capital Group (ICG), Yahoo and others.

The biotechnology index (BTK) is designed to measure the performance of 17 U.S. companies in the biotechnology industry that are primarily involved in the use of biological processes to develop products or provide services. This group includes Amegen, Biogen, Celera Genomics, Chiron Corp., Human Genome Sciences, Immunex Corp., Protein Design Labs, and Vertex Pharmaceuticals.

As Figures 14-7 and 14-8 have shown, the unprecedented stock market surge in all the four industry indexes and the NASDAQ composite index really started in October of 1998. The NASDAQ index bottomed out on October 8, 1998 and began the first stage of a bull-run that lasted for about 10 months and raised the NASDAQ index by 75.5% from 1,419 on 10/08/1998 to 2,490 on 8/10/1999, which was the beginning of the second stage of this bull-run. On March 10, 2000, the NASDAQ reached its peak of 5,048, representing a 102.8% rise from 2,490 at the beginning of the second stage, and a 255.8% rise from 1,419 at the beginning of the first stage.

Table 14-12 provides the values of the NASDAQ composite index and the four industry indexes at the beginning days of each stage and the day on which the NASDAQ index reached its all-time high.

Table 14-12: The NASDAQ Composite Index and Industry Indexes
(1998.10-2000.03)

| Indexes | Index Value | | | Percent Changes % | | |
|---|---|---|---|---|---|---|
| | 10/08/ 1998 | 8/10/19 99 | 03/10/ 2000 | $1^{st}$ stage 10 months | $2^{nd}$ stage 7 months | Total change 17 months |
| **NASDAQ** | 1419.1 | 2490.1 | 5048.6 | 75.47% | 102.75% | 255.76% |
| **High Tech** | 234.7 | 574.5 | 1210.7 | 144.79 | 110.74 | 415.87 |
| **Semiconductor** | 189.9 | 499.1 | 1332.7 | 162.80 | 167.05 | 601.81 |
| **Internet** | 96.6 | 254.0 | 674.8 | 162.98 | 165.65 | 598.59 |
| **Biotechnology** | 123.9 | 241.6 | 688.9 | 95.09 | 185.09 | 456.18 |

The right side of Table 14-12 provides the percentage changes for each stage and the total percentage change over the 17-month period for the five indexes. These results clearly indicate that all of the indexes had a spectacular surge in those two stages of roaring stock markets. The four industry indexes had grown much faster than the NASDAQ composite index had in both the two stages. In particular, the semiconductor industry index and the Internet industry index grew at a rate twice as larger as the NASDAQ index's growth rate.

Indeed, it was the Internet industry that led the stock market's surge in 1999. In the first stage of this bull market, the Internet industry index increased quickly and established its first peak, 358, on 4/26/99, which was a 271% rise from its value 96.59 on 10/08/1999. This brought a quick correction in the Internet industry index, which plunged from its first peak 358 to 254 on 8/10/1999, a 29% drop in three and a half months.

In the second stage of the bull market, the Internet industry index accelerated its momentum and reached its second peak 688.5 on 3/27/2000, which was its all time high and represented a 171% rise from the beginning of the second stage. All the other indexes had followed the Internet industry index increase, but only the semiconductor industry and the biotechnology industry seemed to lag behind in the first stage. In December 1999 the semiconductor industry index began to speed up, and accelerated in the first two months of 2000; it reached its all time high 1,332 on the same day, 3/10/2000, with the NASDAQ composite index's all time high 5,048.

The biotechnology industry index was lagging behind the semiconductor industry index. It took off in January of 2000, and accelerated in February, but it quickly reached its peak 794.5 on 3/6/2000 before other indexes did. However, it quickly plunged by 49% from its peak in about a month, and then rallied back to its all time high of 800.6 on 9/28/2000, when all the other indexes had already started to decrease.

The descending paths for those indexes in the bear market were as steep as their ascending paths in the bull market. In the time period of 3/10/2000 – 9/01/2000, all the indexes declined and bounced back several times attempting to restore their bull run, but eventually lost momentum. This first stage can be viewed as a normal market correction. The sharp decline of the U.S. stock markets really started on 9/01/2000. So far one can identify the four stages of the abrupt fall in the bear market of 2000-2002. At each stage the NASDAQ composite index found its low and attempted to rebound and failed to do so. Then the next stage's low became lower than the previous stage's low. According to the daily trading data, those lows were established on 10/12/00, 1/2/01, 4/4/01, and 9/25/02, which are used to identify the stages of bear market of 2000–2002.

The upper panel of Table 14-13 provides the values of the NASDAQ composite index and the four industry indexes on six specific days, which divided the bear market into five stages so far. The lower panel of Table 14-13 provides percentage changes over the five sub-periods for these indexes.

On 3/10/00 the NASDAQ and semiconductor indexes reached their all time high, the Internet and high technology indexes were close to their all time high, while the biotechnology index was already pulled back from its peak established on 3/6/2000. In the first stage of normal correction, four indexes declined by less than 20%, while the biotechnology index rose by 14%, reflecting its efforts of to jump back.

Table 14-13: The NASDAQ Composite and Industry Indexes in
The Bear Market of 2000-2002

| Indexes | Index Value | | | | | |
|---|---|---|---|---|---|---|
| | 3/10/00 | 9/01/00 | 10/12/00 | 1/2/01 | 4/4/01 | 9/25/02 |
| **NASDAQ** | 5048.62 | 4234.33 | 3074.68 | 2291.86 | 1638.80 | 1222.29 |
| **High Tech** | 1210.70 | 1153.00 | 825.83 | 633.74 | 489.70 | 298.82 |
| **Semiconductor** | 1332.73 | 1142.57 | 689.11 | 570.34 | 463.49 | 256.45 |
| **Internet** | 674.77 | 559.73 | 414.68 | 245.93 | 136.77 | 67 |
| **Biotechnology** | 688.88 | 785.96 | 642.58 | 589.07 | 413.72 | 333.08 |
| | Percentage Changes | | | | | |
| **Indexes** | 3/10/00 - 9/10/00 6 months | 9/1/00 - 10/12/00 1 1/2 months | 10/12/00 -1/2/01 2.5 months | 1/02/01 - 4/4/01 3 months | 4/4/01 - 9/25/02 18 months | 3/10/00- 9/25/02 31.5 months |
| **NASDAQ** | -16.13% | -27.39% | -25.46% | -28.49% | -25.42% | -75.79% |
| **High Tech** | -4.77 | -28.38 | -23.26 | -22.73 | -38.98 | -75.32 |
| **Semiconductor** | -14.27 | -39.69 | -17.24 | -18.73 | -44.67 | -80.76 |
| **Internet** | -17.05 | -25.91 | -40.69 | -44.39 | -51.01 | -90.07 |
| **Biotechnology** | 14.09 | -18.24 | -8.33 | -29.77 | -19.49 | -51.65 |

In the following sub-periods, all indexes plunged sharply and quickly. Particularly, the Internet industry index suffered the worst beating, plunging by nearly 85% over the 18.5-month old bear market at the end of September 2001. The biotechnology index showed a 39.4% decline on 9/21/2001 from its value 688.9 on 3/10/2000. However, compared with its all time high of 800.6 reached on 9/28/2000, the biotechnology index has declined by 47.8%. So far the biotech industry has not been hit as hard as the other technology industries in the 2000-2001 bear market.

Many technology companies' share prices increased spectacularly during the bull market of 1989 - 1999 and then fell miserably during the bear market of 2000-2001. To illustrate how serious the change in technology companies' share prices was we list 20 representative technology companies' stock prices in Tables 14-14.1 – 14-14.4 for some specific dates during the time period from the beginning of 1997 through the end of September 2001. These companies are top-ranked in their industries; all their share prices are the market close prices on the days specified in the table and these prices are adjusted for stock share splits during the time period of 1997 - 2001.

The two bottom rows of 14-14.1 – 14-14.4 denote percentage changes of stock prices for the 20 technology companies. The percentage change of the all time high price relative to the low prices of 1997 (or to the adjusted initial public offering prices for 4 Internet companies) represents how quickly the individual stock price ran up in the bull market. The percentage change of the market closing price on 9/21/01 relative to its all-time high denotes how much the individual stock price fell in the bear market.

The reason why the date 9/21/01 is chosen is due to the opinion that date may represent the bottom of this bear market.[8] U.S. stock markets plunged quickly and severely after the unprecedented terrorist attacks on the World Trade Center in New York City and the Pentagon in Washington on September 11, 2001. The horror of the terrorist attacks and the devastating destructions on Wall Street firms resulted in the close of the U.S. stock markets for four days, while stock markets around the world all plunged severely. When U.S. stock markets reopened on September 17, 2001, the Fed announced its eighth interest rate cut in 2001 to stimulate the U.S. economy. Even though patriotic spirit surged across the United States in response to the terrorist attacks, horrified investors still decided to sell U.S. shares, which sent Dow Jones industrial average down by 14.3% and the NASDAQ composite index down by 16.1% in the reopening week ended on 9/21/2001.

---

[8] As a matter of fact, the U.S. stock markets broke this temporary bottom and generated a new five-year low in October 2002.

Before the terrorist attacks, the U.S. economy was already very weak, struggling on the verge of a recession with increasing number of layoffs and declining revenues and profits of American corporations. September 11 brought all negative factors together in the U.S. stock markets and created the greatest uncertainties for economic conditions, political reactions around the global, military retaliation, and future terrorist attacks. The great fears of investors were reflected in plunging stock prices, which made the following week after the terrorist attacks the worst week for U.S. stock markets since 1929.

On Friday, September 21, 2001, U.S. stock markets rose gradually with the Dow Jones industry average and the NASDAQ composite index closed at 8,236 and 1,423 respectively after hitting as low as 7,927 and 1,387 in intra-day trading. Since then, investors' confidence on the U.S. economy has been boosted by the Bush Administration's proposal of the 60-75 billion economic stimulus package intended to prevent a deep recession in the U.S. economy. On October 2, 2001, the Federal Reserve authority, for the ninth time in 2001, took the action of reducing the federal funds rate by another 0.5%, which put the federal funds rate at its lowest level, 2.5%, since 1962. We believe that monetary and fiscal policies as well as U.S. government's efforts to build the worldwide coalition against terrorists will work together to reenergize the U.S. economy and to restore consumers and investors' confidence. Hopefully, U.S. stock markets put the worst behind them, and the markets began to move slowly in upwards direction.

Tables 14-14.1 – 14-14.4 indicate that in the bull market of 1997-2000, all 20 technology stocks' prices increased dramatically; they have all established their all time highs in the late 1999 or 2000 with the 2 - 16 folds of increases from their 1997's low prices. An astonishing rise occurred for some Internet stocks, such as Yahoo! (a leading Internet portal) and CMGI Inc. (an Internet operating and incubating company) whose share-split-adjusted prices reached an all-time high, $237 and $163 respectively on January 3rd of 2000, compared with their share prices of only $1.46 for Yahoo! and $0.98 for CMGI at the beginning of 1997. Their share prices increased more than 160-fold in nearly three years.

During this bull phase of US stock markets, investors bought almost anything even vaguely associated with the Internet, regardless of valuation or prices. They were incited by bullish reports and recommendations from the Wall Street firms and media, which pushed Internet stock prices skyrocketing.

## Table 14-14.1: Stock Prices ($/share) of High-Tech Companies

| Date | IBM | Microsoft | EBay | America Online | Dell Computer |
|------|-----|-----------|------|----------------|---------------|
| 1/2/97 | 38.08 | 20.41 | $7.90* 9/24/98 | 2.05 | 3.2 |
| 3/2/98 | 50.66 | 41.66 | NA | 7.35 | 16.95 |
| 4/26/99 | 104.3 | 88 | 104.5 | 81 | 44.81 |
| 3/10/00 | 104.61 | 101 | 96.63 | 58.63 | 51.25 |
| All Time high | 132.97 on 9/1/00 | 119.13 on 12/27/99 | 121.88 on 3/24/00 | 94.0 on 12/13/99 | 58.13 on 3/22/00 |
| 9/1/00 | 132.97 | 70.19 | 62.88 | 57.75 | 43.06 |
| 10/12/00 | 102.62 | 54.38 | 51.13 | 51 | 23.19 |
| 1/2/01 | 84.5 | 43.38 | 30.19 | 32.39 | 17.5 |
| 4/4/01 | 91.77 | 51.94 | 30.38 | 35.15 | 22.19 |
| 9/21/01 | 90.5 | 49.71 | 43.79 | 29.85 | 16.63 |
| % change from 1997's low to all time high | 249.19% | 483.68% | 1442.72% | 4485.37% | 1716.56% |
| % change from all-time high to low on 9/21/01 | -31.94% | -58.27% | -64.07% | -68.24% | -71.39% |

* indicates the split-adjusted IPO share price and IPO date.

## Table 14-14.2: Stock Prices ($/share) of High-Tech Companies

| Date | Intel | Applied Material | Qual Comm | Texas Instruments | Oracle |
|------|-------|------------------|-----------|-------------------|--------|
| 1/2/97 | 16.21 | 8.81 | 4.81 | 7.81 | 4.67 |
| 3/2/98 | 21.79 | 17.72 | 6.06 | 13.73 | 4.02 |
| 4/26/99 | 32.08 | 30.38 | 25.43 | 27.29 | 7.17 |
| 3/10/00 | 59.93 | 96.53 | 136 | 90.11 | 40.81 |
| All Time high | 74.7 on 8/31/00 | 114.88 on 4/7/00 | 179.31 on 1/3/00 | 93.54 on 3/3/00 | 46.31 on 9/1/00 |
| 9/1/00 | 73.77 | 84.81 | 59.25 | 66.85 | 46.31 |
| 10/12/00 | 37.04 | 48.06 | 64.38 | 39.47 | 31.5 |
| 1/2/01 | 31.01 | 39.5 | 70.88 | 46.23 | 26.38 |
| 4/4/01 | 22.6 | 38.81 | 43.88 | 27.65 | 13.66 |
| 9/21/01 | 19.3 | 29.24 | 44.89 | 23 | 10.76 |
| % change from 1997's low to all time high | 360.83% | 1203.97% | 3627.86% | 1097.70% | 891.65% |
| % change from all-time high to low on 9/21/01 | -74.16% | -74.55% | -74.97% | -75.41% | -76.77% |

## Table 14-14.3: Stock Prices ($/share) of High-Tech Companies

| Date | Micro Technology | Hewlett Packard | Cisco Systems | Sun Microsystems | Amazon |
|---|---|---|---|---|---|
| **1/2/97** | 14.88 | 24.82 | 6.99 | 3.34 | 1.73* 5/16/97 |
| **3/2/98** | 17.19 | 32.15 | 10.88 | 5.72 | 6.35 |
| **4/26/99** | 18.06 | 39.17 | 29.41 | 16.36 | 103.59 |
| **3/10/00** | 53.19 | 72.4 | 68.19 | 47.1 | 66.88 |
| **All Time high** | 96.56 on 7/14/00 | 76.87 on 4/7/00 | 80.06 on 3/27/00 | 64.32 on 9/1/00 | 106.69 on 12/10/99 |
| **9/1/00** | 78.31 | 61.61 | 68.56 | 64.32 | 41.5 |
| **10/12/00** | 35.56 | 41.31 | 49.81 | 48.97 | 25.13 |
| **1/2/01** | 35.38 | 29.94 | 33.31 | 25.44 | 13.88 |
| **4/4/01** | 34.6 | 27.25 | 13.69 | 13.86 | 8.4 |
| **9/21/01** | 21.11 | 14.96 | 12.09 | 7.96 | 7.48 |
| % change from 1997's low to all time high | 548.92% | 209.71% | 1045.35% | 1825.75% | 6067.05% |
| l% change from all-time high to low on 9/21/01 | -78.14% | -80.54% | -84.90% | -87.62% | -92.99% |

* indicates the split-adjusted IPO share price and IPO date.

## Table 14-14.4: Stock Prices ($/share) of High-Tech Companies

| Company | Juniper Networks | JDS Uniphase | Yahoo! | CMG Information Services | Exite@Home |
|---|---|---|---|---|---|
| **1/2/97** | NA | 3.08 | 1.46 | 0.98 | $8.50* 7/11/97 |
| **3/2/98** | $16.48 IPO on 6/25/99 | 4.77 | 9.15 | 3.47 | 16.5 |
| **4/26/99** | | 15.11 | 96.13 | 70.25 | 80.28 |
| **3/10/00** | 141.22 | 138 | 178.06 | 136.44 | 28.56 |
| **All Time high** | 230.5 on 9/26/00 | 146.52 on 3/06/00 | 237.5 on 1/3/00 | 163.22 on 1/3/00 | 94.66 on 4/12/99 |
| **9/1/00** | 221.63 | 123.81 | 113.94 | 45.81 | 14.5 |
| **10/12/00** | 199.61 | 86.31 | 56.63 | 18 | 9.13 |
| **1/2/01** | 102.56 | 39.25 | 28.19 | 4.63 | 4.56 |
| **4/4/01** | 29.19 | 13.73 | 12.44 | 1.87 | 3.33 |
| **9/21/01** | 11.1 | 5.36 | 8.68 | 1.09 | 0.32 |
| % change from 1997's low to all time high | 1298.67% | 4657.14% | 16167.10% | 16555.10% | 1013.65% |

In 2000, however, it became clear that many Internet companies don't have a path to profitability and too many money-losing Internet companies were crowded in the market. According to the New York-based security data firm Commscan[9], 34 Internet IPOs in 1997 raised a total of $1 billion, including high quality companies such as Yahoo! and Amazon. In 1998 there were 45 Internet IPOs, raising $2 billion in funds from U.S. stock markets. In 1999 the number of Internet IPOs roared to 292, and the capital funds they collected from US stock markets exploded to $24.1 billion. The large volumes of IPOs and the huge amount of money flowing into U.S stock markets created the latest stock market bubble, the so-called Internet bubble, in the time period from 1997 through 1999.

Investors demanded profits and earnings from Internet companies, and they found that few are able to deliver their promises. As investors have finally realized that some Internet companies' business models are flawed, they began to sell Internet stocks to lock in lucrative profits gained during the formation of the Internet bubble. The collapse of the dot.com stocks started in the Spring of 2000, share prices of Internet stocks were plunging in a free fall. One share of Yahoo! stock that was worth $237 dollars 21 month earlier was sold at only $8.68 on September 21, 2001. The share price of CMGI plunged to $1.09 dollar from its peak $163 dollars. Similarly, another Internet stock, Excite@Home, a leading provider of broadband Internet access, saw its share price soaring to $94.66 from $8.50 in less than three years and then falling miserably to 32 cents on September 21, 2001.

Only two Internet stocks, America Online (an Internet media company) and Ebay (an Internet auction house), seemed to stand relatively firm, but still saw their share prices decline by 64-68% from their all-time highs, when the Internet bubble busted.

Technology companies that are major suppliers of the Internet infrastructure of networking equipment such as routers, hubs and switchers, and of working stations, storage hardware and software had all enjoyed a spectacular ride in the bull market and then were beaten down and wounded severely in the following bear market. Cisco Systems Inc., the favored shining star whose shares have been owned by many institutional investors, saw its share price rise by more than 10 times, from share split adjusted price of $6.99 on January 2nd of 1997 to the all time high $80 on 3/27/00. However, its share was worth only $12 dollars in the trading on 9/21/01, reflecting a nearly 85% drop from its all time high. There are only two technology stocks

---

[9] The $1.7 Trillion Dot.com Lesson, by Staff Writer David Kleinbard, CNN, November 9, 2000.

in Tables 14-14.1 – 14-14.4, IBM and Microsoft, whose share prices had declined less than 60% from their all time highs in this bear market, while their share prices rose by 2.5–4.8 times in the 1997-2000 bull market. Technology powerhouse companies like Intel, Dell Computer, and Hewlett Packard all suffered a 70–80% plunge in less than one and a half years.

Cisco's market value dropped from its peak, $586.8 billion, to $88.6 billion at the end of September 2001, losing $498.2 billion in market value. Yahoo! lost $131 billion of its market value and CMGI lost $56.1 billion, from their peaks till the end of September 2001. According to the report from CNN[10], the combined market values of the 280 stocks in the Bloomberg U.S. Internet Index had fallen to $1.193 trillion in the beginning of November 2000 from $2.948 trillion at their peak, a loss of $1.755 trillion, which mainly includes losses between March and September of 2000, but doesn't include continuous losses in the last two months of 2000 and the first nine months of 2001.

From the price movements depicted in 14-14.1–14-14.4 for the popular 20 technology companies one can easily see that trillions of dollars would be generated by U.S. stock markets for those individual and institutional investors who bought technology shares in the early 1997 and 1998 and sold them in the early 2000. In contrast, trillions of dollars could be wiped out for those investors who bought technology shares at the all time highs and were forced to sell at new low prices in 2000 and 2001.

Besides the enormous wealth creation and destruction for investors in the unprecedented three years of roaring bull phase followed by a devastating bear phase, many technology companies had to bear huge losses through reckless acquisitions and investments made during the 1997-1999 expansion. The expected demand and market for Internet related technologies and products had suddenly disappeared and the projected revenues and profits had never been materialized. U.S. technology companies have to downsize their operations via mass layoffs and by reducing capital investment. Many technology companies, even some well-established large companies like Lucent Technologies Inc, have to sell those acquired assets at much lower prices in 2000 and 2001 in order to reduce their debts to levels that were required by the tightening lending standards from investment banks.

Many emerging Internet companies have gone through the process of layoffs, filling for bankruptcy, and eventually ceasing operations. Among the web companies who filed for bankruptcy include an Internet highflier

---

[10] The $1.7 Trillion Dot.com Lesson, by Staff Writer David Kleinbard, CNN, November 9, 2000.

Exite@Home, E-tail pioneers Egghead.com and eToys, and Webvan Group inc, which was the online pioneer that aimed to revolutionize the grocery industry but ended up losing $830 million. The Internet companies' failure has contributed to the large increase in number of public bankruptcies in 2000. As a report from the Turnaround Letter indicates[11], 2000 has been a record year for corporate bankruptcies; about 176 publicly traded companies filed for Chapter 11, which was more than the bankruptcy number of 123 for 1991. The total assets of these companies going into bankruptcy reached $94.786 billion in 2000, which beat the record set in 1991, $93.624 billion.

Some remaining Internet companies saw their equity shares becoming dollar stocks or even penny stocks, struggling on the brink of survival. One of the NASDAQ stock market's minimum requirement rules is that a company's shares trade for at least $1 dollar. If a company's shares trade for less than $1 dollar longer than 10 consecutive days, it is given a month to get the price up. Otherwise, a process begins to unlist the company from the NASDAQ market. According to Bloomberg Markets, 126 companies traded on the major exchanges had shares below the $1 mark at the end of June 2001. This number grew to 336 companies at the end of September 2001.

The terrorist attacks on September 11 caused a dramatic slide in U.S. stock markets; many high tech companies traded on the NASDAQ saw their share prices suffer a steep decline. On September 27, 2001, the authority of the NASDAQ stock market decided to temporarily suspend some rules in order to help struggling companies in danger of being unlisted. This will give some of the technology companies who were hit the worst more time to recover without the threat of being thrown off the NASDAQ market. In fact, many remaining Internet companies have already traded close to $1 for some time before September 11, such as CMGI, BroadVision Inc, PuchasePro.com, Akamai Technologies, Ariba Inc, Commerce One Inc, Data Returns Corp, InfoSpace Inc, VerticalNet, and others. Those companies traded at nearly $1 per share may well be on the way toward bankruptcy or acquisition.

---

[11] The Turnaround Letter, Volume 15, Number 7, January 2001.

## 14-6   Bull and Bear Markets of the United States Since 1929

In this section we will summarize the historical changes in U.S. stock markets by listing in Table 14-15 all time periods in which the Dow Jones industrial average or the NASDAQ composite index changed more than 10% in both either directions. The 10% change is not an official definition for bull or bear markets, but it allows us to capture all of the significant changes in the U.S. stock markets through historical data as well as the latest data on daily trades in both NYSE and the NASDAQ markets.

In each row of Table 14-15, there are two parts: decreases of more than 10% on the left and more than 10% increases on the right. We list the high values of two indexes and the date on which that high indexes occurred. The measure of decreases starts from the index high and ends at the index low. The percent change represents the reduction of index low as a percentage of the index high. The duration denotes the time frame from the index high to the index low. In general, a large decrease was followed by a large increase in the U.S. stock markets. The increase starts on the day of the index low, and ends at the index high. Therefore the right-side index low is identical to the left-side index low in the same row, while the right-side index high is identical to the left-side index high in the next row, with some exceptions.

Row 11 on the right side of 14-15 indicates that both indexes closed at their highs on 7/15/75. In the following two and a half months the NASDAQ composite index had a (-16%) correction while the Dow Jones industrial average did not. So both indexes started with their relative lows on 12/15/75 and rallied in the different time frames as showed on rows 12 and 13. On 1/10/77, the Dow Jones index started a 15-month declined and bounced back to a relative high 903.8 on 2/08/80 (row 14). In this time frame, however, the NASDAQ composite index had experienced two short-term corrections and run back to its relative high 165.3 on 2/08/80 (rows 15 and 16).

Row 20 of Table 14-15 indicates that in the time frame of 7/07/86 – 12/31/86 the NASDAQ composite index suffered a 15.5% decline, while the Dow Jones index did not. In the time period of 10/19/87 – 12/04/87 both indexes did not have a more than 10% movement in either direction, and on 12/04/87 the indexes began to move higher for the following two years. Because these two indexes do not agree on the time frames for movement in either direction, we have to list their changes separately. Rows 23-27 and 30-32 represent increases and decreases of the NASDAQ composite index, and rows 27-29 represent the movements of the Dow Jones industrial average.

Table 14-15: Significant Movements of Dow Jones Industrial Average and NASDAQ Composite Index (1929-2001 Q3)

| More than 10% decrease | | | | More than 10% increase | | | | Row |
|---|---|---|---|---|---|---|---|---|
| Index high | Index low | % | N* | Index low | Index high | % | N* | |
| 09/03/29 381.2 | 07/08/32 41.2 | -89% | 34 | 07/08/32 41.2 | 08/16/37 189.3 | 359% | 61 | 1 |
| 8/16/37 189.3 | 3/31/38 99 | -48% | 7 | 5/01/41 115.3 | 2/05/46 206.6 | 79% | 57 | 2 |
| 2/05/46 206.6 | 10/09/46 163.1 | -21% | 8 | 10/09/46 163.1 | 1/05/53 293.8 | 80% | 75 | 3 |
| 1/05/53 293.8 | 9/04/53 255.5 | -13% | 8 | 9/04/53 255.5 | 8/02/56 521 | 104% | 35 | 4 |
| 8/02/56 521 | 10/22/57 419.8 | -19% | 15 | 10/22/57 419.8 | 12/31/59 679.4 | 62% | 26 | 5 |
| 12/31/59 679.4 | 10/25/60 566.1 | -17% | 10 | 10/25/60 566.1 | 12/13/61 731.1 | 29% | 14 | 6 |
| 12/13/61 734.9 | 6/26/62 535.8 | -27% | 6 | 6/26/62 535.8 | 2/09/66 995.2 | 86% | 43 | 7 |
| 2/09/66 995.2 | 10/7/66 744.3 | -25% | 8 | 10/7/66 477.3 | 12/13/68 981.3 | 32% | 26 | 8 |
| 12/13/68 981.3 | 5/26/70 631.2 | -36% | 17 | 5/26/70 631.2 | 4/28/71 950.8 | 51% | 11 | 9 |
| 4/28/71 950.8 | 11/23/71 798.0 | -16% | 7 | 11/23/71 798.0 100.3* | 1/11/73 1051.7 136.8* | 32% 36% | 14 | 10 |
| 1/11/73 1051.7 136.8* | 12/6/74 577.6 58.2* | -45% -58% | 23 | 12/6/74 577.6 58.2* | 7/15/75 881.1 88.0* | 53% 51% | 8 | 11 |
| 7/15/75 88.0* | 10/01/75 73.8* | -16% | 2.5 | 12/15/75 818.8 | 9/28/76 994.9 | 22% | 9 | 12 |
| | | | | 12/15/75 74.5* | 9/13/78 139.3* | 87% | 33 | 13 |
| 1/10/77 986.9 | 4/03/78 751.0 | -24% | 15 | 4/03/78 751.0 | 2/08/80 903.8 | 20% | 16 | 14 |
| 9/13/78 139.3* | 11/29/78 114.1* | -18% | 2 | 11/29/78 114.1* | 10/08/79 150.9* | 32% | 10 | 15 |
| 10/8/79 150.9* | 10/31/79 135.5* | -10% | 1 | 10/31/79 135.5* | 2/08/80 165.3* | 22% | 3 | 16 |
| 2/8/80 903.8 165.3* | 3/27/80 760.0 124.1* | -16% -25% | 2 | 3/27/80 760.0 124.1* | 6/11/81 1007.4 222.3* | 33% 79% | 15 | 17 |
| 6/11/81 1007.4 222.3* | 8/13/82 788.1 159.1* | -22% -28% | 14 | 8/13/82 788.1 159.1* | 6/24/83 1286.6 328.9* | 63% 107% | 10 | 18 |
| 6/24/83 1286.6 328.9* | 7/25/84 1097 225.3* | -15% -32% | 13 | 7/25/84 1097 225.3* | 7/07/86 1839 411.2* | 68% 83% | 23 | 19 |

Table 14-15 Continued

| More than 10% decrease | | | | More than 10% increase | | | | Row |
|---|---|---|---|---|---|---|---|---|
| Index high | Index low | % | N* | Index low | Index high | % | N* | |
| 8/25/87 2722 455.8* | 10/19/87 1739 291.9* | -36% -36% | 2 | 12/04/87 1767 292.9* | 10/09/89 2791 485.7* | 58% 66% | 22 | 21 |
| 10/09/89 2791 485.7* | 10/16/90 2381 325.4* | -15% -33% | 12 | 10/16/90 2381 | 7/17/98 9338 | 292 % | 93 | 22 |
| | | | | 10/16/90 325.4* | 6/05/96 1249.2* | 284 % | 76 | 23 |
| 6/05/96 1249.2* | 7/24/96 1042.4* | -17% | 2 | 7/24/96 1042.4* | 1/31/97 1379.9* | 32% | 6 | 24 |
| 1/31/97 1379.9* | 4/02/97 1201* | -13% | 2 | 4/02/97 1201* | 10/09/97 1745.9* | 45% | 6 | 25 |
| 10/09/97 1745.9* | 1/09/89 1503.2* | -14% | 3 | 1/09/89 1503.2* | 7/17/98 2008.8* | 34% | 7 | 26 |
| 7/17/98 9338 2008.8* | 10/08/98 7732 1419.1* | -17% -29% | 2.5 | 10/08/98 7732 | 8/25/99 11326 | 47% | 11 | 27 |
| 8/25/99 11326 | 10/15/99 10020 | -12% | 2 | 10/15/99 10020 | 1/14/00 11723 | 17% | | 28 |
| 1/14/00 11723 | 9/21/01 8236 | -30% | 20 | | | | | 29 |
| 1/14/00 11723 | 10/10/02 7181 | -39% | 32 | | | | | 30 |
| | | | | 10/08/98 1419.1* | 7/19/99 2830* | 99% | 9.5 | 31 |
| 7/19/99 2830* | 8/10/99 2490.1* | -12% | 1 | 8/10/99 2490.1* | 3/10/00 5048* | 103 % | 7 | 32 |
| 3/10/00 5048* | 9/21/01 1423* | -72% | 18 | | | | | 33 |
| 3/10/00 5048* | 10/10/02 1108 | -78% | 30 | | | | | 34 |

* NASDAQ composite index; N denotes the duration of index increase or decrease in month

If we consider the left side of Table 14-15 as representing bull markets and the right side as denoting bear markets, one can clearly see that the bull markets have been the dominating phenomenon in the U.S. stock market since 1929, in terms of percentage changes and durations.

On the left side of Table 14-15, there are 29 rows that indicate the more than 10% downward movements of the Dow Jones industrial average or the NASDAQ composite index or both of the indexes. Among those 29 time periods since 1929, there are 7 time periods in which both of the indexes decreased simultaneously by more than 10%. In other time periods only one index decreased more than 10% while the other index did not exist (such as the NASDAQ index before 1971) or failed to decline by more than 10%.

On the right side of Table 14-15, there are 30 rows of data to show increases of the Dow Jones industrial average and the NASDAQ composite index. Similarly, there are 7 time periods since 1929, over which both the indexes increased by more than 10% simultaneously. In the other 23 time-periods only one index, either Dow Jones or NASDAQ, increased by more than 10%.

From the right side of Table 14-15, one can see the U.S. bull market situation since 1929. Even though the right side rows 1, 2, 3, and 4 of Table 14-15 indicate four long-duration bull runs with large percentage advances during 1932–1956, U.S. stock markets were still in the process of recovering from the shadow of the worst bear market of 1929–1932.

The longest true bull market occurred in the time period from 10/16/90 through 7/17/98 (row 22 of Table 14-15), in which the Dow Jones industrial average increased by 292.2%. The value of the index on 7/17/98 was nearly 4 times that of the index on 10/16/90. This bull market lasted for 93 months for the Dow Jones industrial average to rise without any significant sizable corrections of more than 10%. In the same time period, the NASDAQ composite index started with 325.4 on 10/16/90, and ended at 1249.2 on 6/05/96, representing a 283.9% rise in 76 months without any significant corrections of more than 10%. In the late phase of this time period, namely from 6/05/96 – 7/17/98, the NASDAQ had gone through three large downside corrections and three strong surges (right side of rows 24, 25, and 26 of Table 14-15) and ended at 2008.8 on 7/17/98, representing a 517.3% rise from the beginning of this bull market on 10/16/90.

The second-longest bull market occurred in the 1960s. It started on 6/26/62 and ended on 2/09/66, with the Dow Jones industrial average rising by 85.7% over a 43-month period (row 7 of Table 14-15). Then in the 1970s, from 12/15/75 through 9/13/78 the NASDAQ composite index rose by 86.8% over a 33-month period without a significant 10% correction (row 13). In the 1980s, from 7/25/84 through 7/07/86, both indexes rose by 67-83% over this 23-month period (row 19). Again on 12/04/87 another bull market began and lasted for 22 months, which raised both the indexes by 58-66% (row 21).

From the left side of Table 14-15, we can see the worst bear market of 1929-1932. It began on 09/03/29 and lasted for 34 months, reaching the market bottom on 7/08/32, when the Dow Jones industrial average plunged by 89% from its peak (left side row 1 of Table 14-15). It took more than 20 years for the index to return to its previous high of 381.2, which had been established on 9/3/29. The 1973-1974 bear market should be ranked as the second worst bear market in terms of Dow Jones industrial average. The left side of row 11 in Table 14-15 shows that this bear market began on 1/11/73 and reached bottom on 12/6/74. It had lasted for about 23 months and knocked down both indexes by 45-57% from their previous highs.

At present, the United States may be experiencing the third worst bear market, which is shown on the left side of rows 29 and 32 of Table 14-15. As of the end of third quarter of 2001, the Dow Jones industrial average reached as low as 8,236, representing a 29.7% decline from its all-time high 11,723, established on 1/14/2000. By the end of September 2001, this bear market had lasted for 20 months and no one had a clear idea where the market's bottom might be. On 10/10/02, the Dow Jones industrial average was as low as 7181, representing a 39% decline from the all time high.

In terms of the NASDAQ composite index, the bear market of 2000 - 2002 should be ranked the second worst as compared to the bear market of 1929–1932. On 3/10/00, the NASDAQ composite index reached its all time high, 5,048. In the following 18 months the index plunged quickly and severely; it ended at 1,423 on 9/21/01, which was close to the previous low of 1,419 established three years earlier on 10/08/98 (left side of row 27 in Table 14-15). The NASDAQ composite index's drop represents a 71.8% decline from its peak over the 18-month period as of the end of September 2001. On 10/10/02, the NASDAQ composite index reached as low as 1,108 (left side of row 34 in Table 14-15), representing a 78% decline in 30 months from its all time high. Compared with the 89% decline in 34 months of the 1929–1932 bear market, the recent perform of the NASDAQ market was not far behind the worst bear market of 1929–1932.

Besides the above-mentioned three bear markets, there were 6 bear markets since 1929 that each lasted for more than 12 months: 1956-57, 1968-70, 1977-78, 1981-82, 1983-84, and 1989-90. The other 20 bear runs of the U.S. stock markets each lasted several months even one or two months as a pause or rest period of previous bull runs.

From Table 14-15 one can see that the bull-run started in different months of a year, but October was the month in which many bear markets ended and the following bull market began. Table 14-16 lists the starting month of the bull market since 1929 until the end of September 2001. As Table 14-16 shows, one third of the bull markets since 1929 began in October, only 5 of them started in the month of December, three of them in July, and none of them started in February.

Table 14-16: Starting Month of Bull Market (1929-2001 Q3)

| Month | Number of bull markets starting in the month |
|---|---|
| January | 1 |
| February | 0 |
| March | 1 |
| April | 2 |
| May | 2 |
| June | 1 |
| July | 3 |
| August | 2 |
| September | 1 |
| October | 10 |
| November | 2 |
| December | 5 |
| Total | 30 |

From the above analysis of U.S. stock markets' performance using historical and present data, one should recognize that during the evolutionary process of the U.S. economic transformation, the stock market has transformed itself substantially. This is evidenced by a dramatically increased size of operation and by a record number of Americans participating in the market, and by its increasing enormous wealth effects, both positively and negatively, on the U.S. economic future. However, the increasing volatility of U.S. stock markets in general, and of the NASDAQ stock market in particular, has become a great challenge to technology industries and companies, to investors, and to economic policy makers on both monetary and fiscal fronts.

# PART SIX

# CONCLUDING REMARKS

Although the structure shift of the U.S. economy analyzed in Parts 10 and 11 is still in an on-going process, the sectors' evolution in the last five decades has already provided a large amount of evidence to demonstrate the fundamental transformation of the U.S. economy. From this evidence we shall draw some conclusions about the effects of structure changes on the U.S. economy and society.

- **Rethinking the Strength of the U.S. Economy**

In the current stage of U.S. economic growth, it is information technology that generates the demand shift of American consumers. Opportunities are created for the services-producing sector to develop various kinds of applications of information technology and other technologies. The U.S. services industries have been growing rapidly in order to meet high mass-consumption for health care, education, entertainment, and financial and personal services by American individuals, corporations, organizations, communities, and governments.

In the world history of economic development, scientific breakthroughs and technology innovations have induced four industrial revolutions; all of them occurred essentially in the goods-producing sector and in the production side of economies. The previous stages of economic growth, such as the take-off and the drive to technological maturity, transformed a large percentage of the working force from agricultural and resource-extractive industries into the manufacturing industries that yielded increasing productivity and higher wages. Consequently, the standard of living in the United States and many developed nations was raised substantially. However, the major direct users of those revolutionary technologies are producers and corporations rather than consumers and individuals.

In the stage of high mass-consumption, which started in the early 20th century in the U.S. and is still occurring, the focus of the economy and society has been changed. As pointed out by W.W. Rostow, "In a quite technical sense, the balance of attention of the society, as it approached and went beyond maturity, shifted from supply to demand, from problems of production to problems of consumption, and of welfare in the widest sense[1]".

The fourth Industrial Revolution, beginning in the mid-1970s, and the present information technology revolution have accelerated this shift and put the services-producing sector into the driver's seat for economic growth. Consequently the goods-producing sector, which contains many traditional leading sub-sectors and industries in the previous industrial revolutions, has become a declining component of the national economy in terms of its contribution shares to GDP and employment. As chapters 10–14 indicate, the IT-producing industries and the services-producing sector, which consists of many IT-using industries, have become the pillars of the U.S. economy, on which economic growth and social progress rely. Many people, including some policy-makers, have had a hard time comprehending this new reality of structure changes that have already put down roots in the U.S. economy.

For example, not long ago in the debate over Japanese steel producers' dumping in the U.S. market, some politicians asked for the federal government's protection, arguing that it is the steel industry that makes America strong! Obviously this argument was true for the 1950s and 1960s when the metal industry was one of the leading sectors during The Second and Third Industrial Revolutions for the drive to maturity stage and beyond.

---

[1] W.W. Rostow, *The Stages of Economic Growth,* second edition, Cambridge University Press, 1971, p. 73.

The metal industry provided tremendous growth and job opportunity for Americans in the early 20th century. But its contribution to the U.S. economy has decreased significantly and continues to do so. Both its GDP- and labor-shares systematically decreased in the last five decades, from about 4.1% in 1948 to a tiny 1.6% in 2000. One could hardly imagine how this continuously diminishing industry with marginal contribution to the U.S. economy would make America stronger in the future, regardless of furious competition from European, Japanese, Brazilian, Russian, and Chinese steel producers.

By the nominal term, the value-added of the U.S. metal industry increased 15 fold, from $11 billion in 1948 to $162 billion in 2000, its employment, however, decreased from 2.8 million in 1970 to 2.2 million in 2000. The metal industry was unable to create new jobs, and its increasing value-added is completely dependent on rising productivity and trade protection.

U.S. trade protection may help the metal industry in the short term but not in the long term. The structure shift and global competition have created great pressures on U.S. corporations to constantly look for business opportunities. The potential for business expansion and profit already disappeared in those old leading sectors because U.S. domestic demand has been switching to cheaper goods from low cost producers abroad. Therefore the metal industry's contribution to U.S. economy may continue to decline unless future scientific breakthroughs and technology innovations bring the industry back to the leading sectors for economic growth.

Many industries in the manufacturing sector share a similar development pattern to that of the U.S. metal industry during the transitional process. In the durable-goods manufacturing sectors, motor vehicle and transportation equipment, lumber and wood products, furniture and fixture, as well as industrial machinery have all experienced declining contribution shares to GDP and employment for the last five decades. They were all leading sectors during the second and third industrial revolutions when the U.S. economy was in the stage of drive to maturity and in the early phase of mass consumption. One exception in durable-goods manufacturing is the industry of electric and electronic equipment and instrument, which has demonstrated increasing GDP- and labor-shares. This sector contains many IT-producing industries such as computer hardware and software, consumer electronics, semiconductor industry, communications equipment and services industries; they have been growing rapidly as a new leading sector for the fourth industrial revolution, particularly for the current information revolution.

In non-durable-goods manufacturing, food and tobacco products, textile, paper, printing and publishing have reduced their contributions to GDP and employment, while the chemical industry has held a flat GDP-share and a slightly declining employment share. Individual firms in the basic industries such as metal, paper, wood products, petroleum and chemical industries might be still doing well, particularly during the down turn of technology development cycle. But these industries have not shown growth momentum since 1985. As domestic demand has largely shifted to services and cheaper imported goods, the cyclical basic industries have to penetrate foreign markets in order to survive and expand. Similar to U.S. steel companies, other U.S. basic industrial companies also encounter fierce competitions from producers in Japan, Europe, and the newly industrialized countries in Asia and South America.

Clearly, the whole U.S. manufacturing sector has experienced a dramatic shift. Its highest GDP- and labor-shares (contributions to GDP and employment), 29.62% and 27.50%, occurred in 1953. Those shares, however, were almost halved in 2000, dropping to 15.88% and 13.68%. The number of manufacturing workers decreased from 20.175 million in 1980 to 18.511 million in 2000, but its nominal value-added more than doubled from $587 billion in 1980 to $1.567 trillion, thanks to the extraordinary productivity gain in the manufacturing. The U.S. manufacturing sector stopped creating new jobs after 1980. As a matter of fact, 1.5 million manufacturing jobs were eliminated in the last two decades. The U.S. manufacturing sector is no longer a creator of jobs, which leads to skepticism of how long manufacturing production can go up while the number of manufacturing workers goes down.

Not only the manufacturing sector, but the whole goods-producing sector has significantly reduced its GDP- and labor-shares, from 44.4% and 46.2% in 1948 to 23.2% and 22.7% in 2000. The net 3.8 million jobs were added into the goods-producing sector in the last fifty years, compared with the nearly 51 million jobs created by the services-producing sector in the same time period.

All the evidence provided in this volume points out that the structure changes have been taking place not just in a few industries and sectors, but in the whole U.S. economy. The changing aggregate demand has largely reduced the consumption share for durable and non-durable goods, and enormously raised effective demand for a variety of services, which yield a foundation for the rapid growth in output of the services-producing sector. The consumption-driven U.S. economy has led to a radical structure change, in which the old leading sectors for economic growth in the 1950s and earlier have diminished and will continue to decline, and new leading sectors are created in the IT-producing industry and in the services-producing sector.

Finance, insurance, and real estate were the fastest growing industries in the U.S. during the last fifty years; their contribution to GDP rose from 9.8% in 1948 to 19.6% in 2000, which surpassed the GDP-share of the entire manufacturing sector, 15.9%, in 2000. The sub-industry of banking and credit agency alone made a greater contribution to GDP than that of the combined industries of metal, motor vehicle and transportation equipment all together. Now, the great creators of job and wealth in the U.S. economy also include business services, health services, education, legal and social services, as well as other professional services. Nearly 20 million Americans engaged in business services and health services in 2000, about 14.8% of the total U.S. employment, compared with the 18.5 million Americans who were employed by the entire U.S. manufacturing sector in 2000.

The new reality is that for the first time in history, the U.S. economy is no longer dominated by goods-producing activities. Now, more Americans are delivering services than producing goods. The United States can feed, house, and clothe its citizens with only a small portion of its population engaged in goods production, and with the expansion of international trade.

In retrospect, we see that the U.S. economy allocated more than 75% of its working force into agriculture for its traditional society before the take-off in 1843-60. In 1910, the number of U.S. farm workers reduced to 13.6 million, accounting for 35% of U.S. working force and 15% of the U.S. population[2]. Today, the number of U.S. agriculture workers is about 3.3 million, accounting for 2.5% of total U.S. employment and a tiny 1.1% of the U.S. population in 2000. The U.S. agricultural sector, however, has not only supported the increasing U.S. population, but also become the largest exporter to the rest of the world, thanks to the advanced U.S. technology and the extraordinarily increased agriculture productivity.

The systematic and substantial declines in the GDP- and labor-shares of the manufacturing sector lead us to believe that the U.S. manufacturing sector may begin to experience a transition similar to that of U.S. agriculture in different degrees. To date, the U.S. agricultural sector has taken more than 150 years to transform from the traditional era to the modern age. The present transition of U.S. manufacturing, which probably started in the early 1980s (the Fourth Industrial Revolution just began in the middle of the 1970s), will have a long way to go. To predict its transitional course and its effects on the U.S. economy and society would be a great challenge to researchers and observers, since we are all at the very beginning

---

[2] U.S. Farm Workers, by Type, 1910-2000, National Agricultural Statistics Services (NASS), U.S. Department of Agriculture.

of another great economic transformation in human history. Consulting historical experiences, we can be sure that the current transformation will create the next economy and society in ways that will be different from what most people expect[3].

A successful economic transition must go with sustained economic growth. With the diminishing share of manufacturing, the major source of growth for value-added and job creation must be found in the services industries. Presently the services industries include two kinds of industries: the great creator of wealth and the great creator of jobs. The industry of finance, insurance, and real estate is an example of the great wealth creator, with its GDP-share of 19.6% and labor-share of 5.8% in 2000. The industry of retail trade and the industry of education, legal and social services are examples of the great creator of jobs, with their GDP-shares of 9.1% and 2.8%, while labor-shares of 15.8% and 6.5% in 2000 respectively.

Consequently, the services industries acting as the great creator of wealth demonstrate very high productivity, while the services industries acting as the great creator of jobs have very low productivity. In between these two polarized situations come business services, health services, amusement and motion picture, and professional services, all with their productivity below the average of the U.S. economy. An essential task of the U.S. economy during this transition is to boost productivity of many services industries that have a great share of employment. Only upon the fulfilling this task can the majority of U.S. population have an opportunity to substantially raise their income and standard of living in the 21st century.

Like previous economic transitions, the current one requires a large scale of technology diffusion through which the leading sectors can grow rapidly and their spillover effects can reach every other sector of the economy and every aspect of the society. The IT-producing industry has demonstrated its capability to create new technologies and to promote various applications for both goods and services productions as well as for consumers.

The Internet bubble that burst in 2000 and 2001 through stock market crashes has caused the extreme pessimism on the Internet industry in particular and the IT-producing industry in general. When the dust settles, people will find that the IT-industry and the Internet are necessary infrastructures critical to the functioning of the economy and to national security, including security of financial networks, power supply networks, telecommunications systems, transportation networks, and government operations.

---

[3] Peter Drucker, The Next Society, *The Economist*, November 3, 2001.

Consumers keep spending money and time on the Internet and communications. They keep buying new technology products such as camcorders, digital cameras, PDAs (Personal Digital Assistants) on steroids, and play-stations, because the prices of these products have dropped to the affordable level for many Americans. Thanks to the new technology that significantly reduces manufacturing cost and price of microprocessors, which are increasingly built into PCs and other smart consumer electronic products. It is foreseeable that the IT industry will continue generating momentum for U.S. economic transformation.

The IT-producing industry provides not only excellent growth by itself, but also the means and methods to address the core issue of promoting productivity for the services industries. Some smart U.S. technology companies have discovered the huge markets for IT and Internet products and services that serve the low-productivity services industries. For example, Dell Computer Corporation has grasped this growth opportunity to help services providers. With its high cost-efficiency and effective direct-selling, Dell has aggressively offered its PCs, notebooks, servers, storage, network and other IT products and services at the lowest price and highest satisfaction level to schools, universities, retail stores, health care organizations, as well as government agencies. The great potential in the U.S. services industries allows Dell to continue its expansion, with rapidly increasing market share even in the recent years of the down turn in the technology sector.

A fundamental change in the present economic transition, which may touch everyone in the society, is to turn the blue-collar workers into what have been called as knowledge workers in the creative and innovative class, as we described in Chapter 9. Along with declining manufacturing, many manual jobs on assembling lines and factory floors have been eliminated quickly. The dominance of manufacturing workers has been replaced by the dominance of knowledge workers, or professionals, in the U.S. labor market. Knowledge workers must have formal education and specialty of knowledge, who act as doctors, nurses, lawyers, teachers, accountants, financial analysts, engineers, computer technicians, software designers, data processing staff members, project managers, technologists, and consultants and so on. As Peter Drucker points out,

"The next society will be a knowledge society. Knowledge will be its key resource, and knowledge workers will be the dominating group in its workforce[4]."

The United States could be the first nation in the world to successfully transform its current economy into the next economy in the 21st century. Even though not many people know what the next economy will look like, emerging evidences in this volume have pointed out the direction: the continuation of declining manufacturing and increasing services, and the continuation of the rising creative and Innovative class and the falling working class.

The U.S. economy has been in this dynamic transition process for some time. Now only 23 out of every 100 U.S. workers produce goods, and the other 77 deliver services, including government jobs, compared with 46 on goods production and 54 on services developing in 1948. Particularly since 1980, this transition has proceeded quickly in the U.S. with the help of the information technology revolution. Many new IT industries and new services industries have been created, providing more than 50 million new jobs for Americans in the last five decades. This is a massive transition involving so many people in so many different corporations, industries, and sectors.

The strength of the U.S. economy is demonstrated by such a large-scale economic structure change that has been proceeding with a minimum of labor turbulence and disruption. The performance of the U.S. economy was exceptional (as described in Chapter 12 of this book). The longest economic growth in U.S. history was recorded in the last thirty years, which was interrupted by only two serious recessions, 1974–1975 and 1981–1982, both were caused by the external factors, the world oil crisis.

The flexibility, adaptability, and capability of the U.S. economy to manage economic transition are the intrinsic factors for strength and success; these factors are well reflected in a remarkable example. During the 1970s and early 1980s, a swath of formerly smoke-shrouded Midwestern cities, so called the Rust Belt with big factories, big autos and big steel, suffered high unemployment, increasing crime, declining wages, and net emigration. In the 1990s, however, the Rust Belt area rebounded with a decreasing unemployment rate, reducing crime rate, increasing wages, rising population, and rapidly growing exports. The state of Michigan has made a concentrated effort to diversify its economy away from being auto dependent, and the

[4] Peter Drucker, The Next Society, *The Economist*, November 3rd, 2001.

whole region has followed the rest of the country in shifting from a goods-based economy to one based on services[5]. The revival of Midwest economy has transformed the Rust Belt to the Growth Belt, which represents an extraordinary economic transition.

During this on-going economic transition, American workers have to acquire professional knowledge through formal education and training in order to turn themselves from blue-collar workers into professionals for the growing services industries. They also have to be engaged in continuous education and training to update their knowledge in order to retain their jobs. In the United States, individuals, corporations, organizations, communities, and governments have collaboratively made tremendous endeavors dedicated to nurturing creativity, innovation, and the emerging creative and innovative class, which will be the dominating force for the next economy of the 21st century. The emerging new class represents the advanced means of production, the real strength and competitive advantage of the U.S. economy in the changing global economic and political arena.

The growth potential of the IT-producing industry and the services sector is not limited to U.S. domestic markets; it exists globally. As we discussed in Section 10-4 of Chapter 10, international trade by the services sector generated a surplus for the U.S. economy as much as $100 billion in 1998 versus $251 billion of deficit in goods-trade. The United States obviously enjoys a strong competitive advantage in the creation and dissemination of advanced technologies and services. This advantage is rooted in the rising role of the technology industries and services-producing sector in the U.S. economy.

Rethinking where the strength of the U.S. economy comes from, one should also recognize the powerful competitive advantages of U.S. technologies and services in global markets. It is crucial for U.S. industries and companies to strengthen their leadership in technology innovation and service creation in domestic and global markets in order to sustain economic growth.

---

[5] Business News: Population returning to Revitalized Rust Belt, *Naples Daily News,* February 16, 1999.

## • Reshaping Relationships among Economic Variables

The changing structure of the U.S. economy is breaking the promises of conventional economic thinking. For example, high growth leads to high inflation. This is a famous doctrine in economics, and is explained as follows. In an economic boom, banks lend out more money, firms and consumers spend heavily, and new jobs push the work force toward full employment. All these factors generate price pressure from the demand side. Eventually interest rates rise, which make some investments unprofitable, and demand for increasing wages exceeds gains in productivity, which increases the costs of labor and other input factors. To maintain profit margins, businesses have to raise the prices of their products, which generates price pressure from the supply side. The demand-pull and supply-push cause increasingly higher prices and inflation sets in.

The U.S. economy grew at about 3% of real GDP during the 1990s, while CPI-inflation rate remained under 3%. A significant sign of wage pressure has not been found and, after a decade of waiting, the thread of price inflation has yet to emerge. Monetary policy decision-makers at the Federal Reserve have particularly worried about the tightening labor market, constantly warning the public of the risk of running out of workers and increasing the pressure on raising nominal wages that inevitably leads to price inflation.

This puzzling conflict of steady growth and low inflation versus conventional economic thinking may have something to do with the changed economic structure. Increased prices usually start in the goods-producing sector when prices of energy and raw material as well as wages of labor rise, which will eventually be transmitted into rising prices of final goods in all sectors of the economy. In the inflationary environment, those companies that command the greatest price power are producers of oil, steel, paper, lumber, chemicals and other staple commodities. As indicated by the evolution of industries and sectors, the basic commodity-producing industries, such as mining, metal, wood products, food, paper, and textile, have largely reduced their contributions to GDP and employment. Consequently their price power and influence on the overall economy is declining. Under the challenge of foreign producers' competition, prices of staple commodities will likely be dictated by global market conditions rather than by domestic producers' desire. The diminishing influence of the basic industries on the U.S. economy has altered the inflation picture of the U.S. economy.

Another important factor to contain inflation is viewed as the widely adopted information technologies that cross all of the industries and sectors of the U.S. economy. Information technologies allow American corporations to implement innovative ways of conducting business, which reduces cost and enhances efficiency and productivity. As Table 11-1.3 of Chapter 11 indicates, the proxy measure of productivity rose from $50,410 per person in 1990 to $72,941 per person in 2000 (a 45% rise) for the overall economy, and from $51,629 to $74,463 (a 44% rise) for the private sector.

In the goods-producing sector, the electric and electronic equipment and instruments industry, which consists of semiconductor, computer and communications equipment manufacturing, has shown a significant productivity gain in terms of both absolute and relative measures of productivity over 1990-2000. In the services-producing sector, the industries of communications, banking and credit agency, security and commodity brokers, insurance carriers and services, have all registered a large productivity gain. These industries are the heavy users of information technologies. Indeed, information technologies have brought about a significant productivity gain to the overall U.S. economy that has offset the increasing wage pressure and prevented output prices from rising steeply over time.

According to the latest report by the U.S. Department of Commerce[6], the output price of information technology producing industries (i.e. producers of computer hardware and software, communications equipment and services, and instruments) has declined substantially. During both 1996 and 1997, prices of information technology goods and services fell by 7% per year. It was estimated that the information technology producing industries brought overall inflation down to 1.9%; without information-producing industries, the inflation rate would be 2.6%. This 2.6% inflation rate for the non-IT industries also reflects the effect of cost reduction and productivity increase due to using information technologies, which encourage non-IT companies to make profits without hiking the prices of their products and services.

As Table 11-1.2 of Chapter 11 reveals, in 1990-2000 the number of government employees increased by 0.76 million; the number of employees in the private sector increased by 19.47 million, of which 18.11 million belonged to the services-producing sector and only 1.36 million were in the goods-producing sector. As Table 11-9.2 in Section 11-6 of Chapter 11 reveals, the

[6] The Emerging Digital Economy II, Economics and Statistics Administration, U.S. Department of Commerce, 1999.

average wage of the goods-producing sector was $33,111 in 1997, 12% higher than the average wage, $29,598, of the private sector. The average wage of the services-producing sector was $28,361, 4% below the private sector's average wage. It is clear that the tightening labor market has made its appearance in the services-producing sector where wages are still relatively low and the expectation for a rise in pay is also low due to the sector's low productivity.

Unlike the economic boom of the 1950s and 60s, when nearly 3 million additional jobs were created by the manufacturing industries that demanded higher pay, the 1990s' economic expansion has created many new jobs in the low-end services sector where individual workers have not had much bargaining power for high wages. As the employment of all the manufacturing industries actually reduced by 0.6 million over 1990-2000 (Table 11-2.2), the increasing wage pressure has been dampened in those industries by diminishing job opportunities.

The shifting economic strength from goods-producing activities to technology and services-producing activities has weakened the conventional linkage from a tightening labor market through wage pressure to price inflation. This might be one of the sources that create some puzzling phenomena associated with the prolonged economic expansion for the 1990s.

## • Restructuring for a New Phase in the High Mass-Consumption Stage of Economic Growth

The United States was the first of the world's societies to enter the fifth stage of economic growth, the age of high mass-consumption, at the beginning of the twentieth century. Today's U.S. economy as well as entire society has been transforming and restructuring dramatically and moving forward to a new phase in the high mass-consumption stage of economic growth, that is the age of information technology. This phase most likely began in the early 1970s with the transitory period lasting for two decades before leading to the unusually prolonged economic expansion of the 1990s. There are several reasons that lead us to believe that the United States again is the first of the world's societies to move into this new era, and many developed and less developed nations will soon be playing catch up in the march to embrace the age of information technology.

The decade of 1970s was a difficult time period when the quadrupling oil prices shocked the world economy in 1969–1970, 1973, and 1979. At same time, continued poor harvests in 1974 in many countries of the globe pushed world food prices higher, which was followed by the skyrocketing prices of raw materials. Higher costs of fuel and other materials were quickly transmitted into higher prices of manufactured goods. The CPI inflation rate in the United States soared to above 10.5% in 1974, and to nearly 13% in 1980. Meanwhile, the U.S. economy entered a severe recession with the real GDP falling at the annual rate of 0.9% during 1974–1975 and 2.3% in 1982, and the unemployment rate rising to nearly 9%. As both inflation and unemployment were unusually high in those years, economists call the 1973 –1980 era the great stagflation, referring to the coexistence of economic stagnation and high inflation.

The tough macro-economic environment caused many difficulties and problems in the society, but it also created new challenges and opportunities for evolutionary changes to set in, particularly for a swift shift in the sector structure of the U.S. economy.

As we have observed from the previous analyses, the goods-producing sector began to develop a declining trend in the early 1970s. It reduced both GDP- and labor-shares of those manufacturing industries that heavily depend on fuel and other raw materials, such as the metal, auto and transportation equipment, machinery, and wood product industries. Many of them were the leading sectors in the early stage of high mass-consumption; they began to show significant retardation in the 1970s. The technology revolution in the electronics industry, however, brought new leading industries onto the playing ground of the economy. The semiconductor, computer, and communications equipment industries were formed and grew rapidly. These information technology-producing industries became new leading sectors with tremendous growth momentum and greater impacts on the overall economy in the new phase of the high mass-consumption stage. The evidence that old leading industries have given up their leadership to the rapidly growing and newly formed industries bodes well the beginning of a new era in the dynamic process of economic transformation.

The changing leading sectors are the most important indication to identify the stage of economic growth, as Rostow states clearly[7]

At any period of time, the rate of growth in the sectors will

---

[7] W.W. Rostow, *The Stages of Economic Growth*, second edition, Cambridge University Press, 1971.

vary greatly; and it is possible to isolate empirically certain leading sectors, at early stages of their evolution, whose rapid rate of expansion plays an essential direct and indirect role in maintaining the overall momentum of the economy. For some purposes it is useful to characterize an economy in terms of its leading sectors; and a part of the technical basis for the stages of growth lies in the changing sequence of leading sectors. In essence it is the fact that sectors tend to have a rapid growth-phase, early in their life that makes it possible and useful to regard economic history as a sequence of stages rather than merely as a continuum, within which nature never makes a jump.

In this volume we have illustrated the shifting leading sectors of the U.S. economy during the last half century and provided evidence of the old leading sectors' decay and the new leading sectors' rapid expansion. This leads us to believe that the new era has arrived.

Secondly, a new era of economic growth must be upheld by breakthroughs in technology development that allow new leading industries to form and grow. More than two hundred years ago the First Industrial Revolution with the technology breakthrough of Watt's steam engine allowed England to be the first nation in the world to move into the third stage of economic growth—the take-off. In the Second Industrial Revolution, symbolized by the railway revolution, the major technology breakthrough was the discovery of ways to produce cheap steel in large amounts, which created the new leading sectors, such as the steel, machinery, railroad, and transportation industries, for the stage of drive to technological maturity.

A broad range of technology inventions and innovations brought out the Third Industrial Revolution in the internal combustion engine, automobile's moving-assembly line, electricity, and modern chemicals. The leading industries of metal, auto and other transportation equipment, heavy machinery tools, chemicals, oil and petroleum have built the foundations for many currently developed nations that have moved from the technological maturity into the stage of high mass-consumption.

The Fourth Industrial Revolution began with breakthroughs in the information technology industries that produce hardware and software for computers, telecommunications equipment and networks, and consumer electronic products. In the 1970s the semiconductor industry showed its extraordinary success in manufacturing very large scale integrated circuits, which allow a computer's heart—the central processor unit (CPU)—to be crammed onto a single tiny silicon chip. A revolution in the computer industry arrived with personal computers, which began to take the center place of information technology in the 1980s. Computers can process, store, and perform a variety of tasks with increasing volume, speed, accuracy, and continuously declining prices. The explosive growth of computer markets worldwide has generated the greatest momentum for an array of electronics industries across the entire electronic technology chain[8], from advanced materials to sophisticated industrial robots. The Fourth Industrial Revolution has been unfolding into multidimensional sectors, such as laser, new industrial materials, multimedia, genetic engineering, and so on.

A new explosive wave of growth made its first appearance in the middle of the 1990s. This was the beginning of the Internet, which is a sophisticated combination of computer networks and telecommunications networks. Even though the goal of having the Internet enter every business and every home, anytime and anywhere on the globe could be many years away, impressive results of the Internet in the E-business and E-commerce have already demonstrated its astonishing potential to revolutionize the U.S. economy and society.

In our opinion, the era of information technology is a new phase in the stage of high mass-consumption, in which services-production and consumption begin to outweigh goods-production and consumption. People have observed some remarkable changes in this new phase.

First, in the previous three industrial revolutions technology breakthroughs were mainly applied to the manufacturing industries, and the heavy users of those technologies were corporations. Presently, in the Fourth Industrial Revolution, breakthroughs of information technologies are applicable to not only manufacturing industries, but also services industries, not only producers but also consumers, not only corporations but also communities, families, and individuals. This broadening scale and scope of the information technology revolution has not been seen in human history. Its potential and huge effect on economies and societies of the world remain to be exploited.

Secondly, the presently less developed nations of the world, such as China and India, have followed the same stages of economic growth as the United States and other developed nations, but are one or two stages behind. Both China and India accomplished their take-off in the 1950s and currently are in the stage of drive to technological maturity[9]. Due to the huge population burden, the Chinese and Indian economies have little hope to move forward

---

[8] George Kozmetsky and Piyu Yue, *Global Economic Competition, Today's Warfare in Global Electronics Industries and Companies,* Kluwer Academic Publishers, 1997, p. 7.
[9] W. W. Rostow, *The Great Population Spike and After, Reflections on the 21st Century,* 1998, p. 42.

into the mass high-consumption stage in the same way as the U.S. economy did by providing the majority of Americans with single-family homes and two or three cars per family.

In our opinion, the information technology revolution could bring the less developed nations new hopes and opportunities. The nature of the worldwide reach of the Internet allows instant communications across national boundaries to access to information beyond any nation's control. The huge amount of human resources in China and India can be put into work for domestic and foreign companies without any worker actually leaving home. There exists a large probability that the less developed nations may leap forward into the new information technology age. If that happens, the world setting and the balance of power on the globe could alter fundamentally.

Finally, as we have observed in this volume, many services-producing industries still have lower productivity and lower wages, compared with the manufacturing industries. The biggest challenge to the information technology revolution is to raise productivity in a spectrum of service businesses via various applications of information technology. If this challenge could be met in the United States, more than a half of the work force in this country would significantly raise their standard of living. If not, the productivity gain of overall U.S. economy will be limited. Consequently, the probability of raising wages for the majority of workers would be slim.

At the same time education and training become crucial, as the information technology revolution will create new leading industries that require new kinds of workers with knowledge, special skills, and the competence to fulfill new missions. If the U.S. labor market cannot meet the increasing demand for knowledge workers due to poor education and continuous education, American corporations will find it much easier than ever before to fill high skill and high paying jobs with talented people wherever they are found around the globe. That will leave many American workers struggling in some poorly paid low-end services industries with low productivity.

We come to the conclusion that the new phase of the high mass-consumption stage of economic growth requires the rise of the creative and innovative class and mass-education and continuing education as a necessary companion to economic growth. Americans continue to produce goods, to develop services, to shop, to educate and be educated, to entertain and be entertained. Americans have a tradition of optimism and a good can-do attitude. No other country in the world can match the competitive advantage of the creativity and innovation the United States has enjoyed for so many years. Ahead of all other economies in the world, the U.S. economy has been successfully transformed into a high level of economic growth with the changed economic structure and the emerged creative and innovative class. We have every reason to believe that the United States will remain the locomotive that leads the whole world into the new era of information technology and brings peace and prosperity at home and abroad.

# REFERENCES

Amidon, M. Debra, *Innovation Strategy for the Knowledge Economy, The Ken Awakening*, Butterworth-Heinemann, 1997.

Barth, James R., *The Great Savings and Loan Debacle*, Washington, DC: American Enterprise Institute Press, 1991.

Board of Governors of the Federal Reserve System, *Flow of Funds Accounts of the United States*, Washington DC, March 9, 2001.

Bureau of Labor Statistics Bulletin 2178, September 1983.

Calandra, Thom , Analyst Sees Panic Selling ahead, FT MarketWatch.com, Oct. 9, 2000.

Christensen, Clayton, *The Innovator's Dilemma: When New Technologies Cause Great Firms to Fail,* Harvard Business School Press, June 1997.

Christensen, Clayton M., *The Innovator's Dilemma*, Harper Business, An Imprint of Harper Collins Publishers, 2000.

Citigroup, Annual Report, 1999.

Crow, Kenneth, "Achieving Design to Cost Objectives", Product Development Forum Home Page.

Davis, Stan and Jim Botkin, "The Coming of Knowledge-Based Business", Harvard Business Review, September-October, 1994.

Dow Diaries, "The Power of Dow Dividends", http://averages.dowjones.com/ddpower.html.

Drucker, Peter F. *Post-Capital Society*, Harper Business, Harper Collins Publishers, 1993.

Drucker, Peter, "Looking Ahead: Implications of the Present," Harvard Business Review, September-October 1997, pp. 18-24.

Drucker, Peter, The Next Society, A Survey of the Near Future, *The Economists*, November 3rd, 2001.

Flood, D. Mark, The Great Deposit Insurance Debate, *Review*, The Federal Reserve Bank of St. Louis, Vol. 74, No. 4, July/August 1992.

Florida, Richard, *The Rise of The Creative Class and How It's Transforming Work, Leisure, Community and Everyday Life*, Published by Basic Books, 2002.

Gibbons, Michael Gibbons, et al , *The New Production of Knowledge, The dynamics of Science and Research in Contemporary Societies,* Sage Publications, 1994.

Gras, Norman S. B., *Business History of the United States, About 1650 to 1950's*, Edwards Brothers, Inc., 1967.

Greenspan, Alan, "Testimony of Chairman before the Committee on Banking, Housing, and Urban Affairs", U.S. Senate, July 18, 1996.

Greenspan, Alan, "Testimony of Chairman before the Committee on Banking, Housing, and Urban Affairs", U.S. Senate, February 26, 1997.

Greenspan, Alan, "The American Economy in a World Context," At the 35th Annual Conference on bank Structure and Competition of the Federal Reserve Bank of Chicago, Chicago, Illinois, May 6, 1999.

Greenspan, Alan, "Remarks by Chairman Alan Greenspan", at a symposium sponsored by the Federal Reserve Bank of Kansas City, Jackson Hole, Wyoming, August 31, 2001.

Greenspan, Alan, "Remarks by Chairman Alan Greenspan, at the 15th Anniversary Conference of the Center for Economic Research", Stanford University, September 5, 1997.

Greenspan, Alan, "Remarks by Chairman before the New York Association for Business Economics", New York, June 13, 2000.

Grove, Andrew S., *Only the Paranoid Survive*, Doubleday, 1996.

Intel Corp, Interviews with Visionaries: "A History for the Microprocessor", http://www.intel.com

Investor's Business Daily, Bush Widens Lead Among Investors: Can This New Bloc Make A Difference?, October 11th, 2000.

Jorgenson, Dale W., Frank M. Gollop, and Barbara M. Fraumeni, *Productivity and U.S. Economic Growth*, Harvard University Press, Cambridge, Massachusetts, 1987.

Kane, Edward J., *The S & L Insurance Mess: How Did It Happen?* The Urban Institute Press, Washington, D.C., 1989.

Kleinbard, David, "The $1.7 Trillion Dot.com Lesson", CNN, November 9, 2000.

Kozmetsky, George, *Technology Transfer in a Global Context*, the IC2 Institute, the University of Texas, 1994.

Kozmetsky, George and Timothy Ruefli, *Information Technology and Its Impacts*, Graduate School of Business, The University of Texas at Austin, 1971.

Kozmetsky George and Piyu Yue, *Global Economic Competition, Today's Warfare in Global Electronics Industries and Companies*, Kluwer Academic Publishers, 1997.

Kozmetsky, George and Piyu Yue, *Embracing the Global Demographic Transformation, 1950-2050*, an IC2 monograph, 2000.

Lodge, George C., "The Large Corporation and the New American Ideology," in *Corporations and the Common Good*, ed. Robert B. Dickie and Leroy S. Rouner, 1986

Maital, Shlomo, "Future Winners..." *ACROSS THE BOARD*, December 1991.

Market Data, "The NASDAQ Stock Market Five-Year Statistical Review", http://www.marketdata.nasdaq.com

Meulendyke, Ann-Marie, *U.S. Monetary Policy and Financial Markets*, Federal Reserve Bank of New York, 1989.

Murdock, Deroy, "Milton and Rose Friedman Offer Radical Ideas for the 21st Century", GATO, Today's Commentary, December 8, 1999.

Nelson, Richard R., *The Sources of Economic Growth*, Harvard University Press, Cambridge, Mass., 1996.

NYSE, *Summary of 1998 Share Ownership Report*, 1998.

NYSE, *1999 NYSE Fact Book*, http://www.NYSE.com

Park, Sangkyun, *Explanations for the Increased Riskiness of Banks in the 1980s*, Review, Vol.76, No 4, July/August 1994.

Peterson, Robert, Gerald Albaum, and George Kozmetsky, *Modern American Capitalism, Understanding Public Attitudes and Perceptions*, Quorum Books, 1990.

Pimentel, David and Mario Giampietro, *Food, Land, Population and the U.S. Economy*, November, 1994.

Energy Information Administration, *Annual Energy Outlook 1996*, Washington, DC, January 1996

Porter, Michael, *Competitive Advantage: Creating and Sustaining Superior Performance*, The Free Press, 1985.

Ramamoorthy, Chitoor V., "A Study of the Service Industry — Functions, Features and Control", *IEICE Transactions on Communications*, Vol.E83-B, NO. 5, May 2000, pp891.

Robinson, Peter, *Uncommon Knowledge: the New Economy*, Hoover Institution's Television Show, March 10, 2000.

Romer, Paul M., "Increasing Return and Long-Run Growth", *Journal of Political Economy*, 94, 5 (October), 1986.

Romer, Paul M., "Endogenous Technological Change", *Journal of Political Economy*, 98, 5 (October), 1990.

Rostow, W.W., *The Stages of Economic Growth*, second edition, Cambridge University Press, 1971.

Rostow, W.W. *Theorists of Economic Growth From David Hume to the Present, with a Perspective on the Next Century*, Oxford University Press, 1990.

Rostow, W.W., *2050: An Essay on the 21st Century*, January, 5, 1996.

Rostow, W.W. *The Great Population Spike and After, reflections on the 21st Century*, Oxford University Press, 1998.

Satran, Dick, News (Reuters), "Compaq's Shakeup Provides E-Commerce Warning", News (Reuters), April 20, 1999.

Schumpeter, A. Joseph, Capitalism, Socialism and Democracy, New York: Harper, 1975.

Scott, M., *A New View of Economic Growth*, Oxford: Oxford University Press, 1989.

Sloan, P. Alfred, *My Years with General Motor*, Garden City, N.Y., Doubleday, 1964.

Solow, Robert M., "Technical Change and the Aggregate Production Function," *Review of Economics and Statistics*, 39, August 1957.

Soto, Hernando de, *The Mystery of Capital*: *Why Capitalism Triumphs in the West and Fails Everywhere Else,* Published by Basic Books, 2000.

Triplett, Jack, E., "The Solow productivity paradox: what do computer do to productivity?" *Canadian Journal of Economics*, Vol. 32, No. 2, April 1999.

The Turnaround Letter, Volume 15, Number 7, January 2001.

U.S. Bureau of the Census, Internet Release Date: March 9, 1999.

U.S. Department of Commerce, *The Emerging Digital Economy II*, of Economic and Statistics and Administration, U.S. Department of Commerce, July 1999.

U.S. Department of Commerce, *North American Industry Classification System*, March 1999.

U.S. Department of Labor, *Private Pension Plan Bulletin*, Abstract of 1997, Form 5500, Annual Reports, Number 10, Winter 2001, Pension and Welfare Benefits Administration, Office of Policy and Research

U.S. Department of Labor, "Final Report on the National Summit on Retirement Savings", June 4-5, 1998.

# INDEX